DEPTH-PSYCHOLOGICAL UNDERSTANDING

DEPTH-PSYCHOLOGICAL UNDERSTANDING

The Methodologic Grounding of Clinical Interpretations

Philip F. D. Rubovits-Seitz

Routledge
Taylor & Francis Group
LONDON AND NEW YORK

First published 1998 by The Analytic Press, Inc.

Published 2014 by Routledge
2 Park Square, Milton Park, Abingdon, Oxfordshire OX14 4RN
711 Third Avenue, New York, NY 10017

First issued in paperback 2014
Routledge is an imprint of the Taylor & Francis Group, an informa business

Index by Leonard S. Rosenbaum

Library of Congress Cataloging-in-Publication Data

Rubovits-Seitz, Philip F. D., 1921–
Depth-psychological understanding : the methodologic grounding of clinical interpretations / Philip F. D. Rubovits-Seitz.
p. cm.
Includes bibliographical references and index.
ISBN 978-0-88163-279-8 (hbk)
ISBN 978-1-13800-540-2 (pbk)
1. Psychodynamic psychotherapy. 2. Psychoanalysis. I. Title.
[DNLM: 1. Psychoanalytic Interpretation. 2. Psychoanalytic Therapy—methods. WM 460.7 R896d 1998]
RC489.P72R83 1998
616.89'17—dc21
DNLM/DLC
for Library of Congress 98-5988
CIP

To the memories of two fathers,

Charles L. Seitz, M.D.

Frank E. Rubovits, M.D.

Contents

Preface *ix*

I. HISTORICAL BACKGROUND

1 Trouble at the Source: Freud's Methodologic Conflict 3

2 The Postpositivist Turn and the "Lingering Ghost of Positivism" in Interpretive Methodology 21

II. CONTEMPORARY APPROACHES

3 Methodologic Lag in Some Contemporary Models of Interpretive Inquiry 45

4 Some Language-Based Models of Interpretive Methodology: Evaluation of Linguistic, Discourse, and Narrative Models 67

III. NONCLINICAL COMPARISONS

5 Some Nonclinical Methods of Inferring Latent Contents: Comparisons with Clinical Inference and Interpretation 95

6 Evaluation of "Commonsense" (Intentional) Psychology as a Model of Interpretive Inquiry 147

IV. JUSTIFYING INTERPRETATIONS

7 The Probity of Clinical Interpretations in the Light of Grünbaum's Critiques 171

8 Justification of Interpretations: Evaluation of Individual Methods 211

9 Pluralistic, Posttherapeutic Justification of Interpretations: An Illustrative Case 249

V. SUMMARY AND CONCLUSIONS

10 The Methodology of Clinical Interpretation: Problems and Progress 285

Notes *315*

References *343*

Index *431*

Preface

This book deals with what Edward Glover (1952, p. 405) called "the Achilles heel" of psychoanalysis, that is, the uncertainties of inferring latent meanings and determinants in clinical data.[1] Glover chose that metaphor to emphasize the unsolved problems, limitations, and scientifically insecure status of our interpretive methods. We must distinguish in this connection between the methodology and the technique of interpretation. The former, the broader concept, includes both the construal of latent contents, on the one hand, and criteria of communicating depth-psychological information to patients, on the other, with only the latter comprising interpretive "technique." This book focuses specifically on the construal and justification phases of the interpretive process.

Inferring latent contents is the "stock in trade" of psychoanalysts and dynamic psychotherapists, but the literature on this process is surprisingly meager and does not convey its central role in our clinical and investigative work. Because the construal of latent meanings and determinants is crucial to depth-psychological understanding, we must know as much as possible about the nature and functioning of interpretive methods—their modes of operation, capabilities, limitations, problems, and corrective measures. We have taken these methods largely for granted, however (Schimek, 1975, p. 863), and have assumed mistakenly that they are more reliable and accurate than they actually are.[2] This book explores the roots and results of neglecting these problems; evaluates clinical models of construing and justifying latent contents; and reviews both problems and progress in our interpretive methodology.

During the first half-century of psychoanalysis, Freud and his followers assumed that their methods of inferring latent meanings and determinants were scientifically sound. Freud (1905a) claimed confidently and repeatedly that "it is easy to learn how to interpret dreams, to extract from the patient's associations his unconscious thoughts and memories, and to practise similar explanatory arts: for these the patient will always provide the text" (p. 116).[3] When analysts had difficulty agreeing on the interpretation of the same case material, Freud dismissed their disagreements with the ironic comment, "*Quot capita, tot sensa*"—"as many heads, so many opinions."[4] Even at the end of his career, Freud (1937b) continued to insist that psychoanalytic methods of confirming interpretations are "in every respect trustworthy" (p. 263).

The uncertainties of clinical inference and interpretation did not begin to surface in psychoanalysis until the 1950s, when Glover (1952, p. 405) and Thomas M. French (1955, pp. 502–503), working independently of each other and employing different methods of investigation, reported disturbing indications that clinical interpretation may not be as easy or reliable as Freud claimed. French was dismayed to find that individual analysts react differently to the same clinical data, and Glover expressed alarm at the variability of conclusions based upon interpretations.

The reports by Glover and French led a group of psychoanalysts in Chicago to undertake a systematic investigation of the consensus problem. Coordinated by the present writer (Seitz, 1966), the research team attempted to interpret various amounts and kinds of clinical data. We worked together for over three years, but were never able to achieve satisfactory consensus on the blind interpretation of the same case material. Since then, other investigators have documented the consensus problem;[5] and some attempts have been made, though with questionable success, to surmount this limitation of our interpretive methods.[6]

It may be some comfort to clinicians that the consensus problem is not confined to clinical interpretations by psychoanalysts and dynamic psychotherapists, but applies equally to interpretive judgments in other clinical fields,[7] and to the human and social sciences generally (Bernstein, 1988a, pp. 88–89). Since investigators in all of these disciplines have similar difficulties in agreeing on the interpretation of the same data (or texts), our problem does not appear to be that clinical data are unusually obscure; rather, interpretive methods in all fields of human study suffer from limitations of reliability. We should not be surprised, therefore, that questions of how best to infer latent contents and how to formulate and justify interpretive hypotheses in depth-psychological disciplines remain unsolved.[8]

Clinical Interpretation as a Method of Inquiry

Interpretation is an increasingly important aspect of modern thought, part of the movement from metaphysics to epistemology—away from things as they are to how things are known (Coltrera, 1981, pp. 84–85). All branches of science, including the physical sciences, employ interpretive methods of some kind and to some extent (Holt, 1978a, pp. 50–51).[9] In the human and social sciences, interpretive methods are the commonest approach to investigating human beings (Dreyfus and Rabinow, 1983, p. xxvii).[10] Interpretation is thus a general method of inquiry, and clinical interpretation a specific variety of the more general approach.[11] Psychoanalysis and dynamic psychotherapy are relative newcomers to the art and science of interpretation, which began with Aristotle (Ricoeur, 1970, p. 20).

Clinicians tend to think of interpretation mainly in the context of therapeutic interventions—the communication of depth-psychological information to patients;[12] but the interpretive process is first and foremost a form of inquiry—an attempt to gain depth-psychological information and understanding. The philosopher Michael Polanyi (1966) points out that one gains an understanding of the mind through a process of inquiry, which involves picking out clues that have a bearing on something they seem to indicate. "And as in a scientific inquiry, many of the clues will remain unspecifiable and indeed be subliminal" (p. 31).

The therapist's job is thus primarily to learn, not to teach (Schwaber, 1990b, p. 239).[13] During therapy sessions, for example, the clinician's mind is engaged in a continual process of interpretive inquiry, attempting to recognize and understand clues to unconscious meanings and determinants. Conveying depth-psychological information to patients is an important but only sporadic feature of the interpretive process.

Paradoxically, however, a vast literature has accumulated on problems of interpretive "technique," that is, whether, what, when, and how to communicate depth-psychological information to patients, while relatively little attention has been paid to our methods of seeking, construing, formulating, and justifying latent meanings and determinants. This volume, by contrast, focuses specifically on the latter problems—the methods clinicians employ in the process of interpretive inquiry.

With the increasing recognition of relational and interactive factors in the therapeutic process, some clinicians no longer consider interpretation and insight the principal determinants of therapeutic change.[14] Interpretations are viewed as part of a larger interactive process (Greenberg, 1994, p. 12).[15] Yet depth-psychological understanding seems more important than ever, for effective therapeutic interactions and accurate understanding of both patient and therapist appear to depend on and complement each other in the process of cure.[16] Thomä and Kächele (1975, p. 88) note in this connection that scientists often underestimate the role of understanding because they tend to equate it inappropriately with philosophical speculation, whereas in fact understanding is one of the conditions of progress in every field.

The clinical process of interpretive inquiry attempts to identify unconscious determinants as well as meanings. Relations between meanings and determinants are not well understood, however, and often are difficult to distinguish (Shope, 1973, pp. 284, 290, 303).[17] Historically, clinicians have assumed that in causal systems such as psychoanalysis and dynamic psychotherapy, the meanings that one construes often suggest the nature of their determinants (Edelson, 1988, p. 332).[18] The philosopher Adolf Grünbaum (1984, pp. 55–56)[19] maintains, however, that the interpretation of meaning relations in clinical data tells one nothing about underlying causal connections (for example, unconscious motives). This fundamental methodologic question has profound implications for the theory and practice of interpretive inquiry—an issue that is discussed at length in Chapter 7 of this volume.

Interpretive inquiry is an exceedingly complex and incompletely understood process which involves conscious, preconscious, and presumably also unconscious operations (compare Sandler, 1976, and Ogden, 1997, p. 587, n. 1, regarding unconscious "understanding work"), as well as numerous components and several overlapping stages, which include:

1. Various types of *prerequisite knowledge*, including "competences," which are preliminary to but necessary for interpretive work—what Gombrich (1969, p. 71) calls the interpreter's need for a "very well-stocked mind."

2. A set of *basic methodologic (core) concepts*, that is, general background assumptions (in contrast to specific clinical theories) that orient, guide, and inform interpretive inquiry (see, for example, Rapaport, 1944, pp. 182–220).

3. *Data-generating methods*, some applicable to the patient and others to the therapist. The goal of both is to produce as extensive, diverse, and relevant a data base as possible for interpretive inquiry.

4. *Data-gathering methods*, for observing and collecting as large a number and as wide a variety of clinical data as possible from both patient and therapist.

5. *Data-selection methods* and criteria, to reduce the voluminous clinical data to a workable but adequate sample of highly relevant information.

6. *Data-processing methods*, for cognitive transformation of selected clinical data and information into unique personal meanings and determinants that are specific to the individual patient.

7. *Construction* of tentative, alternative interpretive hypotheses.

8. Methods of *checking, revising, and rechecking* alternative constructions in order to determine the most plausible hypothesis.

9. Methods of *justifying* the most plausible interpretive hypothesis employing multiple criteria of evidence and truth.

10. *Reformulating* the hypothesis verbally so that it may be conveyed to and understood by the patient—the technique of interpretation.

11. *Progressive modification* of the interpretation in response to feedback from and "negotiation" (Goldberg, 1987, pp. 122–125) with the patient, as well as from further information as it accrues during the course of the therapeutic process.

12. *Reflection* on one's interpretive understanding of individual patients, which occurs both during and outside of therapy sessions and may lead to the formulation of tentative "working orientations" and "grounded hypotheses" concerning the patient and the patient-therapist dyad (Tuckett, 1994b, pp. 1174–1175).[20]

Organization of the Book

Progress in the methodology of interpretive inquiry has followed a distinctly dialectical course, marked by positivist/antipositivist, objectivist/subjectivist, intrapsychic/interpersonal, doctrinal/

contextual, instinctual drives/object relationships, conflict/deficit, insight/interaction, and other debates (compare, Grolnick, 1982, pp. 697–698). Even the origins of clinical interpretation involved methodologic conflict between Freud's positivist preference for purely observational methods versus his clinical need for a flexibly nonpositivist interpretive approach. Chapter 1 focuses on Freud's attempts to deal with that methodologic conflict; some of his attempts were prescient and productive, while others were not.

Chapter 2 reviews the paradigm shift in general science from a positivist to a postpositivist perspective, compares the two viewpoints, and stresses the compatibility of interpretive inquiry with a postpositivist approach (Nasser, 1994, p. 179). The legacy of Freud's positivism still pervades clinical thinking, however, and interferes in some ways with progress in the further investigation and development of our interpretive methodology.

Chapters 3 and 4 evaluate post-Freudian models of interpretive inquiry, focusing on problems and progress in contemporary approaches. Chapter 5 compares methods of clinical interpretive inquiry with interpretive approaches in nonclinical fields and notes particularly the potential relevance of some nonclinical approaches to the methodology of clinical interpretation. Chapter 6 evaluates a relatively new (nonclinical) model of interpretive inquiry, a depth-psychological extension of "commonsense" (intentional) psychology.

The next three chapters discuss problems and progress in justifying interpretations. There is a great deal more to know about this subject than I have included in these chapters; interested readers can consult the end-notes for suggestions about where to look for further information. Chapter 7 reviews the debate stimulated by Adolf Grünbaum's (1984, 1986, 1993) philosophical critiques of psychoanalysis. The discussion focuses specifically on aspects of the critiques and ensuing debate that bear on the probity of low-level clinical inferences and interpretations, in contrast to higher level theories. Chapter 8 evaluates various methods and models of justification and Chapter 9 presents a clinical case illustrating a pluralistic, posttherapeutic approach to interpretive justification.[21] The final chapter summarizes and attempts to integrate the principal themes and conclusions of the book.

Acknowledgments

I am indebted to many persons who have contributed, directly or indirectly, to this work. In addition to the many teachers, colleagues, students, and patients who have influenced my thinking, Thomas M. French, M.D. (1952, 1954, 1958a, 1970) first stimulated my interest in problems of interpretive methodology. Peter Caws, Ph.D. has provided helpful guidance in the philosophy of science, and has given kind permission to use a table, from his book *Structuralism: The Art of the Intelligible*, that illustrates Lévi-Strauss's method of interpreting myths. I am grateful also to Paul E. Meehl, Ph.D. and Rosemarie Sand, M.D. for permission to quote material from personal communications regarding the "causal controversy." George H. Pollack, M.D., Ph.D., Robert S. Wallerstein, M.D., and Donald P. Spence, Ph.D. have encouraged and advised me regarding publication of this work. The Department of Psychiatry (Jerry M. Wiener, M.D., former Chairman) and the Himmelfarb Medical Library Staff (especially George Paul) of the George Washington University Medical Center have provided intellectual stimulation and collegial support to me during the period of writing this book.

My sons, Chuck Seitz, Ph.D. and Franz Seitz, Ph.D., have been more than generous in their technical assistance and moral support; and I could not ask for a more knowledgeable and helpful editor than John Kerr of The Analytic Press. I am most grateful to Randi Rubovits-Seitz, M.D., who has helped me in countless ways, not least by her forbearance.

PART I

HISTORICAL BACKGROUND

The work of analysis consists of two quite different portions. . . . the person who is being analysed has to be induced to remember something that has been experienced by him and repressed; the dynamic determinants of this process are so interesting that the other portion of the work, the task performed by the analyst, has been pushed into the background.

[Sigmund Freud, 1937b, p. 258]

It is strange indeed that so little emphasis has been laid on the absolutely primal role of methodology in psychoanalysis. . . . methodology is the very essence of psychoanalysis.

[Roland Dalbiez, 1941, p. x]

Even for the practical man of today, whose science is exposed to attacks and revisions which he is supposed to assimilate or reject, some methodological thinking is indispensable.

[David Rapaport, 1967, p. 174]

The formulation of interpretations is performed, as are all of our analytic acts, under the influence of hidden preconceptions. We partly know why we formulate them as we do, and partly we do not. To discover these preconceptions and bring them to consideration is always a useful and widening enterprise.

[Dennis Duncan, 1989, p. 694]

1

Trouble at the Source

Freud's Methodologic Conflict

In one of his encyclopedia articles, Freud (1923a) noted that psychoanalysis began as an "art of *interpretation*," that is, as an attempt to discover hidden meanings in patients' associations (p. 239).[1] As a positivist, Freud would have preferred to use purely observational rather than interpretive methods (see, for example, Freud, 1914b, p. 77); for the scientific goal of positivism is the discovery of absolutely certain knowledge, obtained by rigorous observational methods applied to strictly empirical data. Freud (1937b) was intent on demonstrating that psychoanalysis is a natural science, and that its methods are "trustworthy in every respect" (p. 263). Despite his positivist ideals, however, Freud found it necessary to develop and use nonpositivist interpretive methods, because without such methods he could neither discover nor understand latent contents in his patients' communications (see, for example, Steiner, 1995, p. 437).

The methodologic conflict between Freud's positivist ideals and his clinical need for interpretive methods may have originated when he stopped using suggestion and relied completely on his patients' free associations, for at that point he needed more than a strictly observational method.[2] To understand latent meanings and determinants in such voluminous and seemingly disconnected discourse, he needed a flexible and imaginative form of interpretive methodology. This chapter examines Freud's ambivalence towards interpretive methods, and the ways he attempted to deal with the methodologic conflict. Some of his attempts were prescient and productive; others were not.

Productive Ways of Dealing With the Methodologic Conflict

First, a word about Freud's positivism: He was a positivist in the original meaning of the term—as defined by Auguste Comte (1790–1857), the French sociologist who founded the philosophical school of "Positivism" during the middle of the last century (Frank, 1957; Scharff, 1995). Comte's positivism advocated the application of scientific method not only in the physical sciences but also in human studies, employing the methods of mathematics, logic, observation, and controlled experimentation. Subsequent developments in positivism continued to emphasize the unity of the sciences and the importance of restricting science to the observable. The line of descent in the history of positivism led from Comte to members of the Vienna Circle, who developed "Logical Positivism" (or "Logical Empiricism") during the 1920s (Scriven, 1969, p. 197). Thus "Logical Positivism" did not appear until the next-to-last decade of Freud's life, whereas the influence of Comte's positivism had pervaded his entire scientific training and career. Logical positivism insisted that no hidden entities or causes should be postulated (Lacey, 1986, p. 183), a principle that was antithetical to Freud's thinking and approach. Rather, he embraced Comte's version of positivism, namely, that to carry out observations our minds need some theory. Comte wrote that, if we did not attach our observations to certain principles, we would not be able to recognize them; the facts would remain unnoticed beneath our eyes (Frank, 1957, p. 15).

Some members of the Vienna Circle were sympathetic to Freud's work, however, because it "revealed connections between a great range of new and surprising observed facts" (Frank, 1957, pp. 308–309). Chertok (1968) illustrates Freud's innovative concepts with the following example: Realizing the dangers of erotic complications, investigators of the psychotherapeutic relationship prior to Freud had become very cautious about any affective involvement with female patients. Breuer had become entangled in such a complication and had fled from the problem, giving up his research on hysteria:

> Freud, placed in a similar predicament, confronted the situation. He found a method of defense, which consisted in the belief that the patient was establishing a "false connection," and that her emotional demands were not directed to him personally, but to some person belonging to the patient's more remote past. It is thus that his concern for his own protection led him to a most productive discovery—that of the transference [Chertok, 1968, p. 575].

Despite his lasting commitment to the original form of positivism, Freud's psychological investigations suggest that in some important respects he was able to surmount the methodologic strictures of positivism and to anticipate the development of postpositivist science. Izenberg (1976, p. 13) notes, for example, that it was Freud who broke with the conventional approach of nineteenth-century psychiatry. By postulating hidden intentions, emotions, and beliefs in neurotic behavior, he called into question the prevailing medical model of mental illness.

Additional examples of Freud's (1923a) flexibility and farsightedness in this regard include his leaving a great deal of discretion in clinical interpretation to the individual clinician's tact and skill, rather than applying strict rules to the practice of interpretation (p. 239); his (unacknowledged) breaking of certain technical rules to deal with the conflict between his patients' needs and his own wish to promote the scientific standing of psychoanalysis (Kris, 1994, p. 662); and his occasional, though wavering, acceptance of some limitations regarding the reliability of clinical observations and interpretations, as for example in his acknowledgment that one may sometimes make a wrong surmise, and is never in a position to discover the whole truth (Freud, 1910c, p. 226; see also 1925a, pp. 127–130).

Noting that science does not consist of strictly proved theses, Freud (1915–16, p. 51) also recognized the necessity to employ circumstantial evidence; most scientific propositions have only a variable degree of probability. To Freud, acceptance of such approximations and continuing one's investigative work in the absence of final confirmation indicates a scientific attitude.

During the 1920s, Freud (1923a) acknowledged still further uncertainties regarding his observational and interpretive methods:

> Psycho-analysis is not, like philosophies, a system starting out from a few sharply defined basic concepts, seeking to grasp the whole universe with the help of these and, once it is completed, having no room for fresh discoveries or better understanding. On the contrary, it keeps close to the facts in its field of study, seeks to solve the immediate problems of observation, gropes its way forward by the help of experience, is always incomplete and always ready to correct or modify its theories [p. 253].

Freud still claimed, however, that "with impartiality and practice" it was usually possible to obtain trustworthy results, that is, results confirmed by their repetition in similar cases (p. 239). The latter statement is still tinged with hopes of certainty; but, by use of the qualifying term usually, Freud hinted, at least, that "trustworthy" and "confirmed" knowledge is not always possible with psychoanalytic interpretive methods. In the same paragraph Freud stated that his original interpretive method was still being used, "though with a sense of greater assurance and with a better understanding of its limitations" (p. 239). Mentioning improvement of his interpretive method and also understanding of its limitations in the same sentence illustrates the transitional stage that Freud appears to have reached during the 1920s between a positivist and a postpositivist perspective regarding psychoanalysis and its interpretive methodology.

The same mixture of positivist and postpositivist viewpoints is evident in the last writings published during Freud's lifetime. "Analysis Terminable and Interminable" (Freud, 1937a) emphasizes the limitations of psychoanalysis, whereas "Constructions in Analysis" (Freud, 1937b) alternates between positivist assertions regarding the confirmation of constructions, which Freud insisted were completely trustworthy, and scientifically more tentative statements such as, "We do not pretend that an individual construction is anything more than a conjecture which awaits examination, confirmation, or rejection" (p. 265). Thus the transition between positivist and postpositivist viewpoints that characterized Freud's thinking about psychoanalysis and its interpretive methodology during the 1920s appears to have remained largely unchanged during the final decade of his life.

In addition to the appropriate and useful ways that Freud dealt with the posited methodologic conflict, another set of his reactions appears to have been counterproductive. Clinical necessity forced him to employ interpretive methods, but in compliance with his positivist ideals:

1. He attempted to minimize the role and importance of interpretations in his methodology.
2. He never described his interpretive methods clearly or systematically.
3. He attempted to make his interpretations appear objectively empirical, certain, and reliable, as his positivist ideals demanded.
4. He attempted to shift the task of interpretation to the patient and focused on the fallibility of ancient interpretive methods rather than studying the limitations of his own approach.
5. He ignored the investigations of interpretation by a renowned contemporary hermeneutic scholar, Wilhelm Dilthey, and did not acknowledge his intellectual debt to his teacher, Franz Brentano.
6. He became hypersensitive and overreacted if his empiricism and objectivity were questioned.
7. He devalued methodologists and depreciated their standards of objectivity as excessive.

Minimizing the Role of Interpretations

Perhaps the simplest way for Freud to minimize the role and importance of interpretation in his methodology was to avoid the subject—to say as little as possible about it in his writings. To illustrate, the General Subject Index of the *Standard Edition* (Richards, 1974, pp. 309–310) includes only eleven references to interpretation, most of which deal with the issue of interpreting sensory stimuli. None of the references deals with interpretive methodology. One reference concerns the "ease" of interpreting patients' secret wishes (Freud, 1913a, p. 140); and another refers to the "complete certainty" of interpretations (Freud, 1913b, p. 208).

Another example of Freud's saying very little about interpretation occurs in one of his most important case histories, that of the

Wolf Man (Freud, 1918). In that entire case report Freud mentions only a single, minor interpretation that he communicated to the patient (pp. 89–90). Namnum (1978) asks in this connection: "In his comments on technique, including all the later papers, why did Freud not use the term *interpretation*, which now seems to us so apt, so familiar—indeed, so indispensable?" (pp. 318–319). Namnum notes further that even when Freud did use the term "interpretation" (as in Freud, 1937b, p. 261), "he did so only to criticize that general usage and to propose instead *constructions*, a term with no transitive form" (Namnum, 1978, pp. 318–319). Freud's (1940a) posthumously published "Outline" also does not mention the term interpretation in its discussion of technique, but refers to the "information" we give the patient in the form of a "translation" of his or her associations (p. 174). In his essay on lay analysis, Freud (1926a) refers to interpretation through his imaginary interlocutor, who expostulates, "'Interpret!' A nasty word! I dislike the sound of it; it robs me of all certainty. If everything depends on my interpretation who can guarantee that I interpret right?" (p. 219).

Leavy (1980, pp. 23–24) observes that, except for *The Interpretation of Dreams* (Freud, 1900), Freud was consistently uninformative regarding his method of interpretation. Even his papers on technique avoid the question of how clinicians arrive at their interpretations (Coltrera, 1981, p. 86; Rangell, 1987, pp. 10–11). *The Interpretation of Dreams* itself has surprisingly little to say about how to identify, construe, formulate, and justify latent meanings and determinants. Its 750 pages deal almost entirely with Freud's theory of dream formation, rather than with his methods of interpreting dreams. One comparatively brief chapter focuses on interpretive methods, which Freud illustrates with his "Specimen Dream" of Irma's injection (pp. 96–121); another small section suggests a number of theory-driven interpretive heuristics based upon postulated mechanisms of representation in dream formation (pp. 310–338).

Eissler (1985) suggests that Freud probably fabricated the Specimen Dream in order to demonstrate his thesis that dreams can be interpreted—which may explain the asseverative tone and content of the chapter, in contrast to a more substantive and detailed description of his interpretive methods. Eissler's suggestion also raises the question whether Chapter 2 in *The Interpretation of Dreams* can be considered a true picture of Freud's interpretive approach.

Another example of Freud's taciturnity with respect to interpretive methods is the brief section in one of his encyclopedia articles entitled, "Psychoanalysis as an Interpretive Art" (Freud, 1923a, pp. 238–241). The latter section is a highly condensed overview of clinical interpretation and says very little about the actual methods, strategies, and heuristics that guide interpretive work.

Still another example of Freud's minimizing the role of interpretation in his methodology is his proposal of *lapsus linguae* as the model of psychoanalytic investigation. He suggested that one ask the speaker why he had made the slip and what could the speaker say about it? If the person who made the slip then offered an explanation by saying the first thing that occurred to him, "this small active step and its successful outcome are already a psychoanalysis and are a model for every psychoanalytic investigation" (Freud, 1916–17, pp. 47–48). Note, however, that this model of psychoanalysis does not include interpretation. Freud gives the impression that a person's first association to a slip is transparent, that it provides the unconscious meaning of a slip without interpretation, which overlooks the central role of interpretation in his methodology.[3]

Other writers have noted that Freud sometimes dealt with clinical problems by avoiding or minimizing them. Greenberg (1986, pp. 240–241) observes, for example, that Freud minimized the problem of therapeutic outcome by seldom mentioning it, focusing instead on theoretical issues. Grünbaum (1993, pp. 185–186) points out that Freud was disinclined to attribute therapeutic failure to incorrect interpretations; he considered therapeutic failure compatible with correctness of interpretations and blamed poor therapeutic results on patients' resistances (see, for example, Freud, 1920b, p. 164).

Wax (1995, p. 551) suspects, however, that at some level Freud must have realized the interpretive nature of his clinical work;[4] but the paradox is that, despite his emphasis on constructing the patient's life story, he did not appear to recognize or attempt to deal with the methodologic problems involved in understanding the meanings of their various communications.

By minimizing the role and uncertainties of interpretive methods in clinical practice, Freud set a problematic precedent for psychoanalysis and dynamic psychotherapy which continues to the present day. To illustrate: (1) Although many clinicians would agree that the construal of latent meanings and determinants is an important part of therapeutic work, some may not appreciate just how central and pervasive its importance is; for aside from what a patient actually says and does during therapy sessions, everything else is inferred (Meehl, 1973, p. 117). (2) Like Freud, relatively few clinicians acknowledge in published or presented reports the uncertainty of their interpretations. (3) Descriptions of how clinicians arrive at specific interpretations are rare. (4) Attempts to justify interpretations are virtually nonexistent. (5) Some recent empirical investigations suggest that the average level of interpretive accuracy by clinicians is low (Crits-Christoph, Cooper, and Luborsky, 1988).

Never Describing His Interpretive Methods Clearly or Systematically

Another way that Freud minimized the role and importance of interpretation in his methodology was by not presenting a systematic description of his interpretive approach (compare Kerr, 1994, p. 8, 62–63, 65). His avowed reasons for the omission, mentioned in the Dora case (Freud, 1905a, pp. 11–12), were that a description of interpretive methods would lead to "hopeless confusion," and would distract from his theoretical discussions.

What did Freud mean by that statement? Did he mean that interpretive methods are so complex and poorly understood that they cannot be explicated? Or that interpreters would not be able to agree on methods of construing latent contents? Or did he use "hopeless confusion" and "distraction from theoretical discussions" as rationalizations, to keep from discussing a subject that was problematic for other reasons, for example, its incompatibility with his positivist ideals for psychoanalysis (see, for example, Hertz, 1983)? A possible answer to these questions is suggested later.

In lieu of a clear exposition of his interpretive methods by Freud, Grinstein (1983) has attempted to systematize Freud's "rules" and suggestions regarding dream interpretation. Combing the Freudian corpus for such references, Grinstein found a variety of comments on interpretation scattered throughout Freud's writings. Close reading of Grinstein's text reveals, however, that there really are no hard and fast "rules" of interpretive methodology, rules implying invariant procedures; and there actually is no organized, articulated system of interpretive methods in Freud's approach (see also Hartmann, 1951; Blomfield, 1982, p. 289).

The largely ad hoc nature of interpretation, which varies with each interpreter (Seitz, 1966) and with each change of clinical context (Caston, 1993a; Caston and Martin, 1993) appears to preclude systematization of interpretive methodology (see, for example, Mahoney and Singh, 1979, p. 439). Interpretation is guided by an extensive, loosely knit collection of heuristics rather than by rules (see, for example, Lloyd, 1989, p. 213). The uncertainty of such methods and the unpredictability of their results may well have been the basis of Freud's ambivalence towards interpretation. The "hopeless confusion" of which Freud wrote in justifying the omission of his interpretive methods may have alluded, therefore, to the relatively uncertain nature of interpretive methods and conclusions. To maintain his positivist image and convictions, Freud may have decided not to open that can of worms.

Attempt to Make His Interpretations Appear Empirically Objective and Certain

In keeping with his positivist ideals, Freud (1916–17) attempted to make his interpretations appear as empirically objective, scientific, and certain as possible. He emphasized the role of causation by using terms like "motive," "goal," "intention," and "purpose" in his explanations of symptoms (pp. 61, 107). Shope (1973, p. 276) and Grünbaum (1984, pp. 66–67; 1989, p. 479) also stress Freud's emphasis on "causal continuity" in his concept of meaning. At the same time, however, Freud (1916–17) also referred to the meaning of symptoms in a semantic or communicative sense (p. 36). Wallace (1985) notes in this connection that Freud, "was too good a clinician not to recognize that, however much he longed to theorize in terms of biological tensions, excitations, and drives, in the consulting room he dealt with mental experience and human communication" (p. 161). Wallace concludes that Freud attempted to resolve the tension between his positivism and clinical realities by employing a teleological concept of psychic causation while paying lip service to mechanistic concepts.

Izenberg (1976, pp. 17–19) contrasts Freud's definition of interpretation (for example, 1900, p. 96) to the concepts of *Verstehen* proposed by Dilthey, Simmel, Weber, and Jaspers. *Verstehen* views meaning as immanent in the object to be interpreted, and attempts to draw out the meaning in terms of manifest contextual significance. Freud, on the other hand, replaced the material to be interpreted with another element, which itself was meaningful but causally related to the original material.

Schimek (1975, pp. 845–846) suggests that Freud attempted to reduce his interpretations of meanings mediated by symbolic and linguistic processes to causal connections between "factual" events and the "natural" forces associated with them. By equating interpretations with causal explanations based upon the same types of causal inferences which are fundamental to the natural sciences, Freud presented his methodology as basically observational, supplemented only by necessary causal inferences, and thus an empirical foundation for psychoanalysis. Terwee (1987, p. 362) concludes similarly that Freud attempted to justify his interpretations by appealing to causal laws.

Another strategy for making his interpretations appear objectively empirical was to assert repeatedly his unwavering commitment to empirical observation. Freud wrote (1914b), for example, that speculative ideas are not the foundation on which science rests, that foundation being observation alone (p. 77). Freud's assertions of this kind appear to have convinced some psychoanalysts of his resolute adherence to empirical observation. For example, Gedo et al. (1964, p. 747) and also Meissner (1971, p. 305) present idealized descriptions of Freud's empiricism; but Freud did not always distinguish clearly between observations and inferences (Holt, 1992, pp. 378–379). In one of his writings Freud (1914b) referred to psychoanalysis as, "a science erected on empirical interpretation" (p. 77). Terwee (1987, p. 362) concludes that the level of observation and evidence in Freud's writings is actually the level of clinical interpretation.

Freud was at pains to assure readers that he based his conclusions on extensive clinical observations rather than on interpretations derived from his own theories.[5] The following quotations from various periods of his career illustrate the tone and content of Freud's assertions regarding his empiricism. Only the final example mentions interpretive activity, which he refers to as "drawing undeniable conclusions":

> I can only assure the reader that I approached the study of the phenomena revealed by observation of the psychoneuroses

> without being pledged to any particular psychological system [Freud, 1905a, pp. 112–113].

> I cannot guarantee the completeness of my results, but I can answer for the care taken in arriving at them [Freud, 1908, p. 210].

> I learnt to restrain speculative tendencies and to follow the unforgotten advice of my master, Charcot: to look at the same things again and again until they themselves begin to speak [Freud, 1914a, p. 22].

> Psychoanalysis is founded securely upon the observation of the facts of mental life [Freud, 1926b, p. 266].

> [M]y working hypotheses invariably came about as a direct result of a great number of impressions based on experience [cited by E. Freud, 1960, p. 396].

> [T]he associations give us far more than we need for formulating the latent dream-thoughts—namely, all the explanations, transitions, and connections which the patient's intellect is bound to produce in the course of his approach to the dream thoughts. On the other hand, an association often comes to a stop precisely before the genuine dream thought: it has only come near to it and has only had contact with it through allusions. At that point we intervene on our own; we fill in the hints, draw undeniable conclusions, and give explicit utterance to what the patient has only touched on in his associations [Freud, 1933, p. 12].

Statements of this kind by Freud can be questioned from several standpoints. Is it plausible, for example, that he was theoretically uncommitted to his own psychological system? And is his disavowal of speculation tenable? The construal phase of the interpretive process requires imaginative speculation in search of possible alternative hypotheses. Freud's use of terms like "founded," "invariably," "great number," "facts," "observation," and "direct result" express positivist ideals of empiricism, objectivity, and certainty; but they also suggest a rhetorical intention to persuade. In addition to its exaggerated empirical claims ("the associations give us far more than we need for formulating the latent dream-thoughts"), the final quotation also illustrates Freud's attempt to present clinical interpretation as an essentially observational process which is transparent, objective, and certain—a relatively uncomplicated procedure of filling in hints, "drawing undeniable conclusions," and thus making the patient's allusions explicit.

Freud's frequent and insistent protests regarding his empiricism, his disavowal of allegiance to any theoretical system (including his own), and the relative absence of references to interpretive inferences and conjectures in association with his observations, support the conclusion that he downplayed the role of interpretive methods in psychoanalysis and attempted to put as empirical a face as possible on his methodology.

Freud (1916–1917) was deeply concerned about the charge that interpretations produced their effects through suggestion. In addition to his extensive previous experience with suggestive methods and patient compliance, another important reason for his concern was that "there is a risk that influencing our patient may make the objective certainty of our findings doubtful" (p. 452). Thus, to satisfy positivist criteria of completely certain as well as objective knowledge, Freud attempted to make his interpretations appear as veridical as possible. For example, while discussing the role of inference in psychoanalytic work, he stated unequivocally that psychoanalytic technique "holds its ground against any criticism" (Freud, 1940a, p. 159).

Leaving aside the dogmatic quality and overcompensatory implications of the preceding assertion, Freud's statement suggests that he did not fully appreciate the complexities, uncertainties, and unsolved problems of interpretive methods. For example, unlike strictly natural science approaches, interpretive methodologies do not derive from or depend upon scientific laws, nomic universals, or even a formal theoretical structure. Rather, the only solid referent to interpretive statements is their empirical bearing (McIntosh, 1979, pp. 408–409). The grounding of interpretations is never entirely empirical, however, but relies also on a network of additional, interdependent interpretations which undergo continuous, progressive modification. The same holds true of inferences generally; that is, one induction corrects another induction—we make most inferences not in isolation, but within a network of inductions (Reichenbach, 1951, pp. 240–248). Thus to understand a particular meaning one must turn to wider contexts that precede and follow the data in question (Peterfreund, 1971, pp. 239–241); and since the adjacent contexts must themselves be interpreted, the grounding of individual interpretations is not tied to any single set of observables (Gergen, 1988, p. 35).

The grounding of individual interpretations is thus neither scientific law, nomic universal, formal theoretical structure, nor even purely observed fact, but is largely a shifting, ever-unfolding context of interpreted events (see, for example, Gaudin, 1987, p. xxxiii). Hence the cogent observation by Tuckett (1994a) that, "Interpretations rest on interpretations, rest on interpretations, rest on interpretations, etc." (p. 869). As a result, every possible aspect of interpretation involves an element of uncertainty, an epistemologic gap which must be considered a defining feature of interpretation (Hirsch, 1967, p. 322). And because of these methodologic limitations, depth psychologists must be content to allow latent meanings and determinants to accrue gradually, rather than feeling pressured to make immediate interpretive use of current clinical data (compare Ogden, 1997, p. 570).

Throughout his writings Freud said almost nothing about the methodologic problems and limitations of interpreting clinical data. He minimized the difficulties and fallibility of interpretation, insisting that free association provides a "plentiful store of ideas" that put the therapist on the right track of unconscious processes; and that clinical data contain such "plain and numerous hints" that the therapist is able to guess what is repressed (Freud, 1924, pp. 195–196). He believed and stated that "it is not difficult for a skilled analyst to read the patient's secret wishes plainly between the lines of his complaints and the story of his illness" (Freud, 1913a, p. 140).[6] Thus, to make his interpretive methods appear reliable and his constructions certain, Freud sometimes lapsed into scholasticism. As Shope (1987) observes, "even psychoanalysts sometimes express distress over the extreme confidence that Freud frequently expressed in his interpretations" (p. 209; see also Rubinstein, 1997, p. 563).

Shifting the Task of Interpretation to the Patient, and the Fallibility of Interpretations to Ancient Methods

Freud (1900, p. 98) noted that ancient (Greco-Roman) dream interpretation also employed the principle of association, but in an incorrect way, that is, deriving meanings from what the dream elements brought to the mind of the interpreter. Freud used this historical information tendentiously. Rather than recognizing and acknowledging the problems and limitations of his own interpretive approach, he attributed interpretive fallibility to the ancient interpretive method: "An insuperable source of arbitrariness and uncertainty arises from the fact that the dream-element may recall various things to the interpreter's mind and may recall something different to different interpreters" (p. 98, fn. 1). In describing his own approach, Freud claimed that his procedure eliminated the unreliability of the ancient method. He wrote that his technique

> differs in one essential respect from the ancient method: it imposes the task of interpretation upon the dreamer himself. It is not concerned with what occurs to the *interpreter* in connection with a particular element of the dream, but with what occurs to the *dreamer* [p. 98, fn. 1].[7]

Freud neglected to mention, however, that the patient's associations, by themselves, do not provide the latent contents of a dream; that the therapist responds to the patient's associations with his or her own associations (for example, thoughts, fantasies, memories, feelings, and images); and that the interpretation which results derives from both the patient's and therapist's associations, and from a highly complex process of data processing by the clinician. Freud's attempt to shift the task of interpretation to the patient is misleading, therefore, and does not exempt the clinician from active participation in the construal of latent mental contents.

Ignoring Interpretive Methods and Concepts In Other Disciplines

Interpretive methods became indispensable to Freud's clinical approach, but he lacked expertise in the theory and methodology of interpretation. A few years earlier, when he needed to learn more about the method of hypnosis, he had travelled to Paris to study with Charcot; but when he needed to learn more about interpretive methodology, he did not seek or use some highly relevant knowledge of interpretation that was available to him. He remained self-taught in the theory, methodology, and practice of clinical interpretation.

Freud could have learned a great deal from the work of Wilhelm Dilthey, a German cultural historian and leading contemporary hermeneuticist, who lived from 1833 to 1911. Hermeneutics had expanded rapidly in a number of fields during the latter half of the 19th century, and Dilthey (1958, 1961, 1976) was its principal spokesperson.[8] Dilthey saw in hermeneutics the possibility of a methodologic foundation for the human and social sciences—disciplines which, like psychoanalysis but unlike the natural sciences, attempt to interpret the manifold expressions of the inner life of human beings.

Dilthey and Freud faced similar intellectual tasks, namely, synthesizing disparate epistemologic and methodologic perspectives. Izenberg (1976, p. 13) points out that, independently and almost simultaneously, Dilthey and Freud recognized the need for a genetic and historical approach to psychology. Dilthey's view that study of the individual required a hermeneutic method found a parallel in Freud's use of clinical interpretation (see also Sulloway, 1983, p. xvi).

Dilthey's aim was to develop objectively valid methods of interpretation for the human and social sciences, which conceivably might have interested Freud during the years prior to 1900 when he was engaged in writing his *magnum opus* on the interpretation of dreams; for Freud labored under both inner and outer pressures to make his own interpretations as objectively scientific as possible (Havens, 1973, p. 287).

Another parallel between the two men was Freud's use of a part-whole concept similar to that of hermeneutic methodology, for example, his insistence that the meaning of any fragment depends upon the meaning of the whole (Freud, 1911b, p. 93; 1916–17, pp. 108–109). Both Freudian and hermeneutic approaches to interpretation require the ability to perceive the multiplicities of "part" meanings in the material while simultaneously recognizing the central theme (or "whole" meaning) that runs like an undercurrent through all of the data.

Parallels such as the foregoing led Habermas (1971, p. 214) to conclude that Freud based his interpretation of dreams on the hermeneutic model of philological research;[9] but in a cogent study of Freud and interpretation, Kermode (1985, p. 7) concludes that Freud ignored Dilthey. I concur with Kermode's conclusion: that is, ignoring Dilthey's important work on the methodology of interpretation may have represented yet another way that Freud avoided the subject of interpretation, and by doing so minimized its role and importance in his methodology.

Freud also ignored a seminal contribution by his teacher, Franz Brentano (1874), whose work pointed to a nonpositivist view of psychology. A number of writers[10] have called attention to suggestive parallels between Freud's theory of mind and the theory of intentionality developed by Brentano (see Chapter 6 for a fuller discussion of this issue).

Becoming Hypersensitive to Criticism of His Methodology

A dramatic incident in Freud's relationship with Fliess suggests that Freud may have become hypersensitive and prone to overreact if his empiricism and objectivity were questioned. During their final "Congress" at Achensee, Fliess raised the question whether Freud might be reading his own ideas into his patients' associations. Freud found the question so objectionable that it contributed to his withdrawal from Fliess (Meehl, 1983; see also Mautner, 1994). From the standpoint of the present thesis, Fliess' question may have disturbed Freud's positivist scientific conscience. Freud must have realized at some level that his clinical "observations" were not as pure, uncontaminated by presuppositions, or as certain as his positivism demanded.[11] Interpreting the incident in clinical terms, Freud may have dealt with the inner disturbance produced by Fliess's question by projecting his own overly strict positivist conscience to Fliess, and then withdrawing from Fliess as a demanding and hypercritical superego-figure. Rubinstein (1997, p. 558) cites Sulloway (1979, p. 99) and Jones (1953, p. 255) regarding a similar "completely unreasonable reaction" by Freud to criticism from Breuer.

Devaluing Methodologists

Ekstein (1959, p. 226; see also 1978) reports a possibly related incident in which Freud harshly denounced methodologists as people who spend all of their time cleaning their eyeglasses without ever looking through them. In that instance, Freud may have projected his own demanding positivist conscience to methodologists, whom he then devalued critically for excessive and unproductive standards of objectivity. Again, it may have been Freud's own positivist-empirical ideals that were excessive and in some respects unproductive: for example, they appear to have interfered with full acceptance, investigation, and more complete development of his interpretive methods, compelling him to seek, and at times to overstate, a degree of methodologic reliability and factual certainty which are unattainable with interpretive methods.

Summary

This chapter argues that Freud set a problematic precedent for psychanalysis and dynamic psychotherapy by neglecting problems of interpretive methodology. Freud appears to have struggled with a methodologic conflict between his positivist ideals, on the one hand, and his clinical need for flexible, nonpositivist interpretive methods, on the other. Freud's positivist preferences for pure observation, objectivity, and certainty contributed to his ambivalence towards interpretive methods.

In some respects Freud overcame the excessive strictures of positivism and anticipated the development of postpositivist science, for example, by developing imaginative and productive methods of construing latent meanings and determinants. Some of the ways that he attempted to cope with the methodologic conflict were counterproductive, however. For example, in compliance with his positivist ideals Freud's writings attempted to minimize the role and importance of interpretations in his methodology; he never described his interpretive methods clearly or systematically; he attempted to make his interpretations appear objectively empirical, certain, and reliable; he attempted to shift the task of interpretation to the patient, and emphasized the fallibility of ancient interpretive methods rather than studying the problems and limitations of his own approach; he ignored what might have been useful methods and concepts of interpretation in other disciplines; he became hypersensitive and overreacted if his empiricism and objectivity were questioned; and he devalued methodologists, depreciating their standards of objectivity as excessive.

Freud never fully relinquished his positivist ideals, but erected the above-mentioned compromises in an effort to accomodate both his clinical need for interpretation and his positivist preference for "objective truth." He attempted to make psychoanalysis both a clinical art and a positivist science. His positivist aspirations live on in the scientific lore that underlies psychoanalysis, and contribute to the continuing neglect of problems in our interpretive methodology.

2

The Postpositivist Turn and the "Lingering Ghost of Positivism" in Interpretive Methodology

The positivist model defined knowledge narrowly as empirical, objective, and certain. Positivists evaluated human studies by the same standards, that is, data and methods that produced certain knowledge, or "objective truth" (von Wright, 1971, p. 121). Nagel (1959, pp. 49–50) insisted, for example, that unless data were obtained under carefully standardized conditions, even an extensive collection of data (as in psychoanalysis or dynamic psychotherapy) is an unreliable basis for inference.

By the middle of this century, however, positivism had come under increasing attack from several directions; and by the 1960s, most scientists and philosophers recognized that the logical-empirical paradigm could not provide a secure foundation for absolutely certain knowledge (see, for example, Bonjour, 1978; Bauer, 1992). With the downfall of positivism, a radical shift or "postpositivist turn" has occurred in both the philosophy and the conduct of science (Polkinghorne, 1983, pp. 1–57). Human and social scientists have reexamined their methodologies, leading to broader understanding of science and novel approaches to inquiry (Stent, 1975; Nasser, 1994). The previously vaunted unity of science is no longer widely accepted; science has become increasingly diverse and pluralistic, each domain developing its own terminology, methods, and concepts (Colby and Stoller, 1988, p. 12).

Unlike positivism, postpositivist science questions the notion of certain truth, challenges foundationalism, and holds that human beings, including scientists, have no direct access to truth (Rescher, 1982, pp. 218–219; Beahrs, 1986). Direct, nonpresumptive knowledge is not possible; indirect, inferential, presumptive knowing is the best that we can do (Overman, 1988, p. 335). Lewis Thomas (1978) comments in this connection that the most significant contribution of twentieth century science to human intelligence is recognition of the depth and scope of our ignorance. We are finally getting glimpses of how vast the questions are, and how far they are from being answered. "Because of this, these are hard times for the human mind" (p. 1462; see also Ziman, 1978, p. 148).

Postpositivist science, however, is not a unified school of thought having distinct scientific propositions of its own. It does not seek to replace the positivist paradigm with a single, specific, postpositivist approach. It is primarily an attitude or perspective regarding science and inquiry, namely, that there is no one correct method to follow (Bauer, 1992). Science is not a system of following methodologic rules that lead to acceptable results. Science is a search for better understanding by employing whatever methods are relevant to the problems being studied. One of the investigator's tasks, therefore, is to find or devise methods and strategies that can answer the questions being asked (Polkinghorne, 1983, pp. 3–4; Hull, 1988, p. 516).

Percival Bridgman expressed this attitude bluntly: The scientific method is simply doing one's damnedest with one's mind, no holds barred.[1] Medawar (1969) quips that when scientists are asked about the scientific method, they become "solemn and shifty-eyed" (cited by Colby and Stoller, 1988, p. 19). Feyerabend (1975, p. 28) contends that there is only one methodologic rule in science that applies under all circumstances: "anything goes" (but some limitations of that view are discussed later).

The postpositivist perspective has resulted in a growing trend toward less formalized, more pragmatic, eclectic, qualitative, and problem-oriented approaches to scientific inquiry. In this "new paradigm" which emphasizes qualitative methods, data are collected and analyzed in a more flexible, discovery-oriented, open-ended manner.[2] The qualitative approach does not exclude traditional hypothesis testing, however, but goes beyond it in a number of ways (Stiles, 1994, pp. 158–164; 1993):

1. Results are expressed mainly in words rather than numbers, for example, in dialogues and narratives which may not be coded, rated, or reduced to numbers of any kind.

2. Empathy is used as an interpretive method, emphasizing the meanings, purposes, and significance of what people say and do.

3. Results are interpreted and reported contextually; and since each context is unique, no two events are exactly alike.

4. Recognition is given to the polydimensionality of experience, and to the variations associated with each dimension.

5. Recognition is given also to nonlinear causality, including systems which involve feedback and may behave unpredictably. Such systems can be completely deterministic but impossible to predict more than a few steps ahead because of sensitivity to initial conditions.

The foregoing characteristics make the epistemology of qualitative approaches more pluralistic and tentative than that of traditional hypothesis-testing methodologies. Rather than a single, overarching epistemology, postpositivist science accepts multiple systems of inquiry, each of which contributes progressive approximations to more "truthlike" knowledge. Human and social scientists in particular feel freer to experiment with diverse epistemologic frameworks that are foundationless, relativistic, and pluralistic (MacKay, 1989, p. 2; Wimsatt, 1994, p. 494). Everything is revisable, including common sense (Churchland, cited in Callebaut, 1993, p. 16).

Contrary to positivism, methods in postpositivist science are determined and shaped by the system of inquiry in which they are employed. A method is not an isolated activity operating independently of a system of inquiry. Investigators, including interpreters, often require novel methods designed specifically for a particular problem being studied. An example is the work of Osgood, Suci, and Tannenbaum (1957) on the measurement of meaning. The method they developed, the "Semantic Differential," has no standard concepts or scales, the latter being adapted to whatever specific problem is studied. In other words, the nature of the problem defines the method, rather than the other way around. Single methodological perspectives with clearly defined procedures are understandably tempting to investigators, but they are illusory because they ignore the anomalous aspects of human experience (Polkinghorne, 1983, p. 9).

The relativism (or perspectivism) of postpositivist science recognizes that all of our knowledge is conditional, that is, formulated within particular conceptual systems; but the context-bound character of knowledge does not necessitate a complete relativism. Between the extremes of absolute certainty and absolute uncertainty, alternative knowledge claims within the same conceptual system can be assessed by comparison with each other in relation to available data; thus some interpretive hypotheses (within the same conceptual system) can be accepted and others rejected. Diverse conceptual frameworks within a particular discipline, which generate different interpretations or explanations of the same phenomena, also do not pose a crisis epistemologically or methodologically; for choice of a specific reference frame does not imply that the approach and its results are valid, but only that it is capable of proposing plausible hypotheses to interpret or explain the phenomena (Miller, 1987, p. 501).

On the other hand, the fact that all knowledge is formulated within particular conceptual systems does produce serious problems of communication between colleagues identified with different schools of thought. We tend to translate other theories into our own conceptual framework in an attempt to understand them, but it is important to understand a hypothesis in the context of its own conceptual framework. If we interpret it according to our own way of thinking, we change its meaning, distort it, and interpret only a caricature (Diesing, 1985a, pp. 82–84). Spence (1982a, p. 256) emphasizes the need to adopt a colleague's "metaphor" in order to understand his or her interpretive reasoning and conclusions. And Schwaber (1983a, b, 1986) employs a similar transformation of mental set in relation to patients, that is, adopting the patient's perspective in order to understand his or her psychic reality.

The search for knowledge in the human and social sciences (including psychoanalysis and dynamic psychotherapy) continues to employ two very dissimilar methodologic approaches: one which is research-oriented, positivistic, quantitative, objective, and cumulative; and another which is clinically-oriented and predominantly humanistic, subjective, qualitative, interpretive, pluralistic, and noncumulative (Overman, 1988, pp. vii–xix). Modell (1978a,b) suggests that the two perspectives are related by a principle such as Bohr's complementarity. Some writers (for example, Talley et al., 1994) stress the importance of uniting empirical research and clinical practice, but so far the two camps remain separate and have relatively little influence on each other.

For more detailed descriptions and discussions of positivism, see Achinstein and Barker's (1969) *The Legacy of Logical Positivism—*

especially Michael Scriven's chapter, "Logical Positivism and the Behavioral Sciences" (pp. 195–210) and Achinstein's chapter, "Approaches to the Philosophy of Science" (pp. 259–291). Polkinghorne's (1983) *Methodology for the Human Sciences* is an accessible and informative treatise on the postpositivist perspective in contemporary science. Nasser (1994) discusses the significance of the postpositivist turn for psychoanalysis and dynamic psychotherapy. Leary (1994) and also Seidman (1994) have written useful reviews of the related, but not identical, "postmodern" perspective. Barratt (1993) examines the relation of postmodern views to psychoanalysis.

Table 2-1 presents a schematic comparison of positivist and postpositivist perspectives:

Table 2-1

Comparison of Positivist and Postpositivist Perspectives

Positivism	Postpositivism
Method-oriented	Problem-oriented
Foundationalist	Antifoundationalist
Monistic	Pluralistic
Absolutist	Relativist
Rule-governed	Flexible
Doctrinal, Theory-driven	Data-driven, Context-sensitive, Heuristic, Pattern-seeking
Apodictic knowledge (Neopositivism: Probabilistic)	Assertorial knowledge, Probabilistic
Verification: Correspondence theory, Prediction	Justification: Coherence, correspondence, pragmatic; Multiple methods

Interpretive Methodology and the "Lingering Ghost of Postivism"

Clinical interpretive methods originated during the positivist era, but much of their development has occurred during the postpositivist period. Kermode (1985, pp. 3–4) notes that positivist assumptions began to be questioned during Freud's lifetime. New concepts arose about what constitutes valid interpretation, and natural science approaches began to seem less appropriate for the human sciences. But Freud took little notice of these changes.[3]

Many clinicians since Freud also appear to have taken little notice of these changes. The fact that, like Freud, most psychoanalysts and dynamic psychotherapists in North America are physicians may tend to perpetuate a positivist perspective; for physicians are trained primarily in biological science. As the evolutionary geneticist R. C. Lewontin (1994, p. 479) observes, most biologists are really positivists in their attitudes towards research, evidence, proof, and in the form of their scientific reports. The methodologic preferences and even the case reports of many medically-trained psychoanalysts retain the positivist stamp of their basic training in biology. Leavy (1980, pp. 4–11) also emphasizes the role of the medical setting and of the clinical-historical method in the origins and traditions of clinical interpretive inquiry.

What Spence (1984a) calls the "lingering ghost of positivism" (see also Agassi, 1981) still pervades our thinking, and some of the same positivist-based blind spots that Freud was unable to surmount limit the vision of some contemporary clinicians (compare Reichenbach, 1951, p. 143; Margolis, 1993). Examples of persisting positivist attitudes include the widespread tendency to minimize the difficulties and fallibility of interpretive inquiry, which is a major obstacle to progress in depth-psychological science; the persistent tendency of some clinicians to overvalue initial constructions, which are only conjectures for the most part and thus the most uncertain step in the interpretive process; unsubstantiated claims that continue to be made about uniquely revealing varieties of clinical data and methods of construing unconscious meanings and determinants; and the continued use by clinicians of doctrinal interpretation based upon specific clinical theories (see, for example, Wyss, 1966, pp. 526–527; Eisold, 1994).

Positivist-sounding statements such as the following continue to appear in the clinical literature:

> Psychoanalysis rests on a large and expanding base of verified observations and these are connected in an orderly fashion with certain theoretical constructs. The observations are collected by means of unbiased inquiry; the theoretical generalizations become increasingly certain and the predictions deriving from them increasingly probable, concomitant with the volume of verified observations [Blight, 1981, p. 152].

Herbert Schlesinger (1994) writes that, "despite the manifold possibilities for understanding and intervention, generally only one idea occurs to the analyst as fitting the situation of the moment" (p. 32). Schlesinger also refers to "processes that lead us at a certain juncture to propose to our patient the one (usually right) thing that has come to mind" (p. 36).

Brenner (1968) reports a striking example of anachronous positivist thinking by clinicians regarding the reliability of interpretations. A group of colleagues at an international congress insisted that "if a psychoanalyst has been well analyzed, he will never be mistaken in his interpretations. His every inference concerning the unconscious meaning of his patient's associations will necessarily be correct" (p. 691).[4] With equally misplaced confidence, Goldberg (1988) claims that "reckless interpretations are no more tolerated in psychoanalysis than in physics" (p. 14). Rubinstein (1983/1997), by contrast, emphasized and illustrated "the arbitrariness, because of lack of adequate confirmation, of a great many clinical interpretations" (p. 572). Reichenbach (1951, p. 143) observed wryly that intellectual recognition of our limitations in achieving truth does not give us the strength to resist the deep-seated emotional appeal of seeking certainty.

The "ghost of positivism" sometimes appears during debates, as in a panel discussion of the American Psychoanalytic Association on "Interpretation: Toward a Contemporary Understanding of the Term" (Panel, 1983, p. 244). Brenner emphasized the traditional perspective of psychoanalysis, that is, interpretations are directed at the specific etiology of the patient's psychopathology. Schafer's model of clinical interpretation, by contrast, is that of a narrative transaction, which rests upon a pluralistic (postpositivist) perspective and stresses the inevitably inexact and incomplete nature of interpretations. None of the panel members could accept the pluralistic and relativistic aspects of Schafer's interpretive model.

Brenner attacked Schafer's pluralism as a mixture of empiricism and solipsism which he insisted has nothing to do with psychoanalysis. Other panelists also rejected the epistemologic assumptions of pluralism, and one member stressed the importance of "accurate" reconstructions. Schafer responded that reconstructions by different clinicians result in different accounts shaped by interpreters' preferred paradigms. What Schafer objects to most in the traditional psychoanalytic view of clinical interpretation is the narrow, positivist-like explanation of what is involved in interpretive work. Brenner's description, Schafer argued, is not sufficiently complex and represents only a rudimentary, oversimplified conception of what interpretation is.[5]

The previously described panel discussion illustrates one of the reasons that some psychoanalysts and dynamic psychotherapists are reluctant to give up a positivist perspective, namely, their concern that the ostensibly "firm ground" of genetic and biological "facts" might be lost (compare foundationalism). The panel members reacted to Schafer's emphasis on narrative constructions as a threat to these vaunted, traditional "foundations." It is important to realize, however, that there are very few, if any, really "hard" facts in depth-psychological therapies ("Interpretations rest on interpretations, rest on interpretations, etc."). At the same time, the solution to this methodologic problem is not to go completely narrative and forget all about facts. There are various ways to get at (or near) depth-psychological "facts"; and although our methods are inexact, they are the best we have and are not totally indefensible.

Psychoanalysis and dynamic psychotherapy have been slow to accept the epistemologic and methodologic shift from a positivist to a postpositivist paradigm (compare Margolis, 1993). This epistemologic lag is paradoxical when one recalls that Freud's work was a significant factor in the development of structuralism (Edelson, 1972, p. 250); in the growth of the social sciences (Gardner, 1981, p. 7); in paving the way for pragmatism (Rorty, 1986); and in contributing to the concept of relativism (Holt, 1989, pp. 356–357; Bernstein, 1988a, pp. 88–89). In these ways, the postpositivist legacy of Freud's work is more evident in other disciplines than in psychoanalysis itself.

Combining Positivist and Postpositivist Perspectives

Instructive as it is to contrast positivist and postpositivist models of science, the distinction between the two paradigms is not absolute. A postpositivist approach does not require the elimination of all positivist elements. The pluralism of postpositivist science encompasses multiple epistemologic and methodologic approaches, including some positivist-empirical methods and concepts. Some contemporary philosphers of science and other scholars point out that despite the demise of positivism empiricism retains a place in science as a theory of evidence, though not of truth.[6] Thus modern science emphasizes the search for empirical knowledge not because it rests on a foundation, but because it is a self-correcting process (Williams, 1977, p. 180).[7]

Correspondingly, contemporary neopositivist approaches adopt a probabilistic rather than an apodictic viewpoint. There is no need, therefore, to discard positivism altogether. Meehl (1991, pp. xxv–xxvii; see also Caws, 1994) writes that he still finds the positivist tradition helpful in certain ways; and the philosopher of science Dudley Shapere (1984c) points out that

> the contributions of the positivistic tradition deserve greater appreciation than we might give it if we considered only the deficiencies of so many of its contentions. For, by looking at science carefully in certain ways, it also raised a great many problems regarding the interpretation of science; its answers to those problems, while perhaps far from being all that one would have wished, still provided considerable illumination and insight [p. 376].

One of the advantages of a broader, more encompassing perspective is illustrated by the clinical controversy regarding objectivity. In an essay entitled "Farewell to the Objective Analyst," Arnold Goldberg (1994) maintains that therapists cannot stand outside of the therapeutic relationship and make neutral observations because: (1) they bring presuppositions to the clinical situation; (2) they participate and therefore change as a result of the experience; and (3) they are susceptible to countertransference reactions. Consequently, "our interpretations are never able to be limited to one fixed reading and so the exchange between patient and analyst is always open and continuous" (p. 21).

Goldberg's view is a restatement of arguments by Kuhn (1962), Feyerabend (1975), and other philosophers regarding the theory- and context-bound nature of observations in science. One of the problems with Goldberg's view, however, is its one-sidedness and categorical nature (note for example his use of the terms "never" and "always"). Some philosophers of science and scholars in other fields take a different, more moderate position on the issue of objectivity;[8] and Wallerstein (1988) reports similarly moderate views by clinicians and clinical investigators.

Drawing on the writings of Kordig (1971a, b, c, 1973), Meehl (1983/1991, p. 322) argues that the theory-ladenness of observational statements and associated meaning-variance apply mainly to "cosmological theories" that deal with everything there is. Psychology is different; hence we should not assume uncritically that philosophical arguments about the Copernican hypothesis or relativity theory or quantum mechanics apply equally to depth-psychological therapies and clinical interpretations. Such arguments may apply to astrophysics or to quark theory, Meehl concludes, but not to animal conditioning, or classical psychometrics, or even to psychoanalysis.

The hermeneutic scholar E. D. Hirsch, Jr. (1976) rejects the pure phenomenological form of perspectivism which considers all interpretations or perspectives equally valid, and which denies the possibility of mediating among them.[9] Maquet (1964), a philosopher, concludes that perspectivistic knowledge is not inherently nonobjective; it is partial. It can become nonobjective if it is mistakenly considered global rather than partial.[10]

From considerations such as these it would appear that, as with everything we study, the objectivity of scientific (including clinical) observations and interpretations is not absent but is variable. At times, and under certain conditions, our observations and interpretations may be relatively objective; at other times and in other circumstances, they may be grossly unobjective. We need not throw up our hands, however, and say, "Farewell to objectivity." We can strive to extend and improve it; for clinical interpretive inquiry is a "subjective study of subjectivity struggling to become the objective study of subjectivity" (Stoller, 1979, p. 193). Some clinicians misuse the concept of relativism tendentiously for obscurantist and antiempirical purposes; but, as Meehl (1970/1973) observes, it would be unfortunate if efforts to objectify psychoanalytic inference were abandoned or watered down by a comfortable reliance on generalizations such as, "There is no such thing as a pure observational datum, utterly uninfluenced by one's frame of reference" (p. 116).[11]

The philosopher Shapere (1984a, pp. xvii–xxi) suggests that both the insights and limitations of positivist and postpositivist science are complementary. By taking into account the presuppositions that influence observations and theories, but without adopting a complete relativism, science has developed greater openness to new ideas and at the same time has preserved some degree of objectivity.

Drawing on case studies in the history of science, Shapere concludes that the debate between positivists and their critics represents the continuation of a more general controversy between "absolutist" and "relativist" views that have permeated philosophy since the time of Plato. "The real point of both skepticism and relativism lies in their exposure of shortcomings in our understanding of the nature of knowledge and of the knowledge-seeking process" (pp. xx–xxi). Since both absolutist and completely relativist arguments have been found to be inadequate, the task is to develop a theory of knowledge-seeking that avoids absolutism, on the one hand, but does not collapse into complete relativism, on the other.

The more science learns, the more it is able to learn. The richness of interpretation provided by background information makes it possible for science to develop new ideas. Science is thus a process of building on the best beliefs it has available. Viewed in this way, science can avoid both absolutism and complete relativism (p. xxv; see also Putnam, 1983c, esp. p. 198). The concept of science building on the best beliefs it has available is relevant also to the methodology of clinical interpretation; for inasmuch as the reliability (consistency) of interpretive methods is problematic, and interpretive conclusions are inherently fallible, depth-psychological understanding of patients is based necessarily upon the best constructions available to the clinician, that is, the "most plausible" interpretive hypotheses among various alternative constructions at a given time. This point is discussed further later, in connection with the justification of interpretations (Part IV).

The concepts and procedures involved in science do not come with guarantees, of course. Every aspect of scientific belief involves reasons for doubt; but the mere possibility of doubt is not by itself reason to doubt any particular proposition, or to avoid using best beliefs in seeking further knowledge. Even the doctrine that all knowledge of nature comes from observation of nature has exceptions. Thus the contemporary derivative of classical empiricism is "contingent empiricism." Similarly, we now recognize that things in nature have "relevance-relations" to each other, and that understanding and successful dealing with nature necessitates the use and systematization of such relations

(Shapere, 1984a, pp. xxvi–xxx). The importance of relations and patterns in clinical interpretation is discussed further in Chapter 5.

Eagle (1980b, pp. 371–373) notes that methodologic ambiguities such as the foregoing are reflected in the dual nature of psychoanalytic theory, for example, Freud's preoccupation with both meaning and mechanics, clinical theory and metapsychology. Rubinstein (1976) observed that our discourse about unconscious mental events "straddles two worlds—our everyday human world and the world of natural science" (p. 256; see also Modell, 1978a, b; Strenger, 1986, 1991).

The philosopher of science Gerald Radnitzky (1973, pp. 257–261) draws on concepts of Apel (1965) and on the model of knowledge development in the psychoanalytic situation to argue for an integration of human and natural science perspectives. The two approaches mediate each other so that knowledge develops by a continuous "tacking" between the two perspectives. For example, the human and social sciences, including psychoanalysis and dynamic psychotherapy, need information obtained by naturalistic methods, both as data and as methods of checking; and the natural sciences need information about human psychology obtained by interpretive and other methods of the human and social sciences, in order to deal with psychological and sociological factors that influence scientific investigators and their work (see, for example, studies by the sociologist of science, Karin Knorr-Cetina, 1981, 1984, 1993, p. 180). With respect to the integration of human and natural science perspectives, it is worth noting that one of the earliest and most extensive such integrations was the methodology developed by Freud.

Growing Status of Interpretation as a Method of Scientific Inquiry

The ascendance of postpositivist science has given rise to some belated recognition of and respect for interpretive methodologies—an increased acceptance, even appreciation, of interpretive methods by scientists in many fields, including the philosophy of science. It is now widely accepted that all fields employ interpretation of some kind and to some extent (Holt, 1978a, pp. 50–51; Bernstein, 1988a, pp. 88–89). Ahumada (1994) writes that "from Baconian *interpretatio naturae* onwards interpretation has been part and parcel of empirical science, be it 'exact' or 'observational'" (pp. 697–698). The philosopher Stephen Toulmin (1982, pp. 116–117) asserts that use of an interpretive approach does not diminish the quality of an investigation or relegate its results to the inferior status of subjective opinion, for such a choice remains open to all of the objective possibilities which may be used as rational support for interpretations.

Recognition of the importance and ubiquity of interpretation is attested also by growth of the constructivist viewpoint, that is, that stimuli, such as a patient's productions, acquire meaning through their assimilation into a person's, for example a therapist's, existing knowledge system. The hermeneuticist E. D. Hirsch, Jr. (1983) emphasizes that interpretation is the central activity of cognition; perceived meanings are always interpreted constructs. "We always perceive something other than the language through which we know something. This constructive process is interpretation" (p. 322).[12]

A constructivist viewpoint has begun to appear even in Kohutian self psychology. Contrary to Kohut's singular emphasis on the method of empathy (1984, p. 32), which some critics consider an inappropriately monistic and method-oriented way of attempting to understand the therapeutic dialogue (for example, Hoffman, 1991; Cooper, 1993), some of Kohut's followers (Wolf, 1986, 1989; Goldberg, 1989) now acknowledge the therapist's constructive activities in shaping meanings.[13]

Several recent treatises attempt to establish the central importance of interpretation also for philosophy. Marcia Cavell's (1993) *The Psychoanalytic Mind: From Freud to Philosophy* stresses the importance of interpretation to a theory of mind. *The Need for Interpretation: Contemporary Conceptions of the Philosopher's Task* (Mitchell and Rosen, 1983) attempts to reorient philosophy to interpretation as its central project. An increasing number of younger philosophers believe that philosophy is an interpretive enterprise. *The Interpretive Turn* (Hiley, Bohman, and Shusterman, 1991) argues that the earlier epistemologic and linguistic turns in philosophy have been superseded by an "interpretive turn," characterized by predominant interest in interpretive activities and disciplines. Two authors in the latter collection, Thomas Kent (1991) and Charles Taylor (1991), stress the Russian language philosopher M. M. Bakhtin's (1986) concept that human beings are "constituted in conversation," which places dialogue and its interpretation at the very center of human life.

Interpretation is recognized increasingly, therefore, as a universal feature of all human activities. Dreyfus (1991) refers to human beings in this respect as "interpretation all the way down" (cited by Bohman et al., 1991, p. 7; see also Campbell, 1988, pp. 335–388). Bohman, Hiley, and Shusterman (1991, p. 11) conclude that no experience, meaning, or evidence is independent of or more basic than interpretation.

Although interpretation is a form of practice rather than of theory, Bohman et al. point out that theory always depends upon a background of established interpretive practices which both initiate the theory and continue to influence it. Psychoanalysis illustrates that relationship: for example, Freud acknowledged that psychoanalysis began as an "art of interpretation" (1923a, p. 239). Bohman et al. (1991, p. 11) emphasize that the interpretive turn in philosophy is a practical turn, one that stresses the central role of practice. They offer four reasons why interpretation always involves practical applications: (1) There is always an intentional aspect of interpretation; it is always applied to some intentional object. (2) Interpretation employs a particular perspective which shapes what it interprets. (3) Interpretation is context bound. (4) As purposive agents, we have motives and needs of our own that influence what and how we choose to interpret.

Toward an Epistemology of Interpretive Inquiry

The central argument of this chapter is the relevance of a postpositivist perspective to interpretive inquiry—a pluralistic perspective that accommodates selected methods and concepts of disparate viewpoints, including some (mainly empirical) aspects of positivism. A pluralistic approach, however, does not require unification "into a homogeneous discourse, but rather the recognition of where, when, and how each *mode* of discourse is applicable and appropriate" (Lamm, 1993, p. 33). As Oakeshott (1962) puts it, different universes of discourse "enjoy an oblique relationship which neither requires nor forecasts their being assimilated to one another" (p. 199).

The question arises whether a particular philosophical school, or combination of viewpoints, exists within the postpositivist perspective that might offer an appropriate epistemology of interpretive inquiry—bearing in mind, however, the philosophical complexity of psychoanalysis, and Massicotte's (1995) caveat that "psychoanalysis is not reducible to a subcomponent of any philosophical system" (p. 14). Various continental philosophies and approaches have been proposed in this connection, for example, phenomenology, existentialism, hermeneutics, structuralism, *Verstehen*, Foucault's genealogy—none of which is pluralistic or causally-oriented enough for the present purposes. At the other extreme, Grünbaum (1984, 1993) classifies psychoanalysis as a natural science, pure and simple (see, however, MacKay, 1989, pp. 3–4). Several pluralistic epistemologies have been proposed, for example, Apel's (1965) epistemological-anthropological point of view; Radnitzky's (1973) metatheoretical integration of quasi-naturalistic and hermeneutic approaches; Modell's (1978a,b) and also Phillips's (1987, 1991) concepts of complementarity; Strenger's (1991) epistemology which situates psychoanalysis "between hermeneutics and science"; and Wax's, "richer portrait of psychoanalysis as encompassing interpretive and scientific facets within a normative system" (1995, p. 554; see also 1983).

A promising pluralistic school which some writers have proposed as an epistemology of psychoanalysis is the "New Paradigm," developed by Rom Harré (1960, 1970, 1972) and coworkers.[14] Cheshire and Thomä (1991, pp. 441–442) refer to this paradigm as "scientific realism" because it attempts to describe the methods and concepts of empirical sciences as they are actually used, rather than the ways they are represented in textbooks. Real science, they point out, is characterized methodologically by variety: (1) variety in methods of investigation, observation, and data collection; (2) variety in the types and uses of evidence; (3) variety in the patterns of logical explanation employed; and (4) variety in the logic and methods of validation.

The New Paradigm rejects positivism, but without turning completely to hermeneutics. It emphasizes the role of analogy and conceptual model-building, drawing on the ways that familiar systems work. Cheshire and Thomä (1991, p. 442) note that the New Paradigm employs many types of models, the logic of which tends to be complex. Harré (1970, p. 54) has applied his analysis of such pluralistic logic to some of Freud's explanatory concepts (see also Harré, Clarke, and De Carlo, 1985, p. 6; MacKay, 1989, pp. 88–92). The relation of this approach to psychological (including psychoanalytic) theory is reviewed from various standpoints by Leary (1990a,b; see also Manicas and Secord, 1983; MacKay, 1989, p. 89).

One of the problems with this approach is how to prevent analogies, metaphors, and other figures-of-speech from being used excessively and indiscriminately in their applications to psychological structures and processes (Cheshire and Thomä, 1991, p. 442). A frequent objection to the scientific status of psychoanalysis has been that its metaphors and analogies degenerate into animism and anthropomorphism. To deal with that problem, clinicians must recognize and specify the area of negative analogy, or disanalogy, of a metaphor (Thomä and Kächele, 1987, pp. 30–35; 1990). For example, "to avoid misunderstanding in the kinetic theory of gases, we need to know how the molecules are *not* like bouncing rubber balls as well as how they *are* like them" (Cheshire and Thomä, 1991, p. 445). To his credit, Freud frequently pointed out the disanalogous aspects of his metaphors (Leary, 1990b, p. 45, n. 42).

Another philosophical viewpoint, which does not appear to have been considered previously as a possible (or partial) epistemology of psychoanalysis and interpretive methodology, is that of "naturalism"—also called "naturalized epistemology" or the "naturalistic turn" in the philosophy of science.[15] Naturalized epistemology is associated mainly with the philosopher W. V. O. Quine (for example, 1969), although it has earlier roots in Hume. It is "what results when instead of trying to justify our claims to knowledge we offer a causal account, particularly in terms of evolution, of how we come, and inevitably come, to have the kinds of belief we have" (Lacey, 1986, p. 65).[16]

As an approach to inquiry naturalism has both advantages and disadvantages. The philosopher Daniel Dennett (1984) comments:

> One of the happiest trends in philosophy in the last twenty years has been its Naturalization: since we human beings are a part of nature—supremely complicated but unprivileged portions of the biosphere—philosophical accounts of our minds, our knowledge, our language must in the end be continuous with, and harmonious with, the natural sciences. But while striking the Naturalistic Pose is as agreeable and welcome as it is easy, actually doing naturalized philosophy has proved difficult—indeed a very unnatural act for a philosopher to perform—and contemporary philosophy of meaning, even where it is most brilliant, has been inconstant in its commitment to naturalism [p. ix].

Naturalized epistemology has a number of postpositivist features in common with the New Paradigm (Boyd, 1981); in particular there are similarities regarding the "nonstatement view" of theories, and the role of models in actual scientific work (Suppe, 1977, p. 221; Callebaut, 1993, pp. 219–226). Edelson (1984, pp. 77–108) has applied the nonstatement view to psychoanalysis. According to this view, theories are not considered collections of (hypothetical) statements, but as models of theories. They are closer to descriptions of the actual structures employed by scientists, that is, models that one creates and then interprets, which is similar to the New Paradigm approach. A theory acquires empirical content by finding parts of the world (including, for example, the inner world of a patient) that are like the model—a different kind of fit than the traditional theory of truth as correspondence between belief and fact (Giere, 1988).

In an interesting and unusual volume by Callebaut (1993), *Taking the Naturalistic Turn or How Real Philosophy of Science Is Done*, which includes integrated reports of extensive interviews with scientists as well as philosophers, historians, and sociologists of science, Ronald Giere (in Callebaut, 1993) states that from a naturalistic standpoint there is no necessity to speak about laws:

> In a way, all empirical claims are particular. They are saying, "Here is some real system—do you see it out there? It fits my model, and my model fits it. There are some other systems, and it fits those too." That is how you do science! whereas you don't say: "What we're looking for is a generalization, a universal statement." Forget it. That is the difference: You create models and you apply them to the world [p. 225].

Naturalism has grown rapidly in this country during the past fifteen years as a reaction against objectionable features of both positivism and postpositivist science, although it continues to be influenced by both. The reaction against positivism is directed mainly at foundationalism; naturalism, by contrast, is probabilistic. Its conflict with postpositivist science concerns the issue of relativism. That is, the downfall of positivism and the extreme relativism adopted by radical antipositivists led some postpositivist investigators to conclude that methodology no longer matters, that "anything goes".[17] Some naturalists became concerned that such an extreme relativist position might undermine the determination of investigators to be scientific, and might lead to doubts about whether validity is a rational and reasonable goal.

The social scientist Donald Campbell ([1984] in Overman, 1988, p. 316) notes that the rejection of positivism left the theory of science in disarray. He points out that, "What we should have learned instead is that logical positivism was a gross misreading of the method of the already successful sciences"; and that "properly interpreted, the dethronement of logical positivism should have led to an *increase* in methodological concern rather than its abandonment" (in Overman, 1988, p. 316; see also Callebaut, 1993, p. 232).

That is, precisely because certainty based on infallible methods is unattainable, investigators need to take even greater pains to determine which methods, or combination of approaches, are most likely to produce plausible interpretive hypotheses and probative evidence for them.

Naturalized philosophy of science is interested also in the process of discovery—another feature that recommends it as (part of) an epistemology of clinical interpretive inquiry. For example, naturalized epistemology bears directly on interpretive inquiry by its interest in problems of inductive inference. Kornblith (1993a, pp. 10–11) points out in this connection that everyone has a great deal of inductive knowledge; but since epistemological truths are far from obvious, it is necessary to subject interpretations to empirical tests—which brings epistemology and psychology together in a fruitful interaction.

Positivists and Popperians distinguished carefully between the contexts of discovery and justification in scientific work, but they were interested primarily in justification and paid little attention to the discovery process (Reichenbach, 1951). Thomas Nickles (1980a,b; 1990; and cited in Callebaut, 1993, pp. 207–214), on the other hand, a naturalized philosopher of science, adopts a problem-solving rather than a directly truth-seeking, theory-oriented approach to justification.[18] Nickles (1990) proposes that discovery methods are themselves relevant to justification, though not on the basis of their past results but in the form of their future problem-solving potential. The philosophically informed psychoanalyst Eric Gillett (1990a, p. 295) argues similarly that, since degree of confirmation cannot be measured precisely, there can be no sharp distinction between the heuristic value of a theory and the degree of its confirmation. Nickles suggests further that scientists need to wean themselves from the traditional view of justification employed in foundational epistemology, and turn instead to new models that permit mutual support or even self support—for example, Glymour's (1974/1982), Shapere's (1984b), and other "bootstrap" methods.

Viewpoints such as the foregoing illustrate the postpositivist flexibility and innovative potential of epistemologies such as naturalism, the New Paradigm, and other pluralistic approaches. Despite the ambiguous nature of our discipline and its interpretive methodology, the postpositivist view readily accommodates nontraditional sciences such as psychoanalysis and dynamic psychotherapy; for the postpositivist perspective recognizes that there is no single correct method to follow in research, that science is a creative search to understand better, not a process of following methodologic recipes. In fact, our way of doing science has many parallels with the way scientists in more established fields approach their problems. To illustrate: Karin Knorr-Cetina (1981, 1984), a sociologist of science, goes to scientists' laboratories to observe how they actually do science. Her findings suggest some striking similarities between the processes of scientific discovery in other fields and the psychoanalytic process of interpretive inquiry:

> When you observe scientists in the laboratory, you find processes of negotiation at work, processes of decision-making, which influence what the scientific findings are going to look like. In a sense, the scientific finding is *construed* in the laboratory, by virtue of the decisions and negotiations it incorporates. Of course, these negotiations and decisions are no longer visible once the finding is published and is considered scientific fact. Then the negotiations have disappeared from the surface, but they are embedded in the scientific finding [in Callebaut, 1993, p. 180; emphasis added].

Knorr-Cetina observes further that "a lot of interpretation goes into the production of the scientific fact. Of course, that means if you have many decisions incorporated in such a finding, this also means that these decisions could have been otherwise and might have led to a different scientific fact" (p. 180). Knorr-Cetina adds that scientists "operate in a realm of uncertainty, and within this uncertainty they have to interpret what is going on, what they have got and what they haven't got" (pp. 184–185). She notes further that:

> You also get resistances in the laboratory; but in order for these resistances to make sense, they have to be interpreted. The very

> moment you interpret them, you enter the realm of the social world, you enter the thoughts of previous scientists, of your colleagues in the field, of what you think yourself. The thing becomes contextual, perspectival, dependent, and relative to ruling paradigms (pp. 184–185; see also Wax, 1986, p. 264; Spruiell, 1993; Mayer, 1996).

The similarities between clinical interpretive inquiry and various research strategies in the traditional sciences do not imply, however, that a single (monistic) form of knowledge seeking is involved. Knorr-Cetina's work demonstrates that scientific investigation is epistemologically and methodologically pluralistic; similarly, Modell (1978a) and Strenger (1991) have noted the "mixed discourse," and thus complex epistemology, of psychoanalysis.

The various types of interpretive formulations that clinicians construct in psychoanalysis and dynamic psychotherapy reflect the pluralistic epistemology of interpretive inquiry, for example: (1) some constructions are theoretical constructs, that is, causal-explanatory inferences regarding motivational determinants which are linked to the general theory of psychoanalysis (Mackay, 1989, pp. 88–92); (2) other constructions have less connection with psychoanalytic theory per se than with the therapist's clinical experience with similar patients; (3) still other constructions deal primarily with latent meanings rather than determinants of patients' experiences; (4) some constructions attempt to explicate both latent meanings and determinants; (5) others focus on what a patient may be experiencing at a particular time, rather than on possible meanings or determinants of the experience; and (6) many constructions involve applications of commonsense psychology rather than specifically psychoanalytic theory or previous clinical experience.

Summary

The downfall of positivism, followed by a postpositivist turn in both the philosophy and the conduct of science, has had an emancipating effect upon the human and social sciences. For example, the postpositivist turn has resulted in greater acceptance of interpretive methods, which are so important in many methodologies of these disciplines. Under the continuing influence of Freud's positivism, however, psychoanalysis and dynamic psychotherapy have been slow to accept the shift to a postpositivist perspective. Schafer (1996) observes that psychoanalysis has "lagged behind the times, the logical-positivist orientation still prevails, each psychoanalytic school claiming to be the only one that has got the facts 'right'" (p. 249).

Although no agreement has been reached regarding an epistemology of psychoanalysis and its interpretive methodology, a pluralistic perspective encompassing both postpositivist and natural science approaches seems necessary and appropriate. Some studies in the sociology of science suggest that the process of interpretive inquiry in psychoanalysis and dynamic psychotherapy involves striking but previously unrecognized parallels with knowledge-seeking processes in traditional sciences. Two relatively recent theories of science, the "New Paradigm" and "Naturalized Epistemology," have features that conceivably might provide a basis and beginning for developing an epistemologic model of clinical interpretive inquiry.

One of the unanswered questions regarding the postpositivist paradigm is how to interpret and implement its concept of relativism. The misguided notion that "anything goes" methodologically, that one interpretation is as good as another, and that "truth is only what is experienced as true" (Wolf, 1991, p. 103), goes to the opposite extreme from the previous positivist view that only absolutely certain knowledge is valid. A more balanced, middle ground between the extremes of absolute certainty and absolute relativism recognizes that science builds upon the best beliefs which are available, but leaves all aspects of those beliefs open to revision or rejection. Since both positivist and completely relativist arguments have been found to be inadequate, the task is to develop a theory and methodology of interpretive inquiry that avoids absolutism, on the one hand, but does not collapse into complete relativism, on the other.

PART II

CONTEMPORARY APPROACHES

[W]e have no adequate theory either of the psychoanalyst's act of understanding or of the psychoanalyst's act of making an interpretation.

[Marshall Edelson, 1988, p. 78]

According to Heidegger it is wrong to adopt a simple objective stance, where the primary reality is an objective physical world, and it is likewise wrong to take a simple subjective stance, where your thoughts and feelings are the primary reality. Rather, neither can exist without the other, and you have to consider both together, as a single whole.

[Keith Devlin, 1997, p. 277]

We want the analyst to *discern* the "red thread"; we don't want him to spin it and weave it in.

[Paul Meehl, 1983, p. 360]

[A]nalysts need to be reminded that they are not oracles, not wizards, not linguists, not detectives, not great wise men—but quiet observers, listeners, and occasionally commentators.

[Karl Menninger, 1958, p. 129]

3

Methodologic Lag in Some Contemporary Models of Interpretive Inquiry

Interpretive methodologies differ in the extent to which they reflect the newer, postpositivist perspective. Some interpretive models are almost completely postpositivist in approach, while others retain significant features of the superseded positivist paradigm. "Methodologic lag" refers to the retention of anachronistic positivist features in contemporary models of interpretive inquiry. The term "methodologic lag" differs from Gray's (1982) concept of "developmental lag," the latter referring to ways of listening to and perceiving clinical data that have not kept pace with ego theory.

This chapter discusses some of the most problematic forms of methodologic lag in contemporary models of interpretive inquiry, namely:

1. Monistic and method-oriented rather than pluralistic and problem-oriented approaches.
2. Doctrinal or theory-driven rather than context-sensitive, data-driven approaches.
3. Overconfident and dogmatic attitudes towards interpretations, rather than skeptical and error-correcting approaches.
4. Overgeneralized and rule-governed approaches at one extreme, and radically constructivist methods at the other extreme, rather than flexibly balanced interpretive approaches.

The latter forms of methodologic lag apply particularly to certain language-based models of interpretive inquiry, which are discussed in Chapter 4.

Monistic and Method-Oriented Rather Than Pluralistic, Problem-Oriented Approaches

Investigations based on the positivist model employ only prescribed methods which are capable of producing repeatable (hence presumably certain) results. Methods meeting that criterion are viewed as correct in themselves, and a great deal of positivist research has been based upon the availability of just such accepted methods. An example is the countless number of experiments on maze-learning in rats conducted by behaviorists in psychological laboratories. Another example is the almost obligatory use of significance testing in psychological and social science research (see, for example, Bakan, 1967, pp. 1–29). Meehl (1978/1991) states forcefully that the widespread reliance on refuting the null hypothesis as the standard method of testing theories is basically unsound (p. 817). He points out that there are many areas of both practical and theoretical inference in which nobody knows how to calculate a numerical probability value, or how to determine whether different sources of evidence converge on a particular hypothesis (p. 831). Meehl concludes that it is "vulgar positivism" to insist on such tests (p. 830).

Since the immediate aim of interpretive inquiry is to determine the most plausible construction or reconstruction at a given time, comparisons of alternative hypotheses and implicit probability judgments are necessary (see Hirsch, 1967, p. 174). Most of the probability judgments that interpreters make, however, are not reducible to numerical quantities. Keynes (1962, pp. 34–37) contends, in fact, that it is a fallacy to equate correctness with a numerically precise probability judgment; often, "more" or "less" is the most accurate judgment that one can make (see also Bolles, 1962; Benenson, 1984).

In addition to being method-oriented, the positivist paradigm is also methodologically monistic or exclusivist (Roth, 1987, pp. 5–6). Believing that problems would be solved eventually by one correct method, positivists developed a single-method tradition emphasizing a particular approach, perspective, or variety of data, which largely determined the choice of problems studied as well as the methodology employed in investigating them (Polkinghorne, 1983, pp. 18–19). A recent example of that view in psychoanalysis is Kohut's insistence (1984, p. 32) that empathy is the only useful method of understanding latent mental contents. Not only is such an approach monistic, method-oriented, and positivistic but, in addition, introspections and empathic responses are far from transparent and thus themselves require interpretation.[1] It was psychoanalysis, after all, that challenged the face value of introspection (Malmquist, 1963, p. 11).

Postpositivist science no longer considers methods to be correct in themselves. Particular methods do not stand alone, and are never independent of specific systems of inquiry. Methods are appropriate only in relation to the questions being asked, and no one method is *the* correct method for investigating human beings (Polkinghorne, 1983, pp. 273, 280). Postpositivst approaches are problem- in contrast to method-oriented, and are methodologically pluralistic rather than exclusivistic (Roth, 1987, pp. 5–6; see also Russell, 1987b, pp. 341–350; Watson, 1990). The philosopher David Hull (1988) writes that:

> Epistemological reconstructions of scientific method that portray the scientific process as a prescribed sequence of activities are exceedingly misleading. In the past, epistemologists searched for the epistemic givens upon which all knowledge must be based and the infallible methods that would lead from these firm foundations to certain truth. Any scientific method that incorporates either of these principles is sure to be mistaken. Science by necessity must always be conducted in medias res [p. 516].

The postpositivist perspective emphasizes that science is not a fixed or finished method: its basic agenda is its own improvement. As a science develops and encounters obstacles, it modifies its methods, types of data, and even its basic conceptions to overcome limitations (Polkinghorne, 1983, pp. 118–119; for examples in various disciplines, see Holton, 1973). With regard to methodologic perspectives, Lawrence Friedman (1980, pp. 420–421) suggests that we need a variety of them; for the more such approaches we employ, and the more coherent they are, the closer we come to the individual patient's reality.

Since the subject matter of depth psychology is too complex for any single method of construal,[2] and since pluralistic interpretive methodologies help to identify, clarify, and specify latent meanings and determinants in clinical data, most methods and models of interpretive inquiry have been pluralistic. Gardner (1991, pp. 862–863) notes that even clinicians who stress a single approach "smuggle in" other methods. Freud's interpretive methodology was decidedly pluralistic, comparable with casting a wide net rather than dropping a single line into a large, elusive school of fish (Eissler, 1963; Meissner, 1971; Rubovits-Seitz, 1988a, p. 934)—another way that he anticipated a postpositivist perspective.

Other examples of pluralistic approaches to interpretive methodology include: Ferenczi's (1928/1955) "oscillation" between subjective and objective methods; Levy's (1963) multiple methodologic principles and perspectives; Schafer's (1970) multifaceted "vision of reality"; Modell's (1978a,b) concept of complementarity between different ways of viewing clinical data; Arlow's (1979, 1987) multiple interpretive heuristics; Spence's (1982a) concepts of interpretive pluralism; Peterfreund's (1983) pluralistic perspectives, working models, and strategies; Silverman's (1986) multimodel approach; Horowitz's (1987) "configurational analysis," which attempts to deal systematically with the complexities of clinical data, on the one hand, and the pluralistic methods that interpreters employ, on the other; Pine's (1988) "four psychologies" and multidimensional listening strategies; Wallace's (1988) pluralistic conceptualization of interpretive methodology from realist, correspondence theory, perspectival, interactional, causal, and relativistic standpoints; Chessick's (1989) five listening channels, and his "alternative approaches to understanding" (1992); Hitchcock's (1989) critique of reductively unidimentional interpretive approaches; Samuels's (1989) concepts of the "plural psyche," which he theorizes may mirror the diversity of methods and concepts employed by different schools of depth psychology; Hedges' (1991) four listening perspectives; Pulver's (1993) "eclectic analyst"; Schlesinger's (1994) three modes of listening; Spillius's (1994) multiple methods of arriving at formulations, "none of which should necessarily be privileged" (p. 1121); and others.[3]

A smaller number of interpretive approaches is monistic in type, that is, emphasizes a particular interpretive method, perspective, or variety of data. In addition to Klein's (1975, 1992, 1993) and Kohut's (1959; 1984, p. 32) radically exclusivist method-oriented approaches, other examples of monistic interpretive methods in psychoanalysis and dynamic psychotherapy include Searl's (1936) exclusive focus on resistance analysis; Gray's (1973, 1986, 1990, 1992, p. 325; 1994) preferential focus on the immediacy of the patient's defensive processes[4]; Langs's (1978, pp. 104–105) claim that all of a patient's associations are a commentary on the therapist's behavior, and that all interpretive hypotheses should be validated by viewing the patient's responses to an interpretation from that perspective[5]; Gill's (1982a) and Gill and Hoffman's (1982b) insistent interpretive focus on here-and-now transference phenomena, organized predominantly around behaviors of the analyst; Reiss's (1983) emphasis on sensory illusions in the therapist as the alleged fundamental data around which constructions should be formulated; Schwaber's (1983b, 1986, 1990a,b; 1992) sustained interpretive focus on the patient's perceptual reality, that is, how the patient perceives and experiences relationships and events[6]; Weiss and Sampson's (1986) persistent interpretive focus on "testing behavior" by the patient to disconfirm pathogenic beliefs; Luborsky and Crits-Christoph's (1990) guided inference system for interpreting a single conflictual relationship pattern which they believe affects all of a patient's relationships—contrary to the traditional, unguided interpretive search for sporadically shifting transference conflicts in relation to diverse objects; Etchegoyen's (1991, p. 326) view that the only way to test an interpretation is to communicate it; Greenberg's (1994) privileging of process over content, rather than viewing all varieties of data as potentially useful in providing clues to latent meanings and determinants; and Ogden's (1994; see also Stolorow et al., 1987) focus on intersubjective experiences, which he refers to as the "analytic third[7]".

Emphasizing a single method, perspective, or variety of data can be useful if employed intermittently, as one among a number of approaches; but when applied continually and exclusively, a single method is less capable of identifying, clarifying, and specifying the plurality and interrelations of latent meanings and determinants in clinical data. Diesing (1971, pp. 12–13) notes that overuse of a single method produces a distorted view; and Kaplan (1964, p. 26) observes that if a particular method comes to be regarded as the one avenue to truth, it is truth that suffers.

Thus, a unidimensional interpretive approach that employs mainly or only a single "channel" for generating, gathering, and attempting to process clinical data represents a regressive methodologic shift toward the illusional certainty of monistic, method-based approaches. Bowers (1984) notes that such procedures are often associated with "anointed" methods of inquiry that lead to supposedly warranted claims about the phenomena being investigated. "There is something reassuring about this identification, since it makes the rules of inquiry appear to be entirely rational, explicit, and comprehensible to anyone trained in their use" (pp. 260–261).

Monistic, method-oriented (positivistic) approaches limit the ingenuity and scope of interpretive inquiry. Postpositivist approaches, on the other hand, employ multiple interpretive methods and wide varieties of clinical data, which serve as checks on each other and compensate for the limitations of individual methods and types of data. The interpretation of projective psychological test data illustrates the importance of methodologic pluralism in a closely related field. Bellak (1993, p. 75) points out that a "battery" of tests is needed to assess the various dimensions of personality: no one test can do it all (see also O'Neill, 1993).

Doctrinal Rather Than Data-Driven Approaches

In his perceptive essay "The Refinding of Theory in Clinical Practice," Michael Parsons (1992) observes that it is natural for us to assume that the practice of psychoanalysis is, or should be, derived from theory—that our theory should tell us how to understand the patient's problems and the meanings of his or her communications:

> Our experience, however, seems to belie this. When we are with our patients we seldom work things out so deliberately. We are immediately involved in the interaction with an individual and we do not generally arrive at our interpretations by using theory to deduce what they ought to be. The nature of the connexion between our theory and what we do in the session remains a puzzle [p. 103].

Parsons grants that an, "initial grasp of theory is a necessary starting point, so that our listening is not vacuous. It can show us to some extent what to listen for and how to think about what we hear" (p. 110). However, Parsons adds, there is a risk that the theoretical preconceptions will compromise our free-floating attention and close off possibilities of fresh discovery (p. 110). He concludes that the analyst's use of his or her preconscious is crucial to understanding how clinical practice is informed by theory. "We do not, on this view, determine once for all what our theory is, but continually have to discover it by exploring our preconscious as we watch ourselves at work" (Parsons, 1992, p. 114).

Freud's positivist convictions led him to believe originally that applying his theoretical understanding to patients' associations constituted a sufficient and proper interpretive methodology (Anzieu, 1970, p. 778; cited by Leavy, 1980, p. 12).[8] Grünbaum (1984, 1993) assumes (incorrectly, I believe; see Chapter 7) that Freud continued to base his interpretations largely on the specific clinical theories of psychoanalysis. I have documented elsewhere (1992a, pp. 578–579) that Freud's initial reliance on doctrinal interpretation did not last very long; for already by 1900 he had begun to develop a more sophisticated, inductive approach to interpretation which included an alertness to unanticipated relations and patterns in clinical data. In 1912, for example, he wrote that the most successful results occur when one allows himself to be surprised by any new developments in the data, and responds to such developments with an open mind, free of preconceptions; for if the therapist follows his own expectations he will find only what he already knows (Freud, 1912b, pp. 112, 114). In a letter to Ferenczi during 1915, Freud wrote that theory should remain like a stranger who has not been invited into one's house (cited by Gribinski, 1994, pp. 1011, 1019). Rycroft (1985, pp. 50–57) observes in this connection that although Freud conceived of himself as a scientist, observing and explaining mental phenomena, in practice he did not work that way. If he had, he would have advised analysts to keep theory in mind while working with patients; but instead he advised them to forget about theory until the treatment was finished.

Freud recognized, however, that inevitably observations and interpretations are biased.[9] He even "confessed" that he found himself interpreting whatever interested him most at a particular time (cited by Klauber, 1968, p. 83). Freud (1915b) stated explicitly that even at the descriptive stage one cannot avoid applying certain abstract ideas to the data, and that the source of such ideas is something other than the new observations themselves (p. 117). Thus even one's initial observations and descriptions of phenomena are theory laden to some extent. Deductive reasoning and theoretically informed inductive leaps, therefore, must have continued to play some role in Freud's interpretive approach. Eissler (1963, p. 678) notes, for example, that Freud characteristically drew a large number of conclusions from a single observation.

Freud's shift from a "top-down" (theory-driven) to a more "bottom-up" (data-driven) strategy was thus not the end of doctrinal interpretation in psychoanalysis and dynamic psychotherapy (Peterfreund, 1983, pp. 7–69). Even after turning to a data-driven strategy, Freud occasionally lapsed into a doctrinal approach. For example, as late as 1916–1917, in his lecture on "Analytic Therapy," Freud referred to helping patients overcome resistances, "with the help of suggestion operating in an *educative* sense" (p. 451). In other writings (for example, 1909a, pp. 120–121; 1910a, pp. 141–142) he had described his interpretive technique as giving the patient "the conscious anticipatory idea (the idea of what he may expect to find) and he then finds the repressed unconscious idea in himself on the basis of its similarity to the anticipatory one" (1910a, p. 142). Freud appears not to have recognized the potentially theory-driven and indoctrinating nature of such a procedure.

Various schools of psychoanalysis, including Kleinians[10] and self psychologists[11] rely extensively on theory-driven methodologies of interpretive inquiry. A recent comparative study of psychoanalytic schools by Victoria Hamilton (1993, pp. 70–71) reveals that Kleinian and Kohutian approaches are much less influenced by diverse viewpoints than other schools, which is congruent with their monistic and doctrinal orientations. In his chapter "Epistemological Aspects of Psychoanalytic Interpretation," Gregorio Klimovsky (1991) emphasizes that "freedom of thought favours an aptitude for intepretation. An individual who is prone to stereotyped reactions is not, in general, going to make good interpretations" (p. 491). André Haynal (1993b) writes:

> It is undeniable that theory influences interpretation, as does all the analyst's previous experience, including his reading, his thinking, his personality. However, when it is no longer a thought that arises in a creative movement, but rather, the veneer of a 'cliche'—when, in other words, his alleged preexistent knowledge takes the upper hand—then interpretation is no longer what it should be [p. 81; see also Meissner, 1984; Berger, 1985].

Freud's determined and repeatedly stated efforts not to read is own theories into patients' associations contributed significantly, however, to an important postpositivist trend in clinical interpretation: namely, a heuristic, antidoctrinal strategy of searching for unknown, unanticipated meanings and determinants which are unique to the individual patient and emerge unexpectedly during the therapeutic process. The latter type of interpretive approach, unlike a positivist-inspired, deductive methodology, is predominantly context-oriented, ad hoc, and ex post facto (Mahony and Singh, 1979, p. 439). Ad hoc in this context implies a construal of meanings and determinants that is applicable only to the data studied, rather than representing a more general meaning or determinant derived from a theory. It is ex post facto because such a meaning is construed only after the data have been produced, rather than originating in a preexisting theory prior to data production.

Freud (1923a) came closest to describing an ad hoc, ex post facto interpretive approach in his explanation of how unfocused listening often makes it possible to "catch the drift" of the patient's unconscious thoughts (pp. 238–241). He wrote that unconscious thoughts tend to emerge in the patient's associations like "allusions, as it were, to one particular theme" (p. 239). The analyst then uses the thematic meaning to "guess" what the patient is concealing. That description by Freud pictures his interpretive method as highly context-oriented and heuristic rather than theory-driven; but inevitably, as in any interpretive process, it still leaves room for preconceptions to creep in: for example, in identifying the thematic meaning of "allusions" in the patient's associations, and also in "guessing" what the thematic meaning suggests regarding hidden contents.

Numerous psychoanalytic writers since Freud have emphasized a context-oriented, data-driven approach to clinical interpretation.[12] In the latter methodologies, rather than listening for clinical material that the interpreter "recognizes" as similar to his or her own preferred theories, a data-driven approach attempts to "discover" unknown, unanticipated meanings in the patient's productions and the therapist's reactions.

Thus while a doctrinal approach employs theories that precede and are external to the data, an ad hoc, ex post facto methodology remains focused on and within the data, allowing interrelations among the associations (of both patient and therapist) to dictate the meaning retrospectively (compare Sturrock, 1979, p. 11). Peterfreund (1983, pp. 7–79) referred to these very different interpretive approaches as "stereotyped" in contrast to "heuristic" methods, respectively.

Meissner (1984, pp. 19–20) distinguishes context-oriented from theory-based interpretations this way: At the level of empirical generalization the analyst's freely hovering attention is drawn to certain regularities in the patient's behavior and to patterns of repetition and associative connection.

> It should be noted that such empirical generalizations are essentially nontheoretical; they are simply founded on direct clinical experience and of themselves involve no theory. It is also possible to address such phenomena in terms of low-level interpretations that are essentially nontheoretical. If the analyst were to draw the patient's attention to the fact that feelings of depression and loss seem to come about at times when he is going to be separated from the analyst, this may conceptually involve no more than merely calling attention to an observed regularity of behavior. Such observations or low-level interpretations can serve as the inductive base for theorizing, but of themselves contain no prior commitment to the theoretical level [Meissner, 1984, p. 20].

The context-oriented nature of data-driven interpretations makes such an approach sensitive to subtle, unique, process elements in both the patient's and analyst's associations. As Moss (1985) puts it: "Someone speaks; something happens. This something is the raw material of psychoanalysis: inherently unstable, continually displaced and supplanted by the next word, the next moment. The present tense is only virtual, never fixed, never quite present. The here and now is an imaginary item, an artifice" (p. 21). Spence et al. (1994, p. 44) suggest that processes of this kind are necessarily fleeting because the context of connotations is always changing.

Duncan (1989) describes the "flow" of the construal process in a data-driven approach. The therapist's attention is a continually changing pattern of impression and surmise, which runs like an intermingling current along the flow of the patient's associations: "bits of potential interpretation change kaleidoscopically from moment to moment. They seem equidistant in meaningfulness, and the analyst acts on none of them. Then a working analytic concept enables him to gather them together" (p. 696). The working concept suggests a credible common denominator in the associations; but even then, "we can start an interpretation without quite knowing what we are going to say, be forming an interpretation even while speaking, and surprise ourselves by what we have just said" (p. 696).[13]

Klauber (1980, p. 197) suspects that such spontaneity of interpretation is beneficial therapeutically, and that spontaneity of the therapeutic process is probably enhanced by a data-driven interpretive approach (see also Roche, 1989, p. 345). Another example of useful interpretive spontaneity is Freud's observation (1887–1902) in a letter to Fliess that he probably did his best work early in the development of psychoanalysis, when he did not really know what he was doing (cited by Klauber, 1980, p. 197). In a similar vein, Schwaber (1990b) lays great stress on the analyst's realizing that we truly do not know the patient's inner world (see also Loewenstein, 1957, p. 149; Meltzer, 1978; Margulies, 1989).

Duncan (1989) presents a clinical vignette that nicely illustrates Schwaber's point. The analyst (and patient) literally did not know the basis of a bizarre, recurring, transference disturbance which eventually clarified itself spontaneously through the appearance of unexpected links in the patient's associations (rather than from clinical theory). The following is a slightly abbreviated paraphrase of Duncan's clinical vignette:

> We had come to refer to it as The Funny Thing, not in the sense of comic, but of odd, peculiar. I would say something or fail to say something, fail to understand something or understand something only too well, and suddenly Ms K would totally despair of me as her analyst. There was something irreparably the matter with me. The analysis was hopeless. I would never understand her. It was the same each time. Afterwards, she would not mention it, as though nothing had happened. I never knew what set it off, and it rang no meaningful bell in my emotional self-knowledge. My worry was relieved eventually when, in time, these incidents linked up spontaneously in the material with a delusional aspect of Ms K's mother, who would suddenly take some seemingly neutral event as having aggressive intent, and would put a construction and importance on it that seemed crazy to everybody else. On those occasions her mother was impervious to reason, and would behave in very eccentric ways. All this helped us to understand The Funny Thing as properly inside of Ms. K. As working through occurred, the strange recurring happening gradually went away [p. 693].

Several features of an ad hoc, ex post facto interpretive approach justify classifying it as a postpositivist rather than as a positivist methodology. Such an approach does not depend upon specific methods or "rules" of interpretation, but proceeds on the basis of spontaneously deployed, sometimes improvised, interpretive methods and strategies; it is sensitively data- and context-oriented; and it does not seek certainty. A theory-driven approach to interpretation, on the other hand, is more closely related to the positivist model of inquiry because it emphasizes the application of specific methods and rules, is less resolutely data- and context-oriented, and tends to seek certainty. Edelson (1992a/1994) cautions that infatuation with theory can lead to ignoring details in the clinical material: "Theory banishes what otherwise might be fascinating particulars right out of the picture" (p. 85).

Meehl (1983) puts it this way: "We want the analyst to *discern* the 'red thread'; we don't want him to spin it and weave it in" (p. 360). Meehl (pp. 359–360) lists the following theory-determined errors associated with doctrinal interpretation: (1) content implantation; (2) selective intervention (a more subtle form of implantation); (3) causal inferences based solely on thematic trends in the clinical data (see also Grünbaum, 1989, 1990a; and, Chapter 7); (4) subjective bias in identifying thematic trends.[15] The philosopher of science William Wimsatt (1994) writes that "we have to recognize that our best theories and models are idealizations—deliberate simplifications, usually made with knowledge that they are false" (p. 499). In another essay (1986), Wimsatt discusses the heuristic use of theory.

The advantages of heuristic in contrast to doctrinal approaches apply not only to clinical work but to interpretive methods in all fields (discussed in Chapter 5). To illustrate, the art critic and educator Edmund Feldman (1971) writes that the interpretation of art

> is mainly an empirical enterprise, as opposed to a deductive process. As in a legal proceeding, the process of arriving at a verdict involves the orderly gathering of facts and presentation of evidence and the suspension of judgment until the end. We begin without knowing what the critial judgment will be, and we gradually adduce facts and feelings until a defensible evaluation seems warranted. This is the best way to avoid the pitfalls of excessive subjectivity, of partisanship, and of emotional intoxication. In general, forming conclusions on the basis of 'first principles' or axioms about art—in other words, proceeding *deductively* from premises which may or may not be applicable to the work in question—results in bad art criticism [p. 616].

Heuristically derived interpretations sometimes do, in fact, coincide more or less closely with specific clinical theories—what

Parsons (1992) calls "refinding" theory (see also Casement, 1985); but, methodologically, how one arrives at such interpretations is crucial. If one imposes a particular theory on the data, the interpretation is doctrinal and its plausibility suspect. If, on the other hand, the interpreter reaches a conclusion inductively, employing a discovery-oriented, data-driven approach which holds specific clinical theories in abeyance, the methodology is heuristic and the interpretation correspondingly more plausible. Adherence to a heuristic rather than a doctrinal approach is one of the surest ways to improve interpretation (see, for example, Peterfreund, 1983).

The sheer volume, complexity, and obscurity of clinical data often increase the therapist's temptation to simplify the interpretive task by resorting to use of clinical theories. Spence (1982a, p. 34) writes, for example, that the extent to which background assumptions and theories are employed varies with the "fluency" of the patient's productions. When a therapist cannot understand a patient's latent meanings and determinants by means of a context-oriented approach, he or she is more likely to employ theories in search of an answer. Therapists turn to theory for help when they feel insecure, or lost in the complexities of the clinical data (Friedman, 1988; see also Duncan, 1981).

Paradoxically, the clinician's insecurity about difficult interpretations often leads to the collection of more and more data, despite insufficient time to process further material. Oskamp (1965) reports that additional data increase the clinician's confidence, but not accuracy. The result is inefficiency of inference (Elstein, 1988, p. 30). A related study demonstrates that as the amount of data to be processed increases, accuracy of responses decreases, accompanied by an increase in the construal of illusory correlations based largely upon preconceptions (Lueger and Petzel, 1979).

The latter finding suggests that a data-based approach, which in general increases the effectiveness of interpretive methodology, can itself be overdone. For example, when clinicians have difficulty finding clues to latent mental contents, they often follow Freud's advice (1914a, p. 22) to wait for more associations, on the assumption that sooner or later the data themselves will "begin to speak"—which may turn into a very long wait, however, and the voluminous additional associations may even increase the therapist's confusion. What may be needed at such times is not the amassing of more and more data, but some self-reflection by the therapist about whether he or she is blocking about the patient's productions, and some dialogue with the patient about the opacity of the associations.

A distinction is necessary between occasional, necessary uses of theory, on the one hand, and theory-driven interpretive methodologies, on the other. Observation always requires some background assumptions and basic concepts, and modern science recognizes that such assumptions invariably influence one's observations and conclusions (Polkinghorne, 1983, pp. 94–97; Rosenthal, 1966). For example, since observations involve classifications, and since the latter have theoretical implications, observations cannot be completely independent of theory (Quine, 1953). Observation language and theory language form an interacting system (Hesse, 1980). The inference to be drawn from this, however, is not that one may apply specific theories freely and advantageously to clinical observations and interpretations, which some schools of clinical interpretation maintain (for example, Kohut, 1984, p. 84; Goldberg, 1985, pp. 63–64).[16] It is a long and unwarranted leap from acknowledging that theories contaminate observations and constructions to the conclusion that one may apply clinical theories directly to clinical data, observations, and interpretations.

Knowing how subtly and insidiously background assumptions, personal biases, and clinical theories can influence one's observations and conclusions, clinicians must do what they can to reduce the distorting role of such preconceptions in their interpretive work. Otherwise we fall too easily into the doctrinal trap of imposing rather than discovering meanings; of selectively filtering clinical data for whatever fits one's favored clinical theories; ignoring issues of evidence and justification; and thinking reductively in terms of simplistic, limited, cliché-ridden meanings rather than multiple meanings and determinants that change over time (Peterfreund, 1983, p. 53). Gadamer (1975) stresses the necessity to be aware of one's preconceptions, while remaining open to the discourse of another. One must be sensitive to the discourse's quality of newness. "But this kind of sensitivity involves neither 'neutrality' in the matter of the object nor the extinction of one's self, but the conscious assimilation of one's own fore-meanings and prejudices. The important thing is to be aware of one's own bias" (Gadamer, 1984, p. 238).

Interpretive methodologies necessarily rest upon a relatively small number of basic, very general methodologic concepts, without which interpretation would be impossible (Rapaport,

1944, p. 191). Edelson (1984, p. 130–131) defines a clinical interpretation as an inference or hypothesis about the patient which, combined with a general psychoanalytic hypothesis, appears to follow from what the patient has said. Freud (1915b, p. 117) concluded that the abstract ideas which we impose upon the data constitute the basic general (core) concepts (in contrast to specific clinical theories) of psychoanalysis; that these core concepts do not derive from observations, but are free creations of the human mind; and that although the basic general concepts do not derive from observations, ideally they are related in crucial ways to the empirical phenomena of the field.[17]

According to Rapaport (1944), the basic methodologic concepts that underlie Freud's interpretive system include: the concept of an unconscious mind, continuity, meaning, determinism, overdetermination, instinctual drives, conflict, defense, repetition, transference, and the importance of childhood experiences. What these core concepts of psychoanalysis and interpretive methodology have most in common is their generality, as a result of which they do not give rise to single but to alternative interpretive hypotheses (Applegarth, 1991, p. 743). The methodologist Adriaan De Groot (1969, p. 35) points out that broad, general background assumptions and principles do not force interpretations into preconceived conclusions; new, unique interpretations of the data are possible within the general theoretical framework of a science. By contrast, theory-driven interpretive approaches, which employ highly specific clinical theories, tend to generate single rather than alternative interpretive hypotheses. De Groot comments about theory-driven approaches:

> An obvious advantage of this method is its consistency; an equally obvious disadvantage its one-sidedness. The disadvantage is a serious one and may well assume such proportions that, scientifically, the method is no longer acceptable. This will be the case when there is nothing but continuous theorizing all along the same lines, and no alternative theoretical models and interpretations are ever tried out. If such is indeed the case, the system is no longer a working theory that can be viewed with detachment, and which can be tested. It is bound to develop more and more into a dogma [De Groot, 1969, p. 56].

Thus, theory-driven clinical interpretations often are not applicable to the individual patient, and frequently interfere with the discovery of unique, personal meanings and determinants. Reconstructions are particularly prone to this problem: that is, therapists tend to use a particular model of the infant's early life to guide his or her understanding of a patient's associations (see, for example, Cooper, 1988; and Lichtenberg, 1983). Other examples include Klein's[18] and Kohut's[19] interpretive approaches, both of which are doctrinally driven by their respective genetic theories of pathogenesis. Paniagua (1985, p. 323) cautions that use of specific psychogenetic theories in clinical interpretations all too easily and unsuspectingly becomes indoctrination.

In a trenchant criticism of theory-driven approaches to reconstruction, Arlow (1991) writes that such an approach, "seems alien to me. I had always thought that matters were the other way around, namely, that, from the associations, we get an insight into the early life of the patient" (p. 543). "To me," Arlow continues, "this represents a fundamental error in the psychoanalytic methodology of interpretation. It is what I have called the phenomenological error, a variant of what Hartmann [1959] termed the genetic fallacy, namely, foisting upon the patient's associations an interpretation based upon a model concept of pathogenesis" (p. 544; see also Gergely, 1992).

In a recent essay, "Critical Notes on the Psychoanalyst's Theorizing," Barratt (1994, p. 708) describes a subtle, little recognized, but crucial aspect of the clinician's theorizing which psychologists refer to as "covariational judgments," that is, decisions about "what meaningfully belongs with what." Clinical judgments of that kind are crucial to the therapist's specialized "procedural knowledge," but they are also problematic because clinicians seldom subject this subtle form of theorizing to the necessary process of critical evaluation. Barratt suggests that clinicians be skeptical of their assumptions about what meaningfully belongs with what, because theorizing is everpresent and needs to be treated with suspicion.

Overconfident and Dogmatic Rather Than Skeptical, Error-Correcting Approaches

A central feature of the shift to a postpositivist model of science was the collapse of foundationalism and its associated positivist belief in completely certain (apodictic) knowledge. In place of absolutely certain knowledge the postpositivist perspective substitutes "assertorial" (also called "assertoric") knowledge, that is, the view that some knowledge claims are better than others but that none is beyond question (Polkinghorne, 1983, p. 279). Cheshire's observation (1964, p. 224) that psychoanalytic propositions are "tendency" rather than "categorical" statements exemplifies assertorial knowledge.

In other words, postpositivist science does not claim to discover "truths"; it seeks approximations that move toward but never fully achieve "the truth" (De Groot, 1969, pp. 103–105; see also Hanly, 1990). As Poincaré observed about mathematics, "problems are not solved once and for all; they are only more or less solved" (cited by Colby and Spar, 1983, p. v). Polkinghorne (1983) indicates further that method also does not give "truth," but corrects guesses:

> The logic for justifying assertoric knowledge is different from the deductive logic required for attaining absolute certainty. Assertoric knowledge uses practical reasoning and argumentation. It requires a decision among alternatives, none of which provides certainty. A supporter of a knowledge claim is expected to argue cogently before the apppropriate community, providing evidence pertinent to his or her proposal and defending his or her position as the most likely correct position among various alternatives. Assertoric knowledge is time-bound. It is knowledge that one (or a group) decides for—a particular alternative—in order to act in a given situation. This kind of knowledge is not considered true for all time and for all places, but it does serve as the basis for action [p. 280].

An example of assertorial knowledge serving as a basis for action in the therapeutic situation is the phase of the clinical interpretive process in which the therapist selects a particular construction as the most plausible among alternative hypotheses at a given time, and prepares to convey that tentative depth-psychological understanding to the patient, at an opportune time and in a specific way.

A postpositivist perspective readily comprehends that despite centuries of study by philosophers, hermeneutic scholars, and investigators in many fields, the problems, difficulties, and uncertainties of interpretation persist; that no universally correct methods or categories of interpretation have been established; that general rules or canons of interpretation are of little value in specific instances; that certainty is unattainable, and correctness is only a probability which requires careful checking (Hirsch, 1967). Thus, Kermode (1979, p. 125) refers to interpretation as a necessary but nearly impossible task; and I. A. Richards quipped that the only proper attitude toward a successful interpretation is to view it as a "triumph against odds" (cited by Hirsch, 1967, p. 164).

In contrast to a postpositivist, assertoric, skeptical view of interpretations, which emphasizes the need to justify constructions and reconstructions, exclusivist, method-oriented, theory-driven approaches are more prone to overconfidence and dogmatism regarding their interpretive methods and conclusions. Various reviewers of Kohut's writings, for example, have called attention to his lack of scientific humility and restraint.[20] Moreover, since investigative, including interpretive, methods largely determine the fundamental conceptions of scientific fields,[21] it can be argued that Kohut's overconfidence regarding his interpretive method led inevitably to dogmatic claims regarding his clinical formulations, theories, and therapeutic concepts. In his final volume (Kohut, 1984, p. 53), for example, Kohut spoke of attempting to demonstrate that all forms of psychopathology are based upon defects, distortions, or weaknesses of the self; that all such flaws result from empathic failures by important persons in childhood; and that the "undernourished self" represents the primary basis of all psychopathology (1984, p. 90). In contrast to such sweeping theoretical conclusions, a skeptical, assertoric viewpoint accepts the fact that generalizations in the human and social sciences have a decidedly restricted scope (Fiske and Shweder, 1986, p. 4), and that the complex multidetermined phenomena with which clinicians deal do not lend themselves to all-or-none conceptualizations.

Self psychologists might argue that Kohut's focus on "empathic failures" by the therapist indicates an acceptance of interpretive fallibility—a seemingly cogent argument except for the following: some critics of self psychology (for example, Hoffman, 1991; Cooper, 1993) note that Kohut and some of his followers (for example, Wolf, 1986) conceive of interpretive fallibility only within the narrow bounds of "empathic failure," whereas faulty interpretations occur also for other reasons and in other contexts. The constricted way that self psychologists conceptualize the therapeutic dialogue is reminiscent of a positivist attitude and approach.[22] Lawrence Friedman (1988) observes that:

> Of all people, it is the psychotherapist who has elected to use the subtlest shades of definition to grasp life's immediacies. How dismal, then, that Kohut and his students are able to point to so many ordinary analyses which can only be characterized as extended sales talks for a theoretical schematism [p. 387; see also Stein, 1979].

Abraham (1986) has reviewed the literature on overconfidence in interpretation; and Jelalian and Miller (1984) have reviewed the related literature on persisting beliefs in the face of negative evidence (see also Nagel, 1980; Benedek, 1989). Overconfidence and "confirmation bias" are serious problems in interpretive work because they interfere with the necessary willingness to search for negative evidence. In the presence of overconfidence, disconfirming and discrediting evidence tends to be ignored (Abraham, 1986, p. 67).[23]

Olinick (1980) points out that because of their subjective and regressive character, empathic experiences and impressions are often associated with unwarranted feelings of certainty. Illusory feelings of certainty are not confined to empathic experiences, however: some examples of the latter include Ramzy's (1974, p. 548) oversimplified and dogmatic assertions regarding psychoanalytic inference; Langs' (1978, p. 110) overconfidence regarding his method of validating interpretations; and the pervasive problem of "confirmation bias" in all forms of human inference, reasoning, and judgment (compare Mirsky, 1983, pp. 185–186). Psychoanalysts and dynamic psychotherapists exhibit confirmation bias, for example, in their disinclination to employ justifying procedures for interpretive hypotheses. Gedo (1984c, p. 514) writes that even if such tests were performed, experienced clinicians would refuse to alter their convictions on the basis of the test results, but would continue to base their conclusions on their personal experiences (cited by Eagle, 1986a, pp. 82–83).

Hermeneutic investigators (for example, Hirsch, 1967, pp. 166–167) describe still another source of unwarranted overconfidence in interpreters, that is, the interrelations of part and whole meanings in the interpretive process. The interpreter infers part meanings from individual elements of the clinical data, but also must construct a whole meaning that both specifies and ties together all of the part meanings. The whole is derived from the parts, but the parts are delineated and integrated by the whole—an intrinsically circular process. The inherent circularity of constructions (the "hermeneutic circle") produces an illusion that one's construction is necessarily correct. The illusion results from the fact that most of the evidence for an interpretive hypothesis (in the form of part meanings) derives from, and is generated by, that hypothesis. The construction appears to be correct precisely because it is so internally consistent. Trapped in the hermeneutic circle, the interpreter cannot see that he or she may have misconstrued the whole meaning of the data (see also Wallerstein and Sampson, 1971; Elstein, 1988, pp. 27–28). Macmillan (1991, p. 568) writes that the methodologic problem of circularity is not confined to depth-psychological therapies or to other clinical studies, but is a general problem that affects all investigations (see also Danziger, 1985).

The therapist's biases, which are an integral part of the clinical context, also contribute to illusory feelings of certainty; for the way one observes is as relevant as what one observes. As Leavy (1980, p. xiv) puts it, unless one knows the interpreter's biases, it is difficult to estimate the distortions that he or she introduces.[24] Here Arnoult and Anderson have reviewed a number of useful bias-reducing procedures, including routine construction of alternative hypotheses (Shaklee and Fischoff, 1982); recording interview information and keeping it available for future checking (Arkes, 1981); and continued reevaluation of previous conclusions (Nisbett and Ross, 1980; Ross and Anderson, 1982; Holt, 1988).

A postpositivist approach to interpretive methodology accepts the limitations of interpretive inquiry with respect to both the reliability of its methods and the validity of its results. Such an approach doubts everything that goes into its proof, including its observations, interpretive hypotheses, and how the two fit together (Larrabee, 1964, p. 233). A skeptical attitude starts with alertness to discrepancies between one's constructions, on one hand, and all of the clinical data rather than selected data that support a favored hypothesis, on the other (French, 1958a, pp. 106–197).[25] Natterson (1991) observes that the analyst never knows whether an interpretation is correct, because he or she never knows all of the factors that contribute to the situation. "So the analyst makes a sophisticated guess, prepares for the high probability of error, and expects a flawed but constructive consequence of the interpretation" (pp. 118–119).[26]

Thus, Poland (in Panel, 1986, p. 692) concludes that all interpretations conveyed to the patient are really trial interpretations.

Weich (in Panel, 1986, p. 694) agrees, and proposes the concept of a "good enough therapist" (see also Kumin, 1989). Eagle (1984a, p. 168) suggests the concept of a "good enough interpretation." Freud's concept (1910c, pp. 225–226) that interpretations are good enough if they are "in the neighborhood" of the patient's current conflict, and Hartmann's (1951) view that interpretations have "multiple appeal" in the patient's unconscious, suggest some limitations as well as therapeutic leeway regarding the accuracy of interpretations.

Summary

This chapter emphasizes the advantages of a postpositivist perspective for interpretive methodologies, and illustrates some of the problems produced by persisting features of the positivist paradigm. The advantages of postpositivist models include their idiographic focus, flexibility, ingenuity, scope, spontaneity, openness to alternative hypotheses, scientific tentativeness, and error-detecting/correcting capabilities. The pluralistic, data-driven, and context-sensitive features of postpositivist methodologies increase the probability of understanding the individual patient's reality, and provide checks that compensate for the limitations of particular methods and types of data. For these and other reasons, most methods and models of interpretive inquiry include a substantial number of postpositivist characteristics, although they vary in their pluralism, flexibility, dependence on data rather than theories, self-correcting and justifying procedures. So far, only a few research models of interpretive methodology are systematically justification oriented.

Remnants of the positivist paradigm appear to be involved in some of the commonest and most problematic forms of methodologic lag affecting interpretive inquiry. These include: 1) monistic and method-oriented rather than pluralistic and problem-oriented approaches; 2) doctrinal or theory-driven in contrast to data-driven, context-sensitive approaches; and 3) overconfident and dogmatic attitudes toward interpretations rather than skeptical, error-correcting approaches.

Monistic, method-based approaches emphasize a particular method, perspective, or variety of data—a contemporary clinical example being Kohut's insistence that empathy is the only useful method of construing latent contents. The subject matter of depth psychology is too complex, however, for any single method of interpretive inquiry; latent meanings and determinants elude unilateral investigation.

Doctrinal or theory-driven interpretive methodologies—illustrated for example by Melanie Klein's and Heinz Kohut's approaches—impose preconceived meanings and determinants on the patient's productions, selectively filter the clinical data for whatever fits the interpreter's theory, ignore issues of evidence and justification, and employ reductive, cliché-ridden interpretations. Interpretive methodologies necessarily rest on a relatively small number of basic, very general concepts that, because of their generality, lead to alternative rather than to single interpretive hypotheses. Theory-driven methodologies, on the other hand, employ highly specific clinical theories that tend to generate only single constructions. Thus doctrinal interpretation frequently interferes with the discovery of uniquely personal meanings and determinants, and often is not applicable to the individual patient's reality.

Overconfidence and dogmatism also produce serious problems in interpretive work. These forms of methodologic lag are related to the positivist emphasis on certainty, and as such they interfere with the necessary willingness to search for negative evidence and for alternative hypotheses. Overconfidence contributes also to the pervasive problem of "confirmation bias" in human inference, reasoning, and judgment. A postpositivist perspective, by contrast, accepts the fact that certainty is unattainable, and that "correctness" is only a probability that requires careful checking.

4

Some Language-Based Models of Interpretive Methodology

Evaluation of Linguistic, Discourse, and Narrative Models

The previous chapter considered some major forms of methodologic lag in contemporary models of interpretive inquiry. The present chapter extends that discussion, evaluating some language-based models of clinical interpretation: Lacan's structural linguistic model; examples of rule-governed linguistic and discourse models; a (simulated) discourse model which is not rule-governed; and selected narrative models.

The use of language-based models of interpretation is not new to psychoanalysis. Freud's writings suggest a number of relationships between interpretive methodology and language.[1] Most such comparisons were figurative and illustrative; but at times Freud used language in the processing of clinical data, for example, construing idioms of vernacular speech as thinly disguised expressions of unconscious contents.[2] On one occasion, Freud (1911a, pp. 62–65) employed a language-based model of pathodynamics and interpretive methodology, postulating a series of linguistic transformations underlying the meanings and mechanisms of paranoid symptoms. He proposed that the four clinical types of paranoia result from specific grammatical transformations of the latent homosexual statement, "I [a man] love him" (pp. 64–65). Although he had little knowledge of linguistic rule-ordering as a theoretical device, his use of grammatical transformations was surprisingly similar to that of modern linguistics. Freud's language-based model of interpretive methodology and paranoia was a tour de force, but it may have been somewhat too facile and insufficiently related to the main body of psychoanalytic theory to become established method or doctrine.

Freud (1915c) was understandably reluctant to attempt a theory of language, or even to generalize about the relations of psychoanalysis and interpretive methodology to language.[3] To Freud, words were part of the preconscious, not the unconscious (pp. 201–202; see also Rycroft, 1958). A number of post-Freudian writers, on the other hand, have utilized various aspects of language theory to develop models of mind, of psychopathology, therapy, and interpretive methodology. Wilden (1968, p. 310), agreeing with Lacan, insists (controversially) that psychoanalysis *is* a theory of language. Others argue against equating the unconscious with language;[4] for the mental activity involved in dreams and other unconscious processes is so distinctive that it must be distinguished from what is traditionally referred to as language (Benveniste, 1971, p. 74).

The phrase "rules of interpretation" appears occasionally in clinical writings.[5] Rogers (1981, pp. 434–437) derives a number of "descriptive rules" from Freud's writings on dream interpretation which he classifies as interpretive tactics. He emphasizes that these "descriptive rules" are no more than guidelines or heuristics of dream interpretation. The notion that clinical interpretation might be rule-governed implies a more systematic, orderly, and repeatable process than is actually the case; it appeals to a persisting nostalgia for positivist reliability and certainty.

Paradoxically, Freud (1923a) appears to have assumed a post-positivist attitude towards such rules; for despite his enduring commitment to positivism, he indicated that his method of interpretation was not based on strict rules but left much to the sensitivity, imagination, and judgment of the individual clinician (p. 239). Hartmann (1951) also attempted to dispel the mistaken assumption that a comprehensive set of interpretive rules exists; he stressed the importance of keeping interpretation flexible. Mooij (1991) states that a small number of fundamental rules constitutes the domain of psychoanalysis and makes interpretation of what occurs within that domain possible, but that interpretation itself is not rule-governed. Goldberg (1988, p. 188) agrees that no such set of rules can or should exist.

The following discussions argue that attempts to describe interpretive methodology in terms of linguistic universals, language rules, or, at the other extreme, in terms of radically constructivist narrative models, are questionable. The methodologic advantages of a flexible (postpositivist) interpretive approach are stressed.

Lacan's Structural-Linguistic Model of Clinical Interpretation

Lacan (1956, p. 47)[6] was critical of traditional psychoanalysis for accepting Freud's positivism, and for neglecting Freud's interest in language and the therapeutic dialogue. He objected to the preeminence of experimental method in general science (1966, p. 72), insisting that the "conjectural" (that is, interpretive) human sciences best exemplify "true science" (1978, p. 265). His own approach was nonempirical, mentalistic, and deductive, with some traces of positivism (Shapiro, 1979, p. 125).

Lacan noted Freud's emphasis on the uniqueness of the unconscious, but also his lack of interest in the syntactic structure of language, from which Lacan concluded that the hierarchically-organized syntax of language cannot explain the unique features of the unconscious. Determined to account for the distinctiveness of the unconscious in linguistic terms, Lacan drew upon Saussure's (1915) structural-linguistic concept that language is a system of relations consisting of differences in both the sound images (signifiers) and in the mental concepts (signifieds) that the sounds signify. The combination of signifier and signified comprise the linguistic sign. According to Saussure, two such contingent systems of difference are capable of producing a system of significance, that is, of meaning (Caws, 1988, p. 73). The latter concept gave priority to the signified (mental concepts) over the signifier (sound images, words), which Saussure expressed in the equation: sign = signified/signifier.

Because he was suspicious of the emphasis in psychoanalysis on conscious insight, Lacan could not accept Saussure's giving priority to the ideational concepts of the signified. He believed that searching for the signified, a form of thought, is futile. Instead, he stressed the signifier—the sound, not the meaning, of a word—bits of speech sounds (words) that are idiosyncratic to the individual, which have been repressed and disguised by unconscious operations (Wilson, 1994, p. 153). Thus he inverted Saussure's equation to: sign = Signifier/signified, giving special place (and a capital S) to the Signifier. Lacan insisted that the signifying chain is the proper object of study for both the linguist and the psychoanalyst, and that the relationships within the signifying chain are the best guide to psychic structure. For example, Lacan proposed that Freud's unconscious transformative operations (primary processes) of condensation and displacement are equivalents of the linguistic tropes, metaphor and metonymy. The language scholar Malcolm Bowie (1979) characterizes Lacan's view this way:

> The unconscious, in so far as it becomes visible and audible in speech, symptoms, dreams and involuntary acts of omission and commission, is governed by the same rules as all other systems: the rules which Lacan has expressed in summary form as the "law of the Signifier" (p. 131).

To illustrate Lacan's use of his structual-linguistic approach to interpretation in actual practice, the following examples deal with his methods and concepts of psychoanalytic treatment and of applied psychoanalysis. Edith Kurzweil (1978) observes that, "When he descends from lofty generalizations to psychoanalytic practice, he addreses himself to clinical techniques, to the importance of *Durcharbeiten*, or to the dangers of intellectualizing" (p. 645). She notes also, however, that there are wide gaps between Lacan's lectures on psychoanalysis and his clinical experiences, that he focuses on the language of psychoanalysis rather than on clinical observation, and that his vaunted "return to Freud" relied increasingly on Freud's early studies of hysteria. Ultimately, Kurzweil concludes, Lacan reaches the unconscious via the analysis of dreams:

> Like Freud, he tries to uncover all the relationships between manifest and latent dream content, and all the omissions, pauses, and doubts of the analysand. He is especially concerned with individual speech patterns and with breaks and irregularities in these patterns. Unconscious dream thoughts and free association as well are examined in structuralist fashion: all are part of language; they are semantic condensations of disourse and/or function as syntactic displacements; and unconscious operations such as distortion, reaction formation, denial, and the consideration of representability become equivalents of *metaphor* and *metonymy* (these exist only in "chains of meaning") [Kurzweil, 1978, p. 645].

In his seminar on the psychoses, Lacan (1993) applied his structural-linguistic concepts of interpretation to Schreber's memoirs. Focusing on Schreber's account of his sexual relations with God, Lacan points out that, "the text includes no indication of the slightest presence, the slightest fervor, the slightest real communication that would give us the idea that there really is a relationship here between two beings" (1993, p. 77). Leavy (1996, p. 1274) comments that Lacan's use of the word "fervor" indicates what is missing in Schreber's psychosis, namely, passionate loving feelings toward God. In this example, Lacan bases his interpretation on an absence of affective expression, but the role of signifying chains in deriving this interpretation is not clear. Kurzweil (1980, p. 144) comments that since the unconscious is said to express itself primarily through gaps, irregularities, and lapses, Lacan insisted that he learned more from how a patient talks than from what he or she says—an emphasis on paraverbal rather than on directly verbal clues to latent meanings. The conclusion that Lacan reached regarding Schreber in the preceding example corresponds with a well-known psychoanalytic theory of psychosis (Freud, 1915c), that is, the psychotic's loss of unconscious ties to objects, and restitutive attempts to substitute words about objects for the lost object ties.

The final example is from Lacan's (1966) famous seminar on Edgar Allan Poe's "The Purloined Letter." Unlike most applied psychoanalytic studies of literary works, Lacan focuses on Poe's language rather than on Poe himself. By this move he replaces Poe as the signifier, and puts the narrative in a new context that is said to reveal previously unrecognized meanings. Kurzweil (1980) describes Lacan's analysis this way: "It is full of Lacanisms, of contrapuntal devices, of made-up words, of 'slights' and 'slips of the tongue,' of convolutions that mediate between Poe and Lacan, symbols and signifiers, and the *letter* that is to be understood *to the letter*" (p. 151). Kurzweil continues:

> Letter, it seems, leads to litter, to literally, to Joyce's circle that "played on the homophony of these two words in English," to the letter as refuse handled by the police, to a different seal on a stamp, to makers of handwriting, and on and on. Lacan opposes the possessor to the holder of the letter, ties high treason to the problems of translation, Baudelairisms, the post office, and to the circularity of letters, of social phenomena, and of symbols. He speculates about the emotions, motivations and possible thoughts

> of all the characters, about love and hate, only to get back to Freud, to the fact that sex, the reason for all the commotion, remains hidden [pp. 151-152].

Lacan believed that he had discovered something law-like and universal, and on that basis he made the further claim that there is no mental structure except that of language (Bowie, 1979, p. 131). His modification and clinical use of Saussure's concept involved a double reduction, however, similar to Lévi-Strauss's ill-fated application of structural linguistics to anthropology.[7] Lacan and the other early structuralists failed to recognize the limitations of language as a model of mind (Overman, 1988, p. 391; Rorty, 1985, pp. 103–109). They overlooked the fact that, "the syntax of dreams is too compressed, too discontinuous to be viewed as operating analogously to the syntax of natural language" (Boyd, 1985, p. 112).

Seung (1982a) believes that overgeneralizations of this kind by the early structuralists, including Lacan, contributed to the intellectual reactions of relativism, historicism, and the development of poststructuralism; and as it happens, contemporary structuralists are strongly opposed to universals. Structuralism as originally conceived no longer exists; the posited universal mental structures have not been demonstrated, and investigators no longer search for them (Kurzweil, 1980, p. 10).

Lacan's dismissal of the "signified," or unconscious thought, as an object of clinical interpretation also weakened his theoretical system. Chessick (1992, p. 88) points out that Lacan's unconscious, which consists entirely of signifiers (linguistic chains and networks), resembles Freud's preconscious rather than the unconscious (see also Vergote, 1983). There is no place in Lacan's theory for an autonomous unconscious antedating the acquisition of language.

Since for Lacan the unconscious both consists of and has the structure of language, understanding and interpreting the unconscious depends largely on understanding linguistics. By reformulating Freud's theories as a structural grammar which ostensibly reflects the actual structure of the unconscious, Lacan severely limited Freud's theories, including the theory of the unconscious (Laor and Agassi, 1986, p. 475), and also shortchanged psychoanalytic developmental theory (Weber, 1991, p. 11). In addition, his focus on language to the neglect of affects (Green, 1973) has been criticized as overly intellectual—what Hamburg (1991, p. 360) refers to as the "icy realms" of Lacan's linguistic structures (see also Modell, 1990, p. 18).[8] The limited scope of Lacan's interpretations appears to represent a further consequence of his attempt to reduce the complexities of the unconscious to a few allegedly "law-like" linguistic generalizations.

Lacan's theory of therapy emphasizes making the unconscious conscious, bringing latent signifiers to the surface in the form of full, free speech—a view coinciding with Lacan's focus on early Freud and the topographic model, another oversimplification. Because structural linguistics employs only synchronic but not diachronic analysis, Lacan (1966, p. 856) considered historical reconstructions to be unimportant and unnecessary (see also Weber, 1991, p. 11).

Lacanians rarely intervene, and when they do their interpretations do not attempt to "nail down" meanings but only to "ring bells." The accuracy of interpretations was of little concern to Lacan. As a structuralist he viewed theories and interpretations as attempts to "organize" experience—attempts, he contended, which neither need to be nor can be validated (Laor and Agassi, 1986, pp. 469–470, 485–486).

Lacan's "calculated effort to be unreadable" (Bowie, 1979, p. 147) is well known. Lacan himself asserted that it was a deliberate style, an attempt to depict how the unconscious operates; but Anthony Wilden, one of Lacan's early translators, felt to the contrary that he had in fact become a prisoner of his own style (cited by Leavy, 1979, p. 311).

Considered from the perspective of interpretive methodology and the probity of clinical interpretations, Lacan's approach has little to recommend itself. It exhibits extensive "methodologic lag" in a number of positivistic features: it seeks foundations in alleged linguistic universals, is monistic, method-oriented, absolutist, theory-driven, and apodictic. Lacan does not postulate but proclaims his interpretive formulations; he considers error-detecting and error-correcting measures to be unnecessary. In many ways, therefore, Lacan's methodology is the antithesis of a postpositivist approach.

Edelson's Linguistic Model of Interpretive Methodology

In a series of writings that drew considerable attention at the time, the psychoanalyst Marshall Edelson (1970, 1972, 1975) proposed the concept of linguistic rule-ordering—specifically, Chomsky's (1957, 1965, 1968, 1979) early transformational-generative theory of grammar—as the basis for a theory of clinical interpretation. He drew two principal parallels between Chomskian and Freudian theories: both postulate the presence of deep structures, the existence of which can only be inferred; and both postulate that deep structures are transformed by rule-ordered operations into surface structures. The transformative operations in Freudian theory that Edelson invoked were the primary processes (Edelson, 1975, pp. 126–127). Drawing also on Chomsky's theory of "linguistic competence," Edelson proposed that the principal characteristic of clinical interpretive competence is the interpreter's ability to reconstruct the rule-ordered operations that transform deeper, meaning-bearing structures into surface structures (1975, p. 78).[9]

Edelson's theory of clinical interpretive competence does not lend itself readily to direct clinical examination, however, because linguistic (and, according to Edelson, clinical interpretive) competence involve a detailed knowledge of language of which we are not conscious and which we are unable to explain (1975, pp. 27–28). Thus, the only way that an interpreter might carry out the proposed reconstruction of unconscious rule-ordered operations would be unconsciously. In addition, dynamic, including defensive, processes are excluded in Chomsky's transformational grammar, which limits its clinical applicability still further (Shapiro, 1977, p. 359; 1979, p. 55;). Foulkes (1978) writes:

> The superficially appealing parallels between deep and surface structure, on one hand, and latent and manifest content, on the other, are, when taken too literally, somewhat misleading. The received wisdom of Chomsky and of Freud just don't match up very well. Edelson's theoretical integration is highly instructive, but ultimately unsatisfactory [p. 118].[10]

Chomsky's transformational-generative theory of grammar no longer enjoys the status that it once held among linguists.[11] Psycholinguist Prideaux (1985), for example, concludes that, "There is no real evidence at all that language users invoke a transformational grammar in any sort of step-by-step manner as they either produce or comprehend language" (p. 153). With respect to Edelson's postulated relationship between Chomskian and Freudian theories, Fonagy and Fonagy (1995) point out that

"Chomsky's notion of 'deep structure' has little to do with the psychoanalytic notion of a dynamic unconscious. On the contrary, it is purported to contain the rational kernel of the statement. In the framework of generative grammar, unconscious content may find more ready representation at the level of surface structure, where it would be hidden through the primacy of the conscious content of the utterance (deep structure)" (p. 409).

Since linguistic competence as defined by Chomsky does not appear to account for comprehension of everyday discourse, it cannot be expected to account for understanding of clinical discourse (Reed, 1985, pp. 237–238), It also seems unlikely that interpretive competence is monolithic, as Chomsky's and Edelson's theories imply. The linguists Green and Morgan (1981) argue, for example, that

> a variety of kinds of knowledge and abilities interact to enable discourse production and interpretation. This should hardly be a surprising conclusion. It amounts to claiming that the whole mind is deployed in producing and understanding discourse. It runs counter to common sense, we think, to claim that such mental activities are the product of "strictly linguistic" processing mechanisms [p. 177].[12]

Thus, Edelson's theory of interpretive competence based upon linguistic rule-ordering does not appear to offer a sufficiently promising model of clinical interpretation. In addition to the theory's positivistic appeal to a biological foundation for interpretation, the search for deep structures takes us too far from (surface) content and thus from latent meanings (see Fonagy and Fonagy, 1995, p. 409).

Many present-day linguists regard Chomsky's two-stage theory as merely a first step in the analysis of language (Devlin, 1997, p. 124), that is, a stage of generating deep structure followed by a corrective-transformative process which results in surface structure. From this more limited perspective on Chomskian theory, an essentially descriptive parallel with two major phases of the clinical interpretive process might be justified, namely, the earlier constructive activities of generating interpretive hypotheses, followed by a corrective-transformative phase of checking, revising, and rechecking the constructions.

In recent years Edelson has (partially) modified his earlier views on interpretive competence (see, for example, 1988, pp. xxxiii, 78–88). Still more recently (1992a-b), he has proposed a narrative rather than a formal linguistic (syntactic) model of interpretive methodology and the therapeutic process (discussed later in this chapter).

Schafer's "Action Language" as a Model of Interpretive Methodology

Another example of an extensively rule-governed, language-related model of interpretive methodology is Roy Schafer's "action language" (1973, 1975, 1976, 1978, 1983a). He writes: "Let me remind you that here we are concerned with deciding how to follow the rules of a language; we are not concerned directly or solely with observations" (1975, p. 52). He asserts categorically that, "It is only by means of sets of language rules that we are ever able to achieve a systematic approach to knowing anything, including anything psychoanalytically" (1975, p. 42).

Schafer's language rules are not those of Chomskian syntax but derive from the rules of "language games"[13] described by the later Wittgenstein (1945–1949), which not only communicate but also constitute the object of theoretical meaning.[14] Schafer acknowledges the influence of Wittgenstein and of Ryle (1949), whose views lead to a philosophy of mind without processes or structures.[15] Schafer thus abandons the repressed unconscious and causality, adopting instead Ryle's thesis regarding the primacy of thoughts. As a form of "language game," action language views therapy as a clearing up of confusions in the use or misuse of language, rather than as an exploration of the repressed unconscious. The philosophical assumptions underlying Schafer's argument severely restrict the kinds of psychological questions which can be asked and the kind of theory which might be constructed (Anscombe, 1981, p. 240).

Schafer's aim (1975) is to develop a psychoanalysis without psychodynamics. He proposes that we view all psychological processes, phenomena, and behavior as actions, each action being designated by an active verb; nouns and adjectives for psychological processes should be avoided. Emotions, for example, are not subjective experiences or feeling states, but ways of acting. Emotion is not something one has, but something that one does. He also emphasizes the importance of action language to the interpretive process (1976, pp. 129, 141, 149–152; 1978, p. 185), referring to action language as the "native tongue" of clinical interpretation (1976, p. 211). He insists that we must

> develop and apply this codification tirelessly and unflichingly, for, if we do not obey the rules, we shall not really know or speak the language and in the end we shall not have a single, coherent world to be psychoanalytic about. In the long run, it is one's fidelity to the rules that makes all the difference in systematic thinking. Here one cannot be too faithful or fastidious [1975, p. 43].

The following are two of the many examples that Schafer suggests for translating traditional psychoanalytic statements into action language:

> *Traditional statement*: "His repression of this dangerous impulse was too weak to prevent it from gaining consciousness."
> *Action language*: "By failing to be sufficiently on guard against not doing so, he thought consciously of the action to do so" [1975, p. 49].

> *Traditional statement*: "The conflict between her id and ego was so evenly balanced as to cause a paralysis of thought, affect and behavior."
> *Action language*: "She behaved in a mentally paralyzed fashion; she did not think or perform any actions other than this in any other mode than this. (Putting it this way implies that behaving as though paralyzed is necessarily an action in a certain mode.) She behaved neither in terms of the id class nor in terms of the ego class of those actions and modes of action she had defined. (Both classes could be detailed according to her specific psychological situation or so-called psychic reality.) Having accepted neither class of actions alone and having recognized no satisfactory way of integrating or compromising them, she remained utterly immobile" [Schafer, 1975, p. 49].

Schafer acknowledges that his examples of action language might seem "stilted, fussy or pallid compared to the formulations they would replace" (1975, p. 45); but he attributes such difficulties to unfamiliarity with the action language mode of expressing psychoanalytic statements. He believes that experience in using action language will result in more "graceful" formulations. Since the action language system itself is rigidly rule-governed, however, why should its formulations not also be rigid, cumbersome, and pedantic? Gillett (1993, p. 18) compares the awkwardness of Schafer's action language with trying to explain the operation of an automobile without words for its various parts.[16]

In addition to its theoretical and philosophical differences from psychoanalysis and other depth psychologies, Spence (1982b) points out that, clinically, action language puts patients in an adversarial position; and its emphasis on clarity favors rationality at the expense of groping self-exploration. From the standpoint of interpretive methodology, action language seems surprisingly positivistic in its method-oriented, monistic, and inflexibly rule-governed approach—surprising, because Schafer's later writings dealing with the analytic attitude and the construction of narratives in the interpretive process (for example, 1980a, b, 1983a, b, 1987, 1992) are distinctly postpositivist in tone and perspective.

Labov and Fanshel's Rule-Governed Discourse Model of Clinical Interpretation

In order to extend the scope of linguistic analysis beyond the sentence, sociolinguists have studied the discourse that occurs in various kinds of conversations, including therapeutic discourse between therapists and patients. The latter type of discourse is advantageous to study because it is

> often quite extended, so we have access to a great deal of information about the speakers. The participants become involved in tense and emotional interchanges, which present some of the most difficult problems for understanding of the mechanism of conversation and its coherence. The emotional climate is also an advantage in diminishing the observer effect [Labov and Fanshel, 1977, pp. 353–354].

Scheflen (1973) has reviewed the history of discourse analysis, including pioneering studies by Pittenger et al. (1960) and McQuown et al. (1971). Most such studies employ microanalytic methods to examine both what is said and how the participants say it. In addition to the extensive quantitative data produced by such studies, the following are some general conclusions from the investigation by Pittenger et al. (1960):

1. No matter what else people may communicate about, or think they are communicating about, they are always communicating about themselves, about one another, and about the immediate context of the communication.
2. Indeterminate, "accidental" communications are nonexistent. The only useful working assumption is that every communicative act is determined.
3. The crucial patterns of communication do not occur just once, but over and over again.
4. Understanding of communications involves recognition of what the message is not, as well as what it is.
5. Communication occurs simultaneously in various channels and via multiple systems.
6. Most of the messages that people transmit to others are "packaged," overdetermined. No matter how many contributing factors one may have included, there may still be others that have been overlooked.
7. Communicating and learning to communicate with others go hand in hand. Thus continuous recalibration of communications by participants in conversations is to be expected.
8. People know what they are doing in communicative situations by observing feedback about their own behavior. Feedback requires the same kind of interpretation as any other kind of communication.
9. Focusing on a single communicative event can exaggerate its importance out of proportion to its actual significance.

Discourse models are generally "looser" than formal linguistic (syntactic) models, and usually are not conceptualized as rule governed (Shapiro, 1991, p. 326; but see also Kächele, 1986, p. 244). William Labov (a sociolinguist) and David Fanshel (a clinician) describe an investigation of therapeutic discourse, however, in which they attempt to develop rules of discourse comparable with those of sentence grammar. Their proposed discourse rules are of great generality, are not part of a speaker's or listener's conscious knowledge, and are never represented explicitly in the text of a discourse. In other words, like Chomskian rules of syntax, Labov and Fanshel's (1977) discourse rules are unconscious, invariant, and obligatory (p. 75).

Labov and Fanshel derive their discourse rules from the most crucial step in their analysis of therapeutic discourse, namely, determination of the "speech actions" being performed by the speakers through their utterances. A speech act is an action carried out by means of speech (Austin, 1962; Searle, 1969). "The action is what is *intended* in that it expresses how the speaker meant to affect the listener, to move him, to cause him to respond, and so forth" (Labov and Fanshel, 1977, p. 59). The authors add that, in terms of meaning, the level of interaction in speech acts can be defined as what is really meant, in the deepest sense of "really."

The speech acts interpreted in Labov and Fanshel's study were classified as:

1. *Meta-actions*, which have to do with the regulation of speech itself: for example, initiating, interrupting, redirecting, responding, signaling completion, etc.
2. *Representations* of some state of affairs, for example, assertions such as giving information about specific events and expressing various states of mind about them.
3. *Requests* of various kinds, for example, requests for information, confirmation, attention, approval, action, etc.
4. *Challenges*, defined as any reference to a situation which, if true, would lower the status of the other person: for example, criticisms, attacks, denigrations, insults.

Labov and Fanshel report that the crucial speech acts in therapeutic discourse are not so much requests and assertions, as statements involving challenges which concern the status of the participants, their rights, obligations, and their changing relationships (1977, pp. 58–59).

The rules of discourse proposed by Labov and Fanshel are classified in terms of the preceding speech act categories. For example, under the category of "Requests," they propose rules of Requests, Indirect Requests, Putting off Requests, Relayed Requests, Requests for Information, Reinstating Requests, and Embedded Requests. One kind of Embedded Request is putting off a request by countering with a request for information, for example:

A: How are you today?
B: (with a shrug) How should I be?

For speech acts that involve Challenges, the authors propose rules such as Requests Heard as Critical (including Delayed Requests and Repeated Requests), General Challenges to Competence (for example, Overdue Obligations), Challenging Propositions, and others. An example of a Challenging Proposition would be:

A: It's only three o'clock.
B: Your watch must be a little fast.

In all, Labov and Fanshel propose 24 discourse rules, some of which have corollary subrules, each rule being defined very specifically, for example:

RULE OF REQUESTS

If *A* addresses to *B* an imperative specifying an action *X* at a time *T*, and *B* believes that

1a. *X* should be done (for a purpose *Y*) [*need for the action*]
1b. *B* would not do *X* in the absence of the request [*need for the request*]
2. *B* has the *ability* to do *X* (with an instrument *Z*)
3. *B* has the *obligation* to do *X* or is willing to do it.
4. *A* has the *right* to tell *B* to do *X*, then *A* is heard as making a valid request for action [p. 78].

Perhaps not surprisingly, Labov and Fanshel's discourse rules limit rather than enhance the results of their study. The authors themselves acknowledge that, "In general, we cannot claim a very close correlation between objective evidence and this large body of abstractly stated rules" (1977, p. 357).

Once again, therefore, a positivist-like, method-oriented, rule-governed approach fails to provide an appropriate and effective model of clinical interpretation. This is not to say, however, that discourse analysis has nothing to offer methodologic models of clinical interpretation. On the contrary, the suggestive and potentially useful conclusions mentioned earlier in this section from the study by Pittenger et al. (1960) were based upon discourse analysis—but without the highly questionable feature of discourse "rules," which appears to have limited the results of Labov and Fanshel's investigation.

The next methodology to be discussed also employs a discourse model, but one that is not rule governed. Its results are correspondingly much more promising.

Clippinger's Simulated, Nonrule-Governed Discourse Model

Unlike the previous models, Clippinger (1977) started with the assumption that the rule-ordering of transformational linguistics does not readily apply to higher level cognitive processing. Nor, he reasoned, can discourse, including therapeutic discourse, be represented adequately by a simple sender–receiver model; for knowledge needed to produce and to interpret discourse is not just code determined, but can employ codes in unexpected ways. Discourse is motivated by the need to solve problems. Viewed in this way, discourse provides a "mirror" of the mind, as Freud proposed, offering a rich, natural source of data from which one can draw inferences about underlying mental processes and configurations. Words and sentences alone, however, are incomplete reflections of underlying mental functioning; discourse requires interpretation in terms of more fundamental and complex conceptual structures and processes that operate (as unconscious thought) prior to speech production and understanding. A speaker's intentions to produce specific effects upon listeners, for example, is a major factor in both shaping and understanding discourse.

Clippinger based his artificial intelligence model on actual clinical discourse, which he used to conceptualize possible mental processes underlying and mediating the discourse. He then wrote computer programs for several basic categories of mental processes, categories which have some similarities to the psychoanalytic structural theory: for example, one module perceives and tests reality; another introspects and carries out certain regulatory activities; another selects what is attended to; another develops strategies for solving problems; another represents values and serves as censor; and still another transforms mental processes into verbalizations. Discourse produced by this model results from interactions among the various modules. The processes activated in one module can interrupt, inhibit, modify, or complete processes in other modules. Characteristic patterns of interaction develop among the individual modules, resulting in specific patterns of data processing which eventuate in discourse and/or in interpretive understanding of discourse.

Clippinger's method of testing the adequacy of his discourse model is familiar to cognitive scientists, but perhaps not to all clinicians. He attempts to determine whether clinical discourse can be simulated by a computational program based upon his postulated discourse model. Not only does the program simulate clinical discourse very accurately, but it also includes all of the inconsistencies, self-corrections, qualifications, topic changes, interjections, and partially formed sentences that characterize clinical discourse. Leuzinger-Bohleber and Kächele (1988, p. 292) conclude that the program's ability to produce a text which is virtually identical with that of the psychoanalytic patient whose discourse was used to design the model, provides evidence that the theory upon which the computer program was based adequately simulates some or most of the cognitive processes involved. Testing theories by computer simulation (including psychological theories, as in this case) is one of the techniques employed in the burgeoning field of Artificial Intelligence (see, for example, Teller, 1988).

A discourse model like Clippinger's can generate any number of inferences, and select the ones that best fit the context at a particular time. Some incorrect inferences result from such an approach, but speakers and listeners (including patients and therapists) are accustomed to making mistakes and correcting them as additional information becomes available through dialogue and feedback. Rule-based models, on the other hand, and models based upon postulated linguistic universals, are only as flexible as their rules or universals permit. Rule ordering in particular does not provide an adequate conceptual framework for questions of meaning, context, and intention in actual language use (see Chapter 5, however, for specific though limited ways that syntax is relevant to clinical discourse and interpretation).[17] Since rules and universals are prescriptive, such models restrict the range of possible inferences; and, as Clippinger observes, they are ineffective because a speaker or thinker changes all such constraints according to the effects he or she wishes to achieve (see also Burman and Parker, 1993).

Narrative Models of Interpretive Methodology

Like discourse, to which it is related, narrative also is a universal, transcultural, transhistorical, largely language-based human activity that is not governed by specific rules. Aside from a few constraints on narratives, "almost anything goes" (Lloyd, 1989, p. 225). Narration is of interest not only to literary theorists,[18] but also to cognitive scientists because it involves reasoning. Narrative reasoning is not simply one cognitive heuristic among many, however, but is a basic form of cognition; it informs action by attempting to construct true or likely stories about events represented in perception and memory (Bruner, 1986, 1990; Schank and Abelson, 1977).

Barthes (1975) posited that since narrative is ubiquitous, and because it preceded science as an attempt to make the world intelligible, it may be part of our native endowment. A meta-review of researches on discourse processing and text comprehension suggests that narrative competence is acquired early in life (Mancuso, 1986). After it develops, narrative competence functions as an assimilating structure for organizing and comprehending discourse, reading, and experience generally (Freedman, 1983). Reed (1995, pp. 713–714) emphasizes and illustrates the clinical importance of distinguishing between a patient's narration as a strategy, in contrast to the event narrated—a distinction which views reports of present experience as the product of a narrative strategy developed in the past. The avidity with which human beings assimilate perceptions into narratives is illustrated by experiments in which subjects consistently attributed meanings in narrative form to random, meaningless movements of geometrical figures (Michotte, 1946).

We look for plot, not proof, in narratives; we ask, "What's next?" Kahneman and Tversky (1982) call this the "simulation heuristic," that is, a form of inner narrative in which various possible outcomes are tried in fantasy or thought. Typically, narratives are combinations of actual happenings and imaginings (Sarbin, 1986b, p. 12). Narrative thinking contributes to the interpretation of events by combining what is known about a situation with relevant conjectures to construct a causal pattern (Robinson and Hawpe, 1986). Because narrative adds secondary meanings to real events, Hayden White (1987) questions the adequacy of narrative as a scientific method of representing reality.

One of the few constraints on narrative cognition is a consistent ordering of events in the direction of causality. Another constraint seeks the first plausible conclusion of a narrative rather than considering alternative outcomes, which sometimes leads to premature closure. Narrative cognition typically generates a single, concrete, affirmative explanation; negation and generalization are not part of narrative reasoning. Although the process by which narratives generate conclusions need not be rational, ideally the conclusion itself is.

Narrative case reporting in psychoanalysis and dynamic psychotherapy began very early in Freud's writings (for example, Breuer and Freud, 1893–1895, p. 160). Spence (1982a) comments:

> Freud was a master at taking pieces of the patient's associations, dreams, and memories and weaving them into a coherent pattern that is compelling, persuasive, and seemingly complete, a pattern that allows us to make important discoveries about the patient's life and to make sense out of previously random happenings. Freud's most impressive achievements (in *The Interpretation of Dreams* and in his well-known case histories) are lasting achievements of innovative synthesis, and we have been heavily influenced by this tradition. Freud made us aware of the persuasive power of a coherent narrative [p. 21; see also Spence, 1986b].

According to Polkinghorne (1988, pp. 120–121), Freud's most important contributions to narrative theory are: (1) that an event's meaning can depend on what happens later—a point made also by historians. Since later thinking, feeling, and behavior differ from previous attitudes, an early experience can acquire a different meaning than it had when it occurred (1988, p. 121). (2) Crucial (reported) experiences in a patient's life may not even have occurred—which does not detract, however, from the psychological importance of the reported experiences. Because the self cannot be separated completely from its story (Sprengnether, 1985), all reported events become hypotheses requiring understanding, whether factual or fictional (Polkinghorne, 1988, p. 120). The preceding concepts have raised questions about the traditional (natural science) view that prior events cause subsequent events. Polkinghorne (1988) observes that the narrative operates to find causes for present conditions:

> Freud did not abandon the notion of the primacy of the event in producing the effect, but neither did he abandon the idea that the present operates to reinterpret meaningless past events in order to give them a force of causation that they did not originally have. He maintained that the two logics—one which insists on the causal efficacy of origins and the other which treats events as the products of meanings—must exist side by side [p. 121].

Narrative meaning is a particular type of meaning, which recognizes that something is a part of some whole and that one thing is the cause of something else (Polkinghorne, 1988, p. 6). Narrative thus combines the part–whole concept of hermeneutics with the natural science concept of causality to produce narrative meaning. Some writers argue that since scientific and historical explanations have the same form, the notion that the sciences and humanities occupy mutually exclusive domains is untenable (Blight, 1981, p. 149; Rogers, 1984, p. 42).

A more recent development in psychoanalysis and dynamic psychotherapy, which has roots in both literary theory and historiography, extends the role of narrativity from case reporting to interpretive methodology (Sarbin, 1986a; Edelson, 1992a,b). The historical dimension of clinical interpretations led some historians and philosophers of science to characterize reconstructions and dynamic formulations as "psychoanalytic narratives."[19] Ricoeur (1978) comments in this connection that:

> If Freud can write case histories it is because every scientific experience takes place within a mode of discourse that may be called narrative. The analysand recounts his dreams and the episodes of his past. He recounts what he does not understand until he understands what he recounts [p. 297].

An interpretive narrative is not simply the sum of multiple explanations, however, but serves as an integrating framework for various clinical findings and types of explanations (Thomä and Kächele, 1975, p. 90); for example, the aforementioned cognitive function of narrative competence serves as an "assimilating structure" for organizing and comprehending perceptions (Mancuso, 1986). Understanding of discourse or of any human situation involves building a functional model of it (de Beaugrande, 1983, p. 90)—which patients and therapists do by telling, revising, and retelling patients' stories. Haynal (1993b, pp. 79–80) argues, on the other hand, that although it is fashionable to emphasize the structuring aspect of the narrative, "the advantage of the narrative is its *ambiguity*. The dream narrative is full of 'lacunas,' which provide a chance to 'work' with them" (pp. 79–80). Haynal believes that "this helps to construct a narrative that undoubtedly contains some historic truth but, like a fable, permits the expression of how one feels, how one would like to feel, to be. Its ambiguity is its strength" (1993b, pp. 79–80).

Reviewing his extensive experience in therapeutic process research, Kächele (1992, pp. 9, 12) concludes that the more observational one's approach, the more one needs a narrative form of interpretation in order to highlight interactive aspects of the process. Rogers (1988, p. 168) concludes that clinical narratives derive much of their transformational, interpretive, and persuasive power from the analogical nature of narrativity (see also Cheshire, 1975). The following observations and arguments support that thesis:

1. The functional identity of patients as narrators with what they relate: for example, Freud's recognition that the Rat Man's rats were a "likeness of himself" (1909b, pp. 214, 216).
2. The operational equivalence of the narrative and its meanings: Marcus (1976, p. 441) notes regarding Freud's Dora case (1905a), for example, that such narratives include their own analyses and interpretations.
3. A narrative's systemic wholeness, that is, no part of the story nor any thematic reduction of it can sum up the whole story. For example, referring to the Rat Man as an obsessional neurotic tells very little of his whole story. Rogers (1988) notes in this conection that, "Narratives, as analogs, tend to discount isolated events by linking them with other events in the narrative network, so that what counts most are the relationships generated within the narrative system" (p. 164).
4. Each narrative is *sui generis*, which corresponds with the clinical aim to be guided by the uniquely personal, idiosyncratic details of the individual patient's story.
5. The extreme plasticity and elasticity of the narrative process: the variety of narratives is infinite—which leads Spence (1982a, p. 182) to observe critically that a narrative can accommodate almost any evidence that comes along. Ricoeur (1974, p. 104) and Bouchard (1995, p. 538) argue, on the other hand, that the individual patient's narrative meanings are probably finite; for they are determined largely by the patient's own unconscious structures, as a result of which the same narrative themes tend to repeat themselves, although in varied form. Edelson (1992a/1994, p. 84) further points out that although the principal role of narratives is to suggest themes and to organize the data into coherent stories, narrative evidence can also discredit a theoretical proposition by serving as a counterexample, in the manner of a Popperian falsification.

6. The problem-solving potential of narrativity: for example, even the passive telling of pitiable stories includes a potentially active search for a better solution (Holyoak, 1982).

7. The occurrence of redundant, symbolic versions of the original story in the form of transference relivings.

A relatively small but highly vocal group of clinical writers[20] has attempted to reformulate the therapeutic process, including interpretive methodology, in narrative and radically constructivist terms. On this view, clinical interpreters do not discover actual latent meanings and determinants in the patient's unconscious and past life, but imaginatively construct a story about the patient and his or her past.[21] This group of clinicians and writers considers coherence of the story more important than its accuracy. The therapist contributes to the narrational process by "redescribing, reinterpreting, recontextualizing, and reducing" the patient's life and experiences in terms of certain story lines and subjective experiences based upon psychoanalytic theory (Schafer, 1983a, p. 187). Thus, interpretations involve telling and retelling clinical data along psychoanalytic lines (p. 218). The theory-driven and potentially indoctrinating character of such an approach is all too evident.

In one of his final publications, Freud (1937b) expressed a powerful precedent of the constructivist view. He acknowledged that:

> Quite often we do not succeed in bringing the patient to recollect what has been repressed. Instead of that, if the analysis is carried out correctly, we produce in him an assured conviction of the truth of the construction which achieves the same therapeutic result as a recaptured memory [pp. 265–266].

In his recent and final book, Merton Gill (1994b) described his own transition from an "objective" natural science model of psychoanalysis and interpretive inquiry to a subjective hermeneutic-constructivist-interactive model (see also Wallerstein's [1995] review of Gill's book). Gill recognized, however, that not only positivistic but also relativistic views can go too far, that there is room for both objectivistic and subjectivistic approaches; hence his preference for a pluralistic model which he referred to as "hermeneutic science."

Sherwood's (1969, p. 130) guidelines for a satisfactory psychoanalytic narrative include not only adequacy but also accuracy, whereas the narrational project undertaken by Schafer, Spence, and others deemphasizes the criterion of accuracy. They view such narratives, for the most part, as constructed psychoanalytic fictions. Other writers present arguments and empirical evidence for a relationship between interpretive accuracy and therapeutic outcome.[22] Eagle (1980a, p. 421) points out that most analysts and patients believe, or want to believe, that therapists' interpretations are correct (see also Schlesinger, 1994, p. 36). Eagle (1980a) argues further that the search for self-knowledge, "is not a mere chimera, but involves the identification of real entities" (p. 422). He adds that:

> Freud may have been mistaken in believing that he had demonstrated that psychoanalytic interpretations 'tally with what is real.' But his belief in its importance is not only more consistent than are more recent 'perspectival' formulations with a psychology of self, but also is more consistent with the basic values underlying psychoanalytic theory and therapy, and more likely to lead to an eventual integration between effectiveness and veridicality [p. 423; see also Eagle, 1984b].

With respect to the accuracy of interpretations, clinicians seek as much dynamic and historical truth as they can find, and then extrapolate from these limited kernels of truth to other clinical findings—ideally, always prepared to acknowledge gaps and uncertainties in their interpretations rather than attempting to gloss over incompleteness and inconsistencies by use of narrative smoothing (see Spence, 1986b, for a discussion of distortions produced by narrative smoothing).

Numerous additional arguments have been levelled against the narrative model of interpretation—particularly against the radical constructivist approach.[23] Rogers (1984, p. 51) points out, for example, that the constraints on clinical interpretation are less elastic than clinical narratologists believe; for the therapeutic process is highly redundant, and as recurring patterns accumulate they create increasing constraints on the fit and interpretation of all subsequent data (see also Edelson, 1992a,b).

The radical constructivist narrative model of interpretive methodology has some earmarks of a monistic, method-oriented (hence positivist-like) approach, in contrast to a pluralistic, problem-oriented (postpositivist) methodology. Margaret Hanly (1995) writes, for example, that "a skeptical view concerning the way 'narrative' comes into psychoanalytic discourse is fitting, for human storytelling demands a complex understanding" (p. 35). Rather than viewing the "narratory principle" (Sarbin, 1986) as an overarching model of interpretive inquiry, narrative construction can be conceptualized more simply and modestly as one among many strategies employed in clinical data processing and dynamic formulation. Overemphasizing narrative coherence at the expense of other interpretive strategies is methodologically reductive.

Unlike his earlier (1975) rule-ordered, syntactical theory of interpretive competence, Marshall Edelson (1992a,b) now proposes a narrative approach to interpretive methodology which is more restrained than that of the radical constructivists:

> I believe that psychoanalytic theory will benefit from emphasizing in its core formulations concepts that are closely linked to empirical observations made in the psychoanalytic situation. These will be dramatistic concepts such as wish, defense, conflict, unconscious, fantasy, resistance, and transference, which are necessary for capturing the phenomena observed in the psychoanalytic situation or characterizing the psychoanalytic process. These are, in fact, the concepts most likely to govern the psychoanalyst's way of listening and way of processing what he hears [1992b, p. 121].

Edelson believes also that this approach will help to clarify the nature of psychoanalytic theory, which is not a hierarchical pyramidic set of axioms and universal generalizations having a logico-deductive structure. Rather, psychoanalytic theory appears to be a narrative form, that is, narrative in the sense of being about a protagonist's wants, obstacles to satisfying these wants, and means for coping with these obstacles. For these reasons, Edelson now emphasizes the telling and enacting of stories in psychoanalysis (1992b; see also Edelson's elaboration of this view in the form of a dialogue [1992a/1994, pp. 62–86]).

Kermode (1979, pp. 53–54, 64–65, 72–73, 118) notes that interpreters from disparate schools are united in at least one respect, that is, in the expectation that what one interprets "hangs together." We all seek well-formedness and narrative coherence. We even expect it, just as we expect a riddle to have an answer and a joke to have a point. When we find no manifest relation we look for hidden connections (see Ogden, 1997, p. 588, for a clinical illustration of the sometimes desperate need experienced by therapists for "an anchoring point that could be precisely located and would, if only for a moment, stay put"). By contrast, deconstructionists and radical relativists consider a preference for pattern a sign of bad faith, a flight from "incoherence anxiety"; but Kermode disagrees. He comes down on the side of our need for coherence and closure because "we all seek the center that will allow the senses to rest, at any rate for one interpreter, at any rate for one moment" (1979, pp. 72–73).

Summary

The language-based models of interpretive methodology reviewed in this chapter run the gamut from rule-ordered approaches and a model based on posited linguistic universals, at one extreme, to models having virtually no rules or universals, at the other extreme. Neither extreme describes clinical interpretation fully or convincingly. Rule ordering does not provide an adequate conceptual framework for meaning, context, and intention in actual language use; at the other extreme, the radically constructivist narrative model is overly concerned with coherence at the expense of interpretive accuracy. A more comprehensive and balanced language-based model of interpretive methodology appears to lie somewhere between the two extremes, for example, a non-rule-based discourse model, or a nonradical narrative model similar to Edelson's (1992a,b) recent approach.

Discourse and narrative models may be thought of as rule-described in contrast to rule-ordered or rule-governed systems. Rule description also has limitations, however, and probably cannot capture the particularities, complexities, and subtleties of clinical data. No matter how many descriptive "rules" one might apply, it is doubtful that they could encompass all of the intricate, largely preconscious, cognitive and affective mental activities—including the sensitively empathic, creatively imaginative, and often unsuccessful groping to understand—that characterize our attempts to comprehend latent mental contents. Both the production and understanding of clinical data depend on multiple, uncertain heuristics, rather than on "rules"—hence the need for a flexible (postpositivist) model of interpretive methodology.

The present chapter's critique of various language-based

models of interpretive methodology does not imply that language processes generally are unimportant in interpretive inquiry. Selected language-based models have been questioned because of their positivist-like, method-oriented attempts to reduce the complexities of interpretive methodology to rules, lawlike generalizations, or to a completely constructivist narrative model that views interpretations as clinical fictions—all derived from particular and limited aspects of language theory. Some language processes that are necessary and useful to interpretive methodology are discussed in the section on "Language-Related Disciplines" of the following chapter.

PART III

NONCLINICAL COMPARISONS

Knowledge begins with observation: our senses tell us what exists outside our bodies. But we are not satisfied with what we observe; we want to know more, to inquire into things we do not observe directly. We reach this objective by means of thought operations, which connect the observational data and account for them in terms of unobserved things.

[Hans Reichenbach, 1951, pp. 176–177]

In virtually every domain of human discourse, including the range of natural and human sciences, thinkers following the most diverse pathways have been drawn to reflection on the character, scope, varieties, strategies, and tactics of interpretation.

[Richard Bernstein, 1988a, pp. 88–89]

We have long known how difficult it is to do this kind of cognitive work well; now, thanks to a variety of scattered lines of research, we are beginning to see, in some concrete detail, what kinds of pitfalls await the unwary.

[Robert Holt, 1988, p. 234]

Systematic research in psychoanalysis cannot leave out interpretation.

[John Benjamin, 1961, p. 570]

5

Some Nonclinical Methods of Inferring Latent Contents

Comparisons with Clinical Inference and Interpretation

All branches of science employ interpretation, but scientific disciplines vary in the nature and purposes of their interpretive tasks, in the degree of similarity between the interpreter and what is interpreted, in the types of competences required of interpreters, and in the content of their interpretations. Interpretive methods in diverse disciplines have some features in common, however; and by studying interpretive procedures in other fields we may learn more about the nature, problems, and possibilities of improving the methodology of clinical interpretation.[1]

A recent volume edited by Sander Gilman et al. (1994), *Reading Freud's Reading*, illustrates the possibilities of a comparative approach to problems of interpretive methodology. The volume reports the findings of twelve scholars from diverse fields who studied Freud's literary interests to learn how those interests may have influenced his evolving methods and theories. Stephanie Smith (1997, p. 349), a reviewer of the volume, observes that the various essays provide a rich, multifaceted context of viewpoints, and an opportunity to become acquainted with methods of analysis and interpretation used in other disciplines.

Rather than undertaking a comprehensive review of interpretive methods in all other fields, which would require an entire volume, this chapter focuses on selected examples of interpretation from a limited number of disciplines, emphasizing their similarities and potential relevance to the methodology of clinical interpretation. The disciplines reviewed include:

1. *Relation- and pattern-oriented methodologies,* including the "pattern model" approach, gestalt psychology, system theory, hermeneutics, and structuralism, all of which emphasize relations and patterns rather than things in their respective data.

2. *Language-related disciplines,* including linguistics, psycholinguistics, communication theory, rhetoric, semiotics, literary theory and criticism, and archaeological decipherment.

3. *Cognitive science,* including cognitive psychology, information theory, the computational model of mind, and artificial intelligence.

RELATION- AND PATTERN-ORIENTED METHODOLOGIES

The Pattern Model Approach

In his treatise *The Conduct of Inquiry* (1964), the behavioral science methodologist Abraham Kaplan describes two ways of achieving understanding in science: "Very roughly, we know the reason for something either when we can fit it into a known pattern, or else when we can deduce it from other known truths" (p. 332). The deductive model applies primarily to hierarchical theories, as in the physical sciences, while the "pattern model," as Kaplan calls it, is more applicable to "concatenated" theories whose component parts form a "network of relations that constitute an identifiable configuration or pattern" (1964, p. 298). As examples of concatenated theories, Kaplan lists the "big bang" theory of cosmology, the theory of evolution, and the psychoanalytic theory of neurosis.

The pattern model attempts to understand the phenomena of human behavior by identifying them as specific parts of an overall whole. The unknown is identified with something known by its place in a network of relations. Relations are fundamental, along with some kind of closure (as in the gestalt approach, discussed in the next part of this section). The philosopher Michael Scriven (1962) writes that, "Understanding is roughly the perception of relationships and hence may be conveyed by any process which locates the puzzling phenomena in a system of relations" (p. 193n). Donald Campbell (1966, pp. 88–89), a social scientist, believes that all scientific knowledge is gained by a process of pattern matching. Rosenblatt and Thickstun (1994; see also

Margolis, 1987) suggest that intuition also may be based on a form of preconscious or unconscious pattern matching. When working with individual patients, analysts characteristically "connect events into a pattern and attempt to relate that pattern to other patterns."

The following example of applying a pattern model approach is from a nonclinical study of Andaman Islanders by the social anthropologist, Radcliffe-Brown (1922):

> We have to explain why it is that the Andamanese think and act in certain ways. The explanation of each individual custom is provided by showing its relation to the other customs of the Andamanese and to their general system of ideas and sentiments [p. 230; cited by Diesing, 1971, p. 158].

With respect to the role of interpretation in the pattern model of understanding, Kaplan (1964) distinguishes two types of explanations in science: semantic explanations that clarify the meanings of words and other symbols; and scientific explanations that deal with facts rather than meanings. Kaplan adds, however, that:

> Certain explanations contain as components both semantic and scientific explanations; we may call them *interpretations*. They occur when what is being explained is viewed both as symbol and as fact; a statement has a meaning, but it is also an object or event occurring at a particular time and place. We interpret a speech by explaining its meaning, and by explaining also why it was made by that person who made it, and at that time; we interpret a dream by making manifest its latent content, and by explaining also why the dreamer produced the symbols he did. The scientific explanation may be suggested and supported by the semantic one, as in the case of dream analysis. But the relation between the two components may also be the reverse; we may understand *what* a person says because we know, from the context or in other ways, *why* he is saying it [Kaplan, 1964, p. 328].[2]

Diesing (1971, pp. 162–163) suggests that the pattern model is appropriate when a problem involves numerous and diverse factors of approximately equal importance, when the pattern of relations between these factors is important, and when the relations can be observed fairly directly in the particular case. The principal characteristics of the pattern model approach are: (1) no general laws appear anywhere in the interpretation; (2) in the pattern model one cannot deduce an unknown part of a pattern from a known part; (3) a pattern is rarely if ever finished completely; and (4) any or all of the pattern is subject to change in the course of its development.

The types of relations identified most frequently in the pattern model approach include contextual, part-whole, repetitive, sequential, analogical, transformational, causal, motivational, oppositional, and other kinds of relations. In the clinical situation, repetition of themes and analogical similarities are among the most useful types of relations that facilitate the formation of patterns leading to the construction of latent contents. Rogers (1984, p. 51) points out, for example, that when relations in the form of repetitions are detected, the analyst weaves them together into larger patterns, and those into linking configurations that may extend broadly and deeply in the patient's behavior. As these patterns accumulate, "they create in the very process of their development, additional constraints on the fit of whatever data remain to be interpreted" (1984, p. 51).

Analogies entail imaginative relations among the data which often suggest useful heuristic restructurings of phenomena into unexpected patterns. Cheshire (1975) considers analogical similarities to be the mainstay of our interpretive methodology: for example, it was constructively paradoxical analogizing that led Kekule to visualize benzene molecules as tail-swallowing snakes, and Freud to say, "Look: accidents are like wishes" (p. 113).

Both repetitions and analogies, as well as other types of relations, provide heuristic guides to which data are most relevant, and how to construe the latent meanings of those data. Repetitive relations and patterns also possess a "metainterpretive" potential; that is, recurring parts of the data function as commentaries on each other (Rogers, 1981, p. 441; see also Freud, 1918, p. 11). To illustrate, Freud (1911b, p. 94) observed that several successive scenes in a dream may have essentially the same content, the latent meanings of which become increasingly clear in later versions of the series. Not only dream series, but also the data of individual therapy sessions and the therapeutic process as a whole, tend towards increasing clarity of recurring contents—illustrated, for example, in the case report presented in Chapter 9.

Specific observable relations become the basis of both constructions and evidence in the pattern model approach. Objectivity of the method consists essentially of this: "the pattern can be indefinitely filled in and extended: as we obtain more and more knowledge it continues to fall into place in this pattern, and the pattern itself has a place in a larger whole" (Kaplan, 1964, p. 335). Diesing (1971) adds to Kaplan's statement that, "To be sure, it is rarely the case that new facts fit directly into a pattern without changing it, but Kaplan is stating the ideal. Note also that the pattern model of explanation is somewhat similar to the coherence theory of truth; in both cases, truth comes in large packages" (p. 160).

Diesing (1971) points out that contextual relations contribute not only to the formulation but also to the justification of interpretations: "Since the participant observer or clinican always has several different kinds of evidence available, he can always assess the validity of a kind or piece of evidence in the context of others" (p. 147). He continues:

> I am discussing the use of evidence in a method of discovery, in which a test is always a check point that serves to tell the researcher whether he is moving in the right direction. Every scientific method I have studied has check points built into it, each checking some detail of the developing theory or description against some sort of possible error. When there are many check points no one need be infallible and conclusive, since later checks can catch errors that escaped earlier ones. The researcher builds redundancy into his checks as a substitute for individual infallibility. Consequently there is no need for a single grand test [Diesing, 1971, p. 149].

(Use of multiple justifying tests for clinical interpretations is discussed in Chapter 8 and illustrated with a clinical case in Chapter 9.)

Since none of the evidence employed in the pattern model approach is absolutely dependable, contextual validation must be used more or less continuously on nearly all of the evidence gathered (Diesing, 1971, p. 149; 1985b, p. 557). With respect to the role of relations and patterns in justification, it should be noted that the choice of one theory or interpretation over others is based upon relative overall goodness of fit rather than upon absolute degree of fit (Campbell, 1966, pp. 96–102).

Levy (1963) and Spence (1976, 1982a) distrust the evidential value of pattern matching. Spence (1982a, p. 385) claims that it is simple to find pattern-matches, but difficult to find nonmatches. Cheshire (1975, p. 193) argues, however, that mistakes made in attributing structural properties to relations which are only descriptive does not invalidate pattern-matching approaches themselves.[3]

Gestalt Psychology

Like all of the methodologies included in this section, Gestalt psychology also emphasizes relations and patterns.[4] Relations are fundamental, along with the concept of closure, that is, integration and unity (Wertheimer, 1945). The relative strength of a structure, system, pattern model, or gestalt depends upon the complexity and coherence of integrative links between and among the parts: the more complex and coherent the interrelations of parts, the more stable the entity is (Inhelder, 1983, pp. 134–135). Ekstein (1959, p. 233) traces an early clinical application of gestalt theory to Bernfeld (1934), who proposed that the patient's productions acquire meaning for the therapist by being placed in a *Gesamptzusammenhang*, a total structure or gestalt.

The basic principle of the gestalt approach is that a whole cannot be understood by an analysis of parts; a whole is more than the sum of its parts. The parts of a gestalt have no meaningful identity apart from their function in the whole. This principle is similar to concepts of part–whole relations in systems and hermeneutic theories (discussed below), although the hermeneutic view does not privilege wholes as clearly as gestalt theory does. Like the systems approach, gestalt theory recognizes "emergent" characteristics of wholes. Allport (1955) notes, in fact, that development of the systems approach coincided with studies of perception and thinking by gestalt psychologists during the 1930s.

Gestalt psychologists have extended their original investigations of perception to other problems, including thinking, learning, problem solving, social psychology, motivation, and personality. The extensions carried with them the basic gestalt concepts of "relational determinism" and "good form or figure"—"good" implying properties such as regularity, symmetry, simplicity, and "closure." Goodness of form or figure in gestalt psychology has a counterpart in the methodology of clinical interpretation, namely, goodness of fit, internal consistency, and coherence between an interpretive hypothesis and all (or at least most) of the clinical data. Max Wertheimer's (1945) concepts of "productive thinking" also seem relevant to the clinical interpretive process. Michael Wertheimer (1968, p. 371) describes "productive thinking" as going from a situation whose structure hides the solution, to a state in which relations, at first unrecognized, become central, so that with appropriate reorganization the solution emerges. This description is similar to what in clinical data processing would be called the heuristic of "restructuring." (See also the section below on Language-Related Disciplines, for Wolfgang Iser's [1978] application of gestalt concepts to the reading process, which has important parallels with clinical inference and interpretive inquiry.)

Gestalt psychologists continue to study the problems of how insight and understanding occur. In their essay "The Legacy of Gestalt Psychology," Rock and Palmer (1990, p. 89) suggest that listening is not enough, for the listener must achieve the same cognitive structure as the speaker in order to recognize the essential relations among the relevant facts. Listeners do not have to employ the same creative process as the speaker to achieve understanding, but their eventual state of comprehension must be similar (compare Edelson's [1975] theory of clinical interpretive competence, reviewed in Chapter 4).

In their recent volume *Psychoanalysis as Science* (1993), Bellak and Walkup propose that Gestalt psychology constitutes the relevant and appropriate "ground" for the "figures" of psychoanalytic theory and therapy (see also Lamm, 1995, pp. 442–443). Like psychoanalysis, Gestalt psychology is concerned with problems of structure, coherence, and qualitative transformation—issues that academic psychology has ignored for the most part. Bellak and Walkup believe that a reconceptualization of psychoanalysis along Gestalt lines would further the development of psychoanalysis as science.

System Theory

The concepts of "system" and "structure" are closely linked (Caws, 1988, p. 198). A structure is a set of interrelations within a system. A system is a set of interdependent entities that function together at a higher level of organization. In system approaches, understanding depends largely upon the recognition of relations, the most significant of which may be "relations between relations" (Wilden, 1980, p. 329).[5]

One of the most characteristic features of open (living) systems is their complexity, which the linear, one-way causality of classical science cannot deal with adequately; but "organized complexity" is exactly what system theory is designed to study (Rogers, 1986a, p. 4). When two systems interact, certain features and functions appear that cannot be attributed to the summation of the two original systems, but represent properties of a new emergent system (Riggs, 1977, p. 65). In the therapeutic situation, for example, the patient and therapist do not respond only to each other, but also to the relationship and to the therapeutic process, which develop as emergent systems generated by interactions of the patient and therapist.[6]

Systems themselves are complex and consist of multiple, interrelated subsystems. In the methodology of clinical interpretation, for example, the roles of patient, therapist, clinical data, and context are coequal in producing meanings, each representing an integral subsystem of the therapeutic system as a whole (Rogers, 1982, p. 45; 1987b). Kernberg (1976, 1980) employs this aspect of system theory in his concepts of internalized object relations.[7] Rosenblatt and Thickstun (1977) conclude that most human behavior is organized into purposeful sequences, and that the organizing process that underlies and produces such sequences is a behavioral system.

The interdependent unity of all components in a system has a counterpart in the continuity principle of psychoanalysis (de Beaugrande, 1980, pp. 67–69; Rogers, 1987a, pp. 102–105). When clinicians fail to apply that basic methodologic concept consistently, that is, if they do not interpret all of the data as a unified whole, the result is often the formulation of several dynamically different themes that are strung together like a run-on sentence—what T. M. French (1958b) called the "and . . . and . . . and" fallacy:

> The analyst should not be content with fragmentary bits of insight. His constant aim should be to understand how different trends and themes in the patient's associations fit together into a single intelligible context. Trying to understand a patient's associations is like trying to piece together a jigsaw puzzle. This kind of fitting together into a single intelligible cognitive structure is our only reliable immediate check on the correctness of our interpretations. Consequently, we should not be complacent but actively puzzled if the pieces do not fit together intelligibly [French, 1958b, p. 207].

The processing strategy of thematization, the postulate that a single dynamic theme runs like an undercurrent through all of the data during a specific therapy session, is the best antidote to discontinuous, incompletely integrated, run-on interpretations. Freud (1923a, p. 239) observed that the patient's associations emerge like allusions to one particular theme; and Klauber (1980, p. 196) noted that therapists routinely and actively search for a thematic pattern that gives "interdependent relevance" to everything the patient says. What appear to be disconnected contents are parts of an overall pattern or system. Robert Waelder commented in this connection that:

> Sooner or later you discover that these varied and disconnected contents are part of a pattern that characterizes the patient's whole personality. They fit together, complete each other, support one another, make each other possible. Finally you realize that all these pieces are held together by something they have in common: they serve the same purpose, or they fight against the same danger, or they express the same desire or hope or fear. And once you have seen that, you discover this common denominator everywhere [cited by Guttman and Guttman, 1987, p. 61].

Like any generally useful interpretive heuristic, however, the search for thematic unity in clinical data can be misused. In theory-driven approaches, for example, doctrinal interpretations may be imposed upon the data but rationalized as a unifying theme. Two countermeasures help to guard against that problem: (1) use of a data-driven interpretive methodology; and (2) systematic checking to determine whether a construction accounts both coherently and comprehensively for all, or at least most, of the data. Doctrinal interpretations often betray themselves by accounting for only a few suggestive elements of the clinical material while ignoring a large part of the data (see Abraham, 1986, p. 59. For a clinical illustration of this common error, see Rubovits-Seitz, 1988a, pp. 947–950).

Hermeneutics

Hermeneutics is a very old methodology, comprising the art and science of interpreting meanings in texts of all kinds, including spoken communications (as in psychoanalysis and dynamic psychotherapy).[8] Hermeneutic scholars have studied the principles, methods, and problems of interpretation for centuries. Saint Augustine, for example, developed a method of biblical interpretation that emphasized relations in the form of internal consistency, that is, interpreting a particular passage by its relations to the text as a whole. Thus Augustine searched for parallels from other parts of the Bible to clarify the verse at hand (Pelikan, 1968, p. 951)—a method used in hermeneutics, clinical interpretation, and numerous other interpretive disciplines to this day.

Hermeneutics focuses particularly on the interdependent relations of part and whole meanings: that is, the whole is derived from and constituted by the parts, the latter being delineated and integrated by the whole. Freud (1911b, p. 93) employed the part-whole principle in his concept that the meaning of any fragment depends upon the meaning of the whole. He subsumed part-whole relations in clinical data under the principle of determinism, however, rather than associating it with hermeneutics (1916–17, pp. 108–109). Kermode (1985, p. 7) believes that Freud ignored the discipline of hermeneutics, which is consistent with the view expressed in Chapter 1 that Freud largely avoided issues and problems of interpretive methodology (see also Steiner, 1995, pp. 440–441).

Hermeneutic theory views part meanings as "implications" of the overall meaning; that is, the whole meaning implies certain part meanings but not others. Drawing of correct implications depends upon a correct "guess" about the posited whole meaning. Although most of the practical problems of interpreation are problems of implication, the uncertainty of interpretations results from the necessity to guess initially about the overall meaning.

I have suggested elsewhere (Rubovits-Seitz, 1986a, pp. 17–21; 1991a, pp. 575–576) that the hermeneutic concept of part-whole relations may be applicable to the interpretation of conflict/defense relations in clinical data. That is, in the course of each therapy session the clinical interpreter gains impressions about the general type of conflict that predominates at the time: for example, possibly a dependency conflict, a conflict about control, or about loss; or perhaps a sexual or aggressive type of conflict. The therapist uses the type conception heuristically, scanning the patient's associations for possible relations between the postulated conflict and the actual clinical data. If the tentatively constructed conflict corresponds fairly closely with the patient's current inner conflict, one may be able to understand the patient's associations as part meanings or "implications" of that specific type of conflict. Some associations may represent disguised expressions of the thematic (principal current) conflict itself. Most of the associations, however, allude to various defenses against and attempted solutions of the "focal" conflict. Still other associations may allude to secondary conflicts which occur in response to ego-alien aspects of the defenses themselves. The kinds of defensive compromise formations that one identifies in the patient's associations should represent plausible, even expected, "implications" of that particular type of conflict.

The following clinical anecdote illustrates the postulated parallel between hermeneutic whole and part meanings, on the one hand, and clinical conflicts and defenses, on the other:

> During one of the recurrent phases of dependent transference in a male patient's analysis, the patient anticipated a vacation of the analyst's with growing separation anxiety and increasingly regressive defenses. He began asking the analyst for guidance about a number of reality problems. Then he requested additional appointments. When his questions and requests were not gratified, frustration and rage mounted, but were repressed. At that point he complained that his anxiety was intolerable and that he would have to be hospitalized. In the course of further therapeutic work, a fantasy emerged that the analyst would cancel his vacation in order to stay with and care for the patient. The thematic conflict (or whole meaning) during this period appeared to be: hostility (oral aggression) toward the analyst (as a mother figure) for frustrating his dependence versus fear (separation anxiety) of losing the mother figure completely by harming or alienating him. The conflict was defended against by a series of increasingly dependent regressions, which appeared to represent part meanings (or "implications") of the thematic conflict as whole meaning. Dynamically, the regressions represented compromise formations which attempted to conceal his aggression in ways that sought to secure rather than jeopardize his dependence.

Another potential contribution of hermeneutics to clinical interpretation concerns the justification of interpretations. The father of modern hermeneutics, Wilhelm Dilthey (1976), observed that the epistemologic implications of interpretive justification are much greater than is generally realized—the reason being that human studies rely so extensively on interpretive methods, and valid interpretation is essential to the correctness of all subsequent inferences and theoretical conclusions of such studies. The same principle applies to clinical interpretation, which Freud (1940a) recognized in his statement that, "the certainty of our science rests on these inferences" (p. 159).

The hermeneutic scholar E. D. Hirsch, Jr. (1967, pp. 181–182) emphasizes the importance of relevant evidence in the justification of interpretations. The best hypothesis usually accounts for the most evidence, but relevance of evidence is as important as quantity. Hermeneutic criteria of evidence include: (1) evidence that helps to define and narrow the whole meaning of the data; (2) evidence that increases the number of data accounted for by the whole (thematic) meaning; and (3) "small-scale" evidence, that is, coherence of interrelations among part meanings associated with individual elements of the data, and between part and whole meanings.[9] (The relevance of these criteria to the justification of clinical interpretations is discussed in Chapter 8.)

Two of the most appealing features of hermeneutics are that it makes no claim to have developed a permanently valid methodology of interpretation, and that it is nonreductive—although attempts by some writers to reformulate psychoanalysis as an acausal hermeneutics are reductive.[10] That is, clinical interpretation attempts to construct both unconscious meanings and determinants, so focusing on latent meanings to the exclusion of causal factors is reductive. Hermeneutics emphasizes the complexities, inevitable difficulties, and limitations of the interpretive process. It recognizes that there can never be a method or model of correct construction, because the psychology of understanding cannot be reduced to a systematic procedure, and there is no way of assuring a right "guess" by means of rules and principles (Hirsch, 1967, p. 170). It is worth noting that Freud also used the term "guess" (*zu erraten*) when writing about construction (Gribinski, 1994, pp. 1012–1015)—imaginative guessing or conjecturing being a necessary step in the constructive phase of the interpretive process. Gribinski (1994, pp. 1014–1015) suggests that Strachey's translations of *zu erraten* attempted to downplay the role of guesswork in clinical interpretation, substituting euphemistic terms such as "to detect and explain," "to divine," and "to make out," in place of "to guess."

Structuralism

Structuralism is a methodology that originated in Saussure's (1915) structural linguistic concept that language is a system of relations between the sound images and the mental concepts that comprise the linguistic sign. The early structuralists including Lévi-Strauss in anthropology, Piaget in child development, Barthes in literary criticism, Althusser in Marxism, and Lacan in psychoanalysis were intrigued by the notion of "systems of relations" and attempted to apply that concept in their own fields of study. As it developed, structuralism became a methodology for investigating the human mind, its structures, meanings, and products. It attempts to discover the relational structures involved in mental activities, to delineate how such structures are generated, and to describe how they transform into one another. Structuralists approach human phenomena with the expectation of finding relational structures, much as natural scientists expect to find causal correlations (Caws, 1988, p. 143). They assume that structures underlie all mental functioning, that such structures have cohesiveness, meaning, and generality, and that one can discover underlying structures through analysis (Gardner, 1981, p. 10).

In his definitive yet accessible treatise on structuralism, the philosopher Peter Caws (1988, pp. 248–249) notes that human beings have a talent for apposition, for putting things together and remembering that they have done so, that is, for making and learning relations. Our education involves assimilating myriad preformed examples of such relations, and our social individuality is a product of the relations into which we enter. Kinship patterns, for example, which have been studied by Lévi-Strauss (1969) and others, illustrate this point: "Because occupying a place in a kinship structure is a matter of being related in definite ways to other people who occupy neighboring places in it, individuation in such a structure requires that there be a unique set of relations for each person" (Caws, 1988, p. 249).

To illustrate the application of structuralist methodology in a nonclinical field, the work of Lévi-Strauss in anthropology provides some of the best known and clearest examples. In his empirical compilation and interpretive analyses of myths, for example, Lévi-Strauss's general strategy was: (1) selecting a "reference myth" from among the many examples collected in his field work; (2) delineate the code (for example, culinary) of the group to which the reference myth belonged; (3) demonstrate how within that code other myths could be derived from the reference myth by a series of transformations; and (4) show how myths in other groups are homologous with myths in the first group (Caws, 1988, pp. 117–118).

To illustrate the interrelatedness of his myths, the following examples are from Lévi-Strauss's *The Raw and the Cooked* (1969, pp. 99–104; cited by Caws, 1988, pp. 118–119):

> Three myths about the origin of tobacco have been recounted, M23 and M24 from the Toba and Tereno respectively, and M26 from the Borona. They are full of details that distinguish them quite starkly from one another; the first begins with a woman and her husband going to catch parakeets, the second with a sorceress who defiles plants with menstrual blood and feeds them to her husband, the third with men returning from the hunt who whistle to their wives to come and help them carry game [Caws, 1988, p. 119].

Caws notes further that Lévi-Strauss's interpretive analysis and reorganization of these myths produces a "strictly symmetrical" rendering illustrated in Table 5-1.

Caws (1988) comments critically about Lévi-Strauss's interpretive analysis and conclusions:

> In this highly selective process most of the content of the myths is suppressed; as one small example among many others, the "son snake" of M26 is conceived miraculously (his mother picks up a piece of boa her husband has killed and its blood penetrates and fertilizes her) before Lévi-Strauss's plot summary even begins. The symmetry is thus purchased at what some critics reasonably feel is a rather high price [p. 119].

This example from Lévi-Strauss's work illustrates the structuralist methodology of seeking "systems of relations" in various types of data; but it also suggests some of the potential problems and limitations of such an approach. What psychoanalysis and dynamic psychotherapy can learn from this example is: (1) to focus primarily on relatively limited segments of the therapeutic process (for example, individual therapy sessions), rather than over-reaching interpretively in an attempt to explain overly extensive areas of the patient's history, personality, and functioning;

Table 5-1

Transformation Schema for Myths (Lévi-Strauss, 1969); from Caws (1988, p. 118)

M_{23}–M_{24}	M_{26}
A husband (affinal relationship)	A mother (blood relationship)
has a wife jaguar	has a son snake
destructive through the mouth	protective through the vagina
of a husband who has climbed a tree	of a son who has climbed a tree
looking for animals (birds)	looking for vegetable food (fruit)
that the wife ought not to eat (but does)	that the mother ought to eat (but does not)
disjunction through the agency of the husband	disjunction through the agency of the mother
mother killed by affines (= children, in the case of patrilineal descent) ↘	↙ son killed by relatives (= maternal uncles, in the case of matrilineal descent)

burning of the victim,
origin of tobacco

(2) the ever-present problem of "confirmation bias," that is, the universal human tendency towards overcommitment to favored ideas, neglecting to question the correctness of such ideas, becoming intent upon confirming them, and ignoring disconfirmatory data.[11]

Structuralism and the structural viewpoint in psychoanalysis, though not identical, have important similarities (see also Pulver, 1988, pp. 178–183, for differences as well as similarities between the two). Platt (1983) points out, for example, that "there is a shared assumption among structuralists that the determining reality exists at an empirically unobservable level." Thus structuralists attempt to "cut through the observed reality to formulate a more fundamental one" (Platt, 1983, p. 616). The basic thesis of structuralism, that underlying structures are fundamental while surface features are changeable, coincides closely with Freud's conclusion that a wide variety of surface psychological phenomena including symptoms, dreams, fantasies, character traits, parapraxes, jokes, myths, superstitions, religion, art, and literature can represent diverse transformations of the same unconscious configuration or structure.

Not everything that refers to "structure" is structuralist; structuralism, for example, takes no interest in physical structures. Structuralist investigation applies specifically and exclusively to the human mind (Caws, 1988, p. 48). Structuralism has important connections with clinical interpretation because, by definition, structured mental contents are meaningful (Garner, 1962). When applied to clinical data, structuralism becomes a hermeneutic strategy for understanding and validating meanings in terms of interrelations among interdependent elements, rather than between self-contained entities. Wisdom (1956/1963) defines clinical interpretation in just such terms, that is, the construal of unconscious meanings implies that the therapist, "sees in the associations a relationship between networks of ideas" (p. 153).

Structuralism does not claim, however, that discovering the underlying structure of mind holds the key to complete understanding of meanings; no single approach can do that. Like clinical interpretation, structuralism focuses primarily on limited episodes of significance such as affective relations between people, which do not require general psychological principles to be understood as meaningful and relevant (Caws, 1988, p. 38). Structuralism contributes also to the justification of interpretations, because the posited relation or pattern can be filled in and extended indefinitely; and as more and more detailed findings accrue, they continue to fit into the pattern, and the pattern itself has a place in a still larger whole (Kaplan, 1964, p. 355; Peterfreund, 1983, pp. 212–217).

Clinicians employ structuralist methods, usually without realizing it, every time they attempt to infer latent meanings from clues in the form of relations and patterns in clinical data. Freud hit on the interpretive heuristic of pattern finding very early in the development of psychoanalysis. Describing his analysis of Elisabeth von R. (Breuer and Freud, 1893–1895), he reported a number of relational patterns in the patient's associations, for example:

1. He reported a session in which the patient produced numerous scenes from her early childhood. The scenes seemed to have in common some injury done to her, against which she felt unable to defend herself (p. 172).
2. Freud found that the fluctuations of her symptoms consistently occurred in association with some disturbing recent event (p. 149).
3. He noted the patient's resistance in connection with recalling memories, so he began making a careful record of the occasions on which the resistance was particularly marked (p. 154).

By 1900, pattern finding was well established in Freud's interpretive methodology. Discussing the dream of Irma's injection, for example, he quoted Schiller to the effect that:

> "Looked at in isolation, a thought may seem very trivial or very fantastic; but it may be made important by another thought that comes after it, and in conjunction with other thoughts that may seem equally absurd, it may turn out to form a most effective link" [1900, p. 103].

By 1915–1916 Freud viewed relations and patterns in clinical data as ubiquitous: "everything is related to everything, including small things to great" (p. 27; see also Glymour, 1993, p. 480).

The identification of relations and patterns in clinical data as clues to latent contents continues to serve as a major method of interpretive inquiry in psychoanalysis and dynamic psychotherapy. Arlow (1979, p. 203), for example, describes a number of heuristics employed in the methodology of clinical interpretation, all of which involve relations and patterns of various kinds: context, contiguity, congruence (usually analogical similarity), contrast, configuration (form and sequence of associations), convergence, and recurrence of themes. Often the process of formulating constructions starts with the recognition of a single relation within the data, goes on to additional pattern finding, and proceeds still further by means of pattern building or narrative formation.

Anything that facilitates the recognition of relations and patterns in clinical data contributes to the construal of latent contents (Rogers, 1981, p. 440; Hayek, 1994, pp. 55–56).[12] Repetition of themes and patterns, and analogical similarities, are among the most frequent types of relations that therapists employ in formulating constructions. Both provide heuristic guides to the most relevant data, and how to construe the latent meanings within those data.[13]

In addition to Lacan and his followers, a number of other psychoanalysts have attempted to apply structuralist concepts and methods to psychoanalysis.[14] For example, Kuper (1979, 1986) and Kuper and Stone (1982) applied Lévi-Strauss's structuralist method of investigating myths to the analysis of Freud's (1900) Specimen Dream; but they reported only a cognitive connection between the dream and Freud's scientific ideas at the time (see also Van Velzen, 1988). Most such efforts to integrate structuralism and psychoanalysis have attempted to build theoretical bridges between the two fields; but the principal parallels between structuralism and psychoanalysis appear to be methodologic—specifically, methodologic aspects of clinical inference and interpretation. Thus Kurzweil (1980) observes that structuralism's complex methodology, "continues to inspire. It has inscribed itself on a number of disciplines" (p. 10).

LANGUAGE-RELATED DISCIPLINES

Linguistics: Syntactical Clues to Latent Mental Contents

Chapter 4 included a critique of formal linguistic (rule-ordered, syntactical) models of interpretive methodology, but acknowledged that syntax sometimes does provide clues to unconscious meanings and determinants. Makari and Shapiro (1993) claim, for example, that therapists are able to "hear unconscious data" conveyed by language, including syntax, as well as by paralinguistic and nonverbal cues (see also Smith, 1978). Dahl et al. (1978b) describe various examples of syntactical choices illustrating warded-off wishes, emotions, and concealed intentions. One therapist's intervention, for example, included a phrase having no underlying subject, which he expressed in the passive voice—an "agentless passive" form of syntax. Clinicians studying the session concluded that the therapist's countertransference had in effect eliminated the patient. Another linguistic device called "foregrounding" gives greatest importance to material at the beginning of a communication, and next most importance to material at the end. Applying the heuristic of foregrounding, a therapist's long rambling interpretation reduced to: "I think that you make me mad" (1978b, p. 355). Other investigators who have employed the foregrounding heuristic report that patients' associations at the beginning of a therapy session may "telegraph" the focal (thematic) conflict of the session, and may reveal distinct correlations with the content of dreams reported during the session (Seitz, 1955; Lipton, 1958).

The preceding examples illustrate that syntactical clues to latent contents do occur in the clinical situation, but they do not appear to be a frequent or compelling source of such clues. The subtlety of syntactical clues suggests that their detection may be largely subliminal rather than conscious, and for that reason may need to be studied by specialized microanalytic methods.

Psycholinguistics

Psycholinguistics is the psychological study of language, an interdisciplinary field which includes linguistics, cognitive psychology, and cognitive science (Simon and Kaplan, 1989, pp. 15–18).[15] Psycholinguistic investigation of language processing is particularly relevant to the methodology of clinical interpretation because of parallels with clinical data processing.[16] There is much more to language processing than just syntax and its transformations (Prideaux, 1985, pp. 123–124). We draw upon all of the information that we can muster to produce and comprehend language (Slobin, 1979, p. 53). Both speakers and listeners employ a complex battery of strategies and heuristics to process language. Green and Morgan (1981, p. 177) maintain that the whole mind is involved in producing and understanding discourse—a methodologic principle that applies equally to the interpretive processing of clinical discourse.

Another similarity between language processing and the processing of clinical data is that listeners in both activities preconsciously construct rather than merely extract meanings from what is perceived. The role of construction in language processing is illustrated by the ubiquity of paraphrase: we usually recall the gist or a paraphrase rather than the exact wording of a sentence (Prideaux, 1985, pp. 183–186). We also recall more than we actually hear, because the meaning representations that we construct include not only the sentences we have heard but also the inferences we have drawn from the sentences. We fill in the blanks automatically and preconsciously to produce a complete and coherent meaning (Bransford and Franks, 1971); and once inferences have been placed in memory, they cannot be distinguished from that part of the meaning representation which was based upon the actual original sentences—a psycholinguistic finding that has important implications for misunderstandings in the clinical interpretive process.

Psycholinguistic studies of ordinary conversation reveal further similarities between clinical and nonclinical listening. When an utterance cannot be understood literally in everyday speech, the listener typically reinterprets what has been said in a way that makes the utterance meaningful. A common form of reinterpretation is to consider whether the remark might mean the opposite, as in irony (Searle, 1979b, p. 120; see also Rothenberg, 1971, who describes the same heuristic in clinical listening). Analogously, one of the earliest language-based models of clinical interpretation compared clinical observation and inference with ordinary conversation (Bernfeld, 1941).[17]

As in ordinary conversation, a patient (as speaker) counts on the therapist (as listener) to fill in and understand his or her meanings. Listeners in both everyday and clinical situations perceive speech conceptually: they infer meanings from what the speaker says, does not say, and how he or she says or does not say it. In this process, listeners decode the speaker's symbols into patterns and reform the patterns into meaningful gestalts, while conveying understanding by nodding, murmuring "I see," and by other signals including silence. Although similar to ordinary conversation in these ways, clinical listening is unlike it in other respects. Certain features of the therapeutic situation such as free association and the therapist's relatively greater silence are calculated to prevent the therapeutic interaction from becoming a social conversation. For example, participants in ordinary conversation are expected to make their remarks brief, relevant, unambiguous, and true (Grice, 1975); but the freely associating patient is not expected to follow any of those "rules" of conversation consistently: "The basic rule is a paradox. It is a rule that no rules be followed" (Smith, 1988, p. 406).

The methodologic rationale of freely hovering attention by depth psychological therapists gains support and possible explanation from a series of investigations by Spence (1968, 1981) and coworkers (Spence and Gordon, 1967; Spence and Grief, 1970; Spence and Lugo, 1972; Spence, Lugo, and Youdin, 1974). Quantitative investigations revealed that freely hovering attention facilitates preconscious perception and processing of latent meanings and determinants. A possible explanation of this phenomenon is that freely hovering attention entails partial listening (called "listening away" in psycholinguistics), which increases preconscious subliminal perception of cues that are too subtle to be observed consciously (Spence and Grief, 1970). Polanyi (1966) refers to this form of knowing as "tacit knowledge," based on, "interiorizing particulars to which we are not attending and which, therefore, we may not be able to specify" (p. 24). Spence and Grief (1970) found that "listening away," that is, paying less attention to manifest content, as in unfocused listening, increases the therapist's sensitivity to latent themes. Focused attention facilitates encoding and recall of manifest but not of latent contents. Spence and Lugo (1972) report, on the other hand, that the mode of attending, that is, whether characterized by linear or parallel processing, may be more important than the amount of attention (linear processing is associated primarily with manifest content, parallel processing with latent themes).

The methodology of clinical interpretation is most, but not exclusively, concerned with the semantic aspect of language and thus with the ambiguous concept of meaning. Semantics is both the heart of language and also its most elusive aspect. No less than sixteen definitions of semantic meaning have been proposed (Ogden and Richards, 1946, p. 248)—a number that spawned the following limerick by one of Richards's students at Harvard[18]:

> The Professor was quite overweening,
> As he expounded the meaning of meaning;
> In semantics he basked,
> 'Til a brash student asked,
> For the meaning of meaning of meaning.

The contextual definition of meaning is clearly compatible with clinical inference and interpretation: it combines associational and mediational definitions so that, as Rapaport (1944) puts it, "The meaning of an event is the psychological continuity into which it fits" (p. 216).[19] The representational aspect of meaning, on the other hand, reinforces the tendency to conceive of interpreted meanings as tangible entities existing in the mind of the patient. Interpreted meanings, however, are abstractions, depth-psychological hypotheses of the therapist's, which attempt to conceptualize what might be occurring in the mind of the patient. Laffal (1965, p. 20) points out that we tend to think of meaning as a phenomenon, a fact of life, so we assume that it is up to the linguist, the psychologist, and the philosopher to indicate where it is located and how it functions. Meaning, however, is essentially a theory applied to a set of data which defines some point of view about the relation of those data to their users.

A related aspect of meaning concerns its "multiplace locations" (Rogers, 1982, pp. 33, 45; 1984a, p. 320; 1986, p. 207), which in the clinical situation includes the patient, the therapist, the clinical data, the context, and the process—all of which must be taken into account by clinical interpreters.

Although meanings are carried largely in relations between words, that is, in the contexts of utterances, every therapist has had the experience of a single word seeming to provide the principal clue to understanding the latent theme of a therapy session. Bion's (1967, p. 127) concept of the "selected fact" applies in this conection: a therapist's attention is arrested by a particular word or phrase of the patient's, which results in a large number of apparently unrelated phenomena coming together with a meaning and coherence that they had lacked previously.[20]

Dynamically conspicuous words do not stand alone, of course, but acquire their foreground character against a contextual background of related but less suggestive or revealing words. In addition, so-called "key words," that is, those most closely related to the patient's principal (thematic) conflict at a particular time, tend to recur; and typical kinds of related words appear in close contiguity with key words (Laffal, 1965, pp. 125–128). A clinical investigation by Spence (1980a,b) provides an example of this phenomenon. Based upon carefully designed studies of words related to death, dying, and malignancy in cancer patients, Spence found that clinicians are often alerted to the possibility of a malignancy by specific words in the patient's discourse. "Lexical leakage" of this kind may be the commonest form of speech fault; but it is difficult to identify because, unlike slips of speech, lexical leakage affects only the choice of words without violating the surface structure of the sentence.

Wilson and Weinstein (1992a,b) have reviewed Vygotzky's (1962, 1987) perspective on language development, which includes still another form of meaning called "word meaning." Vygotzky (1987, p. 244) proposes that the concurrence of language and thought creates meanings, and that word meanings are central to the development of mind (p. 49). The possible relevance of Vygotzky's concept to the methodology of clinical interpretation is that word meaning becomes manifest and communicable through a word's linkages with its unique referents, the latter being idiosyncratic for each individual.[21]

Another aspect of psycholinguistics that is relevant to clinical inference and interpretation is "speech-act" theory (Austin, 1962; Searle, 1969). Speech acts include a speaker's intentions, and the effects of the speaker's intentions on the person who hears the utterance. Speech acts include statements, requests, warnings, threats, promises, and so forth. Extralinguistic conventions also transmit intentions. Every message includes an intention as well as grammatical form. Traditionally, intentions have been viewed as conscious; but some investigators (for example, Shapiro, 1979, p. 98) believe that intentions may include unconscious motivations as well (this question is discussed more fully in Chapter 6). In the clinical situation, for example, the therapist assumes that much of what the patient says contains allusions to the transference, the latter including wishful fantasies of influencing the therapist in various ways. The therapist's interventions also carry both conscious and unconscious intentions, especially in interpretations of resistance. Speech-act concepts thus constitute a powerful psycholinguistic model of how words carry "force," and influence both patients and therapists.

Another important area of psycholinguistic research that is relevant to clinical inference and interpretation is verbal accompaniments. The latter include paralinguistic, including prosodic cues, and nonverbal phenomena such as gestures and other body movements. One of the pioneer investigators in this field of study is George Mahl (1961, 1987a,b; Mahl and Schulze, 1964). A number of his investigations have focused on the vocal phenomenon of "flustered" speech, which is extralinguistic, that is, not part of the linquistic code and thus without semantic function, but a useful indicator of anxiety—more so, in fact, than manifest content (Mahl, 1987a, p. 192). Even a relatively weak indicator of speech disturbance such as sentence incompletion can indicate anxiety and repressed conflict (pp. 194–196; see also Fonagy and Fonagy, 1995, for a model of speech "styles").

The major paralinguistic phenomena studied by psycholinguists are the prosodic features of tone, pitch, and melody.[22] Since each adult draws differently from the repertoire of paralinguistic devices, generalizations about these phenomena are risky; thus therapists must learn the characteristic paralinguistic patterns of each individual patient. As they listen, therapists also emit prosodic signals, which do not necessarily interrupt the patient's speech but may serve as reinforcements, encouraging the patient to continue talking (Labov and Fanshel, 1977, p. 47). Considerable study has gone into this area: for example, Spence et al. (1994) describe mutual subliminal reinforcers in the verbal interactions of patient and therapist, while Greenspoon's (1955, 1962) classic experiments demonstrate how subtley and subliminally paralinguistic cues can influence patients' associations, and Gedo (1979, 1986) emphasizes that prosodic and other paralinguistic phenomena serve as one of the major sources of clues to latent meanings.

With respect to nonverbal behavior, psycholinguistic investigators distinguish between two types: actions having a primarily communicative function (Birdwhistell, 1970; Morris et al., 1979; McNeill, 1992), and another group which are idiosyncratic, that is, personal-expressive. Clinicians are more interested in the latter group because they often reveal inner mental states by a process called "nonverbal leakage" (Ekman, 1957, 1964, 1965). Freud (1905a) noticed, for example, that Dora repeatedly opened her handbag and slipped her finger into it. He concluded that the action betrayed childhood masturbation, of which Dora had no memory. On that basis Freud reasoned that what cannot be remembered can reappear as an action (1914c). Investigations by Mahl and coworkers suggest, however, that many symptomatic acts are not merely alternative ways of remembering, but are integral to recollection and verbalization. The following is an example abstracted from Mahl:

> While expressing inferiority feelings as a housewife, a woman placed her fingers over her mouth briefly. Later she mentioned that her inferiority feelings began as a child when she felt unattractive because of protruding front teeth. In this case, the gesture of putting her fingers over her mouth was not an alternative to, but anticipated and may even have facilitated, the memory of embarrassment about her teeth in childhood [1987a, pp. 75–96].

Mahl (1987a, pp. 97–107) also investigated the interpretive problem of whether idiosyncratic movements such as Dora's putting her finger in her purse was autistically masturbatory, or whether it expressed a fantasied interpersonal relationship, that is, an unconscious wish for intercourse with Freud (see also Freud, 1905a, p. 9; and Panel, 1969). Mahl's investigations suggest that autistically appearing movements and gestures often represent embodiments of fantasied interpersonal relationships. In a similar vein, Breuer and Freud (1893–1895) recognized that hysterical symptoms are often disguised enactments of fantasied interpersonal experiences (see also Freud's letter to Fliess dated December 22, 1897, in Masson, 1985, pp. 288–289; and see also Jacobs, 1973, 1994).

Communication Theory

George A. Miller's (1967) widely quoted analysis of ordinary communication suggests a number of parallels with therapeutic discourse and interpretation (see also Watzlawick et al., 1967; Wachtel, 1993). Miller emphasizes the necessity for a listener (or therapist) to thematize continually what is heard in order to surmount the limitations of working memory, which ordinarily has a capacity of only six or seven items. Since we remember better what fits together, the thematizing process groups data into increasingly larger and more coherent units. Informationally rich symbols such as words, concepts, and images, which facilitate the formation of themes, make the most efficient use of our limited memory span. Miller's concept applies equally to interpretive inquiry, in which clinicians make continual use of thematization to deal with the voluminous data of the therapeutic process.

In the language of communication theory, the perception, assimilation, and understanding of messages involves a process of recoding, which is involved also in the interpretive processing of clinical data. One form of recoding groups the information thematically, applies a new name to it, and then remembers the new name rather than the original information. Recoding is thus a powerful method of increasing the amount and complexity of information that can be processed. Because recoding must be accomplished rapidly, it cannot be carried out consciously but must be performed pre- or unconsciously. The commonest kind of recoding is translation into a verbal code, rephrased in "one's own words." Sasso (1993; cited by Speziale-Bagliacca, 1995, p. 133) postulates a specialized form of decoding which may be applied to latent meanings, the latter being carried like anagrams inside other words. Compare, in this connection, Freud's interest in anagrams: for example, his interpretation that the Rat Man's compulsive utterance of the neologistic term "*Glejisamen*" during masturbation contained the words "Gisela," his beloved, and "Samen," semen (Freud, 1909b, pp. 280–281).

Another common form of recoding utilizes imagery. Leavy (1973) writes:

> The act of interpretation is imagination in a very complex sense. Let us consider its more literal sense first: images appear in the analyst's mind, claiming special attention, having been instigated in the first place by some discontinuity in the patient's discourse. Secondly, these images are rooted in the private memories of the analyst. At any time the images may be elaborate, fluctuating, evanescent, but interpetation becomes possible when the images persist and demand to be noticed [p. 314; see also Gardner, 1983, p. 50ff].

Arlow (1979, p. 200) writes similarly that, sooner or later, the therapist's initially passive-receptive mode of listening changes, due to the intrusion of a fantasy-image, thought, or feeling which the therapist notices because at first it seems to differ from what the patient had been saying. Shortly after experiencing the response, however, the therapist often recognizes a meaningful relation between the intruding content and the patient's associations (see Ross and Knapp, 1962; Kern, 1978, for clinical examples).

Paivio (1971, pp. 166–167) notes the advantages of image processing in interpretive work. The synchronous (composite) rather than sequential nature of image representation makes image processing flexible and efficient in the search for relevant information, and for storage in and retrieval from long-term memory. Gardner (1983) writes that, "The visual ranges far ahead, scouting what is to come, and to be come upon, while the main body of verbal thinking plods along until, when possible, word catches up" (p. 72)

Miller (1967) points out that the adeptness of human beings in communicating with each other cannot be attributed to their speed of processing information, which is relatively slow, or to memory, which is relatively limited:

> It is my own opinion that man's peculiar gift as a component in a communication system is his ability to discover new ways to transform, or to recode, the information which he receives. It seems to me that the very fact of our limited capacity for processing information has made it necessary for us to discover clever ways to abstract the essential features of our universe and to express these features in simple laws that we are capable of comprehending in a single act of thought. We are constantly taking information given in one form and translating it into alternative forms, searching for ways to map a strange new phenomenon into simpler and more familiar ones. The search is something we call "thinking"; if we are successful, we call it "understanding" [p. 49].

Still another parallel between the psychology of communication and therapeutic discourse is the uncertainty of construction in the interpretive process. Miller (1967, pp. 75–77) describes the listener's task in ordinary communication this way (the rapidity of the process suggests that it goes on preconsciously for the most part): The listener begins with a guess about the input information, on the basis of which he or she generates a matching internal signal. The first guess is often wrong, which leads to another such guess. The cycle of guessing, mismatches, and corrected guesses recurs until a satisfactory match is obtained. The efficiency of this process depends largely upon the quality of the initial guess. If the initial guess is close, the iterative process is completed rapidly; if not, the listener may not be able to keep up with the flow of speech. Initial guesses are like predictive hypotheses about what incoming messages will turn out to be. Advance postulates make it possible to attune one's apperception to certain interpretations while rejecting others—illustrating again the crucial role of context in listening and understanding. It is important to note, however, that although context is necessary to understanding, at times it can be biasing and misleading.

Another aspect of communication theory and research deals with kinesics, that is, nonverbal communication through body movements and gestures.[23] Birdwhistell's (1970, p. 157) investigations have demonstrated the extreme repetitiveness of some kinesic phenomena: for example, the same motor pattern may be repeated hundreds of times in a twenty-minute period. Study of gestures has led to one of the most important findings of kinesic research, namely, the discovery of parallels between kinesic and language structures. The kinesic system employs forms which are very similar to words in language. There are body behaviors that function like sounds, combine into complex units like words, or into longer structures like sentences or even paragraphs. Like words, the same body movement can be used to communicate different meanings; thus a specific movement has no one constant meaning.

Rhetoric is another aspect of communication theory that is highly relevant to clinical interpretation. Rhetoric is communication that attempts to persuade.[24] In the case of therapeutic discourse, rhetorical devices are employed by both patient and therapist, each attempting to persuade the other to see things in a particular way. Some common rhetorical devices described by Hairston (1978) are employed in both ordinary and clinical communication: (1) Connotation, which operates by triggering associations, including stereotypes, personal needs, and fears. (2) Figurative language which, like connotation, operates by triggering associations. (3) Tone of voice, for example, assuming a confident, hypermasculine, conciliatory, humble, self-critical, injured, casual, familiar, or other tone calculated to influence the listener in specific ways. (4) Certain modes of argument also may be used as rhetorical devices, for example, the argumentum ad hominem which diverts discussion from facts to the personality of the other person; and the argumentum ad baculum, which appeals to human fears and may contain an implicit threat (Runes, 1983, p. 34).

Stanley Fish (1989) argues that since interpretations have no independent grounds but are the products of other interpretations, rhetoric is inevitable and ubiquitous in psychoanalysis and dynamic psychotherapy. Other writers (for example, Maranhão, 1990; see also Margolis, 1990) maintain that psychoanalysis and dynamic psychotherapy are both science and rhetoric, and as such may be at the forefront of developments in science. Maranhão (1990, p. 116) suggests that combining the two approaches reduces the differences between invention/discovery and explanation/interpretation, thus making indirect persuasion an instrument of treatment, inquiry, and scholarly demonstration. Donald Spence (1994a) argues, on the other hand, that psychoanalysis is characterized by a disproportion of rhetoric to evidence. He notes particularly the use of rhetorical "sleight-of-hand"; rhetoric masquerading as explanation; overreliance on the rhetorical figure of metalepsis, that is, invoking causative factors from the distant past to account for present states; and other examples of bad science disguised by empty rhetoric. (See also Rubovits-Seitz [1995b] for a review and critique of Spence's views on the "rhetorical voice" of psychoanalysis.)

Semiotics

Semiotics, the science of signs, is part of the larger field of communication. It is concerned not only with language but with all aspects of communication, including physical signs such as dark clouds signifying rain, smoke as a sign of fire, and so forth. Semiotics shares certain basic features with structuralism (discussed previously); for example, both are relation- and pattern-centered rather than thing-oriented systems (Hawkes, 1977). Unlike structuralism, however, semiotics is not a methodology but a point of view regarding the actions of signs, the perspective that all human experience, from sensation to understanding, is a network of sign relations (Eco, 1989, pp. 177–179; Deely, 1990, p. 5; see also Litowitz and Epstein, 1991).

Interpretation is a defining feature of semiotics, because the essential function of a sign is referral, that is, representing or standing for something other than itself; and the meaning of a sign, what it stands for, must be interpreted by the receiver of the sign. A thermometer, for example, is a type of sign because it stands not only for itself but for something besides itself, namely, the surrounding temperature. When the thermometer is read, a third factor enters in, that of interpretation. Eco (1989, p. 177) notes that an essential feature of signs is that they stimulate their own interpretations; and Cherry (1957) observes that "every sign requires another 'to interpret it'" (p. 264).

Semiotics holds that the world is made up not of facts but of signs about facts, which human beings encode and decode endlessly. All understanding depends upon codes, and to make sense of an event or experience one needs a system of thought or code. A code channels relations among objects and events according to patterns in a publicly accessible way (Deely, 1990, pp. 65–66, 74–76). In human beings the code includes meanings and meaning relations. Understanding of complex codes requires the use of multiple codes simultaneously (Scholes, 1982, p. 143). Codes modify, determine, and even generate meaning, much as language imposes its own mediating pattern on perception and thought. Shands (1970) comments that, "In the epistemological revolution of the twentieth century we have come to understand that what is is what can be communicated in some coded form" (p. 319; emphasis omitted).

One can observe the operation of coding and recoding in the clinical situation as it unfolds over time: during early phases of the therapeutic process, for example, the patient is relatively unfamiliar with the code of clinical interpretation; but as the therapeutic dialogue proceeds, the patient gradually learns the interpretive code, becomes increasingly able to anticipate the therapist's interpretations and to apply the code to his or her own associations (see, for example, Schlessinger and Robbins, 1975, pp. 776–778; 1983, pp. 37–40, 64–66).[25]

Of the various language-related disciplines, semiotics is perhaps the most relevant to clinical interpretation. The historiographer Carlo Ginzburg (1989) notes in this connection that during the 1870s a method emerged in the human sciences that was based upon semiotics, on the deciphering of signs of various kinds. The method was essentially an interpretive approach that relied upon "clues" suggested by inconspicuous details in human science data. Ginzburg includes Freud's interpretive methodology among the disciplines that employed such an approach. Freud (1914d) wrote, for example, that psychoanalysis attempts to interpret "secret and concealed things from despised and unnoticed features, from the rubbish-heap, as it were, of our observations" (p. 222). Ginzberg describes Freud's approach as a method in which minor details serve as clues that are interpreted as signs of crucial, concealed aspects of the mind.

The relation between semiotics and interpretive methodology is only beginning to be explored, but holds considerable promise. Eugene Brody (1990) writes that the psychoanalytic dialectic "involves from the beginning a semiotic attempt to deconstruct the signs that are involved in conscious and unconscious systems of signification" (p. 36). Johansen (1986) believes that both Freud (1900, Chapter 7) and Hartmann (1959, pp. 342–343) recognized the semiotic nature of mental processes. Johansen observes that the psychic apparatus

> can transform inputs from the outside and from the body into different sign systems, store this information, recall it, combine it,

> select from it, transform it from one type of sign system to another, create new meaningful chains of signs on the basis of what is stored, and so on [1986, pp. 520–521].

Hartmann (1959, pp. 342–343) pointed out that much psychoanalytic work involves the use of signs as "indications of mental processes." As such, the psychoanalytic method constitutes a semiotic process of interpretation (Shapiro, 1991, p. 324). The translation into words of symbolic entities such as reported feelings and dream images that stand for something else, illustrates the central role of semiotics in our interpretive methodology. The therapist attempts to rethink, reimage, reunderstand the rebuslike relations of the patient's reported images and feelings, translating them into common thought. Our clinical interpretive methodology may be viewed in large part, therefore, as a semiotic process.[26]

A suggestive convergence of concepts regarding semiotics and interpretive methodology appears variously in the writings of Rosen (1969/1977, pp. 186–189), Gedo (1979, 1981, 1984a), and Killingmo (1990). Rosen theorized that the principal form of communication between parent and infant is a signal-sign system, which includes the cry of hunger, the smiling response, and gestural, babbling, and mimetic behavior, all of which are superseded but not replaced completely by the later development of language.[27] Thus Gedo and Killingmo conclude that it may not be possible to activate or modify affects deriving from presemantic levels solely by the verbal content of interpretations. It may be necessary to approach such affects by intonation and enactments, which may serve as presemantic "semiotic supplements" to verbal-symbolic interpretations.[28]

Another illustration of how usefully semiotics can be applied to depth psychology and interpretive methodology is Rogers' (1987c) reinterpretation of Freud's concepts of repetition. Contrary to Freud's later view (1920a) that the repetition-compulsion is an instinctual process, his earlier essay, "Remembering, Repeating, and Working Through" (1914c), emphasized the representational value of repetition as a source of information for clinical interpretation, that is, repetition as a semiotic signifying process. From the standpoint of semiotics, repetition *is* meaning, because repetition is a sign that represents and points to a particular meaning. Thus, Rogers concludes that the true significance of the repetition-compulsion does not derive from its drivelike qualities, but from "its force as meaning, not its meaning as force" (1987c, p. 584).

Literary Theory and Criticism

In addition to studying the nature of texts, literary scholars also study various methods and models of interpreting texts.[29] Poetic texts in particular share with clinical data the characteristic of concealed meanings which are largely implicit.[30] Clarifying information is often lacking in both poems and clinical data, requiring interpreters to supply additional context from surrounding data or texts. Parallels have been proposed by some writers between poetic license, on the one hand, and both the fundamental rule and confidentiality, on the other.[31]

Numerous writers have noted the similarities between literary and clinical interpretation.[32] The parallels between clinical and literary discourse have been attributed to the subjective viewpoints of both, inner significance replacing correspondence with external reality (Johansen, 1986, p. 535). As a result, clinicians and literary scholars sometimes turn to each other for better understanding of interpretation. A psychoanalyst confided to Coen (1983, p. 169), for example, that he learned more about interpretation from literary critics than from other psychoanalysts.

To the extent that the methodology of clinical interpretation is data driven rather then doctrinal in approach, it can be compared with the New Criticism which became very influential in American literature half a century ago: that is, viewing the object of interpretation as an autonomous whole which is studied in and for itself, without reference to possible external contexts. Historical and causal explanations were replaced by internal analysis in an attempt to demonstrate how a text's various parts contribute to a thematic unity (Culler, 1981, p. 4). The New Criticism's ideal of a self-contained encounter between a reader and an autonomous text is unrealistic, however, because reading always involves relations with other texts,[33] just as the clinical interpreter inevitably draws heuristically to some extent upon his or her experiences with previous patients in order to understand each new patient.

Turning to the history of modern literary theory and its continuing debates about the nature and sources of meaning, we find that the various schools of literary theory acknowledge that neither textual data nor the interpretive act alone can account for meaning—yet they persist in attempting to do so (Ray, 1984; Abrams, 1989). A clinical counterpart of these debates is the perennial controversy between objectivist versus subjectivist approaches to clinical interpretation, that is, disagreements about whether the patient's productions, the interpreter's subjective responses, or both, provide the principal source of meanings for clinical interpretations. Both literary and clinical interpretation have evolved gradually towards a dialectical-dialogic-interactive model of meaning and interpretation (see, for example, Bakhtin's [1986] concept of "the dialogic," described by Brooks [1994, p. 881]). According to the latter view, meaning as structure (within a text or clinical data) and meaning as interpretive act (by a literary or clinical interpreter) are conceived of as mutually constitutive.

Additional parallels between the methodologies of clinical and literary interpretation include the pluralistic, relativistic, and progressive nature of both approaches. Barthes (1970, p. 18; cited by Ray, 1984, pp. 176–177) described interpretation, for example, as a diachronic, shifting, evolving, plurivocal configuration of meanings in complex interrelationships with each other, which fluctuate dynamically, change in figure-ground relations, evolve in form and content, vary in completeness, and remain indefinitely open ended. De Man's (1979; cited by Ray, 1984, p. 194) ironic reference to the "steady ground of provisional conclusion," which gives way inevitably to further interpretation, also expresses a relativistic and progressive view of interpretation.[34]

Literary theory requires interpretations to correlate with specific data, and to enrich and illuminate the particulars of those data (Ray, 1984, p. 197). Similar criteria apply to clinical interpretation: for example, Freud's observation that "intimate details" are necessary to make psychoanalytic formulations conclusive (cited by Nunberg and Federn, 1962, p. 172); Edelson's (1984, pp. 135–137) assertion that highly specific, circumstantial, idiosyncratic details provide the most probative evidence for interpretations; Hirsch's (1967) emphasis on "small-scale" evidence; Cheshire's (1975) concept of "organized interlocking microstructures" underlying interpretations; and Friedman's (1983, p. 215) observation that particularity is possible only in a discursive form of therapy such as psychoanalysis, because its discursive form allows the reconstructed life history to be nuanced endlessly without becoming lost in generalities. Brenneis (1994) writes in this connection that he needs to listen for particulars, whether in the form of speech, fantasies, recurrent characters, or shifts in affect. If "a patient tells me that he is angry with his brother and wants to get back at him, this is too abstract for me. Angry how? Get back at him how? What are the details?" (pp. 34–37).

In both clinical and literary interpretation, constructions are expected to correlate not only with particular data, but also with all (or at least most) of the data in a specific text or unit of therapy. The principal criterion for all interpretation, literary or psychoanalytic, is how completely the interpreter has accounted for all of the details in the narrative (Pearce, 1965, p. 311).[35]

One of the most striking parallels between the methodologies of clinical and literary interpretation is the emphasis of both on repetition of contents. Both follow Hume's Principle of the Uniformity of Nature, that is, "the observation of past regularities provides grounds for predicting that the same regularities will recur in the future" (Kukla, 1989, p. 791). Barthes (1977, pp. 79–124) observed that the basic unit of narrative organization is a sequence, and that although a reader perceives a linear progression of ideas, the sequences are interwoven and the narrative structure is recurrent. Rifferterre (1973, p. 44) notes that poetic texts also seem to progress from image to image, but in fact keep repeating the same information. Suleiman (1980) describes multiple forms of redundancy in literature, which are equally applicable to redundant images observed in clinical narratives. Among the literary examples given are: (1) more than one character experiencing the same event; (2) a single character experiencing the same event repeatedly; (3) several characters possessing the same qualities, or serving similar functions; (4) one character remaining the same through time; (5) one character performing the same function several times; (6) a context metonymically redundant with a character, for example, a baker in his bakery; (7) an event that is redundant with interpretive comments made about it by one or more characters. Redundancies of this kind in literature have numerous counterparts in clinical data and interpretations (see, for example, Freud, 1911b, p. 94; French, 1952, 1954, 1958a; Kelman, 1975).

In addition to the aforementioned parallels between the methodologies of clinical and literary interpretation, the latter has contributed some novel ways of looking at clinical interpretation and at depth-psychological concepts, history, and writings. For example, nineteenth century novels may have contributed to

Freud's understanding of hysterical symptoms and dreams, because literary fictions made certain psychoanalytic theories imaginable (Thomas, 1990, pp. 9, 14).[36] Moreover, by focusing on literary and structural aspects of Freud's writings, the methods of literary criticism have been applied to psychoanalytic literature and to clinical interpretation itself.[37]

Studies of the reading process are among the most important contributions of literary theory to the methodology of clinical interpretation. The argument has been made, however, that clinical interpretation is more like creative writing than like reading because of the many revisions that interpretations undergo. Reader-response theory is particularly apposite to interpretive inquiry in the clinical situation. A reader, for example, is always trying to "make sense" of the text, much as the clinician's mind is engaged in a continual process of attempting to construe latent meanings and determinants in the patient's associations (Fish, 1980).[38] Both reading and interpreting involve the merging of one's consciousness with the flow of a text or a patient's discourse. A somewhat trancelike state occurs in both activities, the personal identity of the reader or clinical interpreter being subordinated to the reading or clinical construal process (Ray, 1984, p. 11).[39] Boyd (1985) writes that "Freud's 'Interpretation of Dreams' sets the model for the connection between literature and psychoanalysis as shared symbol systems, reading the patient as text, the text as patient" (p. 108). He adds:

> Such a procedure is perfectly legitimate as long as we remember that the analogy between the patient and text is based on the extended metaphorical sense of "read" (understand or interpret), as when we speak of reading someone's face or mind, reading a situation, reading between the lines. In this sense of the word, we read both patient and text the same way—namely, semiotically, as an organization of signs to be decoded [Boyd, 1985, p. 108].

Among the various theories of reading that have been proposed, and which are accessibly reviewed by Ray (1984), Iser's (1978) concepts are among the most relevant and applicable to clinical interpretation. Iser's model draws extensively upon gestalt concepts, and his explanation of how each new "fact" is integrated into an evolving gestalt (or whole meaning) employs a temporal (time/change) model of progressive dialectical revisions. Tentatively erected whole meanings are prevented from becoming reified by the ongoing nature of the reading process, which is called "textual extension." The latter confronts the reader with a constant stream of new meanings (or, more correctly, information) that require interpretation. Integration of the previous with the new information gives meaning to the new data. An increasingly inclusive principle of coherence is required to reconcile and integrate old and new constructions, as well as various thematic levels of the text. Iser calls these increasingly comprehensive patterns of meaning "continual gestalt formations." Successive groupings of textual elements find their meanings in the gestalten (compare Rapaport's [1944] psychoanalytic definition of meaning: "the meaning of an event is the continuity into which it fits").

Archaeological Decipherment

Freud compared the therapeutic process with archaeological excavation and restoration (1905a, p. 12; 1937b, pp. 259–260), and clinical interpretation with the decipherment of ancient scripts (1913c, p. 177). He did not elaborate on the analogies, but the methodologies of both archaeology and archaeological decipherment reveal a number of parallels with the methodology of clinical interpretation—parallels which are both suggestive and problematic. In particular, archaeology requires an extensive amount of inference, weighing of imponderables, and a good deal of scientific imagination (Herskovits, 1948, p. 97; cited by Heizer, 1959, p. xv); and it is generally recognized that interpretation is the most difficult part of analyzing artifacts (Anderson, 1984, p. 80), just as it is the most uncertain part of depth-psychological work.

Despite the difficulties and limited scope of their data, however, some archaeologists continue to engage in a search for theories that they hope will make it possible to extend their interpretive conclusions (Trigger, 1978, pp. 134–137). Yet critics charge that theorizing of this kind has actually been a deterrent to progress in archaeology because it produces a one-sided, theory-bound approach to interpretation, and because focusing on a favored theory has had a constricting effect upon other possible avenues of approach by suppressing data that do not fit a favored theory or interpretation (Anderson, 1984, p. 80). To some critics, the basic methodologic problem is "the disinclination of archaeologists to consider the inner core of their intuitive procedure" (Clarke, 1978, p. 25; compare the disinclination of clinicians, beginning with Freud, to investigate the problems and limitations of their interpretive methods).

According to Clarke (1978), archaeological investigation

> has rather dishonestly and inconsistently operated at two levels. A theoretical level of interpretation in terms of rigid monothetic groupings and a practical level of groupings by broad affinity or similarity assessed on an intuitive basis. This schizophrenic division has seriously impaired the development of prehistoric studies, in which lip-service has been paid to a theoretical model of demonstrable inadequacy, whilst actual practical advance has been accomplished by rather furtive groping—with the results subsequently presented as having been achieved by intelligent theorizing [p. 37].

As in all scientific work, archaeological observations are influenced by the observer's frame of reference and personal idiosyncracies. The observer selects the data, and no two observers necessarily report the same perceptions or interpretations of them (Clarke, 1978, pp. 14–15; compare the ubiquity of the consensus problem in all of the human and social sciences [Bernstein, 1988a, pp. 88–89]). Archaeological "facts" are of two kinds: 1) directly observed and described attributes; and 2) the most useful, frequent, but also most "dangerous" kind, namely, inferred or induced "facts." Barber's textbook of archaeological decipherment (1974, pp. 235–236) recognizes the methodologic problems of interpretation and suggests that archaeologists and decipherers look for useful methods in other fields.

Cyrus Gordon's (1982) treatise on deciphering ancient scripts stresses the need for flexibility on the part of interpreters and their methods. Recognition of discrepancies and acceptance of errors are crucial. Darwin (1888, p. 83) wrote, for example, that he could not recall a single hypothesis that did not have to be modified or abandoned eventually. As in clinical interpretation, "the deciphererer can make inferences which may be right because they fit into some pattern inherent in the text" (Gordon, 1982, p. 13); Gordon cautions, however:

> Guesses of this kind are necessary, but they cannot be off the top of one's head; to be successful, they must reckon with the realities, or at least the probabilities, of the text to be deciphered.

> Even then most of the guesses are wrong, so that a prime quality of the cryptanalyst or decipherer is flexibility. Wrong guesses are usually exposed as incorrect by the fact that they lead to impossible combinations when applied elsewhere in the text to be deciphered [1982, pp. 13–14].

Gordon (p. 14) concludes that decipherment without flexibility is impossible. Guesses must be made, but for every guess that turns out to be correct, many wrong ones must be scrapped—a conclusion that is equally relevant to the constructive phase of the clinical interpretive process.

COGNITIVE SCIENCE

Cognitive science is an interdisciplinary field which encompasses psychology (especially cognitive and social psychology), psycholinguistics, information theory, computing science including artificial intelligence, neurobiology, and even psychopharmacology (Harré and Lamb, 1983, p. 95).[40] Modern cognitive psychology began with the pioneering investigations of Bartlett (1932), who developed a dynamic theory of memory. Piaget's (1952, 1973; Piaget and Inhelder, 1973) investigations of cognitive development became another milestone, one familiar to most clinicians. Currently, cognitive science has occupied itself with the revolutionary advances in information theory. The cognitive movement did not really begin to take hold in the behavioral sciences until around 1960, when human beings began to be seen as information-seeking, information-processing organisms who not only process environmentally presented information about physical objects and people but also process and reshape a continuing flow of inner stimulation from the long-term memory system (Singer, 1988a, pp. 298–299).

The Shared Concept of Representations in Psychodynamics and Cognitive Science

Recognizing the need for some sort of internal representation of reality, cognitive psychologists during the 1960s became increasingly interested in the symbolic function, how human beings represent the world symbolically.

Fodor (1983, p. 85–86) points out that the mind is essentially a symbol processing device; thought in general is a matter of deploying these symbols in some disciplined way. Meanwhile, Fodor continues, mental processes have gone underground: cognitive science now assumes that the most interesting thought processes are unconscious.

A similar paradigm shift was occurring at approximately the same time (around 1960) in social psychology, which began to explore organized meaning structures as fundamental to social behavior.[41] As early as 1943, Kenneth Craik had proposed that thinking involves the manipulation of internal representations of the world; but the concept of representations did not become established in cognitive science until the information processing paradigm appeared in the 1960s (Simon, 1981, p. 153). Long before the aforementioned changes, the concept of "psychic representations" had been an integral part of psychoanalytic theory. With the growth of object relations theory, once again during the 1960's, psychoanalytic interest in the "representational world" increased still further.[42]

Just as there are multiple simultaneously ongoing mental processes, there is also presumably a multiplicity of representations. For any one object, various modes of representation—in fact, several of each kind—may exist: lexical, iconic, imagistic, semantic, propositional, enactive, motoric, and others. For example, cognitive investigations of motor representations (which had been recognized earlier by Freud, Reich, and others) have demonstrated the activity of the motor system during mental processes of encoding and retrieval (Zajonc, 1988, pp. 353–356; Zajonc and Markus, 1984). To illustrate: in face recognition, at which human beings excel, when perceiving another's face one's own face is not passive but engages in low-voltage muscular activities which tend to match the face of the other person (Dimberg, 1982). In other words, we imitate faces in encoding them.[43]

It is often taken for granted that what one remembers are traces of stimuli—words, pictures, and so forth. We tend to assume that remembering depends more on properties of the stimulus than on one's own reactions to it. On the basis of the previous experiments and others, however, it now appears that retrieval involves reinstatement of one's original muscular reactions. It seems, therefore, that the self must have important representational and mnesic functions in the encoding, processing, and retrieving of information. One does not necessarily remember a particular passage in a book, for example, but may remember him- or herself reading the passage and reacting to it. Zajonc (1988) writes:

> Thus a part of the self is very much involved in the trace. It might be only the part that observed the object or event, perhaps only the part that processed the information, or perhaps only the part that reacted. But any combination of these elements may be retrieved [p. 357; see also Marcel, 1983].

The preceding observations and concepts are relevant to the importance that depth-psychological therapists attach to observations of their own responses to patients' material. Among other purposes served by that strategy, it may also facilitate important functions for the therapist of encoding, processing, and subsequently being able to retrieve memories of the patient's latent meanings and determinants. This leads to the further suggestion that since retrieval may be enhanced by reinstating the self-activity that was present when an object or event was encoded originally, it might be useful if one attempted first to retrieve the self-structure (self-schema) of the earlier experience: "Primed in that way, the events that occurred might be viewed in their original perspective and reported more accurately" (Zajonc, 1988, p. 358). This concept (and possible method) may be relevant also to the methodologic strategy of controlled therapeutic regression in psychoanalysis, that is, regression in the service of retrieving self-schemas of early experiences.

Relation of Schema Theory to Problems of Interpretive Methodology

A number of attempts have been made in recent years to integrate psychodynamics and cognitive science.[44] Psychodynamic formulations deal with why clinical phenomena occur; cognitive theories and investigations attempt to elucidate how they take place, the specific mental processes involved.

Since most mental processes are not introspectable, the investigation of cognitive processes necessarily depends upon communication. In the clinical situation, patients do most of the communicating, so productive processing by patients receives much more investigative attention than receptive (that is, interpretive) processing by therapists. On the other hand, receptive processing may employ the same operations as productive processing, though in the opposite direction (Charles Stinson, 1992, personal communication). Presumably, however, the mental contents of cognitive processing by patients and therapists may differ in certain respects, even though their respective processing operations may be similar.

Areas of joint concern shared by psychodynamics and cognitive science include emotionality and control processes, particularly how a person regulates emotionality in an interpersonal situation. Cognitive scientists recognize increasingly that emotions, the cognitive system, and the information processing sequence are closely linked. Singer (1988a) writes:

> A key concept in the paradigm shift from a stimulus-response (S-R) to a cognitive perspective in psychology is the notion of a temporally extended, if very rapid, "sequence" in information processing. Cognitive psychologists like to draw flow charts representing the interplay of anticipation, identification of features, "gating out" or filtering of irrelevancies or threatening material, retention in short-term memory, movement of new material (under the direction of some kind of executive or rule-making system) to long-term memory for further rehearsal, and so forth [p. 300].

Correspondingly, the growth of an object relations perspective in psychoanalysis and dynamic psychotherapy has increased the interest of clinicians in cognitive processing. After all, the core concepts of psychodynamics imply a distinctly "intelligent" unconscious, capable of "a great deal of computation within a dynamic sector of unconscious mental processes" (Horowitz, 1988, p. 6). For example, an understanding of the dynamic unconscious from an information processing point of view includes unconscious capabilities such as the anticipation and avoidance of unpleasant or overwhelming mental states by preventing potentially disturbing thoughts and emotions from attaining conscious representation.

A major area of convergence between cognitive psychology and psychodynamics is schema theory, the prototype of which in psychodynamics is Freud's (1912a) theory of transference (Horowitz, 1989, p. 263).[45] Schemas are organized mental structures that integrate and encapsulate knowledge about oneself and the world. They operate both consciously and unconsciously to organize thought, mood states, self-appraisal, and interpersonal behavior. They also function defensively as control processes by foregrounding a neutral schema to avoid the instantiation (activation) of a dreaded person schema. The term "person schema" refers to schemas of self and other, in contrast to schemas of nonhuman objects (Horowitz, 1991a,b).

Person schemas of self interacting with others are called "role relationship models" (Horowitz, 1988, pp. 11–12, 65–66); they are related to "script theory," that is, action sequences that play themselves out automatically in particular real world situations (Schank and Abelson, 1977).[46] Scripts about important interpersonal interactions may develop as a result of specific childhood experiences associated with intense positive or negative emotions, called "scenes" (Tomkins, 1979). Affective scenes of that kind and their resulting scripts influence the individual's interpretation of new information as well as behavior (Carlson, 1981; Carlson and Carlson, 1984).

Self schemas are a special variety of knowledge and beliefs about one's self (Segal and Blatt, 1993). Different self schemas develop in the same person as a result of experiencing diverse roles in relation to others. To integrate such a diversity of self schemas, supraordinate schemas of disparate self schemas tend to develop. Nested hierarchies of such self schemas produce self-organization. Self schemas develop in part from genetics, the biology of temperament, and in part from the meaning structures passed on by or otherwise internalized from family and culture (Emde, 1989, 1993).

Evidence for the existence of schemas comes mainly from experimental research on memory (Singer and Salovey, 1991, p. 36). Although schema theory is a point of convergence between psychodynamics and cognitive science, "it is the most speculative domain in either set of theories" (Horowitz, 1988, p. 14; emphasis omitted). Some clinical counterparts of schema theory include the psychodynamic concepts of unconscious fantasy, self and object representations, imagoes, and transference. The closest conceptual equivalent of person schemas and role relationship models in psychoanalysis is object relations theory.[47]

Each person's schematic organizers of meaning comprise a repertoire of person schemas which includes archaic elements that are probably ineradicable (Horowitz, 1988, pp. 11–13). Early schemas of self and other are held in check by later-developed, more mature schemas that modulate, contain, and integrate immature schemas. Earlier schemas continue to respond to current events, however, employing parallel primitive pathways of association and sequencing, as in primary process thinking. Contradictory schemas having opposing roles, traits, or characteristics also exist, producing intrapsychic conflict.

Another important type of schema is called a "working model" (Bowlby, 1969, 1973, 1980), which integrates information from current real situations with past knowledge contained in person schemas and associative networks of ideas. A similar concept, which is highly relevant to interpretive methodology, is Greenson's hypothesis (1960, pp. 421–423) that the therapist develops an inner working model of the patient which is modified and enlarged as the treatment proceeds. Some additional aspects of schemas that are relevant to interpretive methodology include the following propositions (Benjamin and Friedrich, 1991):

1. Underlying schemas of self and other are suggested by statements such as "I believe . . . "; "That is typical of me . . . "; "I always . . . "; "My father invariably . . . "; "Bosses always . . . "; and so forth (Horowitz, 1988, 1991a).

2. The relative strengths of schemas are suggested by the repetitiveness of specific themes.

3. Person schemas are linked to our emotional and instinctive functions, and as such provide a conative-affective background for experience. Just as the emotional dimension of experience has pervasiveness, concreteness, tenacity, urgency, simultaneity of multiple events, and plasticity (that is, the ability to be shifted, and to slip in and out of awareness), self-other schemas also share these same qualities (Knapp, 1991, pp. 91–92).

4. Person schemas are built up of individual "episodes." At a certain point the episodes are brought together as a "category." Still further organization leads to abstract concepts such as, "Don't get involved with authorities." Thus schemas involve generalizations of progressively greater abstraction.

5. Being well-organized mental structures, schemas change very slowly (the "conservatism" of schemas); but they are not entirely static. They are subject to constant reexamination and reshaping during the ongoing information processing of waking life, and also as a result of conscious ruminations about dreams. (Palombo [1978, 1980, 1984] maintains that processing and revising of schemas is the basic function of dreaming.) Similarly, the

"objects" of object relations theory are not crystallized in their original infantile form, but undergo later elaboration as a result of conscious ruminations, reminiscences, mental "rehearsals," and transference enactments of daily life (Singer, 1988a, p. 332).

Clinical applications of schema theory include a number of problems and limitations. For example, schema theory is highly theoretical, even speculative. In addition, most of its concepts deal with postulated explanations of productive mental processing in patients. Very little attention has been given to the receptive data processing that therapists might use to identify patients' schemas. D'Andrade (1991) comments in this connection:

> No matter how compelling and elegant schema theory may be, and no matter how firm the experimental findings which support this theory, such a theory will have little value for clinicians if there is no way to determine in naturalistic settings, such as therapy sessions, the content of the patient's schemas [p. 279].

Some consensus appears to have developed in linguistics and anthropology regarding methods of identifying schemas; but the problem is more difficult in psychoanalysis and dynamic psychotherapy because the kinds of schemas studied in the clinical situation are "looser," less clearly bounded, and more susceptible to repression and other disguising transformations. Therapists' long hours of listening to patients increase their familiarity with patients' patterns of thought, making it possible to guess the content of some schemas whose conscious derivatives occur only in disguised form; but, as D'Andrade cautions, "the problem of operationalizing this type of schema identification seems formidable" (1991, p. 300; see also Kihlstrom and Cunningham, 1991, pp. 311–312, 331–332).

Another cause for caution regarding the relation of schema theory to clinical interpretation is that information inferred from postulated schemas is used frequently to fill in information that is missing in patients' associations. This practice facilitates rapid perception and processing of clinical data, but also can produce recurrent errors in interpretation, for example, failure to recognize stimuli that differ from schemas. Rumelhart (1980) illustrates this problem in the following way:

> Once we have accepted a configuration of schemata, the schemata themselves provide a richness that goes far beyond our

> observations. For example, upon deciding that we have seen an automobile, we assume that it has an engine, headlights, and all of the standard characteristics of an automobile. We do this without the slightest hesitation. We have complete confidence in our little theory [p. 38].

A related problem is that information which accords well with schemas is organized more rapidly than poorly matching information. Schemas thus enhance data that fit the existing structure, but impede the perception and processing of data that do not fit. In other words, schemas are inherently biasing in favor of existing knowledge and beliefs. In addition, each clinician brings his or her own schemas to the tasks of observing patterns and inferring schemas; for potentially biasing schemas are part of one's culture, including even the language we use (Horowitz, 1991b, pp. 302–304).

Investigations of Problem Solving: Relations to Interpretive Methodology

Some additional parallels between the methodology of clinical interpretation and modern cognitive psychology include: the relation of research in problem solving to making complex clinical judgments; the acquisition of skills and the nature of expert performance, including pattern recognition; the capacity to combine "declarative" knowledge (knowing that) and "procedural" knowledge (knowing how); the capacity for self-monitoring and self-correcting of one's own performances; heuristic methods employed in problem solving; and others.[48]

Cognitive research in problem solving illustrates the distinction between method- and problem-oriented approaches to interpretive methodology (discussed in Chapter 2). Cognitive scientists in the field of artificial intelligence (AI) assumed originally that a few powerful, general mechanisms would be capable of solving highly complex problems (a method-oriented approach); but experience taught otherwise. Investigations revealed that general methods alone were incapable of surmounting the degree of complexity involved in such problems (Duda and Shortliffe, 1983). Eventually, AI investigators recognized the need for a very extensive knowledge base, organized in such a way that ready retrieval was possible, which led to a shift from a method-based to an extensive knowledge-based strategy (Goldstein and Papert, 1977, p. 84).

Comparable findings have been reported from studies of clinicians (Elstein, 1988). Expert clinicians not only know more than novices, but their knowledge is more highly organized, retrievable, and applicable to new situations. Expert clinicians are characterized also by flexibility and adaptability. Being problem- rather than method-oriented, they quickly recognize new problems as variants of familiar types; they generate multiple plausible hypotheses rather than focusing narrowly on a single possibility; and they readily change directions if a tentative construction begins to appear less plausible. Despite extensive experience and skills, however, clinical reasoning and judgment are never error-proof, which the expert also knows and makes allowances for.

Adriaan De Groot's (1965) classic study of reasoning in chess players provides another example of a problem- in contrast to a method-oriented approach. De Groot found that grandmasters do not differ from lesser players in their methods of cognition, that is, in their ability to plan farther ahead or to think more deeply. The differences are largely in perception and memory; grandmasters possess a vast, organized long-term memory of specific information about chessboard patterns that takes thousands of hours to build up (Chase and Simon, 1973, p. 279). Comparable findings have been reported regarding problem-solving strategies employed by expert versus average clinicians (Elstein et al., 1978). Differences between the two groups were not found in cognitive methods, such as their planning activities or in their use of heuristics, but only in the extent and variety of their clinical experience, organized and stored in long-term memory. Expertise depends heavily upon a well-organized store of knowledge about clinical problems (Diamond, 1983; compare also the art historian E. H. Gombrich's observation that interpreters need a "very well-stocked mind" [1969, p. 71]). There is some place in the expert's approach for sudden dramatic insights, but they are rare. Most clinical problems are solved by relatively routine methods of processing data.

The preceding research findings can be applied also to problems of interpretive methodology. Knowing the postulated mechanisms which are thought to characterize unconscious mental functioning, and the major posited methods and strategies of construing unconscious meanings, is not enough to produce consistent and probative interpretations of clinical data. Unless the clinician has assimilated, and organized in retrievable form, extensive and specific details of an individual patient's life history, personality patterns, and current psychological functioning, general knowledge of mental functioning and familiarity with interpretive methodology (that is, interpretive competence) are of little help in understanding the patient's highly personal unconscious meanings and determinants at a given time. It is largely the therapist's unique and extensive exposure to, and accessible memory of, innumerable details about the patient that produce the competence to interpret insightfully. Thus, contrary to recent critiques of the single case method in psychoanalytic research (for example, Grünbaum, 1984, 1993; Spence, 1992, 1994a), the insistent idiographic focus of clinical methods provides the richness of clinical details that cognitive science investigations have shown to be essential in solving complex problems (see, for example, Horowitz's [1987] "configurational analysis").

The finding by cognitive scientists that expertise is not based on special methods or unusual speed of processing, but on an extensive, organized, and readily retrievable knowledge base, is particularly relevant to interpretive methodology. Investigators conclude, for example, that expertise in advanced fields requires as long as ten years of concentrated learning—due in part to the sheer amount of knowledge involved, but also to cognitive constraints on the rate at which human beings can process information and acquire knowledge, for example, the limited attention span of working memory (Simon and Kaplan, 1989). Similarly, a clinical study revealed that both expertness and empathy are significantly more highly developed in therapists having ten or more years of clinical experience (Chevron et al., 1983; see also Spence et al., 1974, and Diamond, 1983). These findings may be relevant to the length of time that depth-psychological treatments require; the difficulties that clinicians (and patients) face in attempting to process the voluminous amounts and varieties of data generated during therapy sessions; and the problems involved in maintaining the ever-increasing amounts of information regarding each patient in an organized, retrievable state for ongoing use in the understanding of current and future material.

One of the ways that therapists retain, organize, and retrieve such extensive amounts of information is by constructing an internal "working model" of each patient's life history and psychological functioning. The model can be added to and modified as needed, providing relatively rapid and accurate recall of patterns already learned about the patient.[49] In the clinical situation, retrieval of stored information, and hence learning, is facilitated also by the method of free association. How free associations contribute to the retrieval of stored information has been explained in various ways. Freud (1925c, p. 41) believed that if the therapist remained relatively detached and silent, the patient's associations would tend to flow freely without guidance from the therapist, and repressed contents would emerge spontaneously. Colby (1963, p. 197) also concluded that when associations flow relatively freely, unconscious wishes sometimes emerge into consciousness spontaneously, explicitly, and in detail—making it unnecessry in such circumstances for the therapist to infer the latent contents. Edelson (1988, p. 322) indicates further that free association involves a special state of mind in which connections among mental contents are more extensively influenced by primary mental processes than in ordinary states of consciousness.

Usually, however, the recovery of latent contents necessitates inferences from the data of free associations, dreams, and other varieties of clinical data. Wallace (1986, pp. 384–385) points out that what is important in such inferences is not whether a particular association represents a specific memory; the therapist bases most inferences on recurrent themes and patterns observed in the associations as a whole. In her perceptive chapter "The Process of Clinical Inference," Audrey O'Neill (1993) notes the widely held but erroneous view that

> thinking by association is quite separate from logical reasoning; that association is natural and undisciplined, whereas logic is artificial and rule-bound. People overlook their similar function in thinking. Associational processes serve the same purpose as syllogisms and induction—linking the particular instance with the general class—which is the essential feature of any practical art that employs scientific principles [p. 75].

Another cogent observation on how free associations facilitate the retrieval of latent contents and thus promote learning is suggested by Fred Levin (1995), who describes the clinician's processing of free associations this way:

> The patient's spontaneous thoughts activate a variety of feeling states and their related working memories; when the analyst

> pays attention to the patient's immediate feeling state, the analyst is able to invite new learning primarily by building from what the patient already knows, rather than building from what is novel to what the patient knows. When we build from what we know, the associated working memory (needed for learning) will always be activated and will contain the relevant data. In contrast, when we try to build to what is known (from some novel piece of data), our working memory will not necessarily be activated, and we will have difficulty comprehending the new information [pp. 429–430; emphases omitted].

The findings of cognitive science regarding expertise suggest that, compared with less intensive dynamic psychotherapies, some of the crucial methodological features of a specifically psychoanalytic interpretive approach include the frequency, continuity, and extended number of therapy sessions involved—all of which contribute to the "years of concentrated learning" required for expertise (Simon and Kaplan, 1989; Bachrach, 1993, p. 288)—that is, "expertise" in relation to each individual patient.

The domain of psychoanalysis is the idiosyncratic world of the individual patient, rather than the study of human beings and human behavior generally—the latter being the scientific province of psychology (Caws, 1986, p. 230). Each individual patient is a new world to be explored, which is one of the reasons that psychoanalytic treatment takes so long. Freud's development of such a protracted and intensive idiographic approach suggests again a prescient, postpositivist predilection in his conception of psychoanalysis and clinical interpretation.

Summary

This chapter is guided by the premise that the more we know about how other scientists work and what methods they employ, the more we shall be able to spell out our own methods and realize our own methodologic assets and liabilities (Ramzy, 1963a, pp. 74–75). With that in mind, various methods and concepts of interpretation employed in a number of nonclinical fields have been compared with clinical methods of construing latent contents. The nonclinical disciplines include: (1) relation- and pattern-oriented methodologies (for example, the pattern-model approach, Gestalt psychology, system theory, hermeneutics, and structuralism); (2) language-related disciplines (for example, linguistics, psycholinguistics, communication theory, semiotics, rhetoric, literary theory and criticism, and archaeologic decipherment); and (3) cognitive science (for example, cognitive psychology, information theory, the computational model of mind, and artificial intelligence).

All five of the methodologies included in the pattern-seeking approaches share with clinical interpretation an emphasis on identifying relations rather than things within their respective data—relations which serve as clues to unobservable entities. Relational patterns take various forms: repetitive, analogical, sequential, thematic, part–whole, causal, oppositional, and others, including "relations between relations." All provide heuristic guides to the most relevant data, and to the construal of latent contents within those data. The widespread use of pattern matching and meaning relations in interpretive methodologies has been criticized by some writers (Spence, 1982a; Grünbaum, 1993), but the vast majority of clinicians and scholars in related disciplines continue to feel confidence in and to employ these methods. The philosopher Donald Davidson (1986) points out, for example, that, "As interpreters, we work our way into the whole system, depending much on the pattern of interrelationships" (p. 314).

Among the language-related disciplines, psycholinguistic studies of language processing suggest a number of possible parallels with clinical data processing, for example, the necessity to construct rather than merely extract meanings from what is observed. We tend to conceive of meanings as tangible entities in the mind of a patient; but the meanings that we interpret are actually abstractions, depth-psychological hypotheses of the therapist's—attempts to infer or to guess what might be occurring in the mind of the patient.

Semiotics is perhaps the most relevant of the language-related disciplines to clinical interpretation. Interpretation, in fact, is a defining feature of semiotics; correspondingly, the methodology of clinical interpretation can be conceptualized as a semiotic process, that is, the use of signs as indicators or markers of underlying mental processes. The methodology of clinical interpretation needs to be studied more systematically and thoroughly from the conceptual standpoint of semiotics.

Comparing clinical and literary approaches to interpretation, both disciplines have evolved towards a dialectical-dialogic-interactive model of meaning and interpretation. Studies of the reading process are among the most relevant contributions of literary theory to interpretive methodology. Iser's (1978) model of the reading process draws extensively on gestalt concepts, which some writers (for example, Bellak and Walkup, 1993; Lamm, 1995, pp. 442–443) consider an appropriate ground for psychoanalytic theory, therapy, and interpretive methodology, because it deals directly with issues that are central to psychoanalysis, namely, structure, organization, coherence, and qualitative transformation. The discipline of deciphering ancient scripts emphasizes the need for flexibility on the part of both interpreters and their interpretive methods. Recognition of discrepancies and acceptance of errors are crucial, because for every correct inference, many wrong ones must be given up—a viewpoint which is applicable as well to the methodology of clinical interpretation.

The disciplines that comprise cognitive science share with psychodynamics the concept of mental representations. The importance that depth-psychological therapists attach to observations of their own responses to patients' material has a counterpart in cognitive science investigations and concepts. Although we tend to assume that remembering depends more on the nature of the stimulus than on our reactions to it, a part of the self is always involved in the trace. Thus observations by clinicians of their own responses to patients facilitate their encoding, processing, and ability to retrieve memories of patients' latent mental contents. Attempting to retrieve the self-structure of earlier experiences can be useful, therefore, to both patients and therapists.

One of the principal areas of correspondence between cognitive science and psychodynamics is schema theory, the prototype of which in psychoanalysis is the concept of transference. Other clinical counterparts of schema theory include the concepts of unconscious fantasy, self and object representations, imagoes, and inner working models. So far, however, schema theory has been applied primarily to productive mental processing in patients, rather than to the receptive data processing carried out by therapists in their attempts to identify patients' schemas.

Cognitive studies of problem solving reveal a number of parallels with psychoanalysis and interpretive methodology, for example, the finding that reliable methods alone cannot solve highly complex problems. The latter require a very extensive knowledge base, organized in a way that facilitates ready retrieval of information. Investigations of clinicians reveal comparable findings: that is, differences between expert and average clinicans do not result primarily from the methods they use, but from the extent and variety of their clinical experience, organized and stored in long-term memory. It is largely the therapist's unique and extensive exposure to, and accessible memory of, innumerable details about the patient that produce the competence to interpret insightfully. Frequency, continuity, and an extended number of therapy sessions are crucial factors in acquiring such detailed knowledge of each patient.

With the decline of behaviorism during the past half-century, modern cognitive psychologists (as well as social psychologists and philosophers of mind) have become increasingly interested in "commonsense psychology"—particularly its role in human reasoning, relating, and communicating. The relation of commonsense (or intentional) psychology to the methodology of clinical interpretation is discussed and evaluated in the following chapter.

6

Evaluation of "Commonsense" (Intentional) Psychology as a Model of Interpretive Inquiry

This chapter continues the comparisons of clinical and nonclinical interpretive methods by focusing on "commonsense" (or intentional) psychology, which has attracted the interest of some cognitive psychologists, social psychologists, and philosophers of mind, as well as a few psychoanalysts. Commonsense psychology is a model, scheme, or "theory" of human behavior having both ancient and more recent roots. In *De Anima* (Book 3: 1), Aristotle referred to a "general sensibility" or common sense which functions as a "coordinating faculty of the mind" (Oursler et al., 1968, pp. 166–167). Aristotle also proposed a "practical syllogism" connecting desires and beliefs, which can serve as a type of motivational cause (Moore, 1980): for example, a person desires a drink of water, believes the desire can be satisfied by drinking water, and on the basis of that desire and belief fills a glass with water and drinks it.

More recently, with the decline of behaviorism, a functionalist concept has emerged, proposing that people share a commonsense "theory" of mind which is learned from experience and from elders during childhood, and which they use to infer states of mind in themselves and others. Commonsense psychology is also called "folk psychology," "vernacular psychology," and "desire/belief psychology."[1] Interest has focused particularly on: (1) the body of beliefs and cognitive processes involved in commonsense knowledge, including how such desires, beliefs, and cognitions are structured; and (2) the role of commonsense psychology in human reasoning, relating, interpreting, and communicating.

Fodor (1993, pp. 222–224) observes that commonsense psychology mediates our relationships with one another; and when this understanding of others is incomplete or inaccurate, relationships falter or may break down. Usually, however, commonsense psychology works so well that people do not even realize its role in their lives. Moreover, it works not only with people one knows intimately, but even with absolute strangers.

Commonsense psychology is knowledge of everyday life. It assumes that people view each other as basically rational, purposive creatures who seek what they desire in the light of their beliefs about the world. The assumption of rationality is also one of commonsense psychology's greatest weaknesses: it has difficulty dealing with irrational, abnormal, aberrant behavior (Wilkes, 1993, p. 180; see also Stich, 1983, for additional arguments against commonsense psychology).

Commonsense psychology often makes it possible to interpret what other people say and do as expressions of their desires and beliefs—a skill that is related to "psychological-mindedness" (Brook, 1992, p. 281).[2] For that reason, commonsense psychology has been characterized as an interpretive method that has evolved because it works; it became indispensable because it helped human beings survive and proliferate (Dennett, 1993, p. 126; Graham, 1993, p. 201). The social scientist Donald Campbell (1975) believes that naturalistic commonsense observation is our only route to knowledge; and Grossman (1995, p. 887) notes that both Einstein and Freud considered scientific observation a further development and refinement of commonsense everyday thinking (see also Morton, 1982).

Common sense in general is knowledge based upon experience rather than on formal education. Carlo Ginzburg (1989) stresses that:

> The ability to identify a defective horse by the condition of its hocks, an impending storm by sudden changes in the wind, a hostile intention in a sudden change of expression, was certainly not to be learned from a farrier's manual or meteorological or psychological treatises. Knowledge of this sort in each instance was richer than any written codification; it was learned not from books but from the living voice, from gestures and glances; it was based on subtleties impossible to formalize, which often could

> not even be translated into words; it was shared by all social classes. These insights were bound by a subtle relationship: they had all originated in concrete experience [p. 15].

Ginzburg adds that the concreteness of commonsense psychology gave this knowledge its force, but also is responsible for its major limitation: an inability to make use of abstraction (1986, p. 15).

Fodor (1987, p. x) concludes that the theory of commonsense psychology is probably true because it explains far more of the facts about behavior than any alternative theory. He questions, in fact, whether a plausible alternative theory exists. If commonsense psychology were to collapse, it would be a human catastrophe. People cannot get along without it because the predictive power of commonsense psychology makes it possible to infer people's intentions from what they say and do. Commonsense explanations are not based on platitudes, as some critics maintain, but when made explicit can be seen to involve the deductive structure of scientific explanations (Fodor, 1987, p. 7).

At the same time, Fodor acknowledges that some of what commonsense psychology proposes about beliefs and desires is probably false because, contrary to common sense, much of the mind is unconscious, and much of it is unlearned (1987, p. 15). Despite these constraints, however, Fodor's main thesis is that, "We have no reason to doubt—indeed, we have substantial reason to believe—that it is possible to have a scientific psychology that vindicates commonsense belief/desire explanation" (1987, p. 16; emphasis omitted).

Another influential view of commonsense psychology by the philosopher Adam Morton (1980, 1982) holds that beliefs are structured as an implicit, high-level "theory" of personality shared by everyone in a particular culture (1980, pp. 7–13). The body of commonsense beliefs and desires is very extensive, including a potential infinity of emotions, moods, character traits, and so forth. Our numerous beliefs and desires do not appear to be learned individually, however, but are parts of a general scheme which encompasses far more beliefs and desires than one could ever describe or express. Thus Morton writes:

> The most striking thing about commonsense psychology in this connection is the combination of a powerful and versatile explanatory power with a great absence of powerful or daring

> hypotheses. When one tries to come up with principles of psychological explanation generally used in everyday life one only finds dull truisms, and yet in particular cases interesting, brave, and acute hypotheses are produced, about why one person, sometimes one group of people, act in some particular way. Somewhere in the works there has to be something very general and systematic, to back up these hypotheses [1980, p. 28].

As research in cognitive science has progressed, models of the commonsense psychological "theory" have become steadily more complex. Even a simple experience such as viewing a photograph involves a great deal of complicated (and mainly unconscious) reasoning, inferential activity, recall of previous experiences, reasoning by analogy, plausible guesses, construction of hypotheses, and methods of self-correction. One cannot assume, however, that complex commonsense reasoning of that kind is necessarily sound and productive of correct conclusions. The work of various investigators on inductive inference suggests, in fact, that human beings have a strong natural tendency to reason very badly.[3] Yet other writers argue that a pessimistic view of human inference is not well supported (Kornblith, 1993a, p. 9). More recent research provides evidence of ways in which inductive inference and other psychological mechanisms are well adapted to the causal structure of the world (Kornblith, 1993a, pp. 9, 61–107; 1993b).

Psychological explanations based upon common sense differ from natural science explanations which appeal to laws (Hempel, 1965). Typically one does not state a law in psychological explanations. Another difference is that scientific psychology attempts to explain and predict generally, while commonsense psychology tries to explain the particular. Wilkes (1993) comments, for example, that, "Commonsense psychology wants to know, roughly, why *this* X did exactly *that* action O at exactly *that* time, and in *this* manner" (p. 171). By contrast, there are very few commonsense principles which assert that if a person is in a specific mental state he or she will act in a certain way. The person's total state must be taken into account, and psychological explanation must be expandable: that is, grounds for explaining why a person acted in a particular way may have to be expanded to account for why some persons do the opposite. In addition, commonsense psychology necessarily bases its explanations on possible rather than invariable transitions between mental states, situations, and actions (Morton, 1980, p. 39).

Another strategy of commonsense explanation which entails expandability is explanation by motives. Viewing a person's behavior from the standpoint of his motives makes his actions intelligible to us, for much of what we refer to as meaning is understood in terms of motives. Each desire and belief, however, is accompanied by many others with which it is connected in content; consequently, we understand a single action as arising from an expandable network of reasons or motives. In this context, the philosopher James Hopkins (1991) suggests that explanation and interpretation are complementary activities: "Our most basic and familiar way of understanding the activities of persons—either our own, or those of others—is by interpreting them as actions resulting from motives, including beliefs and desires" (p. 88). Hopkins adds:

> It is at once interpretive and explanatory. It is interpretive because, as such examples illustrate, assigning motives enables us to make sense of what people say and do. It is explanatory because we take the motives we thus assign to be causes within persons which prompt their actions, and which, therefore, serve to explain them [1991, p. 88].[4]

For motive explanations to be adequate, they must be able to indicate not only that desire brings about the action, but how it does so. To do that requires an understanding of how a desire or intention influenced the person, and how his beliefs guided him. In addition, one needs enough explanations to account for the range of motivational processes, but few enough that the operative motives can be identified (Morton, 1980, p. 42).

Commonsense psychology systematically exploits the similarities between people, and employs imagination to interpret mental states that underlie the actions of oneself or others (Morton, 1980, pp. 52–53; see also Edelson, 1988, p. xxiv). Thus one of the constraints on psychological explanations is that the underlying mental states must be imaginable—that is, capable of being conceptualized as sequences which one can learn to interpret in oneself or others by simulating the sequences in one's imagination. We interpret speech, for example, not only by its content, but also in terms of its manner and intention of production (Morton, 1980, pp. 54–57; see also Wollheim, 1968, 1969).

Relation of Commonsense Psychology to Intentionality

Commonsense psychology is a variety of intentional psychology, the latter defining the psychological in terms of "intentionality." Intentionality is a property of consciousness that points beyond itself, that is, consciousness *of* something. The "intentional object" need not exist or be real, but is what an intentional mental state is *about*, and thus is closely linked with content or meaning. The philosopher John Searle (1994) points out that mental states such as beliefs and desires are intrinsically intentional:

> Mental states have intrinsic intentionality, material objects in the world that are used to represent something have *derived* intentionality. The most important form of derived intentionality is in language and there is a special name in English for this form of intentionality. It is called 'meaning' in one of the many senses of that word [p. 386].

A distinction must be made between the terms "intention" and "intentionality" (Dennett, 1978, p. 257). The former refers to what one plans to do, while intentionality refers to the fact that, due to their structure, mental states are inevitably directed at some object or state of affairs. The specific structures of mental states that make such directedness toward objects possible are *representations* of objects, which are intrinsic to mental states. Representations provide the contents of intentional states, while the thing or state of affairs in the external world at which the mental state is directed by way of its content is the object of the mental state. The kind of relationship the person has to the object, that is, whether belief, desire, fear, or whatever, is the mode of the intentional state (Wakefield, 1992a, pp. 78–79; 1992b).

The term intentionality originated in medieval scholasticism, but was revived and modified during the 1870's by the philosopher Franz Brentano in his treatise on *Psychology from an Empirical Standpoint* (1874). For much of his career Brentano's principal interest was psychology, which he considered an important factor in all science and knowledge. By psychology Brentano meant specifically the investigation of internal psychic phenomena (Barclay, 1964, p. 11). His method of investigation was not that of internal observation or introspection, however, but observation of psychological manifestations in other persons as they reveal themselves in various ways; for example, he considered the association of ideas a valuable source of information regarding mental states (Barclay, 1964, pp. 13–14; see also the following).

Brentano attempted to identify the defining features of the psychological by contrasting psychic and physical phenomena. He concluded that:

1. Psychic processes lack extension, that is, do not occupy physical space.
2. Psychic phenomena are always based on representations: "Nothing can ever be judged, nothing can be desired, nothing can be hoped or feared, unless it has first been represented" (Brentano, 1874, p. 121).
3. Every psychic phenomenon involves a relationship to an object.
4. Psychic phenomena are distinguished by intentionality.[5]

Freud, Brentano, and the Question of Intentionality in Psychoanalytic Theory

A number of writers have called attention to the similarity between Brentano's concept of intentionality and Freud's psychological stance.[6] Freud never acknowledged that he had been influenced by Brentano; but while a student at the University of Vienna Freud took five elective courses in philosophy, all taught by Brentano; and four years after Freud had completed those courses Brentano recommended him to Theodore Gomperz as a translator—which suggests a personal relationship between Freud and Brentano (Merlan, 1945, 1949).

Brentano was one of the most popular lecturers in Vienna. Barclay (1964, p. 10) writes that he was considered a scholar of sterling integrity, and was well loved by his students. Students often followed him home from the lecture hall, and Brentano held many long discussions with students in his home which lasted until early hours of the morning. Freud's correspondence with his friend Silberstein (Freud and Silberstein, 1872–1875) indicates that Freud was invited to Brentano's home for such discussions on at least two occasions. Freud described Brentano to Silberstein as, "this remarkable man and in many respects ideal human being (he is a believer in God, a teleologist (!) and Darwinian and a damned clever fellow, indeed one of genius)" (March 7, 1875). Freud confided further that, "under Brentano's influence the determination has ripened within me to pursue a Ph.D. in philosophy and zoology. Further negotiations are in progress to bring about my enrollment in the philosophy faculty either next semester or next year" (March 7, 1875). In another letter to Silberstein, Freud wrote:

> I have never before enjoyed the lovely feeling which one calls academic bliss and which, for the most part, consists in the awareness of sitting at the source from which knowledge pours forth in its greatest purity and taking a good deep drink of it [April 11, 1875].

Freud appears to have been attracted to Brentano's ideas because Brentano considered the method of philosophy to be identical with that of science. In addition to Freud, Brentano attracted many other outstanding students including Edmund Husserl, who became the founder of phenomenological philosophy; Thomas Masaryk, who founded the Czechoslovakian Republic; Alexius Meinong, who established the first psychological laboratory in Austria; the experimental psychologist, Franz Hillebrand; the sexual ethicist, Christian von Ehrenfels; Carl Stumpf, the teacher of Gestalt psychologist Wolfgang Köhler; and others (McGrath, 1986, pp. 9–10). While most of these former students openly expressed their intellectual debt to Brentano, Freud did not. McGrath (p. 11) comments that whatever their relationship may have been, both Freud and Brentano went to their graves without speaking of their relationship.

Brentano's influence on Freud and psychoanalysis was more implicit than explicit (Barclay, 1964, p. 23). Freud believed, for example, that it is possible to formulate theoretical statements about mental functioning from careful, systematic observation—a methodologic principle that coincided exactly with Brentano's approach. Freud stated also (1915c, p. 173) that what differentiated his method from descriptive psychology was mainly the dynamic aspect of his findings—a claim that Brentano had made about his own system. Additional methodologic parallels between Brentano's and Freud's approaches include emphasis on the association of ideas, which Brentano applied to dreams, insanity, and to other bizarre mental states; the importance of psychological development, which Brentano discussed in terms of stages beginning with primitive, instinctual, self-centered states; and the prominent role of ambivalence in personality development (McGrath, 1986, pp. 122–124).

Barclay (1964) concludes from a comparison of their views on the nature of psychology and the methodology appropriate to it that, "Freud was in substantial agreement with the viewpoint of Brentano" (pp. 25–26). McGrath (1986), a historian, states more specifically that "the method Brentano recommended, a scientific working back and forth between the evidence of the inner 'subjective' world and the outer 'objective' world, was in fact exactly what Freud so often did as a mature scientist" (p. 115). McGrath concludes, therefore, that "Brentano's methodology provided the foundation for Freud's whole approach to psychological investigation" (1986, p. 115).

With respect to Brentano's concept of intentionality, Ricoeur (1970) stresses its importance in Freud's thought. Siegler (1967) interprets Freud's use of the term "intentions" to mean that unconscious intentions exist, but Shope (1970, p. 149) maintains that Freud usually took care not to speak of unconscious intentions. McIntosh (1993, pp. 685–686) makes the interesting observation that Freud's concept of cathexis is similar to intentionality in its implication that mental states are always "about" something. The two concepts appear to overlap, but are not completely equivalent. Brook (1992, pp. 282–284) suggests that Freud made extensive use of everyday psychology, but would have denied that psychoanalysis and interpretive methodology depend upon common sense. Freud usually presented psychoanalysis as a nonintentional (natural) science; but his clinical inferences, reasoning, interpretations, explanations, and vocabulary were often those of intentional psychology.[7]

What most defines an intentional psychology is its distinctive vocabulary, that is, being *about* something, having an *object*: "A belief is about whatever is believed; a desire is about whatever is desired; a fantasy is about whatever it is directed at" (Brook, 1992, p. 283). By drawing on and extending the intentionality of commonsense psychology, psychoanalysis and dynamic psychotherapy are able to employ a distinctive type of interpretation and explanation, namely, interpreting and explaining psychological states (including actions) in terms of reasons for them (Brook, 1992, pp. 285–287). Grünbaum (1988a) considers reasons a variety of cause, which is discussed further in Chapter 7. Phenomena such as energies and neurons which lack intentionality cannot be explained by reasons, but intentional phenomena like desires and beliefs can.

Psychoanalysis and Its Interpretive Methodology as Possible Extensions of Commonsense (Intentional) Psychology

A commonsense (intentional) model of psychoanalysis and interpretive methodology began to attract attention in the 1970s as an alternative to metapsychology (Brook, 1995b, pp. 520–523; Morton, 1980, pp. 135–139; 1982). Rycroft's (1966) proposal of semantic rather than mechanistic explanations in psychoanalysis may have played a part in this development. Since that time, intentional psychology has gained increasing acceptance as a possible or partial model of psychoanalysis, dynamic psychotherapy, and interpretive methodology, while metapsychology has become considerably less relevant. Still further interest in commonsense psychology has developed during the past decade as a counterargument to Grünbaum's philosophical critiques of psychoanalysis (discussed in Chapter 7).[8]

The commonsense model of psychoanalysis and its interpretive methodology has an identifiable link with both hermeneutics and *Verstehen* psychology, all three emphasizing the interpretation of meanings—a feature of the intentional model which has generated controversy with the traditional view of psychoanalysis as a causally-oriented natural science. Some advocates of the intentional model consider psychoanalysis both interpretive and causal.[9] Thus Brook (1995b, p. 525), contrary to Grünbaum (1984, 1993), argues that the framework for thinking about psychoanalysis should not be causality *versus* interpretation of meaning, but causality *via* interpretation of meaning. Wollheim (1984, p. 126) maintains that the cause of a psychological state is often traceable through its intentionality to its effect.

A number of writers including philosophers, psychoanalytically-informed scholars, and psychoanalysts have proposed that psychoanalysis is an extension rather than a direct application of commonsense psychology.[10] The psychoanalytic extension of commonsense psychology includes not only the addition of unconscious intentions, but also unconscious skills for inferring psychological states (Brook, 1992, p. 273). Thus the relationship between commonsense psychology and psychoanalysis is based less upon their respective beliefs than on the interpretive methodology that commonsense psychology provides.

Commonsense psychology applies particularly and specifically to the theory of interpretation, and hence to the theory of therapy, rather than to psychoanalytic theories of the unconscious, psychopathology, and personality development (Johansen, 1986). The interpretive resources of commonsense psychology upon which we depend are nontheoretic with respect to psychoanalysis, that is, what we take for granted and do not need psychoanalysis to understand (Edelson, 1984, p. 83; 1988, pp. 245, 254–255). Our dependence on commonsense psychology is illustrated by the crucial process of

> establishing and maintaining the intersubjective, communicative field between analyst and analysand. When we interpret another's words and understand the simple, immediate intentions they are trying to communicate, we do not use anything specifically psychoanalytic to do so. Yet if we could not rely on this communicative field's being there and quietly working away, we could not bring the special knowledge of psychoanalysis to bear at all [Brook, 1992, pp. 278–279].

Inference-making is another aspect of psychoanalysis and its interpretive methodology which is dependent upon commonsense psychology. Many of the inferences that we make clinically are not specifically psychoanalytic; in fact, some people who have had no psychoanalytic training are very astute in their psychological inferences. Our ability to "read" psychological states such as affects from a speaker's tone of voice is an example. Commonsense psychological ability is closely related in this way to what we call "psychological mindedness" (Brook, 1992, pp. 280–281).

The basic interpretive strategy or heuristic of commonsense psychology is that, based upon what one can infer about a person's desires and beliefs, it would be rational for the person to act as he or she does. Freud appears to have adopted that strategy, but he extended it in several ways: (1) Being more interested in psychological states than actions, he extended the commonsense heuristic to symptoms, dreams, parapraxes, and phantasies. (2) He also extended the strategy from actions intended to satisfy a desire to psychological states that only imagine the fulfillment of a wish. (Shope [1967] notes perceptively that the psychoanalytic concept of wish fulfillment differs significantly from ordinary notions of expressing or fulfilling wishes.)

Wollheim (1993b) adds that Freud also deepened the explanatory scheme of commonsense psychology, suggested variations on it, and contextualized it. Freud deepened the commonsense conception of mind by including unconscious desires and beliefs—examples of which can be seen most clearly in his *Psychopathology of Everyday Life* (1901, for example pp. 227–228). Wollheim (1993b) describes and illustrates several variations on desire/belief explanation, one being the substitution of unconscious phantasy for what would ordinarily be a belief. An example is the Rat Man's conscious fantasy of winning his father's love by his dead father returning as a ghost and being pleased to find the Rat Man hard at work after midnight (Freud, 1909b, pp. 204, 303). Freud (1909b) came to realize, however, that unconscious phantasies do not function in exactly the same way as conscious beliefs, and thus require new and different forms of explanation, which he introduced as variations on the traditional form. One such variation is displaced action in which, for some internal reason, a person is unable to carry out an intended action but performs instead an associated action. An example is the Rat Man's jealousy of his sweetheart's cousin: his murderously jealous phantasies were displaced to actions in which the Rat Man made dangerously excessive attempts to lose weight—the intermediary links in the chain of associations including the cousin's nickname, Dick, which is similar to the German word for fat; thus getting rid of his fat = getting rid of his phantasied rival (pp. 188–189). Freud also used this variant form of explanation for symptomatic actions, and for a type of neurotic symptom affecting the patient's sexual activities.

Another explanatory variation described by Wollheim (1993b) involved an internal mechanism which is sensitive to circumstances and frequently is triggered by anxiety, which Freud (1926a, p. 138) later called a "danger signal." A desire combined with the danger signal mechanism (rather than with a belief or phantasy) can cause a person to perform a certain action: for example, Freud's description (1923c, pp. 142–145) of a young boy's anxiety on seeing a girl's genitalia. The boy defensively denied what he saw, replacing it with the conviction that the girl had a penis. The desire in this case was to feel that his own penis was completely safe, and his disavowal of the perceived sexual differences took the place of a belief or phantasy that his penis was safe.

A third explanatory variant, according to Wollheim (1993b), does not involve a belief, phantasy, or danger signal mechanism, but appeals to an unconscious desire combined with some facilitating factor which allows outlet for the desire. The action produces an imagined or hallucinated satisfaction of the desire which is repeated frequently. This form of explanation applies to dreams, to neurotic symptoms which are not displaced actions, to errors which are not unconsciously motivated actions, and to acting out.

Freud also contextualized commonsense explanations. In addition to the large number of psychological explanations that he proposed in which a psychological factor included both a desire and a belief—or a phantasy, chain of associations, mechanism of defense, or combination of these factors—Freud also constructed a developmental theory of the individual consisting of different stages organized in terms of specific body parts or zones. The developmental stages themselves are not explanatory; what makes them explanatory is that they entail particular desires, chains of associations, mechanisms of defense, and specific phantasies. Bringing these stages together with explanations based upon psychological factors produces a contextualization of explanation (Wollheim, 1993b).

Edelson's (1988) version of the relationship between psychoanalysis and commonsense psychology suggests that psychoanalysis and its interpretive methodology sprang from multiple forms of everyday discourse and multiple interpretive heuristics of commonsense psychology, rather than exclusively from the classical model of desire/belief/action. Edelson believes that psychoanalysis has extended all forms of explanation in commonsense psychology. Rather than extending just the logic of commonsense psychology, psychoanalysis has extended its range of application to areas such as infantile sexuality, stages of psychosexual development, unconscious as well as conscious wishes and fantasies, primary as well as secondary processes, latent as well as manifest contents, and bizarre as well as acceptable wishes, desires, and affects (1988, pp. 327–328).[11]

Edelson (1988) describes two general analogies that commonsense psychology provides for psychoanalytic explanation:

1. Finding the causes of psychological states by studying how content is conveyed along a causal chain: for example, a desire for $x \rightarrow$ a belief that y is the way to secure $x \rightarrow$ an intention to secure $x \rightarrow$ an action that attempts to secure x by doing y. The common content of each link in this causal chain is x. Similarly, a wish for $x \rightarrow$ a wishfulfilling fantasy of obtaining $x \rightarrow$ guilt feelings from not being entitled to x, all sharing the same content of x (pp. 331–332).

2. The process of conveying content involves thematic affinities between causes and effects, which Edelson considers central to both the explanatory strategies and the domain of psychoanalysis (1988, p. 332).

Shope (1987, p. 216, fn. 13) argues that mixing causal and intentional factors is a non sequitur. Elsewhere (1991, p. 104), Edelson questions the causal relevance of thematic affinities.

Andrew Brook (1992) observes that the relationships between psychoanalysis and commonsense psychology described by Jim Hopkins (1986) and Marshall Edelson (1988) are based on wishes, which are forward looking, whereas clinical interpretive inquiry is usually retrospective, looking back to earlier psychological states associated with disturbing experiences, memories (including repressed memories), and fantasies about earlier experiences. Brook (1992, pp. 293–294) maintains that psychoanalytic interpretations and explanations require a substructure of commonsense psychological interpretations before they can even get started. Consequently, many psychoanalytic explanations necessitate a restoring of the intentionality of psychological states where processes of defense have rendered the true intentionality obscure or invisible rather than forward-looking in terms of desire satisfaction or wish fulfillment.

Some of Brook's (1992) arguments that psychoanalysis is an extension of commonsense psychology overstate the probity of clinical inference and interpretation. He claims, for example, that we can decide when the probability of a thematic affinity is the result of a causal connection by interpreting reasons (p. 295). He asserts further:

> Any suggestion that in principle case studies cannot reveal causes of behavior would have to be wrong; for vast reaches of ordinary human existence and most of the time, they can. If untutored commonsense can do this well, surely psychoanalytic case studies will often do much better [p. 296].

Brook claims also that both commonsense psychology and psychoanalysis usually generate good predictions and explanations, allowing a "principled generation and resolution of disagreements" (p. 299). All three of these arguments overlook the consensus problem in clinical (and other forms of) interpretation. And Brook's further claim that background commonsense psychological knowledge is "a huge control and one that has been thoroughly tested" (p. 299), ignores the pervasive problem of confirmation bias in scientific, including interpretive, inquiry.

A number of cognitive psychologists and psychoanalytic theorists suggest that Freud's approach is best understood as a theory of dynamic interaction among intentional states.[12] An example is the view that defense is a process of intentional manipulation of one's own cognitive states (Wakefield, 1992a, p. 95). Erdelyi (1990) theorizes that repression may involve intentional self-manipulation of cognitions. This (controversial) viewpoint considers psychoanalytic theory and its interpretive methodology extensions of commonsense psychology, and thus exempt from the usual forms of scientific testing (Gardner, 1993, pp. 10, 226).

The notion that clinical interpretations are exempt from testing is unsupportable, however (see, for example, Grünbaum, 1984, 1993). Gardner (1993, p. 243) counters with the argument that commonsense psychological practice establishes motivational causes interpretively, using methods which are prior to neo-Baconian canons; and that it is not even clear how such canons could be used, or how inductive methods could replicate commonsense interpretations. This ongoing, unsettled controversy is discussed further in Chapter 7.

Hopkins's Theory of Interpretive Methodology, Based on the Model of Commonsense Psychology

In a series of essays published during the past fifteen years (1982, 1988, 1991, 1992), the philosopher of psychoanalysis, Jim Hopkins, has developed a commonsense-based theory of clinical interpretation that attempts to integrate semantic meanings, causal processes, and psychological understanding. Hopkins views psychoanalysis as a form of interpretive inquiry that deals with both meanings and causes. His theory of interpretation involves a concept of "causal semantics," the model for which he attributes to commonsense psychology. He believes that the interpretation of psychological meanings is closely related to the interpretation of semantic meanings, and that interpretation of psychic states such as motives is an inquiry into causes. The causal explanation of human behavior thus shares methodological features with the interpretation of language. A summary of Hopkins's reasoning follows:

Everyday interpretation of language occurs spontaneously, without reflection; but the same process can be carried out using explicit hypotheses, for example, employing a dictionary or grammar to understand a foreign language. The latter is called theoretical interpretation, which can be used to understand what is involved in natural, ordinary language comprehension. Combinatory semantic theories are well known, and their use in theoretical interpretation well established, for example, to interpret codes, artificial languages, and even natural language itself.

The interpretation of human discourse seeks meanings that provide the best fit with the motives of the person(s) who produced the discourse—which is similar to scientific theories proposing causal explanations that best account for specific data; both processes involve "inference to the best explanation," or what C. S. Peirce called "abduction."[13]

The principal question that Hopkins's theory attempts to answer is how knowledge of semantic connections is related to causal processes and to psychological understanding. Hopkins argues that we use language in a highly specific way to articulate the contents of the mind, that is, by the use of words and phrases that describe motives, on the one hand, and the objects of perception (in the world), on the other. Hopkins (1992) writes:

> A phrase or sentence used in this way fits its motive like a glove; the relation of the phrase or sentence to the world seems precisely adapted to specify a corresponding relation on the part of the motive. So such description makes explicit the intentionality, or object-directedness, of motives, representing our minds as engaged with worldly correlates (or potential correlates) of our words, phrases, and sentences. Linguistic articulation thus provides us with a powerful tool for psychological understanding. It allows us, in effect, to make a double use of language: first in describing the world, and then in describing the mind in its engagement with the world as described. This in turn enables us to make use of our grasp of semantic connections for describing

> and understanding the working of motive, and hence in the explanation of behavior [p. 16].

Hopkins continues, emphasizing that

> this mode of description serves to encode the working of motives linguistically. It enables us to map causal connections which hold as among motives, or as between motives and reality, by semantic connections involved in our understanding of language interconvertible in practice with knowledge of the dynamics of motive. So this use of language gives us, in our commonsense psychology, a sort of natural system for the linguistic—or semantic, or hermeneutic—representation of psychological causal role [1992, p. 17].

Hopkins adds that "semantic encoding of causal role is so simple and direct that we may not even notice it" (p. 17). He suggests the analogy that the mind (or brain) is like "a semantic engine; that is, a device which draws information from the environment and transforms this into motive with environment-directed conditions of satisfaction" (1992, p. 22). In support of his argument, Hopkins submits that, according to his theory, understanding of commonsense psychology should set in at approximately the same age as language development—a prediction which is borne out by recent research indicating that three-year-old children are already adept at belief-desire explanation (Wellman, 1990). He concludes that Freud was the first psychologist to extend systematically and to employ this commonsense, causal-semantic system of understanding, and that this extension of commonsense psychology is grounded in a form of inference that has the power, scope, and cogency to provide strong support for Freud's basic claims (Hopkins, 1992, p. 23).

Edelson (1991, p. 105) and Brook (1995a, pp. 415–416) agree that Hopkins's arguments support the view that psychoanalysis is an extension of commonsense psychology. Brook suggests further that by using the model of commonsense psychology Hopkins has succeeded in integrating the psychoanalytic interpretation of semantic meanings, causal processes, and psychological understanding (Brook, 1995a, p. 416). Edelson appears to vacillate, however, on the issue of whether semantic meaning-relations (thematic affinity) provide evidence of causal connections. He acknowledges that such is the case in commonsense psychology, but he seems to have changed his mind about its cogency in psychoanalysis. In his 1988 volume, Edelson writes, "Reasoning by appeal to thematic affinity is not only central in the explanatory strategies of psychoanalysis. It plays an important role in the definition of the domain of psychoanalysis" (p. 332; see also pp. 135–136). In a later review of Hopkins's theory, however, Edelson (1991) states:

> Thematic affinity is not likely to provide convincing warrant for the scientific credibility of these special assumptions and the causal claims arising from them. Indeed, the point of psychoanalytic explanation is often just to show why there is a lack of thematic affinity between the putative unconscious desires and beliefs of a person and the manifestations of these in the form of phenomena (e.g., symptoms, dreams) that "do not make sense" given the conscious desires and beliefs of that person. A psychoanalytic explanation achieves this aim by inferring from previously unnoticed or undiscovered material the existence, and causal role, of: a) wishes quite unlike those inferred in the commonsense psychology of everyday life; b) unconscious fantasies, in which such wishes are imagined as fulfilled; c) mental operations, acting upon the contents of such wish fulfillments, which are quite unlike the operations that are used in processes of rational inference and action. (It is just these features of psychoanalytic thought that are ordinarily ignored in philosophical—and other—critiques of psychoanalytic theory, fatally so, in my opinion, for the relevance of the methodologic strictures applied in such critiques) [pp. 104–105].

Grünbaum (1993, p. 112) is outspoken in his objections to commonsense psychology as a model of psychoanalytic theory and interpretation. He acknowledges that some aspects of psychoanalytic practice are grounded in commonsense psychology, even adding that the latter may have better warrant than formal psychoanalytic theories; but he is highly critical of any attempt to reformulate psychoanalysis as a commonsense or intentional psychology. In a personal communication to Edelson, Grünbaum writes:

> I no more think that psychoanalytic theory is an extension of commonsense psychology than I think theoretical physics is an extension of common-sense "physics." What commonsense man believes a table is mostly empty space between particles? That is

> why Eddington spoke of two tables. If psychoanalytic theory were the extension of common sense you depict, why did it encounter so much disbelief? And why was it so counterintuitive that the "ego is not master in its own house?" It is utterly incredible common-sensically that horror dreams should be wishfulfilling [cited by Edelson, 1988, p. 330; emphasis omitted].

Edelson (1988, p. 330) responds that Grünbaum appears to confuse the features of the commonsense model with the theoretical extension that psychoanalysis proposes to account for observations that would be counterintuitive in terms of the model alone. With respect to the very frightening effects of some wishes (as in nightmares), psychoanalysis postulates a separate class of wishes, unconscious wishes, and the occurrence of highly disturbing unconscious conflicts about such wishes, as well as a unique set of mechanisms, the primary processes, to account for the unpleasant effects of wishes in nightmares.

Another counterargument to Grünbaum's views regarding "bad dreams" is that commonsense itself includes examples suggesting that forbidden wishes can produce frightening effects. Lord Byron wrote that "dreams in their development have breath, and tears, and tortures, and the touch of joy." And in *Richard III* we read: "Oh! I have pass'd a miserable night, So full of ugly sights, of ghastly dreams, That, as I am a Christian faithful man, I would not spend another such a night, Though 'twere to buy a world of happy days." In his book *The World of Dreams*, Havelock Ellis (1922, p. 99) mentioned that nightmares often include images of inability to move or speak. He reported an example of a colleague who dreamed that he put his hand on the knee of a woman patient. She asked him to remove his hand, but he was unable to move it and "he awoke in horror from this unprofessional situation" (pp. 180–181).

The debate about commonsense psychology as a possible model of psychoanalytic theory and interpretation has spawned some unnecessarily categorical viewpoints on this issue. Rather than considering commonsense psychology the single most cogent model of psychoanalysis and interpretive methodology, it seems more appropriate to view it as one among a number of models which have contributed—individually, variously, partially, and jointly—to the interpretive and explanatory capabilities of psychoanalysis and clinical interpretation. The arguments that psychoanalysis is an extension of commonsense psychology are persuasive, but an extension is neither confined to nor the same as the model itself. Depth-psychological interpretation is a pluralistic art and science, both conceptually and methodologically, and as such appears to rest upon multiple models from the arts, sciences, and everyday life.

Summary

This chapter explores and evaluates commonsense psychology as a recently proposed model of psychoanalysis and its interpretive methodology. Commonsense psychology is knowledge of everyday life which is shared by all members of a culture, making it possible to interpret what other people say and do as expressions of their desires and beliefs—a skill related to "psychological-mindedness." The body of commonsense desires and beliefs is very extensive, including myriad emotions, moods, character traits, and so forth. Some advocates of this viewpoint believe that commonsense psychology, or at least much of it, is probably true because it explains more of the facts about behavior than any alternative theory.

Unlike scientific explanations which are based upon laws and attempt to explain generally, commonsense psychology focuses upon and attempts to explain the particular—an approach which is consonant with an idiographic method such as psychoanalysis. One of the most important strategies of commonsense psychology is explaining behavior in terms of a person's motives, a method of understanding that is both interpretive and explanatory—interpretive because it makes sense of what people say and do, and explanatory because motives are causal processes. Commonsense interpretation also exploits the similarities among people, and employs imagination to understand mental states that underlie the behavior of oneself and others.

Commonsense psychology is a form of intentional psychology, intentionality being defined as consciousness *of* or *about* something—that is, the "object-directedness" of the mental. An intentional object need not exist or be real, however. What an intentional mental state is about is closely related to content or meaning: for example, desires (motives) and beliefs (about how to fulfill desires) are intrinsically intentional. The concept of intentionality was stressed by one of Freud's favorite teachers,

Franz Brentano, whose views on intentionality were very similar to Freud's subsequent psychological stance. Freud never acknowledged that he had been influenced by Brentano, however.

Freud appears to have extended commonsense psychology to include the interpretation of unconscious mental processes, including symptoms, dreams, parapraxes, and unconscious phantasies. He also extended the scope of commonsense psychology from actions intended to satisfy a desire to psychological states that only imagine the fulfillment of a wish. The relationship of commonsense psychology to psychoanalysis appears to apply primarily to the interpretive methodology of psychoanalysis, rather than to psychoanalytic theories of the unconscious, personality development, and psychopathology. The interpretive resources of commonsense psychology which psychoanalysis has co-opted include inference-making (that is, many of the inferences that we make are not specifically psychoanalytic but commonsensical), and also establishing and maintaining the intersubjective communicative field between analyst and patient—without which we would not be able to bring the special knowledge of psychoanalysis to bear on the patient's discourse and problems.

One of the major controversies concerning commonsense psychology as a model of our interpretive methodology concerns the question of whether semantic meaning-relations (thematic affinities) in clinical data provide evidence of causal connections. This is an important question for psychoanalysis and dynamic psychotherapy, because their interpretive methodologies rely so extensively upon the identification of meaning-relations as clues to latent meanings and determinants. Adolf Grünbaum's philosophical critiques of psychoanalysis, which are discussed in the following chapter, argue unequivocally both against the view that psychoanalysis is an extension of commonsense psychology and against the use of meaning-relations to infer causal connections. The philosopher Jim Hopkins argues, on the other hand, that the interpretation of human discourse, including clinical discourse, seeks meanings that involve the best fit with the motives of the person producing the discourse—which is similar to scientific theories proposing causal explanations that best account for specific data. Both processes rely on the method of "inference to the best explanation." Thus commonsense psychology provides us with a natural system for the linguistic representation of psychological causal role, the semantic encoding of which is so simple and direct that we may not even notice it.

Resolution of these controversies may have to await further consensus regarding the pluralistic nature of psychoanalysis, both conceptually and methodologically. From a pluralistic perspective, commonsense psychology can be viewed as one among a number of models that contributes to the interpretive and explanatory capabilities of psychoanalysis and dynamic psychotherapy.

PART IV

JUSTIFYING INTERPRETATIONS

The maturity test for a discipline is its capability of submitting to systematic doubt the definition of its field and of its methods.

[Umberto Eco, 1985, p. 176]

The interpretation is a new kind of fact whose factuality depends on the accuracy with which evidence has been interpreted and on the completeness of the evidence. Unlike a scientific fact, it cannot be demonstrated.

[H. J. Home, 1966, p. 44]

The essence of science is not so much the existence of a body of facts as the existence of a method, a procedure by which 'facts' can be systematically ascertained and progressively revised.

[Michael Sherwood, 1969, p. 260]

Freud and his disciples acted as though they had no conception of the meaning of the word proof. There, without doubt, is the greatest weakness of psycho-analysis.

[Roland Dalbiez, 1941, p. ix]

The problem here is not limited to questioning Freud's conception and tactics of interpretation. It resonates throughout most of modern philosophy and more generally, modern thought. How are we to discriminate between those opinions that are nothing but blind prejudice from claims that can be legitimately warranted?

[Richard Bernstein, 1988a, p. 89]

7

The Probity of Clinical Interpretations in the Light of Grünbaum's Critiques

During the past two decades, the philospher of science Adolf Grünbaum has mounted a forceful philosophical critique of psychoanalysis and its interpretive methodology.[1] He has summarized his critique in the form of ten major arguments (1986).

1. The suggestibility problem.
2. Problems associated with the method of free association.
3. Drawing unwarranted causal inferences from meaning relations.
4. Failure of Freud's "tally argument."
5. Weakness of Freud's consilience (convergence) argument.
6. The mistaken assumption that introspections by treated patients provide reliable evaluations of causal and therapeutic claims.
7. Post hoc fallacy in retrospective positing of causal claims.
8. Arguments against the repression etiology of psychoneuroses.
9. Unjustified extrapolation of the questionable repression etiology to explain slips and dreams.
10. Misconceived attempts to reformulate psychoanalysis as a hermeneutic rather than a scientific discipline.

The first seven of these arguments are most relevant to the methodology of clinical interpretation, so they will be discussed in more detail. The latter three arguments will be considered only briefly, although pertinent references are cited. Before turning to the various arguments themselves, Grünbaum's method of philosophical analysis will be reviewed and evaluated.

Grünbaum's Method of Philosophical Analysis

Grünbaum evaluates Freud's methods and theories by means of eliminative inductivism, a modern version of the inductivist methods proposed by Francis Bacon (1561–1626) and John Stuart Mill (1806–1873). Grünbaum refers to his philosophical approach as Millian or neo-Baconian methods of validating causal hypotheses. He evaluates Freud's methods, theories, and reasoning as Freud wished them to be considered, namely, as empirical methods and causal hypotheses of a natural science. Having acknowledged that Freud's methods and theories are amenable to empirical study by traditional methods and thus are in principle scientific, Grünbaum then holds Freud's feet to the fire, insisting that his methods and causal hypotheses must be evaluated by the same strict standards that apply to all empirical sciences. He describes the modern version of his Millian methods this way:

> A causal hypothesis asserts that some factor *X* is causally relevant to some occurrence *Y*. This means that *X* makes a certain kind of difference to the occurrence of *Y* in some reference class C. To validate such a claim, we must first divide the reference class C into two subclasses, the *X*'s and the non-*X*'s. And then we must show that the incidence of *Y*'s among the *X*'s is different from what it is among the non-*X*'s. Patently, this requirement is essentially neutral as to the subject matter or field of knowledge. It applies alike in the human and the physical sciences [1994, p. 157; emphasis omitted. See also Edelson, 1984, pp. 42–46].

Grünbaum (1993) presents the following examples to illustrate his method of determining causal relevance: "Thus I can validate by means of these methods a supposed causal link between my conscious awareness of a derogatory remark and my introspectively experienced anger by noting, over a period of time and repeatedly, that the presence vs. the absence of insults *makes a difference* statistically to my becoming angry" (p. 164). In another example, Grünbaum writes that "When Breuer and Freud claimed therapeuticity for lifting repressions, they should have used Mill's methods to rule out the rival hypothesis of placebo effect by also noting the results from treatment in which no repressions were lifted" (1993, p. 165).

In the continuing debate about Grünbaum's method of evaluating psychoanalysis, a recurring argument maintains that human nature does not lend itself to the same kinds of codification and formalization employed in the physical sciences, because the contextual complexity of phenomena studied in the human and social sciences is so much greater. The human science methodologist Donald Polkinghorne (1983) notes, however, that

> the original question concerning the nature of a methodology for the human sciences was put forth in clear form by Mill: Should human science adopt the methodology of the physical sciences? Mill took the affirmative side of the question, while Dilthey took the negative side. Those who have stood with Mill have won the debate, and their position has been adopted as the standard methodology for the human sciences by university departments, textbooks, and journals [p. 59].

Grünbaum is identified with a group of philosophers who believe it is possible to study theories and methods in any field by using the same philosophical method (Kitcher, in Callebaut, 1993, p. 75). According to that view, the fact that traditional philosophy of science focused primarily on physics does not detract from its relevance to other sciences. Grünbaum (1993, p. 165) states, for example, that he found no difficulty in applying ideas he had gained from a study of physics to his investigation of psychoanalysis; but another group of philosophers, as well as scholars in other fields, maintain that the model one chooses for such a study is very important.[2] Bruner (1986, p. 90) argues, for example, that clinicians employ a different strategy than physical scientists: rather than focusing on general tendencies, they take account of the specific context in which behavior occurs (see also Hayek, 1994).

Carlo Strenger (1986, pp. 258–259) believes that Grünbaum's use of the same logical method for studying both physics and psychoanalysis contributes to an oversimplified conception of psychoanalytic method and theory.[3] For example, Grünbaum focuses primarily on *etiologic* causes in Freud's theories; but philosophers recognize different kinds of causes. Drawing on concepts of Salmon (1984, pp. 269–270, 275), Edelson (1986b, pp. 99–101; 1988, p. 288) argues that many psychoanalytic explanations entail a *constitutive* rather than an etiologic type of causal relationship, that is, explaining a symptom in terms of internal interrelations among diverse motives.[4] Hopkins (1991, p. 129) suggests another form of oversimplification that results from Grünbaum's use of Millian methods to evaluate psychoanalysis, namely, that Millian canons are insensitive to the extensive range of meaning relations that carry information about the functioning of motives (discussed later).

The severest critics of Grünbaum's approach attack his method of philosophical analysis as perfectionistic, idiosyncratic, self-refuting, superseded, defensive, and unable to be justified.[5] Inductivists agree that the justification of induction is an unsolved problem in philosophy, and that a completely formal inductive logic is impossible. The philosopher Hilary Putnam (1983c) comments that "there is always a need for judgments of reasonableness" (p. 198; see also J. O'Neill, 1993). On the other hand, the principles of scientific reasoning are accepted almost universally by working scientists, and are not a major source of controversy—largely, perhaps, because no satisfactory alternative to the scientific (inductive) method has been found.

In addition to the numerous critical reviews of Grünbaum's philosophical method of evaluating psychoanalysis, one finds also a substantial number of favorable reactions.[6] The Russian philosopher Valerii Leibin (1986) sums up the conflicting responses to Grünbaum's inductivist method by observing that "no matter what arguments are adduced, either in defense of or against the evaluation of psychoanalysis as a science, in the final analysis, each researcher is left with his own opinion" (p. 246). Wimsatt (1994), also a philosopher, asks similarly, "Does *anyone* give up their theories in the face of contrary evidence? No one surrenders gracefully—if at all—in today's philosophy of science" (p. 493; see also Bos and Maier, 1992, for an informative social psychological analysis of the Grünbaum debates).

The remainder of this chapter reviews and evaluates the ten major arguments in Grünbaum's critiques of psychoanalysis and its interpretive methodology. The discussion that follows does not attempt to be exhaustive, nor does it attempt to follow either Grünbaum's logical arguments or the counterarguments of his critics in great detail. Rather, I present the essence of Grünbaum's position, and then indicate various counterarguments that have been raised against his views. I include also my own areas of agreement and disagreement with both Grünbaum, on some points, and his adversaries, on others.

The Suggestibility Problem

Grünbaum contends that clinical data are massively contaminated by: 1) the therapist's interpretive suggestions, which he believes are based on a theoretically biased selection of the patient's material[7]; and 2) by the patient's compliance, which is heightened by positive transference.[8] He concludes that such contamination deprives clinical data of any epistemic value and necessitates extraclinical testing of causal hypotheses (1984, pp. 130–135; see also Levy, 1996, p. 130, fn. 2). It is not entirely clear, however, whether Grünbaum applies the extraclinical testing requirement to low-level, idiographic, interpretive hypotheses, as well as to higher level clinical theories.

Grünbaum's views regarding the contamination of clinical data have given rise to a great deal of debate, examples of which follow. A philosopher points out that in every field, "all data are epistemically contaminated" (Flax, 1981, p. 563).[9] Other philosophers observe that the suggestibility problem is only a general, always-present *doubt* that science deals with by acknowledging the problem, attempting to make it testable, and if it is not testable, then bracketing the problem as a possibility and proceeding with the work.[10] Farrell (1986, pp. 236–237), a philosopher of psychoanalysis, concludes that the factor of suggestion is variable; if it is small, some degree of truth may still be possible.[11]

The philosopher-psychoanalyst Charles Hanly (1988) asks: "If clinical evidence is sufficiently objective to falsify, why is it too contaminated by suggestion to confirm?" (p. 527).[12] Some additional counterarguments by psychoanalysts include Edelson's assertions (1984, pp. 136–137; 144–153, esp. p. 144) that psychoanalytic hypotheses can be and have been tested in the clinical situation; and that what carries special weight with both patient and analyst is the emergence of *circumstantial details* which neither had thought of previously. Spence (1995) and coworkers (Spence and Owen, 1990; Spence, Dahl, and Jones, 1993; Spence, Mayes, and Dahl, 1994) report experiments in which the role of suggestion was minimized, yet highly significant correlations were found between specific interpretations and particular discourse markers.

Experimental investigations by other psychoanalysts have demonstrated that, contrary to therapists' expectations, and whether the therapeutic alliance was positive or not, clinical data and the therapeutic process appeared to be relatively independent of influence by the therapist (Horowitz, 1976); predictions based upon intraclinical data correlated significantly with extraclinical measures (Luborsky, 1986, pp. 247–249); and accurate interpretations had therapeutic effects (Crits-Christoph et al., 1988). Empirical research findings of this kind tell against Grünbaum's conclusion that therapeutic responses to interpretations are largely placebo effects induced by interpretive suggestions and patient compliance. The patient, after all, Lamm (1993) points out, "is always leading the analyst, moment-to-moment, session-by-session, and the analyst (though 'theoretically informed') lacks a premeditated design or plan" (p. 260; see also Strupp, 1986, pp. 260–261; Vaughan and Roose, 1995, p. 351).

Still other writers emphasize that suggestibility is an empirical problem that needs to be, can be, and has been studied.[13] Along similar lines, the philosopher Arnold Davidson (1994, p. 317) notes that the historiographer Carlo Ginzburg (1989) suggests a relevant methodologic principle, namely, that one need not reject a distorted source of evidence outright simply because it is distorted. Ginzburg attempts to develop interpretive procedures that make compelling evidence possible from nonobjective sources; for distorted evidence, though problematic, is not hopeless—contrary to Grünbaum's conclusions regarding clinical data. Davidson (1994) writes that "we must follow Ginzburg's lead in this area and not let inherent distortion of the evidence pass us by, as it so easily can, without further examination" (p. 320).[14]

Wisdom (1956–1957) wrote long ago that, "Until the possibility of the influence of suggestion is refuted in a clear and decisive way, the technology of interpretation must be, from a methodologic point of view, uncertain" (pp. 156–157). For a number of reasons, however, including the inherent circularity of the interpretive process, interpretations would be uncertain even if patients were not suggestible. Moreover, the suggestibility of human beings is a fact of life, not something to be "refuted": suggestibility "is actually an irreducible, primitive phenomenon, a fundamental fact in the mental life of man" (Freud, 1921, p. 89). Consider, for example, Greenspoon's classic experiments (1955, 1962), demonstrating how subtley and subliminally suggestive effects can be communicated from therapist to patient.

The therapist is suggestible, too, sometimes being "taken in" by the patient—or by the therapist's own need to hear what he or she wants to hear (Glover, 1931; Editor, 1986). The therapist's alertness to both the patient's and his or her own suggestibility is part of the therapist's clinical and interpretive competence.[15] Raphling (in Panel, 1995b) observes that the ideal of neutral interpretation is unattainable in therapeutic work: "it is difficult for a patient not to experience an interpretation as advocating something, and equally difficult for the analyst to frame an interpretation that in fact is not" (p. 545). Raphling adds: "But if a patient's transference-based susceptibilities to an interpretation's rhetorical power and conditioning influence can be analyzed, there is a chance that insight can be gained without strings attached" (p. 545).

Suggestibility, therefore, is not just worthless or harmful epistemologic chaff that must be eliminated; it is grist for the therapeutic mill. And to the extent that it is an interpretable part of the data, suggestibility cannot be said to invalidate such data. Greenberg (1994, pp. 11–12) notes in this connection that suggestion is only part of a much larger context associated with the patient-therapist interaction. Suggestibility can become a therapeutic and epistemologic problem, however, if the therapist overlooks, encourages, or exploits this factor in either partner of the therapeutic dyad (Hanly, 1992a, p. 300; Wallace 1985, pp. 103–104, fn. 9). Thus Grünbaum's critique applies primarily to adverse scientific as well as therapeutic consequences of *unrecognized* and *unresolved* undercurrents of suggestibility in the patient-therapist interaction.

Problems Related to the Method of Free Association

Freud (1925c, p. 41) believed that by remaining relatively detached and silent and allowing the patient's associations to flow freely without guidance from the therapist, repressed contents would emerge spontaneously, uncontaminated by suggestion. He believed also that free associations could retrieve repressed memories of traumatic experiences, thereby establishing that repression of such memories caused neuroses (1923a, pp. 246, 251). Grünbaum (1984, pp. 240–245, 269–272) argues, however, that in addition to free associations being irremediably contaminated by suggestion, and the related epistemic problem of selection bias in the therapist's tendency to focus on associations that agree with his or her theory, the validity of free association as a method rests logically and historically on therapeutic success; but since Freud (1926a, p. 154; 1937a) subsequently downplayed and eventually retracted his earlier therapeutic claims, the method of free association is left epistemically unsupported.

Grünbaum (1984, pp. 233–234) also draws upon Glymour's (1983) critique of a reputed causal reversal fallacy in free association to argue against the use of free associations to discover and validate repressed (motivational) causes. Freud (1900) had theorized regarding the free associations to a dream that "the great bulk of the thoughts which are revealed in analysis were already active during the process of forming the dream" (pp. 280–281, 528). He referred to his dream of the botanical monograph (1900, pp. 169ff) as an example of this concept. Glymour and Grünbaum argue, however, that this theory reverses the temporal order of cause and effect exhibited by the free associations. That is, Freud's theory proposes that the manifest dream elements, which represent effects of a repressed motivational cause, precede and initiate the free associations—cause and effect thus being reversed (see also Sand, 1993, pp. 530–533). Grünbaum (1986, p. 278) maintains that the fallacy of causal reversal is involved whenever a psychoanalyst claims that free associations have revealed the cause of a neurotic symptom, a dream wish, or the motive of a slip. He insists rhetorically that "not even the tortures of the thumbscrew or of the rack should persuade a rational being that free association can *certify* pathogens or other causes" (1984, p. 180).

Debate about Grünbaum's argument that free associations are hopelessly contaminated by suggestion has been reviewed in the preceding section of this chapter. His additional critique that therapists tend to focus on associations that agree with their preferred theories (selection bias) is related to the more generic problem of confirmation bias—a universal and apparently ineradicable tendency in human beings, including scientists, to overvalue their own beliefs and to resist giving up favored viewpoints.[16] The universal nature of that tendency argues against its being a methodologic defect specific to free association; and although the occurrence of selection and confirmation bias calls for remedial measures, it no more disqualifies the method of free association than it does other scientific procedures which are susceptible to the same problem.

Edelson (1984, pp. 134–135; 1986a, pp. 232–234) offers the most detailed counterarguments to Grünbaum's critique of free association. He starts by questioning the notion that focal themes in therapy sessions emerge at the prompting of the therapist.

Edelson disputes Grünbaum's implication that clinical interpreters have no criteria other than their preferred theories for selecting among associations (see also Luborsky and Mintz, 1975; French, 1958a,b). On the contrary, therapists distinguish between associations that flow relatively unimpeded, as opposed to those that are carefully monitored, controlled, and organized by the patient—thereby isolating and identifying data contaminated by the patient's selectiveness (see also Colby, 1963, p. 197). In associations that flow relatively freely, unconscious wishes sometimes emerge into consciousness spontaneously, explicitly, and in detail, making it unnecesary in those circumstances for the therapist to infer the latent contents.

According to Edelson (1988, pp. 337–339), Freud attempted to justify the method of free association in five ways: (1) by analogy with commonsense measures used to facilitate the confiding of secrets (see also Glymour, 1993, p. 479); (2) by analogy with hypnosis, during which a person can provide information of which he or she is unaware when not hypnotized; (3) by analogy with the effects of the "talking cure" (Breuer and Freud, 1893–1895); (4) by analogy with word-association experiments; and (5) by analogy with literature, autobiography (for example, the Schreber case), art, jokes, and so forth. Edelson (1988) notes that "none of these justifications is unassailable by itself, but together they provide strong warrant for the credibility of clinical causal inferences in psychoanalysis" (p. 339; see also Levy, 1996, pp. 138, 163).

In response to Grünbaum's and Glymour's critiques of a "causal reversal fallacy" in free association, Edelson (1988, pp. 322–323) presents the following counterargument:

1. Free associations that follow a dream, slip, or symptom often refer to events which occurred before or at the same time as the dream, slip, or symptom.
2. The free associations are manifestations generated by a causal entity, the latter being an enduring propensity, not an isolated event. Both the dream, slip, or symptom and the free associations are connected to the causal entity by the same network of causal processes.
3. The cause of the dream, slip, or symptom is freed to some extent by the method of free association, as a result of which it manifests itself more directly (1988, pp. 348–349).

Edelson (1988, p. 322) notes also that critics of free association tend to overlook the fact that this method involves a special state of mind in which connections among mental contents are much more extensively influenced by primary mental processes than in ordinary states of consciousness.

In response to Grünbaum's insistence that the method of free association does not provide information about antecedent causes, Wallace (1986, pp. 384–385) points out that causal attribution is always an inferential process; and what is important to the analyst is not whether a particular association represents a specific memory emerging from repression. The analyst is concerned with the pattern (including recurrent themes) of all the associations. The associations themselves are not considered recovered causes, but are data from which antecedent causes may sometimes be inferred (see also Symposium, 1995, pp. 429–430). Freud (1900, p. 200) emphasized, for example, that the cause of the dream, slip, or symptom must be inferred from the total material produced by free association.

The psychoanalyst Rosemarie Sand (1993) suggests in this connection that free associations are shaped by (1) the person's enduring character (personality), on the one hand, and (2) the situation in which the associations are produced, which may include transference, on the other. Although by themselves free associations do not appear to provide direct etiologic warrant for prior events, their sources in enduring personality features and in situational factors that may include transference—both of which may have been causal in shaping prior events—give free associations a potentially indirect role in the identification of prior events.

In a cogent chapter on clinical inference, A. O'Neill (1993) argues against the common but mistaken view that

> thinking by association is quite separate from logical reasoning; that association is natural and undisciplined, whereas logic is artificial and rule-bound. People overlook their similar function in thinking. Associational processes serve the same purpose as syllogisms and induction—linking the particular instance with the general class—which is the essential feature of any practical art that employs scientific principles [p. 75].

Drawing Unwarranted Causal Inferences from Meaning Relations

This part of Grünbaum's critique has special relevance to the widely used methods of relation- and pattern-seeking in interpretive methodology.[17] Grünbaum focuses on Freud's view that symptoms have "meanings" by virtue of their motivational causes, in contrast to Jaspers, Ricoeur, and hermeneutically oriented psychoanalysts like Klein and Schafer who attempt to replace the causal sense in which symptoms have meanings with the semantic sense in which texts have meanings.[18] Grünbaum (1989, p. 478) maintains that, by themselves, meaning relations *never* indicate causal linkages. He refers to the confusion of meaning relations with causal connections as the "thematic affinity fallacy," arguing that interpreting symptoms is not the same as interpreting texts (1989, p. 477).

Jaspers and the hermeneutic phenomenologists claimed that Freud paid too little attention to meaning relations, but Grünbaum (1989, p. 479) argues just the opposite—that Freud gave far too much causal-explanatory weight to mere meaning kinships.[19] Grünbaum (1993) notes also that meaning relations vary in kind and degree; but even when they are of very high degree they do not warrant the inference of a causal linkage between the semantically related events: "Narratives replete with mere hermeneutic elucidations of thematic affinities are explanatorily sterile or bankrupt; at best they have literary or reportorial value; at worst, they are mere cock-and-bull stories" (1993, p. 139).

Grünbaum's argument that clinical interpreters mistakenly employ mere meaning relations to posit causal connections bears directly on the question of interpretive probity; for the identification of various types of thematic relations and patterns in clinical data is one of the most widely used methods in depth-psychological inquiry (Cheshire, 1975). Traditionally, clinicians have assumed that meaning relations suggest the nature of their determinants.[20] Grünbaum's argument that meaning relations never indicate their causal (that is, motivational) origins thus challenges a basic methodologic concept and long-established interpretive practice in psychoanalysis and dynamic psychotherapy. This aspect of Grünbaum's critique is not confined to psychoanalysis and dynamic psychotherapy, however; it "spells a major general moral for the human sciences, including history, but also has instructive counterparts in biology and even in physics" (Grünbaum, 1990a, p. 561; emphasis omitted).

Some clinical writers have reached conclusions similar to Grünbaum's regarding the problem of inferring causal connections from meaning relations alone. The clinician and investigator Paul Meehl (1983) writes, for example, that construction of a causal inference "does not follow immediately from correct detection of a theme in the associations" (pp. 359–360). And Donald Spence's (1982a, p. 144–148) critique of pattern-matching in interpretive work includes some examples of clinicians drawing causal inferences from formal (thematic) similarities in patients' material. One of the examples is a case reported by Ramzy (1974), in which the patient became disturbed about the possibility of losing his cleaning lady at a time when a separation from the analyst was imminent. Ramzy suspected that the patient's disturbance about losing the cleaning lady was a displacement from (and thus caused by) deeper concern about the coming separation from the analyst. The thematic kinships on which Ramzy based that inference were some suggestive parallels between the cleaning woman and the therapist: both were in the paid service of the patient; both carried out "cleansing" services for the patient; and both seemed to be leaving the patient. Spence cautions, however, that "we should be careful not to assume that our selected link is either 'demanded' by the material or is the only choice available. It is, more precisely, *our* association to the patient's material which, by virtue of our position, we can raise to the status of an interpretation" (1982a, p. 150; emphasis added).

To his credit in the example cited, Ramzy's interpretation to the patient was stated tentatively rather than authoritatively. Later in the same session he said to the patient: "Your earlier thoughts about the cleaning lady which occurred to you on the way here, and your worry about losing her, make me think that they may be connected with my upcoming absence for the next two weeks" (Ramzy, 1974, p. 546). The psychoanalyst Rosemarie Sand (personal communication, 1997) emphasizes that viewing and treating interpretations as hypotheses lessens the problem of thematic affinity fallacies.

Turning to the debate about Grünbaum's claim that clinicians draw unwarranted causal inferences from meaning relations: Coltrera (1981) notes that Freud (1900, pp. 310–338) employed two models or definitions of interpretation which were inconsistent. One was a "critical" model (as in literary criticism) which derives "meaning from meaning," that is, by thematic affinity. The other, a formal definition of interpretation, emphasized the causal dynamics and genetics of dream-formation. The inconsistency was resolved (partially, at least) in the metapsychological papers, in which Freud (1915d, p. 166) postulated a relationship between instinctual drives and their ideational representatives, the latter being cognate forms of instinctual drive-wishes which can be interpreted as meanings (see also Marks, 1992, pp. 35–41).

Edelson (1991) agrees with Grünbaum that thematic affinity is insufficient warrant for the *validation* of clinical interpretations; but he argues further that by inferring unconscious wishes, psychoanalytic explanations often show why there is a lack of thematic affinity between the manifest features of symptoms and dreams, on the one hand, and the patient's conscious desires and beliefs, on the other. The affinity is between *latent* mental processes and the symptom or dream: "It is just these features of psychoanalytic thought that are ordinarily ignored in philosophical—and other—critiques of psychoanalytic theory, fatally so, in my opinion, for the relevance of the methodologic strictures applied in such critiques" (Edelson, 1991, pp. 104–105).

Grünbaum's conclusion (1993, p. 15) that the psychoanalytic meaning of a symptom, dream, or slip is constituted solely and essentially by its unconscious (motivational) cause illustrates Strenger's observation (1986, pp. 258–259) that Grünbaum sometimes oversimplifies psychoanalytic concepts—in this case adopting a narrow, linear, unidimensional view of latent meanings. Shope (1973, esp. p. 290), by contrast, delineates at least four or possibly five uses of the term "meaning" in Freud's writings: (1) that for which a mental phenomenon substitutes; (2) intention or purpose: its position in a psychic continuity; (3) intention or purpose plus the "significance" of the mental phenomenon; (4) the unconscious (causal) motives behind the phenomenon; and possibly also (5) the "impressions" and "experiences" that give rise to meaning, which overlaps the other definitions. Grünbaum (1984, pp. 66–67, 70–71, 77–78) focuses tendentiously on Shope's fourth meaning; but Shope (1973) does not say that Freud *equated* meaning with cause; he states only that Freud *included* the unconscious causal nexus in his account of meaning (p. 303). In regard to Freud's use of the term meaning, Shope adds that "in view of the great ambiguity of the term in ordinary speech, it is understandable that Freud should have shifted as he did from one concept of meaning to another" (1973, p. 284).

The causal-motivational dimension of unconscious meaning that Grünbaum emphasizes—I would say overemphasizes—was clearly an important part of Freud's thinking; but it was not his only concept of unconscious meaning, nor is it the only viewpoint of most presentday clinicians, scholars, and investigators.[21] Grünbaum (1993, pp. 121–129, 136–137, 141–151) oversimplifies further in the examples of "thematic affinity fallacies" that he attributes to Freud. His examples are drawn largely from early writings by Breuer and Freud (1893–1895, 1895b, 1896, 1909b), when psychoanalytic methods and concepts were in a formative stage, undergoing frequent changes. Even in the "Studies on Hysteria" (1893–1895), however, it is questionable whether Freud based causal inferences on thematic affinity alone.[22]

Grünbaum (1993) acknowledges his dislike of the term "meaning": "I deplore and regret the use of the term 'meaning' in this context, because it is ambiguous and lends itself to misleading use" (p. 121)—an attitude that may contribute to his singular focus on causal connections in interpretive inquiry, relegating latent meanings to little more than a synonym of unconscious motivational cause.[23]

Grünbaum's critique of "thematic affinity fallacies" does not correspond very closely with how clinicians actually use meaning relations in their interpretive work. Clinicians do not assume, for example, that one event in a thematic kinship necessarily causes the other, for example, that punishment for childhood biting causes adult obsessions concerned with biting. If two such manifest contents appear contiguously during the same therapy session, or repetitively in ongoing sessions, the clinician might view the similarity of content (that is, biting) as a possible clue to an as-yet-unidentified latent content which ideally might account dynamically for both elements of the pattern. Grünbaum (1990a, p. 565) recognizes and acknowledges that clinicians do deal with meaning relations—"sometimes," he says—in the manner just described.

Matthias Kettner (1991, pp. 172–177) proposes a defense of thematic kinships based upon Peirce's concept of abduction.[24] In abductive reasoning one infers the best or most plausible explanation from a set of data or facts. Inferences of this kind are employed commonly in everyday life, as well as in medical diagnosis, scientific theory formation, and interpretive inquiry (see, for example, Josephson and Josephson, 1994). Kettner argues that if one employs the premise that meaning relations are causally embedded in the interpretive processes of the individual patient's causally-connected mental life, it would blunt the criticism that psychoanalysts base causal inferences on thematic inferences alone.[25]

Abductive inference is closely related to, if not identical with, a method of weighing evidence and making inferences called

"Inference to the Best Explanation." According to the latter model, our inferences are guided by our explanatory practices, that is: "Beginning with the evidence available to us, we infer what would, if true, provide the best explanation of that evidence."[26] Edelson (1988, pp. 355–359, 363–364) points out that psychoanalysts rely extensively on inference to the best explanation. He spells out the criteria of what counts as the best explanation, and argues that Freud often employed causal reasoning of this kind in his case histories.

In his treatise *Mental Content*, the philosopher Colin McGinn (1989) argues against the view that content (meaning) is only an epiphenomenon. He suggests a possible explanation of how content (meaning-) relations can have causal relevance, basing his argument on the teleology of mental states: "What the causal objection forgets is that mental states have an environment-directed *purpose*, and that specifying that purpose tells us something important about them" (p. 144). McGinn maintains that focusing exclusively on the causal mechanisms that underlie contentful states will never reveal the functions that such mechanisms serve, because "the *purpose* of a causal mechanism is not contained in the way it works" (pp. 149–150).

The language philosopher Jerry Fodor (1993, pp. 236–239) proposes yet another basis for a significant relationship between causes and meanings (see also Fodor, 1975, 1987). He notes that the representational theory of mind provides a plausible mechanism for a parallel, though not a connection, between causal and semantic relations among mental states. The computational theory of mind (or "computer metaphor"), on the other hand, suggests how the semantic and causal properties of symbols may be connected—which leads to a possible model of causal and semantic properties being connected in thoughts. The model, in turn, suggests a theory that explains how there can be semantic content relations among causally related thoughts. Fodor (1987, pp. 19–20) stresses that this sort of problem cannot even be stated, let alone solved, unless we suppose that there are mental states having both semantic contents and causal roles. Edelson (1988, pp. xxii–xxiv) discusses the relevance of this view to psychoanalysis and its interpretive methodology (see also Rorty, 1993, for a summary of dissenting views to Fodor's position; and Loar, 1981, for the complexities, controversies, and incomplete knowledge about causal and semantic properties of mind).

The behavioral science methodologist Abraham Kaplan (1964) refers to interpretations as hypotheses that contain both semantic and scientific explanations:

> We interpret a dream by making manifest its latent content, and by explaining also why the dreamer produced the symbols he did. The scientific explanation may be suggested and supported by the semantic one, as in the case of dream analysis. But the relation between the two components may also be the reverse: we may understand *what* a person says because we know, from the context or in other ways, *why* he is saying it [p. 328].

Brook (1995b, p. 527) believes that thematic affinities constitute evidence that psychological content has been conveyed (transferred) between earlier and later psychic states, and as such provide evidence for psychological explanations in terms of content. Other writers who view conveyance of content as a central form of psychoanalytic explanation include Wollheim (1984), Hopkins (1988), and Edelson (1988, p. 332). Edelson (1988, p. 115), following Wollheim, refers to this mechanism as "ideogenic causality," that is, the ideational content of a psychological state is causative in this form of etiology (compare the concept that meanings can become causes).

Wallace (1989b, pp. 500–501) argues for a continuity between causes and meanings in human behavior, while Bruss (1986, p. 130) notes that Grünbaum's critique ignores the basic psychoanalytic concept of psychic continuity. Bruss suggests that the principal mode of induction employed by clinical interpreters is reconstruction of the psychic continuity, so that every element of the patient's symptoms and associations fit together in a structured network, "without overlap, redundancy, or other logical inconsistencies" (1986, pp. 138–139).

Some additional counterarguments to Grünbaum's position include the following: Wallace (1989b, pp. 507–508) notes that themes are patterns, correlations, regularities; and as such they are similar to the data used for causal inferences in any discipline. Gillett (1995, p. 119) observes that the role of metaphor in language attests the causal significance of thematic kinships; and Malan (1979) maintains that events in a patient's life, particularly precipitating factors, suggest the nature of unconscious determinants underlying a symptom. Rosemarie Sand (1993, pp. 544–545), who has supported most of Grünbaum's views (for example,

Sand, 1983), includes thematic affinity in a proposal for a revised approach to dream interpretation. Cheshire (1975, pp. 20–27) notes that the concept of latent meaning implies that personality, behavior, and psychopathology can be understood and formulated not only as effects of antecedent causes, but also as "expressions" (in the sense of language) of covert causal processes such as wishes, urges, feelings, conflicts, and defenses (see also Searle, 1979a). Thus clinicians often formulate interpretations by viewing clinical data as expressive in nature, and by appealing to their meanings (Cheshire, 1975, p. 163; see also Rycroft, 1966).

Grünbaum (1990a) asks, "But what are the so-called 'meaning connections' in this context? And just what are their relations to *causal* connections" (p. 562). His answers to these questions are confusing, however. on the one hand, he conflates the two by defining psychoanalytic meaning narrowly in terms of motivational cause. Yet elsewhere he refers to the two as separate but "compatible." And in still another connection he suggests that under certain conditions—for example, if supplemented by Mill's methods of controlled inquiry—meaning relations can lead to causal connections. By contrast, psychoanalytic theory conceives of latent meanings and psychic determinants as unequivocally though complexly related, a viewpoint which is consonant with: (1) its core concept of continuity, that is, that all aspects of mental functioning are connected; (2) its nonlinear logic of psychic reality (which Grünbaum questions in a recent [1997] essay); and (3) the additional concepts that subsequent experiences can influence earlier (mental) events, that meanings can become causes, that motivations function as both causes and meanings, and that meanings suggest the nature of their determinants. With regard to the last point, Dalbiez (1941, Vol. 1, pp. 207–210) concluded over half a century ago that Freud's discovery of "unconscious affective thematism" in spontaneous associations resulted from the fact that causality was Freud's guiding concept. Every effect is a sign of its cause; and by applying the principles of determinism and continuity, the psychoanalyst can recognize the affective theme in the patient's associations.

The philosopher Hilary Kornblith (1993b) writes:

> We form our concepts in ways which presuppose the existence of an underlying, explanatory essence; we presuppose that superficial, observable properties are only a rough and ready guide to the real structure of the world, but that these properties are the

> causal consequences of deeper similarities, the details of which we are frequently ignorant about [p. 78; see also Levy, 1996, pp. 160–164].

The main question of the present discussion is whether thematic meaning relations, which are interpretable in clinical data, represent consequences of and thus serve as "rough and ready guides" to a deeper, causally explanatory structure of the mind. Grünbaum says no; but for various reasons numerous other writers, including some philosophers, disagree. Can these differences be reconciled?

In recent writings, Grünbaum appears to have softened his assertion that meaning relations "never" indicate their causal origins, and that "most" clinical interpretations entail a thematic affinity fallacy (see, for example, 1990a, p. 565; 1993, pp. 116–117, 120, 129, 138–139). Edward Erwin (1993, p. 443), one of Grünbaum's staunchest supporters, also writes more tentatively that thematic affinity by itself "is not *generally*" evidence of a causal connection: "In some cases of thematic affinities there is evidence of a causal connection, but it is supplied by *background evidence*" (see also Brook, 1992, pp. 296–298). "Background evidence," however, is an important part of the context that clinicians employ in interpretive work. Clinicians rely on context more than on any other factor in the process of interpretive inquiry.[27] Freud (1900, p. 98 fn. 1, and p. 353) recognized early in the development of psychoanalysis that a correct interpretation can be arrived at only from the context at the time (see also Cavell, 1988, pp. 869–871).

It is important to recognize that Grünbaum's critique of thematic affinity fallacies in clinical interpretations focuses on the question of "establishing" or "warranting" causal inferences based upon meaning relations, rather than on the latter serving as clues during the discovery phase of the interpretive process to as-yet-unidentified latent meanings and determinants. Grünbaum states consistently that "mere" meaning relations or thematic affinities "alone" do not and cannot *warrant* causal inferences. Something in addition to thematic relations is needed to demonstrate that a posited causal correlation is not due to chance. In keeping with his inductivist methodology, Grünbaum suggests that "the warrant can be gotten essentially by the use of J. S. Mill's joint method" (1989, p. 486).

Another way of describing Grünbaum's position is that to

establish a causal connection empirically, in contrast to merely considering or postulating such a relationship, one must demonstrate a constant conjunction between an antecedent (causal) factor and a consequent occurrence. Otherwise one risks the fallacy of "confirming the consequent." If the antecedent is hidden, as in the construal of repressed conflicts, defenses, fantasies, and memories, a causal relation can only be conjectural rather than warranted or established (Peter Caws, personal communication, 1997). Since most such inferences in depth-psychological therapies are necessarily conjectural, it follows that interpretations of causal connections such as unconscious motives are more usefully and honestly treated as tentative hypotheses rather than as authoritative statements.

Recently, Paul Meehl has clarified his earlier-stated view that a causal inference "does not follow immediately from correct detection of a theme in the associations" (1983, pp. 359–360). He explains that

> I did not mean to deny that it is a plausible inference from the associations to an unconscious guiding process. I myself have considerable faith in the validity of such a causal inference on those occasions in which the associative network is relatively rich with numerous cross-connections. My point was not that such inferences can't be valid, nor even that they usually are not valid, but that *since* they don't directly follow—that is, the discernment of thematic relations is not *ipso facto* a discernment of a regnant unconscious cause—we have a problem of how *strong* that inference can be under usual psychoanalytic circumstances. The warrant for making the inference to a guiding, unconscious regnancy from the way the associations flow is, in my view, the same as the warrant for any other causal hypothesis outside of psychoanalysis, or outside of psychology generally, namely, "inference to the best explanation." But the problem is, "How do we convince a skeptic that it *is* the 'best explanation'" [Personal communication, 1997].

The inability to establish a causal inference at a particular time does not mean, of course, that important causal connections are not present. Grünbaum (1989) acknowledges, for example, that "Freud should not be faulted for asserting, in principle, that some mental events can be linked both thematically and causally" (p. 491; emphasis omitted)—though one is not entitled to infer the latter from the former alone.

One is entitled, however, to consider thematic kinships as possible clues to as-yet-unidentified latent meanings and determinants, and to pursue such clues further in the course of an ongoing therapeutic process and interpretive inquiry. Moreover, if a particular type of thematic relation occurs *repeatedly* during the course of a therapeutic process in association with a specific and *recurrent* pathodynamic constellation (the latter including a consistent type of precipitating factor), the possibility of a posited causal-thematic relationship's being owed to chance decreases correspondingly (for clinical examples, see Chapter 9).

The recurrence of specific dynamic constellations associated with particular types of thematic patterns offers a methodologic approach to studying regularities in the conjunction of possible antecedent (causal) factors and consequent meaning relations. The identification of such regularities may make it possible, in turn, to estimate the relative probabilities of posited causal relationships suggested by the recurring causal-thematic conjunctions.

Compare, in this connection, Grünbaum's illustration of employing Millian methods to determine causal relevance (1993, p. 164): he validates a possible causal link between two events by noting "*over a period of time and repeatedly*" (emphasis added) that the presence versus the absence of one event "makes a difference statistically" to the occurrence of the other event. Applying the same reasoning to the clinical interpretation of a possible causal-thematic link: a specific, recurring, unconscious motivational factor may function as an antecedent causal entity that gives rise to various consequent events including a particular and repetitive type of thematic kinship—the latter possibly conveying and thus reflecting the underlying causal entity in the form of symbolic verbal and/or nonverbal expressive behavior.

Freud's concept of pathodynamic recurrences—that is, "the return of the repressed" (1896a, pp. 169–170; 1907, p. 35; 1915c, p. 154)—combined with Mill's joint method, suggests a mixed (psychoanalytic and inductivist) model of repetitive causal-thematic links and their evaluation. One of Freud's many references to "return of the repressed" has special relevance in this connection: "A return like this of what has been repressed is to be expected *with particular regularity*" (1907, p. 35; emphasis added)—an observation that coincides with the aforementioned repetitive dynamic constellations, including the recurrences of unconscious motivational configurations and associated thematic patterns.

Although the model suggested here includes a modified version of Mill's methods, Grünbaum probably would not agree with this attempt to reconcile opposing viewpoints regarding causal and meaning connections; for in addition to his continuing, though somewhat softened, insistence that causes and meanings do not mix, Grünbaum also maintains that the suggestibility problem and other methodologic defects of individual case studies deprive clinical data of epistemic value, and necessitate extraclinical testing of clinical hypotheses.

Failure of the Tally Argument

Freud claimed at one point (1915–1917, p. 452) that since only accurate interpretations affect the patient's psychopathology, the truth of an interpretation can be determined by the therapeutic effectiveness of the intervention—a validating strategy that Grünbaum (1984, pp. 135–172) has dubbed the "tally argument." Grünbaum has an important point to make here, namely, that if repressed thoughts or feelings cause a symptom, and if the therapist's intervention causes the repressed contents to become conscious—that is, if the interpretation tallies with the unconscious cause of the symptom—then according to Freud's logic the symptom should remit. And, in fact, Grünbaum argues that this is a scientifically reasonable claim, one that allows for disproof. In addition, insofar as patient improvement does occur in response to interpretation, this observation is relevant to Freud's overall theories of neurosogenesis and of psychoanalytic treatment.

Grünbaum notes that early in the development of psychoanalysis, Freud asserted the preceding logic, which exonerates him from Popper's later charge that Freud's interpretations were circular and thus could never be disproved. By focusing on this aspect of Freud's reasoning, Grünbaum takes the position that Freud was a better scientist than some critics have realized. Thus, on this point at least, Grünbaum enters the debate as a demonstrably "fair critic." Grünbaum then proceeds to argue, however, that: (1) Freud did not stick to his original line of reasoning, which depends inter alia on patient improvement; and (2) more generally the tally argument is insufficient on other grounds to warrant Freud's claims.

Observing patients' responses to interventions continues to be one of the most widely-used methods of attempting to justify interpretations (discussed further in Chapter 8). Grünbaum (1984, pp. 127–129) argues, however, that the therapist's interpretive suggestions, combined with the compliant patient's suggestibility, deprive clinical data of epistemic value, and render the tally argument null and void. Further weakening of the tally argument resulted from Freud's retraction of therapeutic claims, and from investigations which compared the therapeutic effectiveness of psychoanalysis with other psychological treatments. The results of psychoanalytic therapy were found to be no better than those of other treatments. Grünbaum concludes, therefore, that the therapeutic results of psychoanalysis probably represent placebo effects. Although the tally argument was only one among a number of methods that Freud proposed for justifying interpretations, Grünbaum's critique of this validating strategy is relevant to the question of interpretive probity.

Much of the debate about the tally argument consists of disagreements with Grünbaum regarding Freud's attitude towards this validating method. A number of writers maintain that Grünbaum overstates Freud's dependence upon and commitment to the tally argument.[28] Others (for example, Grant and Harari, 1990) believe that Grünbaum has misread Freud regarding the tally argument, and has misunderstood his meaning. Paradoxically, however, although Grünbaum's emphasis on the tally argument appears to overestimate its importance in Freud's thinking, his critique nevertheless carries some weight because observation of patients' responses to interpretations, which is the central feature of the tally argument, is still one of the most widely used, though not very probative, methods of attempting to justify interpretations. That is, if used alone a patient's reaction to an interpretation is not a very reliable method of justification, because the patient's responses themselves must be interpreted.[29] To test one interpretation by another (untested) interpretation is unacceptable methodologically (Wisdom, 1967, p. 46). And since inexact interpretations are sometimes therapeutic,[30] the criterion of "beneficial effects" cannot be considered a very reliable test of interpretive validity.[31]

One of the most original contributions to the debate about this problem is Wilma Bucci's attempt (1985, 1988, 1989; see also Paivio, 1986) to revise and reconstruct Freud's tally argument in terms of a dual coding theory. The theory is based upon cognitive research, and proposes that verbal and nonverbal information is encoded in different symbolic forms and in separate systems which are specialized for the differing representations involved—verbal representations in the case of verbal information, imagistic representations in the case of perceptual-motivational-emotional (PME) information. The two codes are connected, however, by a complex set of referential links (1988, pp. 33–34).

Employing the dual coding model, Bucci (1985, pp. 597ff) postulates that the basis of effectivenes for one clinical interpretation over another is the directness and strength of interpretive linkages to nonverbal (PME) representations stored in the patient's memory. Evidence that an interpretation has connected with imagistic schemata is based upon the patient's associations following the interpretation: for example, reports of actions, emotions, and actually experiencing emotions in the therapy session; also vivid descriptions of images, fantasies, and dreams in concrete, specific terms. Even if the content of the patient's responses is not the same as the content of the interpretation, associations reflecting nonverbal schemata suggest that the interpretation is "on target." By contrast, verbal-narrational coherence in response to an interpretation is not considered good evidence, and may even represent counter-evidence. Bucci summarizes her theory this way:

1. If perceptual-motivational-emotional (PME) indicators appear in the patient's associations following a particular interpretation, it is probable that referential connections to the important nonverbal, in contrast to the verbal, system of representations have been made.
2. If an interpretation makes referential connections with the nonverbal system, the interpretation is probably accurate.
3. If the patient improves, not only is it likely that connections with the nonverbal system have been made, but also it is probable that PME schemata of the nonverbal system have been changed.

Research methods for applying the dual coding model to clinical data include the use of manuals, trained judges, and rating scales that

> provide a means of external and shared validation of the presence of private and internal emotional representations. Thus we are not confined within the hermeneutic circle, but can point to evidence for emotional structures that are present independent of their verbal report, and that are detected by observers rather than constructed by them [1988, p. 49].

Bucci's dual coding theory may provide cognitive psychological support and a possible explanation for the widely held clinical concept that verbal-intellectual "insight" is more defensive than curative, whereas interpretations that promote experiencing and understanding of latent emotional problems are more likely to be therapeutic. Some problematic aspects of Bucci's thesis must be considered, however. First, there is the question whether dichotomizing verbal and emotional schemata so sharply is consistent with the extensive referential connections that she describes between these two types of representations. One may question also whether such an approach actually escapes the hermeneutic circle, and replaces the subjective activity of construction with objective methods of "detection." For example, the kinds of confirmatory PME responses that Bucci describes are not self-evident observables, but themselves require interpretation. Finally, Bucci's approach to validation of interpretations is methodologically monistic rather than pluralistic, the limitations of which have been discussed in Chapter 3.[32]

Weakness of Freud's Consilience Argument

Another method of validation that Freud employed (for example, 1937b, pp. 262–265) was consilience of inductions from diverse data, the latter being used to cross-validate the patient's acceptance or rejection of interpretations. Grünbaum (1984, pp. 273–278) argues once again, however, that all clinical data are epistemically disqualified by the therapist's interpretive suggestions and the patient's compliance, so that convergent sources of data all share the problem of contamination. Appeal to consilience fails also, Grünbaum contends, because each convergent finding is a product of free association, the validity of which cannot be supported without the tally argument and therapeutic success.

Most of the debate about consilience as a method of justifying interpretations involves disagreements with Grünbaum's argument that data contamination precludes the use of a convergence strategy.[33] With respect to the method of consilience itself, the methodologist Adriaan De Groot (1969, pp. 320ff) emphasizes that various methods of testing hypotheses by internal evidence are used in the case study method, but that it is above all their convergence which supports an interpretation:

> The convergence principle can be seen to operate in a number of variations throughout all forms of interpretation. John Stuart Mill's canons of inductive methods also can be regarded as a specific elaboration of the same principle [De Groot, 1969, p. 323].

The range and diversity of validating methods proposed by Freud is noteworthy, because the more numerous and diverse the methods used, the greater their convergent capability for confirming or disconfirming interpretive hypotheses.[34]

Edelson (1992a/1994, p. 85) presents a striking clinical example of consilience in which multiple varieties of evidence, each providing weak inductive support, add up to relatively strong convergent evidence (see also Edelson, 1985, 1986a,b). Edelson argues also (1988, pp. 341–342; see also Salmon, 1959, pp. 258–259) that inferences from dreams, slips, and symptoms are based upon analogies to different models which are justified in different ways; thus when inferences from these diverse clinical phenomena converge, our confidence in the inferences justifiably increases. Edelson (1988, pp. 343–344; see also 1991, p. 105) considers Darwin's methodology for making causal inferences about history a particularly relevant parallel with the use of consilience to justify clinical interpretations. Stephen Jay Gould (1986) notes in this connection that

> Darwin, so keenly aware of both the strengths and limits of history, argued that iterated pattern, based on types of evidence so numerous and so diverse that no other coordinating interpretation could stand—even though any item, taken separately, could not provide conclusive proof—must be the criterion for evolutionary inference [pp. 64–65; cited by Edelson, 1988, p. 344].

(Grünbaum's disagreements with Edelson appear in Chapter 6, pp. 229–256, of Grünbaum's 1993 monograph.)

Grünbaum's critique of the consilience argument is also a vote of no confidence in the case study method. The philosopher Edward Erwin (1988, pp. 213–214) agrees with Kazdin (1981), however, that an investigation should not be dismissed as worthless simply because it is a case study. The quality of case studies can be improved: for example, by using objective measures, making several different assessments, and by combining comparable cases.[35] Eagle (1980a, p. 418; see also Levy, 1996, pp. 130–131) points out that it is both possible and advantageous to combine intra- and extraclinical testing. Shapiro (1978) reviews some of the diverse extraclinical methods which have been used to test psychoanalytic hypotheses and concludes that each method provides something unique. And Richard Miller (1987), a philosopher of science, notes:

> There is one other current general answer to the question of how to rate causal accounts. It is contained, above all, in Kuhn's least relativist writings. In this proposal, explanations are to be rated according to a diverse catalogue of virtues: good fit with the data, depth, fruitfulness, congruence with received general theories, and (perhaps) simplicity. All such lists are roughly similar and seem roughly right [pp. 196–197].

Grünbaum's conclusion regarding the weakness of Freud's consilience argument rests primariy on the suggestibility issue, and secondarily on the fact that convergent findings would be based upon free associations, which Grünbaum contends are unsupportable without the tally argument and therapeutic success. Grünbaum has overstated the suggestibility issue in his reductio ad absurdum argument that therapists "coach, coax, persuade, prompt, prod, browbeat, and brainwash" patients to accept their interpretations. Counterarguments to his critique of free association and the tally argument weaken his position still further. This leaves little reason to believe that convergence of findings from diverse data cannot be used to cross-validate clinical interpretations (see also Wallace, 1986, p. 382).

The Unwarranted Assumption that Treated Patients' Introspections Provide Reliable Evaluations of Causal and Therapeutic Claims

Freud (1915–17, pp. 285, 452) claimed that when patients' repressions, other defenses, underlying conflicts, and traumatic memories have been resolved by treatment, their introspections can then be considered accurate and thus can be used to evaluate the correctness of interpretations (see also Fliess, 1948, pp. xv–xvi; Waelder, 1962/1976, pp. 629–630). Arguing against that claim, Grünbaum (1984, pp. 147–148; 1993, pp. 204–219) cites the work of Nisbett and Wilson (1977) and Nisbett and Ross (1980), whose findings on the mechanisms and limitations of human inference suggest that introspection of causal connections between one's inner mental states is equally as susceptible to theory-induced errors as causal inferences about external events (see also Eagle, 1982). Nisbett and Wilson conclude that "Subjective reports about higher mental processes are sometimes correct, but even the instances of correct report are not due to direct introspective awareness. Instead, they are due to the incidentally correct employment of a priori causal theories" (1977, p. 233).

Citing Judd Marmor's (1962) observation that "depending upon the point of view of the analyst, the patients of each school seem to bring up precisely the kind of phenomenological data which confirm the theories and interpretations of their analysts" (p. 289), Grünbaum (1993) concludes that patients are under the suggestive influence of the therapist when they make such introspective evaluations, which argues further against the reliability of their judgments. Thus it would seem, Grünbaum continues, "that Freud *persuaded* his male patients they harbored a fear of castration dating back to infancy. Then they furnished *spurious* introspective validation of the putative insight he had given them into the supposed origins and later *effects* of their hypothesized castration anxiety" (p. 217). Grünbaum cites another study comparing experiences of patients with therapists from different schools (Heine, 1953), and further concludes that "the purported insight achieved by the patient is not the product of a process of veridical *self-discovery*, but rather reflects the patient's *conversion* to the therapist's interpretation" (Grünbaum, 1993, p. 218).

Grünbaum's critique of treated patients' introspective access has evoked relatively little debate, however, perhaps in part because many psychoanalysts and dynamic psychotherapists consider the argument something of a straw man. Well-trained, scientifically minded therapists recognize the fallibility of their own introspections, so why would they consider the introspections of treated patients more accurate than their own? Some clinicians and clinical investigators even suggest that Nisbett and Wilson's and Nisbett and Ross' findings may apply more generally to the widespread use of subjective (that is, introspective-empathic, countertransference-oriented, and intersubjective) approaches to clinical interpretive inquiry.[36]

Grünbaum may misinterpret the nature of insight in psychoanalysis and dynamic psychotherapy. He appears to define insight as knowledge about causal relations, whereas actually it represents a restructuring of experience (Strenger, 1991, p. 19). In addition, theory-driven interpretations of the type that Grünbaum describes (for example, "persuading" the patient that he has castration anxiety) are not part of the therapeutic dialogue, because they would not be helpful to either the patient or the process (Edelson, 1984, pp. 136–137). Edelson further argues that what clinicans focus on, and what both patients and therapists find most helpful therapeutically are unexpected, highly specific, circumstantial details that neither the patient nor analyst had known or thought of before.

Marie Cardinal's autobiographical novel, *The Words to Say It* (1983), which is based on her own seven-year analysis, provides striking illustrations of such details. Cardinal began her analysis after escaping from a mental hospital. She suffered from overwhelming anxiety attacks, belief that she was insane, and unremitting menorrhagia. Her narrative description of the analytic experience contains scenes within scenes, and stories within stories: for example, the story her mother told her of hating and blaming the patient's father so bitterly for the death of a previous daughter that she attempted unsuccessfully to abort the patient. Robert Rogers (1988) summarizes the following illustrative anecdote, with its wealth of suggestive, idiosyncratic details, from her analysis:

> "Tube." What does "tube" make you think of, asks the doctor. This image leads to the recovery of the story of a very little girl trying to go peepee in a railway-train lavatory. "I looked between my legs and saw the bottom of a shallow bowl, at the end of a large round shiny pipe with its nasty contents, the ground with its surface of crushed stone speeding dizzily away. I was afraid, afraid. I was afraid of being sucked into this hole, possessed by my own peepee, and after being shoved through the disgusting tube full of excrement, shattered on the brightly lit tracks" (p. 150). This episode, which reflects numerous problems the patient experiences with regard to the orifices and contents of her body, leads eventually to another memory from the same early period involving a violent physical attack on her father as he playfully films his tiny daughter trying to go peepee outdoors on a subsequent occasion, a scene in which the clicking of the movie camera apparently triggers the child's recollection of the clickety-click of the railway train [pp. 162–163].

Bion's (1962) concept of the "selected fact" (after Poincaré) also stresses the importance of unanticipated findings which give new meaning and order to previously unexplained data.[37]

With respect to Grünbaum's persistent critique that the patient is under the therapist's intimidating influence, and that the therapist "coaches, coaxes, persuades, prompts, prods, browbeats, and brainwashes" patients to accept his or her theories, Wallace (1986) observes:

> Grünbaum's argument endows the analyst with an extraordinary epistemological power and the analysand with an equally remarkable capacity for submission. Are patients passive receptacles, ready to receive any and all nonsense that the analyst is willing to pour into them? Or do they have minds of their own, minds capable of rational and critical operations, and minds filled, moreover, with all manner of resistance and capacity for negative transference? [p. 382].

The Post Hoc Fallacy in Retrospective Causal Claims

Grünbaum (1984, pp. 177–189, 251–256; 1993, pp. 311–342) argues that the interpreter's suggestions and the patient's compliance make the accuracy of early memories questionable; and even if one could confirm the occurrence of an infantile trauma, such confirmation would not establish a *causal* role of the trauma in producing a neurosis. Such an inference would constitute a post hoc fallacy. Grünbaum concludes that the therapeutic setting does not provide supportive evidence for the postdiction that a particular childhood experience even occurred during infancy. Rather than relying on retrospective clinical case studies, therefore, Grünbaum proposes that long-term prospective investigations employing control groups are needed to test theories of pathogenesis: "data from the couch *acquire* probative significance when they are independently corroborated by extraclinical findings, or inductively concur with such findings by pointing to the same hypothesis" (Grünbaum, 1993, p. 342; see also Erwin, 1993, pp. 436–442).

Freud (1920b, pp. 167–168) recognized that attempting to specify the relative importance of multiple causal factors is very difficult, so that often no inference is possible until the outcome is known. Frequently, therefore, only post hoc inferences can be made. Our retrospective approach to interpretation has circularity built into it, so the relative strengths of causal factors cannot be measured adequately (Wallerstein and Sampson, 1971). This problem is not confined to psychoanalysis and dynamic psychotherapy, or to other types of clinical studies, however, but is a general problem affecting even the simplest of investigative problems (Macmillan, 1991, p. 568; see also Danziger, 1985).

Grünbaum's critique is most telling, therefore, with respect to genetic formulations of causal links between childhood experiences and adult psychopathology. As Wallace (1989) observes: "The skeptic can still maintain that, at best, we only uncover regularities between *present fantasies* about the past and adult psychological structures" (p. 518; see also pp. 502–503, 514–525). Wallace suggests, however, that Grünbaum's arguments against the intraclinical testing of genetic hypotheses can be rebutted indirectly. He points out that clinicians focus primarily on dynamic relations, that is, on currently operating mental activities. The therapist deals with history as it is represented in the patient's present life: current thoughts, feelings, fantasies, and actions are viewed as traces of prior events. From that perspective, it would be arbitrary to divide the genetic and the dynamic, since each involves the other (Wallace, 1989b, pp. 515–517).

Edelson (1984, pp. 59–76; 1988, pp. 309–364) presents detailed arguments against Grünbaum's charge that psychoanalysis commits post hoc fallacies in its retrospective causal claims. Edelson's counterarguments emphasize the value of single subject research designs, not only heuristically but also in the context of justification. He stresses the variety of forms that single case research designs can take, some being well-suited to the justification of interpretations (1984, pp. 60–61). Edelson acknowledges, however, that although statements of remote etiology are part of psychoanalytic theory, case studies provide stronger evidence for "constitutive" explanations based upon current and recent events, than for pathology having remote causes. Examples of the former type of explanation include formulations of current symptoms expressing or caused by currently active conflicts; and current responses of the patient to recent etiologic events such as an interpretation during the preceding therapy session (Edelson, 1986b, p. 111). (Grünbaum's responses to Edelson's arguments appear in Chapter 6, pp. 229–255, of his 1993 monograph.)

Along similar lines, Thomä and Kächele (1975, pp. 86–87) argue that interpretations applied to a single case, including genetic interpretations and reconstructions, become theoretical statements with respect to that case. Specific predictions can be derived from such theoretical statements regarding causal conditions that must be resolved in order to produce therapeutic change. A decrease in the specified internal causal conditions—for example, pathogenic dispositions such as unconscious fantasies—can be assessed in relation to therapeutic changes in symptoms and behavior.

Arguments Against the Repression Theory of Neurosis

The causal-explanatory importance of unconscious mental activity in Freud's theories rests upon two crucial inductive inferences: that repression of traumatic experiences plays a decisive role in symptom formation; and that lifting of pertinent repressions produces therapeutic improvement. To counter the alternative hypothesis of placebo effects, Breuer and Freud (1893–1895) emphasized that each symptom was removed separately by lifting pertinent repressions individually.

Grünbaum (1984, pp. 177–189) presents the following arguments against the postulated repression etiology of neuroses: (1) separate removal of individual symptoms does not rule out a placebo effect; (2) Breuer and Freud did not offer cogent evidence for the *initiation* of pathogenesis by repression; (3) failure to achieve lasting remissions weakened the therapeutic claim of lifting repressions; and (4) Freud's (1925c, p. 27) subsequent recognition that the patient's relationship to the therapist was a more potent causal factor than the entire cathartic process further weakened the postulated etiologic role of repression. Grünbaum (1993) thus concludes that "Even if the patient's clinical responses *could* be taken at face value as epistemologically uncontaminated, the moral of several chapters in this monograph would remain: Freud's principal clinical arguments for his cornerstone theory of repression are fundamentally flawed" (p. 323).

Grünbaum's critique of repression as a major causal factor in neurosogenesis bears only indirectly on the question of interpretive probity, so debate about this part of his critique is reviewed only briefly. Some writers note that Grünbaum views psychoanalytic theory inappropriately as a single, coherent theory; thus he assumes that if repression were invalidated the entire theoretical structure would collapse (see, for example, Kline, 1986, pp. 245–246). Psychoanalysis, however, is actually a loose collection—or, as Kaplan (1964) calls it, a "loosely concatenated set"—of theories. Strenger (1991) notes that "Psychoanalysis has become the most complex theory of twentieth century psychology, covering an enormous scope. At present it is impossible to isolate single etiological hypotheses from this body of thought without distorting its nature" (p. 17).

Furthermore, according to Edelson (1984, p. 151), psychoanalysis does not consider repression to be the pathogen. Intrapsychic conflict, along with a variety of defenses, only one of which may be repression, is viewed as pathogenic. Grünbaum may err, therefore, when he implies that the psychoanalyst justifies his inferences from free association by appealing to the causal role of repression in neurosis (Edelson, 1984, p. 134).

Grünbaum's focus on Freud's earliest formulations, which postulated that repression of traumatic events caused neuroses, may account for his skeptical view of repression (Wachtel, 1986, pp. 263–264; Levin, 1978). His emphasis on evaluating psychoanalysis in terms of etiology and pathogenicity also applies mainly to the earlier stages of psychoanalytic theory, and thus may not do justice to the theories of conflict and compromise formation. Grünbaum realizes, however, that psychoanalysis has changed since the 1890's, and he argues cogently that what matters is the structure of its hypotheses rather than their changing content; but Strenger (1991, pp. 16–17) points out that the structure as well as the content of psychoanalytic theory has changed over the years, from a set of etiological hypotheses to a theory of human nature in general (see also Wollheim, 1993a,b). Yet the vague and overextended conceptualization of psychoanalysis as a general theory of human nature is also debatable (see, for example, Eagle's [1993, pp. 392–404] critique of Strenger's view; and Edelson, 1988, p. xxii).

In fairness to Grünbaum, it should be noted that his emphasis on the repression theory of neurosis comes straight from Freud (1914a), who insisted that repression is the "cornerstone" of psychoanalysis and that, "the theory of repression is a product of psychoanalytic work, a theoretical inference legitimately drawn from innumerable observations" (pp. 16–17). Moreover, like Freud, Grünbaum's (1993) use of the term "repression etiology" includes the concepts of traumatic memories, psychic conflicts, and compromise formations. And Grünbaum has been at pains to emphasize that "According to Freud's etiologies and principle of 'causal overdetermination,' repression is only a *necessary* rather than both a necessary and sufficient condition for neurosogenesis" (p. 22; see also 1984, pp. 109–110).

Grünbaum (1984) does not say that repression is nonexistent. What he points out is "the momentous epistemologic gap between attesting to the bare *occurrence* of repression, and providing cogent support for its alleged role in neurosogenesis, etc." (p. 188). If future research indicates that Freud overestimated and then clung adamantly to his early theory of repression, we have only to remind ourselves that scientists too are fallible and susceptible to confirmation bias, just as nonscientists are.[38]

Grünbaum (1984), in fact, may be more open-minded on this question than we are: he acknowledges, for example, that "the psychoanalytic method equips its practitioners with a *heuristically* fecund basis for propounding hypotheses, especially in a soaring mind like Freud's" (p. 189). And he states further that although he questions the logical credentials of Freud's repression etiology of neurosis, "Yet I emphatically *allow* for a weighty possibility: Future *extra*clinical evidence (e.g., epidemiologic or experimental findings) *may* turn out to reveal after all that Freud's brilliant intellectual imagination was quite serendipitous for psychopathology and other facets of human conduct" (Grünbaum, 1984, p. 189).

Unjustified Extrapolation of the Questionable Repression Theory to Explain Slips and Dreams

Grünbaum (1984, pp. 190–239) argues that a "thematic relation" between a slip and the postulated content of a repressed wish does not constitute evidence of a *causal* connection between the two, because some kind of thematic relation can be found between any slip and a posited repression. With respect to dreams, Grünbaum argues that Freud's "Specimen Dream" of Irma's injection (1900, p. 96–121) does not support his method of dream interpretation, nor his hypothesis that repressed infantile wishes cause dreams. Grünbaum concludes (1993, pp. 357–382) that Freud's theory of dreams is ill founded, and may in fact be false. Like his arguments against the repression etiology of neuroses, which were discussed in the preceding section of this chapter, this part of Grünbaum's critique is only indirectly relevant to interpretive probity, so debate about this issue is omitted.

Misconceived Attempts to Reformulate Psychoanalysis as a Hermeneutic Discipline

Grünbaum (1984) reserves some of his most caustic criticism for the neglect of causal attributions in psychoanalysis by hermeneutic writers, which he considers "a nihilistic, if not frivolous, trivialization of Freud's entire clinical theory" (p. 58; also pp. 1–95; 1993, pp. 8–19). He argues that acausal hermeneutics would "eviscerate" the causal-scientific core of psychoanalysis; and, paradoxically, that the hermeneutic quest for hidden meanings cannot succeed without methods of causal inquiry (1984, p. 53).

Turning to the debate about Grünbaum's critique of hermeneutics, Phillips (1987) is critical of Grünbaum's views on meaning and causality: that is, one can interpret symptomatic behavior as the effect of multiple causes, but also as "a center of meaning that radiates out in all directions and expresses every dimension of personality, id ego, and superego. Interpretation of the symptom may be less the search for multiple causes than the unraveling of a complex network of meanings" (p. 622; see also pp. 618–622).

Phillips (1991, p. 406) describes a reformulation of hermeneutics stimulated by recent developments in the philosophy of science, and by the increasing number of competing theories in psychoanalysis. Hermeneutics has become a way of dealing with incommensurable discourses in any field. This view of hermeneutics recognizes that although complete epistemological consensus is not possible, clinicians and investigators can seek as much agreement as does exist (see also Steiner, 1995, p. 436).

Roy Schafer is the most articulate spokesperson for the hermeneutic construal of psychoanalysis and clinical interpretation (see, for example, 1970, 1975, 1979, 1983a, 1985a,b, 1987). Although he does not address the Grünbaum critiques directly, a great deal of his writing is relevant to that debate. Schafer asserts, for example, that the entire project of clinical interpretive inquiry is "hermeneutically conceived and executed" (1983a, p. 191); and he objects to narrow, positivist-like conceptions of what is involved in interpretive work—that is, views which are not sufficiently complex, but are only rudimentary, oversimplified notions of what interpretation is (in Panel, 1983, p. 244). He stresses particularly the need to avoid either-or thinking in relation to interpretation (1983a, pp. 7–8).

Grünbaum's assumption that, unlike science, hermeneutics is not interested in the validation of interpretations and theories is an example of either-or thinking; for in fact hermeneutics is divided on the issue of interpretive methodology and validation (see Palmer, 1969, p. 65). Modell (1978a), Strenger (1991), and Bouchard (1995) view the opposition of science and hermeneutics as the central dilemma of psychoanalytic knowledge. A number of influential hermeneuticists[39] agree with Palmer's conclusion that "there is room for a hermeneutics oriented to method and validity, as well as for a hermeneutics focused on the historicality of understanding" (1969, p. 66).

Carlo Strenger (1991) takes a middle position between hermeneutic and scientific conceptions of psychoanalysis, that is, psychoanalysis and clinical interpretation encompass both. A purely hermeneutic conception is inadequate because of its singular focus on internal evidence (mainly coherence). At the same time, interpretive inquiry is central to psychoanalytic science because it has generated most of the concepts and theories of the Freudian system (the heuristic function of clinical interpretation). The assessment of psychoanalysis should not be based exclusively on interpretation, however, but must rely also on extraclinical research which, Strenger maintains (1991, p. 197), already exists to a much greater extent than Grünbaum acknowledges. Bowlby's work (1969, 1973, 1980), for example, utilizes both clinical and extraclinical (ethologic) data (see also Rogers, 1991). To what extent extraclinical research is applicable to low-level inferences and interpretive hypotheses remains a moot question, however.

A hermeneutic conception of psychoanalysis has been used inappropriately by some writers as a defense against the demands of the scientific method, for example, the claim that if psychoanalysis is a hermeneutic discipline it is exempt from the necessity to justify its interpretations and to validate its concepts and theories. Strenger (1991, pp. 40–43) agrees with Grünbaum that narrative coherence is not a sufficient criterion of justification (see also Eagle, 1986b, pp. 231–232). Strenger suggests that hermeneutic confirmation be supplemented by the additional criterion of external coherence: that is, a hypothesis should be consistent with and should cohere with accepted background knowledge in other disciplines (1991, p. 188). Recent research on attachment by Mary Main (1993, p. 240) appears to support Strenger's position; see also Barratt (1976, pp. 462–463). Strenger's view is pluralistic; he assumes that there can be multiple perspectives regarding human nature which need not be reducible to each other. Some constraints are needed, however, to limit the kinds of frameworks which are acceptable. The concept of external coherence attempts to provide such constraints.

Summary

Grünbaum argues persuasively that psychoanalysis is a science, or can be, if pursued within certain constraints. The scientific guidelines that he outlines can be useful to psychoanalysis and dynamic psychotherapy, particularly in interpreting, theorizing about, and attempting to validate causal factors in human personality, development, and psychopathology. Grünbaum reminds us that the burden of proof for our methods and theories rests squarely on our shoulders; that probative evidence supporting our methods and theories is far from satisfactory; and that the search for such evidence is interminable—a never-ending inquiry into unanswered questions and discrepant findings. To improve the science of psychoanalysis, Grünbaum emphasizes the following:

1. Our clinical observations, interpretations, dynamic reasoning, and clinical theories are concerned not only with latent meanings, but also with (motivational) causes. For that reason Grünbaum cautions against adopting an acausal hermeneutic reconstruction of psychoanalytic theory. He recommends use of Mill's methods of controlled inquiry as a scientific approach to justifying interpretations and clinical theories. He suggests also that extraclinical (epidemiologic and experimental) methods will be necessary to validate clinical theories.

2. Unconscious motives are psychological causes and thus are scientifically explanatory. The distinction between reasons and causes, on the other hand, is a false contrast; reasons, too, have causal relevance and are explanatory.

3. There are different types and strengths of causal relations: for example, the differences between necessary and sufficient causes, and the logically weaker and methodologically less demanding relation of "causal relevance."

4. "Meaning relations" or "thematic patterns" in clinical data do not automatically, or by themselves, provide evidence of unconscious causal motives. To establish (in contrast to merely positing) a causal connection based upon thematic relations necessitates an additional measure, such as Mill's method of controlled inquiry, to demonstrate that the postulated causal relationship is not due to chance. Since most such inferences in depth-psychological therapies are only conjectural rather than established, they are best viewed by therapists and conveyed to patients as tentative hypotheses rather than as authoritative statements.

5. At the present stage of scientific development in psychoanalysis and dynamic psychotherapy, our methods and theories are mainly of heuristic value rather than representing validated propositions and procedures. (On the other hand, as Gillett [1990a, p. 295] observes, since it is impossible to measure degree of confirmation precisely on the basis of evidence, there may be no sharp dividing line between the heuristic value of a theory and its validation.) The methodologist Abraham Kaplan (1964) points out that

> at every stage of inquiry the scientist does what he can with the resources available; if it is objected that this thinking makes the acceptance of a particular theory only a temporary expedient, the reply immediately presents itself that all acceptances are only more or less temporary. Truth may be eternal, but science requires no more of a theory than that it be sufficient unto the day [p. 315].

Not everything that Grünbaum writes about psychoanalysis is relevant and applicable to our science: for example, his singular focus on causal-correlational hypotheses and his insistence on use of group-comparison methods to satisfy the canons of eliminative inductivism—methods that are inherently problematic in disciplines such as psychoanalysis and dynamic psychotherapy (Fonagy, 1982, p. 128; Edelson, 1984, p. 65; Grünbaum, 1986, p. 269). The following are some of the principal counterarguments to Grünbaum's critique:

1. It is not entirely clear to what extent Grünbaum's critique applies to interpretive hypotheses in contrast to higher-level clinical theories (see, for example Wollheim, 1993b, p. 105). This aspect of Grünbaum's critique needs clarification.

2. Grünbaum tends to oversimplify some psychoanalytic concepts, particularly regarding changes in the structure of psychoanalytic hypotheses, and the necessity to take such changes into account for purposes of testing clinical theories.

3. Grünbaum overstates the role and problem of suggestion in the interpretive process in his exaggerated descriptions of therapists "coaching, coaxing, persuading, prompting, prodding, browbeating, and brainwashing" patients. His arguments regarding therapists' suggestions and patients' compliance must be considered, however, in relation to subtle, unrecognized, and unresolved undercurrents of suggestibility.

4. Grünbaum's critique of drawing causal inferences from meaning relations is one of the most original and thought provoking of his arguments, but one that calls for further consideration and investigation, not foreclosure. His conception of the relationship between latent meanings and motivational causes is not entirely clear; some of the counterarguments to Grünbaum's views in this regard suggest much closer relations between causes and meanings than Grünbaum describes (for example, McGinn, 1989; Hopkins, 1992; Marks, 1992; Fodor, 1993). On the whole, therapists are more latent-meaning oriented than determinant oriented. It is possible that an increased investigative focus on causal factors in patients' symptoms, dreams, free associations, fantasies, and slips would further the development of depth-psychological science; but whether such a focus would improve our interpretive methodology and facilitate the therapeutic process is another question (see, for example, Whitehorn, 1947).

5. Grünbaum's emphasis on the tally argument overestimates Freud's dependence upon and commitment to that justifying criterion. Paradoxically, however, the observation of patients' responses to interventions, which is the central feature of the tally argument, is still one of the most widely used, though not very probative, methods of attempting to validate interpretations. (This issue is discussed further in Chapter 8.)

6. Grünbaum's conclusion regarding the weakness of Freud's consilience argument is one of the least convincing of his critiques. The keystone of his argument is the suggestibility issue. Remove it and there is no reason, by Grünbaum's own standards, that consilience of inductions cannot be used to cross-validate clinical interpretations (Wallace, 1986, p. 382).

7. Grünbaum's unsparing critique of hermeneutics tendentiously supports his focus on causal relations; but it is difficult to

understand why he impugns hermeneutics so totally—an approach that has contributed much to scholarly work in many fields, and currently is recognized increasingly by some philosophers (for example, Toulmin, 1982; Mitchell and Rosen, 1983; Hiley et al., 1991). His strategy in mounting such an uncompromising critique may be to cut off any retreat to a hermeneutic position that would exempt psychoanalysis from empirical accountability (Eagle, 1986a, p. 84). His categorical rejection of hermeneutics is unnecessary, however; for his argument against a wholesale hermeneutic reformulation of psychoanalysis and clinical interpretation can be made effectively without attempting to discredit the entire hermeneutic enterprise. Edelson (1986b), for example, integrates the causal orientation of the natural sciences with the pattern model approach, producing a "causal pattern model paradigm." Strenger (1991) situates psychoanalysis and interpretive inquiry epistemologically between science and hermeneutics. Gill (1991, 1994b), Marks (1992), and Brook (1995b, p. 519) conceive of psychoanalysis as a "hermeneutic science"—hermeneutic in that it interprets meanings, and scientific because the meaning relations which it interprets may involve causal connections as well.

8. Finally, despite the severity of Grünbaum's critiques, one should not overlook the implicit positive message in his writings, namely, that the scientific methodologies of psychoanalysis, dynamic psychotherapy, and clinical interpretation can be better; they are improvable (compare Diesing, 1985b, p. 555).

8

Justification of Interpretations

Evaluation of Individual Methods

Roland Dalbiez, a French philosopher of science and relatively friendly critic of psychoanalysis, observed over half a century ago that "Freud and his disciples acted as though they had no conception of the meaning of the word proof. There, without doubt, is the greatest weakness of psychoanalysis" (1941, Vol. 1, p. ix). Schmidl (1959, p. 129; see also Kaplan, 1981) noted that Dalbiez's two-volume treatise had virtually no effect on psychoanalytic thinking; and Holzman (1985, p. 765) warns that this basic methodologic problem has not been solved but, if anything, has grown worse—that the failure to develop and use justifying procedures is destroying the science of psychoanalysis. Dalbiez's observation and Holzman's warning are borne out bleakly by Klumpner's (1989) study of sixty frequently cited papers in the psychoanalytic literature, none of which offered direct evidence for the claims being made.

Freud claimed scientific status for psychoanalysis because its explanatory concepts are naturalistic, materialistic, and deterministic, and because it makes proper use of the inductive method. Even during Freud's lifetime, however, when positivism was the reigning theory of science, psychoanalysis did not meet its demands for replicability, objectification, and validation. Freud (1933, p. 12) also defended clinical interpretation, insisting that analysts do not misuse the method to interpret into a patient's associations what they are unable to construe from them. Lothane (1985) points out, however:

> This is the perennial problem of interpretation. How do we know whether we are interpreting from or into? Are we not dignifying the analyst's thoughts, the *analyst's* associations, by the pretentious title of interpretations? How do we know whether patients are alluding to the analyst or talking about themselves? We do not know for sure. But if interpreting is nothing more than entertaining options, it is of service in making further discoveries, subject to the judgment of history. The danger lies in claiming premature validity for interpretations [p. 199].

One of the basic reasons that systematic methods of justifying interpretations are essential scientifically is because interpretations are the first-level inferences, the lowest level of theoretical statements of psychoanalysis and dynamic psychotherapy; and as such they are the only propositions that can be tested by direct empirical evidence, that is, evidence from the case being studied. Higher level theories are tested in other ways. The evidential base of clinical interpretations is a major source of controversy in debates about the scientific status of psychoanalysis (Wolman, 1964, 1984). Without generally accepted criteria of evidence for interpretations, every clinical finding and scientific claim of psychoanalysis and dynamic psychotherapy must be questioned (Peterfreund, 1985, p. 130; see also 1971, p. 335; 1990).

Problems of Clinical Evidence

Evidence consists of the empirical data and logical arguments that support a conclusion. Logical arguments offered as evidence may be inductive, deductive, or both. The best arguments for clinical inferences are nonexperimental and include: (1) arguments by analogy; (2) consilience, that is, inductions from different data converging upon the same conclusion; and (3) abduction, or argument to the best explanation (Edelson, 1991, p. 105; see also Cheshire, 1975, regarding arguments by analogy). Evidence need not be manifest, but may be symbolic; and evidence applies not only to the number of data accounted for but also to their "oddness" or "improbability" (the latter criterion of evidence is further discussed later in connection with Bayesian theory and inference). In a similar vein, hermeneuticists emphasize that relevance of the data accounted for is as important as quantity (Hirsch, 1967, pp. 181–182).

The distinction between evidence and proof is a matter of degree: proof implies convincing support of a proposition. The goal of clinical justification, however, is not merely to confirm or disconfirm a particular hypothesis, but to provide objectively grounded discriminations between alternative interpretations, that is, to demonstrate that a specific interpretation is not only plausible but the most plausible among the various interpretive hypotheses considered. Thus the aim of justification goes beyond "choosing a winner" among competing hypotheses; it attempts to draw objective conclusions about their relative probabilities (Hirsch, 1967, pp. 181–182; see also Waelder, 1960, p. 4).

Problems of clinical evidence are numerous and daunting. Much of the clinical evidence generated by the therapeutic process is "private," that is, not directly observable. The patient cannot report completely and the therapist cannot directly observe the patient's inner experience (Meissner, 1966). To surmount the disjunction between observable and nonobservable evidence, psychoanalysis combines three of its basic methodologic concepts—the unconscious, determinism, and meaning—to postulate *latent* meanings and determinants that are common to both observable and nonobservable types of evidence, thus uniting them as a single coherent theme (Rapaport, 1944). Like any theoretical statement, the posited latent theme attempts to account for as many (and as relevant) clinical data as possible (see Erikson, 1958, for a prototypical example).

The preceding problem is compounded by another difficulty, however: we cannot demonstrate the latent meanings and determinants that unify observational and nonobservational evidence in any simple, direct, empirical way. Both the discovery and justification of latent contents depend upon the identification of subtle, often analogical relations within the data, rather than on observable objects and events. Clinical findings of that kind require interpretation rather than simple observation of empirical data; and as Gergen (1988, p. 34) observes, the anchor point for interpretations is not strictly empirical, but depends on a network of interdependent and continuously modifiable interpretations (see also Connolly and Keutner, 1988, p. 53; Specht, 1988, p. 166).

Thus, there is no satisfactory way of interpreting a segment of clinical data in isolation from the contexts (including other interpretations) that precede and follow it; or, as Edelson (1988, p. 296) puts it, since hypotheses are underdetermined by data, no single set of observables can decide whether a particular hypothesis is correct. In addition, the adjacent contexts themselves must be interpreted. Consequently, to understand and justify a specific latent content, one must evaluate an ever-unfolding context of interpreted events. The latter problem is the methodologic basis and rationale of Freud's insistence that full interpretation of any clinical fragment must await completion of the whole analysis (1937b, p. 265).

Additional problems of clinical evidence arise from the fact that patients' associations are not entirely free and self-generated, but are influenced to a variable extent by the therapist (see, for example, Diesing, 1985b). Still another problem concerns our reliance on relations and patterns in clinical data, which can lead to "soft pattern matches" that may not derive from the patient's inner mental states (Spence, 1976, p. 375). Since meanings differ depending upon context, and because the number of possible contexts is unlimited, we often find ourselves confronted with a bewildering array of alternative interpretations (Spence, 1982a, p. 268). Thus, Wallerstein (1992) concludes "the clinical context, by itself, will never determine which interpretation within which theoretical framework is closest to the mark" (p. 48).

The irreducible subjectivity of interpretive work introduces further problems of inference and evidence (Erikson, 1964, pp. 52–53; Friedman, 1988, p. 458). The therapist's assumptions, values, and perceptions are crucial data that may contribute significantly to interpretive conclusions. Ideally, Renik (1994, p. 1249) observes, reports of interventions need to be what the philosophical tradition referred to as "*pensées pensées*," that is, communications that reveal how the thinker arrived at them (see also O'Shaughnessy, 1994).

Clinical evidence is compromised still further by the fact that intraclinical justification of interpretations utilizes the same pool of clinical data (the therapeutic process of an individual patient), which gave rise to the therapist's interpretive hypotheses in the first place—a potentially circular, self-confirming process. Because of the latter problem, clinical interpretation is in danger of endlessly rediscovering and reconfirming its own basic methodologic concepts. The problem of circularity is not confined to the justification of interpretations, however, but applies to scientific reasoning generally (Rapaport, 1967, p. 172; Danziger, 1985; see also Hirsch, 1967, pp. 166–167, for a related problem associated with the "hermeneutic circle").

Another major limitation of interpretive justification is that one's methods of testing are necessarily paradigm specific, that is, they apply only to the data and interpretations generated by a specific conceptual system of psychoanalysis or dynamic psychotherapy. Some of the individual principles, strategies, and methods of a particular school might be applicable to other systems of clinical interpretation; but in the final analysis the methodologies of interpretive justification employed by different schools must derive from the specific principles, perspectives, and varieties of data on which interpretations in each such conceptual system are based. Diesing (1985a) writes that we

> must understand a hypothesis in the context of its own conceptual framework to devise an adequate test for it. If we interpret it according to our own (different) way of thinking we change its meaning, distort it, and thus test a caricature [p. 82].[1]

Finally, the instrumental (transforming, therapeutic) function of interpretations also compromises their propositional (hypothesis-stating, declarative) function—which interferes, in turn, with determining the truth value of interpretations. Freud (1909a) referred to this problem in the case of Little Hans, whose

> attention had to be turned in the direction for which his father was expecting something to come. This detracts from the evidential value of the analysis; but the procedure is the same in every case. For a psychoanalysis is not an impartial scientific investigation, but a therapeutic measure. Its essence is not to prove anything but merely to alter something [p. 104].

Considering the numerous and serious problems of clinical evidence described previously, it is small wonder that clinical interpretations are error-prone, uncertain, and a major source of disagreements among clinicians (see, for example, Stoller and Geertsma, 1963). Schmidl (1955) was so discouraged by these difficulties that he questioned whether attempting to justify interpretations would be worth the effort. In spite of such problems, however, a number of investigators, methodologists, and philosophers of science believe that clinical interpretations are potentially testable.[2] Discussing the occurrence of certain themes and predictable covariations in clinical data, Meehl (1970/1973) writes: "There are many such clusterings which could in principle be subjected to statistical tests, and my expectation is that, if performed, they would provide rather dramatic support for many of Freud's first-level inferences, and pretty clear refutation of others" (1973, p. 110). Meehl's use of the term "sunport" rather than "proof" is noteworthy, because the postpositivist perspective is less concerned with whether a statement is true or false than with its degree of plausibility, or likelihood of being correct. Thus, interpretive hypotheses are not "proven," but may be more or less "supported" by the evidence (Bell and Staines, 1981, pp. 16–17).

The aforementioned (and other) problems of clinical evidence raise the following basic methodologic questions about the justification of interpretations:

1. Must interpretations really be justified?
2. Can interpretations be justified?
3. Can interpretations be justified intraclinically?
4. What specific methods of justifying interpretations are available?
5. How do the various methods compare with respect to probity?

Must Interpretations Be Justified?

Other than observations, interpretations are the lowest-level, least-generalized scientific statements of psychoanalysis and dynamic psychotherapy. The term "lowest-level" does not necessarily imply a single inference, however; every level of inference can and often does involve a series of inferential steps (Reichenbach, 1951, pp. 240–248; Kaplan, 1964). Interpretive hypotheses are idiographic, applying only to the patient about whom they are constructed. Higher-level theoretical propositions can be thought of as metainterpretations, "interpretations of interpretations," which apply to many or all patients. Epistemologically, interpretations stand midway between observations and higher-level theories, which raises the question: since interpretations are so close to observation, must they really be justified? Is their confirmation or disconfirmation scientifically necessary?

The answer, of course, is yes. Interpretations sometimes appear to be, but never are, purely descriptive and atheoretical.

Similarly, phenomenologic and psychophysiologic studies of perception have demonstrated that not only inferences but observations themselves are theory, method, and perspective bound.[3] Gadamer (1975) notes that to have a method is already to have an interpretation. That is, investigators choose their methods on the basis of already existing interpretations and theories (Faulkoner and Williams, 1985; Meichenbaum, 1988, p. 118). Gardner (1983) writes:

> We find what we are looking for. Of course. All we perceive, all we register, all we recall, all we think, all we imagine, all we feel, all we do, is shaped by what we are looking for [p. 44].

Since subjective bias is inescapable, a major function of scientific methodology is an attempt to objectify observation, inference, and evidence as much as possible. To an interpreter, for example, a construction often seems inevitable, whereas in fact it never is. Hirsch (1967) comments: "Interpretations have a propensity that Pope observed in 18th century watches: none goes just alike, yet each interpreter believes his own" (pp. 166–167).[4]

Elsewhere (Rubovits-Seitz, 1992a) I have reviewed some of the major methodologic problems and limitations that make clinical interpretations fallible and necessitate the use of error-detecting, -correcting, and -justifying procedures. These problems include, among others, reductive selection of data and methods, limitations of interpretive reliability (the consensus problem), and the inherent uncertainty of constructions. Not only interpretive methods but interpreters themselves are fallible, due to cognitive limitations, countertransference distortions, and susceptibility to confirmation bias. Because of the latter problem, for example, a clinician may become overcommitted to an initial construction, fail to question its correctness, become intent upon confirming it, and ignore disconfirming data (see also Rothstein, 1980).

A number of writers representing a variety of viewpoints including hermeneutics, narratology, and radical constructivism, have argued against both the necessity and the possibility of justifying interpretations.[5] They argue that interpretations provide mainly a useful "perspective" on the patient's unconscious and past, and represent a form of myth-making with a therapeutic purpose (for cogent critiques of this view, see Sass and Woolfolk

[1988]; and Nissim-Sabat's [1990, pp. 152–161] critical philosophical review of Spence's [1987] argument for randomness rather than strict determinism in clinical data). Related viewpoints maintain that interpretations are merely "semantic" rather than "propositional" statements, and as such cannot be designated as true or false (Levy, 1963); that interpretations are less concerned with truth than with altering the meaning of the patient's experiences (Gedo, 1979; Cheshire, 1975); and that rather than focusing on the veridicality of constructions therapists are concerned with whether a communicated interpretation stimulates new material and furthers the therapeutic process (Michels, 1983; Reed, 1995, p. 736).

Eagle (1980a, p. 412) raises the question, however, whether and how such "perspectives" differ from giving patients suggestions. An answer frequently heard is that the various perspectives provided by different schools of psychoanalysis offer "multiple aspects of a single complex truth." If the justification of interpretations is ignored, however, then therapeutic effectiveness becomes the empirical claim that must be justified; and there is no evidence that any one perspective, or combination of perspectives, produces better results than others.

Eagle argues further that both outside and certainly inside of the therapy situation, people seek the truth about themselves; and the vast majority of therapists believe that their interpretations are veridical (1980a, p. 421). Thus the search for self-knowledge, "is not a mere chimera, but involves the identification of real entities" (p. 422). Eagle concludes that although Freud may have been wrong about interpretations tallying with what is real in patients, his belief in its importance is more consistent with the basic values underlying psychoanalysis, particularly the value of self-knowledge, than are the recent "perspectival" approaches (1980a, p. 423).[6] Boesky (1990, p. 577) suggests that the patient may benefit not only from the correctness of interpretations but also from the process of mutual, partly successful and partly unsuccessful attempts to understand.

Finally, there is also a very practical reason why interpretations need to be justified. Clinicians must choose between alternative hypotheses, each involving a mixture of epistemic support and liabilities. Making such choices is as indispensable in scientific (including interpretive) work as in everyday life, because of the likelihood that certain choices are better (more plausible, promising, and productive) than others.

Can Interpretations Be Justified?

The philosopher of science W. C. Salmon (1959) concluded long ago that it is possible in principle to state the kinds of evidence that would or would not support psychoanalytic propositions. Another philosopher of psychoanalysis, Michael Sherwood (1969, p. 257), stated more emphatically that his analysis would definitely allow for testing and evaluation (see Eagle, 1973a, for an evaluation of Sherwood's views). Edelson (1977) agrees with Sherwood that the problem is not an inherent inability to test psychoanalytic postulates but their vagueness. In an extended discussion of whether and how interpretations can be justified, Thomä and Kächele (1975) combine the viewpoints of several philosophers,[7] and conclude that clinical interpretations can be justified, though not with the precision or completeness of the physical sciences, and that the principal criterion of justification is change in the patient that can be predicted (within limits).[8]

Whether clinical interpretations can be justified depends also upon when confirmation is undertaken, that is, whether during therapy sessions or after completion of the treatment. Interpretive justification during the treatment of patients is necessarily limited; it consists mainly of attempting to determine the most plausible among alternative constructions at a given time. To that end the therapist checks how much of the data a construction can account for; modifies the construction so that it accounts for more of the data; and rechecks the revised construction to determine whether it now covers most of the data. If not, the original construction is discarded and replaced by a different hypothesis. The process of checking, revising, and rechecking constructions usually generates several promising modified hypotheses. The final step is comparison of these revised alternative hypotheses (De Groot, 1969, pp. 55–56; Edelson, 1988, pp. 99–101)—the principal selection criterion at this phase of justification being internal evidence, that is, which of the alternative hypotheses accounts most consistently, coherently, and comprehensively for the largest number of data.

The foregoing series of justifying operations during therapy sessions is grounded methodologically in three principles of confirmation employed in the human and social sciences: comparison of alternative hypotheses; tests of competing hypotheses against all of the data; and use of disconfirming tests (De Groot, 1969, pp. 309–327; Polkinghorne, 1983, pp. 245–246, 256–257). In the series of operations described above, each revised construction constitutes an alternative hypothesis; competing hypotheses are tested against all of the current data (see, for example, Eissler, 1959; Gedo, 1986); and each discarded construction represents a disconfirmed hypothesis. This is as far as the justifying process usually goes during actual therapeutic work with patients.

The preceding description of partial interpretive justification during therapy sessions has a number of parallels with Hirsch's (1967) hermeneutic method of attempting to justify literary interpretations. It has some features in common also with the "analysis-by-synthesis" model of human perception (see, for example, Neisser, 1967; Dennett, 1991, pp. 12, 134–135). That is, human vision is not just data driven, but shifts rapidly back and forth between centrally generated expectations, on the one hand, and confirmations or disconfirmations based on incoming stimuli, on the other. The continual alternations by clinical interpreters between constructive and checking-revising-rechecking activities are similar to both Hirsch's hermeneutics and the analysis-by-synthesis model of perception: all three activities involve rapid "generate-and-test cycles."

More definitive justification of clinical interpretations requires additional, posttherapeutic investigation based on a record of the entire (completed) therapeutic process, which the therapist or clinical investigator can study retrospectively and systematically in as much detail as necessary. The latter, more extended and detailed justifying process can employ multiple, increasingly exacting justifying procedures, including microanalytic methods of studying the clinical data in the service of justifying interpretations (discussed and illustrated further in this and the following chapters).

Can Interpretations Be Justified Intraclinically?

One of the most controversial questions regarding the justification of interpretations is whether interpretive hypotheses can be justified by intraclinical methods, employing data from the same therapeutic process, or whether extraclinical testing is necessary. Many or perhaps most psychoanalysts, including Freud (1915–1917), have assumed that the only place to test psychoanalytic propositions is within the analytic situation, because no other clinical or experimental setting adequately replicates the subtleties, complexities, and specific dynamic features of the therapeutic relationship and process.[9] To illustrate this methodologic problem in a related field, use of simulated tasks to investigate decision-making have revealed very limited external validity (Elstein, 1988). Shapiro (1978), however, is more optimistic about extraclinical testing of psychoanalytic propositions; he concludes that each such method has its own unique yield and significance.

Some critics of psychoanalysis scoff at the idea that our theories (including interpretations) can be tested objectively within the therapeutic situation (for example, Popper, 1963; Eysenck, 1965; Grünbaum, 1984, 1993). Aside from the controversial issue of suggestibility, however, the actual extent of which is not known, there is another reason why clinical theories (in contrast to lower-level interpretive hypotheses) cannot be tested "on the couch." The hierarchical system of validation employed in case study methodologies stipulates that only the lowest-level theoretical statements, interpretations, can be justified by direct empirical evidence—that is, by clinical data of the case being studied (Diesing, 1971). Higher-level clinical theories are validated by a variety of other, including extraclinical, methods. From this standpoint, the question of whether interpretations can be justified intraclinically must be answered affirmatively; in fact, that is the typical way that interpretations are justified in case study methods.

In addition to the foregoing methodologic rationale of justifying interpretations intraclinically, there is also a compelling practical reason that interpretations are not justified extraclinically, namely, the excessive difficulties of doing so (Meissner, 1982, p. 4). For therapeutic as well as investigative reasons, clinicians need rapid and efficient methods of assessing the relative plausibility of alternative interpretive hypotheses—a "screening" device to rule out quickly those tentative constructions that seem plausible initially but which on further checking are found to have little or no chance of representing the most plausible interpretation at the time.

A further question about the feasibility of intraclinical justification arises from the inherent circularity and self-confirming character of the interpretive process (Hirsch, 1967; Thomä and Kächele, 1975; Meissner, 1982). Circularity refers to the methodologic problem of utilizing the same set of data both to formulate and to validate a hypothesis. Employing the same data for both purposes is self-confirming. A true test attempts to determine whether a hypothesis gains support from new and different data. The question arises, therefore, whether it is feasible methodologically to formulate and justify interpretations using data of the same therapeutic process.

The answer to that important methodologic question depends in part upon what constitutes, or how one defines, "the same data." Does it include only those limited and immediate data on which a construction is based, or does it comprise the data of the entire therapeutic process? If the latter, does "entire therapeutic process" mean all of the data that have been collected up to the time of a particular construction; or does it include all of the data both prior to and following the interpretation?

The construal and formulation of latent contents depend largely (though not completely) on the data of individual therapy sessions. Variable amounts of previous data also contribute to a particular interpretation, for example, data of the immediately preceding sessions, and even earlier data that were especially revealing or contributed to repetitive patterns. Many or most of a therapist's interpretations, however, including some reconstructions, are based largely on relatively circumscribed amounts of clinical data rather than on the total data-base of the therapeutic process (Cheshire, 1975, p. 85). To state this in another way, many data of the therapeutic process are not involved, at least directly, in the discovery phase and formulation of a given interpretation.

The methodologist Adriaan De Groot (1969, pp. 324–327), describes a procedure called "partitioning" of the data which can be used to deal with the problem of circularity (see also Peterfreund, 1983, pp. 205–206). The method involves using one part of the data for the construction of interpretive hypotheses, and another part for hypothesis testing. To illustrate: data from specific sessions upon which an interpretation was based, and earlier data of the therapeutic process which contributed directly to the formulation of an interpretive hypothesis, are excluded from the process of justifying the interpretation. Data that did not contribute directly to the discovery and formulation of a particular hypothesis, and the data of all therapy sessions subsequent to formulation of the hypothesis, may be included in the justifying process.

Another strategy that increases the probity of intraclinical justification is use of a pluralistic approach, that is, employing multiple methods of intraclinical (and sometimes extraclinical) testing of interpretations. The strategy of methodologic pluralism applies to every aspect of the interpretive process, including the justification of interpretations. Postpositivist methodologies characteristically build redundancy into their validity checks as a substitute for the infallibility of individual methods. Diesing (1971, p. 149) writes that every scientific method he has studied includes multiple validity checks, which reduces the need for a single, grand test. Multiple checks reduce errors (Popper, 1959); and two proofs are better than one (Polya, 1945). Thus, a number of writers have proposed pluralistic approaches to make the methodology of justifying clinical interpretations more robust.[10]

Although Freud did not spell out or apply a systematic methodology of justifying interpretations, his basic approach to justification was empirical and pluralistic. He employed all three major theories of truth: correspondence (1933, pp. 170, 176); coherence (1923b, p. 116; 1937b, p. 264); and pragmatic (1915–17, pp. 452–453; 1937b, p. 262). In addition, he proposed multiple methods of empirical testing: (1) internal evidence, mainly coherence, encompassing the vast network of observations and interpretations generated by the entire therapeutic process (1923b, pp. 113, 116; 1937b, p. 265); (2) the patient's (mainly indirect) responses to interpretations, including (a) remission of symptoms (1915–1917; 1937b) and (b) a furthering and deepening of the therapeutic process, leading to clarification and integration of details concerning the patient's life history, personality, and psychopathology (1918, p. 10, 50–52; 1923b, pp. 113, 116; 1937b, p. 262); (3) postdiction (1920b); (4) external validation (1909b; 1937b); (5) similar results in other cases (1922); and (6) cross-validation and convergence of evidence based upon multiple sources and types of data, and use of diverse justifying methods (1923b, pp. 113, 116; 1937b).[11]

Individual Methods of Justifying Interpretations and Their Relative Probity

Psychoanalytic investigators, including Freud, have proposed over a dozen different methods of justifying interpretations. Some of the methods derive in part from the natural sciences, for example, confirmation by observation, prediction, postdiction, external evidence, and quantitative methods. Others have origins in the human and social sciences, for example, various forms of internal evidence such as repetition of themes and patterns, coherence, comprehensiveness, and the patient's responses to an interpretation. The various individual methods of justifying interpretations, in the order of their relative probity, include:

1. Pluralistic methodologies (combinations of the following methods).
2. Cross-validation of independent data samples (from the same treatment).
3. Convergence of evidence (from different validating methods).
4. Organized interlocking microstructures underlying interpretations.
5. "Indirect" postdiction (postdicting classes of antecedent events).
6. "Indirect" prediction (predicting classes of future events).
7. Repetition of themes and patterns.
8. Coherence (internal consistency) and comprehensiveness.
9. The patient's responses to an interpretation.
10. Quantitative methods.
11. External evidence.
12. Justification by observation.
13. Justification by implication.
14. Ruling out the improbable.

In his methodologic treatise on foundations of inference and research in the behavioral sciences, De Groot (1969, pp. 309, 313, 320) notes that "interpretive studies" need not involve the collection of any new data, but usually focus on an existing, closed set of findings (compare the clinical record of a completed case). The investigator attempts to discover relationships within those data, which he or she then subjects to "internal confirmations." De Groot emphasizes the importance of *prestated* justifying criteria, that is, committing oneself to definite confirmation and disconfirmation criteria in advance (1969, pp. 103–105). Doing so reduces the temptation to gloss over or "mold" discrepant findings subsequently; and it subjects the interpretations to a testable prediction that the interpretation will meet the specified justifying criteria. Replication of the justifying tests on additional samples of data demonstrates the predicted outcome repeatedly (cross-validation), providing another of the most probative justifying arguments.

The remainder of this chapter describes and evaluates the various individual methods of justifying clinical interpretations, presented in the order of their relative probity.

Pluralistic Methodologies of Justifying Interpretations

At around the turn of the century, the newly emerging human studies sought to become sciences. One way of achieving that was to draw on the established methods of the natural sciences; another was to make the traditional interpretive methods of those disciplines a scientific procedure. The behavioral sciences adopted the first alternative, the interpretive disciplines the second. Some disciplines including the social sciences, psychoanalysis, and dynamic psychotherapy opted for both alternatives and developed pluralistic methodologies (Seung, 1982a, p. ix). As Meissner (1971) put it: "In developing a method which embraced both objective and subjective data, Freud made of psychoanalysis a scientific hybrid" (p. 305).

Pluralistic methodologies of justifying interpretations follow the heuristics cited above that multiple controls reduce errors, and two proofs are better than one. Edelson (1983), for example, rejects the restrictiveness of traditional validating procedures, preferring less powerful but pluralistic methods of justifying or disconfirming clinical hypotheses. Arlow (1979) proposes a multi-pronged approach to the justification of clinical interpretations:

> Most important is context in which the specific material appears. Contiguity usually suggests dynamic relevance. The configuration of the material, the form and sequence in which the associations appear, represent substantive and interpretable connections. Other criteria are to be seen in the repetition and the convergence of certain themes within the organized body of associations. The repetition of similarities or opposites is always striking and suggestive [p. 203].

Arlow's list of criteria can be paraphrased mnemonically as "The Seven C's of Interpretive Justification": (1) context;

(2) contiguity; (3) configuration; (4) congruence (similarity of content); (5) contrast; (6) convergence; and (7) constancy (repetition of themes).[12]

The more justifying methods one uses, and the more systematically and integratively the various methods are applied and compared, the greater the likelihood of justifying the most plausible interpretation at a given time.[13] Edelson (1984, p. 131) notes that Glymour's (1974, 1980) "pincer-and-bootstrap" strategy of analyzing Freud's (1909a) case report of the Rat Man was based on Kepler's strategy of computing a single theoretical value *by separate routes*. Bruss (1986, p. 151) observes in this connection that by using multiple routes of confirmation, the method becomes a true scientific tool rather than a mere shield against empirical criticism. The batteries of psychological tests employed by clinical psychologists employ a similar heuristic and validating strategy (Little, 1959; Little and Schneidman, 1959, p. 26). By contrast, some therapists focus narrowly on a single preferred criterion rather than employing multiple tests (Michels, 1994, p. 1139); others simply ignore justifying procedures.

Cross-Validation and Convergence of Evidence

Cross-validation compares different samples of data, while convergence compares the results of different justifying methods. Both are referred to as "cross-checking" methods. When different justifying tests are carried out on multiple samples of data, both cross-validation and convergence are involved. Employed together, the two methods comprise a pluralistic approach to the confirmation of interpretations. Labov (1972a) writes, "The value of new data for confirming and interpreting old data is directly proportional to the differences in methods used" (p. 103; see also Chandler et al., 1994).

Malan (1963, p. 269) used cross-checking of qualitative and quantitative methods to test the hypothesis of a correlation between transference interpretations and therapeutic outcome in brief psychotherapy. The results of the two types of tests supported each other. Erikson (1958/1964) noted that the therapist waits to see and compare (cross-validate) further associations; for, "It is, in fact, the gradual establishment of strategic intersections on a number of tangents that eventually makes it possible to locate in the observed phenomena that central core which comprises the 'evidence'" (p. 59). Holt (1978a) writes: "The clinician can and should accomplish something like a cross-validation by dividing the data within the sample available to him" (p. 52). For example, one can collect different kinds of data to verify predictions; and hypotheses based on earlier samples of data can be checked in the course of therapy against later samples.

Barglow et al. (1989) present a cogent example of evidence for clinical interpretations based upon cross-validation and convergence. They studied relations among: (1) clinical reconstructions formulated during the psychoanalysis of a mother; (2) empirical observations of the mother's daughter, made during psychotherapy of the child; and (3) concurrent empirical infant research. The findings from these several sources of data, and from the differing methods of collecting and analyzing the data, converged upon the same conclusion regarding the cause of the child's psychopathology, namely, a form of maternal deprivation. The authors concluded that the "confluence of different sources of evidence, each identified by a different method of investigation, provides one kind of validation for psychoanalytic reconstructions" (1989, p. 401).

Convergence represents a weighing of positive and negative evidence from different methods and sources of data. If the evidence from different methods is contradictory, the investigator is faced with a problem of assessment, because the various methods are not equally weighted with respect to probity: for example, the first half-dozen methods in the present list are much more reliable than the last few tests. If the evidence from the first half-dozen methods were positive, the judgment would be distinctly confirmatory regardless of what the remaining tests indicated. If only one or two of the more reliable indicators were confirmatory, however, the justification of the interpretation would have to be considered equivocal.

Not only do the various methods of confirmation differ in their probity, but also certain types of clinical data tend to be more probative than others. The patient's thoughts, feelings, fantasies, and enactments towards the therapist, that is, data pertaining to the transference, are generally considered the most decisive for purposes of both discovery and justification. As Thomä and Kächele (1975) point out, "At the pivotal point of the transference neurosis, repetition can be observed as nowhere else" (p. 110). Dreams, emotions, urges, impulses, and wishes also rate highly as clinical data, with conscious fantasies, imagery, slips of speech, "lexical leakage" (Spence, 1980a,b; Sharpe, 1940), metaphors, and paraverbal phenomena not far behind in probity. Parallels, contrasts, and contiguities in the clinical data constitute suggestive evidence. Conscious memories and details about everyday events are by no means discounted as clinical data but, taken by themselves, they tend to be somewhat less revealing and probative.

Waelder (1960, pp. 22–25) writes that what we have to do is correct each source of information by comparing data from different sources and cross-checking all of them. For example, we take the data of the patient's self-observation, the data of our own observations in the therapeutic situation, and the observations of others reported by the patient. "We accept none of these sets of data by themselves as necessarily reliable, uncritically, and cross-check each against the others" (1960, p. 23). We find a solution by integrating all of the viewpoints in the eclectic data-base (Waelder, 1960, p. 25).

Demonstration of Organized, Interlocking Microstructures Underlying Interpretations

A convergence of approaches by a hermeneutic scholar, a philosopher of science, and a number of psychoanalytic investigators has led to a promising new approach to the justification of interpretations: the identification of organized, interlocking microstructures underlying interpretations.[14] Michels (1994) notes that in this approach, "validators are closer to the microprocesses than to the macroprocesses of analysis" (p. 1139). Although microstructural analyses are not feasible during the actual treatment of patients, they are well suited to systematic and detailed retrospective investigations employing the record of a completed therapeutic process.

Freud's (1923b, p. 116) jigsaw puzzle model of interpretive justification anticipated the importance of small-scale, microstructural evidence in the justification of interpretations, that is, the complex network of interrelations among individual elements of the clinical data. Freud insisted, for example, that "Our presentation begins to be conclusive only with the intimate detail" (cited in Nunberg and Federn, 1962, p. 172). Cheshire (1975, pp. 156,

178) proposes that an interpretation is most plausible (1) if it integrates phenomena that otherwise would remain isolated and unexplained and (2) by the demonstration of an organized, interlocking microstructure underlying the interpretation. Edelson (1984) states that what is given special weight by both patients and therapists is "the emergence of circumstantial detail having an astonishing degree of specificity and idiosyncratic nuance, in reports of fantasies and interpretations of experience" (pp. 136–137). Edelson adds that, "It is these data that may in the end prove to be the most relevant to the search in the analytic situation for probative evidence providing support for psychoanalytic hypotheses" (1984, p. 137).

Eissler (1959, p. 19) emphasizes similarly that it is the fitting of details into comprehensive contexts that gives probity to our interpretations. And Schafer (1983a, pp. 7–8) notes that clinical interpretation is oriented not only toward increasing complexity, but also toward the greatest degree of particulariy of that which is being explained.

Thomas M. French (see, for example, 1958a, pp. 105–117, 403–405, 411) was a pioneer in the microstructural analysis of the therapeutic process. His discovery of repetitive structures in the form of "Recurrent Dynamic Cycles" pointed the way to a number of contemporary empirical research methods in psychoanalysis, including Luborsky's CCRT approach; Horowitz's configurational analysis; Strupp's cyclical maladaptive patterns; Weiss and Sampson's HMF (Higher Mental Functioning hypothesis); Gill and Hoffman's PERT (Patient's Experience of the Relationship with the Therapist); and Dahl's FRAMES (Fundamental Repetitive and Maladaptive Emotion Structures)—all of which focus on repetitive microstructures in the therapeutic process (Teller and Dahl, 1993, p. 45).[15]

An investigation by Teller and Dahl (1986) illustrates the contemporary method of computer-assisted content analysis in which even very small samples of clinical data yield surprisingly abundant, clear-cut, interrelated patterns of latent contents. In just three paragraphs of clinical data consisting of only 612 words, for example, Teller and Dahl identified an extensive network of recurring microstructural sequences, on the basis of which they were able to make accurate predictions.

Other examples of microanalytic approaches include methods of discourse analysis which have demonstrated microstructural relations between contextual elements and paralinguistic cues in therapy sessions (Pittenger et al., 1960; McQuown, 1971; Labov and Fanshel, 1977). The work of Olinick (1984; 1985, pp. 493, 496) and collaborators (Olinick et al., 1973) focuses on the processes underlying the patient's verbal language, that is, the ways that verbal language is used, including the figures of speech, active and passive voices, shifting of tenses, and the nuances of meanings in the modes of speech. Spence (1980a,b; 1993, 1994b) and coworkers (Spence and Owen, 1990; Spence, Dahl, and Jones, 1993; Spence, Mayes, and Dahl, 1994) employ computer-assisted studies of very subtle "discourse markers" in the speech of a psychoanalytic patient, for example, pronoun co-occurrence and frequency, and also key words. Spence (1994b) suggests the concept of "latent facts," which can be considered a form of organized interlocking microstructure in clinical data, for example:

> The use of pronouns marking the two speakers in the analytic conversation is a fact that is not particularly clinical and, for the most part, is largely out of our awareness as listening analysts. Nevertheless, it turns out that pronoun co-occurrence is a marker of an underlying lawfulness in the analytic situation, which has implications for the understanding of more conventional clinical facts, and a bearing on how they are reported (p. 922). Spence then adds: The thing I wish to emphasize is that there may be a class of latent facts that have the potential for greater reliability and greater falsifiability than the average clinical fact. As clinical accounts are supplemented with this new kind of information, it then becomes possible to have arguments over fact as much as over theory (p. 923).

Indirect Prediction and Postdiction

Unlike its central position in the natural sciences, prediction has a relatively minor role in the methodologies of the human and social sciences. Kaplan's 427-page treatise on methodology for the behavioral sciences (1964) includes only five pages on the subject of prediction, because the highly variable subject matter of the human and social sciences vitiates the predictability of behavior (see also Waelder, 1963). Caws (1988) observes: "All attempts to classify and predict *individual* human behavior quickly encounter limits which show them, in all but a few cases (and all these to some extent pathological), to be futile" (p. 33).

Lacking general laws on which to base predictions, the only grounds for predictions in psychoanalysis, dynamic psychotherapy, and other human and social sciences are empirically based theoretical statements (including interpretations and reconstructions). Being empirically grounded rather than derived from laws, theoretical statements about the individual patient lack the logical force of predictions in the natural sciences. Even if confirmed, empirically based predictions do not carry the weight of predictions derived from general laws. Since clinical interpretations are relatively fallible hypotheses rather than lawlike statements, the uncertainty of predictions based upon interpretations is correspondingly increased.

Some philosophers of science suggest that human and social scientists should not expect themselves to develop theories and explanations having the predictive power of physics and chemistry (Nagel, 1961, p. 349). Partly for that reason, some writers conclude that we should adopt Darwin's rather than Newton's paradigm, that is, an explanatory rather than a predictive science (Demos, 1959; Frank, 1959). Kaplan (1964) comments ruefully that "to arrive at some understanding of what is going on is hard enough, without having also to meet the demand that we anticipate what will happen next" (p. 351).

In spite of the aforementioned problems and limitations of predictions in the human and social sciences, some psychoanalytic investigators have employed predictive strategies in their clinical researches.[16] The Menninger investigators, however, who made the most extensive use of prediction in their long-term project, employed their predictive strategy as much for purposes of data analysis as for the justification of clinical judgments, that is, to compare specific aspects of patients' personalities and behavior before, during, and after therapy (Wallerstein, 1964, pp. 686–687).

Valuable as such investigations are, they illustrate that prediction is by no means the sine qua non of interpretive justification. Attempts to predict the outcome of psychotherapy, for example, have yielded generally poor results (Luborsky et al., 1980). Prediction plays a limited role also in the pattern model approach, the human and social science methodology that seeks understanding by locating puzzling phenomena in a system of relations rather than in general laws. Abraham Kaplan (1964), one of the methodologists who developed the pattern model approach, acknowledges that "knowledge of the pattern as a whole and of some of its parts does not always enable us to predict the others" (p. 347).

Rubinstein (1980) concluded that prediction can be used to test clinical hypotheses indirectly, that is, to predict classes of events rather than specific events. For example, although clinicians cannot predict the occurrence of a specific dream that justifies a particular motive, sometimes it is possible to predict a class of future events that encompasses the motive in question. Rubinstein recognized that an indirect prediction of that kind applies only to the individual patient about whom it is made, and does not support or confirm the general applicability of an interpretation.

Freud (1920b, pp. 167–168) rated postdiction much more highly than prediction for justifying (or disconfirming) interpretive hypotheses. He doubted the value of prediction because of inability to know the relative strengths of overdeterminants beforehand. Peterfreund (1983, pp. 216–217) proposed a similar explanation, namely, that psychoanalysis is a changing, evolving process in which earlier interpretations, rather than being justified as such, require extensive reinterpretation and revision as further information becomes available.[17] Investigators do not, and can not, postdict exactly what the content of antecedent events may have been, but often can make cogent "indirect" postdictions regarding the class of configurations that may be found (Rubinstein, 1975, 1980).

Repetition of Themes and Patterns

According to Hume's Principle of the Uniformity of Nature, "the observation of past regularities provides grounds for predicting that the same regularities will recur in the future" (Kukla, 1989, p. 791). Disciplines such as psychoanalysis and dynamic psychotherapy rely heavily upon this methodologic principle to deal with the wide variability and thus relative unpredictability of human personality and behavior. We employ extensive data bases that include numerous repetitions of phenomena in order to increase the incidence, and thus our chances of discovering, recurrent themes and patterns which provide clues to inner mental states (see, for example, Chassan, 1957, pp. 164–165).

In addition to Hume's Principle, the core psychoanalytic concepts of continuity and the compulsion to repeat also contribute to the methodologic assumption that the patient's major unconscious conflicts and defenses will repeat themselves at intervals throughout the therapeutic process. Therapists are alert, therefore, to discover, formulate, and compare repetitive conflict-defense patterns. Erikson (1958/1964) noted that the therapist "waits to be impressed by recurring themes. These themes will, first faintly but ever more insistently, signal the nature of the patient's message and its meaning" (p. 59; see also Loewald, 1971a,b).

Arguing against Spence's (1982a) claim that pattern matching in psychoanalysis is so "infinitely elastic" that clinical narratives can accommodate "almost any new evidence that comes along" (p. 182), Robert Rogers (1984) emphasizes the constraints on clinical interpretation which result from psychoanalysis being such a redundant process. As repetitive patterns accumulate, "they create, in the very process of their development, additional constraints on the fit of whatever data remain to be interpreted" (p. 51; see also Rogers, 1985, 1987c).

Repetitive phenomena in clinical data thus provide a background and framework for a number of justifying tests: compare, for example, the role of repetition in identifying organized interlocking microstructures. Interpretations of particular conflicts and defenses acquire partial support by demonstrating the repetition of such contents in the clinical data. That is, demonstrating the recurrence of particular conflicts and defenses increases the likelihood that the interpreted contents in question are not merely random occurrences but probably represent abiding configurations within the data.

Why is repetition referred to as only partial confirmation? Some investigators consider repetition a relatively reliable method of justification (for example, Brenner, 1976, pp. 43–45; Rice and Greenberg, 1984), but others do not. Peterfreund (1983) maintained, for example, that repetition "only confirms the hypothesis that the phenomenon tends to be repeated" (p. 42). If utilized as the sole method of justification, therefore, repetition would have to be considered an insufficient justifying measure because of its circular, self-confirming character: that is, seeking repetitive patterns and then defining such patterns as valid because they recur is tautological. In a pluralistic approach to interpretive justification, however, repetition is only one among a number of interrelated criteria that operate synergistically to justify or disconfirm interpretations.

Internal Evidence: Coherence

The phrase "internal consistency and coherence" appears fairly frequently in the psychoanalytic literature, but the distinction between the two terms is not entirely clear. Citing the philosophers Rescher (1973) and Putnam (1983a), Carlo Strenger (1991, p. 190) distinguishes between coherence and consistency: coherence implies consistency, the latter meaning logically compatible. Coherence is the more established term in other fields and is a stronger requirement for justification than consistency.

"External coherence" (or "integration") usually means that one's hypothesis fits well within an established theoretical system; but Strenger (1991) uses the term to mean that a psychoanalytic theory agrees with accepted knowledge outside of psychoanalysis (p. 188). "Internal coherence" refers to observations and inferred meanings fitting well together within an interpretive hypothesis (Kaplan, 1964). Of the two, internal coherence is more important for purposes of justifying interpretations. Rorty (1979) asserts that "nothing counts as justification unless by reference to what we already accept, and thus there is no way to get outside our beliefs and language so as to find some other test than coherence" (p. 178).

In Freud's (1923b) repertory of justifying procedures, the rationale and importance of coherence is suggested by his jigsaw puzzle analogy:

> If one succeeds in arranging the confused heap of fragments, each of which bears upon it an unintelligible piece of drawing, so that the picture acquires a meaning, so that there is no gap anywhere in the design, and so that the whole fits into the frame—if all these conditions are fulfilled, then one knows that one has solved the puzzle and there is no alternative solution [p. 116; see also 1915b, p. 117; and Meissner, 1971, p. 303. For a critique of Freud's jigsaw puzzle analogy, see Meehl, 1983].

Coherence is such a widely used concept in clinical interpretation and justification that some writers classify it as a principle in its own right; others consider it a corollary of the continuity principle (Rapaport, 1944). The popularity of coherence in interpretive work is partly subjective: the satisfaction of a logically consistent and seemingly complete explanation, in contrast to the unsettling effect of ambiguity and incompleteness. Einstein

(1934, p. 43) commented, for example, that being left with two explanations for the same set of phenomena is intolerable to any orderly mind. Booth (1969) observes similarly that, "Perhaps the happiest moment the human mind ever knows is the moment when it senses the presence of order and coherence" (p. 14). By contrast, psychoanalysts and dynamic psychotherapists "live in a nearly constant state of mental disarray, since it is the function of free association to disrupt ordinary continuities and closures" (Leavy, 1980, p. 78). Leavy adds that attempting to construct coherent latent continuities from manifestly disparate data is the essence of clinical interpretation (1980, p. 82).

Coherence contributes significantly both to the discovery phase and to the justification of interpretations. The degree of coherence required for justification is considerably greater than that needed during the phases of construction and progressive revision. Justification of alternative hypotheses is necessarily more systematic and detailed because each hypothesis must be checked against all of the data. In the following, for example, French (1955a) is talking about conflict, but his meaning refers to the interpretation of conflict and its justification:

> To prove that a particular conflict is focal we must show that every detail of a manifest dream can be recognized as a reaction to or defense against that particular conflict. The same principle can also be applied to the free associations of a single interview. If a particular conflict is focal during a psychoanalytic interview, then we should be able to recognize everything that the patient says or does during the interview as a reaction to that particular conflict [p. 1].[18]

Clifford Geertz (1967) maintained that "descent into detail" is necessary both to grasp the essential character of what we are studying, and also for purposes of proof. One of the best places to look for such detailed coherence in the therapeutic process is in so-called "good hours," which Kris (1956a/1975, pp. 255–260) described as seeming "prepared in advance." Peterfreund (1983) evaluated the significance of "good hours" this way: "Good hours are especially important because so many of our sessions are murky, uncertain, confused, and it is often difficult to know what has happened. The good hour is akin to a successful experiment which has given clear-cut, valid, unambiguous results" (pp. 67–68; see also Rubovits-Seitz, 1988b, pp. 186–189, in which the detailed analysis of a good hour is used as evidence in a case study).

Although coherence has been one of the most commonly used justifying methods in psychoanalysis,[19] its effectiveness has been questioned for the following reasons. First, the inherent circularity of the interpretive process produces an illusion of coherence (Hirsch, 1967); and second, the criterion of coherence has been applied unsystematically and almost exclusively to macroscopic aspects of clinical data rather than systematically to small-scale elements—the latter, more detailed approach being necessary for the justification of interpretations.

Spence (1982a, pp. 23–26) has mounted a stern critique of what he refers to as the clinical "bias towards coherence." He cautions against the seductive appeal of coherent explanations. Carried to extreme, the "coherence bias" produces an interpretive tour de force, an overextended, weakly coherent hypothesis that strains to account for all of the data, but in the end ignores details which do not fit. Other investigators argue, however, that although the criterion of coherence does not make a science in the positivist sense, it does contribute to the justification of interpretations within the perspective of postpositivist science (Wallerstein et al., 1956; Colby and Stoller, 1988; Strenger, 1991). Once again, a pluralistic approach to interpretive justification offers some resolution of this controversy: when the criterion of coherence is employed in concert with other justifying methods, its conclusions can be cross-checked by the findings of other tests.

Patients' Responses to Interpretations

Freud's (1915–1917) pluralistic approach to the justification of constructions included inferences drawn from patients' reactions to interpretations. His "tally argument," for example, rested on the criterion of symptom reduction (p. 452; 1937b, 262). Schimek, (1975, pp. 861–862) suggests the following possible rationale for Freud's inclusion of patients' responses to interpretations as a justifying procedure: Because psychoanalysis deals with the past as a psychical reality, the most directly relevant criterion for the justification of an interpretation also should be a psychical phenomenon, namely, the degree to which the interpretation changes the patient's psychical reality, as indicated by responses to an interpretation.

Not long after proposing the tally argument, Freud (1918, pp. 10,

50–52) suggested another justifying criterion that involves patients' responses to interpretations, namely, the furthering and deepening of the therapeutic process, leading to clarification of the smallest details and tying together diverse aspects of the patient's life, history, personality, and psychopathology. Freud (1937b, pp. 262–263) emphasized that direct responses such as agreements or disagreements with an interpretation had no confirmatory value unless followed by indirectly justifying responses such as new memories that extended or completed the interpretation. Freud's list of indirectly supportive responses to interpretations also included expressions of surprise; associations containing something similar or analogous to the content of the construction; a parapraxis which contradicts a denial; and either improvement or exacerbation of symptoms (1937b, pp. 262–263).

Many if not most contemporary psychoanalysts appear to have adopted Freud's emphasis on patients' responses to interpretations, and consider this criterion the principal method of justifying interpretations (Michels, 1994, p. 1136).[20] Psychoanalysts since Freud have suggested numerous, sometimes conflicting, additions to Freud's list of indirectly supportive responses, for example: Isaacs (1939, pp. 153–155) suggested a decrease in anxieties related to the transference, and also the recalling of a dream immediately following an interpretation; Saul (1958, p. 154) and Peterfreund (1990, pp. 9–10) emphasized relief of anxiety generally; Peterfreund (1990, pp. 9–10) also included a change in the direction of the session; Paul (1963b, p. 254) and Peterfreund (1983, p. 125) suggested review and refinement of the interpretation *by the patient* to make it more personally meaningful (these authors maintain that it is primarily the patient rather than the therapist who justifies or disconfirms interpretations, by examining his or her own responses to the interpretation).

Still other suggested responses to interpretations include recovery of memories;[21] paraverbal responses such as gestures and sudden laughter (Brenner, in Panel, 1955a; Paniagua, 1985, p. 314); flushing, startle, jerks of pain, apprehensive movements, facial expressions, and the sudden experiencing of the specific affect or urge referred to in the interpretation (Paul, 1963b, pp. 265–266); a subjective reaction in the therapist of the interpretation "clicking" (Fenichel, 1941, p. 83; see, however, Peterfreund's critique of this criterion, 1983, p. 206); communication between patient and therapist moving constructively to new and unexpected insights (Erikson, 1954; Edelson, 1992a/1994, p. 86); disclosure of a previously withheld secret (Rosen,

1969/1977, pp. 189–190); associations suggesting linkages to nonverbal schemata, that is, associations about actions, emotions, vivid and concrete descriptions of images, fantasies, and dreams (Bucci, 1985, pp. 601–603; 1988; 1989).

In one of the few experimental studies of patients' responses to interpretations, Garduk and Haggard (1972) found that interpretations have more immediate impact than noninterpretive interventions; but the differences were not very relevant to the correctness of interpretations. Since interpretations were more than five times longer than other interventions, and were expressed less often as questions, the investigators could not be certain that interpretive content was the principal factor determining patient responses.

Clinicians and investigators often disagree on the significance of patients' responses to interpretations—which is not surprising, since the meanings of such responses are not self-evident but themselves require interpretation in order to be understood; hence they are as susceptible as any other clinical data and interpretations to the consensus problem. Wisdom (1967) asks, "How does one assess whether a patient's responses confirm or refute an interpretation or clinical hypothesis? That is the basic methodologic problem" (p. 46). He points out:

> The response has itself to be interpreted before we can consider whether it confirms or refutes the interpretation being tested. And this may look like some sort of circular process, because it would hardly seem reasonable to test an interpretation by another one whose truth is just as much open to question [p. 46].

For this and other reasons, some writers (for example, Schmidl, 1955) reject the use of patients' responses to interpretations as a justifying criterion; and others reject the criterion of "beneficial effects" on the grounds that therapeutic improvement can result from inexact interpretations, or from no interpretations at all.[22] Some psychoanalysts believe, however, that patients' responses are potentially probative if clinicians and investigators employ sufficiently stringent criteria in assessing such reactions. Naiman (1968) writes, for example:

> In order to attribute a specific therapeutic role to a particular psychoanalytic interpretation, it must be established that a change has occurred in the patient, that this change is in the direction of

> improvement, that it is due to the interpretation, and that the interpretation produced its effect through insight. It seems reasonable to attribute change to a particular interpretation provided the state of affairs with respect to which change is observed had existed for a sufficiently long time that a spontaneous change is unlikely, that the change occurs within a short time after the giving of an interpretation, that it can be observed in several areas, e.g., behavior, affect, dream, and that there should be no other event, such as a modification in the life situation of the patient, to account for the change [p. 354; see also Loewenstein, 1968; Greenberg, 1994, p. 3].

No matter how stringent the criteria for assessing patients' responses, however, the necessity to interpret such reactions opens the door to confirmation bias and other limitations of interpretive reliability. Here one is reminded of Merton Gill's (1984, pp. 406–411) trenchant critique of Robert Langs's (1978) "validating" approach: Gill notes that Langs draws a series of inferences from the patient's associations which Langs believes are confirmatory of the patient's true unconscious response. Langs is satisfied with the conclusions he draws from amassing inferences in this way; but he "underestimates the ingenuity—and his is striking—with which one can make inferences from manifest associations that seem to validate one's conclusion" (Gill, 1984, p. 407). Gill suggests that Langs damages his own case "by converting inferences too readily into facts" (p. 411).

Quantitative Methods

Some clinical investigations of the therapeutic process employ quantitative methods to justify interpretations.[23] Therapists, on the other hand, can use qualitative methods to some extent during the actual treatment of patients, and to a much greater extent in retrospective, posttherapeutic studies of the records of completed treatments. Meehl (1983/1991, pp. 335–336) points out that disciplines like history rely mainly on qualitative evidence, discernment of intentionality, and convergence.[24] Loevinger (1965) compares qualitative and quantitative approaches this way:

> Measurement in clinical research is beset by paradoxes. First, if one wishes to measure only what is objectively observable and can be formulated on a strictly quantitative basis, one will surely end with nothing but trivialities. If one insists on being concerned only with important traits, one surrenders first strict quantification and then strict objectivity. Second, the clinician seizes on rare symptoms as the keystone of diagnosis; the research worker cannot deal with single or rare instances, but only with frequently replicated symptoms or responses [p. 92].

Loevinger notes further:

> There are no easy or magical formulas for overcoming these dilemmas. In meeting the problems, the standard paraphernalia of the statistical consultant—his factor analysis, analysis of variance, and computer search for patterns—are of as little avail as the unbridled intuition of the clinician. To meet such problems requires evolving a mature science in which measurement, theory, and empirical verification are integral parts of a single enterprise. What the methodologist should bring into the clinical field is not a bag of statistical tricks, but a habit of rigorous and precise thought and a sense of where to look for errors that bias the result [1965, p. 92; see also Meehl, 1958; Wallerstein, 1968, 1975].

The pluralistic perspective of postpositivist science favors the use of all methods that aid in the process of inference and justification (Sharp and Bellak, 1978, p. 54; R. Greenberg, 1986). Thus, qualitative and quantitative methods may be thought of as a continuum rather than as opposing approaches; and one can look for an optimal combination of quantitative methods and sensitive clinical judgment in the justification of interpretations (Holt, 1978, p. 37).[25] The following approaches suggested by Meehl (1983) include some of the more accessible quantitative methods that are available to therapists and clinical investigators:

1. Computer-assisted content analysis (see below).
2. Some simple, straightforward, nonparametric statistics such as chi-square can be applied to test basic, first-level psychodynamic concepts. An example follows:

Metcalf (1956, p. 65) employed chi-square to test the hypothesis that a patient's contact with her mother during the previous 24 hours increased the frequency and duration of her asthma attacks. The chi-square table employs the dimensions of recent contact with mother—no recent contact with mother; and days with asthma—days without asthma:

	Days with asthma	Days without asthma
Contact with mother	9 (60%)	14 (20%)
No recent contact	6 (40%)	56 (80%)

Chi-square significant at the .01 (1%) level

Statistical techniques such as factor and cluster analysis are less applicable to the idiographic subject matter of the therapeutic process.

3. Quantitative methods that are structurally appropriate to the problems of therapy sessions and clinical data: for example, "taxometric methods" which employ psychometric procedures to determine whether an individual exhibits characteristics of a specific class of mental states (Meehl, 1978, pp. 825–826; Meehl and Golden, 1982); and the use of graphs to analyze and present data (Read, 1972, p. 914–958).

4. The Topic Block Theme Tracing Method (Meehl, 1983/1991, pp. 333–335). This method starts by dividing the patient's discourse into blocks of data based on manifest topics rather than on inferred latent motives. The topic blocks are submitted to different groups of psychoanalytic therapists, who record whatever dynamic theme they infer in the specific block of material they have been given. The inferred themes are then given to still another team of clinicians who rank each theme as to its likelihood in a particular block. The rated themes are then arranged in a single table under the several topic block headings. Reading the table left to right reveals whether a particular theme runs through all of the topic blocks, and whether that theme received the highest weightings by clinical raters. A somewhat similar but qualitative method, which can be used by individual clinicians and solo clinical investigators, is described and illustrated in the following chapter of this volume.

5. Bayesian inference offers a method of incorporating prior information with experimental or other investigative forms of evidence to calculate the probability that a particular event is the consequence of some other event. The probability depends upon the number of mutually exclusive events that might conceivably have given rise to the event in question (English and English, 1958, p. 61). This method does not yield actual probability

numbers, but provides some upper and lower limits of likelihood. The advantages of Bayesian inference include its relevance to many forms of inquiry, the formulation and use of prior knowledge, and the fact that nothing of conventional approaches is lost by use of Bayesian analysis. In fact, Lindley (1965) has translated various classical statistical methods into Bayesian terms.

Meehl (1983/1991, p. 314) suggests that clinicians can "think Bayesian," and in doing so can arrive at some reasonable likelihood ratios. For example, Bayesian theory may make it possible to show that a single (for example, a psychoanalytic) hypothesis may explain disparate clinical data better than multiple independent hypotheses. The following example is a paraphrase from Meehl:

> During the same therapy session a woman mentioned 1) that she "accidentally" dropped her wedding ring in the toilet; 2) did not join her husband for the planned celebration of their wedding anniversary due to a severe headache; 3) insisted repeatedly what a fine man her husband is, and how lucky she was to have married him. To determine whether it was more plausible to account for these data by postulating a single psychological explanation, namely, latent ambivalence towards her husband, than by several different hypotheses, Bayes's theorem was applied. It revealed a liklihood ratio of approximately 8 to 1 in favor of the latent ambivalence factor versus the conjunction of multiple separate hypotheses [Meehl, 1991, p. 314].[26]

Meehl's list does not exhaust the quantitative methods that can be used for statistical analysis of idiographic data from an individual patient, therapist, or therapeutic process. Another such method is the Repertory Grid Technique, which was developed originally by George A. Kelly (1955) in connection with his personal construct theory. This method has evolved in the context of psychotherapy as "an attempt to stand in others' shoes, to see their world as they see it, to understand their situation, their concerns" (Fransella and Bannister, 1977, p. 5; compare the psychoanalyst Evelyne Schwaber's [1983a,b, 1990a, 1995a,c] attempts during therapeutic listening to adopt the patient's perspective). To illustrate some of the ways that the Repertory Grid Technique has been used in clinical settings: Ryle and Lunghi (1969) employed this method to study therapeutic change; Ryle and Breen (1972) compared normal and neurotic subjects; Ryle and

Lipshitz (1974) applied the method to therapists in an investigation of countertransference. Other clinical studies employing the Repertory Grid Technique include Bannister, 1965; Fransella and Adams, 1966; Fransella and Bannister, 1977; and Fonagy, 1982.

Procedures used to elicit personal constructs for grids seek to obtain numerous self-descriptions from the subject—from records of therapy sessions, from Q-sort lists of self-descriptive choices, or in other ways. To illustrate, a patient may reveal that she feels the more people know her secrets the less she will be liked. This self-description can be summarized in a chi-square format, which in turn could be the beginnings of Repertory Grid Technique; that is, many such chi-squares can constitute a grid. But the meanings of such self-concepts can be assessed only in terms of their place within the entire network of the patient's myriad personal constructs—a network which changes over time (Fransella and Bannister, 1977, pp. 2–3).

To deal with changes in complex phenomena over time, single case research designs employ "time-series methodologies," which are highly relevant to quantitative, longitudinal investigations of the therapeutic process (see, for example, Moran and Fonagy, 1987). Replying to critics of the single-case method, Meehl (1954) argues that the "uniqueness of the single case is no more fatal to psychology than it is to physics" (p. 129), because of the category- or class-oriented character of concepts and dimensions in descriptive activities generally. That is:

> There is no kind of human knowledge which exhaustively characterizes direct experience by a set of propositions. No set of percentile ranks, no graphical representation of personality components, and no paragraph of characterological description can contain all the richness of our immediate experience. The abstractive or summarizing character of descriptions is shared by differential equations, maps, gossip, novels, and clinical formulations alike [Meehl, 1954, pp. 129–130].

One of the most powerful and flexible methods for studying latent mental contents and converting them into quantitative form for statistical processing, is content analysis (Holt, 1978a, p. 242). The basic operation of content analysis is assigning meanings to categories of behavior. By having different persons carry out that operation, the investigator can develop a method that is objective and reliable. The investigator must also construct a scoring guide or manual, based upon samples of the data to be analyzed (see, for example, Luborsky, 1984; Strupp and Binder, 1984). The investigator must then train judges to do the scoring until interrater agreement reaches a reliable level.

Content analysis also has certain disadvantages. Among other drawbacks, such as difficulty in achieving sufficient sensitivity to "attitudinal-emotional" aspects of therapists' communications (Strupp, 1973, p. 56), content analysis takes so much time that there may be little energy left over for other, including conceptual, aspects of the work. Holt (1978c, pp. 157–159) observes that the frustrations and tediums of content analysis can make an investigator think twice before deciding to "tape everything." In addition, ratings are a notoriously fallible approach to quantification, and are subject to the same errors as other judgments, plus some of their own. Problems of this kind with content analysis led Marsden (1965) to comment that, "System after system has been developed and presented in one or two demonstration studies, only to lie buried in the literature, unused even by its author" (p. 315).

The APA Commission on Psychotherapies (1982) notes still another problem with such methods, namely:

> Most investigators have preferred to develop their own categorical systems, anchoring them to their own psychotherapeutic orientation. This practice effectively precludes comparisons among data collected by therapists of different theoretical persuasions. Some systems, for example Bales's twelve-category system of interaction process analysis (1950) are not restricted to any one theoretical orientation. But these have been considered too general and overinclusive to be of much value for research in psychotherapy (Strupp, 1973). It may be that no one system is capable of encompassing the relevant aspects of the therapeutic process of such theoretically disparate treatments as psychoanalysis and gestalt therapy [p. 42].

Additional references to the extensive literature on quantitative methods are included for the interested reader.[27]

External Methods

In his pluralistic approach to the justification of interpretations and reconstructions, Freud always included the possibility of external validation (Good, 1994, p. 97).[28] In addition to adventitious sources of external evidence such as old diaries (Ezriel, 1951; 1956–1957, p. 118), hospital records (Flumerfelt, 1962), and home movies (Serota, 1964), extraclinical confirmations sometimes result from and converge with intraclinical findings and inferences. For example, Rosen (1955) reported the case of a patient with derealization whose analysis led to the reconstruction that his mother may have committed suicide during his childhood. When the patient became able to confront his father with that possibility, the reconstruction was confirmed. The father's previous denial of the event was a major factor in the pathogenesis of the patient's derealization.

Wolman (1964) reported the case of a young woman who avoided male companionship and maintained that she had never seen a penis, even though she had often taken care of her younger brother. She dreamed of a rapidly growing tree that burst into fire, at which point drops of fluid fell on her naked abdomen. The analyst reconstructed that she may have had sexual relations with a man in her childhood, and suggested that she undergo a pelvic examination. The examination confirmed that she was not a virgin, and further analytic work led to the recovery of memories that she had been raped by her grandfather at the age of 10.

The present writer reported a case of trichotillomania in a young child who pulled hairs from her scalp and tickled her nose with them only when nursing from a bottle (Seitz, 1950). She had been nursed at the breast during the first two weeks of her life. I inferred that her mother might have hirsute nipples, which physical examination confirmed. The child's trichotillomania ceased when hairs were attached to the nipple of her nursing bottle, and returned when the hairs were removed—illustrating external validation combined with experimental manipulation.

Ideally, perhaps, a pluralistic justifying approach would include both intraclinical and external methods (Eagle, 1980a, p. 418). Novey (1968) concluded that in some clinical situations it is crucial to determine whether a past event actually occurred, and that sometimes the patient's investigation of his or her actual past experiences facilitates the therapeutic process. Michael Good (1994, p. 81) reports the surprising observation that he has been unable to find published psychoanalytic case reports in which a patient's memory of early trauma was found to be verifiably false (see, however, Raphling, 1994). On the other hand, Lynda Share's (1994) extensive review of the literature revealed only a handful of cases in which a postulated trauma dating back to infancy had actually been confirmed.

Confirmation by Observation

An interpretation makes assertions about the patient. If the assertion is supported by actual observations, the interpretation may be considered partially justified (Sherwood, 1969, pp. 251ff). On the other hand, Grünbaum (1986, p. 267) stresses the poverty of clinical observations that can count as probative evidence supporting psychoanalytic theory and therapy. Grünbaum argues that in physics as well as in medicine and psychology, empirical data can be used to postulate certain states, but observations alone are not sufficient to justify the posited states. Holt (1989) notes that Freud himself "tended to confuse a replicated observation with a verified theory of the phenomena in question" (p. 68). Edelson (1984) emphasizes the limitations of "enumerative inductivism," that is, the view that any observation entailed by a hypothesis supports that hypothesis, whereas in fact any number of hypotheses can explain the same data. Hirsch (1967, p. 196) draws a similar conclusion from the perspective of hermeneutics.

Justification by Implication

When the patient reports a series of events, certain intervening events can be presumed to have occurred; for example, if the patient lived in one city at age 4 and in another city at age 6, the therapist can presume that the patient moved between ages 4 and 6, even though moving was not a remembered event (Novey, 1968, pp. 31–32).

Ruling Out the Improbable

This type of inference involves ruling out interpretations which, in the light of everything known about the patient, seem impossible or highly improbable. For example:

> A very compulsive young man who was consistently punctual in all aspects of his daily life, including his therapy appointments, began arriving late for his sessions, and on some occasions did not show up at all. Each time he was late or missed an appointment he made the excuse that work pressures were responsible. I noticed that he seemed surprisingly undisturbed about these lapses in his usual punctuality. Asked if the recent pattern of being late or missing appointments was occurring also in other parts of his life, he said no, that it had not happened elsewhere. I commented that since it occurred only in relation to his therapy sessions, and inasmuch as he had always placed such importance on being punctual yet appeared surprisingly undisturbed about being late or missing appointments, it seemed more likely that the recent pattern had something to do with his feelings towards me, rather than being caused by work pressures. He protested that he really had been under a great deal of pressure at work. I asked, "But wouldn't that make you late for other appointments and meetings during the day?" He agreed that it would, and then became puzzled and reflective about why it was happening only in relation to his therapy appointments, and why he wasn't more upset about it.

Conversely, a reconstruction of the past may be accepted in some cases if all other explanations seem extremely improbable. Waelder (1970/1976, pp. 651ff) presents a number of nonclinical (forensic and archaeological) analogies to this form of reasoning and confirmation.

Summary

Clinical interpretations represent the first, most basic level of inference about clinical data. They are the lowest-level theoretical statements of psychoanalysis and dynamic psychotherapy, and thus are the only such propositions tested by direct empirical evidence, that is, by data of the case being studied. Justification of interpretations is crucial, therefore, to the science of psychoanalysis and dynamic psychotherapy.

After considering various problems of evidence and other basic methodologic questions regarding the justification of interpretations, this chapter concludes that interpretations must be justified, can be justified, and can be justified intraclinically, although not as completely or as accurately as theories are confirmed in the physical sciences. A distinction is made between tentative justification of interpretations during the treatment of patients, and more definitive justification or disconfirmation based upon detailed, retrospective, posttherapeutic study of the record of a completed treatment.

Tentative justification during the treatment of a patient represents a "screening" process to rule out initially plausible-appearing constructions which on further checking do not account coherently and comprehensively enough for all (or at least most) of the clinical data. Systematic, retrospective study based upon the record of a completed treatment is capable of employing more varied, complex, detailed, and probative methods of justification. The latter, more definitive approach to justification is analogous to the CPC (Clinical Pathological Conference) tradition in medicine, which carefully checks clinical judgments by detailed review of both clinical and pathological findings, and promotes learning from both the successes and errors of clinicians—an important source of knowledge which psychoanalysis and dynamic psychotherapy have hardly begun to utilize.[29]

Like the interpretive process as a whole, the justification of interpretations is methodologically pluralistic. The most probative methods of justifying interpretations include cross-validation and convergence of evidence, demonstration of organized interlocking microstructures underlying interpretations, indirect prediction and postdiction (of classes of events), and repetition of themes and patterns. The widely used methods of coherence and patients' responses to interpretations are less reliable, especially if used alone—the former because it is circular and the latter because the patient's responses themselves must be interpreted. When these methods operate in concert with other, more probative justifying methods, however, cross-checking of their results can occur. Quantitative methods, including computer-assisted content analysis, also have a place in posttherapeutic investigations of the therapeutic process. Qualitative and quantitative methods can be combined advantageously for both process analysis and the justification of interpretations.

The following chapter illustrates the use of multiple methods of justifying interpretations in a retrospective, posttherapeutic study which employed the record of a completed analysis.

9

Pluralistic, Posttherapeutic Justification of Interpretations: An Illustrative Case

This chapter focuses on the posttherapeutic phase of interpretive justification, in which the record of a completed therapeutic process is studied retrospectively in great detail. The methodology to be described and illustrated, called the "Recurrent Cycles" or RC approach, is an adaptation of French's (1952, 1954, 1958a,b) method of investigating the therapeutic process. French discovered that the therapeutic process follows repetitive dynamic cycles that become steadily shorter (that is, the cycles are completed more rapidly) as the treatment progresses—a form of organized interlocking microstructure that the writer uses in conjunction with other validating methods to justify interpretations and reconstructions. The relationship between interpretations and reconstructions is viewed as reciprocal: each draws upon the other, and both are subjected to similar justifying procedures.

A Brief Description of the Recurrent Cycles (RC) Approach

The RC approach employs records (usually process notes) of the entire therapeutic process from completed treatments. Wolfson and Sampson (1976) compared process notes and tape recordings and found that process notes provide an adequately representative sample of clinical data. Notes jotted down during sessions are very brief; but immediately following each session the therapist dictates further details about what transpired during the session, including the therapist's reactions, impressions, interpretive reasoning, attempts to justify hypotheses, and interventions. For example:

WRITTEN DURING SESSION	DICTATED FOLLOWING SESSION
(seems miffed)	(In the waiting room when I asked him to come in he looked up, made a quick little gesture of tossing his head with lips pursed, and uttered the sound, "Hmf!" He walked into the office with chin held high and hips waggling like a woman tossing her hair angrily, haughtily, disdainfully at a man.)
Wishes didn't have (!) to come today (stiffly).	(His saying "*have* to" seemed to imply that I was forcing him to come. Masochistic defense emerging? Stiffness of posture and speech suggested inhibited anger.)

After a psychoanalysis or dynamic psychotherapy has been completed, the RC approach carries out a form of content analysis on the treatment record. The investigator works backwards, starting at the end of the treatment where conflict-defense patterns are less disguised (Waelder, 1962/1976, p. 263; Mahony and Singh, 1979, p. 442; Leavy, 1980, p. 75), and recurrent dynamic sequences and cycles are much shorter, making them easier to identify. Freud (1918) said about his analysis of the Wolf Man, for example, that all of the information

> which enabled me to understand his infantile neurosis is derived from the last period of the work, during which resistance temporarily disappeared and the patient gave an impression of lucidity which is usually attainable only in hypnosis [p. 11].[1]

Describing their microanalytic FRAME methodology, Teller and Dahl (1986) mention similarly that they compared two sessions that "were picked specifically to include an early session, in which one of the patient's central unconscious wishes was expressed symbolically, and a much later session, in which a similar wish was openly and consciously entertained" (p. 766).

The RC investigator works his way back, session by session, to the beginning of the case. Recurrent dynamic sequences and cycles are formulated for the entire therapeutic process, and are used as part of the evidential base for assessing the probity of the treating therapist's interpretive reasoning and hypotheses. That is, if a latent meaning or determinant which the therapist interpreted during the treatment was accurate, it should be consonant with the specific phase of the patient's recurrent dynamic cycles at that particular time. The RC method also employs the various other justifying methods described in Chapter 8.

The RC approach exploits the decidedly redundant tendencies of the therapeutic process. Freud (1914c, p. 151) concluded that the patient repeats everything in the reservoirs of repressed material, as well as all of his or her symptoms. He theorized (1920a, pp. 18–23) that the source of, and force behind, the compulsion to repeat must be instinctual processes. Hartmann (1939, pp. 95–98) observed, however, that automatized processes are repetitive, too; thus the compulsion to repeat appears to function as a driving force that contributes to both the formation of intrapsychic structures and to reality mastery through learning. Hartmann's ego psychological interpretation of the compulsion to repeat provides a useful theoretical framework for conceptualizing recurrent sequences and cycles in the therapeutic process. The particular forms that such configurations take, in terms of both content and sequence, appear to represent compromise formations based upon a complex interplay of reactivated infantile conflicts, on the one hand, and relatively fixed sequences of specific defenses against the "return" of such conflicts, on the other.

Follow-up studies by a number of psychoanalysts illustrate both the central role of repetition in the therapeutic process and the speeding-up of dynamic cycles as the treatment proceeds. In open-ended, analytic-like follow-up sessions, Pfeffer (1959, 1961, 1963) observed the consistently rapid activation and equally rapid subsidence of transferences similar to those experienced toward the original treating analyst (see also Norman et al., 1976). Schlessinger and Robbins's (1974, 1975, 1983) studies revealed that "a repetition of the analytic process in miniature occurs in the course of a few interviews" (Schlessinger and

Robbins, 1975, p. 761). One patient repeated her basic dynamic cycle twice in a period of only six sessions (1975, p. 771). These observations support French's finding (replicated by the present writer, [Seitz, 1968; Rubovits-Seitz, 1987]) that in a therapeutic process, recurrent cycles become steadily shorter as the treatment progresses—so much so, in fact, that by the end of a therapeutic process the patient's basic dynamic cycle can run its course in just a few days (compare the illustrative case below).

Grinberg et al. (1967, p. 496) describe the therapeutic process as a temporal succession of structuro-dynamic-economic cycles of the patient, in which conflicts are reactivated and repeated. Repetitions of specific sequences, as well as particular contents, have been reported also from investigations of dreams: for example, Trosman (1960) noted the occurrence of identical manifest dream elements in the same positions of the dream sequence on each of several nights. Offenkrantz and Rechtschaffen (1963) observed that the sequence of ego functions in the dreams of a given night were paralleled by similar sequences of defensive activities during the day.

Sequential structures in the therapeutic process appear to be associated primarily with dynamic relations between conflicts and defenses. Thus, during the therapeutic process therapists are particularly alert to dynamic themes which appear to express and disguise a highly activated conflict, on the one hand, and a sequential repertory of defenses against that conflict, on the other. Erikson (1958/1964) noted, for example, that the therapist can rely on the patient to produce a sequence of themes, thoughts, and affects that "seek their own concordance and provide their own cross references" (p. 58).[2]

The RC methodology goes a step further and attempts to identify recurrent *series* of conflict-defense relationships which repeat themselves in much the same sequence throughout the therapeutic process. To identify these recurrent "sequences of sequences," the RC methodology employs a data processing strategy called "template-matching" (Tou and Gonzalez, 1974, p. 17), in which a previously constructed conflict-defense configuration is used as a template, model, or guide to identify similar such dynamic sequences elsewhere in the data of the therapeutic process. De Beaugrande (1980, p. 159) refers to this procedure as "pattern-matching between occurrences" of the same structure, in that one pattern acts as a model for others.

Systematic template-matching in the RC methodology begins

with the formulation of a dynamic cycle near the end of the treatment, where the cycles are shorter and conflict-defense configurations are less disguised, making the identification of cycles easier. As the investigator works backwards towards the beginning of the case, the originally-formulated "template cycle" from the end of the treatment is used as a model and guide to search for similar such dynamic cycles in the case material. As template-matching and the identification of earlier dynamic cycles proceeds, the original template cycle, which comprises only the rough outlines of the patient's basic dynamic cycle, is revised and expanded progressively by the recognition of additional dynamic details in the earlier, longer cycles.

A somewhat similar method was suggested long ago by Susan Isaacs (1939) for validating reconstructions; and more recently Teller and Dahl's microanalytic FRAME methodology (1986, 1993; Dahl, 1988)[3] distinguishes between "Prototypes" and "Instantiations" —the latter representing repetitions of a Prototype. In Teller and Dahl's terminology, "Frames" refer to fixed sequences of events, and a Prototype is the most complete and justified example of a particular Frame. A Prototype also entails the predictive hypothesis that the same fixed sequence will recur. Repetitions (Instantiations) of the Prototype tend to confirm the prediction.

The following case report illustrates the application of the RC methodology in a pluralistic, posttherapeutic approach to the justification of clinical interpretations and reconstructions.

AN ILLUSTRATIVE CASE

The traditional case report attempts to make the therapeutic process as coherent and convincing as possible by use of narrative smoothing, rearrangements of the data, and imposed linearity. We know, of course, that the therapeutic process is not that smooth, linear, or continuous. Both descriptively and psychodynamically the course of the therapeutic process is sporadic, shifting, and repetitious; it proceeds by "fits and starts," changes course unexpectedly, frequenty turning back upon itself to repeat previous patterns. Since the course and psychodynamics of the therapeutic process are not as simple or uncomplicated as we traditionally report them to be, a different kind of case report is needed for investigative purposes and for the justification of interpretations—a method of reporting which is more comprehensive and detailed, and which discloses rather than smooths over the infinite complexities of the process.

The present case report presents both a traditional and an investigative account of a therapeutic process. The reader should not assume that exactly the same clinical material will be found in both versions, or that they differ only in their styles of presentation. The two methods of case reporting differ more extensively than that. The traditional report will seem familiar and relatively easy to follow as it flows along narratively, recounting the week-by-week, month-by-month, and year-to-year developments in the therapeutic process. By contrast, the investigative summary of the treatment will cause the reader more difficulties, partly because of unfamiliarity with its method of reporting, partly because the investigative summary skips around rather than moving along consistently in a straight line, and also because some tabular and diagramatic devices are used to summarize detailed comparisons of data from different parts of the therapeutic process.

Traditional Case Report

Mr. Clark was a 38-year-old married man who had held a relatively minor teaching position without advancement for 10 years. His reasons for consulting a psychoanalyst were that he had felt moderately depressed for over a year following his failure to pass an examination for a higher degree, and because of longstanding feelings of inferiority and dissatisfaction with his accomplishments. Since failing the examination he had not been able to pull himself together emotionally or to start preparing for a re-exam. His wife, who had had an analysis prior to their marriage, suggested to him that he might need therapy. After thinking about her suggestion for several months he decided to seek treatment.

Mr. Clark was a short, slender man with thin hair and thick glasses. His facial expression was an unusual combination of childish innocence and spinsterish primness. He was cooperative and friendly during the initial interviews, in which he sat up and told the story of his life. He was the only child of American-born, Protestant parents who lived in a small, southern agricultural town. He grew up in a protected, indulgent environment consisting (figuratively) of two sets of parents. He and his parents had lived with his maternal grandparents, his mother being the grandparents' only child. Mr. Clark's father had failed in business and had turned to the maternal grandfather for help. His grandfather owned a small grocery store on the edge of town, as well as a large old home on the same property. Evidently the grandparents were as happy to get their daughter back as Mr. Clark's father had been to find a haven for his family. His father went to work for the grandfather in the grocery store, and there was room in the grandparents' home to accommodate both families. The grandfather retired and became something of a small town "gentleman." The arrangement worked so well that it continued until the grandparents' deaths in the patient's late teens. He spent his entire childhood and adolescence in this highly peaceful, protected, and predictable environment.

The childhood family environment was marked by its stability and day-to-day predictability. Meals were served at exactly the same time each day. Local gossip was the main topic of conversation in the home. In this family environment of adults, Mr. Clark felt a sense of belonging in a very special way. It was made quite clear to him by all four "parents" that he was their hope for the future. From an early age he felt and accepted the pressure on him to conform, study hard, and become a "professional man." His grandfather wanted him to become a lawyer because that led to politics. His mother wanted him to be a doctor because that was dignified. His grandfather was against the boy being a doctor because a doctor's life is not his own. His father and grandmother expressed no opinion about what he should be, other than their endorsement of his becoming a "professional man." At times the patient suspected that his father was a little envious of his much-talked-about future, but his father said nothing. Mr. Clark conformed, studied hard, and worked toward becoming what his family expected of him.

Of the four "parents," Mr. Clark was closest to his mother and grandmother. His grandmother doted on him and his mother was like a playmate to him. Mr. Clark's wife once said to him, "Your mother treats you more like a girlfriend than a mother." (Much later in his treatment, Mr. Clark recalled sheepishly that his mother had accompanied his wife and him on part of their honeymoon. Their accommodations on one occasion included only a double bed and a cot. He and his mother slept in the bed while his wife slept on the cot.) He was troubled by the fact that he sometimes made slips of speech in which he called his wife "mother"; and when speaking of his mother he sometimes referred to her as his "wife."

His grandfather had been gruffly affectionate toward him, but he felt least close to his father. At times he would go to the store to be near his father; but he would be sent off after a short time because his presence interfered with the incessant "cracker-barrel" talk among the group of men and older boys who hung around the store.

Mr. Clark slept in the same bedroom with his parents until he was eight years old. A bedroom of his own was then arranged for him by remodelling an attic storage room. Originally he could remember nothing about his experiences of sleeping in the same room with his parents; he "drew a blank" about anything connected with that bedroom. He had no memory of going into the room to sleep, placement of the furniture, seeing his parents in nightclothes, or of anything else associated with going to bed and sleeping for the first 8 years of his life. He remembered vividly the experience of starting to sleep in his own bedroom. He associated the latter bedroom with intense masturbatory activity and with studying. He would study hour after hour in his bedroom, stopping occasionally to masturbate, then returning to his books.

Mr. Clark had only a few playmates and school chums in childhood, being somewhat solitary and shy. He took up music with encouragement from his mother. In his early teens he had a close, fairly intense relationship with a male music teacher who was probably homosexual. At about that time he began having frequent episodes of sex play with certain boy friends, which he initiated and enjoyed, but about which he felt guilty and ashamed. His mother caught him having sex play with another boy and shamed him so severely that afterwards he felt panicky about homosexual desires, fearing that he might be caught again. He was timid toward girls, not even starting to date until he was well into his twenties.

By studying hard he did well in high school, graduating second in his class. He attended college in a nearby town where he did less well due to keener competition. He spent his weekends at home, and his mother visited him frequently at college. The family was very proud of his being in college, none of them having gone beyond high school. He still did not date in college. He spent most of his time studying, which continued to be associated with frequent masturbation. Two gay young men who roomed in the same boarding house tempted him sexually, trying to get him to join in their activities, but he resisted their advances.

His first real experiences away from home began when he was admitted to graduate school in a large, distant city. He had decided upon an academic career because it seemed less competitive than other professions. He was extremely homesick at first and wrote home daily. He continued to be rather solitary, living in single rooms and not having very close friends or belonging to any groups. He studied hard and masturbated, but in graduate school he could barely keep up academically with his fellow students. He had to repeat several courses and go to summer school. He began to feel that graduate school was too much for him, but by dint of almost ceaseless studying he managed to scrape by and to qualify for a Master's degree.

Another factor that contributed to his obtaining a Master's degree was his penchant for attracting the sympathy and support of older male teachers. Ever since he had become involved with the music teacher during his youth, one older man after another—a teacher or an older colleague—had become interested in him and helped him along. At the time he started his treatment, the head of his department at the junior college where he taught had established such a relationship with him. The older man had more or less taken Mr. Clark under his wing and was helping him toward the goal of obtaining a still higher degree.

Mr. Clark began having occasional dates at age 24 while in graduate school, usually with a woman in her late thirties who actively courted him and encouraged him to sleep at her apartment. He had his first intercourse experiences with her, which were uneventful; he felt rather indifferent about it. Once during graduate school he attended a wedding, got drunk, and on the way home with another young man had a sudden urge for sexual relations with him. The experience alarmed him because he thought he had gotten over such interests years before. After graduate school he spent two years in military service. He continued dating only occasionally during that period. He recalled an incident in which he was accused by another officer of being gay because he used a cigarette holder and put his arm around an enlisted man. He became enraged at the accusation and offered to fight the man, but was talked out of it.

After military service he began his academic career, teaching in a small junior college. Once again he met an older colleague who took an interest in him. They had long, involved philosophical discussions that were enjoyable to both. During that period (eight years previous) he met his wife, also a teacher; after six months of courtship they were married. His wife appealed to him because she had such a different, outgoing personality compared with his shyness and introversion. She came from a large family, was sure of herself, wanted marriage and children. Never having been in love with a woman, and wanting to settle down and live a "normal, regular life," he decided to go ahead and get married. His mother was not very friendly toward his wife at first, but later accepted her. Mr. Clark had maintained frequent close contact with his parents, especially his mother. His grandparents had died in his late teens, and he appeared to have grieved normally about their deaths.

His sexual adjustment with his wife was reported as good. They had had frequent sexual relations before marriage, which both enjoyed. During their marriage they had never used contraceptives, ostensibly because his wife wanted to have as many children as possible. Mr. Clark went along with that plan even though he was not certain that he wanted so many children. They had three children at the time he came for treatment, and his wife was pregnant with their fourth child. All three children seemed healthy and normal, both the patient and his wife being devoted parents. Their social life followed a pattern more typical of Mr. Clark than of his wife, that is, very little entertaining or going out. He spent most of his leisure time either playing with the children or watching TV. His wife sometimes complained about the monotony of staying home with the children all the time, but she had not made an issue of it.

Mr. Clark felt that he had been pushed by his wife about several things: obtaining a higher degree, studying for his examinations, having many children, and improving himself socially. She had talked him into enrolling in "success courses" and public speaking groups to build up his confidence. He had gone along with her suggestions, but felt they had not helped much. His attitude about having one child after another was also passive; he had no particular interest in having more children, but had acquiesced to his wife's wishes about it.

His reaction to failing the examination during the previous year had been shock, humiliation, and then depression. His wife sympathized with him and blamed the examiners, which saved some face for him. Shortly afterwards he impregnated his wife with their fourth child. His attitude about the pregnancy was that if his wife wanted more children he was for it too, although he felt they had enough.

Mr. Clark's physical health was good with the exception of occasional painful spasms of the esophagus and rectum. He had had such symptoms for many years; they had begun when he left college and started graduate school (his first sustained experiences away from home). His internist had diagnosed the condition as a gastrointestinal somatization disorder (DSM III: 300.81), and had prescribed chlordiazepoxide, 10 mg as needed, to relieve spasm. The esophageal and rectal symptoms never occurred together, usually lasted for several hours, and the patient was unable to correlate the attacks with life events. Upon questioning, however, he recalled that rectal spasms had occurred as his examination approached, and that esophageal spasms had recurred when his wife became pregnant in recent months.

In addition to the gastrointestinal somatization disorders, his psychiatric diagnoses included a psychoneurotic, reactive-type of depression (*DSM III*: Dysthymic disorder, 300.40), precipitated by failure on the examination and aggravated by ambivalence about his wife's pregnancy. The more acute neurotic symptoms appeared to be engrafted on a character neurosis having passive, masochistic, and latent homosexual features (*DSM III*, Axis II: Other personality disorder, passive-masochistic-latent homosexual, 301.89). The preceding secondary diagnosis refers to a set of largely defensive fantasies and enactments which were in part ego-alien due to conflict with the patient's masculine pride. A dynamic formulation of this kind is not the same as, and does not imply, a state of homosexuality proper—the latter no longer being included as a diagnostic category in our standard nomenclature. I recommended psychoanalysis, which he accepted.

Narrative Summary of the Therapeutic Process

Following the initial interviews, Mr. Clark came four times a week and lay down to free associate. His first dream was of men breaking into his house at night. He was afraid they would attack and harm his youngest child, a daughter about a year old. He fought valiantly to protect his daughter, who was only wounded in the struggle. In his associations to the dream he expressed pride in having defended his daughter. He then recalled fear of possible harm to his wife's pregnancy, which might cause a miscarriage. Although additional meanings of the dream were considered—for example, on a transference level some initial anxieties about his treatment, possibly associated on a deeper level with feminine-homosexual-masochistic fantasies of being assaulted by the analyst—only the most immediately accessible meaning was interpreted to the patient, namely, that he seemed troubled by mixed feelings about his wife's pregnancy. He reacted with a mild protest which lasted only a short time.

During the following several months the theme of ambivalence towards his wife's pregnancy (*vs.* guilt and shame) dominated the treatment. Defenses took the form of self-justifying arguments ("I've already given her three children"), idealizing rationalizations ("It would be nice to have another baby"), and turning the hostility against himself (depression). During this period of the treatment, relatively little in the way of transference to the analyst developed, his emotional ties and conflicts remaining firmly attached to his wife and unborn child. Eventually he expressed the pent-up hostility towards his wife for wanting, demanding, and having "so many children." Upon discussing those feelings with her he was surprised to learn that she had not really wanted the fourth child either, but had gone along with him about it, feeling that he needed a boost to his morale after the failure on his examination.

He became more aware of possessive feelings towards his wife, and expressed resentment at having to share her with "so many other(!) children." When the slip was called to his attention, he admitted sheepishly that he would like to be the new baby, because if he were he wouldn't have to face another examination and the possible, or even likely, humiliation of another failure.

Following the emergence of ambivalence about the pregnancy and hostile-dependent-possessive feelings towards his wife, Mr. Clark's depression began to improve. After about six months of treatment he experienced a return of energy and optimism that had been absent since his failure on the examination. The birth of the new baby was relatively uneventful, although a recurrence of esophageal spasm developed the first time he saw the baby nursing at his wife's breast. He began thinking about preparations for a re-exam, which led to a period of overconfidence, even boasting, about his professional knowledge and ability. Comparisons of himself with colleagues appeared increasingly in his associations, followed by undertones of inferiority feelings.

At that point in the therapeutic process, approximately nine months after starting treatment, a clearcut transference to the analyst developed. In what seemed a slightly forced, offhand manner, he mentioned that he had seen the analyst getting into a taxicab while he himself waited for a bus. Subsequent associations were critical of older, more successful colleagues. A gloomy, irritable mood set in, accompanied by thinly disguised envy of the analyst. When the undercurrent of envy was interpreted to him, he became anxious, recalled fantasies of senior colleagues disapproving of his work, and obsessed about losing his teaching position. In that context he reported a dream of a menacing figure behind him.

The competitive transference activated so much (castration) anxiety that a prolonged regressive defense set in. He developed an exaggerated submissive attitude towards me, which when interpreted to him he rationalized as "being cooperative." Increasingly anal-erotic allusions appeared in his associations and lexical choice, for example, "I have to be 'goosed' to do my best" and "My ass has been itching lately but I don't want anyone to see me scratching it." When the repeated anal references and allusions were called to his attention, he reacted with dreams of men chasing him with guns (erotization of the interpretations as feared wishes for anal penetration).

Intensification of the passive-submissive-homosexual defense was accompanied by relatively anxiety-free dreams of men turning into women, homosexual orgies, and anal intercourse. Recollections of childhood and adolescent experiences of actual and fantasied sex play with other boys occurred. A longstanding scoptophilic compulsion to see graffiti in public toilets increased. He spent more and more time in public toilet booths reading messages from homosexuals, fantasizing trysts with them, and masturbating. The homosexual preoccupations were interpreted to him as displacements of feelings and fantasies about the analyst. An undisguised homosexual transference to the analyst then surfaced, against resistances in the form of pride conflict and fear of exposure. He expressed longings to be held and caressed, and cravings for oral, anal, cutaneous, and genital contact with the analyst. Dreams during that period included images of his father, with whom he yearned for closeness. As a child he had experienced relatively little physical and emotional closeness to his father. While relating an incident of watching urchins play in the street, a wave of sentiment swept over him; he wept for the first time during his treatment as feelings of loneliness and longing for his father welled up in him.

Frustration of the (part wish, part defensive) passive homosexual desires toward me (as father-figure) activated anger; but the hostility was warded off immediately and replaced by a masochistic defense. He became provocative, attempting to start arguments with me. His dreams suggested that he wanted me to get rough with him. Another anal intercourse dream occurred, but this time included anxiety about his shirt-tail in back being bloody. He suffered a severe recurrence of rectal spasm. Fear of injury from anal penetration reached a peak. An outburst of panicky anxiety occurred in connection with obsessive fantasies of throwing himself under the wheels of a train (homosexual panic activated by a disguised masochistic fantasy of soliciting and submitting to rape).

The increasing panic produced by masochistic-homosexual fantasies drove the patient into a still deeper defensive regression—to a passive-dependent mother transference. He felt increasingly helpless and childlike, asking for guidance and comfort from the analyst, requesting extra appointments, and complaining about the length of weekend interruptions. Dreams included images of his mother and grandmother being indulgent and protective towards him. Pride conflict about his dependent longings intensified steadily, however, reaching a peak of shame when colleagues teased him about how much weight he had gained. He suffered a recurrence of esophageal spasm as the conflict between dependence and shame increased.

An almost truculent, swaggering attitude set in as he undertook a strenuous diet and exercise program. He became more assertive towards me and reported some fairly aggressive interchanges with colleagues. The aggressive protest against dependent transference wishes led inevitably to comparisons of himself with other men, which resulted in feelings of inferiority, fantasies of physical and professional inadequacy, and some dreams of himself as "a boy trying to do a man's job." Competitive envy toward colleagues reappeared, followed by a transference of phallic-oedipal rivalry towards me. He read an announcement in the newspaper of a lecture I was scheduled to present to a women's group, following which he felt depressed. That night he dreamed of performing spectacular feats with his musical instrument, which a large audience of women admired, but which men at the "rear" of the hall (analyst) viewed suspiciously.

Further working through of phallic-oedipal conflicts on a transference level included rivalry with me for the admiring favor of my female assistant. Eventually, working through on the level of childhood oedipal objects and conflicts occurred. Memories, feelings, fantasies, and conflicts about surpassing his father and winning his mother's favor surfaced—associated in particular with the notion of becoming "a professional man." Primal scene memories associated with intense sexual excitement and competitiveness (vs. fear, guilt, and shame) were recovered from the formerly amnesic period of sleeping in the same room with his parents for the first eight years of his life.

The analysis was terminated after three years of treatment, totalling approximately 500 appointments. Symptomatic improvements at the time of termination included: (1) he successfully passed the examination for a higher degree; (2) he obtained a more responsible position at a university where he was not dependent on an older man, and where his salary was twice what it had been previously; (3) marked reduction of the previously recurrent esophageal and rectal spasms; and (4) increased energy, assertiveness, and satisfaction in his family, work, and social relationships.

Follow-up studies included two separate consultations during the first ten years following termination. On both occasions (approximately five years apart) he had experienced recurrences of rectal spasms in association with promotions and salary increases. During the follow-up appointments he free-associated well and observed his own associations fairly insightfully. With minimal interpretation from me he was able to recognize the repetition of his old pattern of being "wrecked by success" (Freud, 1916, p. 316). His insight into the dynamics and childhood origins of that pattern was good. His ability to produce, observe, and interpret associations suggested that some development of an "autoanalytic function" (Kramer, 1959; Schlessinger and Robbins, 1983) had occurred.

His personal, family, and work life had continued to be largely satisfying and successful. As yet, however, there had been no really severe, testing traumata in his life since termination—even the two successes were only moderately traumatic! Both parents were still living; and with the exception of one frail child who had some difficulties in school and whom he and his wife had taken to a child psychiatrist, his wife and children were generally healthy and doing well.

This completes the traditional case report, including a narrative summary of the therapeutic process. The next section summarizes a retrospective, posttherapeutic study of the same therapeutic process, employing the Recurrent Cycles (RC) approach. Later sections of this chapter illustrate the use of the RC methodology in conjunction with various other methods (discussed in Chapter 8) to justify interpretations and reconstructions in Mr. Clark's therapeutic process.

Retrospective Investigation of the Therapeutic Process Employing the Recurrent Cycles (RC) Approach

Turning to the end of the case, the rough outlines of a possible dynamic cycle were found in a sequence of fifteen appointments during the final month of treatment (in Figure 9-1, P stands for Patient and T for Therapist; X stands for versus, that is, "in conflict with").

Using the originally formulated cycle as a guide (template-matching), and working backwards from the end of the treatment to the beginning of the case, eight similar cycles were identified in the therapeutic process. Formulating the earlier, longer cycles clarified some unanswered questions about the original (template) cycle, and suggested four more phases (*B*, *D*, *F*, and *H* in Figure 9-2, p. 266) of the patient's Basic Dynamic Cycle.

The lengths of the nine recurring cycles became steadily shorter as the treatment progressed:

Cycle	Number of Months	Number of Appts.
I	9	144
II	6	88
III	5	70
IV	4	55
V	3+	40
VI	3	38
VII	2+	36
VIII	2	30
IX	1	15

The plateauing of cycle durations between Cycles V and VII appeared to be related dynamically to the patient's preparations

Figure 9-1

Rough Outline of a Dynamic Cycle Near the End of the Case

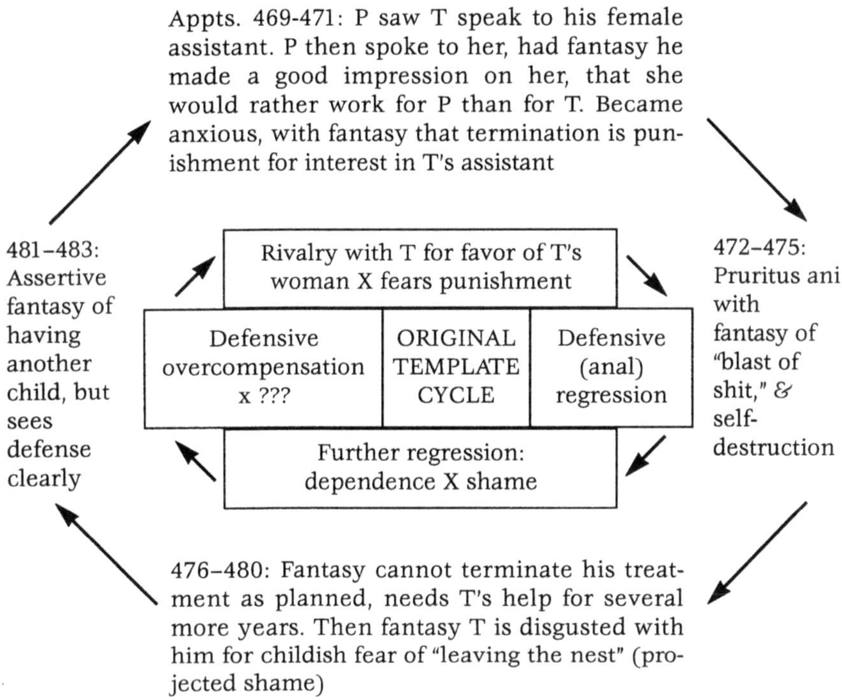

for a reexamination, which was associated with a relative lengthening of two defensive (masochistic and dependent) phases of the cycles.

The tabular summaries (Table 9-1, pp. 268–269) illustrate the recurrences of both thematic contents and sequences that comprise the patient's basic dynamic cycle. The tables compare cycles from early, middle, and late periods of the therapeutic process. The comparisons demonstrate that although essentially the same contents and sequences of conflict-defense configurations recur throughout the therapeutic process, one can also observe in the middle and late cycles the effects of therapeutic working through on defenses, emergence of conflicts, clarification of pathodynamics, and gradual modulation of primitive drive

Figure 9-2

Completed Basic Dynamic Cycle

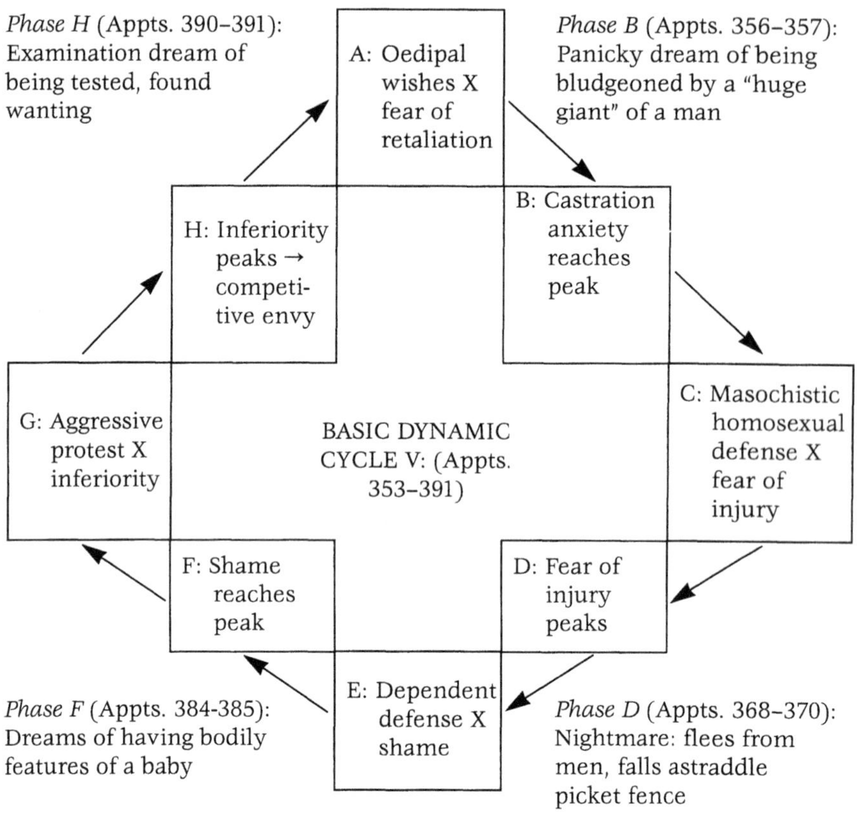

and emotional intensities. These changes are most evident to the clinician in the contents rather than the sequences of the dynamic cycles. Changes in the sequences of dynamic cycles are confined to the less readily observable temporal dimension of duration or length of the sequences, becoming variably but progressively shorter as the treatment proceeds.

The most ego-alien and destructive defense pattern in this patient's pathology was the masochistic component of his defensive anal fixation (Phase C in his Basic Dynamic Cycle). The erotic (latent homosexual) component of this defense produced only moderate conflict, being sublimated to some extent in relationships with male mentors. The masochistic component, however, not only contributed to his failure on the examination, but also had limited his effectiveness in a number of ways throughout his life. For these reasons, the recurrent phases of anal regression are singled out for posttherapeutic study and discussion. I attempted to determine (1) the specific underlying conflict and defense patterns at the times when masochistic trends appeared in the therapeutic process and (2) the sequences of psychodynamic events leading to the emergence of masochistic patterns.

The recurrent masochistic component of the anal regressive phase in the patient's Basic Dynamic Cycle included six fairly distinct dynamic sequences, in the following order of increasingly self-abnegating, self-depreciatory, and self-destructive fantasies or behavior:

C-1: Passive-submissive ("good boy") pattern.
C-2: Passive-feminine (homoerotic) pattern.
C-3: Erotization of nonphysical injury.
C-4: Erotization of physical injury.
C-5: Increasingly provocative masochistic behavior.
C-6: Increasing fear of injury from anal penetration.

Masochistic trends were minimal in the first sequence, consisting merely of somewhat self-abnegating, overly submissive, "good boy" behavior. Much the same could be said about the passive-feminine sequence, although conflict about homoerotic wishes made him overly self-critical about such fantasies. The first indication of a distinctly masochistic tendency appeared during the third dynamic sequence in the form of pleasurizing nonphysical injuries such as imagined or actual criticisms, humiliations, and self-motivated failures (compare his failure on the examination for a higher degree). This form of masochistic

Table 9-1

Comparison of Early, Middle, and Late Cycles (read across)

	Second Cycle Appts. 145–233	Fifth Cycle Appts. 353–391	Ninth Cycle Appts. 469–483
Phase A: Oedipal wishes X fear of retaliation	(145–151) T took cab, P took bus. Critical of older men	(352–355) Read of lecture by T; dream women admire P, but men suspicious	(469–470) Spoke to T's female assistant. Fantasy she prefers P to T
Phase B: Castration anxiety reaches peak	(152–156) Anxiety dream of a menacing man behind him	(356–357) Panic: dream of being tracked down, bludgeoned by huge angry man	(471) Fantasy termination is punishment for craving T's woman assistant
Phase C: Masochistic homosexual defense X fear of injury	(157–185) Anal-erotic dreams become more masochistic	(358–369) Dreams of "spreading cheeks" to men, pinching off penis in rectum; rectal spasm	(472–474) Mild pruritis ani; fantasy of blasting men with "blast of shit"
Phase D: Fear of injury reaches peak	(186) Anxious obsession of throwing self under train	(370) Nightmares of a harpoon rammed in rectum and falling astraddle iron picket fence	(475) Fleeting fantasy of throwing self down garbage chute

(continued)

Table 9-1 *(continued)*

	Second Cycle Appts. 145–233	Fifth Cycle Appts. 353–391	Ninth Cycle Appts. 469–483
Phase E: Defensive regression: Dependence X shame	(187–220) Dependent on T (as mother figure) X Moderate shame	(371–384) Dreams of couch as baby buggy, appts. as nursing at breast X Adult pride	(476–479) Feels can't terminate, needs T longer X Practical and pride conflicts
Phase F: Dependent shame reaches peak	(221) Disgusted with self for dependence on T (mother)	(385) Dream of being nude in public, looking like a baby. Feels humiliated	(480) Projected fantasy that T disgusted with him for his fear of termination
Phase G: Aggressive protest X inferiority feelings	(222–230) Truculent assertive attitude at work	(386–390) Claims does not need more analysis—is ready to "go it alone"	(481–482) Fantasy of having another child after termination
Phase H: Inferiority peaks, leading to competitive envy	(231–233) Compares self with other men, feels inferior, envies them	(391) Examination dream, and woman's vagina too big for him	(483) Realizes having child would just be overcompensation for inferiority

personality and behavior is classified as "moral (or behavioral) masochism," in contrast to "masochistic perversion" (Moore and Fine, 1990, pp. 116–117). The following sequences of dynamic events immediately preceded the appearance of behavioral masochism:

SEQUENCE C-1: PASSIVE-SUBMISSIVE DEFENSE ("GOOD BOY")

C-1-a: Exaggerated submissiveness to father figures.
C-1-b: Dream father-figure pats him approvingly on head.
C-1-c: Frustrated that therapist does not give approval.
C-1-d: Begins to feel anger at lack of approval from T.

SEQUENCE C-2: PASSIVE-FEMININE (HOMOEROTIC) DEFENSE

C-2-a: Becomes playfully flirtatious (like his mother).
C-2-b: Increasingly undisguised homosexual dreams.
C-2-c: Frustrated that T not "aroused" by his dreams.
C-2-d: Angry pique at T's seeming indifference.

SEQUENCE C-3: EROTIZATION OF NONPHYSICAL INJURY (MORAL-BEHAVIORAL MASOCHISM BEGINS)

C-3-a: Fantasy that lack of approval means disapproval.
C-3-b: Martyr-like attitude towards fantasied disapproval.
C-3-c: Secret satisfaction from fantasied disapproval.

One of the most significant aspects of the foregoing sequence is that behavioral masochism began to develop immediately after the patient felt frustrated and angry about the therapist's not expressing approval and thus seeming indifferent toward him. This finding differs somewhat from the usual formulation that behavioral (or moral) masochism is based primarily on regressive erotization of guilt feelings (Moore and Fine, 1990, p. 116), rather than on the reversal and erotization of hostile aggression. The latter dynamic appears again in the next sequence of Phase C, which includes the emergence of "masochistic perversion":

SEQUENCE C-4: EROTIZATION OF PHYSICAL INJURY (MASOCHISTIC PERVERSION BEGINS)

C-4-a: Further submissive and feminine attempts to please T.
C-4-b: Disappointed and frustrated when attempts fail.
C-4-c: Increasing anger at T's (father's) lack of response.
C-4-d: Narcissistic rage at humiliating exposure of his frustrated yearning for T's (father's) love.
C-3-e: Dream of erotized painful anal penetration.

The preceding dynamic sequence partially supports the usual formulation that masochistic perversion in men is associated with passive homosexual tendencies (Moore and Fine, 1990, p. 116). Even more striking, however, is the sequential juxtaposition of rage and a dream of masochistic perversion. The nature and stimulus of the hostility are clear in this sequence: narcissistic rage at the humiliating exposure of self-perceived weaknesses or defects in the form of: a) feeling unloved; and b) vainly yet persistently needing and seeking love that is not returned. More will be said in the section on justification (following) about this dynamic in the pathogenesis of Mr. Clark's masochism.

The central role of hostile aggression in this patient's masochism is illustrated further by the next dynamic sequence of Phase C, in which his masochism becomes increasingly active, overt, and provocative. In fact, by the end of the following sequence, his masochism is transformed into and betrays an underlying sadistic motivation:

SEQUENCE C-5: MASOCHISM BECOMES INCREASINGLY PROVOCATIVE (UNDERLYING SADISTIC FANTASY EMERGES)

C-5-a: More frustrated by lack of loving response from T.
C-5-b: Dream of taunting a "rough character" (T), who then "manhandles" him.
C-5-c: Anal-penetration dream in which he pinches off a large penis in his rectum.

The re-emergence of hostile aggression in the preceding dynamic sequence is short-lived, however. The hostile feelings activate increasingly masochistic defenses in the form of self-destructive fantasies, which precipitate a panicky flight into still deeper defensive regression:

SEQUENCE C-6: FEAR OF INJURY FROM ANAL PENETRATION

C-6-a: Painful rectal spasms recur.
C-6-b: Another dream of anal penetration; but this time his shirt-tail in back is bloody.
C-6-c: Anxiety about physical injury mounts, leading to:

PHASE D: FEAR OF INJURY FROM ANAL PENETRATION PEAKS
which precipitates:

PHASE E: DEEPER REGRESSION TO DEPENDENCE ON MOTHER FIGURES

The preceding formulations of pathodynamic factors contributing to Mr. Clark's masochism are based on detailed comparisons of recurrent and successive dynamic sequences and cycles in his therapeutic process. Detailed comparisons of this kind can be utilized also as organized interlocking microstructures in the justification of interpretations.

Justification of Interpretations Employing the RC Methodology and Multiple Additional Justifying Tests

Drawing upon small-scale evidence in the form of organized interlocking microstructures (that is, the recurrent dynamic sequences and cycles formulated by the RC methodology), and employing various other justifying methods (discussed in Chapter 8), the following examples illustrate some of my attempts to justify specific interpretations and reconstructions in Mr. Clark's therapeutic process:

Example 1: Interpretation Justified by Repetition, Prediction, Coherence, and Convergence.

In the Second Dynamic Cycle (still relatively early in the analysis), Mr. Clark's phallic-oedipal hostility towards me (as father figure) was contained defensively by masochistic fantasies and dreams of anal penetration. As the hostile aggression persisted and threatened to emerge, a corresponding intensification of the masochistic defense occurred, with recurrence of painful rectal spasms and fantasies of increasingly violent anal penetration. (I interpreted to the patient that his fantasies and fears of violent anal penetration were an attempt to conceal hostile feelings towards me.) His immediate reaction to the interpretation was a momentary, last-ditch effort to perpetuate the masochistic defense by an even more self-destructive fantasy of throwing himself under the wheels of a train (a disguised image of actively soliciting and submitting to violent rape). Panicky anxiety about physical injury made the masochistic defense untenable at that point, and precipitated a still further defensive flight into dependent regression.

The preceding (largely constructed) events neither justify nor disconfirm my interpretations. As often happens, justification came later. During the Fifth Dynamic Cycle, the masochistic defense recurred in the predicted dynamic context, and was associated again with anal penetration fantasies and dream images. This time, however, he dreamed of pinching off the penis of a large man who penetrated him anally. The previous interpretation, that the masochistic fantasies attempted to conceal phallic-aggressive feelings towards me (as father figure), now gained support by the criteria of repetition, prediction, coherence, and convergence. The recurrence of symptomatic rectal spasm in association with phallic-competitive conflict and masochistic defense also provides some predictive confirmation of another interpretive hypothesis. At the time of the initial interviews, the patient reported that he had experienced rectal spasms while preparing for the examination which he failed. The therapist made a note at the time to watch for a possible correlation between the examination as a competitive situation and rectal spasm as a symptom of competitive conflict. Still further confirmation of the connection between phallic-oedipal conflict and anal-erotic masochistic defense can be seen in the final phase (Ninth Cycle) of the analysis. The sequence of phallic-aggression followed immediately by masochistic defense is particularly clear in appointments 474–475.

Example 2: Interpretation and Reconstruction Justified by Repetition, Prediction, Postdiction, the Patient's Reactions to an Interpretation, and Convergence.

Sequences C-1 and C-2 of trying to please the therapist (as a father figure), followed by disappointment, chagrin, discouragement, and depression, appears fairly clearly in the recurrent dynamic cycles. The methods of justification in this instance include postdiction, since this sequence was first noticed and postdicted while working backwards on the record. A related reconstruction of this dynamic sequence, that he probably reacted in the same way when unable to please his father, was first noted while working forwards on the record; its recurrence is classified, therefore, as "predicted." (In the RC methodology, the investigator works backwards in attempting to identify sequences and cycles, but forwards in interpreting the therapeutic process within such units.)

Example 3: Transference Interpretation and Reconstruction Justified by Repetition, Postdiction, Organized Interlocking Microstructures, the Patient's Reactions to the Reconstruction, and Convergence.

Sequences C-1, C-2, and C-3 revealed a number of parallels and overlaps in the Second, Fifth, and Ninth Dynamic Cycles. The following transference interpretation and reconstruction were made to the patient during the Fifth Dynamic Cycle: *Transference interpretation*: "Your wish for approval, love, and sexual favor from me came up in the context of fear about how I would react if you competed with me. Your submissiveness and trying to get me to love you thus seem to be ways of relieving anxiety about competitive feelings."

Reconstruction: "Much the same pattern may have occurred during childhood with your father, that is, attempting to cover up any competitive feelings toward him by acting submissive, playing up to him, and trying to mollify him."

The patient's reaction to the interpretation and reconstruction during the Fifth Cycle was an intensification of anal-erotic and masochistic fantasies toward me; but in the corresponding sequence near the end of the treatment (Ninth Cycle), he reported a fantasy of masturbating anally with a long pole that his father had used in the grocery store to reach merchandise on the top shelves. Associations to the long pole included memories of envying his father's long penis; envying his father's status at the grocery store where the men and older boys who hung around the store showed special respect for his father; and envy of his father's special relationship with his mother—how much she must have admired and enjoyed his big penis, judging by her squeals and moans during intercourse (which formerly he had misinterpreted as cries of pain and anguish, thereby avoiding the jealous hurt of realizing how much she enjoyed it). Although the fantasy of masturbating with his father's "long pole" was manifestly homoerotic, a more subtle aspect of the imagery did not escape either the patient or therapist: namely, that in his fantasy he had *gained possession* of his father's "long pole"—the very act of aggression which formerly he had been at such (masochistic) pains to conceal.

The question arises in this connection whether the (partial) emergence of the previously latent phallic-oedipal aggression constitutes probative evidence for the interpretation and reconstruction and, if so, what makes it probative? One factor might be prediction: that is, I had anticipated what might, and eventually did, occur. Grünbaum (1984, 1993) might argue that my interpretation and reconstruction to the patient may have planted the idea in the compliant patient's mind. Another aspect of this evidence is more difficult to discount, however: namely, the context in which it emerged, that is, its position in a relatively fixed and recurrent sequence of mental events.

Close comparisons of Sequences C-1, C-2, and C-3 in the Second, Fifth, and Ninth Dynamic Cycles suggests that what the patient was repeating were not merely isolated memories, emotions, conflicts, and defenses, but a specific series of mental states, each component of which had its own particular and recurrent position in the sequence. The sequence appeared to include a relatively fixed series of defenses against the latent phallic-aggressive feelings towards his father: (1) submissiveness; (2) seductiveness; (3) erotization of nonphysical injury (moral masochism); (4) erotization of physical injury (masochistic perversion); (5) masochism becoming more active, overt, and provocative, with emergence of a sadistic fantasy underlying the masochism; and (6) increasing fear of injury from fantasies of violent anal penetration, leading to deeper defensive (dependent) regression.

Each of these defenses encountered intrapsychic conflict, which appeared to produce a dynamic shift to the next defense in the series. Based on psychodynamic theory, the latent aggression should tend to emerge in less disguised form when the series of masochistic defenses had run their course and come to an end. The fantasies of pinching off a man's penis in his rectum, and of gaining possession of his father's "long pole" occurred, as expected, at the end of such a sequence.

This type of intraclinical evidence is contextually-based. The recurrence of dynamic sequences in which the position of latent entities within the sequences can be inferred or predicted, appears to be a relatively probative type of evidence, a form of organized interlocking microstructure underlying an interpretation or reconstruction. Small-scale evidence of this kind does not stand alone, however, but, as the previous examples illustrate, it operates in concert with various other methods of justification such as cross-validation and convergence of evidence, repetition, prediction, postdiction, coherence, and the patient's responses to interpretations. The more pluralistic the methods of justification, the more probative the support for interpretive hypotheses.

The Progressive Process of Revising Interpretations

Another way that the RC methodology is useful in systematic, retrospective investigations of the therapeutic process is by contributing to the gradual revisions of depth-psychological understanding that lead eventually to more comprehensive formulations of interpretations and reconstructions. To illustrate the process of progressively reshaping interpretations, the numerous revisions and gradual filling in of a major reconstruction in Mr. Clark's analysis will be reviewed and discussed. The reconstruction dealt with his most pathological, self-destructive character pattern, the masochistic defense. To demonstrate the step-wise increases in depth-psychological understanding of this character pattern, interpretive progress on the masochistic defense is divided into four stages: (1) initial impressions based upon the first four dynamic cycles; (2) some additions to the initial reconstruction arising during the fifth cycle; (3) further modifications suggested by the sixth dynamic cycle; and (4) completion of a comprehensive, partially justified reconstruction based upon the last three recurrent cycles.

Initial reconstruction of the masochistic defense (first through fourth dynamic cycles): His father's emotional distance from the patient produced a narcissistic injury and an intensified exhibitionistic urge to attract his father's attention and interest. Partly by trial and error, and partly through identifications with the women in his family, he learned specific methods of attracting his father's attention. His father was not very responsive to the boy's attempts to emulate, play up to, or otherwise please him. He did respond fairly consistently, however, although in critical, scolding, humiliating, and physically punitive ways, to the patient's making a pest of himself at the grocery store, "messing up" on chores that his father assigned to him, and being a

"Momma's boy." Feeling that it was better to be yelled at than ignored, Mr. Clark became adept at "bugging" his father in order to get attention from him. Behavior of that kind also discharged some of his pent-up resentment toward his father for ignoring him. Spankings by his father were common, and may have contributed to the intensification of gluteal-anal eroticism as a compensatory masochistic substitute for the exhibitionistic-narcissistic gratifications that he craved.

Additions to the reconstruction (during the fifth cycle): During the middle phase of the analysis, the relationship of the masochistic defense to conflicts about phallic aggression became increasingly clear. The aggression was directed specifically against father figures, including his transference to the therapist. The nature of the aggression was primarily phallic-competitive, although narcissistic rage from feeling unloved by father figures, or from humiliating exposure of his desire for a father's love, sometimes accompanied the competitive aggression. The narcissistic rage from feeling slighted by a father figure was used additionally as a self-justifying defense against guilt associated with the competitive aggression.

Further modifications of the reconstruction (arising during the sixth cycle): Identifications with his mother and grandmother provided two separate models for the molding of his masochistic defense. Even his characteristic facial expression, an odd mixture of childish innocence and spinsterish primness, replicated his mother's somewhat child-like personality and his grandmother's properness. He internalized his grandmother's submissiveness towards his patriarchal grandfather, which netted him some compensatory, paternal-like attention from his grandfather—and from a long series of mentors in later years. He also internalized his mother's provocativeness towards his father, which contributed to his masochistically exhibitionistic pattern of "bugging" his father.

Completion of the reconstruction (based upon the last three dynamic cycles): He had observed, overheard, and repressed the recollection of his parents' sexual relations during the first eight years of his life. He mistook his mother's moans and cries of passion for pain, which he imagined were caused by his father ramming his huge penis into his mother's rectum and occasionally into her mouth. Recovery of these primal scene memories and fantasies during the last three dynamic cycles of the therapeutic process exposed and weakened the introjection of his mother's supposed pain from "anal" penetration. Much of his anal-erotic imagery had been stimulated and shaped by those experiences and associated fantasies. Their introjection had implanted in him a panic-laden phantasy-wish for violent and painful anal penetration by his father, and for masochistic sexual submission on his own part.

The gradual evolving, broadening, and deepening of the preceding formulations illustrates a number of features and problems associated with the construction and justification of interpretations. First, the sheer numbers and complexities of factors that contributed to the origins of masochism in this patient suggest that attempts to justify clinical interpretations and reconstructions by experimental or other extraclinical methods probably would not be a realistic or productive investigative approach. It is difficult to imagine how such a surplus of subtle, complex meanings and determinants could be replicated or investigated extraclinically. Despite its limitations, therefore, depth-psychological treatments continue to provide our best means of studying, constructing, and attempting to justify interpretations of these exceedingly complex phenomena.

Another strategy of justification which the present examples support is that no one justifying method is applicable to all interpretations and reconstructions. For example, since the reconstructive formulation of Mr. Clark's masochism was changing steadily throughout the therapeutic process, some justifying methods (for example, repetition and prediction) were not always applicable. Demonstration of organized interlocking microstructures underlying each evolving stage of the reconstruction's development was the most consistently effective form of justification in this particular instance. The principle of methodologic pluralism applies to every phase and aspect of psychoanalysis and dynamic psychotherapy, including the formulation and justification of interpretations and reconstructions.

Finally, the present examples illustrate another useful justifying principle, namely, that probability judgments concern only that evidence upon which an interpretation or reconstruction is based (Keynes, 1962; Hirsch, 1967). Since some factors are known and others are unknown, a probability judgment may be correct in relation to the known evidence, but incorrect with respect to the unknown elements. In the case of clinical interpretations and reconstructions, therefore, a construction made earlier in the therapeutic process may be justified insofar as it represents the most plausible and probable interpretation that could be formulated at the time; but later in the treatment, the earlier construction may have to be reassessed as unjustified, or only partially justified, in the light of further clinical evidence. Interpretations and reconstructions always involve a selection and progressive modification of an initially plausible construction, the justification of which is relative at every stage of the interpretive process.

Some Limitations of Interpretive Justification

In order to illustrate the process of posttherapeutic justification as clearly as possible, I have selected and presented a relatively uncomplicated case. Cases involving more severe and complex pathology are also amenable to posttherapeutic investigation of this kind, but they present greater difficulties in identifying recurrent cycles. In addition, the clinical examples of interpretive justification that I have presented largely supported the interpretations to which they were applied; but that is not always, or even usually, the case. Just as often, justifying tests do not support, or may disconfirm, an interpretation. Both therapeutically and scientifically, however, the latter result can be as useful as a confirmation—providing information about where clinical inferences and interpretations may have gone off track. As Kramer (1989) observes, analysis at its best is a process in which mistakes are put to good use.

Another limitation of the present approach is that justifying tests do not overcome or eliminate the consensus problem. Different analysts, including those associated with the same school of psychoanalysis, may disagree on the posttherapeutic formulations of recurrent dynamic cycles, and on the results of various justifying tests. This raises the question, what good are justifying methods if they do not surmount the reliability problem in interpretive work?

First of all, reliability and justification are not equivalent or interchangeable concepts. Reliability is concerned with the consistency of investigative (including interpretive) methods, rather than with the probity of results obtained by such methods. Unlike justification, reliability never refers to hypotheses or theories, but only to methods. Woodard (1993b, p. 150) notes that therapeutic process research has focused primarily on reliability studies rather than on validation, viewing interrater agreement and reliability coefficients as crucial. Yet, "there has often been an inverse relationship between the consensus that could be obtained and the importance of the concept to be judged" (Levine and Luborsky, 1981, p. 501). The more complex the phenomena, the less reliability can be expected; but even highly reliable methods do not guarantee the probity of results. On the other hand, consistently probative results cannot be expected from unreliable methods, and Polya's (1945) work on plausible inference suggests that reliable methods may increase the chances of valid results.

Unlike reliability, justification is directed primarily to hypotheses and theories, attempting to determine their probity. In interpretive work, justifying measures attempt to identify which among alternative constructions is the "most plausible" hypothesis at a given time. The persistence of the consensus problem makes it all the more necessary that we employ whatever justifying measures are available—to check, cross check, and double check the plausibility of our inherently uncertain constructions.

One further caveat must be mentioned in connection with the limitations of interpretive justification. Just as the discovery phase of the interpretive process is perspective-bound, so are the methods of justifying interpretations specific to the particular depth-psychological school or conceptual system of the clinical interpreter. Not only is it necessary to understand an interpretation in the context of its own conceptual framework, but also the justification of interpretations must be carried out within, and also is confined to, the same conceptual system. Ego psychologists, for example, cannot understand or justify Kleinian interpretations by use of ego psychological methods and concepts; and vice versa.

Applying this epistemologic limitation to the interpretations and justifications of the present case: the interpretations that I have posited and attempted to justify do not, and can not, claim to be the "most plausible" formulations that any and all schools of psychoanalysis might propose. The claims for my interpretations and justifications must be considerably more modest and restricted than that, namely: within a (primarily) ego psychological perspective, the interpretations that I have formulated and attempted to justify appear to be the "most plausible" when compared with alternative hypotheses formulated within the same, primarily ego psychological framework.

Summary

Interpretive justification during the treatment of patients is necessarily limited. Therapists attempt to determine the most plausible among alternative constructions at a given time by comparing competing interpretations, testing them against all of the current data, and use of checking, revising, and rechecking procedures. More definitive justification of clinical interpretations requires additional, posttherapeutic, retrospective study employing a record of the entire therapeutic process. The latter, more detailed approach employs multiple justifying tests and criteria, including the identification of organized interlocking microstructures in the clinical data.

The microstructures described in this chapter consist of recurrent dynamic sequences and cycles of conflict-defense configurations which repeat themselves at an increasingly rapid rate as the therapeutic process progresses. Microstructures of this kind were discovered by the late Thomas M. French (1952, 1954, 1958a,b), and have been utilized by the present writer as part of a methodology for justifying interpretations: that is, if an interpretation corresponds well with, or is "in the neighborhood" of, the principal thematic conflict at a particular time, it should be congruent with the specific phase of the patient's underlying recurrent dynamic cycle at that time. Multiple additional justifying methods can be combined with the use of such microstructures to produce a pluralistic methodology of justifying interpretations and reconstructions.

A case report has been presented to illustrate the author's pluralistic approach to justifying interpretations. In addition to a traditional narrative summary of the patient's history and therapeutic process, this chapter has described a systematic posttherapeutic method of investigating the therapeutic process which employs a record of the patient's treatment and attempts to justify (or disconfirm) interpretations and reconstructions. To demonstrate the need for "time change" methods in the formulation and justification of clinical interpretations, the gradual evolving, broadening, and deepening of a major reconstruction in the illustrative case has been traced throughout the entire therapeutic process.

The case report demonstrates that no single method of justification is applicable to all interpretations and reconstructions, and that interpretations, like concepts in general science, invariably change over time in the light of new findings. The strategy of methodologic pluralism applies to every phase and aspect of psychoanalysis and dynamic psychotherapy, including the formulation and justification of interpretations. Interpretations always involve a selection and progressive modification of an initially plausible construction, the justification of which is relative at every stage of the interpretive process.

The pluralistic, problem-oriented, relativistic, and pragmatic aspects of interpretive justification illustrated in this chapter are consonant with the perspectives of postpositivist science, including its more commonsense view of how knowledge is acquired. That is, one need not make final choices between truth and falsity; knowledge claims form a continuum of correctness and incorrectness, and can move in either direction as more information accrues; and since both the methods and logics of postpositivist science are pluralistic, no one method is *the* correct method of formulating and justifying interpretations and reconstructions.

Some inevitable problems and limitations of interpretive justification are also reviewed in this chapter. Although none of the available interpretive hypotheses at a given time may be entirely free of questions and doubts, choosing among them is as common in science as it is in everyday life (Polkinghorne, 1983, pp. 129–131). Holding all hypotheses open to question, attempting to reduce errors by multiple, increasingly exacting tests, and willingness to learn from one's errors,[4] are key elements in a postpositivist approach to interpretive justification.

PART V
SUMMARY AND CONCLUSIONS

What one *observes* in the psychoanalytic session is words, postures, gestures, intonation; everything else is inferred. I think the "lowest level" inferences should be the main object of study for the time being, rather than highly theoretical statements.

[Paul Meehl, 1973, p. 117]

It is necessary to define carefully and to debate the context or perspective from which clinical facts are claimed to have been disclosed and further inferences drawn. This puts the study of the analyst's mind and his observational and inferential methodology at the heart of the accumulation of psychoanalytic knowledge.

[David Tuckett, 1995, p. 659]

We fill in what is omitted by making plausible inferences and translating it into conscious material. In this way we construct, as it were, a sequence of conscious events complementary to the unconscious psychical processes. The relative certainty of our psychical science is based on the binding force of these inferences.

[Sigmund Freud, 1940a, p. 159]

10

The Methodology of Clinical Interpretation

Problems and Progress

To summarize the principal themes of the preceding chapters: Interpretation is an important aspect of modern thought, part of the movement from metaphysics to epistemology—away from things as they are to how things are known. The radical shift in science and philosophy from a positivist to a postpositivist perspective has contributed significantly to the growing interest in interpretation; for interpretive inquiry is very compatible with a postpositivist approach: it does not seek certainty; is problem rather than method oriented, data rather than theory driven; is context sensitive, flexible, relativistic, pattern seeking, pluralistic, probabilistic, and employs multiple methods of justification.

Interpretation is a general method of inquiry, used in various ways and to differing extents in all branches of science. It is the most common form of inquiry in the human and social sciences. Clinical interpretation is a specific and relatively recent variety of the more general interpretive approach. Many nonclinical interpretive methods and concepts are similar and potentially relevant to the methodology of clinical interpretation. Chapter 5 of this volume reviews, illustrates, and compares a number of such methods with clinical interpretation, for example: (1) various relation- and pattern-oriented methodologies such as the pattern model approach, structuralism, system theory, hermeneutics, and gestalt psychology; (2) the methodologies of various language-related disciplines including linguistics, psycholinguistics, communication theory, semiotics, rhetoric, literary theory and criticism, and archaeological decipherment; (3) interpretive methods employed in a number of cognitive science approaches, including cognitive psychology, schema theory, information theory, the computational model of mind, and artificial intelligence; and (4) a recently proposed model of interpretation based upon commonsense (intentional) psychology.

Psychoanalysis and dynamic psychotherapy have followed Freud's example in taking their interpretive methods for granted, in assuming that clinical interpretations are more reliable and accurate than they actually are, and in avoiding problematic aspects of interpretation such as the consensus problem, the circularity of the interpretive process, and confirmation bias. Another tendency among psychoanalysts and dynamic psychotherapists has been the perpetuation of a positivist-like perspective (similar to Freud's) regarding interpretive methodology: for example, seeking certainty in clinical interpretations, which is unattainable (see Barnes, 1988); privileging and overusing single rather than multiple interpretive methods—a positivist-like, method-oriented approach; and assuming incorrectly that clinical interpretations have a secure foundation in psychoanalytic theory and biology—whereas with the partial exception of their empirical bearing, interpretations lack foundations.

To lay the "lingering ghost of positivism" in our interpretive methodology, psychoanalysis and dynamic psychotherapy need to embrace the postpositivist viewpoint more fully—to recognize that it is the most natural and effective scientific perspective for interpretive work. Since the postpositivist viewpoint is pluralistic and eclectic, such a change does not necessitate the elimination of all positivist elements: empiricism, for example, retains a place in science as a theory of evidence, though not of truth. The task is to develop a theory and practice of clinical interpretation that avoids absolutism, on the one hand, but does not collapse into complete relativism, on the other.

For psychoanalysis and dynamic psychotherapy to make scientific claims, some model of justifying interpretations is essential. The accuracy of interpretations depends upon the power of evidence, which consists of empirical data and logical arguments that support or disconfirm a conclusion. Being the first-level inferences, the lowest level theoretical statements of psychoanalysis and dynamic psychotherapy, interpretations are the only propositions that can be tested by direct empirical evidence, that is, data of the case being studied. Higher level clinical theories are tested in other ways.

During the past twenty years the philosopher of science Adolf Grünbaum has mounted a forceful philosophical critique of psychoanalysis and clinical interpretation. He evaluates Freud's methods, theories, and reasoning as Freud wished them to be considered, namely, as empirical methods and causal hypotheses of a natural science. Grünbaum argues persuasively that psychoanalysis is a science, or can be, if pursued within certain constraints. The scientific guidelines that he describes can be useful to psychoanalysis, particularly in interpreting, theorizing about, and attempting to validate causal factors in human development, personality, and psychopathology. He reminds us that the burden of proof for our methods and theories rests squarely on our shoulders, and that probative evidence supporting psychoanalysis and clinical interpretation is far from satisfactory.

Not everything that Grünbaum writes about psychoanalysis is applicable to our science, however: for example, his singular focus on causal-correlational hypotheses, and his insistence upon group-comparison methods to satisfy the canons of eliminative inductivism—methods which are methodologically problematic in disciplines such as psychoanalysis and dynamic psychotherapy. It is unclear to what extent Grünbaum's critique applies to interpretive hypotheses in contrast to higher level theories. His critique of drawing causal inferences from meaning-relations in clinical interpretation is one of the most thought provoking of his arguments, but one that calls for further consideration and investigation, not foreclosure.

Although problems of clinical evidence in psychoanalysis and dynamic psychotherapy are numerous and daunting, the present study concludes that interpretations can be justified, and can be justified intraclinically—though not as completely as theories are confirmed in the physical sciences. The goal of justification is not merely to confirm or disconfirm a particular interpretation, but to discriminate between alternative hypotheses—to determine which among competing hypotheses is the most plausible interpretation.

A distinction is necessary between the relatively limited justification of interpretations during the actual treatment of patients, and more definitive justification based upon retrospective, post-therapeutic study of the record of a completed therapeutic process. The former is essentially a "screening" process to rule out initially plausible-appearing constructions which on further checking do not meet the criteria of accounting both coherently and comprehensively for the largest number of clinical data. Systematic, posttherapeutic analysis based on a record of the entire therapeutic process utilizes more varied, complex, and probative methods of justification. The latter approach has some features in common with the CPC (and autopsy) traditions in medical science: both involve a systematic and thorough review of clinical decisions and procedures; and both promote learning from errors as well as from correct clinical conclusions.

Like the interpretive process generally, the justification of interpretations is methodologically pluralistic. The most probative methods are cross-validation and convergence of evidence, discovery of organized interlocking microstructures in the clinical data which support a particular construction, indirect prediction and postdiction (of classes of events), and repetition of themes and patterns. The widely used methods of coherence and the patient's responses to an interpretation are less reliable, especially if used alone—the former because it is circular, and the latter because the patient's responses themselves must be interpreted. All such methods operate in concert with the more probative justifying procedures, however, making possible a cross-checking of their results. No one method of justification is applicable to all interpretations and reconstructions. Interpretations involve a selection and progressive modification of an initially plausible construction, the justification of which is relative at every stage of the interpretive process.

The pluralistic and relativistic features of clinical interpretive inquiry are consonant with a postpositivist scientific perspective. Although no agreement has been reached regarding an epistemology of psychoanalysis and its interpretive methodology, a pluralistic perspective encompassing both postpositivist and natural science approaches seems necessary and appropriate. A so-called "naturalized" epistemology, for example, bears directly upon interpretive inquiry by its interest in problems of discovery, inductive inference, causality, and empirical justification.

The Nature and Scientific Status of Interpretation as a Method of Inquiry

Philosophers of science have raised a number of questions about the nature and scientific status of interpretation, namely: Are interpretations scientific statements, hypotheses, or reports of special kinds of experiences? Do interpretations actually discover properties in the object, or do they merely impute properties to the object? Can it be demonstrated that interpretive systems such as psychoanalysis are valid? And how can we account for the fact that interpretive practice tolerates a plurality of often incompatible interpretations, yet also assumes that alternative constructions can be compared and choices made among them (Wittgenstein, 1969, p. 212; Barnes, 1988, p. 7)?

Wittgenstein said that to interpret is to think[1]; but that raises the further question, what kind of thinking is involved in interpreting? Wittgenstein claimed that it is easy to recognize when one is interpreting (rather than reporting or describing, for example), because in interpreting we form hypotheses that may turn out to be false (Barnes, 1988, pp. 159, 165–166; see also Reider, 1972). If one is interpreting rather than merely conjecturing, he or she must be able to provide reasons for the interpretation. If one is interpreting rather than describing, it is likely that he or she is not classifying in a way that is easily or generally known. In addition, "interpreting is irreducibly pluralistic: fundamentally diverse activities count as interpreting" (Barnes, 1988, pp. 68, 70).

Concerning the debate about whether interpretations actually discover properties in objects or only impute them, those two alternatives are not mutually exclusive. Imputing properties is not always opposed to discovery, but can be integral to it.[2] Although the interpretive task is not definitively completable, the objects of interpretation have determinate meanings; truth has a place in interpretation; and some interpretations have the status of confirmable or disconfirmable scientific statements (Barnes, 1988, pp. 3, 72). Barnes observes also that the lack of unanimity among interpreters, "the resistance to new interpretations which conflict with entrenched patterns of thought, the desire for novel interpretations, and the always present possibility of error," are characteristic features of interpretation. "They have their parallels in the scientific realm. Such features do not, however, make talk of discovery inappropriate in either realm" (pp. 43–45).

Relatively few interpretations are truth-claiming statements. Most are constructed and offered as plausible hypotheses rather than as true statements; others are inferences about what the patient might be experiencing. Some philosophers argue that interpretations cannot be truth-bearing statements; but the philosopher Nelson Goodman (1978, pp. 120–125) approaches this question by asking whether an interpretation can be refuted.

Refutation of true/false statements is possible in principle, and a relevant counterpossibility is sufficient to discredit such a statement. Citing Goodman's position on whether psychoanalytic interpretations can be validated, Barnes (1988) concludes that:

> I see no reason why in principle we cannot do so. Given that there are alternative hypotheses and that no Archimedian point exists outside the hypotheses from which to judge the relative merits of each, it will often be a difficult task to decide which among competing hypotheses is to be established. Difficulty is not, however, impossibility. We might, for example, have to consider the hypothesis' consistency or coherency, its fecundity, its simplicity or its utility, for these factors, rather than being supplemental to truth, are often used as tests for it [p. 78].

One never knows all of the relevant evidence, however. Thus although an interpretive claim can be true in principle, there are many reasons why in particular cases it may not be possible to establish the truth of a given interpretation (see, for example, the philosopher Colin McGinn, 1989, from whom much of the material for the following section has been drawn).

Mental Content and Interpretive Methodology

Clinicians seldom concern themselves with philosophical questions about mental content, even though the subject is very relevant to clinical interpretation and to the psychoanalytic structural theory. The issue of mental content has been central to the philosophy of mind, which asks questions such as the following: (1) How does attributing content to mental states contribute to our understanding of persons? (2) What is the structural basis of content, the nature of its mechanism? (3) Are contents of the mind essentially independent of the surrounding world, or is there a deep connection between states of mind and conditions of the nonmental world (McGinn, 1989, p. 132; compare also Cavell, 1988)?

Starting with the question of how attributions of content help in the understanding of persons: Both commonsense and scientific psychology refer frequently to content-bearing (representational) states in order to explain mental processes and behavior—which suggests that mental content is not merely an epiphenomenon, but has explanatory (causal) relevance. Commonsense psychology in particular is a distinctly content-based system of interpreting and describing the mental states of others and ourselves. To understand what people want, believe, and do, content is ascribed to their desires, beliefs, and actions.

The principal objection to content-based psychology is the so-called "causal argument," that content and causality do not mix—that content plays no causal role in producing a mental state's intrapsychic or behavioral effects (McGinn, 1989, p. 133; compare Grünbaum's arguments against the causal relevance of "meaning-relations" in interpretive methodology, discussed in Chapter 7). The philosophical basis of the "causal argument," according to McGinn (1989, p. 144), is that contentful states refer to entities outside of the subject's body, which ostensibly rules out their involvement in a causal process, because what takes place at the causal nexus must be intrinsic, local, rather than related to something that exists elsewhere.

McGinn's counterargument to the causal viewpoint invokes the teleology of mental states to suggest how content (meaning-relations) can have causal relevance. He points out that mental states have an environment-directed purpose, and that specifying their purpose tells us something important about such states. In other words, like bodily traits, the powers and properties of the mind are also evolutionary, and as such help the organism adapt to environmental contingencies. Moreover, the content and biological function or purpose associated with mental states are intimately interrelated. Thus the teleological theory answers the causal objection by locating content in a wider context. Specifying the content of a mental state suggests its biological function, which helps to explain why the organism does what it does. This form of explanation has the advantage of making it possible to predict an organism's behavior without knowing the detailed workings of its causal mechanisms (McGinn, 1989, pp. 149–150, 153).[3]

With respect to the structural basis of content, the most widely favored view within philosophy is that of a syntax-driven mechanism such as the "language of thought" hypothesis proposed by Jerry Fodor (1975, 1987). The mechanism underlying content according to that theory is a representational state that manipulates sentences. A rival theory proposes that we generate mental representations by constructing abstract models of the world, the manipulation of which is the mechanistic basis of content.[4] McGinn (1989) distinguishes between sentential and modelling theories this way: "sentences do not simulate what they describe, and models do not describe what they simulate" (p. 181).

Mental models not only simulate (abstractly) the structure of what they represent, but also the operations of what is modelled, that is, how it works. Modelling theory differs from the older image theory of content in that the latter requires literal resemblance between the representational image and what it stands for, whereas a model need not resemble the real object in that way. By themselves, however, modelling structures cannot generate intentionality. They are only the underlying mechanism, which needs a purpose if it is to subserve content.

The question of whether mental content is essentially autonomous with respect to the world, or whether the world enters into the very nature of mental states, is reflected in the current psychoanalytic debate between traditionalists who stress Freud's interpretive focus on intrapsychic contents, and interactivists whose interpretations emphasize "real" patient-therapist interactions. The classic argument for externalism of content is that mental states vary with variations in the environment, and thus the mind must be penetrated and configured by the world. The commitment of psychoanalytic theory to the complemental series encompasses both internalist and externalist views;[5] and from the standpoint of clinical practice, the question arises whether our interpretive focus is or ought to be exclusively either intrapsychic or interactive (Inderbitzin and Levy, 1994, p. 764). McGinn concludes on the basis of philosophical analysis that mental states comprise both internalist and externalist "locations" of mental content (1989, p. 100).

The Role of Interpretation in an Interactivist Approach

The interactive perspective focuses on psychological processes in either patient or therapist that affect psychological processes in the other. The therapeutic process is conceptualized as a series of (often "real") interactions between therapist and patient. The intrapsychic focus of traditional approaches is criticized for ignoring the therapist's conflicts and biases, and for underestimating the patient's recognition of and responses to such attitudes in the therapist (Hoffman, 1983).

On the basis of these views, clinical interactivists no longer consider depth-psychological interpretations and insight the principal factors in therapeutic change.[6] Interpretations to the patient are viewed as part of a larger interactive process. Raphling (1992, 1995) suggests that the trend towards reducing the importance of interpretation is related also to the assertiveness (aggression) necessitated by the interpretive act, which some therapists consider assaultive.

For a number of reasons, however, it seems doubtful that even the most extreme interactive approach could be carried out effectively in the absence, or radical reduction, of depth-psychological interpretive inquiry, that is, attempting to understand the patient in depth. The object or direction of interpretive focus in an interactive approach is said to shift from the traditional patient-centered emphasis on intrapsychic events to "real" interactions between therapist and patient; but interactive psychological processes are themselves far from self-evident, and thus require the usual painstaking interpretive work to be understood. In fact, depth-psychological understanding may be even more important (and difficult) in an interactive approach; for, as Cooper (1993) observes, the therapist is a "participant-observer attempting to understand psychic and multiple realities" (p. 109). A number of writers have noted that effective therapeutic experiences and accurate understanding—not only of the patient, but also of the therapist and of the interactions between them—appear to depend upon and complement each other.[7]

The Role of Theory in Interpretive Methodology

Despite Freud's injunctions against the use of theory in constructing latent mental contents (for example, 1912b, pp. 114–115), doctrinal interpretation persists as a methodologic problem.[8] Rather than employing interpretations heuristically to discover multiple unknown meanings and determinants, such an approach finds mainly what it seeks, and indoctrinates patients with preconceived clinical theories. On the other hand, clinical observation and interpretation cannot do without some concepts and background assumptions. The problem, as Meehl (1970/1973, p. 115) puts it, is how to get the advantages of a skilled observer who knows what to listen for and how to classify it, without the methodologic disadvantage that a person possessing such skill is already theoretically biased by professional training.

The present study suggests that a distinction must be made between two levels and types of theories: a) the general methodologic (core) concepts of psychoanalysis, which are indispensable to clinical interpretation; and b) specific clinical theories, which often are not applicable to the individual patient and frequently interfere with the construction of unique personal meanings and determinants. General methodologic concepts promote the construction of multiple, alternative meanings and determinants, and thus are necessary and useful in interpretive work. The basic general assumptions that underlie Freud's interpretive system include the concepts of an unconscious mind, continuity, meaning, determinism, overdetermination, instinctual drives, conflict, defenses (among which repression has a preeminent place), repetition, transference, and the importance of childhood experiences (Rapaport, 1944). What most characterizes these core concepts of psychoanalysis and clinical interpretation is their generality, because of which they do not force interpretations into preconceived conclusions; new, unique interpretations of the data are possible within the general theoretical (and methodological) framework of a science.

By contrast, interpretive approaches that emphasize specific clinical theories employ highly particular as well as basic general concepts; and to the detriment of interpretive inquiry, specific clinical theories generate only single rather than alternative interpretive hypotheses. For that reason (and others), Loewenstein (1957, p. 149) suggested that psychoanalysis should be conducted as though clinical theory did not exist; and Paniagua (1985) argues that therapists need not even "believe in" the oedipal or other complexes in order to practice effective psychoanalysis and clinical interpretation. For when there is nothing but continuous theorizing all along the same lines, and no alternative theoretical models and interpretations are considered, the approach is no longer a working theory but a dogma (De Groot, 1969, p. 56). Thus the methodology of clinical interpretation must be developed and applied in practice independently of specific clinical theories; for clinical theory does not, cannot, and should not produce a method of interpretation.

Interpretive Heuristics

Rather than relying upon specific clinical theories to interpret latent mental contents, psychoanalysis and dynamic psychotherapy have a wide variety of heuristics available to guide interpretive inquiry. Diesing (1971, p. 15) defines a heuristic as a loosely systematic procedure for investigation or inquiry that gives good results on the whole, but does not guarantee them in any particular instance. Unlike algorithms, heuristics are methods of inquiry and search. The fundamental rule of psychoanalysis, for example, and the basic methodologic (core) concepts of psychoanalysis and interpretive methodology are heuristic strategies that both guide interpretive inquiry and serve as constraints to reduce unfruitful searches. Heuristic strategies collect and organize relevant information, reduce complexity and ambiguity, and increase understanding of what is important at a particular time (Thomä and Kächele, 1987, p. 260; 1990; see also Rogers, 1981, p. 440).

Freud employed numerous heuristics in his interpretive work, many of which have been described by Grinstein (1983), for example: the thematization heuristic, that is, searching for a thread of continuity that links disparate data into a dynamic theme; the fractionation heuristic, used to get behind the secondary elaborations of dreams; the importance of context; focusing strategies—focusing, for example, on the point of sensory intensity in a dream; on affects; on conspicuous omissions and areas of vagueness, which suggest repression; focusing on events of the previous day in search of possible precipitants; focusing on similarities, contrasts, contiguities, and repetitions; and many others.

Peterfreund (1983) also described a large number of heuristic strategies which he found useful in interpretive work, for example: comparing and matching data in different ways; searching not only for discrete but also for general patterns in clinical data—the larger the pattern the better; using error-correcting feedback to test a postulated pattern's goodness of fit; making predictions based upon working models; working inductively from within the data; searching randomly through segments of memory; scanning for the unusual, for phenomena that do not fit the normal flow of experience; and others.

Additional examples of interpretive heuristics described by various authors[9] include: the importance of analogies and metaphors; using all of the data; carrying out observation as a largely unfocused activity, while data processing requires some focusing of attention; narrative building as a heuristic process; the necessity to mobilize memory indirectly, by one content suggesting another; working backwards at times, because latent contents tend to be less disguised toward the end of a therapy session, in later versions of dream series, and at the end of the therapeutic process.

Howard Shevrin (1984, pp. 34–35) presents an instructive clinical vignette illustrating the use of multiple heuristics in arriving at a construction; and a volume edited by Groner et al. (1983), *Methods of Heuristics*, provides a useful review of heuristic methods employed in various other disciplines. The heuristics employed in clinical interpretation include numerous parallels with widely used heuristics in other disciplines—illustrating again some relevant postpositivist methodologic similarities between psychoanalysis and other sciences.

The Difficulties and Fallibility of Clinical Interpretive Inquiry

Contrary to Freud's assertions, clinical interpretation is neither "easy" nor "trustworthy in every respect"; it is difficult and fallible. Numerous factors contribute to the problems and limitations of interpretive methodology: (1) the sheer numbers, complex interrelations, and instability of unconscious meanings and determinants; (2) the obscuring effects of repression and other defenses; (3) the diverse perspectives, background assumptions, and biases from which we view all phenomena (interpretive relativism); (4) special limitations of interpreters' objectivity, including confirmation bias and countertransference distortions; (5) ambiguities inherent in language, paralinguistic and nonverbal cues, imagery, and in our perceptions of all such phenomena; (6) multiple conceptions rather than a unified definition of meaning; (7) several coexisting layers of meaning, producing plurivocality of individual meanings; (8) the multiplace "locations" of meaning—in the patient, the interpreter, the clinical data, and the context; (9) dissimilarities between meanings in the individual case compared with generalizations from other cases; (10) limitations and distortions of memory on the part of both patient and therapist; (11) the circularity and self-confirmability of interpretations; (12) the inherently provisional nature of constructions, necessitating multiple revisions and alternative hypotheses; (13) obstacles to the comparison of alternative constructions; (14) inherent problems in the nature of clinical evidence; and (15) difficulties in justifying interpretations.

Multiplicity, complexity, ambiguity, and obscurity of latent mental contents are among the commonest factors in the preceding list. Spence (1982a, pp. 267–268) notes that there is an irony here, because the importance of ambiguity in the therapeutic process has not been properly addressed by our interpretive method. Even the language we use to discover, formulate, and justify latent mental contents limits as well as facilitates what can be perceived and understood in patients' associations (Viderman, 1974); for language, including paralinguistic and nonverbal cues, serves purposes of concealment as well as revelation. In addition, every person draws differently from the repertory of verbal and paraverbal devices (Labov and Fanshel, 1977). Thus, language can serve as the "persistent seduction, the central resistance" of therapy, because it so readily replaces the patient's primary inner experience with words and paraverbal accompaniments, both of which are inherently ambiguous (Spence, 1982a, p. 62).

The preceding problem is an example of so-called "method effects" in scientific inquiry: that is, the methods we use decisively influence and constrain what we can observe and understand. The methods one uses to solve a scientific (including interpretive) problem are thus an important part of the problem itself. Fox et al. (1963) point out that "often in the history of science, obvious inconsistencies have compelled a critical reexamination of the methods that were used to arrive at contradictory results. It is then that the most startling, even revolutionary, discoveries are made" (p. 7; see also Hooke, 1963; Scriven, 1969, p. 208).

The contextual aspect of meanings is another source of both interpretive understanding and difficulty. Because we have no way of interpreting an isolated segment of clinical data in and of itself, we must turn to wider contexts that precede and follow the data in question (Peterfreund, 1971, pp. 239–241). The adjacent contexts themselves must be interpreted, however, so that to understand any particular meaning we must study an ever-widening and changing context of other interpreted events. A specific interpretation, therefore, is not tied to any single set of observables, but rests upon an extensive array of previous interdependent interpretations—which, in addition, are not static but in a continuous state of dynamic flux (McIntosh, 1979, pp. 408–409; Gergen, 1988, p. 35; Kermode, 1985).

The large amounts and complex varieties of data generated by the clinical situation also confront therapists with both interpretive opportunities and difficulties—the latter because of inability to assimilate and process so much data in a limited period of time. The therapist's attention is necessarily divided between observing and registering the new data that continue to pour in, and at the same time attempting to process the data already generated in the session. Therapists sometimes respond to this problem counterproductively by use of ineffective heuristic "shortcuts," for example, reducing the amount and variety of data, and employing fewer and simpler methods of processing the data (Turk and Salovey, 1988, pp. 2–7; see also Rubovits-Seitz, 1992a, p. 151, for examples of questionable "shortcut heuristics" in clinical interpretation). Therapists' moods and energy levels also influence their interpretive efficiency, producing effects upon memory, attentional focus, selective encoding and retrieval of information, and data processing (Turk and Salovey, 1988, pp. 107–109).

Another source of difficulty for clinical interpreters is the frustrating uncertainty of their conclusions; for no universally valid methods of interpretation or categories of meaning have been discovered; general rules of interpretation are of little value in specific instances; and we lack an agreed-upon methodology and clinical tradition of justifying interpretations. Clinical interpreters thus live, as Leavy (1980, p. 78) observes, "in a nearly constant state of mental disarray," without benefit of ordinary continuities and closures (see also Ogden, 1997, p. 569, who notes that depth-psychological therapists must tolerate the experience of "being adrift").

These and other difficulties argue against the claim that clinical interpretation is "easy" and "trustworthy in every respect." The latter view persists, however, in the widespread tendency to underestimate the difficulties and fallibility of interpretive methodology. I. A. Richards insisted, by contrast, that, "The only proper attitude toward a successful interpretation is to view it as a triumph against odds" (cited by Hirsch, 1967, p. 164); and Kermode (1979, p. 125) observes wryly that interpretation is "impossible but necessary."

Some Common but Avoidable Errors in Interpretive Inquiry

With the growth of postpositivist science, interest in interpretive methods has increased steadily in the human and social sciences, and also in philosophy; but the problems and limitations of interpretive inquiry persist (Watson, 1993, p. 8). Increased knowledge of interpretive methodology does not eliminate errors, but may reduce them—by increasing the clinician's understanding of and confidence in what he is doing, and also by learning the limitations and avoiding the pitfalls of interpretive work. Holt (1988) points out that knowledge of this kind is especialy important to students, "for the trainee has to learn to sharpen and deepen intuition, to develop observational skills, and to act decisively but judiciously, blending caring and ethical concern with hard-headed calculation" (p. 247).

Some errors in interpretive methodology appear to result in part from misleading maxims that live on in the clinical lore of psychoanalysis and dynamic psychotherapy. An example is Freud's aphoristic metaphor that the patient tries to conceal but betrayal oozes from every pore (1905a, pp. 77–78; see also 1901, pp. 230–238; 1913a, p. 140). This aphorism implies that the patient provides "such plain and numerous hints" of latent conflicts that the therapist has no difficulty in recognizing the patient's underlying problems (Freud, 1924, pp. 195–196; see also 1905a, p. 116). If that were actually the case, however, would the consensus problem be so persistent, and "good hours" so infrequent? Peterfreund (1983, p. 68) came closer to the truth in his observation that many sessions are so murky, uncertain, and confused that it is difficult to know what has happened.

A related misconception noted by Spence (1988b, pp. 3–4, 13) is the belief that if a therapist's understanding is clear and convincing, it will be shared by others who hear or read about it—the fallacy that clinical material is transparent, that its interpretation is readily apparent to everyone. Clinicians listen in different ways, however, and often arrive at different conclusions from the same data.

Freud's (1937b, p. 263) overconfident insistence that clinical interpretations are "trustworthy in every respect" has been perpetuated by some of our most highly respected contemporary colleagues. Arlow (1979) writes, for example, that, "Most of the time the intuitive work has been so efficient that a sense of conviction is immediate, gratifying, and accompanied instantly by recollection of the supporting evidence from the patient's productions" (p. 203). Note, however, that the "supporting evidence" which produces such a strong subjective "sense of conviction" is based upon ennumerative (in contrast to eliminative) inductivism, which philosophers of science caution is a weak supporting argument. It is easy to find some facts that are consistent with an interpretation, but a genuine test attempts to refute it. To refute a hypothesis, and thus begin to improve it, one needs negative data that reveal the interpretation's shortcomings (Diesing, 1985a, pp. 81–82). Holt (1996, p. 200) observes that Freud's failure to understand the crucial significance of negative evidence was one of his major scientific weaknesses—a methodologic blind spot that became a problematic precedent for psychoanalysis and dynamic psychotherapy which persists to this day.

Lawrence Friedman (1988, p. 458) concludes that Freud was overly sanguine about the reliability of his method and the validity of its results. Freud's overconfident claims about clinical interpretation have misled several generations of clinicians, reinforcing our tendency towards confirmation bias, that is, becoming overcommitted to a particular interpretation, neglecting to question its correctness, being intent upon confirming it, and ignoring disconfirming data. To reduce confirmation bias, we need to increase our use of alternative hypotheses and disconfirming tests; and the antidote to overconfidence is an increase in scientific skepticism regarding all of our interpretive hypotheses. Paul Meehl (1954, pp. 27–28) reminds us that depth psychologists, of all people, should be highly suspicious of themselves. We have no reason to assume that we are free from ordinary errors.

Disagreements among interpreters and depth-psychological schools are dismissed at times with the reassuring but misleading platitude that disparate viewpoints are merely "parts of a complex truth." A similar convention employed in case conferences and professional meetings attempts to neutralize disagreements regarding interpretations with the accommodating shibboleth, "That, too"—which forces competing constructions into a single eclectic formulation, whether they fit dynamically or not—the so-called "and . . . and . . . and" fallacy, or "run-on" interpretation. To avoid the error of eclecticism, one must realize that each interpretation refers to a separate whole meaning; thus each interpretation must be compared individually with every alternative hypothesis, because each interpretation stands or falls as a whole. One cannot simply select and synthesize plausible elements from disparate interpretions; for that produces merely another, eclectic hypothesis which itself must stand or fall as a whole.

Another misleading maxim that contributes to errors in interpretation is Freud's injunction (after Charcot) to look at the same phenomena repeatedly, "until they themselves begin to speak" (1914a, p. 22). Freud (1900, p. 311, fn. 1, and p. 335) also referred approvingly to Rank's (1910) report of "a dream which interprets itself." Hayek (1994, pp. 55–56) observes, however, that our ability to recognize certain patterns may lead to the erroneous belief that if we look long enough a pattern will always reveal itself.

Like most aphorisms, this one contains a kernel of truth, that is, the value of extended observation in the investigation of complex phenomena; but the metaphorical implication that if one waits and watches long enough the data themselves will provide the answers is misleading in several respects. First, it does not coincide with the kinds of answers we seek, namely, unconscious mental processes. Staring at surface contents cannot provide such answers, no matter how long the observation is continued. In the second place, the data of the clinical surface keep changing, which does not permit sustained observation of the same phenomena. And finally, in its attempt to make our clinical work seem as purely empirical as possible, the Charcot-Freud aphorism leaves out the crucial interpretive aspect of clinical observation.

Diesing (1971) points out that in actual practice the interpreter does not wait for large amounts of data to be collected, processed, and analyzed, but begins to develop his case immediately. His first step is often to watch for recurrent themes that reappear in various contexts. His observations are not entirely passive, however, but may include actively noticing that something is recurrently absent, or that a hypothesis is continually confirmed or disconfirmed, or recognizing a regular contrast with some other situation. Often it is simply a matter of being surprised by something. The interpreter does not rest satisfied with his first guess, but thinks up as many alternative constructions as he can, sometimes quite rapidly. "Each interpretation is tested, and those that survive are tested some more. Testing and revision of interpretations is a continuous process" (pp. 145–146; see also Meehl, 1954, p. 120; Oskamp, 1965, p. 264).

The converse of the preceding error is a tendency, fed by the universal inclination towards confirmation bias, to focus on an early interpretive impression, to assume rather than question its correctness, and to use it as a guide to subsequent data collection and formulation (Shaklee and Fischoff, 1982). Meehl (1960, p. 21) reports that a therapist's image of a patient may crystallize very rapidly, as early as the second to fourth therapy sessions. Other investigators have found that even when an initial impression about a person is completely discredited, many subjects continue to believe their original impressions (Einhorn and Hogarth, 1978; see also Jelalian and Miller, 1984, who have reviewed the psychological literature on the persistence of beliefs in the face of disconfirming evidence).

Most interpretive problems are so complex, however, that correct understanding is seldom achieved by an initial construction; multiple revisions and reformulations of a hypothesis are necessary to reach an adequate understanding (Elstein, 1988, pp. 28–29). Thus Dalbiez (1941, Vol. 2) concludes that "the first quality, indispensible to anyone who claims a really scientific approach to psychoanalysis, is to know how not to draw conclusions" (p. 145; compare Keats's "negative capability" in Beckson and Ganz, 1975, pp. 157–158).[10]

A related methodologic error focuses on some dramatic event in the patient's associations to the exclusion of other material (Abraham, 1986, p. 59). The reasons for this error include the mistaken belief that a few suggestive data provide sufficient evidence, the use of selected data to confirm prior expectations, and misusing postulated dynamic relations as evidence.

Another common but avoidable error in the methodology of clinical interpretation is overuse of a single interpretive method or variety of clinical data. To favor particular interpretive methods and varieties of clinical data is to risk neglecting other useful data and methods. Overuse of a single method produces a distorted view (Diesing, 1971, pp. 12–13). The most extreme example of this error in contemporary psychoanalysis and dynamic psychotherapy is Kohut's claim (1984, p. 32) that empathy is the only useful method for investigating the inner life of man, including his psychopathology. Aside from the well-known problem of empathy's subjectivity, which increases the tendency to read one's own thoughts into the patient's associations, empathy tends to generate only single, separate meanings rather than multiple, interrelated meanings. As a result, Kohut's monistic method cannot construe the plurivocality of overdetermined and complexly interconnected meanings, the surplus meanings in symbols of all kinds, the abstract meanings of metaphors, the opposing meanings involved in conflicts, the complex repertories of defenses against inner conflicts, and the multiple interrelated part meanings associated with individual elements of the clinical data, the latter being essential to the justification of interpretive hypotheses.

Peterfreund (1983) refers to another common error in the use of empathy, a tendency to think that the therapist's empathic experiences are a form of evidence. "Not at all!" Peterfreund writes. "And unless the fallacy of this thinking is recognized, the resultant work may be no better than the stereotyped approaches I have criticized" (p. 206; see also Erle, 1968, p. 637, for a similar view).

The subject matter of depth psychology is too complex and too elusive for unidimensional methods of interpretation; thus, if a particular method comes to be regarded as the one avenue to truth, it is truth that suffers (Kaplan, 1964, p. 26). To cope with the obscure, complexly overdetermined, and unstable nature of latent mental contents and processes, we need multiple interpretive methods, concepts, perspectives, and procedures; for multiple types of methods, employing wide varieties of clinical data, serve as checks on each other and compensate for the limitations of individual methods and varieties of data (Polkinghorne, 1983, pp. 252–254).

Finally, doctrinal interpretation is one of the most prevalent but avoidable methodologic errors of interpretive methodology (see, for example, Bernardi, 1989). Roustang (1982) writes that when clinicians bend the data of therapy sessions to fit their particular clinical theories, true psychoanalysis or dynamic psychotherapy cannot occur. He proposes the paradox that we must know less (for example, less clinical theory) in order to learn more. Andresen (1983) describes the paradox this way: some who are most enthusiastically drawn to the work of Freud may well be those for whom its most important lessons prove elusive. They may never see his finest gift, namely, new ways of looking and knowing. Thus, "one should not look to Freud for all the answers but should cultivate receptivity in therapy sessions" (pp. 141–142).

Some Remedial Strategies for Interpretive Methodology

Because the limitations and uncertainties of clinical interpretation make errors inevitable, "damage control" becomes a necessary and important part of interpretive methodology, that is, systematic use of error-detecting, correcting, and justifying procedures, in conjunction with the basic methodologic strategy of "learning from error" (see, for example, Berkson and Wettersten, 1984; Polkinghorne, 1983, pp. 249–251; Rumelhart et al., 1986a). To deal with errors realistically, we must attempt to recognize mistakes when they occur and, if possible, put them to some use in the interpretive process. For example, we attempt to recognize and utilize countertransference distortions as potential aids to understanding and interpretation. The same basic error-correcting strategy of attempting to undo and to learn from our mistakes applies to all types of methodologic errors (Peterfreund, 1983, pp. 116–117, 172; Waelder, in Guttman and Guttman, 1987, p. 50).

A number of investigators have concluded that the clinical setting provides relatively little opportunity for therapists to improve their interpretive accuracy (Goldberg, 1968, p. 491; Abraham, 1986). Ideally, for such improvement to occur the accuracy of interpretations would have to be linked by systematic feedback to the data and cues that led clinicians to specific constructions. Although we lack such an ideal method, we can employ the indirect approach of learning from error: that is, since errors are inevitable, the interpreter goes ahead and makes mistakes, but then uses the mistakes as error-correcting feedback. Recognizing one's errors thus facilitates progress towards an interpretive goal.

The remedial strategy of recognizing, correcting, and learning from errors starts with the expectation that the interpreter will make mistakes—a mind-set that increases the clinician's alertness to discrepancies between his or her constructions, on the one hand, and all of the clinical data (rather than selected data that support one's hypothesis), on the other (French, 1958a, pp. 106–107; Lomas, 1987; Einhorn, 1988, p. 66). The scientifically skeptical clinician doubts everything that goes into his proof: doubts his facts, his hypotheses, and whether the two fit together as he thinks they do (Larrabee, 1964, p. 233; Hayek, 1994, p. 65).

Recognition of discrepancies and acceptance of errors are crucial strategies not only in clinical work but in all scientific endeavors. Darwin (1988, p. 83) wrote that he could not recall a single hypothesis that did not have to be modified or abandoned eventually.[11] Similarly, initial constructions in clinical interpretation are largely "guesses"; and much of our interpretive methodology has the purpose of correcting these guesses. Polkinghorne (1983) points out in this connection that, "Method does not give truth; it corrects guesses" (p. 249). Unless therapists and clinical investigators realize the ever-present susceptibility of interpretations to error, they tend to assume inappropriately that their interpretations are correct—as a result of which they do not consider alternative formulations, do not bother to justify interpretations, and thus carry their mistakes forward to new material in the therapeutic process.

Conjecturing and the likelihood of errors are inherent in all forms of inquiry. One of the fundamental ways that human beings learn is by trial and error, or conjectures and refutations (Popper, 1959, 1963; see also Radford, 1983). Like developments in science generally, formulation of the "most plausible" interpretation in clinical work is a necessarily gradual process of step-by-step approximations; for the conjectural approach to understanding, although imaginative and creative, is also very fallible. For that reason, the testability of interpretive hypotheses—that is, use of justifying tests that attempt to refute hypotheses—is essential (Lakatos, 1978; see Eccles, 1974, pp. 349–350, for a striking example).

A methodologic school of hermeneutics identified with E. D. Hirsch, Jr. (1967, 1976, 1983) also emphasizes the importance of disconfirming tests. Because constructions begin as "guesses" or conjectures about the "whole" (thematic) meaning of the data being interpreted, Hirsch recommends a series of error-detecting and error-correcting procedures in which the interpreter: (1) checks how much of the data a construction accounts for; (2) revises the construction to account for more of the data; and then (3) rechecks the revised construction to determine whether it now covers most of the data. If not, the original construction is discarded and replaced by an alternative hypothesis which is subjected to the same series of checking procedures.

The principal selection criterion for choosing among competing constructions is the criterion of internal evidence, that is, which of the alternative hypotheses accounts most coherently and comprehensively for the largest number of data (Edelson, 1988, pp. 99–101). Some additional criteria for differentiating among more or less plausible interpretations include: (1) logical soundness; (2) accounting for puzzling data; (3) consistency not only with the data, but also with more general (empirical and theoretical) knowledge; (4) relative credibility in relation to other interpretations in the same case; and (5) surviving falsification tests (Runyon, 1982, p. 128).

More definitive justification of interpretations requires additional, posttherapeutic investigation based on a record of the entire therapeutic process. Studying the record of a completed treatment makes it possible to employ multiple, increasingly probative justifying tests. With respect to the type of record employed in such studies, Wolfson and Sampson (1976) compared different kinds of clinical records and found that process notes provide an adequately representative sample of clinical data. Spence (1982a) and the present writer (1987) believe that for investigative purposes process notes should be "unpacked" immediately following each therapy session.

Another remedial strategy for surmounting the difficulties of interpretive methodology is to search for small-scale, microstructural evidence in the clinical data. Freud emphasized that the probity of our findings depends upon "intimate details" (cited by Nunberg and Federn, 1962, p. 172). Freud's jigsaw puzzle analogy (1923b, p. 116) also implies the fitting together of numerous small details in the clinical data. Edelson (1984, pp. 136–137) observes similarly that the emergence of highly specific, idiosyncratic, circumstantial details in the patient's fantasies, reports of experiences, and in other data provide the most relevant and probative evidence.[12]

The origin of interpretive methods that employ small clues can be traced to a paradigm based upon semiotics and the ability to infer causes from their effects—an approach that emerged in the human sciences during the 1870s (Ginzburg, 1989). Focus on the smallest details suggests an analogy with detective work, as in the frequently noted similarities between Freud's approach and Sherlock Holmes's methods. Freud (1914d) wrote that psychoanalysis attempts to interpret, "secret and concealed things from despised and unnoticed features, from the rubbish heap, as it were, of our observations" (p. 222). Ginzburg (1989) describes Freud's interpretive approach this way:

> It was the idea of a method of interpretation based on discarded information, on marginal data, considered in some way significant. By this method, details usually considered of little importance, even trivial or "minor," provided the key [p. 101].

The methodology of clinical interpretation is not just particularistic, however, but at the same time is holistic—that is, it recognizes that the whole meaning at any given time is greater than the sum, or any combination, of its part meanings. The holistic and particularistic perspectives of interpretive methodology are not contradictory, but complementary. Olinick (1984) notes that "psychoanalysis is an unusual discipline in its insistence that the detail must never, even momentarily, be overlooked for the general nor the general for the detail; both conflate to a meaning that is otherwise incomplete and misleading" (see also Eissler, 1959, pp. 1–2; Forrester, 1980, p. 79; Levenson, 1988, pp. 14–15). Freud's (1909b) analysis of the Rat Man's obsession provides a model of combining holistic and particularistic perspectives in clinical interpretation: he returned repeatedly to the patient's choice of rats, attempting to discover and explain why nothing but rats could fulfill the overdetermined motives and meanings of the patient's obsession (Schafer, 1983a, pp. 7–8).

Interpretation of individual therapy sessions also illustrates the importance of both holistic and particularistic perspectives. The therapist pays close attention to the details of the patient's associations (see Klauber, 1980, p. 196), but also attempts to infer a "whole" (thematic) meaning that ties the various details ("part meanings") together. Schafer (1986, p. 156) invokes the continuity principle to account for the tendency towards thematization in clinical material, and the corresponding holistic aspect of clinical interpretation. Thematization, a corollary of the continuity principle, is thus the postulated mechanism responsible for the "red thread of allusions" that runs like an undercurrent through all of the clinical data in a therapy session.

Thematization of clinical material makes the understanding of latent contents both easier and more difficult—easier because it reduces the "search space" for latent contents to the dynamic theme at a particular time; but more difficult because the dominant theme of a therapy session is the most intensely defended against and its disclosure the most tenaciously resisted. The concept of a thematizing mechanism implies also that not just any interpretation can be considered acceptable, because thematization postulates that only one set of meanings (the dominant dynamic theme of a therapy session) can be considered the most plausible interpretation at a given time.

It should be noted that thematization is not confined to so-called productive processing by the patient's mental activity of free associating, but is employed also as an interpretive heuristic by the therapist in his or her receptive processing which attempts to understand the patient's associations in depth. Both the patient's and the therapist's use of the thematizing heuristic illustrates a postulated general principle of cognitive data processing—that methods of "receptive" (interpretive) processing by a listener (for example, a therapist) often replicate the "productive" processing operations of a speaker.[13]

The importance of methodologic pluralism as a remedial strategy has been mentioned above, but a further word should be said about its applicability in every phase and aspect of the interpretive process. Rather than taking full advantage of the multiple methodologic principles, concepts, strategies, and heuristics of interpretive inquiry, interpreters often utilize only a fraction of the methodologic armamentarium that is available to them. By casting a wide net of data generating, gathering, selection, and processing operations during the discovery phase of the interpretive process, the clinician finds multiple clues that suggest alternative constructions. During the justifying phase, multiple operations of checking, comparing, modifiying, and rechecking alternative hypotheses, and numerous additional justifying procedures during the posttherapeutic phase of justification, help the clinician and clinical investigator to identify the "most plausible" interpretation at given times during the therapeutic process.

The advantages of a pluralistic approach include: (1) each individual method has limitations, for which additional methods compensate; (2) pluralistic approaches provide interpretive versatility for different kinds of patients, psychopathology, and clinical-dynamic circumstances; (3) shifting one's mode of observation, perspective, and methods of data-processing has been shown experimentally to increase interpretive efficiency and thus effectiveness (Spence and Grief, 1970; Spence and Lugo, 1972); and (4) a multilateral approach is more likely to encompass the totality of major dynamic factors interplaying at a particular time.

Gail Reed (1995, p. 727) suggests still another possible advantage of methodologic pluralism, which concerns the use of multiple interpretive hypotheses. She reasons that because one of the functions of clinical interpretation is to reduce the fixity of traumatically induced, repressively maintained latent contents, the therapist's practice of considering alternative meanings and determinants may serve as a model for the patient in overcoming the tendency to focus fixedly on a single (traumatic) meaning, and in regaining the capacity to discriminate between past and present experiences.

The Interpretive Attitude

The clinician's attitude towards the interpretive task, that is, the intellectual and emotional mind-set of the therapist engaged in interpretive inquiry, can both alleviate and aggravate the problems of interpretive methodology. Schafer (1983a) refers to interpretive methodology as "the major cognitive aspect of the analytic attitude" (p. ix). The problems, limitations, and fallibility of interpretive inquiry necessitate a well-developed tolerance of uncertainty, flexibility, open-mindedness, and readiness to recognize errors; but the interpreter also needs a quietly confident attitude regarding the investigative possibilities and therapeutic value of interpretive inquiry. Thus, Jerome Bruner (1987) suggests a "modest" view of interpretation—but one "whose uncertainties are more than counterbalanced by its riches" (p. xvi).

The interpretive attitude is a significant factor in dealing with the methodologic tension between seeking the "most plausible" interpretation, on the one hand, and the realities of interpretive relativism and uncertainty, on the other. An attitude of compromise is needed to integrate these contradictory aspects of the interpretive process—by adopting a more realistic level of expectation regarding the accuracy of interpretations (see, for example, Hayek, 1994, pp. 65–66). The following discussion considers both sides of such a compromise.

Starting with the limitations of interpretive inquiry: Post-positivist science teaches that our truth claims and justifying procedures are constrained by the concepts and perspectives of particular conceptual systems. Since we cannot escape our contexts, the limits of knowledge are contained within individual schools of thought. What each school accepts as knowledge is what agrees with the standards and practices of that school. Thus, there is not one truth which corresponds with reality; there are some truths which hold within various reference frames. Reality is "views," not something that lies behind and causes our views (Ogilvy, 1977; cited by Polkinghorne, 1983, pp. 250–251).

When confronted with differences in systems of inquiry, an open-minded interpretive attitude recognizes that comparison and interaction of contexts offers greater possibilities of understanding than any one point of view. Polkinghorne points out that, "The very acceptance of a possible alternative places one's own assumptions in question" (Polkinghorne, 1983, p. 251; see also Pollock, 1986; Pulver, 1993). A flexible (postpositivist) interpretive attitude no longer thinks in terms of "the" way of knowing, but views each conceptual framework as "a" way of knowing—that is, as a specific and limited context. In a similar vein, Phillips (1991, pp. 371, 406) and Hoit (1995, pp. 29–31) suggest the usefulness of a hermeneutic perspective in understanding phenomena outside the boundaries of individual psychoanalytic schools. Toulmin (1983) has observed in this connection that the general categories of hermeneutics can be applied equally to the natural and human sciences. The aims of interpretation in both are similar: "to be perceptive, illuminating, and reasonable." Thus a successful interpretation "will combine soundness and centrality in its general approach, with relevance and sensitivity in its specific details" (p. 99).

Turning to the side of the interpretive attitude that entails a modest degree of confidence in the investigative possibilities and therapeutic value of interpretive inquiry: Both Hirsch (1967), a hermeneutic scholar, and Diesing (1971), a social science methodologist, call attention to the importance of "meaning types" in interpretive methodology. A type is a simple, low-level variety of theory, a shareable determinate class of meanings which can subsume and represent more than one experience. Types are unifying concepts that integrate individual observations, a capability that accounts for a type's indispensable heuristic function; for, paradoxically, an entity's individual characteristics can be known only through a type. Thus at every stage of coming to know anything in particular, we are brought to our knowledge by the heuristic of type ideas (Hirsch, 1967, p. 272).

In the clinical situation, when an interpreter gains an impression about the type of latent content being expressed (and disguised) in the patient's associations, the type conception is used as a "whole" meaning to provide the basis for understanding specific details. If the individual associations ("part" meanings) do not fit the originally posited type of latent content fairly completely and coherently, the type conception is modified and checking-revising-rechecking operations are initiated and continued until a satisfactory fit is found.

We are never able to revise and refine type conceptions completely enough to achieve a perfect fit; hence the ideal of a completely correct interpretation is not attainable. We are able, however, to construct and often to justify the "most plausible" interpretation among alternative hypotheses at a particular time—that is, the interpretation that resonates with what is dynamically most relevant, hierarchically dominant, affectively charged, evidentially supportable, interpretively accessible, and therefore maximally meaningful to the patient at that time. We are able to do that, and to achieve therapeutic effects by doing so, even though our interpretations are not completely accurate. How is that possible?

The concept of type conceptions suggests that clinical interpretations may not need to be completely accurate. As a type conception, an interpretation applies to an entire class of phenomena. Even such a limited (class-bound) degree of specificity and veridicality may be sufficient, however, to resonate with whatever type of latent disturbance is most emergent in the patient's mind at the time. Since type conceptions are such an important, ubiquitous, and shareable means of communication, the interpretive type conception which the therapist conveys to a patient may be "good enough," both dynamically and therapeutically, by being "in the neighborhood" of the patient's currently thematic latent disturbance (Freud, 1910c, pp. 225–226; see also Busch, 1993). Eagle (1984a, p. 168) proposed the term and concept, "good enough interpretation," but his usage applies mainly to technical aspects of interpretations communicated to patients. It seems appropriate to extend the meaning of this felicitous term to include also the methodologic issue of interpretive accuracy. Weich (1986) has proposed a related concept of a "good enough analyst."

Ricoeur (1970) observes cogently regarding the importance of types in clinical interpretation that

> interpretation is possible because it regularly comes back to the same signifying segments, the same correspondences. These recurrences form a kind of dictionary of preconstituted types [p. 433].

Ricoeur continues:

> Thus analysis is terminable because *certain* singular configurations are discernible; but the singular is discernible, as this and not that, because it carves its singularity out of types that limit the range of possible combinations [p. 433].

The methodologic concept of type conceptions is congruent also with Rubinstein's (1980) proposal of "indirect" prediction and postdiction in psychoanalysis and dynamic psychotherapy, that is, the possibility of predicting or postdicting classes of events, in contrast to specific events (see also Hayek, 1994, p. 63). Discussing the process of clinical inference, A. O'Neill (1993, p. 75) notes similarly that the essential feature of interpretive inquiry is linking particular instances with the general class of such phenomena. Cummins (1989, p. 167, fn. 20) draws on Harman's (1987) views of inference to propose a concept of "rational enough inference," that is, rational enough relative to the situation and circumstances.

The concept of "good enough interpretations" appears to cohere also with Hartmann's (1951) hypothesis regarding the "multiple appeal" of interpretations. He suggests that the process set in motion by an interpretation

> produces not only, so to speak, "local" reactions. It goes beyond the stimulated "area," changing the balance of mental energies and affecting a variety of aspects of the dynamic system. This process activates or sets in a state of preparedness elements functionally and genetically connected with it; its appeal often reaches from one system into the others, and its unconscious side effects may transcend the barriers of countercathexis [p. 41; see also Levin, 1980, for a related concept regarding the way interpretations may work; and Pollock, 1981, regarding reminiscences and insight].

The concept of "good enough" (that is, sufficiently accurate) interpretations differs from Freud's view that our constructions often do not lead to the patient remembering what has been repressed. Instead, Freud proposed, "we produce in him an assured conviction of the truth of the construction which achieves the same therapeutic result as a recaptured memory" (1937b, p. 265)—a conclusion which makes interpretively-facilitated therapeutic change sound suspiciously like a "faith cure" (compare Viederman, 1983). The concept of "good enough" interpretations differs also from the "narrational project" of Schafer, Spence, and others, who deemphasize the criterion of interpretive accuracy and view psychoanalytic narratives as "constructed psychoanalytic fictions." By contrast, the concept of clinical interpretations as type conceptions, the multiple appeal of which may be "good enough" to facilitate therapeutic effects, provides a methodologically grounded basis for a modest degree of confidence in our interpretive methods. Such a view implies, as Eagle (1980a, p. 423) observes, that the clinical construal of latent mental contents "is not a mere chimera, but involves the identification of real entities."[14]

The methodologist Paul Diesing (1985b, p. 555, in response to Von Eckhardt, 1982) suggests still another basis for modest confidence in our interpretive methods. Replying to the criticism that psychoanalysis is "unscientific," Diesing points out that each of the methods that science develops has its own characteristic weaknesses and sources of error—weaknesses that are only gradually but never fully recognized or overcome. Methodologies, therefore, are never completely "scientific" or reliable, but they are improvable. The present work has attempted to demonstrate that despite the numerous and difficult problems of inferring and justifying latent mental contents, and in spite of the epistemologic lag in our acceptance of a postpositivist scientific perspective, slow but significant progress is being made in improving our interpretive methodology, and thus our capacity for depth-psychological understanding.

Notes

Preface

1. Meehl (1979, p. 565) maintains that the critical problem of psychoanalysis is the epistemological-methodological problem of the inference. See also Woodard's (1993a,b) review and empirical study of the psychoanalytic inference process.

2. See, for example, Crits-Christoph et al., 1988a/1990, pp. 181–188; 1993, pp. 375–379; Rubovits-Seitz, 1992a, pp. 154–160.

3. For similar such statements, see also Freud, 1913a, p. 140; 1914a, p. 22; 1915a, p. 159; 1924, pp. 195–196; 1925a, pp. 128–129; 1933, p. 12; 1937b, pp. 263–265; 1940a, p. 159.

4. Cited by Klauber, 1968, p. 81; see also Freud, 1900, p. 98n.

5. Stoller and Geertsma, 1963; Sklansky et al., 1966; Weber et al., 1966; Thomä et al., 1976; Fisher and Greenberg, 1977; Werman, 1979; Runyon, 1981; Spence, 1982a; Peterfreund, 1983; Rosenbaum and Muroff, 1984; Fossage and Loew, 1987; Bernardi, 1989; Etchegoyan, 1989, p. 382; Cooper, 1993.

6. See, for example, Luborsky, 1977; Levine and Luborsky, 1981; Luborsky et al., 1985; Luborsky and Crits-Christoph, 1988, 1990; Crits-Christoph et al., 1988a/1990, 1988b, 1993; Luborsky and Luborsky, 1993; Diamond, 1983; Strupp and Binder, 1984; Caston, 1986, 1993a,b; Caston and Martin, 1993; Rosenberg et al., 1986; Horowitz, 1987; Kächele, 1988; Woodard, 1993a,b. It should be noted in this connection that investigations employing quantitative methods, multistage research designs, and guided inference manuals involve only limited interpretive tasks; the methods employed in such studies differ significantly from the processes, contents, and depths of interpretations formulated in clinical practice (see, for example, Fisher and Greenberg, 1977, p. 296; Peterfreund, 1971, p. 336; Meehl, 1993).

7. See, for example, Arnoff, 1954; Goldberg, 1968; Nisbett and Ross, 1980; Abraham, 1986; Turk and Salovey, 1988.

8. See, for example, Edelson, 1988, p. 78; Barron et al., 1992a, p. 508; Binder et al., 1992; Schlesinger, 1994.

9. See also Toulmin, 1983, pp. 99, 117; Ahumada, 1994, pp. 697–698.

10. See also Martin and McIntyre, 1994, pp. 159–280, for debate about interpretation in these fields.

11. See, for example, Holt, 1961; Kettner, 1991, p. 169.

12. See, for example, the *Glossary of Psychoanalytic Terms* by Moore and Fine, 1990, p. 103; Namnum, 1978, pp. 314–315; Levy, 1984; Giovacchini, 1990; Etchegoyan, 1991, pp. 318–470; Baranger, 1993, pp. 15, 18.

13. See also Laplanche and Pontalis, 1973, pp. 227–229; Schafer, 1983, p. 21; Paniagua, 1985, p. 314; Haynal, 1993b, p. 81.

14. See, for example, Rycroft, 1956; Loewald, 1960; Rangell, 1984, p. 130; Wallerstein, 1986b; Thomä and Kächele, 1987, pp. 7, 44–50; Cooper, 1989; Brody, 1990, p. 2; Meissner, 1991, pp. 151–192; Levine, 1994, p. 665; Friedman, 1995, pp. 517–520; Panel, 1995a,b; Schwaber, 1995b, p. 557.

15. Compare also Cavell, 1988, pp. 859–860. See also, however, Inderbitzin and Levy, 1994, pp. 775–777, for a critical evaluation of the interactional viewpoint and approach.

16. Eagle and Wolitzky, 1981, pp. 364–366; Oremland, 1991, p. 10; Spence et al., 1994a, p. 61.

17. See also Rubinstein, 1976, pp. 332–333; Bell and Staines, 1981, p. 87; Edelson, 1985, p. 87; 1986, pp. 100–104; Whitehorn, 1947, p. 199.

18. See also Friedman, 1988, p. 378; Brook, 1995b, p. 519; Hanly, in Panel, 1996, pp. 640–641.

19. See also Grünbaum, 1989, pp. 489–493; 1990a, pp. 562–567; 1993, pp. 120–123.

20. See also Tuckett, 1993; Glaser and Strauss, 1967, pp. vii–viii.

21. An earlier version of Chapters 8 and 9 was corecipient of the 1987 Serota Award for unpublished research in psychoanalytic reconstructions.

Chapter 1

1. See also Coltrera and Ross, 1967; Meissner, 1971.

2. See, for example, Breuer and Freud, 1893–1895, pp. xvii–xviii, 60 fn. 1, 62 fn. 1; and Glymour, 1993, pp. 479–480.

3. See also Freud, 1900, p. 98, fn. 1; and Shope, 1987, pp. 191–192.

4. See, for example, Breuer and Freud, 1893, p. 227; and Freud, 1923a, p. 239.

5. See, for example, Freud, 1896, p. 205; 1898, p. 266; 1900, pp. xxv, 511; 1905a, pp. 12–13, 112–113; 1905b, pp. 177–78; 1908, p. 210; 1913b, p. 208; 1914a, p. 22; 1914b, p. 77; 1915b, p. 117; 1915c, p. 190; 1916–17, p. 51; 1918, pp. 51–52; 1921, p. 122; 1923a, p. 253; 1926b, p. 266; 1933, pp. 12, 181; 1937b, p. 262; 1940a, pp. 158–159.

6. For similar such statements, see Freud, 1914a, p. 22; 1915a, p. 159; 1925a, pp. 128–129; 1933, p. 12; 1937b, pp. 263–265.

7. See also Freud, 1915–1916, p. 101; and 1918, pp. 50–51, in which he acknowledges the role of construction by the analyst in the interpretive process. Throughout most of the Wolf Man's case report, however, Freud emphasizes the patient's rather than his own activity in formulating interpretations (1918, see esp. pp. 89–90).

8. See also Palmer, 1969, pp. 98–123; Rickman, 1988; Mueller-Vollmer, 1989, pp. 148–164.

9. Forrester, 1980, pp. x, 213–214; see also Junker, 1991 (cited by Bergmann, 1995, p. 589), who notes that Freud interpreted like a hermeneuticist and wrote case histories that sound like short stories.

10. See, for example, Barclay, 1964; McGrath, 1986; Edelson, 1988; Brook, 1992; Wakefield, 1992a,b; McIntosh, 1993; Wollheim, 1993b.

11. See, for example, Freud, 1901, pp. 228–229; 1974, p. 472; and Klauber, 1968, p. 83.

Chapter 2

1. Cited by Conant, 1951, p. 116; for specific examples of this attitude in the history of science, see Holton, 1973, pp. 106–109, 112, 133–142; and Bauer, 1992.

2. See, for example, Elliott, 1984, 1992; Elliott and Morrow-Bradley, 1994, p. 137; Kirk and Miller, 1986; Mahrer, 1988; Packer and Addison, 1989a,b; Patton, 1990; Toukmanian and Rennie, 1992; Bryman and Burgess, 1994.

3. Fonagy (1982, p. 135) maintains, on the other hand, that it would be an oversimplification to assume that Freud was completely unwilling or unable to go beyond the positivist reference frame. As indicated in the previous chapter and elsewhere in the present volume, in some respects Freud anticipated the postpositivist turn.

4. See also Rothstein, 1980; and Arlow's (1995, p. 218) critique of Isakower (1992a,b) regarding the so-called "analyzing instrument."

5. For another example of an oversimplified interpretive model, see Zac, 1972.

6. See, for example, Feigl, 1973; Rescher, 1982; Gholson and Barker, 1985; Roth, 1987. See also Gauld and Shotter, 1977, pp. 199–215, for a discussion of empirical investigations within a hermeneutic psychology.

7. See also the philosopher Bonjour, 1978, who argues that empirical knowledge can have no foundation.

8. See, for example, Shapere, 1984a, pp. xvii–xxxiii, 102–119; 1984c, p. 382, fn. 33; Betti, 1962; Maquet, 1964; Segall et al., 1966; Hirsch, 1976; Kirk and Miller, 1986; Bohman, 1991, Chap. 3; Meehl, 1983/1991, pp. 315–322; Ginzburg, 1994, pp. 294–295; Davidson, 1994, p. 307; Martin, 1994.

9. Cited by Kirk and Miller, 1986, pp. 49–50; see also Curtis, 1992, p. 648; Paniagua, 1995, pp. 368–369. The philosopher Thomas Nagel (1994, p. 38) emphasizes that "the unconscious does not abolish objectivity, even if it makes it more difficult to achieve." Also, "even though like any science psychology relies on imagination to frame its hypotheses, its aim is to discover objective truths about the human mind" (cited by Schwaber, 1995b, p. 563, fn. 3).

10. Cited by Kirk and Miller, 1986, p. 50; see also Segall et al., 1966. M. Hanly (1995) writes that "even if it could be shown that positivism plays no part in contemporary culture, it does not follow that psychoanalysis should

give up its search for objective knowledge." She adds that we "should be willing to consider at least the possibility of an epistemology for psychoanalysis that integrates subjectivity and objectivity" (p. 38). See also Waelder, 1970; C. Hanly, 1992a, p. 293; Elevitch, 1978; Hook, 1959.

11. See also Eagle, 1980a, p. 412; Campbell, 1988, p. 376; Reed, 1995.

12. See also Piaget, 1952; Kelly, 1955; Marcuse, 1955; Rieff, 1959; Neisser, 1967; Ricoeur, 1970, 1977; Habermas, 1971; Loch, 1977; Steele, 1979; Viderman, 1974, 1979; Mancuso and Adams-Webber, 1982; Spence, 1982a; Schafer, 1983a; Stern, 1983, 1985, 1991; Barratt, 1984, 1994; von Glasersfeld, 1984; Gergen, 1985; Protter, 1985; Tenzer, 1985; Schön, 1986; Hoffman, 1987, 1991, 1994; Sass, 1989; Gill, 1994a,b.

13. For a critical evaluation of radical constructivism, see Inderbitzin and Levy, 1994; and Chapter 4 of this volume.

14. Harré and Secord, 1972; Bhaskar, 1978; Harré and De Carlo, 1985; see also Hesse, 1966; Leatherdale, 1974; Reason and Rowan, 1981.

15. See, for example, Kim, 1988; Kornblith, 1993a,b; Callebaut, 1993.

16. For naturalized theories of meaning, intentionality, and mental content, see Millikan (1984) and McGinn (1989). The latter authors base their arguments that meaning (mental content) can have causal relevance on the *teleology* of mental states, that is, that minds have evolved to solve survival problems (compare Freud's references to the relation between meaning and biological "purpose"). Mental states have their own distinctive biological functions; for example, states such as desires and beliefs have environmentally directed functions that help the organism adapt to environmental contingencies. Meaning is thus a concomitant of and is closely interrelated with biological function or purpose (see also Mackay, 1989, esp. p. 2).

17. See, however, Eagle's, (1980a, p. 412); and Polkinghorne's (1983, pp. 150–151) descriptions of a postpositivist perspective that goes beyond the purely relativist view that one interpretation is as good as another.

18. See also Simon (1977, 1992), a pioneer in discovery models and problem-solving methods.

Chapter 3

1. Shane and Shane (1993, p. 780) report that most self psychologists no longer follow Kohut's exclusive reliance on introspection and empathy.

2. Barthes (1977, p. 87) asserted that meaning eludes all unilateral investigation.

3. For example, Schafer, 1973; Kazdin, 1981; Lichtenberg, 1981, p. 128; Freedman, 1983; Buckley et al., 1984; Gedo, 1984b, pp. 137, 139; Gustafson, 1984; Sadow, 1984; Cooper, 1985, 1987, 1994; Wallerstein, 1988; Gardner, 1991; Leon, 1992; Spence et al., 1994, p. 63.

4. Gray does not apply this method in all cases, however.

5. See Gill (1984) for a critique of Langs's approach.

6. Compare, however, Schwaber, 1995c, p. 714.

7. Some critical reviews of the foregoing, variably monistic interpretive approaches include Schafer (1985b, p. 289; 1994a,b) and Paniagua (1995, p. 368) regarding Klein's methodology; Rubovits-Seitz (1979, 1986b, 1988a) regarding Kohut's interpretive method; Thomä and Kächele (1987, pp. 344–345) regarding Weiss and Sampson's methodology; Phillips (1991) and Boesky (in Panel, 1995b, p. 549) regarding Schwaber's perspective; Gill (1984) regarding Langs's monistic concept of validation; Bond et al. (1987), Perry et al. (1989), Woodard (1993a,b), Caston (1993a,b), Caston and Martin (1993), and Waldron (1995) regarding Luborsky and Crits-Christoph's sustained focus on the "Core Conflictual Relationship Theme" (CCRT).

8. For an example of Freud's early theory-driven strategy of interpretation, see Freud, 1900, Vol. 4, pp. 310–338. Coltrera (1981, p. 87) notes in this connection that Freud (1900, pp. 310–338) stressed psychodynamic and psychogenetic explanations of unconscious causality in his theory-based "formal definition" of interpretation.

9. See, for example, Freud, 1901, pp. 228–229; 1915b, p. 117; and Freud's letter to H. Loewy, 1930, cited by E. Freud, 1960, p. 396.

10. See, for example, Klein, 1975, 1992, 1993; Money-Kyrle, 1958; and De Racker, 1961.

11. See, for example, Kohut, 1984; Ornstein and Ornstein, 1980; Goldberg, 1985; Wolf, 1986.

12. See, for example, Reik, 1936, 1948; Kris, 1956a,b; French, 1952, 1954, 1958a; Loewenstein, 1957; Searles, 1960, 1965; Bion, 1962, 1970; Winnicott, 1965, 1971; Meltzer, 1978; Esman, 1979; Klauber, 1980; Olinick, 1980; Spence, 1982a; Peterfreund, 1983; Poland, 1984, 1986, 1988; Schwaber, 1987, 1990a; McLaughlin, 1988; Roche, 1989; Wallace, 1989a; Parsons, 1992; Caston, 1993a; Caston and Martin, 1993; Smith, 1995; and others.

13. See also Bion (1967, p. 127) regarding the role of the "selected fact" in the interpretive process (compare also Skelton, 1995, for Bion's use of modern logic); and Spence (1982a, pp. 81–135) regarding "unwitting interpretations."

14. See also Chapman and Chapman (1967), Goldberg (1968), and Goldberg and Werts (1966) for experimental demonstrations of erroneous observations and interpretations produced by preconceptions.

15. See also Hirsch (1983) regarding the "politics" of competing interpretive theories; Berger's (1985) questions and doubts about the relevance of clinical theory in interpretive practice; Greenwald et al.'s (1986) analysis of conditions under which theory obstructs progress; a volume of *Psychoanalytic Inquiry* edited by Pulver et al. (1987) devoted to the question of how theory shapes technique; and a Panel report (1990) on how theory affects psychoanalytic technique.

16. For a critique of these doctrinal views, see Reed, 1987, p. 433.

17. See also Einstein, 1934, pp. 4–5, 7, 17, 27, 63, who asserted that there is no method that one can learn and apply systematically in order to establish the basic general principles of a science; for there is no logical inductive path to such principles. The basic principles of a science rest upon a sympathetic

understanding of experience, but they cannot be extracted from phenomena; they must be freely invented.

18. Klein, 1975, 1992, 1993; Money-Kyrle, 1958; De Racker, 1961. For more recent and variably modified Kleinian views, see also Aulagnier's (1979) concept of "evenly suspended theorization" (cited by Baranger, 1993, p. 19); Grosskurth, 1986; Joseph, 1989; Petot, 1990, 1991; Spillius, 1992, 1994; Ogden, 1992, 1994; Scharff, 1992; and Gabbard, 1995.

19. Kohut, 1984, p. 84; Ornstein and Ornstein, 1980; Goldberg, 1985; Wolf, 1986.

20. See, for example, Stein, 1979, pp. 677–680; Rothstein, 1980, p. 393; Eagle, 1984a, pp. 64–65.

21. Rapaport, 1944/1967; Danziger, 1985; Fiske and Shweder, 1986, p. 5.

22. See Hoffman, 1991. See also Cooper, 1993, p. 120, for a contrasting example of a flexible, data-driven, pluralistic approach to conceptualizing interpretive fallibility and the therapeutic dialogue.

23. Paniagua (1995) writes that "related also to omniscient claims and other unresolved narcissistic issues in analysts are the interpretive use of psychogenetic equations and formulas, and other grand theorizing; the tendency to assume, instead of demonstrate, conclusions; the belief in the infallibility of countertransferential intuitions; and the propensity to 'enlighten' analysands through interpretations instead of jointly discovering dynamics" (p. 367). See also Rothstein, 1980, for narcissistic issues in psychoanalysts.

24. See also Strupp, 1958; Kiesler, 1966; Rosenthal, 1966; Chapman and Chapman, 1967, 1969; Fisher and Greenberg, 1977, pp. 285–297, 303–305, 411.

25. See also Einhorn, 1988, p. 66; Beres, 1980, p. 16; Etchegoyen, 1989, p. 380.

26. See also Davidson, 1982, pp. 302–303. Nina Coltart (1992, pp. 2–3) reminds us that the heart of our work is a mystery, that we really do not know what we are doing. Schwaber (1995a) emphasizes similarly that "we cannot know 'it' until it has become past tense; we cannot know the meanings in what is yet unconscious until they have entered awareness. Before then, we have only our inferences, however convincing these may seem" (p. 277).

Chapter 4

1. See, for example, Freud, 1900, pp. 277–278, 408–409; 1910a,b; 1911a, pp. 62–65; 1913c, pp. 176–178; 1918, p. 90.

2. See, for example, Freud, 1910a, p. 143; 1910b; Marshall, 1974; Bruss, 1976, p. 72; Heynick, 1981; Grinstein, 1983, pp. 9, 21, 46, 74–75, 79, 159–160, 181.

3. Ricoeur, 1978, p. 322, fn. 21; see also Laffal, 1964; and Coltrera, 1981, pp. 105–107.

4. See, for example, Ricoeur, 1970, pp. 395–403; 1978; Rogers, 1981, p. 453; Boyd, 1985, pp. 111–113; Rubovits-Seitz, 1986a, pp. 35–39.

5. See, for example, Grinstein, 1983; Spruiell, 1983; Reed, 1987; Goldberg, 1988.

6. Other relevant writings by Lacan include: 1956, 1966, 1970, 1972, 1978, 1988a,b. See also Leavy, 1973, 1977, 1979, 1980, 1983a,b, 1990; Bowie, 1979, 1991; Muller and Richardson, 1982; Smith, 1983, Felman, 1987; Muller, 1988; Chessick, 1992, pp. 73–93.

7. The first reduction in the cases of both Lacan and Lévi-Strauss was their insistence on the primacy of language in all matters of significance. The second reduction in both cases was their restrictive selection of data that fit their respective theories. Lacan focused on verbal data to the relative exclusion of affects (see, for example, Leavy, 1996b, p. 1280); and Lévi-Strauss selectively reported contents of myths that made his comparisons of myths appear strictly symmetrical (see Caws, 1988, pp. 115–120).

8. Leavy (1977/1978) replied to these criticisms twenty years ago, asserting that "for Lacan, the emergence in analysis of the signifier, or rather of the chain of signifiers ordered in metaphoric and metonymic linkages, is inseparable from the emergence of the affects" (p. 288). More recently (1996b, p. 1280), however, Leavy acknowledges that affects simply do not fit well with Lacan's theory, due to his exclusive preoccupation with the theory of linguistic signs.

9. A similar theory of literary interpretive competence from the standpoint of poetics, but without appeal to Chomskian linguistics, has been proposed by Ciardi and Williams (1975, esp. p. 12).

10. For additional critiques of Edelson's theory, see Mahoney and Singh, 1975, pp. 222–243; 1979, p. 440; Dahl et al., 1978, pp. 342–343. Foulkes's own proposed "grammar" of dreams has been criticized because the discourse of dreams is not predominantly verbal but employs extensive preverbal and nonverbal elements (Rogers, 1981, p. 433).

11. See, for example, Bates, 1976, p. 354; Litowitz and Litowitz, 1977, pp. 440–443; Shapiro, 1979, pp. 50, 90–91, 98; Labov, 1980, p. vii; Green and Morgan, 1981; Leaffer, 1982, pp. 24–25; Prideaux, 1985, p. 153; Tweney, 1993, p. 339; see also, however, Litowitz, 1978.

12. See also Tweney, in Callebaut, 1993, p. 339; Cherry, 1957, pp. 221–224; Olds, 1994, pp. 583–584.

13. See also Ekstein (1978, p. 339), who attempts to formulate the clinical interpretive process as a "language game."

14. See Meissner, 1979a, p. 100, for a critique of Wittgenstein's theory.

15. For philosophical critiques of Wittgenstein and of Ryle, see Quine, 1960; Putnam, 1975; and Schwartz, 1977.

16. For additional critiques of action language, see Friedman, 1976; Barratt, 1978; Aufhauser, 1979; Frank, 1979; Holt, 1979; Meissner, 1979a,b; Rawn, 1979; Calogeras and Alston, 1980; Anscombe, 1981; Fonagy, 1982, p. 133; Spence, 1982a.

17. See also Dahl and Stengel, 1978; Dahl et al., 1978; Shapiro, 1979, 1986, 1988, 1991; Makari and Shapiro, 1993.

18. See, for example, Scholes, 1974, 1982; Scholes and Kellogg, 1966; Todorov, 1977; Genette, 1980; Prince, 1982.

19. See, for example, Farrell, 1961; Danto, 1965, 1985; Scholes and Kellogg, 1966; Sherwood, 1969; White, 1973; Ricoeur, 1978; Hunter, 1991.

20. Loch, 1977; Viderman, 1979; Schafer, 1976, 1979, 1980, 1983a–d, 1985a,b, 1987, 1992; Bellin, 1984; Spence, 1982a, 1986b, 1987; Hoffman, 1983, 1987, 1991, 1994; Stern, 1983, 1985, 1991; Gill, 1994a,b.

21. See, for example, Rieff, 1959; Ricoeur, 1970; Habermas, 1971; Gergen, 1985; Gergen and Gergen, 1986.

22. See, for example, Garduk and Haggard, 1972; Malan, 1976; Eagle, 1980a, pp. 421–423; 1984b; Marziali, 1984; Thomä and Kächele, 1987, p. 44; 1990; Crits-Christoph et al., 1988a, pp. 492–493; Silberschatz, et al., 1988; Hanly, 1990, 1992a,b; Edelson, 1992a,b; Busch, 1993. See also Sloane et al. (1975), however, who report that in outcome studies comparing psychotherapy and behavior therapy, patients who received more interpretations showed less improvement.

23. See, for example, Schimek, 1975; Barratt, 1984; Meissner, 1979a,b; Eagle, 1980a, 1984b; Viederman, 1983; Rogers, 1984; Scott, 1985; Wetzler, 1985; Leary, 1989; Loewenstein, 1991; Roth, 1989, 1991a,b; Reed, 1995.

Chapter 5

1. See, for example, Barber, 1974, pp. 235–236; Wallace, 1983a,b; 1985; Ramzy, 1963a, pp. 74–75; Kubie, 1975; Holzman and Aronson, 1992.

2. Spence would disagree with Kaplan's (1964, p. 328) view that certain explanations are interpretations. In a polemical essay entitled "When Interpretation Masquerades as Explanation," Spence (1986a) argues that an interpretation suggests what might be true, not necessarily what is true: "It rarely suggests alternative explanations. Its principal goal is to persuade, convince, and bring about insight and change *in the patient*, rather than present a reasoned argument that relies on public data and shared rules of evidence and logic" (p. 5). The philosopher Michael Sherwood (1969) concludes, however, that logically a psychoanalytic narrative explanation is not that different from explanation in other fields. Edelson (1985, p. 87) comments that it is a mistake to assume that because psychoanalysis is concerned with meanings and purposes it is not concerned with causal explanation; for wishes and beliefs are motives, and "motives are among the causes of psychoanalytical phenomena" (1986, p. 102). Jessica Benjamin (1986, p. 484) questions whether the fault lies, as Spence suggests, in the presentation of data: "Usually competing ideas arise because each explains some measure of the truth. The ultimate task of resolving differences is a work of critical understanding rather than of evidential explanation" (p. 486). Grünbaum (1984, 1993) disagrees with Kaplan's (1964) view that "the scientific explanation may be suggested and supported by the semantic one, as in the case of dream analysis" (p. 328). As indicated previously, and discussed more fully in Chapter 7, Grünbaum insists (controversially) that meaning relations tell one nothing about causal connections.

3. In Spence's sustained critique of "soft pattern matches" in clinical interpretation (1982a, 1986a, 1987, 1988, 1990, 1992, 1994b), he claims that pattern matching depends more on analogical reasoning than on clear similarities between events (1987, p. 22). In a more recent report, Spence (1992) criticizes pattern matching as a form of medieval logic dependent on the prescientific "Doctrine of Signatures" (Foucault, 1970). The latter doctrine emphasized outward signs of hidden similarities, which were used as a method of understanding the world: for example, suggestive resemblances between a thunderstorm and an epileptic seizure. Spence ignores a crucial difference, however, between the medieval "Doctrine of Signatures" and present-day psychological pattern matching. The recognition of patterns in interpretive inquiry is based on posited, often repetitive internal relations among the patient's own associations and enactments. The "Doctrine of Signatures," on the other hand, dealt with purported relations between some aspect of a person and ostensibly similar external events.

In still another review, Spence (1991) appears to have reversed himself. Citing Greenwald et al. (1986), he suggests that clinicians should focus on the conditions under which a given phenomenon makes its appearance (for example, a male patient provokes arguments with his father only when his mother is present). Such an approach takes both the clinical episode and its context into account, focusing on a series of patterns rather than a series of events. Spence (1991, p. 283) now claims that the latter form of interpretive inquiry is "native to the consulting room," because by investigating under what conditions a phenomenon (such as a symptom, conflict, or defense) appears, we take the recurrent pattern as our basic unit of clinical significance, and make pattern matching "the essential clinical activity." (See also Brooks, 1994, p. 74, for a further critique of Spence's views on pattern matching.)

4. Michael Wertheimer (1968) has written an accessible introductory essay on gestalt psychology. Standard treatises on the subject include Koffka's (1935) *Principles of Gestalt Psychology* and Kohler's (1970) *Gestalt Psychology*. For some clinically related applications of gestalt concepts, see Max Wertheimer's (1945) *Productive Thinking*; Heider's (1960) "The Gestalt Theory of Motivation;" Asch's (1987) *Social Psychology*; and Bellak and Walkup's (1993) *Psychoanalysis as Science*.

5. See also Meehan, 1968; Sadovsky, 1983, pp. 623–625; Laszlo, 1972. For the relevance of system theory to psychiatry, see Schwartz and Wiggins, 1986. Attempts to integrate system theory and psychoanalysis include works by Charny and Carroll, 1966; Loeb and Carroll, 1966; Peterfreund, 1971; Symposium, 1981; Rosenblatt and Thickstun, 1977. See also Holt, 1989, p. 364, n.10; 1992, p. 398; but see also Plänkers, 1986.

6. Another possible example of an emergent system in the clinical situation may be the "interpersonally decentered subject" or "analytic third" which, according to Ogden (1992a,b) and Green (1993), emerges in the course of the therapeutic interaction.

7. See also Fairbairn, 1952; Bowlby, 1969, 1973; 1980; Klein and Tribich, 1981, p. 37; Rogers, 1991.

8. The introductory chapter of a book by Howard (1982, pp. 1–34) offers a brief, accessible overview of hermeneutics. Treatises by Palmer (1969) and Bleicher (1980) provide in-depth reviews of the subject. Hirsch's (1967) approach, although controversial, is a refreshing challenge to hermeneutics (and to clinical interpretation) because it emphasizes the neglected problem of justification (see also Betti, 1980; Ricoeur, 1976, p. 78; 1977; Martin, 1994).

For methodologic parallels between hermeneutics and clinical interpretation, see Ricoeur (1970, 1974, 1977, 1978); Taylor (1971); Kockelmans, 1975; Steele (1979, 1985); Packer (1985); Rubovits-Seitz (1986a, 1991a); Messer, Sass, and Woolfolk (1988; especially the chapters by Sass and Woolfolk, and Woolfolk and Messer); Van Velzen (1988); Packer and Addison (1989a,b); Chessick (1990, 1992); Phillips (1991); and Strenger (1991). George Klein's (1976) treatise on psychoanalytic theory is written from a hermeneutic perspective; and both Roy Schafer (1975, 1979, 1983c) and Donald Spence (1982a, 1988a) are leading spokespersons for a hermeneutic viewpoint in psychoanalysis, dynamic psychotherapy, and clinical interpretation. In his final book, Merton Gill (1994b) describes his belated turn to hermeneutics.

9. Other hermeneutic writers who have emphasized interpretive justification include Betti, 1980; Palmer, 1969, p. 65; Ricoeur, 1970, 1977, 1982, pp. 263–264; Habermas, 1971; Gauld and Shotter, 1977, pp. 199–215; Rubovits-Seitz, 1986a, pp. 17–21; 1991a, pp. 575–576; Woolfolk, 1986, pp. 265–266; Phillips, 1987, p. 616; Bernstein, 1988b, pp. 169–171, 173.

10. Kermode, 1985, p. 10; Steiner, 1995, pp. 440–441. See also Packer and Addison, 1989a,b; Stiles, 1994, p. 161.

11. Some key references to the rapidly expanding literature on confirmation bias include works by Tversky and Kahneman, 1974; Nisbett and Ross, 1980; Tweney et al., 1981; Kahneman et al., 1982; Kahneman and Tversky, 1982; Anderson, 1983; Faust, 1984; Dallas and Baron, 1985; Turk and Salovey, 1988; Rubovits-Seitz, 1992a, pp. 144–148.

12. Whether such relations in clinical data also contribute to the identification of unconscious determinants (for example, motivational causes) is a moot question. Meehl (1983, pp. 359–360) and Grünbaum (1984, 1989, 1990a, 1993) argue that thematic or meaning relations, by themselves, do not warrant causal inferences. This important methodologic question is discussed more fully in Chapter 7.

13. Freud, 1911b, p. 94; 1918, p. 11; 1937b, p. 268; Cheshire, 1975, p. 113; Rogers, 1981, p. 441; 1988; Gillman, 1987.

14. Levenson, 1972; Calogeras, 1973; Boyer, 1978; Gould, 1978; Kurzweil, 1978; Stolorow, 1978; Kuper, 1979, 1986; Kuper and Stone, 1982; Siomopoulos, 1983; Slap and Saykin, 1983, 1984; Atwood and Stolorow, 1984; Hildebrand, 1988; Rudnytsky, 1988; Holt, 1989, pp. 254–256.

15. See also Clark and Clark (1977) for a useful introduction to psycholinguistics. Slobin's (1979) text is more general and technical. Prideaux's (1985) book focuses on research aspects of psycholinguistics. Spence (1968, 1979), Shapiro (1979), Rosen (1977), and Rieber (1980) attempt to integrate psycholinguistics with psychoanalysis and dynamic psychotherapy.

16. Most of what we know about the processing of clinical data is based on intuitive impressions rather than on systematic investigation (see, for example, Spence, 1979). Olinick (1980) believes that clinical processing operations are introspectable, but Edelson (1980, p. 192) questions that view. From the standpoint of psychoanalytic structural theory, it is conceivable that both language processing and clinical data processing occur in the conflict-free sphere of the preconscious and unconscious ego, which would imply that such operations are partially introspectable and partly not. See also Deese, 1962, 1965; Dixon, 1971, 1981.

17. See also Calef and Weinshel, 1975; Weinshel, 1984; Arlow, 1991, p. 546; 1992, pp. xvii–xviii; 1995, p. 232.

18. Frank Rettenberg (personal communication, 1994).

19. See also Mischler, 1979; and Shope, 1973, who includes causal continuity among Freud's several uses of the term "meaning."

20. See also, however, Britton and Steiner (1994, p. 1070) and Spence (1984a, p. 42), who question "insight" or "discovery" of this kind.

21. Compare Barthes' (1968, p. 21) concept of "ideolectic" (personal) meanings. See also Makari and Shapiro (1993, p. 1009) and Tuckett (1983).

22. See Labov and Fanshel, 1977, p. 380, for a more detailed list of paralinguistic cues. See also Lieberman (1965) and Labov and Fanshel (1977, pp. 42–49) for the difficulties of coding and achieving consensus on paralinguistic phenomena.

23. See, for example, Mahl, 1956, 1959, 1961, 1987a,b; Mahl and Schulze, 1964; Dittman, 1962, 1963; Dittman and Wynne, 1961; Ekman, 1957, 1964, 1965; Scheflen, 1963, 1965, 1973; Sherer and Ekman, 1982. For microanalytic investigations of communicative phenomena during the therapeutic process, see Pittenger, Hockett, and Danehy, 1960; McQuown, 1971; Labov and Fanshel, 1977.

24. See, for example, Hairston, 1978; Prelli, 1989; Margolis, 1990; Simons, 1990a,b; Pera and Shea, 1991; Brooks, 1994, pp. 46–47, 71–72; Spence, 1983b, 1994; Wilcocks, 1994.

25. The fact that patients in well-going analyses and dynamic psychotherapies learn the therapist's interpretive code raises the question whether the therapist's interventions serve as suggestions to the patient regarding the code. If interventions were presented authoritatively as apodictic statements they might well have a suggestive effect; but if interventions are conveyed more tentatively as assertoric possibilities, the likelihood of suggestive influence is reduced. An important part of the interpretive code that the patient needs to learn, both for effective collaboration in the therapeutic relationship and for future self-inquiry, is that depth-psychological interpretation is difficult and fallible and thus calls for a benevolently skeptical attitude. Ideally, therefore, the patient learns the interpretive code not under the pressure of suggestion from or an inner need to please the therapist, but from a process of mutual search for the most plausible interpretation at a given time. If suggestive effects occur in connection with interventions,

those effects themselves become a necessary focus of interpretive inquiry. This issue is discussed further in Chapter 7.

26. Makari and Shapiro (1993) propose a model of psychoanalytic listening based upon semiotics and psycholinguistics. Other examples of applying semiotics to problems of clinical interpretation include: Mahl and Shulze (1964) on extralinguistic phenomena; Rosen (1969) on relations of sign phenomena to unconscious meanings; Martindale (1975) on semiotic reinterpretation of psychoanalytic theory; Bruss (1986) on projective identification; Johansen (1986, pp. 50–53) on semiotic similarities between clinical and literary interpretation; Rogers on repetition (1987c) and types of semantic relationships (1986b); Chinen's (1987) semiotic perspective on object relations; Johnson (1988) on semiotics, transference interpretation, and therapeutic change; Kristeva (1983, p. 85) on the relation of interpretation to semiotics; Barratt (1990) on the "rupture" of the human subject between semiosis and desire; Killingmo (1990) on semiotic aspects of preverbal affects and their interpretation; Olds (1990) on brain-centered psychology; Litowitz and Epstein (1991) on semiotic aspects of clinical theory and practice.

27. Bruss (1986) argues, on the other hand, that theories such as projective identification, which deal with the psychological capacities of infants, are high-order inferences which presuppose phenomena that lie beyond semiotic method.

28. See also Bucci, 1985, 1988, 1989, who postulates that verbal and nonverbal contents are coded and stored separately (see also Paivio, 1986); and Johansen's (1986) proposal of two different semiotic memory systems—one being perceptual, pictorial, or iconic, the other involving symbolic linguistic representations.

29. For accessible introductions to literary theory and criticism, see Hernadi, 1978, 1981.

30. See, for example, Leech, 1969; Edelson, 1975, p. 108; Ricoeur, 1978, p. 310; Jones, 1997. Shoshana Felman (1982) suggests cogently that the relationship between psychoanalysis and literature be considered one of reciprocally implied rather than applied knowledge.

31. Johansen, 1986, pp. 540, 550–553; see also Scholes, 1982, p. 43; Brooks, 1994, pp. 24–25, 35–36. Coltrera (1981, pp. 87–89) notes perceptively that in discussing the posited mechanisms of representation in dreams, Freud (1900, pp. 310–338) employed two definitions of interpretation that are inconsistent with each other. One is a data-driven, "critical" model (as in literary criticism), that is, "deriving meaning from meaning": for example, Freud's (1900, pp. 311, fn. 1; 335) reference to Rank's (1910) report of a "dream that interprets itself," which Freud considered the most complete reported interpretation of a very long dream. At the same time, however, Freud employed a formal, theory-driven model of interpretation in terms of the (postulated) causal dynamics and genetics of dream-formation: that is, he reasoned backwards from his theory of representation in dream-formation to interpret the meanings of some common dream images (compare Edelson's [1975] contro-

versial theory of "interpretive competence," that is, an interpreter's ability to reconstruct the rule-ordered operations that transform deeper, meaning-bearing structures into surface structures—discussed critically in Chapter 4). Coltrera (1981, p. 89) makes the further salient observation that the inconsistency between "critical" and "formal" definitions of interpretation was resolved, at least partially, in Freud's metapsychological papers (see 1915c, p. 166) by his postulating a relationship between instinctual drives and their ideational representatives—the latter being cognate forms of drive-wishes that can be interpreted as meanings.

32. For example, Spence, 1976, p. 370; Skura, 1981; Kurzweil and Phillips, 1983; Krieger, 1988, pp. 8–9, 13; Edelson, 1992b, p. 118. Olinick (1984, p. 636) cites Marcus (1974), Holland (1978), Skura (1981), and Chabot (1982, see esp. pp. 49–75) to illustrate the parallels between reading a literary text and the interpretive "reading" of a patient. See also Taylor, 1971.

33. Comparing legal and historical models of interpretation, Carlo Ginzburg (1994, p. 295) writes similarly that "a purely internal reading of the evidence, without any reference to its referential dimension, is impossible." He suggests that "the fashionable injunction to study reality as a text should be supplemented by the awareness that no text can be understood without a reference to extratextual realities" (p. 295).

34. See also Stanley Fish (1989; cited by Brooks, 1994, p. 46), who argues that there are no grounds for interpretation which are not themselves based on other acts of interpretation. Derrida's strategy of deconstruction (see, for example, Culler, 1982; Ray, 1989, pp. 141–149) shares with Barthes, Fish, and De Man the concept that meaning as structure and as interpretive act are mutually constitutive; but the same authors also emphasize the infinite regress (absolute relativity) of meanings. Gail Reed (1995, p. 725) points out, on the other hand, that clinical work is not predicated on an absolutism of relative meaning, but on a hierarchy of meanings in which latent meanings are assumed to have particularly powerful, persistent, and influential effects upon the patient's experiences and actions. Reed (p. 727) argues further that clinical interpretation cannot be equated simply with deconstruction; for clinical interpretation involves first a process of constructing latent meanings and determinants, followed by the analysis (deconstruction) of the constructed latent contents.

35. See also Eissler, 1959; De Groot, 1969, pp. 309–327; Polkinghorne, 1983, pp. 245–246; Abraham, 1986, p. 59.

36. See also Morton, 1980, pp. 52–53, who notes that one of the constraints on psychological explanations is that underlying mental states must be "imaginable." Steven Marcus (in Gelfand and Kerr, 1992; cited by L. J. Friedman, 1995, p. 181) observes that Wordsworth anticipated Freud by developing a narrative mode which was very similar to the psychoanalytic life history. Unconscious desires and ideas were central; the narrative was circular rather than linear or unidirectional; and it contained multiple, confluent meanings. Edel's (1966) study of symbolism in the writings of Nathaniel Hawthorne contains a striking example of literature anticipating

depth-psychological therapies and clinical interpretation. Hawthorne died half a century before the advent of psychoanalysis, yet a passage in *The Scarlet Letter* describes a therapeutic relationship which bears an uncanny resemblance to psychoanalysis:

> Roger Chillingworth strove to go deep into his patient's bosom, delving among his principles, prying into his recollections, and probing everything with a cautious touch, like a treasure-seeker in a dark cavern. Few secrets can escape an investigator, who has opportunity and license to undertake such a quest and skill to follow it up. A man burdened with a secret should especially avoid the intimacy of his physician. If the latter possesses native sagacity, and a nameless something more—let us call it intuition; if he show no intrusive egotism, nor disagreeably prominent characteristics of his own; if he have the power, which must be born with him, to bring his mind into such affinity with his patient's, that this last shall unawares have spoken what he imagines himself only to have thought; if such revelations be received without tumult, and acknowledged not so often by an uttered sympathy as by silence, an inarticulate breath, and here and there a word, to indicate that all is understood; if to these qualifications of a confidant be joined the advantages afforded by his recognized character as a physician—then, at some inevitable moment, will the soul of the sufferer be dissolved, and flow forth in dark, but transparent stream, bringing all its mysteries into the daylight [Edel, 1966, pp. 108–109].

Grubrich-Simitis (1993, p. 135; cited by Pigman, 1995, p. 93) notes that Freud's reading of classical literature also contributed to his method of interpretation. Freud wrote to Fliess on January 30, 1899, for example, that Jakob Burkhardt's (1898–1902) *History of Greek Culture* contained "unexpected parallels," for example: "For the way in which one should comport oneself in the work of interpretation: *Burkhardt* . . . The result is not at all to be forced . . . ; a gentle attentiveness with regular diligence leads further" (Freud, 1985, p. 342).

37. Felman, 1982a. See also Mahony's (1982, 1984, 1986, 1989) studies of Freud's writing style and case histories; Marcus's (1984) analysis of literary devices in Freud's case histories; and Derrida's (1972) essay, "Freud at the Scene of Writing," in which Derrida proposes that Freud's (1925b) contribution on the mystic writing pad replaced his original hydraulic model of mind with a "graphematic" model.

38. Holland (1978, 1990) observes that "we 'predict' our way through a text, eliminating alternatives to produce a single interpretation" (1978, p. 193). Edelson (1975, p. 141) compares clinical interpretation with the interaction of "anticipations and retrospections" involved in reading; see also Mahony and Singh, 1979, pp. 444–455. Coen (1996) considers Erik Erikson a forerunner of reader response criticism (see, for example, Erikson, 1954).

39. See also Fish (1970, p. 74), who emphasizes the importance of slowing

down the reading process in order to grasp meanings that otherwise would not be evident. Priel (1990, pp. 547–548) applies the same concept to the clinical situation, that is, a slowing down of the interpretive process appears to be essential to the production and understanding of meanings (compare Freud's, 1910c, caution not to "rush"). Priel (1990) applies the reader-response perspective not only to the therapist's "reading" of a patient, but also to the patient's "reading" of the therapist's interpretations: "A reading that searches to fulfill the inevitable gaps that are structured in every interpretation is a mutative element in analytical interpretations. Accordingly, the question is not what the analyst said (that produced therapeutic change), but how what the therapist said affected the patient's creation of meaning" (p. 537). Effective interpretations are those through which new meanings are created by the patient (see also Basch, 1981, p. 172, who maintained that the interpretive tasks of providing both further information and new meaning are performed largely by the patient).

40. See also Hunt, 1982, for an accessible overview of cognitive science; and Osherson and Lasnik, 1990, for the role of language in cognitive science.

41. See, for example, Lewin, 1935, 1951; Heider, 1958; Festinger, 1954, 1957; Kelly, 1967; Abelson et al., 1968.

42. See, for example, Sandler and Rosenblatt, 1962b; Jacobson, 1964; Moore and Fine, 1990; Wakefield, 1990. For a contrary view, see Goldberg, 1990, who draws on the connectionist theory of brain processing (see Olds, 1994; Palombo, 1992) to argue (controversially) for a psychoanalysis without intermediary representations.

43. In one such experiment, Zajonc (1988, p. 356) investigated the role of facial musculature, recorded by means of EMG, in the recognition-memory of faces presented under various conditions. One group of subjects chewed gum while viewing photographs of faces. The assumption was that chewing gum would interfere with mimicry of their facial muscles. The results confirmed that prediction.

44. See, for example, Neisser, 1967, 1976; Rumelhart, 1980; Knapp, 1981, 1988, 1991; Bowers and Meichenbaum, 1984; Bucci, 1985, 1988, 1989; Erdelyi, 1985, 1988; Erdelyi and Goldberg, 1979; Schank, 1982; Reiser, 1984, 1990; Wegman, 1985; Horowitz, 1987, 1988, 1989, 1991a,b, 1993; Horowitz and Zilberg, 1983; Horowitz et al., 1991; Kihlstrom, 1987; Singer, 1988a,b, 1990; Singer and Salovey, 1991; Edelson, 1992a; Segal and Blatt, 1993; Panel, 1994.

45. See also Mandler, 1988; and Horowitz et al., 1991, pp. 180–181, for historical surveys of the schema concept; and Neisser, 1976; Markus, 1977; Hastie, 1981; Taylor and Crocker, 1981; Bandura, 1982; Horowitz and Zilberg, 1983; Horowitz, 1987; and Rumelhart et al., 1986, for additional investigations and concepts related to schema theory.

46. For an opposing view, see Holland et al. (1986), who question the concept of "holistic" internal causal schemata such as scripts, because subsets of beliefs can produce effects independently of other beliefs.

47. See, for example, Fairbairn, 1952; Klein, 1958; Guntrip, 1961; Sutherland, 1963; Jacobson, 1964; Kernberg, 1976; Greenberg and Mitchell, 1983; Mitchell,

1988; Rogers, 1991. Horowitz (1988, pp. 11–12) proposes a "schematic repertoire theory" which attempts to express object relations theory in terms of schema theory; see also Slap and Slap-Shelton (1991) for an accessible treatise on applying schema theory to psychoanalysis.

48. Barron et al., 1992b, pp. 299–312. See also Piaget, 1973; Klein, 1976; Schneider and Shiffrin, 1977; Shiffrin and Schneider, 1977; Basch, 1981; Cohen et al., 1985; Pfeiffer and Leuzinger-Bohleber, 1986; Nelson, 1986; Squire, 1986; Roediger, 1990; Clyman, 1991; Goldman, 1994; Olds, 1994. For a review of heuristic methods employed in various sciences, see Groner et al., 1983. Some parallels between heuristic methods in other sciences and in clinical interpretation are discussed in Chapter 10.

49. See, for example, Schafer, 1959; Greenson, 1960, pp. 421–423; Meehl, 1960, p. 21; Peterfreund, 1975, 1983; Heimann, 1969, 1977; Thomä and Kächele, 1987, pp. 261–262; Horowitz, 1988, 1991b.

Chapter 6

1. Brook (1992) objects to the term "folk" psychology because "we are not talking about something on a par with folk art; we are talking about the stuff of great novels, the raw material of Shakespeare. Even the term *commonsense psychology* is too weak for this store of interpretive skill and wisdom" (pp. 273–274). So far no introductory textbook of commonsense psychology has been written, but Dennett (1993, p. 124) suggests Ryle's *Concept of Mind* (1949) as a substitute. Accessible recent surveys of commonsense psychology include Bogdan (1991), Greenwood (1991), and Christensen and Turner (1993).

2. See Rubovits-Seitz, 1988b, pp. 197–200, for a review of psychological-mindedness.

3. See, for example, Meehl, 1954; Nisbett and Ross, 1980; Kahneman, Slovic, and Tversky, 1982. See also Rubovits-Seitz, 1992a, pp. 144–148, for a review and discussion of the ubiquitous problem of confirmation bias.

4. Hopkins, 1991, p. 88. Spence (1986a) argues against the use of interpretations as explanations; but Grünbaum (1993, pp. 117–118) insists that "Freud's interpretations of the unconscious 'meanings' of symptoms, dreams, and slips are obviously offered as explanatory causal hypotheses" (p. 117). Wollheim (1993b) and Haynal (1993a, p. 72) disagree with Grünbaum on this issue; see also Rycroft (1966).

5. Some philosophers, however (for example, Quine, 1960; Pettit, 1983, pp. 317–318; Lyons, 1995), have raised questions about intentionality. Brentano claimed that all mental phenomena are intentional; but some psychological phenomena such as pain and other sensations appear to be nonintentional. And since intentionality is neither necessary nor sufficient for the psychological, how can it be the distinguishing feature of the mental (Haldane, 1988, p. 136)? Brentano himself later changed his views about intentionality, abandoning the concept around 1905 (Barclay, 1964, p. 18).

For additional philosophical viewpoints on intentionality, see Searle, 1983, 1989, 1994; Dennett, 1987; Dennett and Haugeland, 1987; Caws, 1993.

6. For example, Barclay, 1964; McGrath, 1986; Brook, 1992; and McIntosh, 1993.

7. Wallace (1989b, p. 504) notes, for example, that Freud (1896, p. 193) included the commonsense notions of "suitability" and "proportionality" between cause amd effect as criteria of causality; that is, a postulated traumatic event should possess the relevant suitability and the necessary traumatic force to serve as a determinant. Weston (1992, pp. 38–40) points out in this connection that causal inferences and arguments do not appeal just to the correlation of phenomena, but also explain why it "makes sense" for A to cause B—that is, what makes A a suitable determinant of B.

8. Grünbaum (1984, 1993; see also Chapter 7). Grünbaum (1984, pp. 51, 77–83, 89–90, 93) impugns commonsense psychology for much the same reason that he attacks hermeneutics, because both approaches emphasize the interpretation of meanings. The philosopher J. R. Searle (1989) insists that only conscious psychical processes possess intrinsic intentionality (mental content), all nonconscious processes being physiological. Natsoulas (1992) has examined Searle's arguments and finds them inadequate (see also Hampshire, 1963; Eagle, 1980b, pp. 336, 347–357, 377; Dilman, 1988, pp. 176–177; Horgan and Woodward, 1993, pp. 152–153; Rorty, 1993, p. 400).

9. For example, Hopkins, 1982, 1988, 1991, 1992; Wollheim, 1984, 1993a,b; Edelson, 1988; Gill, 1991; Strenger, 1991; Brook, 1992, 1995b.

10. For example, McIntyre, 1958, pp. 52, 56–57; Sharpe, 1970, 1988, 1993; Morton, 1980, 1982; Farrell, 1981; Hopkins, 1982, 1988, 1991, 1992; Johansen, 1986; Dilman, 1988, pp. 84–85; Edelson, 1988, 1992b; Moore, 1988, p. 142; Sachs, 1989.

11. Brook (1992, p. 292) questions Edelson's claim that psychoanalysis has extended all forms of explanation in commonsense psychology, because Edelson has not specified the multiple varieties of heuristics included in commonsense psychology, nor how psychoanalysis extends them.

12. For example, Wakefield, 1992a, p. 80; see also Gill, 1976, 1983; Holt, 1976, 1989; Klein, 1976. George Klein (1976) referred to the methodology clinical interpretation as a process of "reading intentionality."

13. Peirce, 1931–1958, Vol. 5, pp. 145, 172. See also Harman, 1965; Edelson, 1988; Lipton, 1991.

Chapter 7

1. Grünbaum, 1976, 1977, 1979, 1982, 1983a,b, 1984, 1986, 1988a,b, 1989, 1990a,b, 1991, 1993, 1994.

2. The latter group includes philosophers Alan Nelson, Paul Churchland, Ned Block, and others (cited in Callebaut, 1993, p. 75). See also Putnam, 1981, pp. 190–191; Leibin, 1986, pp. 246–247; Schlesinger, 1985; Watson, 1985; Savodnik, 1986, p. 257; Klimovsky, 1991, p. 493; Emde,

1993, pp. 422–423; Child, 1994; Massicotte, 1995, pp. 20, 26; Wimsatt, 1994, p. 494.

3. See also Wollheim, 1993b, pp. 108–109; Diesing, 1985a, pp. 82–84; Wax, 1995, pp. 552–553; Edelson, 1984, p. 122; Fonagy, 1982, pp. 128–130, 137–140.

4. See also Heil and Mele, 1993. Early in his work Freud recognized the ubiquity of multiple interlocking causes (for example, 1893–1895, pp. 173, 287–290); and he employed different kinds of causal explanations in his case studies.

5. See, for example, Laor, 1985; Spruiell, 1986; Wolfenstein, 1990; Berger, 1993; Robinson, 1993; Wollheim, 1993b; Bowman, 1996, pp. 385–389; Galatzer-Levy, 1996.

6. For example, the philosophers Erwin, 1986, 1988, 1993; von Eckhardt, 1981, 1982, 1985, 1986; and Flanagan, 1986; the psychoanalysts Edelson, 1983, 1984, 1986a,b, 1988; Sand, 1983, 1993; Reiser, 1986; Gillett, 1987, 1995; Kline, 1986, 1988; Hanly, 1992a; Holzman, 1993; and Rubovits-Seitz, 1994a; the psychiatrists Hobson, 1986; Hobson and McCarley, 1977; and Klerman, 1986; and the psychologists Eagle, 1984a, pp. 157, 171, 174, 222; 1986a,b, 1989, 1994; Eysenck, 1965, 1986; Eysenck and Wilson, 1973.

7. To support his argument that the analyst's interpretations are based on a theoretically biased selection of the patient's material, Grünbaum cites Freud's own statements regarding his interpretive technique (for example, Freud, 1910a, pp. 141–142; see also 1909a, pp. 120–121), that is, giving the patient "anticipatory ideas" of what the patient may expect to find in himself—a potentially indoctrinating procedure. He also cites reports by Marmor (1962, 1970); Christiansen (1964); Shapiro and Morris (1978, p. 384); Blanck and Blanck (1974, pp. 320–322); and Peterfreund (1983, pp. 19–61; see esp. p. 52), all of which suggest that selection bias can and does occur. For example, all of the cases reported by Peterfreund "are replete with unabashed coaching and coaxing of the patient to produce stereotypically expected responses" (Grünbaum, 1986, p. 275).

8. To support his argument regarding patient compliance, Grünbaum cites Freud's statements that the analyst must mobilize positive feelings in the patient toward the therapist in order to overcome resistances to interpretations (for example, Freud, 1915–1917, pp. 445–447; see also Collins, 1980). Grünbaum paraphrases Freud's descriptions of patients' positive feelings (1912a, p. 150; 1915–1917, pp. 439–444) as "extravagant in degree as well as grotesque in character"—a state of mind that heightens suggestibility (Grünbaum, 1984, p. 131). Grünbaum (1984) also cites texts by Möller (1976, p. 71) that neurotics are "notoriously suggestible"; Fisher and Greenberg (1977, p. 364), who assert that neurotics will accept "bogus interpretations"; and Heine (1953; cited by Grünbaum, 1993, p. 218), who insists that purported insight is not true self-discovery but conversion to the therapist's theories.

9. See also Cook and Campbell, 1979 (cited by Holt, 1986, pp. 242–244); Shevrin, 1986, pp. 257–259; Tuckett, 1995, p. 658; Levy, 1996, pp. 130–131. Freud used the term "suggestion" to mean a number of things, and was well

aware that patients' associations are not entirely free or self-generated, but are influenced to variable extents by the therapist (see, for example, Freud, 1909a, p. 104; 1911b, p. 96; 1923b, pp. 114–116). The methodologist Paul Diesing (1985b) notes the following sources of influence on social science data, including the data of psychoanalysis and dynamic psychotherapy: (1) data-generating and data-gathering procedures shape the data to some extent (so-called "method effects": compare Fiske and Shweder, 1986, p. 5); (2) the therapist's expectations, including confirmation bias (see Rubovits-Seitz, 1992a, pp. 144–148); (3) the therapist induces responses through interventions, which become part of the data; (4) wittingly or unwittingly, the compliant patient may produce material to please the therapist; (5) narrative smoothing of constructions, reconstructions, and case histories; (6) the therapist's efforts to be impartial and objective are imperfect (for a striking example in Freud's therapeutic approach, see Kris, 1994); and (7) no one theoretical perspective fits a case and its clinical data perfectly.

10. Fine and Forbes, 1986, pp. 237–238; see also Sachs, 1989, p. 355; Wollheim, 1993, pp. 110–111; Erwin, 1993, pp. 422–432.

11. See also Malan, 1979; Eagle, 1980a, p. 406; Luborsky, 1986, pp. 247–249; Spence, 1986c, p. 259; 1995, pp. 706, 711; Wallace, 1986, p. 381. Anton Kris (1994, p. 656) notes that Freud found it necessary to defend psychoanalysis repeatedly against the accusation that its results are the product of suggestion alone.

12. See also Hanly, 1992a, p. 298, for citations of Freud (1915–1917, p. 238; 1923b, p. 114) and Jones (1955, p. 22) regarding the manifest but not latent contents of patients' dreams, that is, the disguise but not the unconscious wish being influenced by the analyst's interpretations. Grünbaum (1984, pp. 237–238) presents a counterargument to Freud's and Hanly's views.

13. See, for example, Vaughan and Roose, 1995; Gauld and Shotter, 1986, pp. 239–240; Caston, 1993a,b; Caston and Martin, 1993.

14. The philosopher Clark Glymour (1982) writes similarly:

> Knowing that clinical evidence is subject to suggestion should make us sensitive to the indicators that the therapist is determining the responses he receives. I do not see, however, that the experimental knowledge we now have about suggestibility requires us to renounce clinical evidence altogether. Indeed, I can imagine circumstances in which clinical evidence might have considerable force [p. 30].

Glymour concludes that knowledge of the suggestibility problem obligates us to use our heads and good judgment in assessing clinical evidence; but, "we would not be using our heads if, for example, we took the evidence to be of the same quality in the Little Hans and the Rat Man cases" (1982, p. 30).

15. Colby (1958/1963) describes some of the ways clinicians determine whether a patient consents to an interpretation only out of transference compliance:

> First, the ideational, affective, and behavioral changes we expect to follow interpretation do not occur even though the patient agrees to the interpretation offered. Second, while the offered interpretations have varying degrees of plausibility, the patient routinely responds with the same unvarying degree of consent and acceptance. And third, there are many other signs of compliance in the patient's behavior besides his responses to interpretation. When an analyst can conclude that the patient is in a phase of transference compliance, he introduces this compliance into the collaborative analytic investigation [p. 197; see also Freud, 1910c, pp. 225–226; Lossy, 1962; Panel, 1983].

16. See, for example, Tweney et al., 1981, pp. 16ff; see also Tversky and Kahneman, 1974; Mahoney and de Monbreun, 1977; Mynatt et al., 1977; Nisbett and Ross, 1980; Kahneman et al., 1982; Kahneman and Tversky, 1982; Anderson, 1982, 1983; Faust, 1984; Jelalian and Miller, 1984; Dallas and Barron, 1985; Abraham, 1986; Turk and Salovey, 1988; Rubovits-Seitz, 1992a, pp. 144–148. See also Platt (1964), Diesing (1985a), and Rubovits-Seitz (1992a, p. 146) for the use of multiple hypotheses and disconfirming tests to reduce confirmation bias.

17. See Grünbaum, 1984, pp. 55–56, 62–63, 198–199, 209–210, 227–229; 1989; 1990a; 1993, pp. 128–134, 136–139, 152.

18. Jaspers, 1974, p. 91; Ricoeur, 1970, p. 359; Klein, 1976; Schafer, 1976.

19. See also Grünbaum, 1989, pp. 479–483, for examples of Freud using meaning relations to infer causes: for example, Freud, 1893–1895, pp. 6–7, 29–30; 1896, pp. 193–194; 1909b, pp. 166, 215–216; see also 1914a, p. 12; 1937b, p. 259, where Freud uses inferences from thematic affinities to justify the theory of transference.

20. See, for example, Whitehorn, 1947; Edelson, 1988, p. 332; Friedman, 1988, p. 378; Brook, 1995b, p. 519.

21. See, for example, Green, 1995; Steiner, 1995, pp. 437–438. See also Waelder, 1930/1976, pp. 73–74; Schilder, 1935, p. 274; Langer, 1948; Meissner, 1966, pp. 249–253; 1995a, p. 256; 1995b, p. 288; Thass-Thienemann, 1968, pp. 11–16, 83; 1973, pp. 3–10; Grossman and Simon, 1969, pp. 99–109; Rosen, 1969/1977, pp. 197–207; Barthes, 1970; Weiss, 1974; Thomä and Kächele, 1975, pp. 63–75; Ekstein, 1978, p. 341; Hardy, 1978; Parkin, 1979; Bruner, 1986, 1987, 1990; Polkinghorne, 1988, p. 121; Holt, 1989, pp. 178, fn. 3, 194–195, 216, 241, fn. 11; 257, fn. 6; 308; Watson, 1993.

22. See, for example, Freud, 1893–1895, pp. 6, 17, 290; 1895b, pp. 135–136; 1896, pp. 196, fn. 1; 196–197, 202–203. See also Brook, 1992, pp. 296–298.

23. Grünbaum (1993, pp. 115–117) oversimplifies both "psychoanalytic meaning" and "semantic meaning" in his statement that "the psychoanalytic meaning of a symptom or a neurosis is essentially constituted by its *unconscious cause*, whereas the semantic meaning of a word is constituted by its sense and referent" (p. 115). By contrast, see Millikan's (1984) more complete and "naturalized" theory of meaning; and the philosophers Daniel Taylor (1970, pp. 110–194); John Searle (1979a); Brian Loar (1981); Sollace Mitchell

(1983, pp. 81–85); and the psychoanalysts Andrew Brook (1995b, pp. 523–525) and Lawrence Friedman (1996, pp. 259–261).

24. See Peirce, 1931–1958, Vol. 5, pp. 145, 172, 180–212, and see esp. p. 189; and Peirce, 1901, pp. 150–156.

25. Erwin (1993, pp. 451–453) reviews Kettner's argument critically, but focuses on whether it can warrant Freud's repression theory rather than on the issue of causal inferences based on meaning relations.

26. Lipton, 1991, pp. 1, 56–74; see also Harman, 1965, 1973, 1986; Brody, 1970; Thagard, 1978; Cartwright, 1983, pp. 4–8, 51–52, 89–91.

27. See also, for example, Bruner, 1986, p. 90; Glymour, 1993, pp. 483–484; and Brook, 1992, pp. 297–298.

28. Cioffi, 1986, 1988, p. 75; Farrell, 1986; Levy, 1988; Sachs, 1989; Meissner, 1990; Robinson, 1993; and others.

29. Wisdom, 1956/1963, p. 156; Pine, 1985, p. 150; Friedman, 1988, p. 133.

30. See, for example, Glover, 1931; Fromm-Reichmann, 1950, pp. 84–85; Mendel 1964; Yorke, 1965, pp. 227–228; Spence, 1982a.

31. See, for example, Kris, 1947, p. 246; Farrell 1976; Rycroft, 1968, pp. 76–77; Cheshire, 1975.

32. For additional debate about the tally argument, see Spence, 1982a; Holzman, 1985; Caplan, 1986; Erdelyi, 1986; Spruiell, 1986; Wallace,1986, 1989b; Wallerstein, 1986b; Phillips, 1987; Richardson, 1990; Strenger, 1991; Berger, 1993; and Erwin, 1993, pp. 409–420; and an unpublished manuscript by Kerz (1987), cited by Bucci, 1989, pp. 253–254.

33. See, for example, Edelson, 1984, pp. 144–153 (see also Glymour, 1974, 1980); 1986a, 1988, 1992a; Bruss, 1986; Cioffi, 1986; Holt, 1986, Strupp, 1986; Wallace, 1986, p. 382; Wax, 1986; Hanly, 1990.

34. Hanly, 1990, p. 380; see also Labov, 1972a, p. 103; Bruss, 1976, p. 73; Edelson, 1988, pp. 340–342; Rubovits-Seitz, 1992a, pp. 159–160.

35. See also Fonagy, 1982, pp. 128–130; Jones and Windholz, 1990, who propose systematic approaches to psychoanalytic case studies. Jones et al. (1993a) suggest that causal effects may be measurable over time in single case studies by use of "time series analyses"; see Moran and Fonagy (1987) for an application of such analyses by psychoanalysts; also Jones, 1993b, and Shapiro, 1993, pp. 160–161. See also Kline (1988) for a counterargument to Erwin's (1988) critique of clinical versus experimental evidence in psychoanalysis and dynamic psychotherapy.

36. See, for example, Jones and Nisbett, 1971; Maltsberger and Buie, 1974, 1980; Shapiro, 1974; Gedo, 1980; Treurniet, 1980, 1983; Buie, 1981; Wallerstein, 1985; Abraham, 1986; Jones, 1986; Reed, 1987; Rubovits-Seitz, 1988a, 1992a.

37. See also Cheshire, 1964, p. 225; De Groot, 1969, pp. 320–321; Klauber, 1980, p. 197; Duncan, 1989, p. 696.

38. See, for example, Geller and Pitz, 1968; Mitroff, 1974; Mahoney and de Monbreun, 1977; Snyder, 1984; Jordan et al., 1988.

39. For example, Hirsch, 1967, 1976; Habermas, 1971; Gauld and Shotter, 1977, pp. 199–215; Betti, 1980; Ricoeur, 1970, 1977, 1982, pp. 263–264;

Woolfolk, 1986, pp. 265–266; Phillips, 1987, p. 616; Bernstein, 1988b, pp. 169–171, 173.

Chapter 8

1. The philosopher of science Richard Miller (1987) observes, however, that different explanatory frameworks in a field, which attribute differing explanations to the phenomena, do not produce an epistemologic crisis. "For accepting a theory, approach, or explanation only requires belief in its adequacy to cope with the phenomena" (1987, p. 501).

2. See, for example, Kubie, 1952; Seeman, 1953; Cheshire, 1964, p. 217; Erikson, 1964, pp. 58–59; Sherwood, 1969, p. 253; Meehl, 1970/1973, p. 110; Klerman, 1982, p. 57; Edelson, 1985; Rubovits-Seitz, 1986a, 1992a.

3. See, for example, Merleau-Ponty, 1962; Arnheim, 1969; Marcel, 1983; Treisman, 1986; Repp, 1991.

4. See also Seitz, 1966; Werman, 1979; Fosshage and Loew, 1987; Bernardi, 1989.

5. See, for example, Viderman, 1974, 1979; Loch, 1977; Schafer, 1976, 1979; Steele, 1979; Spence, 1982a, 1987.

6. See also Thomä and Kächele, 1987, p. 44; 1990; Crits-Christoph et al., 1988a; Silberschatz et al., 1988; and Rubovits-Seitz, 1991a, 1992a, for similar views.

7. Hempel and Oppenheim, 1953; Popper, 1959/1968, 1963; Sherwood, 1969; Stegmüller, 1969; and Habermas, 1971 (see also Nichols, 1972, for a summary of Habermas's views on Freud).

8. For further discussion and debate on this question, see Rapaport, 1960, p. 130; Waelder, 1939/1976, pp. 189–199; Meehl, 1973, pp. 115–117; Gergen, 1981; Jacobson and Parmalee, 1982, p. 204; Spence, 1987, pp. 113–159; Edelson, 1984 (who draws on concepts of Giere, 1979, and Suppes, 1967, 1970, regarding the "nonstatement" view of theory); and Bruss, 1986, pp. 138–139.

9. See, for example, Stengel, Ezriel, and Farrell, 1951; Wisdom, 1967; Thomä and Houben, 1967; Meehl, 1970/1973, p. 117; Edelson, 1983, 1984; Brody, 1990, pp. 47–49; Meissner, 1992.

10. See, for example, Waelder, 1939/1976, p. 198; Ricoeur, 1977, p. 863; Arlow, 1979a, p. 203; Rubovits-Seitz, 1987, 1988a; Boesky, 1988.

11. Additional references to the issue of intraclinical justification include: Kris, 1953; Schmidl, 1955; Chassan, 1956, 1957, 1970, 1979; Farrell, 1961; Fromm and French, 1962; Paul, 1963a,b; French and Fromm, 1964, p. 8; Wolman, 1984; Eagle, 1973a,b; Meehl, 1970; Thomä and Kächele, 1975; Barratt, 1976; Kratochwill, 1978; Kratochwill et al., 1984, 1992; Kazdin, 1981, 1982; Meissner, 1982; Barlow, Hayes, and Nelson, 1984; Barlow and Hersen, 1984; Bellak and Hersen, 1984; Edelson, 1970, 1972, 1977, 1978, 1983, 1984, 1985, 1986a,b, 1988, 1992a; see especially Edelson's writings on single case

studies: 1984, pp. 59–76; 1985, pp. 231–269; 1988, pp. 231–364; Klimovsky, 1991; Hilliard, 1993; Beland, 1994; De Azevedo, 1994; Kernberg, 1994; Kerz-Rühling, 1996.

12. Other examples of pluralistic justifying approaches include Isaacs, 1939; Waelder, 1939; Janis, 1958; Rubovits-Seitz, 1987, 1991a, 1992a; Boesky, 1988.

13. Diesing, 1971, p. 149; Edelson, 1984, p. 158; Boesky, 1988; Knapp, 1988, pp. 103–105; Hanly, 1990.

14. Hirsch, 1967, 1976; Cheshire, 1975; French, 1952, 1954, 1958a; Renneker, 1960; Seitz, 1966, 1969, Rubovits-Seitz, 1986a, 1987, 1991a; Olinick, 1985; Olinick et al., 1973; Edelson, 1984; Teller and Dahl, 1986; Spence, 1995; Spence et al., 1990, 1993, 1994.

15. See also Renneker, 1960; Hoffman and Gill, 1988; Strupp et al., 1988; Horowitz, 1993; Luborsky and Luborsky, 1993; Weiss, 1993; Weiss and Sampson, 1986.

16. See, for example, Benjamin, 1950; Bellak, 1958, 1961; Knapp, 1963; the Menninger Psychotherapy Research Project (Wallerstein, 1964, 1986; Sargent et al., 1968; Kernberg et al., 1972; Horwitz, 1974; Appelbaum, 1977); and the Mount Zion Psychotherapy Research Group (Weiss and Sampson, 1986).

17. See also Horwitz (1963, pp. 427–428), who maintains that postdiction has less explanatory power than prediction, because only the latter is based on both necessary and sufficient conditions. Rapaport and Gill (1959) argue, on the other hand, that theoretically postdiction is as valid as prediction if care is taken not to invoke ex post facto explanations (see also Devereaux, 1951a, and Rubinstein, 1975, 1980).

18. See also Eissler, 1959, pp. 1–2, 19; Fromm and French, 1962; French and Fromm, 1964; Meissner, 1966, p. 249; Seitz, 1966, 1969; Rubovits-Seitz, 1986a, 1987; Hirsch, 1967, p. 196; Cheshire, 1975, p. 178; Schafer, 1983a, pp. 7–8; Edelson, 1984, pp. 136–137; Teller and Dahl, 1986.

19. See, for example, Bernfeld, 1932; Isaacs, 1939; Waelder, 1939; Schmidl, 1955; Ekstein, 1959; French and Fromm, 1964, p. 8; Greenson, 1967; Thomä and Houben, 1967; Thomä and and Kächele, 1987.

20. See also Brenner, in Panel, 1955a, p. 496; Loewenstein, 1957/1963, p. 182; Ezriel, 1956–1957/1963, pp. 118–119; and Symposium, 1994, in which Michels, Beland, Tuckett, and Kernberg express similar views.

21. Waelder, in Guttman and Guttman, 1987, p. 52; see also Kris, 1950, 1951, 1956a,b; Loewenstein, 1951a,b, 1956, 1957; Peterfreund, 1990, pp. 9–10.

22. Glover, 1931; Farrell, 1976; Yorke, 1965; Wisdom, 1967; Rycroft, 1968; Cheshire, 1975; Spence, 1982a.

23. See, for example, Horowitz, 1977; Fonagy, 1982; Meehl, 1983; Greenberg, 1986.

24. Some accessible writings on qualitative methods include: Lazarsfeld and Barton, 1951; Dahl, 1981; Polkinghorne, 1983; Elliott, 1984, 1992; Elliott and Morrow-Bradley, 1994; Kirk and Miller, 1986; Mahrer, 1988; Packer and Addison, 1989a,b; Patton, 1990; Toukmanian and Rennie, 1992; Dey, 1993; Stiles, 1993, 1994, pp. 158–164; Bryman and Burgess, 1994.

25. See also Sandler et al. (1962a), Bolland and Sandler (1965), and Sandler (1989) for an example of the qualitative method of indexing clinical material (the Hampstead Index), which can be used in connection with quantitative methods (compare also the use of textbank systems, described by Mergenthaler, 1985). See also Meehl (1958) for a thoughtful discussion of the pros and cons of qualitative and quantitative methods; and Campbell's (1988), integration of qualitative and quantitative methods in the social sciences. Barglow et al. (1989), report an example of combining qualitative and quantitative methods in the justification of clinical reconstructions.

26. The "bible" of Bayesian inference is a volume by Savage (1954). See also summaries of Bayesian inference for the behavioral sciences by Edwards et al., 1963; and Binder, 1964, 1973, pp. 64–65. See also Jefferey, 1983; Howson and Urbach, 1989; Earman, 1992.

27. Some additional references dealing with quantitative methods include:

1) *Reviews*: Gottschalk and Auerbach, 1966; Kline, 1972; Fisher and Greenberg, 1977; Luborsky and Spence, 1978; Garfield and Bergin,1978; Fonagy, 1982; Rice and Greenberg, 1984; Greenberg and Pinsof, 1986; Masling, 1986; Dahl, Kächele, and Thomä, 1988; Barber and Crits-Christoph, 1993; Shapiro and Emde, 1993; Weiss, 1993; Talley, Strupp, and Butler, 1994; Vaughan and Roose, 1995, see esp. pp. 351–352.
2) *Content analysis*: Hall and Van de Castle, 1966 (on content analysis of dreams); Holsti, 1968, 1969; Marsden, 1971; Kiesler, 1973; Dahl and Stengel, 1978; Gottschalk, 1979; Gottschalk and Gleser, 1969; Russell, 1987a,b.
3) *Computer-assisted content analysis*: Stone et al., 1966; Taylor, 1970; Dahl, 1972, 1974; Kiesler, 1973; Laffal, 1976, 1990; Dahl et al., 1978a,b; Colby, 1981; Lolas et al., 1982; Teller and Dahl, 1986; Merganthaler, 1985; Merganthaler and Kächele, 1988; Spence et al., 1993, 1994; Spence, 1995.
4) *Single-case study methods and designs*: Davidson and Costello, 1969; Waskow and Parloff, 1975; Kratochwill, 1978; Kratochwill et al., 1984, 1992; Chassan, 1979; Kazdin, 1981, 1982; APA Commission on Psychotherapies, 1982; Barlow, Hayes, and Nelson, 1984; Barlow and Hersen, 1984; Edelson, 1984, 1988, pp. 231–363; Grünbaum, 1993, pp. 229–255; Jones, 1993b; Jones et al., 1993b; Moras, Telfer, and Barlow, 1993.
5) *Examples of additional quantitative methods* used for process analysis and justification (see especially the review article by Luborsky and Spence, 1978): Strupp, 1958, 1960, 1973; Endler, 1961; Malan, 1963, 1976, 1979; Fiske et al., 1964; Kiesler et al., 1964; Isaacs and Haggard, 1966; Stollack et al., 1966; Moos and Clemes, 1967; Sargent et al., 1967; Thomä and Houben, 1967; Meltzoff and Kornreich, 1970; Kernberg et al., 1972; DeWitt et al., 1983; Horwitz, 1974; Waskow and Parloff, 1975; Holt, 1978a; Gill, 1982a; Gill and Hoffman, 1982b; Tryon, 1982; Barlow et al., 1984 (see especially pp. 157–289 for time-series methodologies);

Bellack and Hersen, 1984; Bucci, 1985, 1988, 1989; Greenberg, 1986; Weiss and Sampson, 1986; Beitman, 1987; Perry et al., 1989; Jones and Windholz, 1990; Woodard, 1993a,b.

28. See also Kris, 1950; Bonaparte, 1945; Novey, 1968; Harrison, 1970; Wetzler, 1985; Barglow et al., 1989.

29. See, for example, Berkson and Wettersten, 1984; Peterfreund, 1983, pp. 116–117, 172; Polkinghorne, 1983, pp. 249–251; Rubovits-Seitz, 1992a, pp. 153–160.

Chapter 9

1. See also Heinicke's (1993, p. 360) empirical investigations of child analyses. The method of working backwards on data has been reported also by investigators in other fields: for example, Newell, Shaw, and Simon, 1962; Wickelgren, 1974, pp. 137–151; Kermode, 1979, p. 89; Gordon, 1982, pp. 137, 166; Gabler, 1984, p. 306.

2. See also Gauld and Shotter, 1977, p. 5, who point out that hermeneutics has been broadened to include the interpretation of "text-analogues" (Taylor, 1971), that is, any sequence of human activities to which one can assign meanings.

3. Teller and Dahl's FRAME methodology (1986, pp. 780–781) is an adaptation of the cognitive scientist Marvin Minsky's (1975) proposed framework for representing knowledge of people—much of which is highly stereotyped, repetitious, structured, and situation-specific—in the form of computer programs.

4. Berkson and Wettersten's (1984) *Learning from Error: Karl Popper's Psychology of Learning*, is a useful source of information on this important aspect of scientific, including interpretive, work.

Chapter 10

1. Wittgenstein, 1969, p. 212; cited by Barnes, 1988, p. 10. For Wittgenstein's views on the form of psychoanalytic interpretation, see Levy, 1983.

2. Goodman, 1978, p. 22; cited by Barnes, 1988, p. 70. In clinical interpretation, for example, various clues to latent meanings and determinants are suggested by the patient's associations, dreams, paraverbal and nonverbal behavior, which the therapist uses imaginatively to construct possible latent contents—the most plausible of which (partially discovered, partially imputed) may be conveyed to the patient.

3. McGinn draws on the writings of Ruth Millikan (1984, 1993) in developing this argument, which differs from Grünbaum's view of the causal argument. Compare also Freud's writings (1900, pp. 74, 579, 616–617;

1915–17, p. 40) on the relation of meaning and purpose; see also Bowman, 1996, p. 378.

4. McGinn, 1989, pp. 172–208; see also Johnson-Laird, 1983; Craik, 1943. See Tomkins, 1962, 1963; Paivio, 1969, 1971; and Kosslyn, 1980, for the older image theory of content.

5. Freud, 1915–1917, pp. 346–347, 362; see also Laplanche and Pontalis, 1973, pp. 71–72; Gill, 1994, pp. 15, 28; Michels, 1996, p. 621.

6. Coltrera (1981, p. 94) contends (controversially) that only the Kleinians, with their elaborate explanations, still hold to the old faith in the efficacy of interpretation.

7. See, for example, Eagle and Wolitzky, 1981; Oremland, 1991, p. 10; Rubovits-Seitz, 1992b; Spence et al., 1994, p. 61.

8. See, for example, Goldberg, 1985, pp. 63–64; Rubovits-Seitz, 1988a, pp. 652–654; Bernardi, 1989; Schlesinger, 1995, p. 686.

9. Newell, Shaw, and Simon, 1962; Wickelgren, 1974, pp. 137–151; Kermode, 1979, p. 89; Gordon, 1982, p. 137; Gabler, 1984, p. 306.

10. Information theory suggests similarly that the amount of uncertainty in interpretive work is a function of the number of possible (alternative) constructions that might account for the clinical material. That is, the number of hypotheses that could have been but were not selected, rather than the one chosen by the interpreter, determines the amount of information and thus uncertainty involved in an interpretive task (Garner, 1962, p. 7). To focus single-mindedly on an initial construction without considering plausible alternative hypotheses may relieve a sense of uncertainty, therefore, but at the cost of information that might contain crucial clues to the most plausible interpretation.

11. See also Gordon's (1982, pp. 13–14) emphasis on the importance of recognizing errors in deciphering ancient scripts. Sellars (1963, p. 170) notes that science is rational not because it has foundations but because it is a self-correcting enterprise. Kumin (1989, p. 150) concludes that since the nature of clinical inference is inexact, and for other reasons, interpretive errors are unavoidable. Weich (1986, p. 694) believes that all interpretations are relatively imprecise, which is consonant with Poland's (1986, p. 692) view that all interpretations are trial interpretations. Arlow (1987, p. 68) notes the everpresent desire of psychoanalysts and dynamic psychotherapists to improve therapeutic results by making interpretations more precise and thus more effective.

12. See also Hirsch, 1967, p. 196; Seitz, 1968; Cheshire, 1975, p. 178; Davidson, 1986, p. 314; Teller and Dahl, 1986; Rubovits-Seitz, 1987.

13. Some cognitive scientists believe that receptive processing employs the same operations as productive processing, though in the opposite direction (Charles Stinson, 1992, personal communication). Compare also Edelson's (1975) language-based theory of clinical interpretive competence, discussed in Chapter 4.

14. See also Eagle, 1984b; Edelson, 1984, p. 139. Gail Reed (1995) argues persuasively that our interpretive work is not based on an assumption of

absolutely relative mental contents, but on a hierarchy of meanings and determinants. We assume, for example, that latent mental contents affect people's experiences and actions much more than they realize. Additional arguments and evidence for a relationship between interpretive accuracy and therapeutic outcome include: Sherwood, 1969, p. 130; Garduk and Haggard, 1972; Malan, 1976; Marziali, 1984; Rubovits-Seitz, 1987, 1991a, 1992a; Thomä and Kächele, 1987, p. 44; Crits-Christoph et al., 1988a/1990, pp. 492–493; 1993; Silberschatz et al., 1988; Hanly, 1990, 1992a,b; Edelson, 1992a,b; Busch, 1993.

References

ABELSON, R., ARONSON, E. & MCGUIRE, W., eds. (1968), *Theories of Cognitive Consistency*. Chicago: Rand McNally.

ABRAHAM, I. (1986), Diagnostic discrepancy and clinical inference. *Genet. Soc. Gen. Psychol. Monogr.*, 112:41–102.

ABRAMS, M. (1989), *Doing Things with Texts*. New York: Norton.

ABRAMS, S. (1995), "Is memory not the trusted archivist?" *Amer. Psychoanal.*, 29:31.

ACHINSTEIN, P. (1969), Approaches to the philosophy of science. In *The Legacy of Logical Positivism*, ed. P. Achinstein & S. Barker. Baltimore, MD: Johns Hopkins University Press, pp. 259–291.

——— & BARKER, S., eds. (1969), *The Legacy of Logical Positivism*. Baltimore, MD: Johns Hopkins University Press.

AGASSI, J. (1981), Psychoanalysis as a human science. *Brit. J. Med. Psychol.*, 54:295–297.

AHUMADA, J. (1994), Interpretation and creationism. *Internat. J. Psycho-Anal.*, 75:695–707.

ALLPORT, F. (1955), *Theories of Perception and the Concept of Structure*. New York: Wiley.

ANDERSON, A. (1984), *Interpreting Pottery*. New York: Pica Press.

ANDERSON, C. (1982), Inoculation and counterexplanation. *Soc. Cogn.*, 1:126–139.

——— (1983), Abstract and concrete data in the perseverence of social theories. *J. Exper. Soc. Psychol.*, 19:93–108.

ANDERSON, J. (1991), Is human cognition adaptive? *Behav. Brain Sci.*, 14:471–517.

ANDERSON, J. R., ed. (1984), *Cognitive Skills and Their Acquisition*. Hillsdale, NJ: Lawrence Erlbaum Associates.

ANDRESEN, J. (1983), Review of *Dire Mastery: Discipleship from Freud to Lacan*, by François Roustang (1982). *Contemp. Psychiat.*, 2:141–142.

ANSCOMBE, R. (1981), Referring to the unconscious: A philosophical critique of Schafer's action language. *Internat. J. Psycho-Anal.*, 62:225–241.

ANZIEU, D. (1970), Eléments d'une théorie de l'interpretation. *Rev. Franc. Psychanal.*, 34:755–820.

APA COMMISSION ON PSYCHOTHERAPIES (1982), *Psychotherapy Research: Methodological and Efficacy Issues*. Washington, DC: American Psychiatric Press.

APEL, K.-O. (1965), Die Entfaltung der sprachanalytischen Philosophie und das Problem der "Geisteswissenschaften." *Philos. Jahrbk.*, 72:239–289. Also in *Analytic Philosophy of Language and the Geisteswissenschaften: Foundations of Language*, Supplement 5. Dordrecht: Reidel, 1967.

APPELBAUM, S. (1977), *Psychotherapy: The Anatomy of Change*. New York: Plenum.

APPLEGARTH, A. (1991), Review of *Psychoanalysis: A Theory in Crisis*, by M. Edelson (1988). *Internat. J. Psycho-Anal.*, 72:742–745.

ARKES, H. (1981), Impediments to accurate clinical judgment and possible ways to minimize their impact. *J. Consult. Clin. Psychol.*, 49:323–330.

ARLOW, J. (1979), The genesis of interpretation. *J. Amer. Psychoanal. Assn.*, 27(Suppl.):193–206.

—— (1987), The dynamics of interpretation. *Psychoanal. Quart.*, 56:68–87.

—— (1991), Methodology and reconstruction. *Psychoanal. Quart.*, 60:539–563.

—— (1992), Forward. In *Psychotherapy: The Analytic Approach*, ed. M. Aronson & M. Scharfman. Northvale, NJ: Aronson, pp. xv–xix.

—— (1995), Stilted listening. *Psychoanal. Quart.*, 64:215–233.

ARNHEIM, R. (1969), *Visual Thinking*. Berkeley: University of California Press.

ARNOFF, F. (1954), Some factors influencing the unreliability of clinical judgments. *J. Clin. Psychol.*, 44:272–277.

ARNOULT, C. & ANDERSON, G. (1988), Identifying and reducing causal reasoning biases in clinical practice. In *Reasoning, Inference, and Judgment in Clinical Psychology*, ed. D. Turk & P. Salovey. New York: Free Press, pp. 209–231.

ASCH, S. (1987), *Social Psychology*. London: Oxford University Press.

ATWOOD, G. & STOLOROW, R. (1984), *Structures of Subjectivity*. Hillsdale, NJ: The Analytic Press.

AUFHAUSER, M. (1979), Review of *A New Language for Psychoanalysis*, by R. Schafer (1976). *J. Amer. Psychoanal. Assn.*, 27:209–215.

AULAGNIER, P. (1979), *Les Destins du Plaisir*. Paris: Presses Universitaires de France.

AUSTIN, J. (1962), *How to Do Things with Words*. London: Oxford University Press.

BACHRACH, H. (1993), The Columbia Records Project and the evolution of psychoanalytic outcome research. In *Research in Psychoanalysis: Process, Development, Outcome*, ed. T. Shapiro & R. Emde. *J. Amer. Psychoanal. Assn.*, 41(Suppl.):279–297.

BAKAN, D. (1967), *On Method*. San Francisco: Jossey-Bass.

BAKHTIN, M. (1986), The problem of speech genres. In *Speech Genres and Other Late Essays*, ed. C. Emerson & M. Holquist (trans. V. McGee). Austin: University of Texas Press, pp. 60–102.

BALES, R. (1950), *Interaction Process Analysis: A Method for the Study of Small Groups*. Cambridge, MA: Addison-Wesley.
BANDURA, A. (1982), The self and mechanisms of agency. In *Psychological Perspectives on the Self, Vol. 1*, ed. J. Suls. Hillsdale, NJ: Lawrence Erlbaum Associates, pp. 3–39.
BANNISTER, D. (1965), The rationale and clinical relevance of repertory grid technique. *Brit. J. Psychiat.*, 111:977–982.
BARANGER, M. (1993), The mind of the analyst: from listening to interpretation. *Internat. J. Psycho-Anal.*, 74:15–24.
BARBER, F. (1974), *Archaeological Decipherment*. Princeton, NJ: Princeton University Press.
BARBER, J. & CRITS-CHRISTOPH, P. (1993), Advances in measures of psychodynamic formulations. *J. Consult. Clin. Psychol.*, 61:574–585.
BARCLAY, F. (1964), Franz Brentano and Sigmund Freud. *J. Existent.*, 5:1–36.
BARGLOW, P., JAFFE, C. & VAUGHN, B. (1989), Psychoanalytic reconstructions and empirical data. *J. Amer. Psychoanal. Assn.*, 37:401–435.
BARLOW, D. & HERSEN, M. (1984), *Single Case Experimental Designs*, 2nd ed. New York: Pergamon.
—— HAYES, S. & NELSON, R. (1984), *The Scientist Practitioner*. New York: Pergamon.
BARNES, A. (1988), *On Interpretation*. Oxford, UK: Basil Blackwell.
BARRATT, B. (1976), Freud's psychology as interpretation. *Psychoanal. Contemp. Sci.*, 5:443–478.
—— (1978), Critical notes on Schafer's "Action Language." *The Annual of Psychoanalysis*, 6:287–303. New York: International Universities Press.
—— (1984), *Psychic Reality and Psychoanalytic Knowing*. Hillsdale, NJ: The Analytic Press.
—— (1990), Reawakening the revolution of psychoanalytic method. *Psychoanal. Contemp. Sci.*, 13:139–163.
—— (1993), *Psychoanalysis and the Postmodern Impulse*. Baltimore, MD: Johns Hopkins University Press.
—— (1994), Critical notes on the psychoanalyst's theorizing. *J. Amer. Psychoanal. Assn.*, 42:697–725.
BARRON, J., EAGLE, M. & WOLITZKY, D. (1992a), Introduction: the treatment process. In *Interface of Psychoanalysis and Psychology*, ed. J. Barron, M. Eagle & D. Wolitsky.. Washington, DC: American Psychological Association, pp. 503–515.
—— —— —— (1992b), Introduction: psychoanalysis and cognitive psychology. In *Interface of Psychoanalysis and Psychology*, ed. J. Barron, M. Eagle & D. Wolitsky. Washington, DC: American Psychological Association, pp. 299–312.
BARTHES, R. (1968), *Elements of Semiology*. New York: Hill & Wang.
—— (1970), *S/Z*. Paris: Editions du Seuil.

—— (1975), Introduction to the structural analysis of narrative. *New Literary Hist.*, 6:237–277.

—— (1977), *Image, Music, Text*. New York: Hill & Wang.

—— (1982), The third meaning: research notes on some Eisenstein stills. In *A Barthes Reader*, ed. S. Sontag. New York: Hill & Wang, pp. 317–333.

BARTLETT, R. (1932), *Remembering*. Cambridge, UK: Cambridge University Press.

BASCH, M. (1976), Psychoanalytic interpretation and cognitive transformation. *Internat. J. Psycho-Anal.*, 62:151–175.

BATES, E. (1976), *Language and Context: The Acquisition of Pragmatics*. New York: Academic Press.

BAUER, H. (1992), *Scientific Literacy and the Myth of the Scientific Method*. Champaign: University of Illinois Press.

BEAHRS, J. (1986), *Limits of Scientific Psychiatry*. New York: Brunner/Mazel.

BECKSON, K. & GANZ, A. (1975), *Literary Terms*. New York: Farrar, Straus & Giroux.

BEITMAN, B. (1987), *The Structure of Individual Psychotherapy*. New York: Guilford.

BELAND, H. (1994), Validation in the clinical process. *Internat. J. Psycho-Anal.*, 75:1141–1158.

BELL, P. & STAINES, P. (1981), *Reasoning and Argument in Psychology*. London: Routledge & Kegan Paul.

BELLACK, A. & HERSEN, M., eds. (1984), *Research Methods in Clinical Psychology*. New York: Pergamon.

BELLAK, L. (1958), Studying the psychoanalytic process by the method of short-range prediction and judgment. *Brit. J. Med. Psychol.*, 31:249–252.

—— (1961), Research in psychoanalysis. *Psychoanal. Quart.*, 30:519–548.

—— (1993), *The Thematic Apperception Test, The Children's Apperception Test, and the Senior Apperception Technique in Clinical Use*. Boston, MA: Allyn & Bacon.

—— & WALKUP, J. (1993), *Psychoanalysis as Science*. Boston, MA: Allyn & Bacon.

BELLIN, E. (1984), The psychoanalytic narrative: on the transformational axis between writing and speech. *Psychoanal. Contemp. Thought*, 49:3–42.

BENEDEK, L. (1989), *Le Travail Mental du Psychanalyste*. Paris: Editions Universitaires de France.

BENENSON, F. (1984), *Probability, Objectivity, and Evidence*. London: Routledge & Kegan Paul.

BENJAMIN, J. (1961), Comment on "When Interpretation Masquerades as Explanation." *J. Amer. Psychoanal. Assn.*, 34:483–487.

BENJAMIN, J.D. (1950), Methodological considerations in the validation and elaboration of psychoanalytical personality theory. *Amer. J. Orthopsychiat.*, 20:139–155.

——— (1961), In Panel, Research in psychoanalysis, rep. A. Pfeffer. *J. Amer. Psychoanal. Assn.*, 9:562–570.

BENJAMIN, L. & FRIEDRICH, F. (1991), Contributions of structural analysis of social behavior (SASB) to the bridge between cognitive science and a science of object relations. In *Person Schemas and Maladaptive Interpersonal Patterns*, ed. M. Horowitz. Chicago: University of Chicago Press, pp. 379–412.

BENVENISTE, E. (1971), Remarks on the function of language in Freudian theory. In *Problems of General Linguistics*, trans. M. Mack. Coral Gables, FL: University of Miami Press, pp. 65–75.

BERES, D. (1980), Certainty: a failed quest? *Psychoanal. Quart.*, 49:1–26.

BERGER, L. (1985), *Psychoanalytic Theory and Clinical Relevance.* Hillsdale, NJ: Lawrence Erlbaum Associates.

——— (1993), Review of *Validation in the Clinical Theory of Psychoanalysis*, by A. Grünbaum (1993). *Psychoanal. Bks.*, 4:462–469.

BERGMANN, M. (1995), Review of *Von Freud in den Freudianern*, by H. Junker (1991). *J. Amer. Psychoanal. Assn.*, 43:586–590.

BERKSON, W. & WETTERSTEN, J. (1984), *Learning from Error.* La Salle, IL: Open Court.

BERNARDI, R. (1989), The role of paradigmatic determinants in psychoanalytic understanding. *Internat. J. Psycho-Anal.*, 70:341–357.

BERNFELD, S. (1932), Der Begriff der "Deutung" in der Psychoanalyse. *Zeitschr. angew. Psychol.*, 42:488–497.

——— (1934), Die Gestalttheorie. *Imago*, 20:32–77.

——— (1941), The facts of observation in psychoanalysis. *J. Psychol.*, 12:289–305. Also in *Internat. Rev. Psycho-Anal.*, 12:341–351, 1985.

BERNSTEIN, R. (1983), *Beyond Objectivism and Relativism.* Philadelphia: University of Pennsylvania Press.

——— (1988a), Interpretation and its discontents. In *Hermeneutics and Psychological Theory*, ed. S. Messer, L. Sass & R. Woolfolk. New Brunswick, NJ: Rutgers University Press, pp. 87–108.

——— (1988b), A plea for differences: commentary on Adolf Grünbaum. In *Hermeneutics and Psychological Theory*, ed. S. Messer, L. Sass & R. Woolfolk. New Brunswick, NJ: Rutgers University Press, pp. 168–174.

BETTI, E. (1980), Hermeneutics as the general methodology of the *Geisteswissenschaften*. In *Contemporary Hermeneutics*, ed. J. Bleicher. London: Routledge & Kegan Paul, pp. 51–94.

BHASKAR, R. (1978), *A Realist Theory of Science*, 2nd ed. Hassocks, UK: Harvester/Humanities Press.

BINDER, A. (1964), Statistical theory. *Ann. Rev. Psychol.*, 15:277–310.

——— (1973), The statistical method. In *Handbook of General Psychology*, ed. B. Wolman. Englewood Cliffs, NJ: Prentice-Hall, pp. 49–66.

BINDER, J., STRUPP, H. & ROCK, D. (1992), A proposal for improving the psychoanalytic theory of technique. In *Interface of Psychoanalysis and*

Psychology, ed. J. Barron, M. Eagle & D. Wolitzky. Washington, DC: American Psychological Association, pp. 605–625.

BION, W. (1962), *Learning from Experience*. London: Heinemann.

—— (1967), *Second Thoughts*. New York: Aronson.

—— (1970), *Attention and Interpretation*. London: Tavistock.

BIRDWHISTELL, R. (1970), *Kinesics and Context*. Philadelphia: University of Pennsylvania Press.

BLANCK, G. & BLANCK, R. (1974), *Ego Psychology*. New York: Columbia University Press.

BLEICHER, J. (1980), *Contemporary Hermeneutics*. London: Routledge & Kegan Paul.

BLIGHT, J. (1981), Must psychoanalysis retreat to hermeneutics? *Psychoanal. Contemp. Thought.*, 4:147–205.

BLOMFIELD, O. (1982), Interpretation—some general aspects. *Internat. Rev. Psycho-Anal.*, 9:287–301.

BOESKY, D. (1988), Criteria of evidence for an unconscious fantasy. In *Fantasy, Myth, and Reality*, ed. H. Blum, Y. Kramer & D. Richards. Madison, CT: International Universities Press, pp. 111–131.

—— (1990), The psychoanalytic process and its components. *Psychoanal. Quart.*, 59:550–584.

BOGDAN, R., ed. (1991), *Mind and Common Sense*. Cambridge, UK: Cambridge University Press.

BOHMAN, J. (1991), *New Philosophy of Social Science*. Cambridge, MA: MIT Press.

—— HILEY, D. & SHUSTERMAN, R. (1991), Introduction: the interpretive turn. In *The Interpretive Turn*, ed. D. Hiley, J. Bohman & R. Shusterman. Ithaca, NY: Cornell University Press, pp. 1–14.

BOLLAND, J. & SANDLER, J. (1965), *The Hampstead Psychoanalytic Index*. New York: International Universities Press.

BOLLES, R. (1962), The difference between statistical and scientific hypotheses. *Psychol. Reports*, 11:639–645.

BONAPARTE, M. (1945), Notes on the analytic discovery of a primal scene. *The Psychoanalytic Study of the Child*, 1:119–125. New York: International Universities Press.

BOND, J., HANSELL, J. & SHEVRIN, H. (1987), Locating transference paradigms in psychotherapy transcripts. *Psychotherapy.*, 24:736–749.

BONJOUR, L. (1978), Can empirical knowledge have a foundation? *Amer. Philos. Quart.*, 15:1–13.

BOOTH, S. (1969), *An Essay on Shakespeare's Sonnets*. New Haven, CT: Yale University Press.

BOS, J. & MAIER, R. (1992), The name of the game: an analysis of the Grünbaum debate. *Communic. & Cogn.*, 25:295–324.

BOUCHARD, M. (1995), The specificity of hermeneutics in psychoanalysis. *Internat. J. Psycho-Anal.*, 76:533–546.

BOWERS, K. (1984), On being unconsciously influenced and informed. In *The Unconscious Reconsidered*, ed. K. Bowers & D. Meichenbaum. New York: Wiley, pp. 227–272.

—— & MEICHENBAUM, D., eds. (1984), *The Unconscious Reconsidered*. New York: Wiley.

BOWIE, M. (1979), Jacques Lacan. In *Structuralism and Since*, ed. J. Sturrock. Oxford, UK: Oxford University Press, pp. 116–153.

—— (1991), *Lacan*. Cambridge, MA: Harvard University Press.

BOWLBY, J. (1969), *Attachment and Loss, Vol. 1: Attachment*. New York: Basic Books.

—— (1973), *Attachment and Loss, Vol. 2: Separation—Anxiety and Anger*. New York: Basic Books.

—— (1980), *Attachment and Loss, Vol. 3: Loss—Sadness and Depression*. New York: Basic Books.

BOWMAN, M. (1996), On the idea of natural science as a resistance to psychoanalysis. *Psychoanal. Contemp. Thought*, 19:371–402.

BOYD, R. (1981), Scientific realism and naturalistic epistemology. *PSA 1980, Vol. 2*, ed. P. Asquith & R. Giere. East Lansing, MI: Philosophy of Science Association, pp. 613–662.

BOYD, Z. (1985), The grammar of representation in psychoanalysis and literature. In *The Psychoanalytic Study of Literature*, ed. J. Reppen & M. Charney. Hillsdale, NJ: The Analytic Press, pp. 107–124.

BOYER, L. (1978), On aspects of the mutual influences of anthropology and psychoanalysis. *J. Psychol. Anthropol.*, 1:265–296.

BRANSFORD, J. & FRANKS, J. (1971), The abstraction of linguistic ideas. *Cogn. Psychol.*, 2:331–350.

BRENNEIS, C. (1994), Observations on psychoanalytic listening. *Psychoanal. Quart.*, 63:29–53.

BRENNER, C. (1968), Psychoanalysis and science. *J. Amer. Psychoanal. Assn.*, 16:675–696.

—— (1976), *Psychoanalytic Technique and Psychic Conflict*. New York: International Universities Press.

BRENTANO, F. (1874), *Psychology from an Empirical Point of View*, trans. D. Terrell. London: Routledge & Kegan Paul, 1971.

BREUER, J. & FREUD, S. (1893–1895), Studies on hysteria. *Standard Edition*, 2:1–335. London: Hogarth Press, 1955.

BRITTON, R. & STEINER, J. (1994), Interpretation: selected fact or overvalued idea? *Internat. J. Psycho-Anal.*, 75:1069–1078.

BRODY, B. (1970), Confirmation and explanation. In *Readings in the Philosophy of Science*, ed. B. Brody. Englewood Cliffs, NJ: Prentice-Hall, pp. 410–426.

BRODY, E. (1990), *Psychoanalytic Knowledge*. Madison, CT: International Universities Press.

—— & TORMEY, J. (1980), Clinical psychoanalytic knowledge. *Pers. Biol. Med.*, Autumn:143–159.

BROOK, A. (1992), Psychoanalysis and common sense psychology. *The Annual of Psychoanalysis*, 20:273–303. Hillsdale, NJ: The Analytic Press.

—— (1995a), Review of *Psychoanalysis, Mind, and Art: Perspectives on Richard Wollheim*, ed. J. Hopkins & A. Savile (1992). *Internat. J. Psycho-Anal.*, 76:415–416.

—— (1995b), Explanation in the hermeneutic science. *Internat. J. Psycho-Anal.*, 76:519–532.

BROOKS, P. (1994), *Psychoanalysis and Storytelling*. Oxford, UK: Basil Blackwell.

BRUNER, J. (1986), *Actual Minds, Possible Worlds*. Cambridge, MA: Harvard University Press.

—— (1987), Foreword. In *The Freudian Metaphor*, by D. Spence. New York: Norton, pp. ix–xvi.

—— (1990), *Acts of Meaning*. Cambridge, MA: Harvard University Press.

BRUSS, N. (1976), The transformation in Freud. *Semiotica*, 17:69–94.

—— (1986), Validation in psychoanalysis, and "projective identification." *Semiotica*, 60:129–192.

BRYMAN, A. & BURGESS, B., eds. (1994), *Analyzing Qualitative Data*. New York: Routledge.

BUCCI, W. (1985), Dual coding: a cognitive model for psychoanalytic research. *J. Amer. Psychoanal. Assn.*, 33:571–607.

—— (1988), Converging evidence for emotional structures. In *Psychoanalytic Process Research Strategies*, ed. H. Dahl, H. Kächele & H. Thomä. Berlin: Springer, pp. 29–49.

—— (1989), A reconstruction of Freud's tally argument. *Psychoanal. Inq.*, 9:249–281.

BUCKLEY, P., CONTE, H., PLUTCHICK, R., WILD, K. & KARASU, T. (1984), Psychodynamic variables as predictors of psychotherapy outcome. *Amer. J. Psychiat.*, 141:742–748.

BUIE, D. (1981), Empathy: its nature and limitations. *J. Amer. Psychoanal. Assn.*, 29:281–308.

BURKHARDT, J. (1898–1902), *Griechische Kulturgeschichte, Vols. 1–4*, ed. J. Oeri. Berlin: W. Spemann.

BURMAN, E. & PARKER, I., eds. (1993), *Discourse Analytic Research*. New York: Routledge.

BUSCH, F. (1993), "In the neighborhood": aspects of a good interpretation and a "developmental lag" in ego psychology. *J. Amer. Psychoanal. Assn.*, 41:151–177.

CALEF, V. & WEINSHEL, E. (1975), A neglected classic: Siegfried Bernfeld's "The facts of observation in psychoanalysis." *J. Phila. Assn. Psychoanal.*, 2:38–40. Also in *Internat. Rev. Psycho-Anal.*, 12:341–351, 1985.

CALLEBAUT, W., ed. (1993), *Taking the Naturalistic Turn or How Real Philosophy of Science Is Done*. Chicago: University of Chicago Press.

CALOGERAS, R. (1973), Lévi-Strauss and Freud: their structural approaches to myths. *Amer. Imago*, 30:57–79.

——— & ALSTON, T. (1980), On "action language" in psychoanalysis. *Psychoanal. Quart.*, 49:663–696.

CAMPBELL, D. (1966), Pattern matching as an essential in distal knowing. In *The Psychology of Egon Brunswik*, ed. K. Hammond. New York: Holt, Rinehart & Winston, pp. 81–166.

——— (1975), Degrees of freedom and the case study. *Compar. Polit. Studies*, 8:178–193.

——— (1984), Can we be scientific in applied social science? In *Evaluation Studies, Vol. 9*, ed. R. Connor, D. Altman & C. Jackson. Beverly Hills, CA: Sage, pp. 26–49.

——— (1988), *Methodology and Epistemology for Social Science: Selected Papers*, ed. E. Overman. Chicago: University of Chicago Press.

CAPLAN, A. (1986), With a friend like Professor Grünbaum does psychoanalysis need any enemies? *Behav. Brain Sci.*, 9:228–229.

CARDINAL, M. (1983), *The Words to Say It*, trans. P. Goodheart. Cambridge, MA: Van Vactor & Goodheart.

CARLSON, L. & CARLSON, R. (1984), Affect and psychological magnification: derivations from Tompkins's script theory. *J. Personality*, 52:36–45.

CARLSON, R. (1981), Studies in script theory, I: adult analogs of a childhood nuclear scene. *J. Personality Soc. Psychol.*, 4:533–561.

CASEMENT, P. (1985), Theory re-discovered. In *On Learning from the Patient*. London: Tavistock, pp. 216–220.

CASTON, J. (1986), The reliability of the diagnosis of the patient's unconscious plan. In *The Psychoanalytic Process: Theory, Clinical Observations, and Empirical Research*, ed. J. Weiss & H. Sampson. New York: Guilford, pp. 241–255.

——— (1993a), Can analysts agree? The problems of consensus and the psychoanalytic mannequin: I. A proposed solution. *J. Amer. Psychoanal. Assn.*, 41:493–512.

——— (1993b), Mannequins in the labyrinth and the couch-lab intersect. *J. Amer. Psychoanal. Assn.*, 41(Suppl.):51–65.

——— & MARTIN, E. (1993), Can analysts agree? The problems of consensus and the psychoanalytic mannequin: II. Empirical tests. *J. Amer. Psychoanal. Assn.*, 41:513–548.

CAVELL, M. (1988), Interpretation, psychoanalysis, and the philosophy of mind. *J. Amer. Psychoanal. Assn.*, 36:859–879.

——— (1993), *The Psychoanalytic Mind*. Cambridge, MA: Harvard University Press.

CAWS, P. (1986), The scaffolding of psychoanalysis. *Behav. Brain Sci.*, 9:229–230.

——— (1988), *Structuralism: The Art of the Intelligible*. Atlantic Highlands, NJ: Humanities Press International.

—— (1993), Rethinking intentionality. In *Yorick's World: Science and the Knowing Subject*, by P. Caws. Berkeley: University of California Press, pp. 318–331.

—— (1994), Review of *Selected Philosophical and Methodological Papers*, by Paul E. Meehl (1991). *Psychoanal. Bks.*, 5:30–34.

CHABOT, B. (1982), *Freud and Schreber*. Amherst: University of Massachusetts Press.

CHANDLER, J., DAVIDSON, A. & NAROOTUNIAN, H., eds. (1994), Editors' introduction. In *Questions of Evidence*. Chicago: University of Chicago Press, pp. 1–8.

CHAPMAN, L. & CHAPMAN, J. (1967), Genesis of popular but erroneous psychodiagnostic observations. *J. Abnorm. Psychol.*, 72:193–204.

—— & —— (1969), Illusory correlation as an obstacle to the use of valid psychodiagnostic signs. *J. Abnorm. Psychol.*, 74:271–280.

CHARNY, E. & CARROLL, E. (1966), General systems theory and psychoanalysis. *Psychoanal. Quart.*, 35:377–387.

CHASE, W. & SIMON, H. (1973), The mind's eye in chess. In *Visual Information Processing*, ed. W. Chase. New York: Academic Press, pp. 215–281.

CHASSAN, J. (1956), On probability theory and psychoanalytic research. *Psychiatry*, 19:55–61.

—— (1957), On the unreliability of reliability and some other consequences of the assumption of probabilistic patient-states. *Psychiatry*, 20:163–171.

—— (1970), On psychodynamics and clinical research methodology. *Psychiatry*, 33:94–101.

—— (1979), *Research Design in Clinical Psychology and Psychiatry*, 2nd ed. New York: Irvington.

CHERRY, C. (1957), *On Human Communication*. New York: Science Editions, 1961.

CHERTOK, L. (1968), The discovery of the transference: toward an epistemological interpretation. *Internat. J. Psycho-Anal.*, 49:560–576.

CHESHIRE, N. (1964), On the rationale of psychodynamic argumentation. *Brit. J. Med. Psychol.*, 37:217–230.

—— (1975), *The Nature of Psychodynamic Interpretation*. London: Wiley.

—— & THOMÄ, H. (1991), Metaphor, neologism and "open texture": implications for translating Freud's scientific thought. *Internat. Rev. Psycho-Anal.*, 18:429–455.

CHESSICK, R. (1989), *The Technique and Practice of Listening in Intensive Psychotherapy*. Northvale, NJ: Aronson.

—— (1990), Hermeneutics for psychotherapists. *Amer. J. Psychother.*, 44:256–273.

—— (1992), *What Constitutes the Patient in Psychotherapy: Alternative Approaches to Understanding Humans*. Northvale, NJ: Aronson.

CHEVRON, E., ROUNSAVILLE, B. & ROSENBLUM, E. (1983), Selecting psychotherapists to participate in psychotherapy outcome studies. *J. Nerv. Ment. Dis.*, 171:348–353.

CHILD, W. (1994), *Causality, Interpretation, and the Mind.* New York: Oxford University Press.

CHINEN, A. (1987), Symbolic modes in object relations: a semiotic perspective. *Psychoanal. Contemp. Thought*, 10:373–406.

CHOMSKY, N. (1957), *Syntactic Structures.* The Hague: Mouton.

——— (1965), *Aspects of the Theory of Syntax.* Cambridge, MA: MIT Press.

——— (1968), *Language and Mind.* New York: Harcourt, Brace, 1972.

——— (1979), Language and unconscious knowledge. In *Psychoanalysis and Language*, ed. J. Smith. *Psychiatry and the Humanities, Vol. 3.* New Haven, CT: Yale University. Press, pp. 3–44.

CHRISTENSEN, S. & TURNER, D., eds. (1993), *Folk Psychology and the Philosophy of Mind.* Hillsdale, NJ: Lawrence Erlbaum Associates.

CHRISTIANSEN, B. (1964), The scientific status of psychoanalytic clinical evidence. *Inquiry*, 7:47–49.

CIARDI, J. & WILLIAMS, M. (1975), *How Does a Poem Mean?* Boston, MA: Houghton Mifflin.

CIOFFI, F. (1986), Did Freud rely on the tally argument to meet the argument from suggestibility? *Behav. Brain Sci.*, 9:230–231.

——— (1988), "Exegetical myth-making" in Grünbaum's indictment of Popper and exoneration of Freud. In *Mind, Psychoanalysis and Science*, ed. P. Clark & C. Wright. Oxford, UK: Basil Blackwell, pp. 61–87.

CLARK, H. & CLARK, E. (1977), *Psychology and Language: An Introduction to Psycholinguistics.* New York: Harcourt Brace Jovanovich.

CLARKE, D. (1978), *Analytical Archaeology*, 2nd ed. New York: Columbia University Press.

CLIPPINGER, J. (1977), *Meaning and Discourse: A Computer Model of Psychoanalytic Speech and Cognition.* Baltimore, MD: Johns Hopkins University Press.

CLYMAN, R. (1991), The procedural organization of emotions: a contribution from cognitive science to the psychoanalytic theory of therapeutic action. *J. Amer. Psychoanal. Assn.*, 39(Suppl.):349–382.

COEN, S. (1983), Review of *The Literary Use of the Psychoanalytic Process*, by M. Skura (1981). *Rev. Psycho-Anal. Bks.*, 2:169–172.

——— (1996), The passions and perils of interpretation (of dreams and texts): an appreciation of Erik Erikson's dream specimen paper. *Internat. J. Psycho-Anal.*, 77:537–548.

COHEN, N., EICHENBAUM, H. & DEACEDO, B. (1985), Different memory systems underlying acquisition of procedural and declarative knowledge. *Ann. NY Acad. Sci.*, 444:54–71.

COLBY, K. (1958), Causal correlations in clinical interpretation. In *A Skeptical Psychoanalyst.* New York: Ronald Press, pp. 47–59. Also in

Psychoanalytic Clinical Interpretation, ed. L. Paul. New York: Free Press of Glencoe (Macmillan), 1963, pp. 189–199.

——— (1981), Modeling a paranoid brain. *Brain Behav. Sci.*, 4:515–534.

——— & SPAR, J. (1983), *The Fundamental Crisis in Psychiatry: Unreliability of Diagnosis*. Springfield, IL: Thomas.

——— & STOLLER, R. (1988), *Cognitive Science and Psychoanalysis*. Hillsdale, NJ: The Analytic Press.

COLLINGWOOD, R. (1946), *The Idea of History*. London: Oxford University Press.

COLLINS, S. (1980), Freud and the "riddle of suggestion." *Internat. Rev. Psycho-Anal.*, 7:429–437.

COLTART, N. (1992), *Slouching towards Bethlehem. . . .* New York: Guilford.

COLTRERA, J. (1981), On the nature of interpretation: epistemology as practice. In *Clinical Psychoanalysis, Vol. 3*. New York: Aronson, pp. 83–127.

——— & ROSS, N. (1967), Freud's psychoanalytic technique—from the beginnings to 1923. In *Psychoanalytic Techniques: A Handbook for the Practicing Psychoanalyst*, ed. B. Wolman. New York: Basic Books, pp. 13–50.

CONANT, J. (1951). *On Understanding Science—An Historical Approach*. New York: New American Library.

CONNOLLY, J. & KEUTNER, T., eds. (1988), *Hermeneutics versus Science?* Notre Dame, IN: University of Notre Dame Press.

COOK, T. & CAMPBELL, D. (1979), *Quasiexperimentation*. Chicago: Rand McNally.

COOPER, A. (1985), Will neurobiology influence psychoanalysis? *Amer. J. Psychiat.*, 142:1395–1402.

——— (1987), Changes in psychoanalytic ideas: transference interpretation. *J. Amer. Psychoanal. Assn.*, 35:77–98.

——— (1988), Infant research in adult psychoanalysis. Unpublished manuscript. Presented at Workshop for Mental Health Professionals, "On the Significance of the Data of Infant Observational Research for Clinical Work with Children, Adolescents and Adults," Seattle, March 12–13.

——— (1989), Concepts of therapeutic effectiveness in psychoanalysis: a historical review. *Psychoanal. Inq.*, 9:4–25.

——— (1994), The quiet revolution in psychoanalytic theory over the past twenty years. Presented to Chicago Psychoanalytic Society, Oct. 25, 1993. Abstr.: *Bull. Inst. Psychoanal.*, 4:13.

COOPER, S. (1993), Interpretive fallibility and the psychoanalytic dialogue. *J. Amer. Psychoanal. Assn.*, 41:95–126.

CRAIK, K. (1943), *The Nature of Explanation*. Cambridge, UK: Cambridge University Press.

CRITS-CHRISTOPH, P., COOPER, A. & LUBORSKY, L. (1988a), The accuracy of therapists' interpretations and the outcome of dynamic psychotherapy. *J. Consult. Clin. Psychol.*, 56:490–495. Also in *Understanding*

Transference, ed. L. Luborsky & P. Crits-Christoph. New York: Basic Books, 1990, pp. 173–188.

——— LUBORSKY, L., DAHL, L., POPP, C., MELLON, J. & MARK, D. (1988b), Clinicians can agree in assessing relationship patterns in psychotherapy: the core conflictual relationship theme method. *Arch. Gen. Psychiat.*, 45:1001–1004.

——— BARBER, J., BARNACKIE, K. & COOPER, A. (1993), Assessing the therapist's interpretations. In *Psychodynamic Treatment Research*, ed. N. Miller, L. Luborsky, J. Barber & J. Docherty. New York: Basic Books, pp. 361–386.

CULLER, J. (1981), *The Pursuit of Signs*. Ithaca, NY: Cornell University Press.

——— (1982), *On Deconstruction*. Ithaca, NY: Cornell University Press.

CUMMINS, R. (1989), *Meaning and Mental Representation*. Cambridge, MA: MIT/Bradford.

CURTIS, H. (1992), Psychoanalytic ecumenism and varieties of psychoanalytic experience. *J. Amer. Psychoanal. Assn.*, 40:643–663.

DAHL, H. (1972), A quantitative study of a psychoanalysis. *Psychoanal. Contemp. Sci.*, 1:237–257.

——— (1974), The measurement of meaning in psychoanalysis by computer analysis of verbal context. *J. Amer. Psychoanal. Assn.*, 22:37–57.

——— (1988), Frames of mind. In *Psychoanalytic Research Strategies*, ed. H. Dahl, H. Kächele & H. Thomä. Berlin: Springer, pp. 51–66.

——— & STENGEL, B. (1978a), A classification of emotion words: a modification and partial test of de Rivera's decision theory of emotions. *Psychoanal. Contemp. Thought*, 1:269–312.

——— TELLER, V., MOSS, D. & TRUJILLO, M., (1978b), Countertransference examples of the syntactic expression of warded off contents. *Psychoanal. Quart.*, 47:339–363.

——— KÄCHELE, H. & THOMÄ, H., eds. (1988), *Psychoanalytic Process Research Strategies*. Berlin: Springer.

DALBIEZ, R. (1941), *Psychoanalytical Method and the Doctrine of Freud, Vols. 1 & 2*, trans. T. Lindsay. New York: Longmans, Green.

DALLAS, M. & BARON, R. (1985), Do psychotherapists use a confirmation strategy during interviewing? *J. Soc. Clin. Psychol.*, 3:106–122.

D'ANDRADE, R. (1991), The identification of schemas in naturalistic data. In *Person Schemas and Maladaptive Interpersonal Patterns*, ed. M. Horowitz. Chicago: University of Chicago Press, pp. 279–301.

DANTO, A. (1965), *Analytic Philosophy of History*. Cambridge, UK: Cambridge University Press.

——— (1985), *Narration and Knowledge*. New York: Columbia University Press.

DANZIGER, K. (1985), The methodological imperative in psychology. *Philos. Soc. Sci.*, 15:1–13.

DARWIN, C. (1888), *The Life and Letters of Charles Darwin*. New York: Basic Books.

DAVIDSON, A. (1994), Carlo Ginzburg and the renewal of historiography. In *Questions of Evidence*, ed. J. Chandler, A. Davidson & H. Harootunian. Chicago: University of Chicago Press, pp. 304–320.

DAVIDSON, D. (1982), Paradoxes of irrationality. In *Philosophical Essays on Freud*, ed. R. Wollheim & J. Hopkins. Cambridge, UK: Cambridge University Press, pp. 289–305.

—— (1986), A coherence theory of truth and knowledge. In *Truth and Interpretation*, ed. E. LePore. Oxford, UK: Basil Blackwell, pp. 307–319.

DAVIDSON, P. & COSTELLO, C. (1969), *N = 1: Experimental Studies of Single Cases*. New York: Van Nostrand-Reinhold.

DAVIS, W. (1978), *The Act of Interpretation: A Critique of Literary Reason*. Chicago: University of Chicago Press.

DE AZEVEDO, A. (1994), Validation of the psychoanalytic clinical process: the role of dreams. *Internat. J. Psycho-Anal.*, 75:1181–1192.

DE BEAUGRANDE, R. (1980), *Text, Discourse, and Process*. Norwood, NJ: Ablex.

—— (1983), Surprised by syncretism: cognition and literary criticism exemplified by E. D. Hirsch, Stanley Fish, and J. Hillis Miller. *Poetics*, 12:83–137.

DEELY, J. (1990), *Basics of Semiotics*. Bloomington: Indiana University Press.

DEESE, J. (1962), On the structure of associative meaning. *Psychol. Rev.*, 69:161–175.

—— (1965), *The Structure of Associations in Language and Thought*. Baltimore, MD: Johns Hopkins University Press.

DE GROOT, A. (1965), *Thought and Choice in Chess*. The Hague: Mouton.

—— (1969), *Methodology: Foundations of Inference and Research in the Behavioral Sciences*. The Hague: Mouton.

DE MAN, P. (1979), *Allegories of Reading*. New Haven, CT: Yale University Press.

DEMOS, R. (1959), Psychoanalysis: science and philosophy. In *Psychoanalysis, Scientific Method, and Philosophy*, ed. S. Hook. New York: New York University Press, pp. 329–335.

DENNETT, D. (1978), Current issues in the philosophy of mind. *Amer. Philos. Quart.*, 15:244–261.

—— (1984), Foreword. In *Language, Thought, and Other Biological Categories*, by Ruth Millikan. Cambridge, MA: MIT/Bradford, pp. ix–x.

—— (1987), *The Intentional Stance*. Cambridge, MA: MIT/Bradford.

—— (1991), *Consciousness Explained*. Boston, MA: Little Brown.

—— (1993), Three kinds of intentional psychology. In *Folk Psychology and the Philosophy of Mind*, ed. S. Christensen & D. Turner. Hillsdale, NJ: Lawrence Erlbaum Associates, pp. 121–143.

—— & HAUGLELAND, J. (1987), Intentionality. In *The Oxford Companion to the Mind*, ed. R. Gregory. Oxford, UK: Oxford University Press, pp. 383–386.

DE RACKER, G. (1961), On the formulation of the interpretation. *Internat. J. Psycho-Anal.*, 42:49–54.

DERRIDA, J. (1972), Freud and the scene of writing. *Yale French Studies*, 48:73–117.

DEVEREAUX, G. (1951), Logical status and methodological problems of research in clinical psychiatry. *Psychiatry*, 14:327–352.

DEVLIN, K. (1997), *Goodbye Descartes: The End of Logic and the Search for a New Cosmology of the Mind.* New York: Wiley.

DEWITT, K., KALTREIDER, N., WEISS, D. & HOROWITZ, M. (1983), Judging change in psychotherapy: reliability of clinical formulations. *Arch. Gen. Psychiat.*, 40:1121–1128.

DEY, I. (1993), *Qualitative Data Analysis.* New York: Routledge.

DIAMOND, D. (1983), The anatomy of the third ear: clinical experience and the inference process in psychotherapy. Unpublished doctoral dissertation, Department of Psychology, University of Michigan, Ann Arbor.

DIESING, P. (1971), *Patterns of Discovery in the Social Sciences.* Chicago: Aldine.

——— (1985a), Hypothesis testing and data interpretation: the case of Milton Friedman. *Res. Hist. Econ. Thought Methodol.*, 3:61–89.

——— (1985b), Comments on "Why Freud's research methodology was unscientific" by von Eckhardt. *Psychoanal. Contemp. Thought*, 8:551–566.

DILMAN, I. (1988), Intentions and the unconscious. In *Mind, Psychoanalysis, and Science*, ed. P. Clark & C. Wright. Oxford, UK: Basil Blackwell, pp. 169–186.

DILTHEY, W. ([1913–1967] 1958), *Gesammelten Schriften.* Stuttgart: Teubner, 1958.

——— (1961), *Pattern and Meaning in History*, ed. H. Rickman. New York: Harper.

——— (1976), *Dilthey: Selected Writings*, ed. H. Rickman. Cambridge, UK: Cambridge University Press.

DIMBERG, U. (1982), Facial reactions to facial expressions. *Psychophysiology*, 19:643–647.

DITTMAN, A. (1962), The relationship between body movements and moods in interviews. *J. Consult. Psychol.*, 26:480–495.

——— (1963), Kinesic research and therapeutic processes: further discussion. In *Expression of Emotions in Man*, ed. P. Knapp. New York: International Universities Press, pp. 140–147.

——— & WYNNE, L. (1961), Linguistic techniques and the analysis of emotionality in interviews. *J. Abnorm. Soc. Psychol.*, 63: 201–204.

DIXON, N. (1971), *Subliminal Perception.* London: McGraw-Hill.

——— (1981), *Preconscious Processing.* New York: Wiley.

DORPAT, T. (1995), Review of *Doing Supervision and Being Supervised*, by R. Langs (1994). *Psychoanal. Books*, 6:467–471.

DREYFUS, H. (1991), Heidegger's hermeneutic realism. In *The Interpretive*

Turn, ed. D. Hiley, J. Bohman & R. Shusterman. Ithaca, NY: Cornell University Press, pp. 25–41.

——— & RABINOW, P. (1983), *Michel Foucault: Beyond Structuralism and Hermeneutics*, 2nd ed. Chicago: University of Chicago Press.

DUDA, R. & SHORTLIFFE, E. (1983), Expert systems research. *Science*, 220:261–268.

DUNCAN, D. (1981), A thought on the nature of psychoanalytic theory. *Internat. J. Psycho-Anal.*, 62:339–349.

——— (1989), The flow of interpretation: the collateral interpretation force and flow. *Internat. J. Psycho-Anal.*, 70:693–700.

EAGLE, M. (1973a), Sherwood and the logic of explanation in psychoanalysis. *Psychoanal. Contemp. Thought*, 2:331–337.

——— (1973b), Validation of motivational formulations: acknowledgment as a criterion. *Psychoanal. Contemp. Sci.*, 2:265–275.

——— (1980a), Psychoanalytic interpretations: veridicality and therapeutic effectiveness. *Noûs*, 4:405–425.

——— (1980b), A critical examination of motivational explanation in psychoanalysis. *Psychoanal. Contemp. Thought*, 3:329–380.

——— (1982), Privileged access and the status of self-knowledge in Cartesian and Freudian conceptions of the mental. *Philos. Soc. Sci.*, 12:349–373.

——— (1984a), *Recent Developments in Psychoanalysis*. New York: McGraw-Hill.

——— (1984b), Psychoanalysis and "narrative truth": a reply to Spence. *Psychoanal. Contemp. Thought*, 7:629–640.

——— (1986a), Critical notice: A. Grünbaum's *The Foundations of Psychoanalysis: A Philosophical Critique (1984). Philos. Sci.*, 53:65–88.

——— (1986b), Pychoanalysis as hermeneutics. *Behav. Brain Sci.*, 9:231–232.

——— (1989), The epistemological status of psychoanalysis. *Soc. Research*, 56:383–419.

——— (1993), The dynamics of theory change in psychoanalysis. In *Philosophical Problems of the Internal and External Worlds*, ed. J. Earman, A. Janis, G. Massey & N. Rescher. Pittsburgh, PA: University of Pittsburgh Press/Universitatsverlag Konstanz, pp. 373–408.

——— (1994), To the editors. *The New York Review of Books*, April 21, p. 66.

——— & WOLITZKY, D. (1981), Therapeutic influences in psychoanalytic treatment. In *Curative Factors in Psychodynamic Therapy*, ed. S. Slipp. New York: McGraw-Hill, pp. 349–378.

EARMAN, J. (1992), *Bayes or Bust?* Cambridge, MA: MIT/Bradford.

ECCLES, J. (1774), The world of objective knowledge. In *The Philosophy of Karl Popper*, ed. P. Schilpp. LaSalle, IL: Open Court, pp. 349–350.

ECO, U. (1985), Producing signs. In *On Signs*, ed. M. Blonsky. Baltimore, MD: Johns Hopkins University Press, pp. 176–183.

EDEL, L. (1966), Hawthorne's symbolism and psychoanalysis. In *Hidden Patterns*, ed. L. & E. Manheim. New York: Macmillan, pp. 93–112.

EDELSON, M. (1970), Toward a study of interpretation in psychoanalysis. In *Explorations in General Theory in Social Science*, ed. J. Loubser, R. Baum, E. Effrat & V. Lidz. New York: Free Press, 1976, pp. 151–181.

——— (1972), Language and dreams: *The Interpretation of Dreams* revisited. *The Psychoanalytic Study of the Child*, 27:203–282. New Haven, CT: Yale University Press.

——— (1975), *Language and Interpretation in Psychoanalysis*. Chicago: University of Chicago Press (pbk, 1984).

——— (1977), Psychoanalysis as science. *J. Nerv. Ment. Dis.*, 165:1–28.

——— (1978), What is the psychoanalyst talking about? In *Psychoanalysis and Language*, ed. J. Smith. *Psychiatry and the Humanities, Vol. 3*. New Haven, CT: Yale University Press, pp. 99–170.

——— (1980), Language and medicine. In *Applied Psycholinguistics and Mental Health*, ed. R. Rieber. New York: Plenum, pp. 177–204.

——— (1983), Is testing psychoanalytic hypotheses in the psychoanalytic situation really impossible? *The Psychoanalytic Study of the Child*, 38:61–109. New Haven, CT: Yale University Press.

——— (1984), *Hypothesis and Evidence in Psychoanalysis*. Chicago: University of Chicago Press.

——— (1985), The hermeneutic turn and the single case study in psychoanalysis. In *Exploring Clinical Methods for Social Research*, ed. D. Berg & K. Smith. Beverly Hills, CA: Sage, pp. 71–104.

——— (1986a), The evidential value of the psychoanalyst's clinical data. *Behav. Brain Sci.*, 9:232–234.

——— (1986b), Causal explanation in science and in psychoanalysis: implications for writing a case study. *The Psychoanalytic Study of the Child*, 41:89–127. New Haven, CT: Yale University Press.

——— (1988), *Psychoanalysis: A Theory in Crisis*. Chicago: University of Chicago Press.

——— (1991), Review of *Mind, Psychoanalysis and Science*, ed. P. Clark & C. Wright (1988). *Psychoanal. Quart.*, 60:101–108.

——— (1992a), Can psychotherapy research answer the psychotherapist's questions? *Contemp. Psychoanal.*, 28:118–151. Also in *Psychotherapy Research and Practice: Bridging the Gap*, ed. P. Talley, H. Strupp & S. Butler. New York: Basic Books, 1994, pp. 60–87.

——— (1992b), Telling and enacting stories in psychoanalysis. In *Interface of Psychoanalysis and Psychology*, ed. J. Barron, M. Eagle & D. Wolitzky. Washington, DC: American Psychological Association, pp. 99–123.

EDITOR (1986), Editorial commentary. *Behav. Brain Sci.*, 9:266.

EDWARDS, W., LINDMAN, H. & SAVAGE, L. (1963), Bayesian statistical inference for psychological research. *Psychol. Rev.*, 70:193–242.

EINHORN, H. (1988), Diagnosis and causality in clinical and statistical prediction. In *Reasoning, Inference, and Judgment in Clinical Psychology*, ed. E. Turk & P. Salovey. New York: Free Press, pp. 51–69.

—— & HOGARTH, R. (1978), Confidence in judgment: persistence of the illusion of validity. *Psychol. Rev.*, 85:395–416.

EINSTEIN, A. (1934), *Essays in Science*. New York: Philosophical Library.

EISOLD, K. (1994), The intolerance of diversity in psychoanalytic institutes. *Internat. J. Psycho-Anal.*, 75:785–800.

EISSLER, K. (1959), The function of details in the interpretation of works of literature. *Psychoanal. Quart.*, 28:1–20.

—— (1963), Freud and the psychoanalysis of history. *J. Amer. Psychoanal. Assn.*, 11:675–703.

—— (1985), A farewell to Freud's *Interpretation of Dreams*. *Amer. Imago*, 42:111–129.

EKMAN, P. (1957), A methodological discussion of nonverbal behavior. *J. Psychol.*, 43:141–149.

—— (1964), Body position, facial expression, and verbal behavior during interview. *J. Abn. Soc. Psychol.*, 68:295–301.

—— (1965), Communication through nonverbal behavior: a source of information about an interpersonal relationship. In *Affect, Cognition and Personality*, ed. S. Tomkins & C. Izard. New York: Springer, pp. 390–442.

EKSTEIN, R. (1959), Thoughts concerning the nature of the interpretive process. In *Readings in Psychoanalytic Psychology*, ed. M. Levitt. New York: Appleton-Century-Crofts, pp. 221–247.

—— (1966), *Children of Time and Space, of Action and Impulse*. New York: Appleton-Century-Crofts.

—— (1978), Further thoughts concerning the nature of the interpretive process. In *The Human Mind Revisited*. New York: International Universities Press, pp. 329–348.

ELEVITCH, B. (1978), Explanation in psychoanalysis. *Psychoanal. Rev.*, 65:313–325.

ELLIOTT, R. (1984), A discovery-oriented approach to significant change events: interpersonal process recall and comprehensive process analysis. In *Patterns of Change*, ed. L. Rice & L. Greenberg. New York: Guilford, pp. 240–286.

—— (1992), Proposed criteria for evaluating qualitative research. Unpublished manuscript, Department of Psychology, University of Toledo (rev. July 1994).

—— & MORROW-BRADLEY, C. (1994), Developing a working marriage between psychotherapists and psychotherapy researchers: identifying shared purposes. In *Psychotherapy Research and Practice: Bridging the Gap*, ed. P. Talley, H. Strupp & S. Butler. New York: Basic Books, pp. 124–142.

ELLIS, H. (1922), *The World of Dreams*. Boston, MA: Houghton Mifflin.

ELSTEIN, A. (1988), Cognitive processes in clinical inference and decision making. In *Reasoning, Inference, and Judgment in Clinical Psychology*, ed. D. Turk & P. Salovey. New York: Free Press, pp. 17–50.

—— SHULMAN, L. & SPRAFKA, S. (1978), *Medical Problem Solving: An Analysis of Clinical Reasoning.* Cambridge, MA: Harvard University Press.

ELSTER, J. (1989), *Nuts and Bolts for the Social Sciences.* Cambridge, UK: Cambridge University Press.

EMDE, R. (1989), The infant's relationship experience: developmental and affective aspects. In *Relationship Disturbances in Early Childhood,* ed. A. Sameroff & R. Emde. New York: Basic Books, pp. 33–51.

—— (1993), Epilogue: A beginning—research approaches and expanding horizons for psychoanalysis. In *Research in Psychoanalysis: Process, Development, Outcome,* ed. T. Shapiro & R. Emde. *J. Amer. Psychoanal. Assn.,* 41(Suppl.):411–424.

ENDLER, N. (1961), Changes in meaning during psychotherapy as measured by the semantic differential. *J. Consult. Psychol.,* 8:105–111.

ENGLISH, H. & ENGLISH, A. (1958), *A Comprehensive Dictionary of Psychological and Psychoanalytical Terms.* Toronto: Longmans, Green.

ERDELYI, M. (1985), *Psychoanalysis: Freud's Cognitive Psychology.* New York: Freeman.

—— (1986), Psychoanalysis has a wider scope than the retrospective discovery of etiologies. *Behav. Brain Sci.,* 9:234–235.

—— (1988), Issues in the study of unconscious and defense processes: discussion of Horowitz's comments, with some elaborations. In *Psychodynamics and Cognition,* ed. M. Horowitz. Chicago: University of Chicago Press, pp. 81–94.

—— (1990), Repression, reconstruction, and defense: history and integration of the psychoanalytic and experimental frameworks. In *Repression and Dissociation,* ed. J. Singer. Chicago: University of Chicago Press, pp. 1–32.

—— & GOLDBERG, B. (1979), Let's not sweep repression under the rug: toward a cognitive psychology of repression. In *Functional Disorders of Memory,* ed. J. Kihlstrom & F. Evans. Hillsdale, NJ: Lawrence Erlbaum Associates, pp. 355–402.

ERIKSON, E. (1954), The dream specimen of psychoanalysis. *J. Amer. Psychoanal. Assn.,* 2:5–56.

—— (1958), The nature of clinical evidence. *Daedalus,* 87:65–87. Also in *Insight and Responsibility.* New York: Norton, 1964, pp. 49–80.

ERLE, J., rep. (1968), Some aspects of the nature of evidence: report of J. A. Arlow's Section of the Kris Study Group to the New York Psychoanalytic Society, Sept. 26, 1967. *Psychoanal. Quart.,* 37:636–638.

ERWIN, E. (1986), Defending Freudianism. *Behav. Brain Sci.,* 9:235–236.

—— (1988), Psychoanalysis: clinical versus experimental evidence. In *Mind, Psychoanalysis, and Science,* ed. P. Clark & C. Wright. Oxford, UK: Basil Blackwell, pp. 205–223.

—— (1993), Philosophers on Freudianism: an examination of replies to

Grünbaum's *Foundations*. In *Philosophical Problems of the Internal and External Worlds*, ed. J. Earman, A. Janis, G. Massey & N. Rescher. Pittsburgh, PA: University of Pittsburgh Press, pp. 409–460.

ESMAN, A. (1979), On evidence and inference, or the Babel of tongues. *Psychoanal. Quart.*, 48:628–630.

ETCHEGOYEN, R. (1989), On interpretation and its testing. In *The Psychoanalytic Core*, ed. H. Blum, E. Weinshel & F. Rodman. Madison, CT: International Universities Press, pp. 309–398.

—— (1991), *The Fundamentals of Psychoanalytic Technique*. London: Karnac Books.

EYSENCK, H. (1965), *Fact and Fiction in Psychology*. Harmondsworth, UK: Penguin.

—— (1986), Failure of treatment—failure of theory? *Behav. Brain Sci.*, 9:236.

—— & WILSON, G. (1973), *The Experimental Study of Freudian Theories*. London: Methuen.

EZRIEL, H. (1951), The scientific testing of psychoanalytic findings and theory: the psychoanalytic session as an experimental situation. *Brit. J. Med. Psychol.*, 24:30–34.

—— (1956–57), Experimentation within the psychoanalytic session. *Brit. J. Philos. Sci.*, 7:29–48, 342–347. Also in *Psychoanalytic Clinical Interpretation*, ed. I. Paul. New York: Free Press of Glencoe (Macmillan), 1963, pp. 112–142.

FAIRBAIRN, W. (1952), *An Object Relations Theory of the Personality*. New York: Basic Books.

FARRELL, B. (1961), On the character of psychodynamic discourse. *Brit. J. Med. Psychol.*, 34:7–13.

—— (1976), The criteria for a psychoanalytic interpretation. In *The Philosophy of Mind*, ed. J. Glover. Oxford, UK: Oxford University Press, pp. 15–34.

—— (1981), *The Standing of Psychoanalysis*. Oxford, UK: Oxford University Press.

—— (1986), The probative value of the clinical data of psychoanalysis. *Behav. Brain Sci.*, 9:236–237.

FAULKONER, J. & WILLIAMS, R. (1985), Temporality in human action: an alternative to positivism and historicism. *Amer. Psychologist*, 11:1179–1188.

FAUST, D. (1984), *The Limits of Scientific Judgment*. Minneapolis: University of Minnesota Press.

FEIGL, H. (1973), Empiricism at bay? In *Methodological and Historical Essays in the Natural and Social Sciences*, ed. R. Cohen & M. Wartofsky. Boston, MA: Reidel, pp. 1–20.

FELDMAN, E. (1971), *Varieties of Visual Experience*, 2nd ed. Englewood Cliffs, NJ: Prentice-Hall.

FELMAN, S. (1982a), *Literature and Psychoanalysis*. Baltimore, MD: Johns Hopkins University Press.

——— (1982b), To open the question. In *Literature and Psychoanalysis*, ed. S. Felman. Baltimore, MD: Johns Hopkins University Press, pp. 5–10.

——— (1987), *Jacques Lacan and the Adventure of Insight*. Cambridge, MA: Harvard University Press.

FENICHEL, O. (1941), *Problems of Psychoanalytic Technique*. New York: Psychoanalytic Quarterly.

FERENCZI, S. (1928), The elasticity of psychoanalytic technique. In *Final Contributions to the Problems and Methods of Psychoanalysis*. New York: Basic Books, 1955, pp. 87–101.

FESTINGER, L. (1954), A theory of social comparison processes. *Human Relations*, 7:117–140.

——— (1957), *A Theory of Cognitive Dissonance*. Evanston, IL: Row, Peterson.

FEYERABEND, P. (1975), *Against Method*. London: New Left Books.

FINE, A. & FORBES, M. (1986), Grünbaum on Freud: three grounds for dissent. *Behav. Brain Sci.*, 9:237–238.

FISH, S. (1980), Literature in the reader: affective stylistics. In *Reader-Response Criticism*, ed. J. Tompkins. Baltimore, MD: Johns Hopkins University Press, pp. 70–100.

——— (1989), Withholding the missing portion: psychoanalysis and rhetoric. In *Doing What Comes Naturally*, by S. Fish. Durham, NC: Duke University Press, pp. 525–554.

FISHER, S. & GREENBERG, R. (1977), *The Scientific Credibility of Freud's Theories and Therapy*. New York: Basic Books. (New York: Columbia University Press, 1985, pbk.)

FISHMAN, J. (1970), *Sociolinguistics*. Rowley, MA: Newbury House.

FISKE, D. & SHWEDER, R. (1986), *Metatheory in Social Science*. Chicago: University of Chicago Press.

——— CARTWRIGHT, D. & KIRTNER, W. (1964), Are psychotherapeutic changes predictable? *J. Abn. Soc. Psychol.*, 69:418–426.

FLANAGAN, L. (1986), Psychoanalysis as a social activity. *Behav. Brain Sci.*, 9:238–239.

FLAX, J. (1981), Psychoanalysis and the philosophy of science: critique or resistance? *J. Philos.*, 78:561–569.

FLIESS, R., ed. (1948), *The Psychoanalytic Reader*. New York: International Universities Press.

FLUMERFELT, J. (1962), On reconstruction. *Bull. Phila. Assn. Psychoanal.*, 12:53–68.

FODOR, J. (1975), *The Language of Thought*. New York: Thomas C. Crowell.

——— (1981), *Representations*. Cambridge, MA: MIT Press.

——— (1983), Imagery and the language of thought. In *States of Mind*, ed. J. Miller. New York: Pantheon, pp. 82–98.

——— (1987), *Psychosemantics*. Cambridge, MA: MIT Press.

——— (1993), The persistence of the attitudes. In *Folk Psychology and the*

Philosophy of Mind, ed. S. Christensen & D. Turner. Hillsdale, NJ: Lawrence Erlbaum Associates, pp. 221–246.

FOGEL, G., ed. (1991), *The Work of Hans Loewald*. Northvale, NJ: Aronson.

FONAGY, I. & FONAGY, P. (1995), Communication with pretend actions in language, literature and psychoanalysis. *Psychoanal. Contemp. Thought*, 18:363–418.

FONAGY, P. (1982), The integration of psychoanalysis and experimental science. *Internat. Rev. Psycho-Anal.*, 9:125–145.

FORRESTER, J. (1980), *Language and the Origins of Psychoanalysis*. New York: Columbia University Press.

FOSSHAGE, J. & LOEW, C., eds. (1987), *Dream Interpretation: A Comparative Study*, rev. ed. New York: PMA.

FOUCAULT, M. (1970), *The Order of Things*, trans. A. Smith. London: Tavistock.

FOULKES, D. (1978), *A Grammar of Dreams*. Hassocks, Sussex, UK: Harvester; New York: Basic Books.

FOX, R., GARBUNY, M. & HOOKE, R. (1963), *The Science of Science*. New York: Walker.

FRANK, A. (1979), Two theories or one? Or none? *J. Amer. Psychoanal. Assn.*, 27:169–207.

FRANK, P. (1957), *Philosophy of Science*. Englewood Cliffs, NJ: Prentice-Hall.

—— (1959), Psychoanalysis and logical positivism. In *Psychoanalysis, Scientific Method, and Philosophy*, ed. S. Hook. New York: New York University Press, pp. 308–313.

FRANSELLA, F. & ADAMS, B. (1966), An illustration of the use of repertory grid technique in a clinical setting. *Brit. J. Soc. Clin. Psychol.*, 5:51–62.

—— & BANNISTER, D. (1977), *A Manual for Repertory Grid Technique*. London: Academic Press.

FREEDMAN, N. (1983), On psychoanalytic listening: the construction, paralysis, and reconstruction of meaning. *Psychoanal. Contemp. Thought*, 6:405–434.

FRENCH, T. (1952), *The Integration of Behavior, Vol. I: Basic Postulates*. Chicago: University of Chicago Press.

—— (1954), *The Integration of Behavior, Vol. II: The Integrative Process in Dreams*. Chicago: University of Chicago Press.

—— (1955a), Discussion of "Relation of Initial Associations to Focal Conflict in Analytic Interviews," by P. Seitz. Presented to Chicago Psychoanalytic Society, Feb. 22.

—— (1955b), The problem of consensus. Presented to the Panel on "Validation of Psychoanalytic Techniques," rep. J. Marmor. *J. Amer. Psychoanal. Assn.*, 5:496–505.

—— (1958a), *The Integration of Behavior, Vol. III: The Reintegrative Process in a Psychoanalytic Treatment*. Chicago: University of Chicago Press.

—— (1958b), The art and science of psychoanalysis. *J. Amer. Psychoanal.*

Assn., 6:197–214. Also in *Psychoanalytic Clinical Interpretation*, ed. L. Paul. London: Free Press of Glencoe (Macmillan), 1963, pp. 200–219; and in *Psychoanalytic Interpretations: The Selected Papers of Thomas M. French, M.D.* Chicago: Quadrangle, 1970, pp. 408–425.
—— (1970), *Psychoanalytic Interpretations: The Selected Papers of Thomas M. French, M.D.* Chicago: Quadrangle.
—— & FROMM, E. (1964), *Dream Interpretation: A New Approach*. New York: Basic Books.
FREUD, E. (1960), *Letters of Sigmund Freud*. New York: Basic Books.
FREUD, S. (1887–1902), *The Origins of Psychoanalysis: Letters to Wilhelm Fliess*. New York: Basic Books, 1954.
—— (1895a), Project for a scientific psychology. *Standard Edition*, 1:283–430. London: Hogarth Press, 1966.
—— (1895b), A reply to criticisms of my paper on anxiety neurosis. *Standard Edition*, 3:121–140. London: Hogarth Press, 1962.
—— (1896a), Further remarks on the neuro-psychoses of defence. *Standard Edition*, 3:159–188. London: Hogarth Press, 1962.
—— (1896b), The aetiology of hysteria. *Standard Edition*, 3:189–224. London: Hogarth Press, 1962.
—— (1898), Sexuality in the aetiology of the neuroses. *Standard Edition*, 3:261–286. London: Hogarth Press, 1962.
—— (1900), The interpretation of dreams. *Standard Edition*, 4 & 5. London: Hogarth Press, 1953.
—— (1901), The psychopathology of everyday life. *Standard Edition*, 6:1–310. London: Hogarth Press, 1960.
—— (1905a), Fragment of an analysis of a case of hysteria. *Standard Edition*, 7:3–124. London: Hogarth Press, 1956.
—— (1905b), Jokes and their relation to the unconscious. *Standard Edition*, 8:3–258. London: Hogarth Press, 1960.
—— (1907), Delusions and dreams in Jensen's Gradiva. *Standard Edition*, 9:3–96. London: Hogarth Press, 1959.
—— (1908), On the sexual theories of children. *Standard Edition*, 9:205–234. London: Hogarth Press, 1959.
—— (1909a), Analysis of a phobia in a five-year-old boy. *Standard Edition*, 10:3–152. London: Hogarth Press, 1955.
—— (1909b), Notes upon a case of obsessional neurosis. *Standard Edition*, 10:153–318. London: Hogarth Press, 1955.
—— (1910a), The future prospects of psychoanalytic therapy. *Standard Edition*, 11:139–152. London: Hogarth Press, 1957.
—— (1910b), The antithetical meaning of primal words. *Standard Edition*, 11:153–162. London: Hogarth Press, 1957.
—— (1910c), "Wild" psychoanalysis. *Standard Edition*, 11:219–230. London: Hogarth Press, 1957.
—— (1911a), Psychoanalytic notes on an autobiographical account of a case

of paranoia (dementia paranoides). *Standard Edition*, 12:3–84. London: Hogarth Press, 1958.

—— (1911b), The handling of dream-interpretation in psychoanalysis. *Standard Edition*, 12:89–96. London: Hogarth Press, 1958.

—— (1912a), The dynamics of transference. *Standard Edition*, 12:97–108. London: Hogarth Press, 1958.

—— (1912b), Recommendations to physicians practising psychoanalysis. *Standard Edition*, 12:109–120. London: Hogarth Press, 1958

—— (1913a), On beginning the treatment (Further recommendations on the technique of psychoanalysis I). *Standard Edition*, 12:121–144. London: Hogarth Press, 1958.

—— (1913b), On psychoanalysis. *Standard Edition*, 12:205–212. London: Hogarth Press, 1958.

—— (1913c), The claims of psychoanalysis to scientific interest. *Standard Edition*, 13:165–192. London: Hogarth Press, 1955.

—— (1914a), On the history of the psychoanalytic movement. *Standard Edition*, 14:3–66. London: Hogarth Press, 1957.

—— (1914b), On narcissism: an introduction. *Standard Edition*, 14:67–104. London: Hogarth Press, 1957.

—— (1914c), Remembering, repeating, and working-through (Further recommendations on the technique of psychoanalysis II). *Standard Edition*, 12:145–156. London: Hogarth Press, 1958.

—— (1914d), The Moses of Michelangelo. *Standard Edition*, 13:211–236. London: Hogarth Press, 1955.

—— (1915a), Observations on transference love (Further recommendations on the technique of psychoanalysis III). *Standard Edition*, 12:157–171. London: Hogarth Press, 1958.

—— (1915b), Instincts and their vicissitudes. *Standard Edition*, 14:109–140. London: Hogarth Press, 1957.

—— (1915c), Repression. *Standard Edition*, 14:141–158. London: Hogarth Press, 1957.

—— (1915d), The unconscious. *Standard Edition*, 14:159–216. London: Hogarth Press, 1957.

—— (1915–1916), Introductory lectures on psychoanalysis, Parts 1 and 2. *Standard Edition*, 15:9–239. London: Hogarth Press, 1963.

—— (1916–1917), Introductory lectures on psychoanalysis, Part 3. *Standard Edition*, 15:243–496. London: Hogarth Press, 1963.

—— (1916), Some character-types met with in psychoanalytic work, II. Those wrecked by success. *Standard Edition*, 14:309–337. London: Hogarth Press, 1957.

—— (1918), From the history of an infantile neurosis. *Standard Edition*, 17:3–122. London: Hogarth Press, 1955.

—— (1920a), Beyond the pleasure principle. *Standard Edition*, 18:3–144. London: Hogarth Press, 1955.

——— (1920b), The psychogenesis of a case of homosexuality in a woman. *Standard Edition*, 18:145–174. London: Hogarth Press, 1955.

——— (1921), Group psychology and the analysis of the ego. *Standard Edition*, 18:67–144. London: Hogarth Press, 1955.

——— (1922), Some neurotic mechanisms in jealousy, paranoia, and homosexuality. *Standard Edition*, 18:221–234. London: Hogarth Press, 1955.

——— (1923a), Two encyclopaedia articles. *Standard Edition*, 18:235–262. London: Hogarth Press, 1955.

——— (1923b), Remarks on the theory and practice of dream interpretation. *Standard Edition*, 19:109–124. London: Hogarth Press, 1961.

——— (1923c), The infantile genital organization: an interpolation into the theory of sexuality. *Standard Edition*, 19:141–148. London: Hogarth Press, 1961.

——— (1924), A short account of psychoanalysis. *Standard Edition*, 19:191–212. London: Hogarth Press, 1961.

——— (1925a), Some additional notes on dream-interpretation as a whole. *Standard Edition*, 19:125–140. London: Hogarth Press, 1961.

——— (1925b), A note upon the "mystic writing pad." *Standard Edition*, 19:227–234. London: Hogarth Press, 1961.

——— (1925c), An autobiographical study. *Standard Edition*, 20:3–76. London: Hogarth Press, 1959.

——— (1926a), Inhibitions, symptoms and anxiety. *Standard Edition*, 20:77–178. London: Hogarth Press, 1959.

——— (1926b), Psychoanalysis. *Standard Edition*, 20:259–270. London: Hogarth Press, 1959.

——— (1930), Letter to H. Loewy. In *Letters of Sigmund Freud*, ed. E. Freud. New York: Basic Books, p. 396.

——— (1933), New introductory lectures on psychoanalysis. *Standard Edition*, 22:3–184. London: Hogarth Press, 1964.

——— (1937a), Analysis terminable and interminable. *Standard Edition*, 23:209–254. London: Hogarth Press, 1964.

——— (1937b), Constructions in analysis. *Standard Edition*, 23:255–270. London: Hogarth Press, 1964.

——— (1940a), An outline of psychoanalysis. *Standard Edition*, 23:141–208. London: Hogarth Press, 1964.

——— (1940b), Some elementary lessons in psychoanalysis. *Standard Edition*, 23:279–286. London: Hogarth Press, 1964.

——— (1985), *The Complete Letters of Sigmund Freud to Wilhelm Fliess, 1887–1904*, ed. J. Masson. Cambridge, MA: Harvard University Press.

——— & SILBERSTEIN, E. (1872–1875), Correspondence. Freud Collection, D-2; Library of Congress, Washington, DC.

FRIEDMAN, L. (1976), Problems of an action theory of the mind. *Internat. Rev. Psycho-Anal.*, 3:129–138.

——— (1980), Kohut: a book review essay. *Psychoanal. Quart.*, 49:393–422.

—— (1983), Reconstruction and the like. *Psychoanal. Inq.*, 3:189–222.

—— (1988), *The Anatomy of Psychotherapy*. Hillsdale, NJ: The Analytic Press.

—— (1995), Two panels on interaction: an introduction. *J. Amer. Psychoanal. Assn.*, 43:517–520.

FRIEDMAN, L.J. (1995), Review of *Freud and the History of Psychoanalysis*, ed. T. Gelfand & J. Kerr (1992). *Psychoanal. Quart.*, 64:181–184.

FROMM, E. & FRENCH, T. (1962), Formation and evaluation of hypotheses in dream interpretation. *J. Psychol.*, 54:271–283.

FROMM-REICHMANN, F. (1950), *Principles of Intensive Psychotherapy*. Chicago: University of Chicago Press.

GABBARD, G. (1995), Countertransference: the emerging common ground. *Internat. J. Psycho-Anal.*, 76:475–485.

GABLER, H. (1984), The synchrony and diachrony of texts: practice and theory of the critical edition of James Joyce's Ulysses. In *Text: Transactions of the Society of Textual Scholarship*, ed. D. Greetham & W. Hill. New York: AMS, pp. 305–326.

GADAMER, H.-G. (1975), *Truth and Method*. New York: Crossroad, 1984.

—— (1976), *Philosophical Hermeneutics*, trans. D. Linjer. Berkeley: University of California Press.

GALATZER-LEVY, R. (1996), Review of *Validation in the Clinical Theory of Psychoanalysis*, by A. Grünbaum (1993). *J. Amer. Psychoanal. Assn.*, 44:594–598.

GARDNER, H. (1981), *The Quest for Mind: Piaget, Lévi-Strauss, and the Structuralist Movement*. Chicago: University of Chicago Press.

GARDNER, M. R. (1983), *Self Inquiry*. Boston, MA: Little Brown.

—— (1991), The art of psychoanalysis: on oscillation, and other matters. *J. Amer. Psychoanal. Assn.*, 39:851–870.

GARDNER, S. (1993), *Irrationality and the Philosophy of Psychoanalysis*. Cambridge, UK: Cambridge University Press.

GARDUK, E. & HAGGARD, E. (1972), *Immediate Effects on Patients of Psychoanalytic Interpretations*. New York: International Universities Press.

GARFIELD, S. & BERGIN, A., eds. (1978), *Handbook of Psychotherapy and Behavior Change*. New York: Wiley.

GARNER, W. (1962), *Uncertainty and Structure as Psychological Concepts*. New York: Wiley.

GAUDIN, C. (1987), Introduction. In *On Poetic Imagination and Reverie*. Dallas, TX: Spring, pp. xxxi–lix.

GAULD, A. & SHOTTER, J. (1977), *Human Action and Its Psychological Investigation*. London: Routledge & Kegan Paul.

—— & —— (1986), Warranting interpretations. *Behav. Brain Sci.*, 9:239–240.

GEDO, J. (1979), *Beyond Interpretation*, rev. ed. Hillsdale, NJ: The Analytic Press, 1993, (pbk).

——— (1980), Reflections on some current controversies in psychoanalysis. *J. Amer. Psychoanal. Assn.*, 28:363–383.

——— (1981), *Advances in Clinical Psychoanalysis*. New York: International Universities Press.

——— (1984a), *Psychoanalysis and Its Discontents*. New York: Guilford.

——— (1984b), Discussion of J. Lichtenberg's "The empathic mode of perception and alternative vantage points for psychoanalytic work." In *Empathy II*, ed. J. Lichtenberg, M. Bornstein & D. Silver. Hillsdale, NJ: The Analytic Press, pp. 137–141.

——— (1984c), Letter to the editor. *Rev. Psychoanal. Bks.*, 3:511–515.

——— (1986), Relevance or reductionism in interpretation: a reprise of the psychoanalysis of Kleist's puppet theater. In *Conceptual Issues in Psychoanalysis*. Hillsdale, NJ: The Analytic Press, pp. 186–199.

——— SABSHIN, M., SADOW, L. & SCHLESSINGER, N. (1964), "Studies on hysteria": a methodological evaluation. *J. Amer. Psychoanal. Assn.*, 12:734–751.

GEERTZ. C. (1967), The impact of the concept of culture on the concept of man. *Reflections*, 2:42–55.

GELFAND, T. & KERR, J. eds. (1992), *Freud and the History of Psychoanalysis*. Hillsdale, NJ: The Analytic Press.

GELLER, E. & PITZ, G. (1968), Confidence and decision speed in the revision of opinion. *Organiz. Behav. Human Perform.*, 3:190–201.

GENETTE, G. (1980), *Narrative Discourse: An Essay in Method*. Ithaca, NY: Cornell University Press.

GERGELY, G. (1992), Developmental reconstructions: infancy from the point of view of psychoanalysis and developmental psychology. *Psychoanal. Contemp. Thought*, 15:3–56.

GERGEN, K. (1981), The meagre voice of empiricist affirmation. *Person. Soc. Psychol. Bull.*, 7:333–337.

——— (1985), The social constructionist movement in modern psychology. *Amer. Psychol.*, 40:266–275.

——— (1988), If persons are texts. In *Hermeneutics and Psychological Theory*, ed. S. Messer, L. Sass & R. Woolfolk. New Brunswick, NJ: Rutgers University Press, pp. 28–51.

——— & GERGEN, M. (1986), Narrative form and the construction of psychological science. In *Narrative Psychology*, ed. T Sarbin. New York: Praeger, pp. 22–44.

GHOLSON, B. & BARKER, P. (1985), Kuhn, Lakatos, and Laudan: Applications in the history of physics and psychology. *Amer. Psychol.*, 40:755–769.

GIERE, R. (1979), *Understanding Scientific Reasoning*. New York: Holt, Rinehart & Winston.

——— (1988), *Explaining Science: A Cognitive Approach*. Chicago: University of Chicago Press.

GILL, M. (1976), Metapsychology is not psychology. In *Psychology versus Metapsychology*, ed. M. Gill & P. Holzman. Madison CT: International Universities Press, pp. 77–105.

—— (1982a), *Analysis of Transference: Vol. I, Theory and Technique*. New York: International Universities Press.

—— (1983), The point of view of psychoanalysis: energy discharge or person? *Psychoanal. Contemp. Thought*, 6:523–552.

—— (1984), Robert Langs on technique: a critique. In *Listening and Interpreting*, ed. J. Raney. New York: Aronson, pp. 395–413.

—— (1991), Merton Gill speaks his mind. *Amer. Psychoanal.*, 25:17–21.

—— (1994a), Letter to the Editor: Comments on "Neutrality, Interpretation, and Therapeutic Intent." *J. Amer. Psychoanal. Assn.*, 42:681–684.

—— (1994b), *Psychoanalysis in Transition*. Hillsdale, NJ: The Analytic Press.

—— & HOFFMAN, I. (1982b), *Analysis of Transference: Vol. II, Studies of Nine Audio-recorded Psychoanalytic Sessions*. New York: International Universities Press.

GILLETT, E. (1987), The problem of scientific perfectionism. *Psychoanal. Contemp. Thought*, 10:299–315.

—— (1990a), A strategy for the clinical validation of psychoanalytic theory. *Psychoanal. Contemp. Thought*, 13:289–310.

—— (1990b), The problem of unconscious affect: signal anxiety versus the double-prediction theory. *Psychoanal. Contemp. Thought*, 13:551–600.

—— (1993), The confusion over personification and reification. *Psychoanal. Contemp. Thought*, 16:3–42.

—— (1995), Review of *Philosophical Problems of the Internal and External Worlds*, ed. J. Earman, A. Janis, G. Massey & N. Rescher (1993). *J. Nerv. Ment. Dis.*, 183:119–120.

GILLMAN, R. (1987), Dreams as resistance. In *The Interpretation of Dreams in Clinical Work*, ed. A. Rothstein. Madison, CT: International Universities Press, pp. 27–36.

GILMAN, S., BIRMELE, J., GELLER, J. & GREENBERG, V., eds. (1994), *Reading Freud's Reading*. New York: New York University Press.

GINZBURG, C. (1989), *Clues, Myths, and the Historical Method*, trans. J. & A. Tedeschi. Baltimore, MD: Johns Hopkins University Press.

—— (1994), Checking the evidence: the judge and the historian. In *Questions of Evidence*, ed. J. Chandler, A. Davidson & H. Harootunian. Chicago: University of Chicago Press, pp. 290–303.

GIOVACCHINI, P. (1990), Interpretations, an obscure technical area: comments on Winnicott's "Interpretation in Psycho-Analysis." In *Tactics and Techniques in Psychoanalytic Therapy, Vol. III*, ed. P. Giovacchini. Northvale, NJ: Aronson, pp. 71–89.

GLASER, B. & STRAUSS, A. (1967), *The Discovery of Grounded Theory: Strategies for Qualitative Research*. London: Weidenfeld & Nicholson.

GLOVER, E. (1931), The therapeutic effect of inexact interpretation: a contri-

bution to the theory of suggestion. *Internat. J. Psycho-Anal.*, 12:397–411.
—— (1952), Research methods in psychoanalysis. *Internat. J. Psycho-Anal.*, 33:403–409.
GLYMOUR, C. (1974), Freud, Kepler, and the clinical evidence. In *Freud: A Collection of Critical Essays*, ed. R. Wollheim. Garden City, NY: Anchor, pp. 285–304. Also in *Philosophical Essays on Freud*, ed. R. Wollheim & J. Hopkins. Cambridge, UK: Cambridge University Press, 1982, pp. 12–31.
—— (1980), *Theory and Evidence*. Princeton, NJ: Princeton University Press.
—— (1983), The theory of your dreams. In *Physics, Philosophy, and Psychoanalysis*, ed. R. Cohen & L. Laudan. Dordrecht: D. Reidel, pp. 57–71.
—— (1993), How Freud left science. In *Philosophical Problems of the Internal and External Worlds*, ed. J. Earman, A. Janis, G. Massey & N. Rescher. Pittsburgh, PA: University of Pittsburgh Press, pp. 461–487.
GOLDBERG, A. (1985), The definition and role of interpretation. In *Progress in Self Psychology, Vol. 1*, ed. A. Goldberg. New York: Guilford, pp. 62–65.
—— (1987), Psychoanalysis and negotiation. *Psychoanal. Quart.*, 56:109–129.
—— (1988), *A Fresh Look at Psychoanalysis: The View from Self Psychology*. Hillsdale, NJ: The Analytic Press.
—— (1989), A shared view of the world. *Internat. J. Psycho-Anal.*, 7:16–20.
—— (1990), *The Prisonhouse of Psychoanalysis*. Hillsdale, NJ: The Analytic Press.
—— (1994), Farewell to the objective analyst. *Internat. J. Psycho-Anal.*, 75:21–30.
GOLDBERG, L. (1968), Simple models or simple processes: some research on clinical judgments. *Amer. Psychol.*, 23:483–496.
—— & WERTS, C. (1966), The reliability of clinicians' judgments: a multitrait-multimethod approach. *J. Consult. Psychol.*, 30:199–206.
GOLDMAN, A. (1994), *Readings in Philosophy and Cognitive Science*. Cambridge, MA: MIT Press.
GOLDSTEIN, I. & PAPERT, S. (1977), Artificial intelligence, language, and the study of knowledge. *Cogn. Sci.*, 1:84–123.
GOMBRICH, E. (1969), The evidence of images. In *Interpretation: Theory and Practice*, ed. C. Singleton. Baltimore, MD: Johns Hopkins University Press, pp. 35–104.
GOOD, M. (1994), The reconstruction of early childhood trauma: fantasy, reality, and verification. *J. Amer. Psychoanal. Assn*, 42:79–102.
GOODMAN, N. (1978), *Ways of Worldmaking*. Indianapolis, IN: Hackett.
GORDON, C. (1982), *Forgotten Scripts*. New York: Basic Books.
GOTTSCHALK, L. (1979), *The Content Analysis of Verbal Behavior—Further Studies*. New York: SP Med. & Sci. Bks. Spectrum.
—— & AUERBACH, A., eds. (1966), *Methods of Research in Psychotherapy*. New York: Appleton-Century-Crofts.

—— & GLESER, G. (1969), *The Measurement of Psychological States Through the Content Analysis of Verbal Behavior*. Berkeley: University of California Press.

GOULD, N. (1978), The structure of dialectical reason: a comparative study of Freud's and Lévi-Strauss' concepts of the unconscious mind. *Ethos*, 6:187–211.

GOULD, S. (1986), Evolution and the triumph of homology, or why history matters. *Amer. Scient.*, 74:60–69.

GRAHAM, G. (1993), The origins of folk psychology. In *Folk Psychology and the Philosophy of Mind*, ed. S. Christensen & D. Turner. Hillsdale, NJ: Lawrence Erlbaum Associates, pp. 200–220.

GRANT, D. & HARARI, E. (1990), Misreading Freud—some thoughts on Adolf Grünbaum's "tally argument." *Psychoanal. Contemp. Thought*, 13:311–319.

GRAY, P. (1973), Psychoanalytic technique and the ego's capacity for viewing intrapsychic activity. *J. Amer. Psychoanal. Assn.*, 21:474–494.

—— (1982), "Developmental lag" in the evolution of technique for psychoanalysis of neurotic conflict. *J. Amer. Psychoanal. Assn.*, 30:621–655.

—— (1986), On helping analysands observe intrapsychic activity. In *Psychoanalysis: The Science of Mental Conflict*, ed. A. Richards & M. Willick. Hillsdale, NJ: The Analytic Press, pp. 245–262.

—— (1990), The nature of therapeutic action in psychoanalysis. *J. Amer. Psychoanal. Assn.*, 38:1083–1097.

—— (1992), Memory as resistance, and the telling of a dream. *J. Amer. Psychoanal. Assn.*, 40:307–326.

—— (1994), *The Ego and Analysis of Defense*. Northvale, NJ: Aronson.

GREEN, A. (1973), *Le Discours Vivant*. Paris: Presses Universitaires de France.

—— (1993), Discussion of "The inner experiences of the analyst," and a response from Theodore Jacobs. *Internat. J. Psycho-Anal.*, 74:1131–1136, 1140–1145.

—— (1995), *La Causalité Psychique*. Paris: Jacob.

GREEN, G. & MORGAN, J. (1981), Pragmatics, grammar, and discourse. In *Radical Pragmatics*, ed. P. Cole. New York: Academic Press, pp. 167–181.

GREENBERG, J. (1994), Psychotherapy research: a clinician's view. In *Psychotherapy Research and Practice: Bridging the Gap*, ed. P. Talley, H. Strupp & S. Butler. New York: Basic Books, pp. 1–18.

—— & MITCHELL, S. (1983), *Object Relations in Psychoanalytic Theory*. Cambridge, MA: Harvard University Press.

GREENBERG, L. & PINSOF, W., eds. (1986), *The Psychotherapeutic Process: A Research Handbook*. New York: Guilford.

GREENBERG, R. (1986), The case against Freud's cases. In Précis of *The Foundations of Psychoanalysis: A Philosophical Critique*, with open peer commentary. *Behav. Brain Sci.*, 9:240–241.

GREENSON, R. (1960), Empathy and its vicissitudes. *Internat. J. Psycho-Anal.*, 41:418–424.

——— (1967), *The Technique and Practice of Psychoanalysis, Vol. I.* New York: International Universities Press.

GREENSPOON, J. (1955), The reinforcing effect of two spoken sounds on the frequency of two responses. *Amer. J. Psychol.*, 68:409–416.

——— (1962), Verbal conditioning and clinical psychology. In *Experimental Foundations of Clinical Psychology*, ed. A. Bachrach. New York: Basic Books, pp. 510–553.

GREENWALD, A., PRATKANIS, A., LEIPPE, M. & BAUMGARDNER, M. (1986), Under what conditions does theory obstruct research progress? *Psychol. Rev.*, 93:216–229.

GREENWOOD, J., ed. (1991), *The Future of Folk Psychology*. Cambridge, UK: Cambridge University Press.

GRIBINSKI, M. (1994), The stranger in the house. *Internat. J. Psycho-Anal.*, 75:1011–1021.

GRICE, H. (1975), Logic and conversation. In *Syntax and Semantics, Vol. 3: Speech Acts*, ed. P. Cole & J. Morgan. New York: Academic Press, pp. 41–58.

GRINBERG, L., LANGER, M., LIBERMAN, D. & RODRIGUÉ, E. & G. (1967), The psychoanalytic process. *Internat. J. Psycho-Anal.*, 48:496–503.

GRINSTEIN, A. (1983), *Freud's Rules of Dream Interpretation*. New York: International Universities Press.

GROLNICK, S. (1982), The current psychoanalytic dialogue: its counterpart in renaissance philosophy. *J. Amer. Psychoanal. Assn.*, 30:679–699.

GRONER, R., GRONER, M. & BISCHOF, W., eds. (1983), *Methods of Heuristics*. Hillsdale, NJ: Lawrence Erlbaum Associates.

GROSSKURTH, P. (1986), *Melanie Klein: Her World and Her Work*. New York: Knopf.

GROSSMAN, W. (1995), Psychological vicissitudes of theory in clinical work. *Internat. J. Psycho-Anal.*, 76:885–899.

——— & SIMON, B. (1969), Anthropomorphism: motive, meaning, and causality in psychoanalytic theory. *The Psychoanalytic Study of the Child*, 24:78–111 (see esp. pp. 99–109). New York: International Universities Press.

GRUBRICH-SIMITIS, I. (1993), *Zurück zu Freuds Texten: Stümme Dokumente Sprechen Machen*. Frankfurt: S. Fischer.

GRÜNBAUM, A. (1976), Is falsifiability the touchstone of scientific rationality: Karl Popper versus inductivism. In *Essays in Memory of Imre Lakatos*, ed. R. Cohen, P. Feyerabend & M. Wartofsky. Dordrecht: Reidel, pp. 213–252.

——— (1977), How scientific is psychoanalysis? In *Science and Psychotherapy*, ed. R. Stern, L. Horowitz & J. Lynes. New York: Haven, pp. 219–254.

——— (1979), Epistemological liabilities of the clinical appraisal of psychoanalytic theory. *Psychoanal. Contemp. Thought*, 2:451–526.

——— (1982), Can psychoanalytic theory be cogently tested "on the couch?" Parts I & II. *Psychoanal. Contemp. Thought*, 5:155–255; 311–436.

——— (1983a), Logical foundations of psychoanalytic theory. In *Theories of Psychopathology and Personality*, ed. T. Millon. New York: Holt, Rinehart & Winston, pp. 193–216.

——— (1983b), Retrospective versus prospective testing of aetiologic hypotheses in psychoanalytic theory. In *Testing Scientific Theories*, ed. J. Earman. *Minnesota Studies in the Philosophy of Science, Vol. X.* Minneapolis: University of Minnesota Press, pp. 315–347.

——— (1984), *The Foundations of Psychoanalysis: A Philosophical Critique*. Berkeley: University of California Press.

——— (1986), Précis of *The Foundations of Psychoanalysis: A Philosophical Critique*, with open peer commentary. *Behav. Brain Sci.*, 9:217–228, 266–281. Also in *Mind, Psychoanalysis and Science*, ed. P. Clark & C. Wright. Oxford, UK: Basil Blackwell, 1988, pp. 3–32.

——— (1988a), Are hidden motives in psychoanalysis reasons but not causes of human conduct? In *Hermeneutics and Psychological Theory*, ed. S. Messer, R. Sass & R. Woolfolk. New Brunswick, NJ: Rutgers University Press, pp. 149–167, 175–181.

——— (1988b), The role of the case study method in the foundations of psychoanalysis. *Can. J. Philos.*, 18:623–658.

——— (1989), Why thematic kinships between events DO NOT attest their causal linkage. In *An Intimate Relation*, ed. J. Brown & J. Mittelstrass. Boston, MA: Reidel, pp. 477–493.

——— (1990a), Meaning connections and causal connections in the human sciences. The poverty of hermeneutic philosophy. *J. Amer. Psychoanal. Assn.*, 38:559–577.

——— (1990b), The psychoanalytic enterprise in scientific perspective. In *Scientific Theories*, ed. C. Savage. Minneapolis: University of Minnesota Press, pp. 41–58.

——— (1991), Etiology and therapy in psychoanalytic theory. *Behav. Brain Sci.*, 14:729–732.

——— (1993), *Validation in the Clinical Theory of Psychoanalysis*. Madison, CT: International Universities Press.

——— (1994), Letter to the Editor: Reply to Louis Berger's review of *Validation in the Clinical Theory of Psychoanalysis* (1993). *Psychoanal. Bks.*, 5:154–167.

——— (1997), Is the concept of "psychic reality" a theoretical advance? *Psychoanal. Contemp. Thought*, 20:245–268.

GUNTRIP, H. (1961), *Personality Structure and Human Interaction*. London: Hogarth Press.

GUSTAFSON, J. (1984), An integration of brief dynamic psychotherapy. *Amer. J. Psychiat.*, 141:935–944.

GUTTMAN, S. & GUTTMAN, I., eds. (1987), Robert Waelder on psychoanalytic technique: five lectures. *Psychoanal. Quart.*, 56:1–67.

HABERMAS, J. (1971), *Knowledge and Human Interests*, trans. M. Shapiro. Boston, MA: Beacon.

—— (1974), *Theory and Practice*, trans. J. Viertal. London: Heinemann.

HAIRSTON, M. (1978), *A Contemporary Rhetoric*, 2nd ed. Boston, MA: Houghton Mifflin.

HALDANE, J. (1988), Psychoanalysis, cognitive psychology and self-consciousness. In *Mind, Psychoanalysis and Science*, ed. P. Clark & C. Wright. Oxford, UK: Basil Blackwell, pp. 113–140.

HALL, C. & VAN DE CASTLE, R. (1966), *The Content Analysis of Dreams*. New York: Appleton-Century-Crofts.

HAMBURG, P. (1991), Interpretation and empathy: reading Lacan with Kohut. *Internat. J. Psycho-Anal.*, 72:347–361.

HAMILTON, V. (1993), Truth and reality in psychoanalytic discourse. *Internat. J. Psycho-Anal.*, 74:63–79.

HAMPSHIRE, S. (1963), Disposition and memory. *Internat. J. Psycho-Anal.*, 74:59–68.

HANLY, C. (1988), Review of *The Foundations of Psychoanalysis: A Philosophical Critique*, by Adolf Grünbaum (1984). *J. Amer. Psychoanal. Assn.*, 36:521–528.

—— (1990), The concept of truth in psychoanalysis. *Internat. J. Psycho-Anal.*, 71:375–383.

—— (1992a), Inductive reasoning in clinical psychoanalysis. *Internat. J. Psycho-Anal.*, 73:293–301.

—— (1992b), *The Problem of Truth in Applied Psychoanalysis*. New York: Guilford.

—— (1995), On facts and ideas in psychoanalysis. *Internat. J. Psycho-Anal.*, 76:901–908.

HANLY, M. (1995), The "narrative" topic in psychoanalysis. *Internat. Psychoanal.*, 4:33–35.

HARDY, W. (1978), *Language, Thought, and Experience*. Baltimore, MD: University Park.

HARMAN, G. (1965), The inference to the best explanation. *Philos. Rev.*, 74:88–95.

—— (1973), *Thought*. Princeton, NJ: Princeton University Press.

—— (1987), *Change of View*. Cambridge, MA: MIT/Bradford.

HARRÉ, R. (1960), *An Introduction to the Logic of the Sciences*. London: Macmillan.

—— (1970), *The Principles of Scientific Thinking*. London: Macmillan.

—— (1972), *The Philosophies of Science*. London: Oxford University Press.

—— & SECORD, P. (1972), *The Explanation of Social Behavior*. Oxford, UK: Basil Blackwell.

—— & LAMB, R., eds. (1983), *Encyclopedic Dictionary of Language*. Cambridge, MA: MIT Press.

—— CLARKE, D. & DE CARLO, N. (1985), *Motives and Mechanisms.* London: Methuen.

HARRIS, Z. (1952), Discourse analysis. *Language,* 28:1–30.

HARRISON, S. (1970), Psychoanalysis, our science? *J. Amer. Psychoanal. Assn.,* 18:125–149.

HARTMANN, H. (1939), *Ego Psychology and the Problem of Adaptation,* trans. D. Rapaport. New York: International Universities Press, 1958.

—— (1951), Technical implications of ego psychology. *Psychoanal. Quart.,* 20:31–43, 1951. Also in *Essays in Ego Psychology.* London: Hogarth Press, 1964, pp. 142–154.

—— (1959), Psychoanalysis as a scientific theory. In *Essays in Ego Psychology.* New York: International Universities Press, 1964, pp. 318–350.

HASTIE, R. (1981), Schematic principles in human memory. In *Social Cognition: The Ontario Symposium,* ed. E. Higgins, C. Harman & M. Zama. Hillsdale, NJ: Lawrence Erlbaum Associates, pp. 39–88.

HAVENS, L. (1973), *Approaches to the Mind.* Boston, MA: Little, Brown.

HAWKES, T. (1977), *Structuralism and Semiotics.* London: Methuen.

HAYEK, F. ([1964] 1994), The theory of complex phenomena. In *Readings in the Philosophy of Social Science,* ed. M. Martin & L. McIntyre. Cambridge, MA: MIT Press, pp. 55–70.

HAYNAL, A. (1993a), *Psychoanalysis and the Sciences,* trans. E. Holder. Berkeley: University of California Press.

—— (1993b), Text-context interpretation. In *Psychoanalysis and the Sciences,* trans. E. Holder. Berkeley: University of California Press, pp. 71–82.

HEDGES, L. (1991), *Listening Perspectives in Psychotherapy.* Northvale, NJ: Aronson.

HEIDER, F. (1958), *The Psychology of Interpersonal Relations.* New York: Wiley.

—— (1960), The gestalt theory of motivation. In *Nebraska Symposium on Motivation, 1960,* ed. M. Jones. Lincoln: University of Nebraska Press, pp. 145–172.

HEIL, J. & MELE, A. (1993), *Mental Causation.* Oxford, UK: Clarendon.

HEIMANN, P. (1969), Gedanken zum Erkenntnisprozess des psychoanalytikers. *Psyche,* 23:2–24.

—— (1977), Further observations on the analyst's cognitive process. *J. Amer. Psychoanal. Assn.,* 25:313–333.

HEINE, R. (1953), A comparison of patients' reports on psychotherapeutic experiences with psychoanalytic, nondirective, and Adlerian therapists. *Amer. J. Psychother.,* 7:16–23.

HEINICKE, C. (1993), Integrating experientially based concepts and behavioral observations in developmental and intervention research. *J. Amer. Psychoanal. Assn.,* 41(Suppl.):353–368. Also in *Research in Psychoanalysis,* ed. T. Shapiro & R. Emde, Madison, CT: International Universities Press, 1995, pp. 353–368.

HEIZER, R., ed. (1959), *The Archaeologist at Work*. New York: Harper & Row.

HEMPEL, C. (1965), *Aspects of Scientific Explanation and Other Essays in the Philosophy of Science*. New York: Free Press.

—— & OPPENHEIM, P. (1953), The logic of explanation. In *Readings in the Philosophy of Science*, ed. H. Feigl & M. Brodbeck. New York: Appleton-Century-Crofts, pp. 319–352.

HERNADI, P., ed. (1978), *What Is Literature?* Bloomington: Indiana University Press.

—— ed. (1981), *What Is Criticism?* Bloomington: Indiana University Press.

HERSKOVITS, M. (1948), *Man and His Works*. New York: Knopf.

HERTZ, N. (1983), Dora's secrets, Freud's techniques. *Diacritics*, 13:65–83.

HESSE, M. (1966), *Models and Analogies in Science*. South Bend, IN: University of Notre Dame Press.

—— (1980), *Revolutions and Reconstructions in the Philosophy of Science*. Bloomington: Indiana University Press.

HEYNICK, F. (1981), Linguistic aspects of Freud's dream model. *Internat. Rev. Psycho-Anal.*, 8:299–314.

HILDEBRAND, H. (1988), The other side of the wall: a psychoanalytic study of creativity in later life. *Internat. Rev. Psycho-Anal*,. 15:353–363.

HILEY, D., BOHMAN, J. & SHUSTERMAN, R., eds. (1991), *The Interpretive Turn*. Ithaca, NY: Cornell University Press.

HILLIARD, R. (1993), Single-case methodology in psychotherapy process and outcome research. *J. Consult. Clin. Psychol.*, 61:373–380.

HIRSCH, E. (1967), *Validity in Interpretation*. New Haven, CT: Yale University Press.

—— (1976), *The Aims of Interpretation*. Chicago: University of Chicago Press.

—— (1983), The politics of theories of interpretation. In *The Politics of Interpretation*, ed. W. Mitchell. Chicago: University of Chicago Press, pp. 321–333.

HITCHCOCK, J. (1989), Review of *Psychoanalytic Treatment: An Intersubjective Approach*, by R. Stolorow, B. Brandchaft, & G. Atwood, (1987). *Psychoanal. Quart.*, 58:666–671.

HOBSON, J. (1986), Repressed infantile wishes as the instigators of all dreams. *Behav. Brain Sci.*, 9:241–242.

—— & MCCARLEY, R. (1977), The brain as a dream state generator: an activation-synthesis hypothesis of the dream process. *Amer. J. Psychiat.*, 134:1335–1348.

HOFFMAN, I. (1983), The patient as interpreter of the analyst's experience. *Contemp. Psychoanal.*, 19:389–422.

—— (1987), The value of uncertainty in psychoanalytic practice (discussion of E. Wittenberg). *Contemp. Psychoanal.*, 23:205–215.

—— (1991), Discussion: toward a social-constructivist view of the psychoanalytic situation. *Psychoanal. Dial.*, 1:74–105.

—— (1994), Dialectical thinking and therapeutic action in the psychoanalytic process. *Psychoanal. Quart.*, 63:187–218.

—— & GILL, M. (1988), A scheme for coding the patient's experience of the relationship with the therapist (PERT): some applications, extensions, and comparisons. In *Psychoanalytic Research Strategies*, ed. H. Dahl, H. Kächele & H. Thomä. New York: Springer, pp. 67–98.

HOIT, M. (1995), The influence of hermeneutic philosophy on psychoanalysis. *The Annual of Psychoanalysis*, 23:13–32. Hillsdale, NJ: The Analytic Press.

HOLLAND, J., HOLYOAK, K. & NISBETT, R. (1986), *Induction: Processes of Inference, Learning, and Discovery*. Cambridge, MA: MIT Press.

HOLLAND, N. (1978), What can a concept of identity add to psycholinguistics? In *Psychoanalysis and Language*, ed. J. Smith. New Haven, CT: Yale University Press, pp. 171–234.

—— (1990), *Holland's Guide to Psychoanalytic Psychology and Literature-and-Psychology*. New York: Oxford University Press.

HOLSTI, O. (1968), Content analysis. In *Handbook of Social Psychology*, ed. G. Lindzey & E. Aronson. Reading, MA: Addison-Wesley, pp. 596–692.

—— (1969), Introduction of Part II. In *The Analysis of Communication Content*, ed. G. Gerbner, O. Holsti & K. Krippendorf. New York: Wiley, pp. 109–121.

HOLT, R. (1961), Clinical judgment as a disciplined inquiry. *J. Nerv. Ment. Dis.*, 133:369–382.

—— (1976), Drive or wish? A reconsideration of the psychoanalytic theory of motivation. In *Psychology versus Metapsychology*, ed. M. Gill & P. Holzman. Madison CT: International Universities Press, pp. 158–197.

—— (1978a), *Methods in Clinical Psychology* (2 vols.). New York: Plenum.

—— (1978b), Clinical and statistical prediction: a reformulation and some new data. In *Methods in Clinical Psychology, Vol. 2*. New York: Plenum, pp. 19–37.

—— (1978c), Experimental methods in clinical psychology. In *Methods in Clinical Psychology, Vol. 2*. New York: Plenum, pp. 139–186.

—— (1979), Review of *Language and Insight*, by R. Schafer (1978), *Psychoanal. Quart.*, 48:496–500.

—— (1986), Some reflections on testing psychoanalytic hypotheses. *Behav. Brain Sci.*, 9:242–243.

—— (1988), Judgment, inference, and reasoning in clinical perspective. In *Reasoning, Inference, and Judgment in Clinical Psychology*, ed. D. Turk & P. Salovey. New York: Free Press, pp. 233–249.

—— (1989), *Freud Reappraised*. New York: Guilford.

—— (1992), The contemporary crises of psychoanalysis. *Psychoanal. Contemp. Thought*, 15:375–398.

—— (1996). Letter to the editor: reply to Newton. *Psychoanal. Bks.*, 7:299–301.

HOLTON, G. (1973), *Thematic Origins of Scientific Thought*. Cambridge, MA: Harvard University Press.

HOLYOAK, K. (1982), An analogical framework for literary interpretation. *Poetics*, 11:105–126.

HOLZMAN, P. (1985), Psychoanalysis: is the therapy destroying the science? *J. Amer. Psychoanal. Assn.*, 33:725–770.

—— (1993), Introduction. In *Validation in the Clinical Theory of Psychoanalysis*, by Adolf Grünbaum. Madison CT: International Universities Press, pp. xvii–xxii.

—— & ARONSON, G. (1992), Psychoanalysis and its neighboring sciences: paradigms and opportunities. *J. Amer. Psychoanal. Assn.*, 40:63–88.

HOME, H. (1966), The concept of mind. *Internat. J. Psycho-Anal.*, 47:42–49.

HOOK, S., ed. (1959), *Psychoanalysis, Scientific Method, and Philosophy*. New York: New York University Press.

HOOKE, R. (1963), *Introduction to Scientific Inference*. San Francisco: Holden-Day.

HOPKINS, J. (1982), Introduction: philosophy and psychoanalysis. In *Philosophical Essays on Freud*, ed. R. Wollheim & J. Hopkins. Cambridge, UK: Cambridge University Press, pp. vii–xlv.

—— (1988), Epistemology and depth psychology: critical notes on *The Foundations of Psychoanalysis*. In *Mind, Psychoanalysis and Science*, ed. P. Clark & C. Wright. Oxford, UK: Basil Blackwell, pp. 33–60.

—— (1991), The interpretation of dreams. In *The Cambridge Companion to Freud*, ed. J. Neu. Cambridge, UK: Cambridge University Press, pp. 86–135.

—— (1992), Psychoanalysis, interpretation, and science. In *Psychoanalysis, Mind, and Art*, ed. J. Hopkins & A. Savile. Oxford, UK: Basil Blackwell, pp. 3–34.

HORGAN, T. & WOODWARD, J. (1993), Folk psychology is here to stay. In *Folk Psychology and the Philosophy of Mind*, ed. S. Christensen & D. Turner. Hillsdale, NJ: Lawrence Erlbaum Associates, pp. 144–166.

HOROWITZ, M. (1976), Two classes of concomitant change in a psychotherapy. Presented to conference on "Communicative Structures and Psychic Structures." Brooklyn, NY: Downstate Medical Center, Jan. 15–17.

—— (1977), The quantitative line of approach in psychoanalysis: a clinical assessment of its current status. *J. Amer. Psychoanal. Assn.*, 25:559–580.

—— (1987), *States of Mind: Configurational Analysis of Individual Psychotherapy*. Northvale, NJ: Aronson.

—— ed. (1988), *Psychodynamics and Cognition*. Chicago: University of Chicago Press.

—— (1989), Relationship schema formulation. *Psychiatry*, 52:260–274.

—— ed. (1991a), *Person Schemas and Maladaptive Interpersonal Patterns*. Chicago: University of Chicago Press.

—— (1991b), Converging several methods for inferring person schemas. In

Person Schemas and Maladaptive Interpersonal Patterns, ed. M. Horowitz. Chicago: University of Chicago Press, pp. 303–310.

——— (1993), Defensive control of states and person schemas. *J. Amer. Psychoanal. Assn.*, 41(Suppl.):67–90.

——— & ZILBERG, N. (1983), Regressive alterations in the self concept. *Amer. J. Psychiat.*, 140:284–289.

——— FRIDHANDLER, B. & STINSON, C. (1991), Person schemas and emotion. *J. Amer. Psychoanal. Assn.*, 39(Suppl.):173–208.

HORWITZ, L. (1963), Theory construction and validation in psychoanalysis. In *Theories in Contemporary Psychology*, ed. M. Marx. New York: Macmillan, pp. 413–434.

——— (1974), *Clinical Prediction in Psychotherapy*. New York: Aronson.

HOWARD, R. (1982), *Three Faces of Hermeneutics*. Berkeley: University of California Press.

HOWSON, C. & URBACH, P. (1989), *Scientific Reasoning: The Bayesian Approach*. LaSalle, IL: Open Court.

HULL, D. (1988), *Science as a Process*. Chicago: University of Chicago Press.

HUNT, M. (1982), *The Universe Within*. New York: Simon & Schuster.

HUNTER, K. (1991), *Doctors' Stories: The Narrative Structure of Medical Knowledge*. Princeton, NJ: Princeton University Press.

INDERBITZIN, L. & LEVY, S. (1994), On grist for the mill: external reality as defense. *J. Amer. Psychoanal. Assn.*, 42:763–788.

INHELDER, B. (1983), On generating procedures and structuring knowledge. In *Methods of Heuristics*, ed. R. Groner, M. Groner & W. Bischof. Hillsdale, NJ: Lawrence Erlbaum Associates, pp. 131–139.

ISAACS, K. & HAGGARD, E. (1966), Some methods used in the study of affect in psychotherapy. In *Methods of Research in Psychotherapy*, ed. L. Gottschalk & A. Auerbach. New York: Appleton-Century-Crofts, pp. 226–239.

ISAACS, S. (1939), Criteria for an interpretation. *Internat. J. Psycho-Anal.*, 20:148–160.

ISAKOWER, O. (1992a), Preliminary thoughts on the analyzing instrument. *J. Clin. Psychoanal.*, 1:184–194.

——— (1992b), The analyzing instrument: states of consciousness and the dream psychology of Dr. Bertram Lewin. *J. Clin. Psychoanal.*, 1:204–208.

ISER, W. (1978), *The Act of Reading*. Baltimore, MD: Johns Hopkins University Press.

IZENBERG, G. (1976), *The Existential Critique of Freud*. Princeton, NJ: Princeton University Press.

JACOBS, T. (1973), Posture, gesture and movement in the analyst: cues to interpretation and countertransference. *J. Amer. Psychoanal. Assn.*, 21:77–92.

——— (1994), Nonverbal communication: some reflections on their role in the psychoanalytic process and psychoanalytic education. *J. Amer. Psychoanal. Assn.*, 42:741–762.

JACOBSON, A. & PARMELEE, D., eds. (1982), *Psychoanalysis: Critical Explorations in Contemporary Theory and Practice.* New York: Brunner/Mazel.

JACOBSON, E. (1964), *The Self and the Object World.* New York: International Universities Press.

JANIS, I. (1958), The psychoanalytic interview as an observational method. In *Assessment of Human Motives*, ed. G. Lindzey. New York: Grove Press, pp. 149–181.

JASPERS, K. (1974), Causal and "meaningful" connections between life history and psychosis. In *Themes and Variations in European Psychiatry*, ed. S. Hirsch & M. Shephers. Charlottesville: University of Virginia Press, pp. 80–93.

JEFFEREY, R. (1983), Bayesianism with a human face. In *Testing Scientific Theories*, ed. J. Earman. Minneapolis: University of Minnesota Press, pp. 133–156.

JELALIAN, E. & MILLER, A. (1984), The perseverance of beliefs: conceptual perspectives and research developments. *J. Soc. Clin. Psychol.*, 2:25–56.

JOHANSEN, J. (1986), Strategies of understanding. *Psychoanal. Contemp. Thought*, 9:497–561.

JOHNSON, F. (1988), Transference-interpretation, semiotics, and psychotherapeutic change: some observations on subjective dealienation. *Psychoanal. Contemp. Thought*, 11:57–116.

JOHNSON-LAIRD, P. (1983), *Mental Models.* Cambridge, UK: Cambridge University Press.

JONES, A. (1997), Experiencing language: some thoughts on poetry and psychoanalysis. *Psychoanal. Quart.*, 66:683–706.

JONES, E. (1953), *The Life and Work of Sigmund Freud, Vol. 1.* New York: Basic Books.

——— (1955), *The Life and Work of Sigmund Freud, Vol. 2.* New York: Basic Books.

JONES, EDWARD (1986), Interpreting interpersonal behavior: the effects of expectancies. *Science*, 234:41–46.

——— & NISBETT, R. (1971), *The Actor and the Observer.* New York: General Learning Press.

JONES, ENRICO (1993a), How will psychoanalysis study itself? *J. Amer. Psychoanal. Assn.*, 41(Suppl.):91–108.

——— & WINDHOLZ, M. (1990), The psychoanalytic case study: toward a method of systematic inquiry. *J. Amer. Psychoanal. Assn.*, 38: 985–1015.

——— GHANNAM, J., NIGG, J. & DYER, J. (1993b), A paradigm for single-case research: the time-series study of a long-term psychotherapy for depression. *J. Clin. Consult. Psychol.*, 61:381–394.

JORDAN, J., HARVEY, J. & WEARY, G. (1988), Attributional biases in clinical decision making. In *Reasoning, Inference and Judgment in Clinical Psychology*, ed. D. Turk & P. Salovey. New York: Free Press, pp. 90–106.

JOSEPH, B. (1989), *Psychic Equilibrium and Psychic Change*, ed. M. Feldman & E. Spillius. London: Routledge.

JOSEPHSON, J. & JOSEPHSON, S. (1994), *Abductive Inference*. New York: Cambridge University Press.

JUNKER, H. (1991), *Von Freud in den Freudianern*. Tübingen, Germany: Edition Diskord.

KÄCHELE, H. (1986), Validating psychoanalysis: what methods for what task? In Précis of *The Foundations of Psychoanalysis*, by Adolf Grünbaum (1984), with open peer commentary. *Behav. Brain Sci.*, 9:244–245.

—— (1988), Clinical and scientific aspects of the Ulm process model of psychoanalysis. *Internat. J. Psycho-Anal.*, 69:65–71.

—— (1992), Narration and observation in psychotherapy research. *Psychother. Research*, 2:1–15.

KAHNEMAN, D., SLOVIC, P. & TVERSKY, A., eds. (1982a), *Judgment under Uncertainty*. New York: Cambridge University Press.

—— & TVERSKY, A. (1982), The simulation heuristic. In *Judgment Under Uncertainty*, ed. D. Kahneman, P. Slovik & A. Tversky. New York: Cambridge University Press, pp. 201–208.

KAPLAN, A. (1964), *The Conduct of Inquiry*. New York: Crowell.

KAPLAN, A. H. (1981), From discovery to validation: a basic challenge to psychoanalysis. *J. Amer. Psychoanal. Assn.*, 29:3–26.

KAZDIN, E. (1981), Drawing valid inferences from case studies. *J. Consult. Clin. Psychol.*, 49:183–192.

—— (1982), *Single-Case Research Designs*. New York: Oxford University Press.

KELLY, G. (1955), *The Psychology of Personal Constructs*. New York: W.W. Norton.

KELMAN, H. (1975), The "day precipitate" of dreams: the Morris hypothesis. *Internat. J. Psycho-Anal.*, 56:209–218.

KENT, T. (1991), Hermeneutics and genre: Bakhtin and the problem of communicative interaction. In *The Interpretive Turn*, ed. D. Hiley, J. Bohman & R. Shusterman. Ithaca, NY: Cornell University Press, pp. 282–303.

KERMODE, F. (1979), *The Genesis of Secrecy*. Cambridge, MA: Harvard University Press.

—— (1985), Freud and interpretation. *Internat. Rev. Psycho-Anal.*, 12:3–12.

KERN, J. (1978), Countertransference and spontaneous screens: an analyst studies his own visual images. *J. Amer. Psychoanal. Assn.*, 26:21–47.

KERNBERG, O. (1976), *Object-relations Theory and Clinical Psychoanalysis*. New York: Aronson.

—— (1980), *Internal World and External Reality*. New York: Aronson.

——— (1994), Validation in the clinical process. *Internat. J. Psycho-Anal.*, 75:1193–1200.

——— BURSTEIN, E., COYNE, L., APPELBAUM, A., HORWITZ, L. & VOTH, H. (1972), Psychotherapy and psychoanalysis: final report of the Menninger Foundation's Psychotherapy Research Project. *Bull Menn. Clin.*, 36:3–275.

KETTNER, M. (1991), Peirce's notion of abduction and psychoanalytic interpretation. In *Semiotic Perspectives on Clinical Theory and Practice*, ed. B. Litowitz & P. Epstein. Berlin: Mouton, pp. 163–179.

KEYNES, J. (1962), *A Treatise on Probability*. New York: Torchback.

KIESLER, D. (1966), Some myths of psychotherapy research and the search for a paradigm. *Psychol. Bull.*, 65:110–136.

——— (1973), *The Process of Psychotherapy: Empirical Foundations and Systems of Analysis*. Hawthorne, NY: Aldine.

——— MATHIE, P. & KLEIN, M. (1964), Sampling from the recorded therapy interview: a comparative study of different segment lengths. *J. Consult. Psychol.*, 28:349–357.

KIHLSTROM, J. (1987), The cognitive unconscious. *Science*, 237:1445–1452.

——— & CUNNINGHAM, R. (1991), Mapping interpersonal space. In *Person Schemas and Maladaptive Interpersonal Patterns*, ed. M. Horowitz. Chicago: University of Chicago Press, pp. 11–36.

KILLINGMO, B. (1990), Beyond semantics: a clinical and theoretical study of isolation. *Internat. J. Psycho-Anal.*, 71:113–126.

KIM, J. (1988), What is "naturalized epistemology?" *Philos. Perspect.*, 2:381–405.

KIRK, T. & MILLER, M. (1986), *Reliability and Validity in Qualitative Research*. Newbury Park, CA: Sage.

KLAUBER, J. (1968), On the dual use of historical and scientific method in psychoanalysis. *Internat. J. Psycho-Anal.*, 49:80–88.

——— (1980), Formulating interpretations in clinical psychoanalysis. *Internat. J. Psycho-Anal.*, 61:195–201.

KLEIN, G. (1976), *Psychoanalytic Theory: An Exploration of Essentials*. New York: International Universities Press.

KLEIN, M. (1958), *Contributions to Psychoanalysis*. London: Hogarth Press.

——— (1975, 1992, 1993), *The Writings of Melanie Klein, Vols. 1–4*, ed. R. Money-Kyrle. London: Karnac Books.

KLEIN, MILTON & TRIBICH, D. (1981), Kernberg's object-relations theory: a critical evaluation. *Internat. J. Psycho-Anal.*, 62:27–43.

KLERMAN, G. (1982), Testing analytic hypotheses: do personality attributes predispose to depression? In *Psychoanalysis: Critical Explorations in Contemporary Theory and Practice*, ed. A. Jacobson & D. Parmelee. New York: Brunner/Mazel, pp. 56–73.

——— (1986), The scientific tasks confronting psychoanalysis. *Behav. Brain Sci.*, 9:245.

KLIMOVSKY, G. (1991), Epistemological aspects of psychoanalytic interpretation. In *The Fundamentals of Psychoanalytic Technique*, by R. Etchegoyen. London: Karnac Books, pp. 471–493.

KLINE, P. (1972), *Fact and Fancy in Freudian Theory*. London: Methuen.

——— (1986), Grünbaum's philosophical critique of psychoanalysis: or what I don't know isn't knowledge. *Behav. Brain Sci.*, 9:245–246.

——— (1988), Freudian theory and experimental evidence: a reply to Erwin. In *Mind, Psychoanalysis, and Science*, ed. P. Clark & C. Wright. Oxford, UK: Basil Blackwell, pp. 225–232.

KLUMPNER, G. (1989), Interview with Chairman, Committee on Scientific Activities. American Psychoanalytic Association. *Amer. Psychoanal.*, 22:13.

KNAPP, P. (1963), Short-term psychoanalytic and psychosomatic predictions. *J. Amer. Psychoanal. Assn.*, 11:245–280.

——— (1981), Core processes in the organization of emotions. *J. Amer. Acad. Psychoanal.*, 9:415–434.

——— (1988), Steps toward a lexicon: discussion of "Unconsciously Determined Defense Strategies." In *Psychodynamics and Cognition*, ed. M. Horowitz. Chicago: University of Chicago Press, pp. 95–114.

——— (1991), Self-other schemas: core organizers of human experience. In *Person Schemas and Maladaptive Interpersonal Relations*, ed. M. Horowitz. Chicago: University of Chicago Press, pp. 81–102.

KNORR-CETINA, K. (1981), *The Manufacture of Knowledge*. New York: Pergamon.

——— (1984), The fabrication of facts: toward a microsociology of scientific knowledge. In *The Sociology of Knowledge*, ed. N. Stehr & V. Meja. New Brunswick, NJ: Transaction Books, pp. 223–244.

——— (1993), Comments on the sociology of science. In *Taking the Naturalistic Turn or How Real Philosophy of Science Is Done*, ed. W. Callebaut. Chicago: University of Chicago Press, p. 180.

KOCKELMANS, J. (1975), Toward an interpretive or hermeneutic social science. *Graduate Faculty Philosophy Journal: New School for Social Research*, 5:73–96.

KOFFKA, K. (1935), *Principles of Gestalt Psychology*. New York: Harcourt, Brace.

KOHLER, W. (1970), *Gestalt Psychology*. London: Liveright.

KOHUT, H. (1959), Introspection, empathy, and psychoanalysis: an examination of the relationship between mode of observation and theory. *J. Amer. Psychoanal. Assn.*, 7:459–483.

——— (1984), *How Does Analysis Cure?* ed. A. Goldberg & P. Stepansky. Chicago: University of Chicago Press.

——— & SEITZ, P. (1963), Concepts and theories of psychoanalysis. In *Concepts of Personality*, ed. J. Wepman & R. Heine. Chicago: Aldine, pp. 113–141.

KORDIG, C. (1971a), The theory-ladenness of observation. *Rev. Metaphys.*, 24:448–484.

——— (1971b), The compatibility of scientific theories. *Philos. Sci.*, 38:467–485.

——— (1971c), *The Justification of Scientific Change*. Dordrecht: D. Reidel.

——— (1973), Discussion: observational invariance. *Philos. Sci.*, 40:558–569.

KORNBLITH, H. (1993a), *Naturalizing Epistemology*. Cambridge, MA: MIT Press.

——— (1993b), *Inductive Inference and Its Natural Ground*. Cambridge, MA: MIT/Bradford.

KOSSLYN, S. (1980), *Image and Mind*. Cambridge, MA: Harvard University Press.

KRAMER, M. (1959), On the continuation of the analytic process after psychoanalysis (a self observation). *Internat. J. Psycho-Anal.*, 40:17–25.

KRAMER, P. (1989), *Moments of Engagement*. New York: Norton.

KRATOCHWILL, T., ed. (1978), *Single-Subject Research: Strategies for Evaluating Change*. New York: Academic Press.

——— MOTT, S. & DODSON, C. (1984), Case study and single-case research in clinical and applied psychology. In *Research Methods in Clinical Psychology*, ed. A. Bellack & M. Hersen. New York: Pergamon, pp. 55–99.

——— & LEVIN, J., eds. (1992), *Single-Case Research Design and Analysis*. Hillsdale, NJ: Lawrence Erlbaum Associates.

KRIEGER, R. (1988), *Words about Words about Words*: Baltimore, MD: Johns Hopkins University Press.

KRIS, A. (1994), Freud's treatment of a narcissistic patient. *Internat. J. Psycho-Anal.*, 75:649–664.

KRIS, E. (1947), The nature of psychoanalytic propositions and their validation. In *Freedom and Experience*, ed. S. Hook & M. Konwitz. Ithaca, NY: Cornell University Press, pp. 239–259. Also in *Selected Papers of Ernst Kris*. New Haven, CT: Yale University Press, 1975, pp. 3–23.

——— (1950), On preconscious mental processes. *Psychoanal. Quart.*, 19:540–560. Also in *Selected Papers of Ernst Kris*. New Haven, CT: Yale University Press, 1975, pp. 217–236.

——— (1951), Ego psychology and interpretation in psychoanalytic therapy. *Psychoanal. Quart.*, 20:15–30. Also in *Selected Papers of Ernst Kris*. New Haven, CT: Yale University Press, 1975, pp. 237–251.

——— (1953), Validation of psychoanalytic propositions. In *Readings in Philosophy of Science*, ed. P. Wiener. New York: Scribners, pp. 236–257.

——— (1956a), On some vicissitudes of insight in psychoanalysis. *Internat. J. Psycho-Anal.*, 37:445–455. Also in *Selected Papers of Ernst Kris*. New Haven, CT: Yale University Press, 1975, pp. 252–271.

——— (1956b), The recovery of childhood memories in psychoanalysis. *The Psychoanalytic Study of the Child*, 11:54–88. New York: International Universities Press. Also in *Selected Papers of Ernst Kris*. New Haven, CT: Yale University Press, 1975, pp. 301–340.

KRISTEVA, J. (1983), Psychoanalysis and polis. In *The Politics of Interpretation*, ed. W. Mitchell. Chicago: University of Chicago Press, pp. 83–98.

KUBIE, L. (1952), Problems and techniques of psychoanalytic validation and progress. In *Psychoanalysis as Science*, ed. E. Hilgard, L. Kubie & E. Pumpian-Mindlin. Stanford, CA: Stanford University Press, pp. 46–124.

—— (1975), The language tools of psychoanalysis: a search for better tools drawn from better models. *Internat. Rev. Psycho-Anal.*, 2:11–24.

KUHN, T. (1962), *The Structure of Scientific Revolutions*. Chicago: University of Chicago Press.

KUKLA, A. (1989), Nonempirical issues in psychology. *Amer. Psychol.*, 44:785–794.

KUMIN, I. (1989), The incorrect interpretation. *Internat. J. Psycho-Anal.*, 70:141–152.

KUPER, A. (1979), A structural approach to dreams. *Man*, 14:645–662.

—— (1986), Structural anthropology and the psychology of dreams. *J. Mind Behav.*, 7:333–344.

—— & STONE, A. (1982), The dream of Irma's injection: a structural analysis. *Amer. J. Psychiat.*, 139:1225–1234.

KURZWEIL, E. (1978), Structuralist psychoanalysis: review of *Écrits: A Selection*, by Jacques Lacan. *Partisan Rev.*, 45:642–646.

—— (1980), *The Age of Structuralism*. New York: Columbia University Press.

—— & PHILLIPS, W., eds. (1983), *Literature and Psychoanalysis*. New York: Columbia University Press.

LABOV, W. (1972a), Some principles of linguistic methodology. *Language in Society*, 1:97–119.

—— (1972b) *Sociolinguistic Patterns*. Philadelphia: University of Pennsylvania Press.

—— ed. (1980), Introduction. In *Locating Language in Time and Space*. New York: Academic Press, pp. i–xx.

—— & FANSHEL, D. (1977), *Therapeutic Discourse: Psychotherapy as Conversation*. New York: Academic Press.

LACAN, J. (1956), *Language of the Self*, trans. A. Wilden. Baltimore, MD: Johns Hopkins University Press.

—— (1966), *Écrits, A Selection*, trans. A. Sheridan. New York: Norton, 1977.

—— (1970), The insistence of the letter in the unconscious, trans. J. Miel. In *Structuralism*, ed. J. Ehrmann. Garden City, NY: Doubleday/Anchor, pp. 101–137.

—— (1972), On structure as an inmixing of an otherness prerequisite to any subject whatsoever. In *The Structuralist Controversy*, ed. R. Macksey & E. Donato. Baltimore, MD: Johns Hopkins University Press, pp. 186–200.

—— (1978), *The Four Fundamental Concepts of Psychoanalysis*, trans. A. Sheridan. New York: Norton.

—— (1988a), *The Seminar of Jacques Lacan, Book 1: Freud's Papers on Technique, 1953–1954*, trans. J. Forrester. New York: Norton.

—— (1988b), *The Seminar of Jacques Lacan, Book 2: The Ego in Freud's*

Theory and in the Technique of Psychoanalysis, 1954-1955, trans. S. Tomaselli. New York: Norton.

——— (1993), *The Seminar of Jacques Lacan: Book 3. The Psychoses, 1955-1956*, ed. J.-A. Miller (trans. R. Grigg). New York: Norton.

LACEY, A. (1986), *A Dictionary of Philosophy*. London: Routledge (pbk, 1990).

LAFFAL, J. (1964), Freud's theory of language. *Psychoanal. Quart.*, 33:157–175.

——— (1965), *Pathological and Normal Language*. New York: Atherton.

——— (1976), Schreber's memories and content analysis. *J. Nerv. Ment. Dis.*, 162:385–390.

——— (1990), *A Concept Dictionary of English with Computer Programs for Content Analysis*. Essex, CT: Gallery Press (with two diskettes).

LAKATOS, I. (1978), Falsification and the methodology of scientific research programmes. In *The Methodology of Scientific Research Programmes*. Cambridge, UK: Cambridge University Press, pp. 8–101.

LAMM, L. (1993), *The Idea of the Past: History, Science, and Practice in American Psychoanalysis*. New York: New York University Press.

——— (1995), Review of *Psychoanalysis as a Science*, by L. Bellak & J. Walkup (1993). *Psychoanal. Bks.*, 6:440–444.

LANGER, S. (1948), *Philosophy in a New Key: A Study in the Symbolism of Reason, Rite, and Art*. New York: Mentor.

LANGS, R. (1978), Validation and the framework of the therapeutic situation: thoughts prompted by Hans H. Strupp's "Suffering and Psychotherapy." *Contemp. Psychoanal.*, 14:98–124.

LAOR, N. (1985), Psychoanalysis as science: the inductivist's resistance revisited. *J. Amer. Psychoanal. Assn.*, 33:149–166.

——— & AGASSI, J. (1986), The scientific status of psychoanalysis: Lacan contra Freud. *Psychoanal. Contemp. Thought*, 9:465–492.

LAPLANCHE, J. & PONTALIS, J.-B. (1973), *The Language of Psychoanalysis*, trans. D. Nicholson-Smith. New York: Norton.

LARRABEE, H. (1964), *Reliable Knowledge*. Boston, MA: Houghton Mifflin.

LASZLO, E. (1962) *Introduction to Systems Philosophy*. New York: Gordon & Breach.

LAZARSFELD, P. & BARTON, A. (1951), Qualitative measurement in the social sciences: classification, typologies, and indices. In *The Policy Sciences*, ed. D. Lerner & H. Lasswell. Stanford, CA: Stanford University Press, pp. 145–165.

LEAFFER, T. (1982), Applications to psychoanalysis and psychotherapy. In *Linguistics and the Professions*, ed. R. DiPietro. Norwood, NJ: Ablex, pp. 13–25.

LEAR, J. (1995), The shrink is in. *The New Republic*, 213:18–25, Dec. 25.

LEARY, D., ed. (1990a), *Metaphors in the History of Psychology*. Cambridge, UK: Cambridge University Press.

——— (1990b), Psyche's muse. In *Metaphors in the History of Psychology*, ed.

D. Leary. Cambridge, UK: Cambridge University Press, pp. 1–78.

LEARY, K. (1989), Psychoanalytic process and narrative process. a critical consideration of Schafer's "narrational project." *Internat. Rev. Psycho-Anal.*, 16:179–190.

—— (1994), Psychoanalytic "problems" and postmodern "solutions." *Psychoanal. Quart.*, 63:433–465.

LEATHERDALE, W. (1974), *The Role of Analogy, Model and Metaphor in Science*. Amsterdam: North Holland.

LEAVY, S. (1973), Psychoanalytic interpretation. *The Psychoanalytic Study of the Child*, 28:305–330. New Haven, CT: Yale University Press.

—— (1977), The significance of Jacques Lacan. *Psychoanal. Quart.*, 46:201–219. Also in *Psychoanalysis and Language*, ed. J. Smith. New Haven, CT: Yale University Press, 1978, pp. 271–292.

—— (1979), Review of *Écrits*, by J. Lacan. *Psychoanal. Quart.*, 48:311–317.

—— (1980), *The Psychoanalytic Dialogue*. New Haven, CT: Yale University Press.

—— (1983a), The theme and the word: further reflections on Jacques Lacan. In *Interpreting Lacan*, ed. J. Smith. New Haven, CT: Yale University Press, pp. 3–20.

—— (1983b), Speaking in tongues: linguistic approaches to psychoanalysis. *Psychoanal. Quart.*, 52:34–55.

—— (1990), Lacan's words. *Psychoanal. Quart.*, 59:437–443.

—— (1996a), Review of *The Seminar of Jacques Lacan, Book 3: The Psychoses*, 1955–1956 (1993). *J. Amer. Psychoanal. Assn.*, 44:1269–1276.

—— (1996b) Review of *The Seminar of Jacques Lacan, Book 7: The Ethics of Psychoanalysis*, 1959–1960 (1992). *J. Amer. Psychoanal. Assn.*, 44:1276–1281.

LEECH, G. (1969), *A Linguistic Guide to English Poetry*. London: Longmans.

LEIBIN, V. (1986), Psychoanalysis: science or hermeneutics? *Behav. Brain Sci.*, 9:246–247.

LEON, I. (1992), The psychoanalytic conceptualization of perinatal loss: a multidimensional model. *Amer. J. Psychiat.*, 149:1464–1472.

LEUZINGER-BOHLEBER, M. & KÄCHELE, H. (1988), From Calvin to Freud: Using an artificial intelligence model to investigate cognitive changes during psychoanalysis. In *Psychoanalytic Process Research Strategies*, ed. H. Dahl, H. Kächele & H. Thomä. Berlin: Springer, pp. 291–305.

LEVENSON, E. (1972), *The Fallacy of Understanding*. New York: Basic Books.

—— (1988), The pursuit of the particular: on the psychoanalytic inquiry. *Contemp. Psychoanal.*, 24:1–16.

LEVIN, D. (1992), *Forms of Uncertainty*. Charlottesville: University Press of Virginia.

LEVIN, F. (1980), Metaphor, affect, and arousal; how interpretations might work. *The Annual of Psychoanalysis*, 9:231–249. Madison, CT: International Universities Press.

——— (1995), Notes on Psyche '94, International Symposium on Mind-Body Problems, Oct.6–7, 1994. *Psychoanal. Quart.*, 64:429–432.

LEVIN, K. (1978), *Freud's Early Psychology of the Neurosis*. Hassocks, UK: Harvester Press.

LEVINE, F. & LUBORSKY, L. (1981), The core conflictual relationship theme—a demonstration of reliable clinical inference by the method of mismatched cases. In *Object and Self*, ed. A. Tuttman, C. Kaye & M. Zimmerman. New York: International Universities Press, pp. 501–526.

LEVINE, H. (1994), The analyst's participation in the analytic process. *Internat. J. Psycho-Anal.*, 75:665–676.

LÉVI-STRAUSS, C. ([1958] 1967), *Structural Anthropology*, trans. C. Jacobson & B. Schoepf. Garden City, NY: Doubleday/Anchor, 1967.

——— (1964) *The Raw and the Cooked*, trans. J. & D. Weightman. New York: Harper & Row, 1969.

——— (1969) *The Elementary Structure of Kinship*, trans. J. Bell, J. Sturmer & R. Needham. Boston, MA: Beacon Press.

LEVY, D. (1983), Wittgenstein on the form of psychoanalytic interpretations. *Internat. Rev. Psycho-Anal.*, 10:105–109.

——— (1988), Grünbaum's Freud. *Inquiry*, 31:193–215.

——— (1996), *Freud Among the Philosophers*. New Haven, CT: Yale University Press.

LEVY, L. (1963), *Psychological Interpretation*. New York: Holt, Rinehart & Winston.

LEVY, S. (1984), *Principles of Interpretation*. New York: Aronson.

LEWIN, K. (1935), *A Dynamic Theory of Personality*. New York: McGraw-Hill.

——— (1951), *Field Theory in Social Science*. New York: Harper.

LEWONTIN, R. (1994), Facts and factitious in natural sciences. In *Questions of Evidence*, ed. J. Chandler, A. Davidson & H. Harootunian. Chicago: University of Chicago Press, pp. 478–491.

LICHTENBERG, J. (1981), The empathic mode of perception and alternative vantage points for psychoanalytic work. *Psychoanal. Inq.*, 1:329–355.

——— (1983), *Psychoanalysis and Infant Research*. Hillsdale, NJ: The Analytic Press.

LIEBERMAN, P. (1965), On the acoustic basis of the perception of intonation by linguists. *Word*, 21:40–54.

LINDLEY, D. (1965), *Introduction to Probability and Statistics from a Bayesian Viewpoint, 2. Inference*. London: Cambridge University Press.

LIPTON, P. (1991), *Inference to the Best Explanation*. London: Routledge.

LIPTON, S. (1958), A note on the connection between preliminary communications and subsequently reported dreams. *J. Amer. Psychoanal. Assn.*, 6:237–241.

LITOWITZ, B. (1978), On overdetermination. In *Psychoanalysis and Language*, ed. J. Smith. New Haven, CT: Yale University Press, pp. 355–394.

——— & EPSTEIN, P., eds. (1991), *Semiotic Perspectives on Clinical Theory and Practice*. New York: Mouton de Gruyter.

——— & LITOWITZ, N. (1977), The influence of linguistic theory on psychoanalysis: a critical, historical survey. *Internat. Rev. Psycho-Anal.*, 4:419–448.

LITTLE, K. (1959), Problems in the validation of projective techniques. *J. Proj. Tech.*, 23:287–290.

——— & SHNEIDMAN, E. (1959), Congruencies among interpretations of psychological test and anamnestic data. *Psychol. Monogr.*, 73:1–42.

LLOYD, D. (1989), *Simple Minds*. Cambridge, MA: MIT/Bradford.

LOAR, B. (1981), *Mind and Meaning*. Cambridge, UK: Cambridge University Press.

LOCH, W. (1977), Some comments on the subject of psychoanalysis and truth. In *Thought, Consciousness, and Reality*, ed. J. Smith. New Haven, CT: Yale University Press, pp. 217–225.

LOEB, F. & CARROLL, E. (1966), General systems theory and psychoanalysis: II. Application to psychoanalytic case material (Little Hans). *Psychoanal. Quart.*, 35:388–398.

LOEVINGER, J. (1965), Measurement in clinical research. In *Handbook of Clinical Psychology*, ed. B. Wolman. New York: McGraw-Hill, pp. 78–94.

LOEWALD, H. (1960), On the therapeutic action of psychoanalysis. *Internat. J. Psychoanal.*, 41:16–33. Also in *Papers on Psychoanalysis*. New Haven, CT: Yale University Press, 1980, pp. 221–256.

——— (1971a), Some considerations on repetition and repetition compulsion. *Internat. J. Psycho-Anal.*, 52:59–66. Also in *Papers on Psychoanalysis*. New Haven, CT: Yale University Press, 1980, pp. 87–101.

——— (1971b), On motivation and instinct theory. *The Psychoanalytic Study of the Child*, 26:91–128. New Haven, CT: Yale University Press. Also in *Papers on Psychoanalysis*. New Haven, CT: Yale University Press, 1980, pp. 102–137.

LOEWENSTEIN, E. (1991), Psychoanalytic life history: is coherence, continuity, and aesthetic appeal necessary? *Psychoanal. Contemp. Thought*, 14:3–28.

LOEWENSTEIN, R. (1951a), The problem of interpretation. *Psychoanal. Quart.*, 20:1–14.

——— (1951b), Ego development and psychoanalytic technique. *Amer. J. Psychiat.*, 107:617–622.

——— (1956), Some remarks on the role of speech in psychoanalytic technique. *Internat. J. Psycho-Anal.*, 37:460–467.

——— (1957), Some thoughts on interpretation in the theory and practice of psychoanalysis. *The Psychoanalytic Study of the Child*, 12:127–150. New York: International Universities Press. Also in *Psychoanalytic Clinical Interpretation*, ed. L. Paul. London: Free Press of Glencoe (Macmillan), 1963, pp. 162–188.

——— (1968), Discussion of "Short-term effects as indications of the role of interpretation in psychoanalysis," by James Naiman. *Internat. J. Psycho-Anal.*, 49:356–357.

LOLAS, F., MERGENTHALER, E. & VON RAD, M. (1982), Content analysis of verbal behavior in psychotherapy research: a comparison between two methods. *Brit. J. Med. Psychol.*, 55:327–333.

LOMAS, P. (1987), *The Limits of Interpretation.* Northvale, NJ: Aronson.

LOSSY, F. (1962), The charge of suggestion as a resistance in psychoanalysis. *Internat. J. Psycho-Anal.*, 43:408–467.

LOTHANE, Z. (1985), Robert Langs: The communicative approach. In *Beyond Freud: A Study of Modern Psychoanalytic Theorists*, ed. J. Reppen. Hillsdale, NJ: Lawrence Erlbaum Associates, pp. 175–201.

LUBORSKY, L. (1977), Measuring a pervasive psychic structure in psychotherapy. In *Communicative Structures and Psychic Structures*, ed. N. Freedman & S. Grand. New York: Plenum, pp. 367–395.

——— (1984), *Principles of Psychoanalytic Psychotherapy: A Manual for Supportive-Expressive Treatment.* New York: Basic Books.

——— (1986), Evidence to lessen Professor Grünbaum's concern about Freud's clinical inference method. *Behav. Brain Sci.*, 9:247–249.

——— & MINTZ, J. (1975), What sets off momentary forgetting during a psychoanalysis? *Psychoanal. Contemp. Sci.*, 3:233–268.

——— & SPENCE, D. (1978), Quantitative research on psychoanalytic psychotherapy. In *Handbook of Psychotherapy and Behavior Change*, ed. S. Garfield & A. Bergin. New York: Wiley, pp. 331–368.

——— MINTZ, J., AUERBACH, A., CRITS-CHRISTOPH, P., BACHRACH, H., TODD, T., JOHNSON, M., COHEN, M. & O'BRIEN, C. (1980), Predicting the outcome of psychotherapy: findings of the Penn Psychotherapy project. *Arch. Gen. Psychiat.*, 37:471–481.

——— MELLON, J., VAN RAVENSWAAY, P., CHILDRESS, A., COHEN, K., HOLE, A., MING, S., CRITS-CHRISTOPH, P., LEVINE, F. & ALEXANDER, K. (1985), A verification of Freud's grandest clinical hypothesis: the transference. *Clin. Psychol. Rev.*, 5:231–246.

——— & CRITS-CHRISTOPH, P. (1988), Measures of psychoanalytic concepts—the last decade of research from "the Penn studies." *Internat. J. Psycho-Anal.*, 69:75–86.

——— & ——— (1990), *Understanding Transference: The Core Conflictual Relationship Theme Method.* New York: Basic Books.

——— & LUBORSKY, E. (1993), The era of measures of transference: the CCRT and other measures. In *Research in Psychoanalysis: Process, Development, Outcome*, ed. T. Shapiro & R. Emde. *J. Amer. Psychoanal. Assn.*, 41(Suppl.):329–351.

LUEGER, R. & PETZEL, T. (1979), Illusory correlation in clinical judgment: effects of amount of information to be processed. *J. Consult. Clin. Psychol.*, 47:1120–1121.

LYONS, W. (1995), *Approaches to Intentionality*. New York: Oxford University Press.

MACKAY, N. (1989), *Motivation and Explanation: An Essay on Freud's Philosophy of Science*. Madison, CT: International Universities Press.

MACMILLAN, M. (1991), Psychoanalysis as method. In *Freud Evaluated: The Completed Arc*. Amsterdam: North-Holland, pp. 549–576.

MAHL, G. (1956), Disturbances and silences in the patient's speech in psychotherapy. *J. Abn. Soc. Psychol.*, 53:1–15.

—— (1959), Measuring the patient's anxiety during interviews from "expressive" aspects of his speech. *Trans. New York Acad. Sci.*, 21:249–257.

—— (1961), Measures of two expressive aspects of a patient's speech in two psychotherapeutic interviews. In *Comparative Psycholinguistic Analysis of Two Psychotherapeutic Interviews*, ed. L. Gottschalk. New York: International Universities Press, pp. 91–114.

—— (1987a), *Explorations in Nonverbal and Vocal Behavior*. Hillsdale, NJ: Lawrence Erlbaum Associates.

—— (1987b), Everyday disturbances of speech. In *Language in Psychotherapy*, ed. R. Russell. New York: Plenum, pp. 213–230.

—— & SCHULZE, G. (1964), Psychological research in the extralinguistic area. In *Approaches to Semiotics*, ed. T. Sebeok, A. Hayes & M. Bateson. The Hague: Mouton, pp. 51–124.

MAHONEY, M. & DE MONBREUN, B. (1977), Psychology and the scientist: an analysis of problem-solving bias. *Cogn. Ther. Res.*, 1:229–238.

MAHONY, P. (1982), *Freud as a Writer*. New York: International Universities Press.

—— (1984), *Cries of the Wolf Man*. New York: International Universities Press.

—— (1986), *Freud and the Rat Man*. New Haven, CT: Yale University Press.

—— (1989), *On Defining Freud's Discourse*. New Haven, CT: Yale University Press.

—— & SINGH, R. (1975), *The Interpretation of Dreams*, semiology, and Chomskian liguistics: a radical critique. *The Psychoanalytic Study of the Child*, 30:221–241. New Haven, CT: Yale University Press.

—— & —— (1979), Some issues in linguistics and psychoanalysis: reflections on Marshall Edelson's *Language and Interpretation in Psychoanalysis*. *Psychoanal. Contemp. Thought*, 2:437–446.

MAHRER, A. (1988), Discovery-oriented psychotherapy research: rationale, aims, and methods. *Amer. Psychol.*, 43:694–702.

MAIN, M. (1993), Discourse, prediction, and recent studies in attachment: implications for psychoanalysis. *J. Amer. Psychoanal. Assn.*, 41(Suppl.): 209–244.

MAKARI, G. & SHAPIRO, T. (1993), On psychoanalytic listening: language and unconscious communication. *J. Amer. Psychoanal. Assn.*, 41:991–1020.

MALAN, D. (1963), *A Study of Brief Psychotherapy*. London: Tavistock.
——— (1976), *Toward the Validation of Dynamic Psychotherapy*. New York: Plenum.
——— (1979), *Individual Psychotherapy and the Science of Psychodynamics*. London: Butterworths.
MALCOLM, J. (1987), Reflections: *J'appele un chat un chat. The New Yorker*, 20:84–107 (April).
MALMQUIST, C. (1963), Problems of methodology and theory construction in psychoanalysis. *Psychoanal. Rev.*, 50:3–23.
MALTSBERGER, J. & BUIE, D. (1974), Countertransference hate in the treatment of suicidal patients. *Arch. Gen. Psychiat.*, 30:625–633.
——— & ——— (1980), The devices of suicide: revenge, riddance and rebirth. *Internat. Rev. Psycho-Anal.*, 7:61–72.
MANCUSO, J. (1986), The acquisition and use of narrative grammar structure. In *Narrative Psychology: The Storied Nature of Human Conduct*, ed. T. Sarbin. New York: Praeger, pp. 91–110.
——— & ADAMS-WEBBER, J., eds. (1982), *The Construing Person*. New York: Praeger.
MANDLER, C. (1988), Problems and directions in the study of consciousness. In *Psychodynamics and Cognition*, ed. M. Horowitz. Chicago: University of Chicago Press, pp. 21–47.
MANICAS, P. & SECORD, P. (1983), Implications for psychology of the new philosophy of science. *Amer. Psychologist*, 38:399–413.
MAQUET, J. (1964), Objectivity in anthropology. *Current Anthropol.*, 5:47–55.
MARANHÃO, T. (1990), Psychoanalysis: science or rhetoric? In *The Rhetorical Turn*, ed. H. Simons. Chicago: University of Chicago Press, pp. 116–144.
MARCEL, A. (1983), Conscious and unconscious perception: an approach to the relations between phenomenal experience and perceptual processes. *Cogn. Psychol.*, 15:238–300.
MARCUS, S. (1974), Freud and Dora. *Partisan Rev.*, 41:12–23, 89–108.
——— (1976), Freud and Dora: story, history, case history. *Psychoanal. Contemp. Sci.*, 5:389–442.
——— (1984), *Freud and the Culture of Psychoanalysis*. Boston, MA: George Allen & Unwin.
MARCUSE, H. (1955), *Eros and Civilization*. Boston, MA: Beacon Press.
MARGOLIS, H. (1987), *Patterns, Thinking, and Cognition*. Chicago: University of Chicago Press.
——— (1993), *Paradigms and Barriers*. Chicago: University of Chicago Press.
MARGOLIS, J. (1990), Reconciling realism and relativism. In *The Rhetorical Turn*, ed. H. Simons. Chicago: University of Chicago Press, pp. 308–319.
MARGULIES, A. (1989), *The Empathic Imagination*. New York: Norton.
MARKS, L. (1992), Freud and Fechner, desire and energy, hermeneutics and psychophysics. In *Cognition, Information Processing, and Psychophysics*, ed. H.-G. Geissler, S. Link & J. Townsend. Hillsdale, NJ: Lawrence Erlbaum Associates, pp. 23–42.

MARKUS, H. (1977), Self-schemas and processing information about the self. *J. Pers. Soc. Psychol.*, 35:63–78.

MARMOR, J. (1962), Psychoanalytic therapy as an educational device. In *Psychoanalytic Education*, ed. J. Masserman. New York: Grune & Stratton, pp. 286–299.

—— (1970), Limitations of free association. *Arch. Gen. Psychiat.*, 22:160–165.

MARSDEN, G. (1965), Content-analysis studies of therapeutic interviews: 1954 to 1964. *Psychol. Bull.*, 63:298–321.

—— (1971), Content-analysis studies of psychotherapy: 1954 through 1968. In *Handbook of Psychotherapy and Behavior Change*, ed. A. Bergin & S. Garfield. New York: Wiley, pp. 345–407.

MARSHALL, J. (1974), Freud's psychology of language. In *Freud: A Collection of Critical Essays*, ed. R. Wollheim. New York: Doubleday/Anchor, pp. 349–365.

MARTIN, M. (1994), Taylor on interpretation and the sciences of man. In *Readings in the Philosophy of Social Science*, ed. M. Martin & L. McIntyre. Cambridge, MA: MIT Press, pp. 259–279.

—— & MCINTYRE, L., eds. (1994), *Readings in the Philosophy of Social Science*. Cambridge, MA: MIT Press.

MARTIN, W. (1986), *Recent Theories of Narrative*. Ithaca, NY: Cornell University Press.

MARTINDALE, C. (1975), The grammar of altered states of consciousness: a semiotic reinterpretation of aspects of psychoanalytic theory. *Psychoanal. Contemp. Thought*, 1:331–354.

MARZIALI, E. (1984), Prediction of outcome of brief psychotherapy from therapist interpretive interventions. *Arch. Gen. Psychiat.*, 41:301–304.

MASLING, J., ed. (1986), *Empirical Studies of Psychoanalytic Theories, Vols. 1 & 2*. Hillsdale, NJ: The Analytic Press.

MASSICOTTE, W. (1995), The surprising philosophical complexity of psychoanalysis (belatedly acknowledged). *Psychoanal. Contemp. Thought*, 18:3–31.

MASSON, J., ed. (1985), *The Complete Letters of Sigmund Freud to Wilhelm Fliess, 1887–1904*. Cambridge, MA: Harvard University Press.

MAUTNER, B. (1994), Freud's "lost" dream and the schism with Wilhelm Fliess. *Internat. J. Psycho-Anal.*, 75:321–333.

MAYER, E. (1996), Changes in science and changing ideas about knowledge and authority in psychoanalysis. *Psychoanal. Quart.*, 65:158–200.

MCGINN, C. (1989), *Mental Content*. Oxford, UK: Basil Blackwell.

MCGRATH, W. (1986), *Freud's Discovery of Psychoanalysis*. Ithaca, NY: Cornell University Press.

MCINTOSH, D. (1979), The empirical bearing of psychoanalytic theory. *Internat. J. Psycho-Anal.*, 60:405–431.

—— (1993), Cathexes and their objects in the thought of Freud. *J. Amer. Psychoanal. Assn.*, 41:679–709.

MCINTYRE, A. (1958), *The Unconscious*. London: Routledge & Kegan Paul.

MCLAUGHLIN, J. (1988), The analyst's insights. *Psychoanal. Quart.*, 57:370–389.

MCNEILL, D. (1992), *Hand and Mind*. Chicago: University of Chicago Press.

MCQUOWN, N., ed. (1971), *The Natural History of an Interview*. Microfilm Collection of Manuscripts in Cultural Anthropology. Chicago: University of Chicago Library.

MEDAWAR, P. (1969), *Induction and Intuition in Scientific Thought*. Philadelphia: American Philosophy Society.

MEEHAN, E. (1968), *Explanation in Social Science: A System Paradigm*. Homewood, IL: Dorsey.

MEEHL, P. (1954), *Clinical vs. Statistical Prediction*. Minneapolis: University of Minnesota Press.

—— (1958), When shall we use our heads instead of the formula? In *Concepts, Theories, and the Mind-Body Problem. Minnesota Studies in the Philosophy of Science, Vol. 2*, ed. H. Feigl, M. Scriven & G. Maxwell. Minneapolis: University of Minnesota Press, pp. 498–506.

—— (1960), The cognitive activity of the clinician. *Amer. Psychologist*, 15:19–27.

—— (1970), Some methodological reflections on the difficulties of psychoanalytic research. In *Minnesota Studies in the Philosophy of Science, Vol. 4. Analyses of Theories and Methods of Physics and Psychology*, ed. M. Radner & S. Winokur. Minneapolis: University of Minnesota Press, pp. 403–416. Also in *Psychoanalytic Research: Three Approaches to the Experimental Study of Subliminal Processes*, ed. M. Mayman. New York: International Universities Press, 1973, pp. 104–117; rev. & exp. version in *Selected Philosophical and Methodological Papers* (of Paul E. Meehl), ed. C. Anderson & K. Gunderson. Minneapolis: University of Minnesota Press, 1991, pp. 272–283.

—— (1978), Theoretical risks and tabular asterisks: Sir Karl, Sir Ronald, and the slow progress of soft psychology. *J. Consult. Clin. Psychol.*, 46:806–834. Also in *Selected Philosophical and Methodological Papers*, ed. C. Anderson & K. Gunderson. Minneapolis: University of Minnesota Press, 1991, pp. 1–42.

—— (1979), A funny thing happened on the way to the latent entities. *J. Pers. Assess.*, 43:564–581.

—— (1983), Subjectivity in psychoanalytic inference: the nagging persistence of Wilhelm Fliess's Achensee question. In *Testing Scientific Theories*, ed. J. Earman. Minneapolis: University of Minnesota Press, pp. 349–411. Also in *Selected Philosophical and Methodological Papers*, ed. C. Anderson & K. Gunderson. Minneapolis: University of Minnesota Press, 1991, pp. 284–337.

——— (1991), *Selected Philosophical and Methodological Papers*, ed. C. Anderson & K. Gunderson. Minneapolis: University of Minnesota Press.

——— (1993), If Freud could define psychoanalysis, why can't the ABPP do it? *Psychoanal. Contemp. Thought*, 16:299–326.

——— & GOLDEN, R. (1982), Taxometric methods. In *Handbook of Research Methods in Clinical Psychology*, ed. P. Kendall & J. Butcher. New York: Wiley, pp. 127–181.

MEICHENBAUM, D. (1988), What happens when the "brute data" of psychological inquiry are meanings: nurturing a dialogue between hermeneutics and empiricism. In *Hermeneutics and Psychological Theory*, ed. S. Messer, L. Sass & R. Woolfolk. New Brunswick, NJ: Rutgers University Press, pp. 116–130.

MEISSNER, W. (1966), The operational principle and meaning in psychoanalysis. *Psychoanal. Quart.*, 35:233–255.

——— (1971), Freud's methodology. *J. Amer. Psychoanal. Assn.*, 19:265–309.

——— (1979a), Methodological critique of the action language in psychoanalysis. *J. Amer. Psychoanal. Assn.*, 27:79–105.

——— (1979b), Critique of concepts and therapy in the action language approach to psychoanalysis. *Internat. J. Psycho-Anal.*, 60:291–310.

——— (1982), The history of the psychoanalytic movement. In *Psychoanalysis: Critical Explorations in Contemporary Theory and Practice*, ed. A. Jacobson & D. Parmelee. New York: Brunner/Mazel, pp. 3–28.

——— (1984), Models in the mind: the role of theory in the psychoanalytic process. *Psychoanal. Inq.*, 4:5–32.

——— (1990), Foundations of psychoanalysis reconsidered. *J. Amer. Psychoanal. Assn.*, 38:523–557.

——— (1991), *What Is Effective in Psychoanalytic Therapy*. Northvale, NJ: Aronson.

——— (1992), The concept of the therapeutic alliance. *J. Amer. Psychoanal. Assn.*, 40:1059–1088.

——— (1995a), The economic principle in psychoanalysis: II. regulatory principles. *Psychoanal. Contemp. Thought*, 18:227–261.

——— (1995b), The economic principle in psychoanalysis: III. motivational principles. *Psychoanal. Contemp. Thought.*, 18:261–292.

MELTZER, D. (1978), Routine and inspired interpretations. *Contemp. Psychoanal.*, 14:210–225.

MELTZOFF, J. & KORNREICH, M. (1970), *Research in Psychotherapy*. Chicago: Aldine (see esp. pp. 403–483).

MENDEL, W. (1964), The phenomenon of interpretation. *Amer. J. Psychoanal.*, 24:184–189.

MENNINGER, K. (1958), *Theory of Psychoanalytic Technique*. New York: Basic Books.

MERGENTHALER, E. (1985), *Textbank Systems: Computer Science Applied in the Field of Psychoanalysis*. Berlin: Springer.

——— & KÄCHELE, H. (1988), The Ulm textbank management system: a tool for psychotherapy research. In *Psychoanalytic Process Research Strategies*, ed. H. Dahl, H. Kächele & H. Thomä. Berlin: Springer, pp. 195–211.

MERLAN, P. (1945), Brentano and Freud. *J. Hist. Ideas*, 6:375–377.

——— (1949), Brentano and Freud, a sequel. *J. Hist. Ideas*, 10:451.

MERLEAU-PONTY, M. (1962), *Phenomenology of Perception*. New York: Humanities Press.

MESSER, S., SASS, L. & WOOLFOLK, R., eds. (1988), *Hermeneutics and Psychological Theory*. New Brunswick, NJ: Rutgers University Press.

METCALF, M. (1956), Demonstration of a psychosomatic relationship. *Brit. J. Med. Psychol.*, 29:63–66.

MICHELS, R. (1983), Contemporary psychoanalytic views of interpretation. In *Psychiatry Update, Vol. 2*, ed. L. Grinspoon. Washington, DC: American Psychiatric Press, pp. 61–70.

——— (1994), Validation in the clinical process. *Internat. J. Psycho-Anal.*, 75:1133–1140.

——— (1996), Book review essay: Gill, Gray, Mitchell and Reed on psychoanalytic technique. *Internat. J. Psycho-Anal.*, 77:615–623.

MICHOTTE, A. (1946), *The Perception of Causality*, trans. T. & E. Miles. London: Methuen, 1963.

MILLER, G. (1967), *The Psychology of Communication*. New York: Basic Books.

MILLER, R. (1987), *Fact and Method*. Princeton, NJ: Princeton University Press.

MILLIKAN, R. (1984), *Language, Thought, and Other Biological Categories*. Cambridge, MA: MIT/Bradford.

——— (1993), Explanation in biopsychology. In *Mental Causation*, ed. J. Heil & A. Mele. Oxford, UK: Clarendon Press, pp. 211–232.

MINSKY, M. (1975), A framework for representing knowledge. In *The Psychology of Computer Vision*, ed. P. Winston. New York: McGraw-Hill, pp. 211–277.

MIRSKY, M. (1983), Jokes and the logic of the cognitive unconscious. In *Methods of Heuristics*, ed. R. Groner, M. Groner & W. Bischof. Hillsdale, NJ: Lawrence Erlbaum Associates, pp. 171–193.

MISCHLER, E. (1979), Meaning in context: is there any other kind? *Harvard Educ. Rev.*, 49:1–19.

MITCHELL, S. (1983), Post-structuralism, empiricism, and interpretation. In *The Need for Interpretation*, ed. S. Mitchell & M. Rosen. London: Athlone, pp. 54–89.

——— & ROSEN, M., eds. (1983), *The Need for Interpretation*. London: Athlone.

MITROFF, I. (1974), *The Subjective Side of Science*. Amsterdam: Elsevier.

MODELL, A. (1978a), The nature of psychoanalytic knowledge. *J. Amer. Psychoanal. Assn.*, 26:641–658.

——— (1978b), Affects and the complementarity of biologic and historical meaning. *The Annual of Psychoanalysis*, 6:167–180. Madison, CT: International Universities Press.

—— (1990), *Other Times, Other Realities*. Cambridge, MA: Harvard University Press.

MÖLLER, H. (1976), *Methodische Grundprobleme der Psychiatrie*. Stuttgart: W. Kohlhammer-Verlag.

MONEY-KYRLE, R. (1958), On the process of psychoanalytic inference. *Internat. J. Psycho-Anal.*, 39:129–133.

MOOIJ, A. (1991), *Psychoanalysis and the Concept of a Rule*. Berlin: Springer.

MOORE, B. & FINE, B., ed. (1990), *Psychoanalytic Terms and Concepts*. New Haven, CT: Yale University Press.

MOORE, M. (1980), The nature of psychoanalytic explanation. *Psychoanal. Contemp. Thought*, 3:459–543.

—— (1988), Mind, brain and unconscious. In *Mind, Psychoanalysis and Science*, ed. P. Clark & C. Wright. Oxford, UK: Basil Blackwell, pp. 141–165.

MOOS, R. & CLEMES, S. (1967), Multivariate study of the patient-therapist system. *J. Consult. Psychol.*, 31:119–130.

MORAN, G. & FONAGY, P. (1987), Psychoanalysis and diabetic control: a single-case study. *Brit. J. Med. Psychol.*, 60:357–372.

MORAS, K., TELFER, L. & BARLOW, D. (1993), Efficacy and specific effects data on new treatments: a case study strategy with mixed anxiety-depression. *J. Consult. Clin. Psychol.*, 61:412–420.

MORRIS, D., COLLETT, P. & MARSH, P. (1979), *Gestures*. New York: Stein & Day.

MORTON, A. (1980), *Frames of Mind: Constraints on the Commonsense Conception of the Mental*. Oxford, UK: Clarendon Press.

—— (1982), Freudian commonsense. In *Philosophical Essays on Freud*, ed. R. Wollheim & J. Hopkins. Cambridge, UK: Cambridge University Press, pp. 60–74.

MOSS, D. (1985), What you see is what you get: empiricism, psychoanalytic theory, and brief therapy. *Psych-Critique*, 1:21–34.

MUELLER-VOLLMER, K. (1989), *The Hermeneutics Reader.*. New York: Continuum.

MULLER, J. (1988), Lacan's transmission. *Psychoanal. Contemp. Thought*, 11:483–533.

—— & RICHARDSON, W. (1982), *Lacan and Language*. New York: International Universities Press.

MYNATT, C., DOHERTY, M. & TWENEY, R. (1977), Confirmation bias in a simulated research environment: an experimental study of scientific inference. *Quart. J. Exper. Psychol.*, 29:85–95.

NAGEL, E. (1959), Methodological issues in psychoanalytic theory. In *Psychoanalysis, Scientific Method, and Philosophy*, ed. S. Hook. New York: New York University Press, pp. 38–56.

—— (1961), *The Structure of Science*. New York: Harcourt, Brace & World.

NAGEL, T. (1980), *The Limits of Objectivity*. Salt Lake City: University of Utah Press.

——— (1994), Freud's permanent revolution. *New York Rev. Bks.*, May 12, p. 38.

NAIMAN, J. (1968), Short term effects as indicators of the role of interpretations in psychoanalysis. *Internat. J. Psycho-Anal.*, 49:353–356.

NAMNUM, A. (1978), Psychoanalytic interpretation: a historical perspective. In *The Human Mind Revisited*. New York: International Universities Press, pp. 313–327.

NASSER, A. (1994), Psychoanalysis after representation: the philosophical framework. *Psychoanal. Contemp. Thought*, 17:179–214.

NATSOULAS, T. (1992), Freud and consciousness: VI. A present-day perspective. *Psychoanal. Contemp. Thought*, 15:305–348.

NATTERSON, J. (1991), *Beyond Countertransference*. Northvale, NJ: Aronson.

NEISSER, U. (1967), *Cognitive Psychology*. Englewood Cliffs, NJ: Prentice-Hall.

——— (1976), *Cognition and Reality*. San Francisco: Freedman.

NELSON, K., ed. (1986), *Event Knowledge*. Hillsdale, NJ: Lawrence Erlbaum Associates.

NEWELL, A., SHAW, J. & SIMON, H. (1962), The processes of creative thinking. In *Contemporary Approaches to Creative Thinking*, ed. H. Gruber, G. Terrell & M. Wertheimer. New York: Atherton, pp. 63–110.

NICHOLS, C. (1972), Science or reflection: Habermas on Freud. *Philos. Soc. Sci.*, 2:261–270.

NICKLES, T. (1980a), *Scientific Discovery, Logic, and Rationality*. Dordrecht: Reidel.

——— (1980b), *Scientific Discovery: Case Studies*. Dordrecht: Reidel.

——— (1990), Discovery logics. *Philosophica*, 45:7–32.

NISBETT, R. & WILSON, R. (1977), Telling more than we know: verbal reports on mental processes. *Psychol. Rev.*, 84:321–259.

——— & ROSS, L. (1980), *Human Inference*. Englewood Cliffs, NJ: Prentice-Hall.

NISSIM-SABAT, M. (1990), Review of *The Freudian Metaphor*, by D. Spence (1987). *Psychoanal. Bks.*, 1:143–161.

NORMAN, H., BLACKER, K., OREMLAND, J. & BARRETT, W. (1976), The fate of the transference neurosis after termination of a satisfactory analysis. *J. Amer. Psychoanal. Assn.*, 24:471–498.

NOVEY, S. (1968), *The Second Look*. Baltimore, MD: Johns Hopkins University Press.

NUNBERG, H. & FEDERN, E., eds. (1962), *Minutes of the Vienna Psychoanalytic Society, Vol. 1*. New York: International Universities Press.

OAKESHOTT, M. (1962), *Rationalism in Politics*. New York: Basic Books.

OFFENKRANTZ, W. & RECHTSCHAFFEN, A. (1963), Clinical studies of sequential dreams, I. A patient in psychotherapy. *Arch. Gen. Psychiat.*, 8:497–508.

OGDEN, C. & RICHARDS, I. (1946), *The Meaning of Meaning*. New York: Harcourt, Brace.
OGDEN, T. (1992a), The dialectically constituted/decentered subject of psychoanalysis, I. The Freudian subject. *Internat. J. Psycho-Anal.*, 73:517–526.
—— (1992b), The dialectically constituted/decentered subject of psychoanalysis, II. The contributions of Klein and Winnicott. *Internat. J. Psycho-Anal.*, 73:613–626.
—— (1994), The analytic third: working with intersubjective clinical facts. *Internat. J. Psycho-Anal.*, 75:3–19.
—— (1997) Reverie and interpretation. *Psychoanal. Quart.*, 66:567–595.
OGILVY, T. (1977), *Many Dimensional Man*. New York: Oxford University Press.
OLDS, D. (1990), Brain-centered psychology: a semiotic approach. *Psychoanal. Contemp Thought*, 13:331–364.
—— (1994), Connectionism and psychoanalysis. *J. Amer. Psychoanal. Assn.*, 42:581–611.
OLINICK, S. (1980), *The Psychotherapeutic Instrument*. New York: Aronson.
—— (1984), Psychoanalysis and language. *J. Amer. Psychoanal. Assn.*, 32:617–653.
—— (1985), The primary data of psychoanalysis. *Contemp. Psychoanal.*, 21:492–500.
—— POLAND, W., GRIGG, K. & GRANITIR, W. (1973), The psychoanalytic work ego: process and interpretation. *Internat. J. Psycho-Anal.*, 54: 143–151.
O'NEILL, A. (1993), The process of clinical inference. In *Clinical Inference: How to Draw Meaningful Conclusions from Psychological Tests*. Brandon, VT: Clinical Psychology Publishing Company, pp. 65–148.
O'NEILL, J. (1993), Popper, Grünbaum, and induction. *Can. J. Psycho-Anal.*, 1:105–130.
OREMLAND, J. (with M. Gill) (1991), *Interpretation and Interaction: Psychoanalysis or Psychotherapy?* Hillsdale, NJ: The Analytic Press.
ORNSTEIN, P. & ORNSTEIN, A. (1980), Formulating interpretations in clinical psychoanalysis. *Internat. J. Psycho-Anal.*, 61:203–211.
OSGOOD, C., SUCI, G. & TANNENBAUM, P. (1957), *The Measurement of Meaning*. Urbana: University of Illinois Press.
O'SHAUGHNESSY, E. (1994), What is a clinical fact? *Internat. J. Psycho-Anal.*,75:939–947.
OSHERSON, D. & LASNIK, H. (1990), The study of cognition. In *Language: An Invitation to Cognitive Science*, ed. D. Osherson & H. Lasnik. Cambridge, MA: MIT Press, pp. xi–xix.
OSKAMP, S. (1965), Overconfidence in case study judgments. *J. Consult. Psychol.*, 29:261–265.
OURSLER, W., ATTLEE, C. & THE EDITORS (1968), Common sense; philosophy of common sense. *Encyclopaedia Britannica*, 6:166–177.

OVERMAN, E., ed. (1988), *Methodology and Epistemology for Social Science: Selected Papers of Donald T. Campbell*. Chicago: University of Chicago Press.

PACKER, M. (1985), Hermeneutic inquiry in the study of human conduct. *Amer. Psychol.*, 40:1081–1093.

—— & ADDISON, R., eds. (1989a), *Entering the Circle: Hermeneutic Investigation in Psychology*. Albany: State University of New York Press.

—— & —— eds. (1989b), Introduction. In *Entering the Circle: Hermeneutic Investigation in Psychology*. Albany: State University of New York Press, pp. 13–36.

PAIVIO, A. (1969), Mental imagery in association learning and memory. *Psychol. Rev.*, 76:241–260.

—— (1971), *Imagery and Verbal Processes*. New York: Holt, Rinehart & Winston.

—— (1986), *Mental Representations: A Dual Coding Approach*. New York: Oxford University Press.

PALMER, R. (1969), *Hermeneutics: Interpretation Theory in Schleiermacher, Dilthey, Heidegger, and Gadamer*. Evanston, IL: Northwestern University Press.

PALOMBO, S. (1978), *Dreaming and Memory*. New York: Basic Books.

—— (1980), The cognitive act in dream construction. *J. Amer. Acad. Psychoanal.*, 8:185–201.

—— (1984), Deconstructing the manifest dream. *J. Amer. Psychoanal. Assn.*, 32:405–420.

—— (1992), Connectivity and condensation in dreaming. *J. Amer. Psychoanal. Assn.*, 40:1139–1159.

PANEL (1955a), Validation of psychoanalytic theory, rep. H. Brosin. *J. Amer. Psychoanal. Assn.*, 3:489–495.

—— (1955b), Validation of psychoanalytic techniques, rep. J. Marmor. *J. Amer. Psychoanal. Assn.*, 3:496–505.

—— (1961), Research in psychoanalysis, rep. A. Pfeffer. *J. Amer. Psychoanal. Assn.*, 9:562–570.

—— (1969), Nonverbal communication in the analysis of adults, rep. A. Suslick. *J. Amer. Psychoanal. Assn.*, 17:955–967.

—— (1983), Interpretation: toward a contemporary understanding of the term, rep. A. Rothstein. *J. Amer. Psychoanal. Assn.*, 31:237–245.

—— (1986), Clinical aspects of language, rep. M. Weich. *J. Amer. Psychoanal. Assn.*, 34:687–698.

—— (1990), Effects of theory on psychoanalytic technique and the development of the psychoanalytic process, rep. E. Schwaber. *J. Amer. Psychoanal. Assn.*, 38:221–233.

—— (1994), Psychoanalysis and cognition, rep. A. Wilson. *Internat. J. Psycho-Anal.*, 75:775–784.

——— (1995a), Toward a definition of the term and concept of interaction, rep. K. Hurst. *J. Amer. Psychoanal. Assn.*, 43:521–537.

——— (1995b), Interpretive perspectives on interaction, rep. S. Purcell. *J. Amer. Psychoanal. Assn*, 43:539–551.

——— (1996), Meaning in the clinical moment, rep. B. Opatow. *J. Amer. Psychoanal. Assn.*, 44:639–648.

PANIAGUA, C. (1985), A methodological approach to surface material. *Internat. Rev. Psycho-Anal.*, 12:311–325.

——— (1995), Common ground, uncommon methods. *Internat. J. Psycho-Anal.*, 76:357–371.

PARKIN, S. (1979), Meaning and mechanism in psychoanalysis. *Internat. J. Psycho-Anal.*, 60:481–487.

PARSONS, M. (1992), The refinding of theory in clinical practice. *Internat. J. Psycho-Anal.*, 73:103–115.

PATTON, M. (1990), *Qualitative Evaluation and Research Methods*. Beverly Hills, CA: Sage.

PAUL, L., ed. (1963a), *Psychoanalytic Clinical Interpretation*. London: Free Press of Glencoe (Macmillan).

——— (1963b), The logic of psychoanalytic interpretation. In *Psychoanalytic Clinical Interpretation*, ed. L. Paul. London: Free Press of Glencoe (Macmillan), pp. 249–272.

PEARCE, R. (1965), Robin Molineux on the analyst's couch: a note on the limits of psychoanalytic criticism. In *Psychoanalysis and American Fiction*, ed. I. Malin. New York: Dutton, pp. 309–316.

PEIRCE, C. (1901), Abduction and induction. In *Philosophical Writings of Peirce*, ed. J. Buchler. New York: Dover, 1955, pp. 150–156.

——— (1931–1958), *Collected Papers, Vols. 1–8*, ed. C. Hartshorne, P. Weiss & A. Burks. Cambridge, MA: Harvard University Press.

PELIKAN, J. (1968), Exegesis and hermeneutics, biblical. *Encyclopaedia Britannica*, 8:949–954.

PELLER, L. (1966), Freud's contribution to language theory. *The Psychoanalytic Study of the Child*, 21:448–467. New York: International Universities Press.

PERA, M. & SHEA, W., eds. (1990), *Persuading Science: The Art of Scientific Rhetoric*. Canton, MA: Science History.

PERRY, J., AUGUSTO, F. & COOPER, S. (1989), Assessing psychodynamic conflicts: I. Reliability of the Idiographic Conflict Formulation method. *Psychiatry*, 52:289–301.

PETERFREUND, E. (1971), *Information, Systems, and Psychoanalysis*. New York: International Universities Press..

——— (1975), How does the psychoanalyst listen? On models and strategies in the psychoanalytic process. *Psychoanal. Contemp. Sci.*, 4:59–101.

——— (1983), *The Process of Psychoanalytic Therapy*. Hillsdale, NJ: The Analytic Press.

——— (1985), The heuristic approach to psychoanalytic therapy. In *Analysts at Work*, ed. J. Reppen. Hillsdale, NJ: The Analytic Press, pp. 127–143.

——— (1990), On the distinction between clinical process and clinical content theories. *Psychoanal. Psychol.*, 7:1–12.

PETOT, J.-M. (1990), *Melanie Klein: Vol. 1*. Madison, CT: International Universities Press.

——— (1991), *Melanie Klein: Vol. 2*. Madison, CT: International Universities Press.

PETTIT, P. (1983), Intentionality. In *Encyclopedic Dictionary of Psychology*, ed. R. Harré & R. Lamb. Cambridge, MA: MIT Press, pp. 317–318.

PFEFFER, A. (1959), A procedure for evaluating the results of psychoanalysis. *J. Amer. Psychoanal. Assn.*, 7:418–444.

——— (1961), Follow-up study of a satisfactory analysis. *J. Amer. Psychoanal. Assn.*, 9:698–718.

——— (1963), The meaning of the analyst after analysis: a contribution to the theory of therapeutic results. *J. Amer. Psychoanal. Assn.*, 11:229–244.

PFEIFER, R. & LEUZINGER-BOHLEBER, M. (1986), Applications of cognitive science methods to psychoanalysis: a case study and some theory. *Internat. Rev. Psycho-Anal.*, 13:221–240.

PHILLIPS, J. (1987), Grünbaum on hermeneutics. *Psychoanal. Contemp. Thought*, 10:585–626.

——— (1991), Hermeneutics in psychoanalysis: review and reconsideration. *Psychoanal. Contemp. Thought*, 14:371–424.

PIAGET, J. (1952), *The Origins of Intelligence in Children*. New York: International Universities Press.

——— (1973), The affective unconscious and the cognitive unconscious. *J. Amer. Psychoanal. Assn.*, 21:249–261.

——— & INHELDER, B. (1973), *Memory and Intelligence*. New York: Basic Books.

PIGMAN, G. (1995), Review of *Reading Freud's Reading*, ed. S. Gilman, J. Birmele, J. Geller & V. Greenberg (1994). *Psychoanal. Bks.*, 6:92–98.

PINE, F. (1985), The interpretive moment. In *Developmental Theory and Clinical Process*. New Haven, CT: Yale University Press, pp. 148–159.

——— (1988), The four psychologies and their place in clinical work. *J. Amer. Psychoanal. Assn.*, 36:339–357.

——— (1990), *Drive, Ego, Object and Self*. New York: Basic Books.

PITTENGER, R., HOCKETT, C. & DONEHY, J. (1960), *The First Five Minutes: A Sample of Microscopic Interview Analysis*. Ithaca, NY: Paul Martineau.

PLÄNKERS, T. (1986), On the relationship between psychoanalysis and systems theory. *Psyche*, 40:678–708.

PLATT, G. (1983), Structuralism. In *Encyclopedic Dictionary of Psychology*, ed. R. Harré & R. Lamb. Cambridge, MA: MIT Press, pp. 615–617.

PLATT, J. (1964), Strong inference. *Science*, 146:347–353.

POLAND, W. (1984), The analyst's words: empathy and countertransference. *Psychoanal. Quart.*, 53:421–424.

—— (1986), The analyst's words. *Psychoanal. Quart.*, 55:244–272.

—— (1988), Insight and the analytic dyad. *Psychoanal. Quart.*, 57:341–369.

POLANYI, M. (1966), *The Tacit Dimension*. Garden City, NY: Doubleday.

POLKINGHORNE, D. (1983), *Methodology for the Human Sciences*. Albany: State University of New York Press.

—— (1988), *Narrative Knowing and the Human Sciences*. Albany: State University of New York Press.

POLLOCK, G. (1981), Reminiscences and insight. *The Psychoanalytic Study of the Child*, 36:279–287. New Haven, CT: Yale University Press.

—— (1986), Is there a "two-cultures" model for psychoanalysis? *Behav. Brain Sci.*, 9:253–254.

POLYA, G. (1945), *How to Solve It*. Princeton, NJ: Princeton University Press.

POPPER, K. (1959), *The Logic of Discovery*. New York: Basic Books. London: Hutchinson, 1968.

—— (1963), *Conjectures and Refutations*. New York: Harper.

—— (1986), Predicting overt behavior versus predicting hidden states. *Behav. Brain Sci.*, 9:254–255.

PRELLI, L. (1989), *A Rhetoric of Science*. Columbia: University of South Carolina Press.

PRIDEAUX, G. (1985), *Psycholinguistics: The Experimental Study of Language*. New York: Guilford.

PRIEL, B. (1990), The effectiveness of interpretations: a reader-response perspective on psychoanalytic cure. *Psychoanal. Contemp. Thought*, 13:535–550.

PRINCE, G. (1986), *Narratology*. New York: Mouton.

PROTTER, B. (1985), Toward an emergent psychoanalytic epistemology. *Contemp. Psychoanal.*, 21:208–227.

PULVER, S. (1988), Psychic structure, function, process, and content: toward a definition. *J. Amer. Psychoanal. Assn.*, 35(Suppl.):165–189.

—— (1993), The eclectic analyst, or the many roads to insight and change. *J. Amer. Psychoanal. Assn.*, 41:339–357.

—— ESCOLL, P. & FISCHER, N., ed. (1987), How theory shapes technique: perspectives on a clinical study. *Psychoanal. Inq.*, 7:141–299.

PUTNAM, H. (1975), *Mind, Language and Reality*. Cambridge, UK: Cambridge University Press.

—— (1981), *Reason, Truth and History*. Cambridge, UK: Cambridge University Press.

—— (1983a), *Realism and Reason*. Cambridge, UK: Cambridge University Press.

—— (1983b), Why reason can't be naturalized. In *Realism and Reason: Philosophical Papers, Vol. 3*. Cambridge, UK: Cambridge University Press, pp. 229–247.

—— (1983c), Philosophers and human understanding. In *Realism and Reason: Philosophical Papers, Vol. 3*. Cambridge, UK: Cambridge University Press, pp. 184–204.

QUINE, W. (1951), Two dogmas of empiricism. *Philos. Rev.*, 60:20–43.

——— (1953), *From a Logical Point of View*. Cambridge, MA: Harvard University Press. New York: Harper & Row, 1963.

——— (1960), *Word and Object*. Cambridge, MA: MIT Press.

——— (1969), Epistemology naturalized. In *Ontological Relativity and Other Essays*. New York: Columbia University Press, pp. 69–90.

RADCLIFFE-BROWN, A. (1922), *The Andaman Islanders*. Cambridge, UK: University Press.

RADFORD, M. (1983), Psychoanalysis and the science of problem-solving man: an appreciation of Popper's philosophy and a response to Will (1980). *Brit. J. Med. Psychol.*, 56:9–26.

RADNITZKY, G. (1973), *Contemporary Schools of Metascience*. Chicago: Henry Regnery.

RAMZY, I. (1963), Research aspects of psychoanalysis. *Psychoanal. Quart.*, 32:58–76.

——— (1974), How the mind of the psychoanalyst works: an essay on psychoanalytic inference. *Internat. J. Psycho-Anal.*, 55:543–550.

——— & SHEVRIN, H. (1976), The nature of the inference process in psychoanalytic interpretation: a critical review of the literature. *Internat. J. Psycho-Anal.*, 57:151–159.

RANGELL, L. (1984), The analyst at work. The Madrid Congress. Synthesis and critique. *Internat. J. Psycho-Anal.*, 65:125–140.

——— (1987), Historical perspectives and current status of the interpretation of dreams in clinical work. In *The Interpretation of Dreams in Clinical Work*, ed. A. Rothstein. Madison, CT: International Universities Press, pp. 3–24.

RANK, O. (1910), Ein Traum der sich selbst deutet. *Jahrb. Psychoanal. Psychopath. Forsch.*, 2:465–490.

RAPAPORT, D. (1944), The scientific methodology of psychoanalysis. In *Collected Papers of David Rapaport*, ed. M. Gill. New York: Basic Books, 1967, pp. 165–220.

——— (1960), *The Structure of Psychoanalytic Theory*. New York: International Universities Press.

——— & GILL, M. (1959), The points of view and assumptions of metapsychology. *Internat. J. Psycho-Anal.*, 40:153–162.

RAPHLING, D. (1992), Some vicissitudes of aggression in the interpretive process. *Psychoanal. Quart.*, 61:352–369.

——— (1994), A patient who was not sexually abused. *J. Amer. Psychoanal. Assn.*, 42:65–78.

——— (1995), Interpretation and expectation: the anxiety of influence. *J. Amer. Psychoanal. Assn.*, 43:95–111.

RAWN, M. (1979), Schafer's "action language": a questionable alternative to metapsychology. *Internat. J. Psycho-Anal.*, 60:455–465.

RAY, W. (1984), *Literary Meaning*. Oxford, UK: Basil Blackwell.

READ, R. (1972), *A Methodological Background for Economists and Social Scientists*. Englewood Cliffs, NJ: Prentice-Hall.

REASON, P. & ROWAN, J., eds. (1981), *Human Inquiry: A Sourcebook of New Paradigm Research*. New York: Wiley.

REED, G. (1985), Psychoanalysis, psychoanalysis appropriated, psychoanalysis applied. *Psychoanal. Quart.*, 54:234–269.

—— (1987), Rules of clinical understanding in classical psychoanalysis and in self psychology: a comparison. *J. Amer. Psychoanal. Assn.*, 35:421–446.

—— (1995), Clinical truth and contemporary relativism: meaning and narration in the psychoanalytic situation. *J. Amer. Psychoanal. Assn.*, 43:713–739.

REICHENBACH, H. (1951), *The Rise of Scientific Philosophy*. Berkeley: University of California Press.

REIDER, N. (1972), Metaphor as interpretation. *Internat. J. Psycho-Anal.*, 53:463–569.

REIK, T. (1948), *Listening with the Third Ear*. New York: Farrar, Strauss.

REISER, M. (1984), *Mind, Brain, Body*. New York: Basic Books.

—— (1986), Grünbaum's critique of psychoanalytic evidence: a sheep in wolf's clothing? *Behav. Brain Sci.*, 9:255–256.

—— (1990), *Memory in Mind and Brain*. New York: Basic Books.

REISS, D. (1983), Illusion as a tool in psychoanalytic investigation. *Psychoanal. Contemp Thought.*, 6:331–402.

RENIK, O. (1994), Publication of clinical facts. *Internat. J. Psycho-Anal.*, 75:1245–1250.

RENNEKER, R. (1960), Microscopic analysis of sound tape: a method of studying preconscious communication in the therapeutic process. *Psychiatry*, 23:347–355.

REPP, B. (1991), Toward an emancipation of the "weaker sense." *Psychol. Sci.*, 2:382–386.

RESCHER, N. (1973), *The Coherence Theory of Truth*. Oxford, UK: Oxford University Press.

—— (1982), *Empirical Inquiry*. Totowa, NJ: Rowman & Littlefield.

RICE, L. & GREENBERG, L., eds. (1984), *Patterns of Change: Intensive Analysis of Psychotherapy Process*. New York: Guilford.

RICHARDS, A., compiler (1974), Indexes and bibliographies. *Standard Edition*, 24. London: Hogarth Press.

RICHARDSON, R. (1990), The "tally argument" and the validation of psychoanalysis. *Philos. Sci.*, 57:668–678.

RICKMAN, H. (1988), *Dilthey Today*. New York: Greenwood.

RICOEUR, P. (1970), *Freud and Philosophy: An Essay on Interpretation*, trans. D. Savage. New Haven, CT: Yale University Press.

—— (1974), *The Conflict of Interpretations*, ed. D. Ihde. Evanston, IL: Northwestern University Press.

—— (1976), *Interpretation Theory*. Fort Worth: Texas Christian University Press.

——— (1977), The question of proof in Freud's psychoanalytic writings. *J. Amer. Psychoanal. Assn.*, 24:835–871.

——— (1978), Image and language in psychoanalysis. In *Psychoanalysis and Language*, ed. J. Smith. New Haven, CT: Yale University Press, pp. 293-324.

——— (1982), *Hermeneutics and the Human Sciences*, ed. J. Thompson. Cambridge, UK: Cambridge University Press.

RIEBER, R., ed. (1980), *Applied Psycholinguistics and Mental Health*. New York: Plenum.

RIEFF, P. (1959), *Freud: The Mind of the Moralist*. Chicago: University of Chicago Press.

RIFFATERRE, M. (1973), The self-sufficient text. *Diacritics*, 3:39–45.

RIGGS, B. (1977), Resistance and transference: a general systems formulation. *J. Amer. Acad. Psychoanal.*, 5:65–77.

ROBINSON, J. & HAWPE, L. (1986), Narrative thinking as a heurisitic process. In *Narrative Psychology: The Storied Nature of Human Conduct*, ed. T. Sarbin. New York: Praeger, pp. 111–125.

ROBINSON, P. (1993), *Freud and his Critics*. Berkeley: University of California Press.

ROCHE, R. (1989), Notes for an epistemology of psychoanalysis. *Internat. Rev. Psycho-Anal.*, 16:339–347.

ROCK, I. & PALMER, S. (1990), The legacy of gestalt psychology. *Sci. Amer.*, 263:84–90.

ROEDIGER, J. (1990), Implicit memory. *Amer. Psychol.*, 45:1043–1056.

ROGERS, R. (1981), Textuality in dreams. *Internat. Rev. Psycho-Anal.*, 8:433–447.

——— (1982), Amazing reader in the labyrinth of literature. *Poetics Today*, 3:31–46.

——— (1984a), Science, psychoanalysis, and the interpretation of literature. *Poetics*, 13:309–323.

——— (1984b), Historical, narrative, and other half-truths: problems in psychoanalytic interpretation. *Internat. Forum Psychoanal.*, 1:37–52.

——— (1985), Three times true: redundancy in ambiguous texts. *Poetics Today*, 6:591–605.

——— (1986a), System theory and psychoanalysis. Presented to Benjamin C. Riggs Symposium, Department of Psychiatry and Behavioral Science, Medical University of South Carolina, Charleston.

——— (1986b), Semiotic matrices: fundamental types of semantic relationships. *Semiotica*, 60:193–209.

——— (1987a), General system theory and literary texts. Part I, The reading process: from diversity to equifinality. *J. Lit. Semant.*, 16:94–112.

——— (1987b), General system theory and literary texts. Part II, The nonsummativity of non-literal texts. *J. Lit. Semant.*, 16:182–199.

——— (1987c), Freud and the semiotics of repetition. *Poetics Today*, 8:579–590.

——— (1988), Structure in psychoanalytic interpretation: narrative as analogue. *Psychoanal. Contemp. Thought*, 11:145–170.

——— (1991), *Self and Other: Object Relations in Psychoanalysis and Literature*. New York: New York University Press.

RORTY, R. (1979), *Philosophy and the Mirror of Nature*. Princeton, NJ: Princeton University Press (pbk, 1980).

——— (1985), Epistemological behaviorism and the de-transcendentalization of analytic philosophy. In *Hermeneutics and Praxis*, ed. R. Hollinger. Notre Dame, IN: University of Notre Dame Press, pp. 89–121.

——— (1986), Freud and moral reflection. In *Pragmatism's Freud*, ed. J. Smith & W. Kerrigan. Baltimore, MD: Johns Hopkins University Press, pp. 1–27.

——— (1993), Consciousness, intentionality, and pragmatism. In *Folk Psychology and the Philosophy of Mind*, ed. S. Christensen & D. Turner. Hillsdale, NJ: Lawrence Erlbaum Associates, pp. 388–404.

ROSEN, V. (1955), Reconstruction of a traumatic childhood event in a case of derealization. *J. Amer. Psychoanal. Assn.*, 3:211–221.

——— (1969), Sign phenomena and their relationship to unconscious meaning. *Internat. J. Psycho-Anal.*, 50:197–207. Also in *Style, Character, and Language*, ed. S. Atkin & M. Jacovy. New York: Aronson, 1977, pp. 171–194.

——— (1977), *Style, Character, and Language*, ed. S. Atkin & M. Jacovy. New York: Aronson.

ROSENBAUM, M. & MUROFF, M., eds. (1984), *Anna O: Fourteen Contemporary Reinterpretations*. New York: Free Press.

ROSENBERG, S., SILBERSCHATZ, G., CURTIS, J., SAMPSON, H. & WEISS, J. (1986), A method of establishing reliability of statements from psychoanalytic case formulations. *Amer. J. Psychiat.*, 143:1454–1456.

ROSENBLATT, A. & THICKSTUN, J. (1977), *Modern Psychoanalytic Concepts in a General Psychology*. New York: International Universities Press.

——— & ——— (1994). Intuition and consciousness. *Psychoanal. Quart.*, 63:696–714.

ROSENTHAL, R. (1966), *Experimenter Effects in Behavioral Research*. New York: Appleton-Century-Crofts.

ROSS, D. & KAPP, F. (1962), A technique for self-analysis of countertransference. *J. Amer. Psychoanal. Assn.*, 10:643–657.

ROSS, L. & ANDERSON, C. (1982), Shortcomings in the attribution process: on the origins and maintenance of erroneous social assessments. In *Judgment under Uncertainty*, ed. D. Kahneman, A. Slovic & A. Tversky. New York: Cambridge University Press, pp. 129–152.

ROTH, P. (1987), *Meaning and Method in the Social Sciences: A Case for Methodological Pluralism*. Ithaca, NY: Cornell University Press.

——— (1989), How narratives explain. *Soc. Res.*, 56:449–478.

——— (1991a), Truth in interpretation: the case of psychoanalysis. *Philos. Soc. Sci.*, 21:175–195.

——— (1991b), Interpretation as explanation. In *The Interpretive Turn*, ed. D. Hiley, J. Bohman & R. Shusterman. Ithaca, NY: Cornell University Press, pp. 179–196.

ROTHENBERG, A. (1971), The process of Janusian thinking in creativity. *Arch. Gen. Psychiat.*, 24:195–205.

ROTHSTEIN, A. (1980), Psychoanalytic paradigms and their narcissistic investment. *J. Amer. Psychoanal. Assn.*, 28:385–395.

ROUSTANG, F. (1982), *Dire Mastery: Discipleship from Freud to Lacan*, trans. N. Lukachev. Baltimore, MD: Johns Hopkins University Press.

RUBINSTEIN, B. (1975), On the clinical psychoanalytic theory and its role in the inference and confirmation of particular clinical hypotheses. *Psychoanal. Contemp. Sci.*, 4:3–58.

—— (1976), On the possibility of a strictly clinical psychoanalytic theory: an essay in the philosophy of science. In *Psychology versus Metapsychology*, ed. M. Gill & P. Holzman. New York: International Universities Press, pp. 229–264.

—— (1980), The problem of confirmation in clinical psychoanalysis. *J. Amer. Psychoanal. Assn.*, 22:418–444.

—— (1983), Freud's early theories of hysteria. In *Physics, Philosophy and Psychoanalysis*, ed. R. Cohen & L. Laudan. Dordrecht: Reidel, pp. 169–190. Also in *Psychoanalysis and the Philosophy of Science: Collected Papers of Benjamin B. Rubinstein, M.D.*, ed. R. Holt. Madison, CT: International Universities Press, 1997, pp. 551–575.

—— (1997), *Psychoanalysis and the Philosophy of Science: Collected Papers of Benjamin B. Rubinstein, M.D.*, ed. R. Holt. Madison, CT: International Universities Press.

RUBOVITS-SEITZ, P. (1979), Review of *The Psychology of the Self: A Casebook*, ed. A. Goldberg (1978). *J. Nerv. Ment. Dis.*, 167:454–456.

—— (1983a), Interpretation: fact or fiction? *J. Nerv. Ment. Dis.*, 171:397–399.

—— (1983b), Review of *Analysis of Transference, Vol. 1: Theory and Technique*, by M. Gill (1982a); and *Analysis of Transference, Vol. 2: Studies of Nine Audio-Recorded Psychoanalytic Sessions*, by M. Gill & I. Hoffman (1982b). *J. Nerv. Ment. Dis.*, 171:513–516.

—— (1986a), Clinical interpretation, hermeneutics, and the problem of validation. *Psychoanal. Contemp. Thought*, 9:3–42.

—— (1986b), Review of *How Does Analysis Cure?* by H. Kohut (1984). *J. Nerv. Ment. Dis.*, 174:432.

—— (1987), The validation of interpretations and reconstructions. La Jolla, CA: Herman M. Serota Foundation. Unpublished manuscript.

—— (1988a), Kohut's method of interpretation: a critique. *J. Amer. Psychoanal. Assn.*, 36:933–959.

—— (1988b), Intelligence and analyzability. *The Annual of Psychoanalysis*, 16:171–216. Madison, CT: International Universities Press.

—— (1991a), Interpretive methodology, validation, and structuralist hermeneutics. *Psychoanal. Contemp. Thought*, 14:563–593.

—— (1991b), Review of *Understanding Transference: The Core Conflictual Relationship Theme Method*, by L. Luborsky & P. Crits-Christoph (1990). *J. Nerv. Ment. Dis.*, 179:706.

——— (1992a), Interpretive methodology: some problems, limitations, and remedial strategies. *J. Amer. Psychoanal. Assn.*, 40:139–168.

——— (1992b), Review of *Interpretation and Interaction: Psychoanalysis or Psychotherapy?* by J. Oremland (1991). *J. Nerv. Ment. Dis.*, 180:137.

——— (1994a), Review of *Validation in the Clinical Theory of Psychoanalysis: A Study in the Philosophy of Psychoanalysis*, by Adolf Grünbaum (1993). *J. Nerv. Ment. Dis.*, 182:188–189.

——— (1994b), The fallibility of interpretations (Letter to the Editor). *J. Amer. Psychoanal. Assn*, 42:1310–1312.

——— (1995a), Research in psychoanalysis: an historical note (Letter to the Editor). *J. Amer. Psychoanal. Assn.*, 43:651–652.

——— (1995b), Review of *The Rhetorical Voice of Psychoanalysis: Displacement of Evidence by Theory*, by D. Spence (1994). *J. Nerv. Ment. Dis.*, 183:118–119.

RUDNYTZKY, P., ed. (1988), *The Persistence of Myth: Psychoanalytic and Structuralist Perspectives*. New York: Guilford.

RUMELHART, D. (1980), Schemata: the building blocks of cognition. In *Theoretical Issues in Reading Comprehension*, ed. R. Spira, B. Bruce & W. Brewer. Hillsdale, NJ: Lawrence Erlbaum Associates, pp. 33–58.

——— HINTON, G. & WILLIAMS, R. (1986a), Learning internal representations by error propagation. In *Parallel Distributed Processing*, Vol.1, ed. D. Rumelhart & J. McClelland. Cambridge, MA: MIT Press, pp. 318–362.

——— MCCLELLAND, J. & THE PDP RESEARCH GROUP (1986b), *Parallel Distributed Processing, Vol. 1*. Cambridge, MA: MIT Press.

RUNES, D., ed. (1983). *Dictionary of Philosophy*, rev. ed. Totowa, NJ: Rowan & Allanheld, 1984.

RUNYON, W. (1981), Why did Van Gogh cut off his ear? The problem of alternative explanations in psychobiography. *J. Person. Soc. Psychol.*, 40:1070–1077.

——— (1982), *Life Histories and Psychobiography*. New York: Oxford University Press.

RUSSELL, R., ed. (1987a), *Language in Psychotherapy: Strategies of Discovery*. New York: Plenum.

——— (1987b), Psychotherapeutic discourse: future directions and the critical pluralist attitude. In *Language in Psychotherapy: Strategies of Discovery*, ed. R. Russell. New York: Plenum, pp. 341–350.

RYCROFT, C. (1956), The nature and function of the analyst's communication. *Internat. J. Psycho-Anal.*, 37:469–472.

——— (1958), An enquiry into the function of words in psychoanalysis. *Internat. J. Psycho-Anal.*, 39:408–415.

——— (1966), Introduction: causes and meaning. In *Psychoanalysis Observed*, ed. C. Rycroft. London: Constable, pp. 7–22.

——— (1968), *A Critical Dictionary of Psychoanalysis*. London: Nelson.

—— (1985), *Psychoanalysis and Beyond*, ed. P. Fuller. London: Hogarth Press/Chatto & Windus.

RYLE, A. & LUNGHI, M. (1969), The measurement of relevant change after psychotherapy: use of repertory grid technique. *Brit. J. Psychiat.*, 115:1297–1304.

—— & BREEN, D. (1972), Some differences in the personal constructs of normal and neurotic subjects. *Brit. J. Psychiat.*, 120:483–489.

—— & LIPSHITZ, S. (1974), Towards an informed counter-transference: the possible contribution of repertory grid technique. *Brit. J. Med. Psychol.*, 47:219–225.

RYLE, G. (1949), *The Concept of Mind*. London: Hutchinson.

SACHS, D. (1989), In fairness to Freud: a critical notice of the *Foundations of Psychoanalysis*, by Adolf Grünbaum (1984). *Philos. Rev.*, 98:349–378.

SADOVSKY, V. (1983), Systems theory. In *The Encyclopedic Dictionary of Psychology*, ed. R. Harré & R. Lamb. Cambridge, MA: MIT Press, pp. 623–625.

SADOW, L. (1984), Two modes of psychoanalytic thought. In *Psychoanalysis: The Vital Issues, Vol. 1*, ed. J. Gedo & G. Pollock. New York: International Universities Press, pp. 413–429.

SALMON, W. (1959), Psychoanalytic theory and evidence. In *Psychoanalysis, Science, and Philosophy*, ed. S. Hook. New York: New York University Press, pp. 252–267.

—— (1984), *Scientific Explanation and the Causal Structure of the World*. Princeton, NJ: Princeton University Press.

SAMUELS, A. (1989), *The Plural Psyche*. London: Routledge.

SAND, R. (1983), Confirmation in the Dora case. *Internat. Rev. Psycho-Anal.*, 10:333–357.

—— (1993), On a contribution to a future scientific study of dream interpretation. In *Philosophical Problems of the Internal and External Worlds*, ed. J. Earman, A. Janis, G. Massey & N. Rescher. Pittsburgh, PA: University of Pittsburgh Press, pp. 527–547.

SANDLER, J. (1976), Dreams, unconscious fantasies and "identity of perception." *Internat. Rev. Psycho-Anal.*, 3:33–42.

—— (1989), The Hampstead Index as an instrument of psychoanalytic research. *Internat. J. Psycho-Anal.*, 43:287–291.

—— KAWENOKA, M., NEURATH, L., ROSENBLATT, B., SCHNURMANN, A. & SIGAL, J. (1962), The classification of superego material in the Hampstead Index. The *Psychoanalytic Study of the Child*, 17:107–127. New York: International Universities Press.

—— & ROSENBLATT, B. (1962), The concept of the representational world. *The Psychoanalytic Study of the Child*, 17:128–145. New York: International Universities Press.

SARBIN, T., ed. (1986a), *Narrative Psychology: The Storied Nature of Human Conduct*. New York: Praeger.

—— (1986b), The narrative as a root metaphor for psychology. In *Narrative Psychology*, ed. T. Sarbin. New York: Praeger, pp. 3–21.

SARGENT, H., COYNE, L., WALLERSTEIN, R. & HOLTZMAN, W. (1967), An approach to the quantitative problems of psychoanalytic research. *J. Clin. Psychol.*, 23:243–291.

—— HORWITZ, L., WALLERSTEIN, R. & APPELBAUM, A. (1968), *Prediction in Psychotherapy Research: A Method for the Transformation of Clinical Judgments into Testable Hypotheses*. New York: International Universities Press.

SASS, L. (1989), Humanism, hermeneutics, and humanistic psychoanalysis: differing conceptions of subjectivity. *Psychoanal. Contemp. Thought*, 12:433–504.

—— & WOOLFOLK, R. (1988), Psychoanalysis and the hermeneutic turn: a critique of *Narrative Truth and Historical Truth*. *J. Amer. Psychoanal. Assn.*, 36:429–454.

SASSO, G. (1993), *La Mente Intralinguistica: L'instabilto del Segno. Anagrammi e Parole Dentro Le Parole*. Genova: Marietti.

SAUL, L. (1958), *Technique and Practice of Psychoanalysis*. Philadelphia: Lippincott.

SAUSSURE, F. (1915), *Course in General Linguistics*, ed. C. Bally & A. Sechehaye (trans. W. Baskin). New York: McGraw-Hill, 1966.

SAVAGE, L. (1954), *The Foundations of Statistics*. New York: Wiley.

SAVODNIK, I. (1986), Some gaps in Grünbaum's critique of psychoanalysis. *Behav. Brain Sci.*, 9:257.

SCHAFER, R. (1959), Generative empathy in the treatment situation. *Psychoanal. Quart.*, 28:342–373.

—— (1970), The psychoanalytic vision of reality. *Internat. J. Psycho-Anal.*, 51:279–297. Also in *A New Language for Psychoanalysis*. New Haven, CT: Yale University Press, 1976, pp. 22–56.

—— (1973), Action: its place in psychoanalytic interpretation and theory. *Internat. J. Psycho-Anal.*, 51:279–297. Also in *A New Language for Psychoanalysis*. New Haven, CT: Yale University Press, 1976, pp. 22–56.

—— (1975), Psychoanalysis without psychodynamics. *Internat. J. Psycho-Anal.*, 56:41–55.

—— (1976), *A New Language for Psychoanalysis*. New Haven, CT: Yale University Press.

—— (1978), *Language and Insight*. New Haven, CT: Yale University Press.

—— (1979), The appreciative analytic attitude and the construction of multiple histories. *Psychoanal. Contemp. Sci.*, 2:3–24.

—— (1980a), *Narrative Actions in Psychoanalysis*. Worcester, MA: Clark University Press, 1981.

—— (1980b), Narration in the psychoanalytic dialogue. *Crit. Inq.*, 7:29–53. Also in *The Analytic Attitude*. New York: Basic Books, 1983, pp. 212–239.

—— (1982), The imprisoned analysand: an essay on interpretation. The

32nd Freud Anniversary Lecture, New York, April 13. Abstract in *Psychoanal. Quart.*, 52:662–664. Also in *The Analytic Attitude*. New York: Basic Books, 1983, pp. 257–280.

——— (1983a), *The Analytic Attitude*. New York: Basic Books.

——— (1983b), Construction of the psychoanalytic narrative: an introduction. *Psychoanal. Contemp. Thought*, 6:403–404.

——— (1985a), The interpretation of psychic reality, developmental influences, and unconscious communication. *J. Amer. Psychoanal. Assn.*, 33:537–554.

——— (1985b), Wild analysis. *J. Amer. Psychoanal. Assn.*, 33:275–299.

——— (1986), Discussion of transference and countertransference in brief psychotherapy. In *Between Analyst and Patient*, ed. H. Meyers. Hillsdale, NJ: The Analytic Press, pp. 149–157.

——— (1987), Self-deception, defense, and narration. *Psychoanal. Contemp. Thought*, 10:319–346.

——— (1992), *Retelling a Life*. New York: Basic Books.

——— (1994a), One perspective on the Freud-Klein controversies 1941–1945. *Internat. J. Psycho-Anal.*, 75:359–365.

——— (1994b), The contemporary Kleinians of London. *Psychoanal. Quart.*, 63:409–432.

——— (1996), Authority, evidence, and knowledge in the psychoanalytic relationship. *Psychoanal. Quart.*, 65:236–253.

SCHANK, R. (1982), *Dynamic Memory: A Theory of Reminding and Learning in Computers and People*. New York: Cambridge University Press.

——— & ABELSON, R. (1977), *Scripts, Plans, Goals, and Understanding*. Hillsdale, NJ: Lawrence Erlbaum Associates.

SCHARFF, J. (1992), *Projective and Introjective Identification and the Use of the Therapist's Self*. Northvale, NJ: Aronson.

SCHARFF, R. (1995), *Comte after Positivism*. Cambridge, UK: Cambridge University Press.

SCHEFLEN, A. (1963), Communication and regulation in psychotherapy. *Psychiatry*, 26:126–136.

——— (1965), Quasi-courtship behavior in psychotherapy. *Psychiatry*, 28: 245–257.

——— (1973), *Communicational Structure: Analysis of a Psychotherapy Transaction*. Bloomington: Indiana University Press.

SCHILDER, P. (1935), Psychoanalysis and philosophy. *Psychoanal. Rev.*, 22:274–287.

SCHIMEK, J. (1975), The interpretation of the past: childhood trauma, psychical reality, and historical truth. *J. Amer. Psychoanal. Assn.*, 23:845–865.

SCHLESINGER, G. (1985), *The Range of Epistemic Logic*. Aberdeen, Scotland: Aberdeen University Press.

SCHLESINGER, H. (1994), How the analyst listens: the pre-stages of interpretation. *Internat. J. Psycho-Anal.*, 75:31–37.

—— (1995), The process of interpretation and the moment of change. *J. Amer. Psychoanal. Assn.*, 43:663–688.

SCHLESSINGER, N. & ROBBINS, F. (1974), Assessment and follow-up in psychoanalysis. *J. Amer. Psychoanal. Assn.*, 7:418–444.

—— & —— (1975), The psychoanalytic process: recurrent patterns of conflict and change in ego functions. *J. Amer. Psychoanal. Assn.*, 23:761–782.

—— & —— (1983), *A Developmental View of the Psychoanalytic Process: Follow-up Studies and Their Consequences*. New York: International Universities Press.

SCHMIDL, F. (1955), The problem of scientific validation in psychoanalytic interpretation. *Internat. J. Psycho-Anal.*, 36:105–113.

—— (1959), Psychoanalysis as science. *J. Amer. Psychoanal. Assn.*, 7:127–145.

SCHNEIDER, W. & SHIFFRIN, R. (1977), Controlled and automatic processing: I. *Psychol. Rev.*, 84:1–66.

SCHOLES, R. (1974), *Structuralism in Literature*. New Haven, CT: Yale University Press.

—— (1982), *Semiotics and Interpretation*. New Haven, CT: Yale University Press.

—— & KELLOGG, R. (1966), *The Nature of Narrative*. London: Oxford University Press.

SCHÖN, D. (1986), Making meaning: an exploration of artistry in psychoanalysis. *The Annual of Psychoanalysis*, 14:301–316. Madison, CT: International Universities Press.

SCHWABER, E. (1983a), Psychoanalytic listening and psychic reality. *Internat. Rev. Psycho-Anal.*, 10:379–392.

—— (1983b), A particular perspective on analytic listening. *The Psychoanalytic Study of the Child*, 38:519–546. New Haven, CT: Yale University Press.

—— (1986), Reconstruction and perceptual experience: further thoughts on analytic listening. *J. Amer. Psychoanal. Assn.*, 34:911–932.

—— (1987), Review of *Kohut's Legacy: Contributions of Self Psychology*, ed. P. Stepansky & A. Goldberg (1984). *J. Amer. Psychoanal. Assn.*, 35:743–750.

—— (1990a), The psychoanalyst's methodological stance: some comments based on a response to Max Hernandez. *Internat. J. Psycho-Anal.*, 71:31–36.

—— (1990b), Interpretation and the therapeutic action of psychoanalysis. *Internat. J. Psycho-Anal.*, 71:229–240.

—— (1992), Countertransference: the analyst's retreat from the patient's vantage point. *Internat. J. Psycho-Anal.*, 73:349–361.

—— (1995a), The psychoanalyst's mind: from listening to interpretation—a clinical report. *Internat. J. Psycho-Anal.*, 76:271–281.

—— (1995b), Towards a definition of the term and concept of interaction. *Internat. J. Psycho-Anal.*, 76:557–564.

—— (1995c), A particular perspective on impasses in the clinical situation: further reflections on psychoanalytic listening. *Internat. J. Psycho-Anal.*, 76:711–722.

SCHWARTZ, M. & WIGGINS, O. (1986), Systems and the structuring of meaning: contributions to a biopsychosocial medicine. *Amer. J. Psychiat.*, 143:1213–1221.

SCHWARTZ, S., ed. (1977), *Naming, Necessity, and Natural Kinds*. Ithaca, NY: Cornell University Press.

SCOTT, W. (1985), The historical truth of psychoanalytic reconstructions. *Internat. Rev. Psycho-Anal.*, 12:187–197.

SCRIVEN, M. (1962), Explanations, predictions, and laws. In *Scientific Explanation, Space, and Time*, ed. H. Feigl & G. Maxwell. Minneapolis: University of Minnesota Press, pp. 170–230.

—— (1969), Logical positivism and the behavioral sciences. In *The Legacy of Logical Positivism*, ed. P. Achinstein & S. Barker. Baltimore, MD: Johns Hopkins University Press, pp. 195–210.

SEARL, M. (1936), Some queries on principles of technique. *Internat. J. Psycho-Anal.*, 17:471–493.

SEARLE, J. (1969), *Speech Acts*. Cambridge, UK: Cambridge University Press.

—— (1979a), *Expression and Meaning*. Cambridge, UK: Cambridge University Press.

—— (1979b), Metaphor. In *Metaphor and Thought*, ed. A. Ortony. Cambridge, UK: Cambridge University Press, pp. 92–123.

—— (1983), *Intentionality*. Cambridge, UK: Cambridge University Press.

—— (1989), Consciousness, unconsciousness, and intentionality. *Philos. Topics*, 17:193–209.

—— (1994), Intentionality. In *A Companion to the Philosophy of Mind*, ed. S. Guttenplan. Oxford, UK: Basil Blackwell, pp. 379–386.

SEARLES, H. (1960), *The Non-Human Environment*. New York: International Universities Press.

—— (1965), *Collected Papers on Schizophrenia and Related Subjects*. London: Hogarth Press.

SEEMAN, W. (1953), Discovery and justification in psychotherapy. *Psychiatry*, 16:81–86.

SEGAL, Z. & BLATT, S., eds. (1993), *The Self in Emotional Distress*. New York: Guilford.

SEGALL, M., CAMPBELL, D. & HERSKOVITS, M. (1966), *The Influence of Culture on Visual Perception*. Indianapolis, IN: Bobbs-Merrill.

SEIDMAN, S., ed. (1994), *The Postmodern Turn*. New York: Cambridge University Press.

SEITZ, P. (1950), Psychocutaneous conditioning during the first two weeks of life. *Psychosom. Med.*, 12:187–188.

—— (1955), Relation of initial associations to focal conflict in analytic interviews. Presented to the Chicago Psychoanalytic Society, Feb. 22.

—— (1966), The consensus problem in psychoanalytic research. In

Methods of Research in Psychotherapy, ed. L. Gottschalk & A. Auerbach. New York: Appleton-Century-Crofts, pp. 209–225.

—— (1968), Cycles and subcycles in the analytic process. Presented to the Chicago Psychoanalytic Society, May 28. Abstr: *Bull. Phila. Assn. Psychoanal.*, 19:97–100, 1969.

—— (1978), Review of *The Bipersonal Field*, by R. Langs (1976). *J. Nerv. Ment. Dis.*, 166:374–375.

SELLARS, W. (1963), *Science, Perception, and Reality*. London: Routledge & Kegan Paul.

SEROTA, H. (1964), Home movies of early childhood: correlative developmental data in the psychoanalysis of adults. *Science*, 143:1195.

SEUNG, T. (1982a), *Structuralism and Hermeneutics*. New York: Columbia University Press.

SHAKLEE, H. & FISCHOFF, B. (1982), Strategies of information search in causal analysis. *Memory & Cognition*, 10:520–530.

SHANDS, H. (1970), *Semiotic Approaches to Psychiatry*. The Hague: Mouton.

—— (1974), Language and psychiatry. In *Current Trends in Linguistics, Vol. 12, Part 4*, ed. T. Sebeok. The Hague: Mouton, pp. 2657–2708.

SHANE, M. & SHANE, E. (1993), Self psychology after Kohut: one theory or many? *J. Amer. Psychoanal. Assn.*, 41:777–798.

SHAPERE, D. (1984a), Introduction. In *Reason and the Search for Knowledge*. Dordrecht: Reidel, pp. xiii–xlv.

—— (1984b), Meaning and scientific change. In *Reason and the Search for Knowledge*. Dordrecht: Reidel, pp. 58–101.

—— (1984c), Notes toward a post-positivistic interpretation of science, Parts I & II. In *Reason and the Search for Knowledge*. Dordrecht: Reidel, pp. 102–119, 342–382.

SHAPIRO, A. & MORRIS, L. (1978), The placebo effect in medical and psychological therapies. In *Handbook of Psychoanalysis and Behavior Change*, 2nd ed., ed. S. Garfield & A. Bergin. New York: Wiley, pp. 369–410.

SHAPIRO, D. (1989), *Psychotherapy of Neurotic Character*. New York: Basic Books.

SHAPIRO, T. (1970), Interpretation and naming. *J. Amer. Psychoanal. Assn.*, 18:399–421.

—— (1974), The development and distortions of empathy. *Psychoanal. Quart.*, 43:4–25.

—— (1977), Epilogue. In *Style, Character, and Language: Victor H. Rosen, M.D.*, ed. S. Atkin & M. Jucovy. New York: Aronson, pp. 351–360.

—— (1978), On the verification of psychoanalytic concepts by extraclinical techniques. *Internat. J. Psychoanal. Psychother.*, 7:586–594.

—— (1979), *Clinical Psycholinguistics*. New York: Plenum.

—— (1991), Words and feelings in the psychoanalytic dialogue. *J. Amer. Psychoanal. Assn.*, 39(Suppl.):321–348.

—— (1993), Discussion: the clinician and the scientist. *J. Amer. Psychoanal. Assn.*, 41(Suppl.):153–164.

——— & EMDE, R., ed. (1993), Research in Psychoanalysis: Process, Development, Outcome. *J. Amer. Psychoanal. Assn.*, 41 (Supplement): 1–424.

SHARE, L. (1994), *If Someone Speaks, It Gets Lighter: Dreams and the Reconstruction of Infant Trauma.* Hillsdale, NJ: The Analytic Press.

SHARP, V. & BELLAK, L. (1978), Ego function assessment of the psychoanalytic process. *Psychoanal. Quart.*, 47:52–72.

SHARPE, E. (1940), Psycho-physical problems revealed in language: an examination of metaphor. *Internat. J. Psycho-Anal.*, 21:201–213.

SHARPE, R. (1988), Mirrors, lamps, organisms and texts. In *Mind, Psychoanalysis and Science*, ed. P. Clark & C. Wright. Oxford, UK: Basil Blackwell, pp. 187–261.

——— (1993), The very idea of folk psychology. In *Folk Psychology and the Philosophy of Mind*, ed. S. Christensen & D. Turner. Hillsdale, NJ: Lawrence Erlbaum Associates, pp. 188–199.

SHERER, K. & EKMAN, P. (1982), *Handbook of Methods in Nonverbal Behavior Research.* Cambridge, UK: Cambridge University Press.

SHERWOOD, M. (1969), *The Logic of Explanation in Psychoanalysis.* New York: The Academic Press.

SHEVRIN, H. (1984), The fate of the five metapsychological principles. *Psychoanal. Inq.*, 4:33–58.

——— (1986), An argument for the evidential standing of psychoanalytic data. *Behav. Brain Sci.*, 9:257–259.

SHIFFRIN, R. & SCHNEIDER. W. (1977), Controlled and automatic human information processing: II. *Psychol. Rev.*, 84:127–190.

SHOPE, R. (1967), The psychoanalytic theories of wish-fulfillment and meaning. *Inquiry*, 10:421–438.

——— (1970), Freud on conscious and unconscious intentions. *Inquiry*, 13:149–159.

——— (1973), Freud's concepts of meaning. *Psychoanal. Contemp. Sci.*, 2:176–303.

——— (1987), The prospects for psychoanalysis: a discussion review. *Psychoanal. Contemp. Thought.*, 10:155–298.

SIEGLER, F. (1967), Unconscious intentions. *Inquiry*, 10:251–267.

SILBERSCHATZ, G., CURTIS, J., FRETTER, P. & KELLY, T. (1988), Testing hypotheses of psychotherapeutic change processes. In *Psychoanalytic Process Research Strategies*, ed. H. Dahl, H. Kächele & J. Thomä. New York: Springer, pp. 129–145.

SILVERMAN, D. (1986), A multi-model approach: looking at clinical data from three theoretical perspectives. *Psychoanal. Psychol.*, 3:121–132.

SIMON, H. (1977), *Models of Discovery and Other Topics in the Methods of Science.* Dordrecht: Reidel.

——— (1981), *The Science of the Artificial.* Cambridge, MA: MIT Press.

——— (1992), Scientific discovery as problem-solving. *Internat. Stud. Philos. Sci.*, 6:1–14.

—— & KAPLAN, C. (1989), Foundations of cognitive science. In *Foundations of Cognitive Science*, ed. M. Posner. Cambridge, MA: MIT Press, pp. 1–47.

SIMONS, H., ed. (1990a), *The Rhetorical Turn*. Chicago: University of Chicago Press.

—— (1990b), The rhetoric of inquiry as an intellectual movement. In *The Rhetorical Turn*, ed. H. Simons. Chicago: University of Chicago Press, pp. 1–34.

SINGER, J. (1988a), Sampling ongoing consciousness and emotional experience: implications for health. In *Psychodynamics and Cognition*, ed. M. Horowitz. Chicago: University of Chicago Press, pp. 297–346.

—— (1988b), Psychoanalytic theory in the context of contemporary psychology. *Psychoanal. Psychol.*, 5:95–125.

—— ed. (1990), *Repression and Dissociation*. Chicago: University of Chicago Press.

—— & SALOVEY, P. (1991), Organized knowledge structures and personality: person schemas, self schemas, prototypes, and scripts. In *Person Schemas and Maladaptive Interpersonal Patterns*, ed. M. Horowitz. Chicago: University of Chicago Press, pp. 33–79.

SIOMOPOULOS, V. (1983), *The Structure of Psychopathological Experience*. New York: Brunner/Mazel.

SKELTON, R. (1995), Bion's use of modern logic. *Internat. J. Psycho-Anal.*, 76:389–397.

SKLANSKY, M., ISAACS, K., LEVITOV, E. & HAGGARD, E. (1966), Verbal interaction and levels of meaning in psychotherapy. *Arch. Gen. Psychiat.*, 4:158–170.

SKURA, M. (1981), *The Literary Use of the Psychoanalytic Process*. New Haven, CT: Yale University Press.

SLAP, J. & SAYKIN, A. (1983), The schema: basic concepts in a nonmetapschological model of mind. *Psychoanal. Contemp. Thought*, 6:305–325.

—— & —— (1984), On the nature and organization of the repressed. *Psychoanal. Inq.*, 4:107–124.

—— & Slap-Shelton, L. (1991), *The Schema in Clinical Psychoanalysis*. Hillsdale, NJ: The Analytic Press.

SLOANE, R., STAPLES, F., CRISTOL, A., YORKSTON, N. & WHIPPLE, K. (1975), *Psychotherapy versus Behavior Therapy*. Cambridge, MA: Harvard University Press.

SLOBIN, D. (1979), *Psycholinguistics*. Glenview, IL: Scott, Foresman.

SMITH, H. (1995), Analytic listening and the experience of surprise. *Internat. J. Psycho-Anal.*, 76:67–78.

SMITH, J., ed. (1978), *Psychoanalysis and Language*. New Haven, CT: Yale University Press.

—— ed. (1983), *Interpreting Lacan*. New Haven, CT: Yale University Press.

—— (1988), Psychoanalysis and psychotherapy: comments on the analytic attitude. *Brit. J. Psychother.*, 4:401–411.

SMITH, S. (1997), Review of *Reading Freud's Reading*, ed. S. Gilman, J. Birmele, J. Geller & V. Greenberg (1994). *Psychoanal. Quart.*, 66:348–349.

SNYDER, M. (1981), Seek and you shall find: testing hypotheses about other people. In *Social Cognition: The Ontario Symposium, Vol. 1*, ed. E. Higgins, C. Harman & M. Zanna. Hillsdale, NJ: Lawrence Erlbaum Associates, pp. 277–303.

SPECHT, E. (1988), Literary-critical interpretation—psychoanalytic interpretation. In *Hermeneutics versus Science?* ed. J. Connolly & T. Keutner. Notre Dame, IN: Notre Dame University Press, pp. 153–169.

SPENCE, D. (1968), The processing of meaning in psychotherapy: some links with psycholinguistics and information theory. *Behav. Sci.*, 13:349–361.

——— (1976), Clinical interpretation: some comments on the nature of the evidence. *Psychoanal. Contemp. Sci.*, 5: 367–388.

——— (1979), Language in psychotherapy. In *Psycholinguistic Research*, ed. D. Aronson & R. Rieber. Hillsdale, NJ: Lawrence Erlbaum Associates, pp. 471–496.

——— (1980a), Lawfulness in lexical choice: a natural experiment. *J. Amer. Psychoanal. Assn.*, 28:115–132.

——— (1980b), Lexical leakage. In *Applied Psycholinguistics and Mental Health*, ed. R. Rieber. New York: Plenum, pp. 139–175.

——— (1981), Psychoanalytic competence. *Internat. J. Psycho-Anal.*, 62:113–124.

——— (1982a), *Narrative Truth and Historical Truth*. New York: Norton.

——— (1982b), On some clinical implications of action language. *J. Amer. Psychoanal. Assn.*, 30:169–184.

——— (1983a), Narrative persuasion. *Psychoanal. Contemp. Thought*, 6:457–481.

——— (1983b), Ambiguity in everyday life. *Psychoanal. Inquiry*, 3:255–278.

——— (1984a), Perils and pitfalls of free-floating attention. *Contemp. Psychoanal.*, 20:37–59.

——— (1984b), The lingering ghost of positivism. *Internat. Forum Psychoanal.*, 1:293–301.

——— (1986a), When interpretation masquerades as explanation. *J. Amer. Psychoanal. Assn.*, 34:3–22.

——— (1986b), Narrative smoothing and clinical wisdom. In *Narrative Psychology*, ed. T. Sarbin. New York: Praeger, pp. 211–232.

——— (1986c), Are free associations necessarily contaminated? *Behav. Brain Sci.*, 9:259.

——— (1987), *The Freudian Metaphor*. New York: Norton.

——— (1988a), Tough and tender-minded hermeneutics. In *Hermeneutics and Psychological Theory*, ed. S. Messer, L. Sass & R. Woolfolk. New Brunswick, NJ: Rutgers University Press, pp. 62–84.

——— (1988b), Guidelines for case presentations: toward a new genre of case reporting. Report to Committee on Scientific Activities, American Psychoanalytic Asociation. Unpublished manuscript.

——— (1990), The rhetorical voice of psychoanalysis. *J. Amer. Psychoanal. Assn.*, 38:579–603.

——— (1991), Review of S. Goldberg's, *Two Patterns of Rationality in Freud's*

Writings (1988). *Internat. Rev. Psycho-Anal.*, 18:281–283.
—— (1992), Interpretation: a critical perspective. In *Interface of Psychoanalysis and Psychology*, ed. J. Barron, M. Eagle & D. Wolitzky. Washington, DC: American Psychological Assn., pp. 558–572.
—— (1993), Beneath the analytic surface: the analysand's theory of mind. *Internat. J. Psycho-Anal.*, 74:729–738.
—— (1994a), *The Rhetorical Voice of Psychoanalysis*. Cambridge, MA: Harvard University Press.
—— (1994b), The special nature of psychoanalytic facts. *Internat. J. Psycho-Anal.*, 75:915–925.
—— (1995), When do interpretations make a difference: a partial answer to Fliess' *Achensee* question. *J. Amer. Psychoanal. Assn.*, 43:689–712.
—— & GORDON, C. (1967), Activation and measurement of an early oral fantasy: an exploratory study. *J. Amer. Psychoanal. Assn.*, 15:99–129.
—— & GRIEF, B. (1970), An experimental study of listening between the lines. *J. Nerv. Ment. Dis.*, 151:179–186.
—— & LUGO, M. (1972), The role of verbal clues in clinical listening. *Psychoanal. Contemp. Sci.*, 1:109–131.
—— & OWEN, K. (1990), Lexical co-occurrence and association strenth. *J. Psycholing. Res.*, 19:317–330.
—— DAHL, H. & JONES, E. (1993), Impact of interpretation upon associative freedom. *J. Clin. Consult. Psychol.*, 61:395–402.
—— LUGO, M. & YOUDIN, R. (1974), Cardiac correlates of cognitive processing. *Psychosom. Med.*, 36:420–435.
—— MAYES, L. & DAHL, H. (1994), Monitoring the analytic surface. *J. Amer. Psychoanal. Assn.*, 42:43–64.
SPEZIALE-BAGLIACCA, R. (1995), Letter from Genoa. *Psychoanal. Bks.*, 6:136–138.
SPILLIUS, E. (1992), Clinical experiences of projective identification. In *Clinical Lectures on Klein and Bion*, ed. R. Anderson. London: Tavistock/Routledge, pp. 59–73.
—— (1994), On formulating clinical fact to a patient. *Internat. J. Psycho-Anal.*, 75:1121–1132.
SPRENGNETHER, M. (1985), Ghost writing: a meditation on literary criticism as narrative. In *The Psychoanalytic Study of Literature*, ed. J. Reppen & M. Charney. Hillsdale, NJ: The Analytic Press, pp. 37–49.
SPRUIELL, V. (1983), The rules and frames of the psychoanalytic situation. *Psychoanal. Quart.*, 52:1–33.
—— (1986), The foundations of psychoanalysis: an essay on a philosophical book by Adolf Grünbaum. *Internat. Rev. Psycho-Anal.*, 14:169–183.
—— (1993), Deterministic chaos and the sciences of complexity: psychoanalysis in the midst of a general scientific revolution. *J. Amer. Psychoanal. Assn.*, 41:3–44.
SQUIRE, L. (1986), Mechanisms of memory. *Science*, 232:1612–1619.

STEELE, R. (1979), Psychoanalysis and hermeneutics. *Internat. Rev. Psycho-Anal.*, 6:389–911.

—— (1985), Paul Ricoeur: reporting, reading, and interpreting. In *A Study of Modern Psychoanalytic Theorists*, ed. J. Reppen. Hillsdale, NJ: The Analytic Press, pp. 311–327.

STEGMÜLLER, W. (1969), *Probleme und Resultate der Wissenschaftstheorie und Analytischen Philosophie, Vol. 1.* Berlin: Springer.

STEIN, M. (1979), Review of *The Restoration of the Self*, by H. Kohut (1977). *J. Amer. Psychoanal. Assn.*, 27:665–680.

STEINER, R. (1995), Hermeneutics or Hermes-mess? *Internat. J. Psycho-Anal.*, 76:435–445.

STENGEL, E., EZRIEL, H. & FARRELL, B. (1951), The scientific testing of psychoanalytic findings and theory. *Brit. J. Med. Psychol.*, 24:26–29.

STENT, G. (1975), Limits to the scientific understanding of man. *Science*, 187:1052–1057.

STERN, D. (1983), Unformulated experience: from familiar chaos to creative disorder. *Contemp. Psychoanal.*, 19: 71–99.

—— (1985), Some controversies regarding constuctivism and psychoanalysis. *Contemp. Psychoanal.*, 21:201–208.

—— (1991), A philosophy for the embedded analyst: Gadamer's hermeneutics and the social paradigm of psychoanalysis. *Contemp. Psychoanal.*, 27:51–80.

STICH, S. (1983), *From Folk Psychology to Cognitive Science*. Cambridge, MA: MIT/Bradford.

STILES, W. (1993), Quality control in qualitative research. *Clin. Psychol. Rev.*, 13:593–618.

—— (1994), Views of the chasm between psychotherapy research and practice. In *Psychotherapy Research and Practice: Bridging the Gap*, ed. P. Talley, H. Strupp & S. Butler. New York: Basic Books, pp. 154–166.

STOLLACK, G., GUERNEY, B. & ROTHBERG, M. (1966), *Psychotherapy Research: Selected Readings*. Chicago: Rand-McNally.

STOLLER, R. (1979), *Sexual Excitement: Dynamics of Erotic Life*. New York: Pantheon.

—— & GEERTSMA, R. (1963), The consistency of psychiatrists' clinical judgments. *J. Nerv. Ment. Dis.*, 137:58–66.

STOLOROW, R. (1978), The concept of psychic structure: Its metapsychology and clinical psychoanalytic meanings. *Internat. Rev. Psycho-Anal.*, 5:313–320.

—— BRANDCHAFT, B. & ATWOOD, G. (1987), *Psychoanalytic Treatment: An Intersubjective Approach*. Hillsdale, NJ: The Analytic Press.

STONE, J., DUNPHY, D., SMITH, M. & OGILVIE, M. (1966), *The General Inquirer: A Computer Approach to Content Analysis*. Cambridge, MA: MIT Press.

STRENGER, C. (1986), Review of *The Foundations of Psychoanalysis*, by A.

Grünbaum (1984). *Internat. J. Psycho-Anal.*, 67:255–260.

—— (1991), *Between Hermeneutics and Science*. Madison, CT: International Universities Press.

STRUPP, H. (1958), The performance of psychoanalytic and client-centered therapists in an initial interview. *J. Consult. Psychol.*, 22: 265–274.

—— (1960), *Psychotherapists in Action*. New York: Grune & Stratton.

—— (1973), *Psychotherapy: Clinical, Research, and Theoretical Issues*. New York: Aronson.

—— (1986), Transference: one of Freud's basic discoveries. *Behav. Brain Sci.*, 9:260–261.

—— & BINDER, J. (1984), *Psychotherapy in a New Key*. New York: Basic Books.

—— SCHACHT, T. & HENRY, W. (1988), Problem-treatment-outcome congruence: a principle whose time has come. In *Psychoanalytic Process Research Strategies*, ed. H. Dahl, H. Kächele & H. Thomä. New York: Springer, pp. 1–14.

STURROCK, J. (1979), *Structuralism and Since*. New York: Oxford University Press.

SULEIMAN, S. (1980), Redundancy and the "readable" text. *Poetics Today*, 1:119–142.

SULLOWAY, F. (1979), *Freud, Biologist of the Mind: Beyond the Psychoanalytic Legend*. New York: Basic Books.

SUPPE, F. (1977), *The Structure of Scientific Theories*. Urbana: University of Illinois Press.

SUPPES, P. (1967), What is a scientific theory? In *Philosophy of Science Today*, ed. S. Morgenbesser. New York: Basic Books, pp. 56–67.

—— (1970), *A Probabilistic Theory of Causality*. Amsterdam: North-Holland.

SUTHERLAND, J. (1963), Object relations theory and the conceptual model of psychoanalysis. *Brit. J. Med. Psychol.*, 36:109–124.

SYMPOSIUM (1981), Emmanuel Peterfreund on information and systems theory. *Psychoanal. Rev.*, 68:159–190.

—— (1994), The conceptualisation and communication of clinical facts in psychoanalysis, ed. D. Tuckett. *Internat. J. Psycho-Anal.*, 75:865–1266.

—— (1995), Psyche '94: International Symposium on Mind-Body Problems, rep. F. Levin. *Psychoanal. Quart.*, 64:429–432.

TALLEY, P., STRUPP, H. & BUTLER, S., eds. (1994), *Psychotherapy Research and Practice: Bridging the Gap*. New York: Basic Books.

TAYLOR, C. (1971), Interpretation and the sciences of man. *Rev. Metaphysics*, 25:3–34. Also in *Readings in the Philosophy of Social Science*, ed. M. Martin & L. McIntyre. Cambridge, MA: MIT Press, 1994, pp. 181–211.

—— (1991), The dialogical self. In *The Interpretive Turn*, eds D. Hiley, J. Bohman & R. Shusterman. Ithaca, NY: Cornell University Press, pp. 304–314.

TAYLOR D. (1970), *Explanation and Meaning*. Cambridge, UK: Cambridge University Press.

TAYLOR, K. (1970), *Computer Applications in Psychotherapy: Bibliography and Abstracts*. Washington, DC: NIMH.

TAYLOR, S. & CROCKER, J. (1981), Schematic bases of social information processing. In *Social Cognition: The Ontario Symposium*, ed. E. Higgins, C. Herman & M. Zanna. Hillsdale, NJ: Lawrence Erlbaum Associates, pp. 89–134.

TELLER, V. (1988), Artificial intelligence as a basic science for psychoanalytic research. In *Psychoanalytic Process Research Strategies*, ed. H. Dahl, H. Kächele & H. Thomä. Berlin: Springer, pp. 161–177.

——— & DAHL, H. (1981), The framework for a model of psychoanalytic inference. *Proceedings of the 7th International Conference on Artificial Intelligence*, 1:394–400.

——— & ——— (1986), The microstructure of free association. *J. Amer. Psychoanal. Assn.*, 34:763–798.

——— & ——— (1993), What psychoanalysis needs is more empirical research. In *Research in Psychoanalysis: Process, Development, Outcome*, ed. T. Shapiro & R. Emde. *J. Amer. Psychoanal. Assn.*, 41(Suppl.):31–49.

TENZER, A. (1985), Constructing new truths. *Contemp. Psychoanal.*, 21:228–236.

TERWEE, S. (1987), Grünbaum's *Foundations of Psychoanalysis*. *Psychoanal. Contemp. Thought*, 10:347–372.

THAGARD, P. (1978), The best explanation: criteria for theory choice. *J. Philos.*, 75:76–92.

THASS-THIENEMANN, T. (1968), *The Interpretation of Language: 1. Understanding the Symbolic Meaning of Language*. New York: Aronson.

——— (1973), *The Interpretation of Language: 2. Understanding the Unconscious Meaning of Language*. New York: Aronson.

THOMÄ, H. & HOUBEN, A. (1967), Ueber die Validierung psychoanalytischer Theorien durch die Untersuchung von Deutungsaktionen. *Psyche*, 21:664–692.

——— & KÄCHELE, H. (1975), Problems of metascience and methodology in clinical psychoanalytic research. *The Annual of Psychoanalysis*, 3:49–119. Madison, CT: International Universities Press.

——— GRÜNZIG, H., BÖCKENFÖRDE, H. & KÄCHELE, H. (1976), Das Konsensus Problem in der Psychoanalyse. *Psyche*, 30:978–1027.

——— & KÄCHELE, H. (1987), *Psychoanalytic Practice: 1. Principles*. New York: Springer.

——— & ——— (1990), *Psychoanalytic Practice: 2. Clinical Studies*. New York: Springer.

THOMAS, L. (1978), Hubris in science? *Science*, 20:1459–1462.

THOMAS, R. (1990), *Dreams of Authority*. Ithaca, NY: Cornell University Press.

TODOROV, T. (1977), *The Poetics of Prose*. New York: Basil Blackwell.

TOMKINS, S. (1962), *Affect, Imagery, Consciousness, Vol. 1: The Positive Affects*. New York: Springer.

—— (1963), *Affect, Imagery, Consciousness, Vol. 2: The Negative Affects*. New York: Springer.

—— (1979), Script theory: differential magnification of affects. In *Nebraska Symposium on Motivation*, ed. H. Home & R. Dienstbier. Lincoln: University of Nebraska Press, pp. 210–236.

TOU, J. & GONZALEZ, R. (1974), *Pattern Recognition Principles*. Reading, MA: Addison-Wesley.

TOUKMANIAN, S. & RENNIE, D., eds. (1992), *Psychotherapy Process Research: Paradigmatic and Narrative Approaches*. Newbury Park, CA: Sage.

TOULMIN, S. (1953), *The Philosophy of Science*. London: Hutchinson; New York: Harper & Row, 1960.

—— (1972), *Human Understanding*. Princeton, NJ: Princeton University Press.

—— (1982), The construal of reality criticism in modern and postmodern science. *Critical Inq.*, 9:93–111. Also in *The Politics of Interpretation*, ed. W. Mitchell. Chicago: University of Chicago Press, pp. 99–117, 1983.

—— (1990), *Cosmopolis*. Chicago: University of Chicago Press.

TREISMAN, A. (1986), Features and objects in visual processing. *Sci. Amer.*, 255:114–125.

TREISMAN, A.M. (1965), Verbal responses and contextual constraints in language. *J. Verb. Learn. Verb. Behav.*, 4:118–128.

TREURNIET, N. (1980), On the relation between the concepts of self and ego in Kohut's psychology of the self. *Internat. J. Psycho-Anal.*, 61:325–333.

—— (1983), Psychoanalysis and self-psychology: a metapsychological essay with a clinical illustration. *J. Amer. Psychoanal. Assn.*, 31:59–100.

TRIGGER, B. (1978), *Time and Tradition: Essays in Archaeological Interpretation*. New York: Columbia University Press.

TROSMAN, H., RECHTSCHAFFEN, A., OFFENKRANTZ, W. & WOLPERT, E. (1960), Studies in psychophysiology of dreams, IV. Relations among dreams in sequence. *Arch. Gen. Psychiat.*, 3:602–607.

TRYON, W. (1982), A simplified time series analysis for evaluating treatment interventions. *J. Appl. Behav. Anal.*, 15:423–429.

TUCKETT, D. (1983), Words and the psychoanalytic interaction. *Internat. Rev. Psycho-Anal.*, 10:407–413.

—— (1993), Some thoughts on the presentation and discussion of the clinical material of psychoanalysis. *Internat. J. Psycho-Anal.*, 74:1175–1189.

—— (1994a), The conceptualisation and communication of clinical facts in psychoanalysis: Foreword. *Internat. J. Psycho-Anal.*, 75:865–870.

—— (1994b), Developing a grounded hypothesis to understand a clinical process: the role of conceptualisation in validation. *Internat. J. Psycho-Anal.*, 75:1159–1180.

—— (1995), Editorial afterthoughts: the conceptualisation and communication of clinical facts in psychoanalysis. *Internat. J. Psycho-Anal.*, 76:653–662.

TURK, D. & SALOVEY, P,. eds. (1988), *Reasoning, Inference, and Judgment in Clinical Psychology*. New York: Free Press.

TVERSKY, A. & KAHNEMAN, D. (1974), Judgment under uncertainty: heuristics and biases. *Science*, 185:1124–1131.

TWENEY, R., DOHERTY, M. & MYNATT, C., eds. (1981), *On Scientific Thinking*. New York: Columbia University Press.

VAN DEN DAELE, L. (1974), Discussion of M. Rendon's "Structuralism in psychoanalysis." *Amer. J. Psychoanal.*, 39:353–357.

VAN VELZEN, H. (1988), Irma's rape: the hermeneutics of structuralism and psychoanalysis compared. *The Psychoanalytic Study of Society*, 12:1–36. Hillsdale, NJ: The Analytic Press.

VAUGHAN, S. & ROOSE, S. (1995), The analytic process: clinical and research definitions. *Internat. J. Psycho-Anal.*, 76:343–356.

VERGOTE, A. (1983), From Freud's "other scene" to Lacan's "other." In *Interpreting Lacan*, ed. J. Smith. New Haven, CT: Yale University Press, pp. 193–222.

VIDERMAN, S. (1974), Interpretation in the analytical space. *Internat. Rev. Psycho-Anal.*, 1:467–480.

——— (1979), The analytic space: meaning and problems. *Psychoanal. Quart.*, 48:257–291.

VIEDERMAN, M. (1983), The psychodynamic life narrative: its implications as the transference cure. *Psychiatry*, 46:236–246.

VON ECKARDT, B. (1981), On evaluating the scientific status of psychoanalysis. *J. Philos.*, 78:570–572.

——— (1982), Why Freud's research methodology was unscientific. *Psychoanal. Contemp. Thought*, 5:549–574.

——— (1985), Adolf Grünbaum and psychoanalytic epistemology. In *Beyond Freud: A Study of Modern Psychoanalytic Theorists*, ed. J. Reppen. Hillsdale, NJ: The Analytic Press, pp. 353–403.

——— (1986), Grünbaum's challenge to Freud's logic of argumentation: a reconstruction and an addendum. *Behav. Brain Sci.*, 9:262–263.

VON GLASERSFELD, E. (1984), An introduction to radical constructivism. In *The Invented Reality*, ed. P. Watzlawick. New York: Norton, pp. 17–40.

——— & VON WRIGHT, G. (1971), *Explanation and Understanding*. Ithaca, NY: Cornell University Press.

VYGOTZKY, L. (1962), *Language and Thought*. Cambridge, MA: MIT Press.

——— (1987), *The Collected Papers of L. V. Vygotsky, Vol. 1*, ed. R. Rieber & A. Carton. New York: Plenum.

WACHTEL, P. (1986), Early Freud, late Freud, conflict and intentionality. *Behav. Brain Sci.*, 9:263–264.

——— (1993), *Therapeutic Communication*. New York: Guilford.

WAELDER, R. (1930), The principle of multiple function: observations on overdetermination. In *Psychoanalysis: Observation, Theory, Application. Selected Papers of Robert Waelder*, ed. S. Guttman. New York: International Universities Press, 1976, pp. 68–83.

—— (1939), The criteria of interpretation. In *Psychoanalysis: Observation, Theory, Application. Selected Papers of Robert Waelder*, ed. S. Guttman. New York: International Universities Press, 1976, pp. 189–199.

—— (1960), *Basic Theory of Psychoanalysis*. New York: International Universities Press.

—— (1962), Psychoanalysis, scientific method, and philosophy. *J. Amer. Psychoanal. Assn.*, 10:617–637. Also in *Psychoanalysis: Observation, Theory, Application. Selected Papers of Robert Waelder*, ed. S. Guttman. New York: International Universities Press, 1976, pp. 248–274.

—— (1963), Psychic determinism and the possibility of predictions. *Psychoanal. Quart.*, 32:15–42. Also in *Psychoanalysis: Observation, Theory, Application. Selected Papers of Robert Waelder*, ed. S. Guttman. New York: International Universities Press, 1976, pp. 283–307.

—— (1970), Observation, historical reconstruction, and experiment: an epistemological study. In *Psychoanalysis and Philosophy*, ed. C. Hanly & M. Lazerowitz. New York: International Universities Press, pp. 280–326. Also in *Psychoanalysis: Observation, Theory, Application. Selected Papers of Robert Waelder*, ed. S. Guttman. New York: International Universities Press, 1976, pp. 635–675.

WAKEFIELD, J. (1990), Why instinctual impulses can't be unconscious: an exploration of Freud's cognitivism. *Psychoanal. Contemp. Thought*, 13:265–288.

—— (1992a), Freud and cognitive psychology: the conceptual interface. In *Interface of Psychoanalysis and Psychology*, ed. J. Barron, M. Eagle & D. Wolitzky. Washington, DC: American Psychological Association, pp. 77–98.

—— (1992b), Freud and the intentionality of affect. *Psychoanal. Psychol.*, 9:1–23.

WALDRON, S. (1995), Review of *Understanding Transference*, by L. Luborsky & P. Crits-Christoph (1990). *Psychoanal. Quart.*, 64:398–402.

WALLACE, E. (1983a), Historiography in history and psychoanalysis. *Bull. Hist. Med.*, 57:247–266.

—— (1983b), *Freud and Anthropology*. Philadelphia: Lea & Febiger.

—— (1985), *Historiography and Causation in Psychoanalysis*. Hillsdale, NJ: The Analytic Press.

—— (1986), The scientific status of psychoanalysis: a review of Grünbaum's *The Foundations of Psychoanalysis* (1984). *J. Nerv. Ment. Dis.*, 174:379–386.

—— (1988), What is "truth"? *Amer. J. Psychiat.*, 145:137–147.

—— (1989a), Toward a phenomenological and minimally theoretical psychoanalysis. *Annual Psychoanal.*, 17:17–69.

—— (1989b), Pitfalls of a one-sided image of science: Adolf Grünbaum's *Foundations of Psychoanalysis (1984). J. Amer. Psychoanal. Assn.*, 37:493–529.

WALLERSTEIN, R. (1964), The role of prediction in theory building in psychoanalysis. *J. Amer. Psychoanal. Assn.*, 12:675–691.

—— (1968), Discussion of G. Engel's "Some obstacles to the development of research in psychoanalysis." *J. Amer. Psychoanal. Assn.*, 16:215–222.

—— (1975), *Psychotherapy and Psychoanalysis: Theory, Practice, Research.* New York: International Universities Press.

—— (1985), How does self psychology differ in practice? *Internat. J. Psycho-Anal.*, 66:391–404.

—— (1986a), *Forty-Two Lives in Treatment.* New York: Guilford.

—— (1986b), Psychoanalysis as a science: a response to the new challenges. *Psychoanal. Quart.*, 55:414–451.

—— (1988), One psychoanalysis or many? *Internat. J. Psycho-Anal.*, 69:5–21.

—— ed. (1992), *The Common Ground of Psychoanalysis.* Northvale, NJ: Aronson.

—— (1994), Borderline disorders: report on the 4th IPA research conference. *Internat. J. Psycho-Anal.*, 75:763–774.

—— (1995), Review of *Psychoanalysis in Transition: A Personal View*, by M. Gill (1994). *J. Amer. Psychoanal. Assn.*, 43:595–600.

—— & SAMPSON, H. (1971), Issues in research in the psychoanalytic process. *Internat. J. Psycho-Anal.*, 52:11–50.

—— ROBBINS, L., SARGENT, H. & LUBORSKY, L. (1956), The psychotherapy research project of the Menninger Foundation: rationale, method, and sample use. First report. *Bull. Menn. Clin.*, 20:221–278.

WASKOW, I. & PARLOFF, M., eds. (1975), *Psychotherapy Change Measures.* Rockville, MD: NIMH.

WATSON, W. (1990), Types of pluralism. *The Monist*, 73:350–366.

—— (1993), *The Architectonics of Meaning: Foundations of the New Pluralism.* Chicago: University of Chicago Press.

WATZLAWICK, P., BEAVIN, J. & JACKSON, D. (1967), *Pragmatics of Human Communication.* New York: Norton.

WAX, M. (1983), How Oedipus falsifies Popper: psychoanalysis as a normative science. *Psychiatry*, 46:95–105.

—— (1986), Psychoanalysis: conventional wisdom, self knowledge, or inexact science? *Behav. Brain Sci.*, 9:264–265.

—— (1995), How secure are Grünbaum's *Foundations? Internat. J. Psycho-Anal.*, 76:547–556.

WEBER, J., ELINSON, J. & MOSS, L. (1966), The application of ego strength scales to psychoanalytic clinic records. In *Developments in Psychoanalysis at Columbia University*, ed. G. Goldman & D. Shapiro. New York: Hafner, pp. 215–281.

WEBER, S. (1991), *Return to Freud: Jacques Lacan's Dislocation of Psychoanalysis*, trans. M. Levine. Cambridge, UK: Cambridge University Press.

WEGMAN, C. (1985), *Psychoanalysis and Cognitive Psychology*. New York: Academic Press.

WEICH, M. (1986), The good enough analyst. In Panel: Clinical Aspects of Language, Chm. T. Shapiro. *J. Amer. Psychoanal. Assn.*, 34:692–694.

WEINSHEL, E. (1984), Some observations on the psychoanalytic process. *Psychoanal. Quart.*, 53:63–92.

WEISS, F. (1974), Meaning and dream interpretation. In *Freud: A Collection of Critical Essays*, ed. R. Wollheim. Garden City, NY: Anchor/Doubleday, pp. 53–69.

WEISS, J. (1993), Empirical studies of the psychoanalytic process. *J. Amer. Psychoanal. Assn.*, 41(Suppl.):7–29.

——— & SAMPSON, H. (1986), *The Psychoanalytic Process: Theory, Clinical Observations, and Empirical Research*. New York: Guilford.

WELLMAN, H. (1990), *The Child's Theory of Mind*. Cambridge, MA: MIT Press.

WERMAN, D. (1979), Methodologic problems in the psychoanalytic interpretation of literature: a review of studies of Sophocles' Antigone. *J. Amer. Psychoanal. Assn.*, 27:451–478.

WERTHEIMER, M. (1945), *Productive Thinking*. New York: Harper, 1959.

WERTHEIMER, M.M. (1968), Gestalt psychology. *Encyclopaedia Britanican*, 10:370–371.

WESTON, A. (1992), *A Rulebook for Arguments*. Indianapolis, IN: Hackett.

WETZLER, S. (1985). The historical truth of psychoanalytic reconstructions. *Internat. Rev. Psycho-Anal.*, 12:187–197.

WHITE, H. (1973), *Metahistory*. Baltimore, MD: Johns Hopkins University Press.

——— (1987), *The Content of the Form*. Baltimore, MD: Johns Hopkins University Press.

WHITEHORN, J. (1947), The concepts of "meaning" and "cause" in psychodynamics. *Amer. J. Psychiat.*, 151:199–202, 1994.

WICKELGREN, W. (1974), *How to Solve Problems*. London: Tavistock (pbk).

WILCOCKS, R. (1994), *Maelzel's Chess Player: Sigmund Freud and the Rhetoric of Deceit*. Lanham, MD: Rowan & Littlefield.

WILDEN, A. (1968), Lacan and the discourse of the other. In *The Language of the Self: The Function of Language in Psychoanalysis*, by J. Lacan. Baltimore, MD: Johns Hopkins University Press, pp. 157–311.

——— (1980), *System and Structure: Essays in Communication and Exchange*. London: Tavistock.

WILKES, K. (1993), The relationship between scientific psychology and common sense psychology. In *Folk Psychology and the Philosophy of Mind*, ed. S. Christensen & D. Turner. Hillsdale, NJ: Lawrence Erlbaum Associates, pp. 144–187.

WILLIAMS, M. (1977), *Groundless Belief.* New Haven, CT: Yale University Press.

WILSON, A. & WEINSTEIN, L. (1992a), An investigation into some implications of a Vygotzkian perspective on the origins of mind: psychoanalysis and Vygotzkian psychology, Part I. *J. Amer. Psychoanal. Assn.*, 40:349–379.

——— & ——— (1992b), Language and the psychoanalytic process: psychoanalysis and Vygotzkian psychology, Part II. *J. Amer. Psychoanal. Assn.*, 40:725–760.

WILSON, M. (1994), Review of *Arguing with Lacan: Ego Psychology and Language*, by J. Smith (1991). *Psychoanal. Quart.*, 63:150–154.

WIMSATT, W. (1986), Heuristics and the study of behavior. In *Metatheory in Social Science*, ed. D. Fiske & R. Shweder. Chicago: University of Chicago Press, pp. 293–314.

——— (1994), Lewontin's evidence (that there isn't any). In *Questions of Evidence*, ed. J. Chandler, A. Davidson & H. Harootunian. Chicago: University of Chicago Press, pp. 492–503.

WINNICOTT, D. (1965), *The Maturational Processes and the Facilitating Environment.* London: Hogarth Press.

——— (1971), *Playing and Reality*. London: Tavistock.

WISDOM, J. (1956), Psychoanalytic technology. *Brit. J. Philos. Sci.*, 7:15–29. Also in *Psychoanalytic Clinical Interpretation*, ed. L. Paul. London: Free Press of Glencoe (Macmillan), 1963, pp. 143–161.

——— (1967), Testing an interpretation within an analytic session. *Internat. J. Psycho-Anal.*, 48:44–52.

WITTGENSTEIN, L. (1945–1949), *Philosophical Investigations*, trans. G. Anscombe. New York: Macmillan, 1953.

——— (1969), *Philosophical Investigations*, New York: Macmillan.

WOLF, E. (1986), Discrepancies between analysand and analyst in experiencing the analysis. In *Progress in Self Psychology, Vol 2*, ed. A. Goldberg. New York: Guilford, pp. 84–94.

——— (1989), Therapeutic experiences. In *Dimensions of Self Experience: Progress in Self Psychology, Vol. 5*, ed. A. Goldberg. Hillsdale, NJ: The Analytic Press, pp. 105–119.

——— (1991), The personal myth and the history of the self. In *The Personal Myth in Psychoanalytic Theory*, ed. P. Hartocollis & I. Graham. Madison, CT: International Universities Press, pp. 89–107.

WOLFENSTEIN, E. (1990), A man knows not where to have it: Habermas, Grünbaum and the epistemological status of psychoanalysis. *Internat. Rev. Psycho-Anal.*, 17:23–45.

WOLFSON, A. & SAMPSON, H. (1976), A comparison of process notes and tape recordings—implications for therapy research. *Arch. Gen. Psychiat.*, 33:558–563.

WOLLHEIM, R. (1968), Thought and passion. *Proceedings of the Aristotelian Society*, 68:1–24.

——— (1969), The mind and the mind's image of itself. *Internat. J. Psycho-Anal.*, 50:209–220.

——— (1971), *Sigmund Freud*. New York: Viking, 1971; Cambridge, UK: Cambridge University Press, 1981.

——— ed. (1974), *Freud: A Collection of Critical Essays*. Garden City, NY: Doubleday/Anchor.

——— (1984), *The Thread of Life*. Cambridge, MA: Cambridge University Press.

——— (1993a), *The Mind and Its Depths*. Cambridge, MA: Harvard University Press.

——— (1993b), Desire, belief, and Professor Grünbaum's Freud. In *The Mind and Its Depths*. Cambridge, MA: Harvard University Press, pp. 91–111.

——— & HOPKINS, J., eds. (1982), *Philosophical Essays on Freud*. Cambridge, UK: Cambridge University Press.

WOLMAN, B. (1964), Evidence in psychoanalytic research. *J. Amer. Psychoanal. Assn.*, 12:717–733.

——— (1984), *Logic of Science in Psychoanalysis*. New York: Columbia University Press.

WOODARD, G. (1993a), The Psychoanalytic Inference Process. Unpublished manuscript. Department of Psychology, University of Michigan, Ann Arbor.

——— (1993b), The Phenomenology of the Third Ear: An Empirical Investigation of the Psychoanalytic Inference Process. Unpublished doctoral dissertation, Department of Psychology, University of Michigan, Ann Arbor.

WOOLFOLK, R. (1986), Hermeneutics and psychoanalysis. *Behav. Brain Sci.*, 9:265–266.

WYSS, D. (1966), *Depth Psychology*, trans. G. Onn. New York: Norton.

YORKE, C. (1965), Some metapsychological aspects of interpretation. *Brit. J. Med. Psychol.*, 38:27–42.

ZAC, J. (1972), An investigation of how interpretations arise in the analyst. *Internat. J. Psycho-Anal.*, 53:315–320.

ZAJONC, R. (1988), Prolegomena for the study of access to mental events: notes on Singer's chapter. In *Psychodynamics and Cognition*, ed. M. Horowitz. Chicago: University of Chicago Press, pp. 347–359.

——— & MARKUS, H. (1984), Affect and cognition: the hard interface. In *Emotions, Cognitions and Behavior*, ed. C. Izard, J. Kagan & R. Zajonc. Cambridge, UK: Cambridge University Press, pp. 73–102.

ZIMAN, J. (1978), *Reliable Knowledge*. Cambridge, UK: Cambridge University Press.

Author Index

A

Abelson, R., 84, 136, 329n.
Abraham, I., 63, 103, 302, 304, 315n., 327n., 334n., 335n.
Abrams, M., 127
Achinstein, P., 24
Adams, B., 243
Adams-Webber, J., 318n.
Addison, R., 317n., 324n., 337n.
Agassi, J., 26, 72, 73
Ahumada, J., 32, 315n.
Allport, F., 100
Alston, T., 321n.
Anderson, C., 324n., 334n.
Anderson, G., 64
Anderson, J. R., 130
Andresen, J., 303
Anscombe, R., 76, 321n.
Anzieu, D., 51
Apel, K.-O., 32, 35
Appelbaum, S., 337n.
Applegarth, A., 59
Arkes, H., 64
Arlow, J., 48, 60, 111, 120, 225–6, 299–300, 317n., 325n., 336n., 340n.
Arnheim, R., 336n.
Arnoff, F., 315n.
Aronson, E., 322n.
Asch, S., 323n.
Atwood, G. E., 324n.
Auerbach, S., 338n.
Aufhauser, M., 321n.
Aulagnier, P., 320n.
Austin, J., 80, 117

B

Bachrach, H., 143
Bakan, D., 46
Bakhtin, M. M., 33, 127
Bales, R., 244
Bandura, A., 329n.
Bannister, D., 242, 243
Baranger, M., 316n., 320n.
Barber, F., 131, 322n.
Barber, J., 338n.
Barclay, F., 152–5, 317n., 330n., 331n.
Barglow, P., 227, 338n., 339n.
Barker, S., 24, 317n.
Barlow, D., 336n., 338n.
Barnes, A., 286, 289, 290, 339n.
Baron, R., 324n.
Barratt, B., 25, 60, 206, 318n., 321n., 322n., 326n., 336n.
Barron, J., 315n., 330n., 334n.
Barthes, R., 84, 127–8, 318n., 325n., 334n.
Bartlett, R., 132
Barton, A., 337n.
Basch, M. F., 329n., 330n.
Bates, E., 321n.
Bauer, H., 21, 22, 317n.
Beahrs, J., 21
Beckson, K., 302
Beitman, B., 339n.
Beland, H., 337n.
Bell, P., 216, 316n.
Bellack, A., 339n.
Bellak, L., 50, 101, 145, 240, 323n., 336n., 337n.

Bellin, E., 322n.
Benedek, L., 63
Benenson, F., 46
Benjamin, J., 93, 137, 322n.
Benjamin, J. D., 337n.
Benjamin, L., 137
Benveniste, E., 68
Beres, D., 320n.
Berger, L., 52, 319n., 332n., 335n.
Bergin, A., 338n.
Bergmann, M., 317n.
Berkson, W., 304, 339n.
Bernardi, R., 303, 315n., 336n., 340n.
Bernfeld, S., 100, 114, 337n.
Bernstein, R., x, 28, 32, 93, 131, 169, 324n., 336n.
Betti, E., 317n., 324n., 335n.
Bhaskar, R., 318n.
Binder, A., 338n.
Binder, J., 244, 315n.
Bion, W., 116, 198, 319n.
Birdwhistell, R., 118, 121
Blanck, G., 332n.
Blanck, R., 332n.
Blatt, S., 136, 329n.
Bleicher, J., 324n.
Blight, J., 27, 86
Blomfield, O., 11
Boesky, D., 218, 319n., 336n., 337n.
Bogdan, R., 330n.
Bohman, J., 33–4, 317n.
Bolland, J., 338n.
Bolles, R., 46
Bonaparte, M., 339n.
Bond, J., 319n.
Bonjour, L., 21, 317n.
Booth, S., 235
Bos, J., 174
Bouchard, M., 87, 205
Bowers, K., 49, 329n.
Bowie, M., 70, 72, 73, 321n.
Bowlby, J., 137, 205, 323n.
Bowman, M., 332n., 340n.
Boyd, R., 37
Boyd, Z., 72, 129, 320n.
Boyer, L., 324n.
Bransford, J., 114
Breen, D., 242
Brenneis, C., 127–8
Brenner, C., 27–8, 233, 237, 337n.
Brentano, F., 18, 152–5, 167, 330n.
Breuer, J., 5, 85, 110–11, 119, 179, 184, 201, 316n.
Bridgman, P., 22
Britton, R., 325n.
Brody, B., 336n.
Brody, E., 124, 316n.
Brook, A., 148, 155–7, 160–1, 163, 186, 188, 209, 316n., 317n., 330n., 331n., 334n., 335n.
Brooks, P., 127, 323n., 325n., 327n.
Bruner, J., 84, 173, 309, 334n., 335n.
Bruss, N., 186, 226, 320n., 326n., 335n., 336n.
Bryman, A., 317n., 337n.
Bucci, W., 192–4, 238, 326n., 329n., 335n., 339n.
Buckley, P., 318n.
Buie, D., 335n.
Burgess, B., 317n., 337n.
Burkhardt, J., 328n.
Burman, E., 83
Busch, F., 311, 322n., 341n.
Butler, S., 338n.

C

Calef, V., 325n.
Callebaut, W., 23, 37–9, 173, 318n., 321n., 331n.
Calogeras, R., 321n., 324n.
Campbell, D., 34, 38, 96, 99, 148, 318n., 332n., 338n.
Caplan, A., 335n.
Cardinal, M., 198
Carlson, L., 136
Carlson, R., 136
Carroll, E., 323n.
Cartwright, D., 335n.
Casement, P., 57
Caston, J., 11, 315n., 319n., 333n.
Cavell, M., 33, 188, 290, 316n.

Caws, P., 29, 69, 101, 107–10, 143, 189, 230, 321n., 331n.
Chabot, B., 327n.
Chandler, J., 226
Chapman, J., 319n., 320n.
Chapman, L., 319n., 320n.
Charny, E., 323n.
Chase, W., 140
Chassan, J., 232, 336n., 338n.
Cherry, C., 123, 321n.
Chertok, L., 4–5
Cheshire, N., 35–6, 87, 98–9, 127, 181, 187, 212, 218, 222, 228–9, 324n., 335n.–337n., 340n.
Chessick, R., 48, 72, 321n., 324n.
Chevron, E., 141
Child, W., 332n.
Chinen, A., 326n.
Chomsky, N., 74–5
Christensen, S., 330n.
Christiansen, B., 332n.
Ciardi, J., 321n.
Cioffi, F., 335n.
Clark, E., 324n.
Clark, H., 324n.
Clarke, D., 35, 131
Clemes, S., 338n.
Clippinger, J., 82–3
Clyman, R., 330n.
Coen, S., 126, 328n.
Cohen, N., 330n.
Colby, K., 21, 22, 61, 142, 179, 236, 333n., 334n., 338n.
Collins, S., 332n.
Coltart, N., 320n.
Coltrera, J., xi, 8, 182, 316n., 326n., 327n., 340n.
Comte, A., 4
Conant, J., 317n.
Connolly, J., 213
Cook, T., 332n.
Cooper, A., 10, 33, 60, 62, 293, 316n., 318n.
Cooper, S., 293, 315n., 320n.
Costello, C., 338n.
Craik, K., 133, 340n.
Crits-Christoph, P., 10, 49, 176, 315n., 319n., 322n., 336n., 338n., 341n.
Crocker, J., 329n.
Culler, J., 126, 327n.
Cummins, R., 312
Cunningham, R., 138
Curtis, H., 317n.

D

Dahl, H., 112–13, 175, 229–30, 250–1, 253, 321n., 337n.–340n.
Dalbiez, R., 1, 169, 187, 211, 302
Dallas, M., 324n., 334n.
D'Andrade, R., 138
Danehy, J., 325n.
Danto, A., 322n.
Danziger, K., 64, 200, 214, 320n.
Darwin, C., 131, 305
Davidson, A., 176, 317n., 320n., 338n., 340n.
Davidson, D., 144
De Azevedo, A., 337n.
de Beaugrande, R., 86, 102, 252
De Carlo, N., 35, 318n.
De Groot, A., 59, 61, 140, 194–5, 219, 222, 224, 294, 327n., 335n.
De Man, P., 127
de Monbreun, B., 334n., 335n.
De Racker, G., 319n., 320n.
Deely, J., 123
Deese, J., 325n.
Demos, R., 231
Dennett, D., 36, 148, 152, 220, 330n., 331n.
Derrida, J., 328n.
Devereaux, G., 337n.
Devlin, K., 75
DeWitt, K., 338n.
Dey, I., 337n.
Diamond, D., 140, 141, 315n.
Diesing, P., 24, 49, 97, 99, 209, 214–15, 221, 223, 295, 300–2, 310, 313, 332n.–334n.
Dilman, I., 331n.
Dilthey, W., 17, 105
Dimberg, U., 133

Dittman, A., 325n.
Dixon, N., 325n.
Dreyfus, H., xi, 34
Duda, R., 139
Duncan, D., 1, 54–5, 57, 335n.

E

Eagle, M., 32, 63, 65, 89, 195, 197, 202, 205, 209, 218, 219, 245, 311, 313, 316n., 318n., 320n., 322n., 331n.–333n., 336n., 340n.
Earman, J., 338n.
Eccles, J., 305
Eco, U., 123, 169
Edel, L., 327n., 328n.
Edelson, M., xii, 28, 37, 54–6, 59, 73–6, 86–7, 89–91, 127, 142, 151, 159–60, 163–5, 173, 175, 178–80, 183, 185, 186, 195, 198, 200, 202, 207, 209, 212, 213, 219, 225–6, 229, 237, 246, 305–6, 315n.–317n., 321n.–322n., 325n.–329n., 331n., 332n., 334n.–338n., 340n., 341n.
Edwards, W., 338n.
Einhorn, H., 302, 304, 320n.
Einstein, A., 234–5, 319n.
Eisold, K., 26
Eissler, K. R., 8, 48, 51, 220, 229, 307, 327n., 337n.
Ekman, P., 118, 325n.
Ekstein, R., 18, 100, 321n., 334n., 337n.
Elevitch, B., 318n.
Elliott, R., 317n., 337n.
Ellis, H., 164–5
Elstein, A., 57, 64, 140, 221, 302
Emde, R., 136, 331n., 338n.
Endler, N., 338n.
English, A., 241
English, H., 241
Epstein, P., 123, 326n.
Erdelyi, M., 161, 329n., 335n.
Erikson, E. H., 213, 214, 226–7, 233, 237, 252, 328n., 336n.
Erle, J., 303
Erwin, E., 188, 195, 199, 332n., 333n., 335n.
Esman, A., 319n.
Etchegoyen, R., 49, 315n., 316n., 320n.
Eysenck, H., 221, 332n.
Ezriel, H., 245, 336n., 337n.

F

Fairbairn, W. R. D., 323n., 329n.
Fanshel, D., 78–81, 118, 230, 297, 325n.
Farrell, B., 175, 322n., 331n., 335n.–337n.
Faulkoner, J., 217
Faust, D., 324n., 334n.
Federn, E., 127, 228, 306
Feigl, H., 317n.
Feldman, E., 56
Felman, S., 321n., 326n., 328n.
Fenichel, O., 237
Ferenczi, S., 48
Festinger, L., 329n.
Feyerabend, P., 29
Fine, A., 333n.
Fine, B., 269–71, 316n., 329n.
Fischoff, B., 64, 302
Fish, S., 122, 129, 327n., 328n.
Fisher, S., 315n., 320n., 332n., 338n.
Fiske, D., 62, 320n., 333n., 338n.
Flanagan, L., 332n.
Flax, J., 175
Fliess, R., 196
Fliess, W., 18
Flumerfelt, J., 245
Fodor, J., 133, 148–9, 185, 208, 291
Fonagy, I., 74–5, 118
Fonagy, P., 74–5, 118, 207, 243, 317n., 321n., 332n., 335n., 337n., 338n.
Forbes, M., 333n.
Forrester, J., 307, 317n.
Fosshage, J., 315n., 336n.
Foucault, M., 323n.
Foulkes, D., 74, 321n.
Fox, R., 297
Frank, A., 321n.

Frank, P., 4, 231
Franks, J., 114
Fransella, F., 242, 243
Freedman, N., 84, 318n.
French, T. M., x, 64, 102, 128, 179, 229, 235, 249, 281, 304, 319n., 336n., 337n.
Freud, E., 12, 319n.
Freud, S., ix–x, xiv, 1, 3–20, 34, 51–4, 57, 59, 65, 67–8, 71, 85, 87–8, 98, 103–4, 106, 110–12, 118–20, 124–5, 128, 130, 135, 142, 153–5, 158, 159, 161, 167, 176, 177–8, 180, 182, 183, 188, 189–91, 194–6, 199, 201–4, 211, 214–15, 220, 223, 225, 226, 228, 232, 234, 236–7, 250–1, 263, 283, 293, 299, 301, 306, 307, 311–12, 315n.–317n., 319n., 320n., 324n., 326n.–334n., 339n., 340n.
Friedman, L., 47, 57, 62–3, 127, 214, 300, 315n., 316n., 321n., 334n., 335n.
Friedman, L. J., 327n.
Friedrich, F., 137
Fromm, E., 336n., 337n.
Fromm-Reichmann, F., 335n.

G

Gabbard, G., 320n.
Gabler, H., 339n., 340n.
Gadamer, H.-G., 58, 217
Galatzer-Levy, R., 332n.
Ganz, A., 302
Gardner, H., 28, 107
Gardner, M. R., 47, 217, 318n.
Gardner, S., 120, 161
Garduk, E., 238, 322n., 341n.
Garfield, S., 338n.
Garner, W., 110, 340n.
Gaudin, C., 15
Gauld, A., 317n., 324n., 333n., 335n., 339n.
Gedo, J., 12, 63, 118, 125, 218, 220, 318n., 335n.
Geertsma, R., 215, 315n.
Geertz, C., 235
Gelfand, T., 327n.
Geller, E., 335n.
Genette, G., 321n.
Gergely, G., 60
Gergen, K., 15, 213, 298, 318n., 322n., 336n.
Gergen, M., 322n.
Gholson, B., 317n.
Giere, R., 37, 336n.
Gill, M. M., 49, 88, 209, 239, 318n., 319n., 322n., 324n., 331n., 337n., 338n., 340n.
Gillett, E., 38, 78, 186, 207, 332n.
Gillman, R., 324n.
Gilman, S., 95
Ginzburg, C., 124, 148–9, 176, 306, 317n., 327n.
Giovacchini, P., 316n.
Glaser, B., 316n.
Gleser, G., 338n.
Glover, E., ix, x, 176, 335n., 337n.
Glymour, C., 39, 111, 178–9, 226, 316n., 333n., 335n.
Goldberg, A., xiii, 27, 29, 33, 58, 68, 304, 315n., 319n.–321n., 340n.
Goldberg, B., 329n.
Goldberg, L., 319n.
Golden, R., 241
Goldman, A., 330n.
Goldstein, I., 140
Gombrich, E., xii, 140
Gonzalez, R., 252
Good, M., 245
Goodman, N., 289–90, 339n.
Gordon, C., 115, 131–2, 339n., 340n.
Gottschalk, L., 338n.
Gould, N., 324n.
Gould, S. J., 195
Graham, G., 148
Grant, D., 192
Gray, P., 45, 48, 318n.
Green, A., 72, 323n., 334n.
Green, G., 75, 113, 321n.
Greenberg, J., xii, 9, 49, 177, 233, 329n.

Greenberg, R., 240, 315n., 320n., 332n., 337n.–339n.
Greenson, R., 137, 330n., 337n.
Greenspoon, J., 118, 176
Greenwald, A., 319n., 323n.
Greenwood, J., 330n.
Gribinski, M., 51, 106
Grice, H., 114
Grief, B., 115, 308
Grinberg, L., 252
Grinstein, A., 10, 295, 320n., 321n.
Grolnick, S., xiv
Groner, M., 296, 330n.
Groner, R., 296, 330n.
Grosskurth, P., 320n.
Grossman, W., 148, 334n.
Grubrich-Simitis, I., 328n.
Grünbaum, A., xii, xiv, 9, 11, 35, 51, 56, 141, 144, 155, 161, 164–5, 167, 171–209, 221, 246, 275, 287, 316n., 322n., 324n., 330n.–334n., 338n.
Guntrip, H., 329n.
Gustafson, J., 318n.
Guttman, I., 103, 304, 337n.
Guttman, S., 103, 304, 337n.

H

Habermas, J., 17, 318n., 322n., 324n., 335n., 336n.
Haggard, E., 238, 322n., 338n., 341n.
Hairston, M., 122, 325n.
Haldane, J., 330n.
Hall, C., 338n.
Hamburg, P., 72
Hamilton, V., 52
Hampshire, S., 331n.
Hanly, C., 61, 175, 177, 316n., 318n., 322n., 332n., 333n., 335n., 337n., 341n.
Hanly, M., 89–90, 317n.
Hansell, J., 319n.
Harari, E., 192
Hardy, W., 334n.
Harman, G., 312, 331n., 335n.
Harré, R., 35, 132, 318n.
Harrison, S., 339n.
Hartmann, H., 11, 60, 65, 68, 124–5, 251, 312
Hastie, R., 329n.
Haugeland, 331n.
Havens, L., 17
Hawkes, T., 123
Hawpe, L., 84
Hawthorne, N., 328n.
Hayek, F., 112, 301, 304, 309, 312
Hayes, S., 336n., 338n.
Haynal, A., 52, 86, 316n., 330n.
Hedges, L., 48
Heider, F., 323n., 329n.
Heil, J., 332n.
Heimann, P., 330n.
Heine, R., 197, 332n.
Heinicke, C., 339n.
Heizer, R., 130
Hempel, C., 150, 336n.
Hernadi, P., 326n.
Hersen, M., 336n, 338n., 339n.
Herskovits, M., 130
Hesse, M., 58, 318n.
Heynick, F., 320n.
Hildebrand, H., 324n.
Hiley, D., 33, 34
Hilliard, R., 337n.
Hirsch, E., 15, 30, 33, 46, 62, 63, 106, 127, 212–14, 217, 220, 221, 236, 246, 278, 298, 305, 310, 317n., 319n., 324n., 335n., 337n., 340n.
Hitchcock, J., 48
Hobson, J., 332n.
Hockett, C., 325n.
Hoffman, I., 33, 49, 62, 293, 318n., 320n., 322n., 337n., 338n.
Hogarth, R., 302
Hoit, M., 310
Holland, J., 329n.
Holland, N., 327n., 328n.
Holsti, O., 338n.
Holt, R., xi, 12, 28, 32, 64, 93, 227, 240, 243–4, 246, 299–300, 316n., 321n., 323n., 324n., 331n., 332n., 334n., 335n., 338n.

Holton, G., 317n.
Holyoak, K., 88
Holzman, P., 211, 322n., 332n., 335n.
Home, H. J., 169
Hook, S., 318n.
Hooke, R., 297
Hopkins, J., 151, 161–4, 167, 174, 186, 208, 330n., 331n.
Horgan, T., 331n.
Horowitz, M., 48, 135–7, 139, 141, 176, 315n., 329n., 330n., 337n.
Horwitz, L., 337n., 338n.
Houben, A., 336n.–338n.
Howard, R., 324n.
Howson, C., 338n.
Hull, D., 22, 47
Hume, D., 232
Hunt, M., 329n.
Hunter, K., 322n.

I

Inderbitzin, L., 292, 316n., 318n.
Inhelder, B., 100, 132
Isaacs, K., 337n., 338n.
Isaacs, S., 253
Iser, W., 101, 129
Izenberg, G., 5, 11, 17

J

Jacobs, T., 119
Jacobson, A., 336n.
Jacobson, E., 329n.
Janis, I., 337n.
Jaspers, K., 181, 334n.
Jefferey, R., 338n.
Jelalian, E., 63, 302, 334n.
Johansen, J., 124–6, 157, 326n., 331n.
Johnson, F., 326n.
Johnson-Laird, P., 340n.
Jones, A., 326n., 335n.
Jones, Edward, 335n.
Jones, Enrico, 175, 230, 333n., 335n., 338n., 339n.
Jones, Ernest, 333n.
Jordan, J., 335n.
Joseph, B., 320n.
Josephson, J., 184
Josephson, S., 184
Junker, H., 317n.

K

Kächele, H., 36, 79, 83, 86–7, 200, 219, 221, 227, 295, 315n., 316n., 319n., 322n., 330n., 334n., 336n.–338n., 341n.
Kahneman, D., 84, 324n., 330n., 334n.
Kaplan, A., 49, 96–7, 99, 141, 143, 186, 202, 207, 211, 216, 230–2, 234, 303, 322n.
Kaplan, C., 113, 141, 143
Kapp, F., 120
Kazdin, E., 195, 318n., 336n., 338n.
Kellogg, R., 321n., 322n.
Kelly, G. A., 242, 318n., 329n.
Kelman, H., 128
Kent, T., 33
Kermode, F., 17, 26, 62, 90–1, 104, 298, 324n., 339n., 340n.
Kern, J., 120
Kernberg, O., 102, 329n., 337n., 338n.
Kerr, J., 10, 327n.
Kerz, 335n.
Kerz-Rühling, 337n.
Kettner, M., 184, 316n.
Keutner, T., 213
Keynes, J., 46, 278
Kiesler, D., 320n., 338n.
Kihlstrom, J., 138, 329n.
Killingmo, B., 125, 326n.
Kim, J., 318n.
Kirk, T., 317n., 337n.
Klauber, J., 51, 54–5, 103, 307, 315n., 317n., 319n., 335n.
Klein, G., 324n., 331n., 334n.
Klein, M., 48, 60, 66, 319n., 320n., 329n., 330n.
Klein, Milton, 323n.
Klerman, G., 332n., 336n.
Klimovsky, G., 52, 331n., 337n.

Kline, P., 202, 332n., 335n., 338n.
Klumpner, G., 211
Knapp, P., 137, 329n., 337n.
Knorr-Cetina, K., 32, 39–40
Kockelmans, J., 324n.
Koffka, K., 323n.
Kohler, W., 323n.
Kohut, H., 33, 46, 48, 58, 60, 62, 66, 302–3, 319n., 320n.
Kordig, C., 30
Kornblith, H., 38, 150, 187–8, 318n.
Kornreich, M., 338n.
Kosslyn, S., 340n.
Kramer, M., 263
Kramer, P., 279
Kratochwill, T., 336n., 338n.
Krieger, R., 327n.
Kris, A., 5, 333n.
Kris, E., 5, 235, 319n., 333n., 335n.–337n., 339n.
Kristeva, J., 326n.
Kubie, L., 322n., 336n.
Kukla, A., 128, 232
Kumin, I., 65, 340n.
Kuper, A., 112, 324n.
Kurzweil, E., 70–2, 112, 324n., 327n.

L

Labov, W., 78–81, 226, 230, 297, 321n., 325n., 335n.
Lacan, J., 69–73, 321n.
Lacey, A., 4, 36
Laffal, J., 116, 320n., 338n.
Lakatos, I., 305
Lamb, R., 132
Lamm, L., 34, 101, 145, 176
Langer, S., 334n.
Langs, R., 48, 63, 239
Laor, N., 72, 73, 332n.
Laplanche, J., 316n., 340n.
Larrabee, H., 64, 304
Lasnik, H., 329n.
Laszlo, E., 323n.
Lazarsfeld, P., 337n.
Leaffer, T., 321n.
Leary, D., 36
Leary, K., 25, 322n.
Leatherdale, W., 318n.
Leavy, S., 8, 26, 51, 64, 71, 120, 235, 250, 298, 321n.
Leech, G., 326n.
Leibin, V., 174, 331n.
Leon, I., 318n.
Leuzinger-Bohleber, M., 83, 330n.
Levenson, E., 307, 324n.
Lévi-Strauss, C., 107–9, 321n.
Levin, F., 142–3, 310
Levin, K., 202
Levine, F., 280, 315n.
Levine, H., 316n.
Levy, D., 175, 195, 332n., 335n., 339n.
Levy, L., 48, 99, 218
Levy, S., 188, 292, 316n., 318n.
Lewin, K., 329n.
Lewontin, R. C., 26
Lichtenberg, J. D., 318n.
Lieberman, P., 325n.
Lindley, D., 242
Lipshitz, S., 243
Lipton, P., 331n., 335n.
Lipton, S., 113
Litowitz, B., 123, 321n., 326n.
Litowitz, N., 321n.
Little, K., 226
Lloyd, D., 11, 84
Loar, B., 185, 334n.
Loch, W., 318n., 322n., 336n.
Loeb, F., 323n.
Loevinger, J., 239–40
Loew, C., 315n., 336n.
Loewald, H., 233, 316n.
Loewenstein, R., 55, 239, 294, 319n., 322n., 337n.
Loewy, H., 319n.
Lolas, F., 338n.
Lomas, P., 304
Lossy, F., 334n.
Lothane, Z., 211–12
Luborsky, E., 337n.
Luborsky, L., 10, 49, 176, 179, 231, 244, 280, 315n., 319n., 333n., 337n., 338n.

Lueger, R., 57
Lugo, M., 115, 308
Lunghi, M., 242
Lyons, W., 330n.

M

Mackay, N., 22, 35, 36, 40, 318n.
Macmillan, M., 64, 200
Mahl, G., 117–19, 325n., 326n.
Mahoney, M., 321n., 334n., 335n.
Mahony, P., 11, 53, 250, 328n.
Mahrer, A., 317n., 337n.
Maier, 174
Main, M., 206
Makari, G., 112, 321n., 325n.–326n.
Malan, D., 186, 226, 322n., 333n., 338n., 341n.
Malmquist, C., 47
Maltsberger, J., 335n.
Mancuso, J., 84, 86, 318n.
Mandler, C., 329n.
Manicas, P., 36
Maquet, J., 30, 317n.
Maranhão, T., 122
Marcel, A., 134, 336n.
Marcus, S., 87, 327n., 328n.
Marcuse, H., 318n.
Margolis, H., 26, 28, 97
Margolis, J., 325n.
Margulies, A., 55
Marks, L., 183, 208, 209
Markus, H., 133, 329n.
Marmor, J., 197
Marsden, G., 244, 338n.
Marshall, J., 320n.
Martin, E., 11, 319n., 333n.
Martin, M., 315n., 317n., 324n.
Martindale, C., 326n.
Marziali, E., 341n.
Masling, J., 338n.
Massicotte, W., 35, 332n.
Masson, J., 119
Mautner, B., 18
Mayer, E., 40
Mayes, L., 175, 230
McCarley, R., 332n.
McGinn, C., 185, 208, 290–2, 318n., 339n., 340n.
McGrath, W., 154–5, 317n., 331n.
McIntosh, D., 14, 155, 298, 317n., 331n.
McIntyre, A., 331n.
McIntyre, L., 315n.
McLaughlin, J., 319n.
McNeill, D., 118
McQuown, N., 78, 230, 325n.
Medawar, P., 22
Meehan, E., 323n.
Meehl, P., 10, 29–30, 46, 56, 181, 189, 215–16, 234, 239–43, 283, 294, 300–2, 315n., 317n., 324n., 330n., 336n.–338n.
Meichenbaum, D., 217, 329n.
Meissner, W., 12, 48, 52–4, 213, 221, 225, 234, 316n., 321n., 322n., 334n.–337n.
Mele, A., 332n.
Meltzer, D., 55, 319n.
Meltzoff, J., 338n.
Mendel, W., 335n.
Mergenthaler, E., 338n.
Merlan, P., 153
Merleau-Ponty, M., 336n.
Messer, S., 324n.
Metcalf, M., 240
Michels, R., 218, 226, 228, 237, 337n., 340n.
Michotte, A., 84
Mill, J. S., 171, 188–90
Miller, A., 63, 302, 334n.
Miller, G. A., 119–21
Miller, M., 317n., 337n.
Miller, R., 24, 196, 336n.
Millikan, R., 318n., 334n., 339n.
Minsky, M., 339n.
Mintz, J., 179
Mirsky, M., 63
Mischler, E., 325n.
Mitchell, S., 33, 209, 329n., 334n.
Mitroff, I., 335n.
Modell, A., 24, 32, 35, 40, 48, 73, 205
Möller, H., 332n.

Money-Kyrle, R., 319n., 320n.
Mooij, A., 68
Moore, B., 147, 269–71, 316n., 329n., 331n.
Moos, R., 338n.
Moran, G., 243, 335n.
Moras, K., 338n.
Morgan, J., 75, 113, 321n.
Morris, D., 118, 332n.
Morrow-Bradley, C., 317n., 337n.
Morton, A., 148–51, 156, 327n., 331n.
Moss, D., 54
Mueller-Vollmer, K., 317n.
Muller, J., 321n.
Muroff, M., 315n.
Mynatt, C., 334n.

N

Nagel, E., 21, 231
Nagel, T., 63, 317n.
Naiman, J., 238–9
Namnum, A., 8, 316n.
Nasser, A., xiv, 21, 25
Natsoulas, T., 331n.
Natterson, J., 64
Neisser, U., 220, 318n., 329n.
Nelson, K., 330n.
Nelson, R., 336n., 338n.
Newell, A., 339n., 340n.
Nichols, C., 336n.
Nickles, T., 38
Nisbett, R., 64, 196–7, 315n., 330n., 334n., 335n.
Nissim-Sabat, M., 218
Norman, H., 251
Novey, S., 245–6, 339n.
Nunberg, H., 127, 228, 306

O

Oakeshott, M., 34
Offenkrantz, W., 252
Ogden, T., xii, 15, 49, 90–1, 115, 298, 320n., 323n.
Ogilvy, T., 309
Olds, D., 321n., 326n., 330n.
Olinick, S., 63, 230, 307, 319n., 325n., 327n., 337n.
O'Neill, A., 50, 142, 180, 312
O'Neill, J., 174
Oppenheim, P., 336n.
Oremland, J., 316n., 340n.
Ornstein, A., 319n., 320n.
Ornstein, P. H., 319n., 320n.
Osgood, C., 23
O'Shaughnessy, E., 214
Osherson, D., 329n.
Oskamp, S., 57, 301
Oursler, W., 147
Overman, E., 21, 24, 38, 72
Owen, K., 175, 230

P

Packer, M., 317n., 324n., 337n.
Paivio, A., 120, 192, 326n., 340n.
Palmer, R., 101, 205, 317n., 324n.
Palombo, S., 137, 329n.
Paniagua, C., 60, 237, 294, 316n., 317n., 319n.–320n.
Papert, S., 140
Parker, I., 83
Parkin, S., 334n.
Parloff, M., 338n.
Parmalee, D., 336n.
Parsons, M., 50, 57, 319n.
Patton, M., 317n., 337n.
Paul, L., 237, 336n.
Pearce, R., 128
Peirce, C., 184, 331n., 335n.
Pelikan, J., 104
Pera, M., 325n.
Perry, J., 319n., 339n.
Peterfreund, E., 14, 48, 52, 53, 58, 110, 212, 222, 232, 233, 235, 237, 295, 297, 299, 303, 304, 315n., 319n., 323n., 330n., 332n., 337n., 339n.
Petot, J.-M., 320n.
Pettit, P., 330n.
Petzel, T., 57
Pfeffer, A., 251
Pfeiffer, R., 330n.

Phillips, J., 204, 310, 319n., 335n., 336n.
Phillips, W., 324n., 327n.
Piaget, J., 132, 318n., 330n.
Pigman, G., 328n.
Pine. F., 48, 335n.
Pinsof, W., 338n.
Pittenger, R., 78, 79, 81, 230, 325n.
Pitz, G., 335n.
Plänkers, T., 323n.
Platt, G., 109–10, 334n.
Poland, W., 64, 319n., 340n.
Polanyi, M., xi, 115
Polkinghorne, D., 21–3, 46–7, 58, 61, 85–6, 173, 219, 282, 303–5, 309–10, 318n., 327n., 334n., 337n., 339n.
Pollock, G., 310, 312
Polya, G., 223, 280
Pontalis, J.-B., 316n., 340n.
Popper, K., 221, 305, 336n.
Prelli, L., 325n.
Prideaux, G., 74, 113–14, 321n., 324n.
Priel, B., 329n.
Prince, G., 321n.
Protter, B., 318n.
Pulver, S., 48, 109, 310, 319n.
Putnam, H., 31, 174, 234, 321n., 331n.

Q
Quine, W., 36, 58, 321n., 330n.

R
Rabinow, P., xi
Radcliffe-Brown, A., 97–8
Radford, M., 305
Radnitzky, G., 32, 35
Ramzy, I., 63, 143, 182, 322n.
Rangell, L., 8, 316n.
Rank, O., 301, 326n.
Rapaport, D., xiii, 1, 58–9, 115–16, 130, 213, 214, 234, 294, 320n., 336n.–337n.
Raphling, D., 177, 245, 293
Rawn, M., 321n.
Ray, W., 127, 129, 327n.
Read, R., 241
Reason, P., 318n.
Rechtschaffen, A., 252
Reed, G., 75, 84, 218, 308, 318n., 319n., 321n., 322n., 327n., 335n., 340n.
Reichenbach, H., 14, 26–7, 38, 93, 216
Reider, N., 287
Reik, T., 319n.
Reiser, M., 329n., 332n.
Reiss, D., 49
Renneker, R., 337n.
Rennie, D., 317n., 337n.
Repp, B., 336n.
Rescher, N., 21, 234, 317n.
Rettenberg, F., 325n.
Rice, L., 233, 338n.
Richards, A., 7, 115
Richards, I. A., 298
Richardson, W., 321n., 335n.
Rickman, H., 317n.
Ricoeur, P., xi, 86–7, 155, 311, 318n., 320n., 322n., 324n., 326n., 334n.–336n.
Rieber, R., 324n.
Rieff, P., 318n., 322n.
Rifferterre, M., 128
Riggs, B., 102
Robbins, F., 124, 251–2, 263
Robinson, J., 84
Robinson, P., 332n., 335n.
Roche, R., 55, 319n.
Rock, D., 315n.
Rock, I., 101
Roediger, J., 330n.
Rogers, R., 68, 86–7, 89, 98, 102, 112, 116, 125–6, 198, 233, 295, 320n.–324n., 326n., 329n.
Roose, S., 176, 333n., 338n.
Rorty, R., 28, 72, 185, 234, 331n.
Rosen, V., 33, 125, 209, 237, 245, 324n., 326n., 334n.
Rosenbaum, M., 315n.
Rosenberg, S., 315n.
Rosenblatt, A., 96–7, 102, 323n., 329n.
Rosenthal, R., 58, 320n.
Ross, D., 120

Ross, L., 64, 196, 315n., 330n., 334n.
Ross, N., 316n.
Roth, P., 46, 47, 317n., 322n.
Rothenberg, A., 114
Rothstein, A., 217, 317n., 320n.
Roustang, F., 303
Rowan, J., 318n.
Rubinstein, B., 15, 18, 27, 32, 232, 312, 316n., 337n.
Rubovits-Seitz, P., 48, 103–4, 123, 217, 235, 252, 298, 315n., 319n., 320n., 324n., 330n., 332n.–337n., 339n.–341n.. *See also* Seitz, P.
Rudnytzky, P., 324n.
Rumelhart, D., 138–9, 304, 329n.
Runes, D., 122
Runyon, W., 306, 315n.
Russell, R., 47, 338n.
Rycroft, C., 51, 68, 156, 187, 316n., 330n., 335n., 337n.
Ryle, A., 242–3
Ryle, G., 76, 321n., 330n.

S

Sachs, D., 331n., 333n., 335n.
Sadovsky, V., 323n.
Sadow, L., 318n.
Salmon, W., 173, 195, 219
Salovey, P., 136, 298, 315n., 324n., 329n., 334n.
Sampson, H., 49, 64, 200, 249, 306, 319n., 337n., 339n.
Samuels, A., 48
Sand, R., 178, 180, 182, 186–7, 332n.
Sandler, J., xii, 329n., 338n.
Sarbin, T., 84, 86, 90
Sargent, H., 337n., 338n.
Sass, L., 217, 318n., 324n.
Sasso, G., 120
Saul, L., 237
Saussure, F., 69, 107
Savage, L., 338n.
Savodnik, I., 331n.
Saykin, A., 324n.
Schafer, R., 27–8, 41, 48, 76–8, 88, 204–5, 229, 307, 309, 316n., 318n., 319n., 322n., 324n., 330n., 334n., 336n., 337n.
Schank, R., 84, 136, 329n.
Scharff, J., 4, 320n.
Scheflen, A., 78
Schilder, P., 334n.
Schimek, J., ix, 12, 236, 322n.
Schlesinger, G., 331n.
Schlesinger, H., 27, 48, 89, 315n., 340n.
Schlessinger, N., 124, 251–2, 263
Schmidl, F., 211, 215, 238, 336n., 337n.
Schneider, W., 330n.
Schneidman, E., 226
Scholes, R., 123, 321n., 322n.
Schön, D., 318n.
Schreber, D. P., 71
Schulze, G., 117, 325n., 326n.
Schwaber, E., xi, 24, 49, 242, 316n.–320n.
Schwartz, M., 323n.
Schwartz, S., 321n.
Scott, W., 322n.
Scriven, M., 4, 96, 297
Searl, M., 48
Searle, J., 80, 114, 117, 152, 187, 331n., 334n.
Searles, H., 319n.
Secord, P., 36, 318n.
Seeman, W., 336n.
Segal, Z., 136, 329n.
Segall, M., 317n.
Seidman, S., 25
Seitz, P., x, 11, 113, 245, 252, 336n., 337n., 340n. *See also* Rubovits-Seitz, P.
Sellars, W., 340n.
Serota, H., 245
Seung, T., 72, 225
Shaklee, H., 64, 302
Shands, H., 124
Shane, E., 318n.
Shane, M., 318n.
Shapere, D., 29–32, 39, 317n.
Shapiro, A., 332n.

Shapiro, T., 69, 74, 79, 112, 117, 125, 196, 221, 321n., 324n.–326n., 335n., 338n.
Share, L., 245
Sharp, V., 240
Sharpe, E., 228
Sharpe, R., 331n.
Shaw, J., 339n., 340n.
Shea, W., 325n.
Sherer, K., 325n.
Sherwood, M., 88–9, 169, 219, 245, 322n., 336n., 341n.
Shevrin, H., 296, 319n., 332n.
Shiffrin, R., 330n.
Shope, R., xii, 11, 15, 155, 158, 160, 183, 316n., 325n.
Shortliffe, E., 139
Shotter, J., 317n., 324n., 333n., 335n., 339n.
Shusterman, R., 33, 34
Shweder, R., 62, 320n., 333n.
Siegler, F., 155
Silberschatz, G., 322n., 336n., 341n.
Silberstein, W., 153–4
Silverman, D., 48
Simon, B., 334n.
Simon, H., 113, 133, 140, 141, 143, 318n., 339n., 340n.
Simons, H., 325n.
Singer, J., 132, 135, 136, 138, 329n.
Singh, R., 11, 53, 250, 321n., 328n.
Siomopoulos, V., 324n.
Skelton, R., 319n.
Sklansky, M., 315n.
Skura, M., 327n.
Slap, J., 324n., 330n.
Slap-Shelton, L., 330n.
Sloane, R., 322n.
Slobin, D., 113, 324n.
Slovic, P., 330n.
Smith, H., 319n.
Smith, J., 112, 114, 321n.
Smith, S., 95
Snyder, M., 335n.
Spar, J., 61
Specht, E., 213
Spence, D., 24, 26, 48, 54, 57, 78, 85, 87, 89, 99, 115–16, 122–3, 141, 144, 175, 182, 214, 218, 228, 230, 233, 236, 297, 299, 306, 308, 315n., 316n., 318n., 319n., 321n.–325n., 327n., 330n., 333n., 335n.–338n., 340n.
Speziale-Bagliacca, R., 120
Spillius, E., 48, 320n.
Sprengnether, M., 85
Spruiell, V., 40, 321n., 332n., 335n.
Squire, L., 330n.
Staines, P., 216, 316n.
Steele, R., 318n., 324n., 336n.
Stegmüller, W., 336n.
Stein, M., 320n.
Steiner, R., 3, 104, 204, 324n., 325n., 334n.
Stengel, E., 321n., 336n., 338n.
Stent, G., 21
Stern, D., 318n., 322n.
Stich, S., 148
Stiles, W., 22–3, 324n., 337n.
Stinson, C., 135, 340n.
Stollack, G., 338n.
Stoller, R., 21, 22, 30, 215, 236, 315n.
Stolorow, R. D., 49, 324n.
Stone, A., 112, 324n.
Stone, J., 338n.
Strauss, A., 316n.
Strenger, C., 32, 35, 40, 173, 183, 198, 202, 205–6, 209, 234, 236, 324n., 331n., 335n.
Strupp, H., 176, 244, 315n., 320n., 335n., 337n., 338n.
Sturrock, J., 53
Suci, G., 23
Suleiman, S., 128
Sulloway, F., 17
Suppe, F., 37
Suppes, P., 336n.
Sutherland, J., 329n.

T

Talley, P., 24, 338n.
Tannenbaum, P., 23

Taylor, C., 33, 324n., 327n., 339n.
Taylor, D., 334n.
Taylor, K., 338n.
Taylor, S., 329n.
Telfer, L., 338n.
Teller, V., 229, 250–1, 253, 337n.–340n.
Tenzer, A., 318n.
Terwee, S., 12
Thagard, P., 335n.
Thass-Thienemann, T., 334n.
Thickstun, J., 96–7, 102, 323n.
Thomä, H., 35–6, 86, 200, 219, 221, 227, 295, 315n., 316n., 319n., 322n., 330n., 334n., 336n.–338n., 341n.
Thomas, L., 21
Thomas, R., 129
Todorov, T., 321n.
Tomkins, S., 136, 340n.
Tou, J., 252
Toukmanian, S., 317n., 337n.
Toulmin, S., 33, 209, 310, 315n.
Treisman, A., 336n.
Treurniet, N., 335n.
Tribich, D., 323n.
Trigger, B., 130
Trosman, H., 252
Tryon, W., 338n.
Tuckett, D., xiii, 15, 283, 316n., 325n., 332n., 337n.
Turk, D., 298, 315n., 324n., 334n.
Turner, D., 330n.
Tversky, A., 84, 324n., 330n., 334n.
Tweney, R., 321n., 334n.

U

Urbach, P., 338n.

V

Van de Castle, R., 338n.
Van Velzen, H., 112, 324n.
Vaughan, S., 176, 333n., 338n.
Vergote, A., 72
Viderman, S., 297, 318n., 322n., 336n.
Viederman, M., 312, 322n.
von Eckhardt, B., 313, 332n.
von Glasersfeld, E., 318n.
von Wright, G., 21
Vygotzky, L., 117

W

Wachtel, P., 119, 202
Waelder, R., 103, 196, 213, 228, 230, 246, 250, 304, 318n., 334n., 336, 337n.
Wakefield, J., 152, 161, 317n., 329n., 331n.
Waldron, S., 319n.
Walkup, J., 101, 145, 323n.
Wallace, E., 11, 48, 142, 177, 180, 186, 196, 199–200, 208, 319n., 322n., 331n., 333n., 335n.
Wallerstein, R., 30, 64, 88, 200, 214, 231, 236, 240, 316n., 318n., 335n., 337n.
Waskow, I., 338n.
Watson, W., 47, 299, 331n., 334n.
Watzlawick, P., 119
Wax, M., 9, 35, 40, 332n., 335n.
Weber, J., 315n.
Weber, S., 72
Wegman, C., 329n.
Weich, M., 311, 340n.
Weinshel, E., 325n.
Weinstein, L., 117
Weiss, J., 49, 319n., 334n., 337n.–339n.
Wellman, H., 163
Werman, D., 315n., 336n.
Wertheimer, M., 100–1, 323n.
Werts, C., 319n.
Weston, A., 331n.
Wettersten, J., 304, 339n.
Wetzler, S., 322n., 339n.
White, H., 84, 322n.
Whitehorn, J., 208, 316n., 334n.
Wickelgren, W., 339n., 340n.
Wiggins, O., 323n.
Wilcocks, R., 325n.
Wilden, A., 68, 73, 101
Wilkes, K., 148, 150
Williams, M., 29, 321n.

Williams, R., 217
Wilson, A., 117, 197
Wilson, G., 332n.
Wilson, M., 69
Wilson, R., 196–7
Wimsatt, W., 22, 56, 174, 332n.
Windholz, M., 335n., 339n.
Winnicott, D., 319n.
Wisdom, J., 110, 176, 192, 238, 335n.–337n.
Wittgenstein, L., 76, 289, 321n., 339n.
Wolf, E. S., 33, 41, 62, 319n., 320n.
Wolfenstein, E., 332n.
Wolfson, A., 249, 306
Wolitzky, D., 316n., 340n.
Wollheim, R., 151, 156, 158–9, 186, 202, 207, 317n., 330n.–333n.
Wolman, B. B., 212, 245
Woodard, G., 279, 315n., 319n., 339n.
Woodward, J., 331n.
Woolfolk, R., 217, 324n., 336n.
Wynne, L., 325n.
Wyss, D., 26

Y

Yorke, C., 335n., 337n.
Youdin, R., 115

Z

Zac, J., 317n.
Zajonc, R., 133–4, 329n.
Zilberg, N., 329n.
Ziman, J., 21

Subject Index

A

abductive inference ("inference to the best explanation"), 162, 184–5, 189
absolutism, 24, 30–1, 41
action language. *See under* language-based models of interpretation
analogy, 87–8, 115–16
  as argument for clinical inference, 212
  as cognitive transformation, 35–6, 87–8, 98
  in commonsense reasoning, 150
  recognizing disanalogies, 36
"and . . . and . . . and" fallacy (run-on interpretation), 300
apodictic knowledge, 25, 60–2
apodictic viewpoint, 29
archaeological decipherment. *See under* language-related parallels
Aristotle, practical syllogism, 147
assertorial knowledge, 25, 61–2

B

biases
  clinical context and, 64, 121, 293
  coherence, 236
  confirmation, 63, 239, 300, 302, 324n., 324n.11, 330n.
  cultural, 139
  Freud's views, 51, 286
  initial impression, 302
  vs. ostensibly unbiased inquiry, 27
  procedures to reduce, 58, 64, 240, 282, 300, 334n.
  schemas and, 139
  selection, 178, 332n.
  subjective, 56, 217
  theoretical (doctrinal), 56, 175, 332n.
Brentano, Freud, and intentionality, 153–5

C

case study, illustrative, 253–64
  posttherapeutic justification, RC approach, 264–79. *See also* recurrent cycles approach
    basic dynamic cycle, 265–6
    brief description of RC approach, 249–53
    cycle comparisons, 268–9
    cycle lengths, 264
    interpretations, reconstructions, and justification, 272–6, 279–82
    justification, limitations of, 279–80
    original template cycle, 265
    progressive revisions, 276–9
    template matching, 252–3
    working backwards, 250–1
case study method
  critiques and defenses of, 141, 195–6, 200
  history of, 31

justification in, 194–5, 221
single-case studies, 200, 338
use of "good hours" in, 235–6
causal controversy (relations of meanings and causes), 180–91, 291
clinical example, 182
Grünbaum's critiques, 180–9
counterarguments to, 182–91
views supporting, 181–3, 186–9
causal explanations
"best explanation"
criteria for what counts as, 185
inference to, 162
causal controversy and, 291
Freud's views, 17, 183, 330n.
Grünbaum's critique, 181–2, 206–7, 287, 291
counterarguments, 182–9
reconciled view, 190
motives and, 206
in New Criticism, 126
teleologic argument, 291
causal reversal fallacy, 179–80
causality
mental content and, 291
in narrative, 84
causes
Grünbaum's views, 181–2, 206–7, 287, 291
interpretation of, xii
meanings and, 162, 291
motives and, 206
certainty. *See* absolutism; apodictic knowledge; uncertainty
checking, revising, and rechecking constructions, xiii, 219, 281
circularity problem, 63–4, 214–15, 221–2, 236
"partitioning" method for dealing with, 222
clinical data
causal controversy and, 167, 181–91
cognitive processing of, 47–8, 51, 67, 88, 101, 103–4, 110–11, 113, 119, 144, 295–6, 307
complementary ways of viewing, 47–8, 187, 333n.
complexities of, 47, 49, 57, 91, 229
as direct empirical evidence, 221, 247
dual coding method and, 192–4
indexing of, 338n.
justification and, 64, 128, 175–6, 215–16, 220, 228–30, 233, 238–44, 287–8, 303–4
latent contents inferred from, 142
"locations" of meaning and, 116, 296
methodologic pluralism and, 47–8
parallels with poetic texts, 126
problems of interpreting, 15, 58, 91, 175, 213–14, 217–18, 297–8
records of, 244, 249–50, 306
schemas and, 138–9
sources of influence on, 175–6, 332–3n.
structuralism and, 110
varieties of, 26, 49–50, 141, 227–8, 302–3
clinical interpretation. *See* interpretation; interpretation(s)
cognitive science. *See under* parallels with nonclinical interpretive fields
cognitive transformation, xiii. *See also* clinical data, cognitive processing of; data processing methods
commonsense psychology
as an interpretive method, 147–8
Aristotle's practical syllogism, 147
controversies regarding, 167–8
critiques of, 164–5
explanation by motives, 151
Freud and, 153–5, 158–9
Hopkins' commonsense-based theory of interpretation, 161–3, 167
intentionality and, 152–3, 166
Brentano, Freud and, 153–5

commonsense psychology *(cont.)*
limitations of, 148–9
models of, 150
relation to clinical interpretation, 156–61
sources of, 147–9
various analysts' views, 159–61
communication theory. *See under* language-related parallels
complementarity, 20, 307
confirmation bias, 63, 300, 302, 324n.
conflict, 104–5, 251–2, 310
consensus problem, x, 204, 238, 279, 299
consilience argument, 194–6, 226–8, 248, 272–6. *See also under* Grünbaum's critiques
construction, xiii
comparison with model of perception, 220
importance of alternative hypotheses, 305, 308
overemphasis on initial constructions, 302
parallel with literary interpretation, 128
role in language processing, 113
role in ordinary communication, 121
role of "guessing" in, 106, 121, 131–2, 305
uncertainty of, 26, 106, 121, 297
constructivism
in Freud, 88, 312
radical, 88–9
in self psychology, 33
context
evidence, justification and, 99, 188, 200, 229, 275
in Freud's approach, 157–9, 188, 295
interpretive difficulties and, 11, 15, 23–4, 54, 64, 83, 91, 121, 173, 214–15, 280, 291, 297, 309
as interpretive heuristic, 14–15, 23, 30, 34, 41, 45, 53–6, 65, 83, 98, 111, 121, 126, 151, 177, 186, 188, 213–14, 225, 229–30, 261, 274, 285, 297, 309–10, 323n.
meanings and, 71, 102, 115–16, 214, 291
in other fields, 11–12, 53–4, 60, 79, 85, 95, 126, 173
in recurrent dynamic themes and cycles, 274–5, 301
continuity
as basic methodologic concept, 59, 294
between causes and meanings, 186
coherence and, 234
Freud's emphasis on causal, 11, 325
as interpretive heuristic, 102, 120, 143, 186, 233, 295
meaning and, 115, 130, 183
parallel with reading theory, 130
parallel with system theory, 102
thematization and, 307
cross-validation. *See under* justification, individual methods
cycles
communication, 121
perceptual, 220
recurrent dynamic, 249–59

D

damage control, 65, 304–5
data-driven approaches. *See under* methodology
data-gathering methods, xiii
data-generating methods, xiii
data processing methods, xiii. *See also* clinical data, cognitive processing of
clinical aspects of, xiii, 16, 90, 101–3, 296, 298, 308, 325n.
in discovery and justifying phases of interpretive inquiry, 16
draw on data from patient's and

analyst's associations, 16
relation to discourse processing, 113
AI model of discourse, 82
relation to language processing, 75, 113
Freud's use of language in processing clinical data, 67
importance of construction in, 113, 144
relation to narrative construction, 90
relation to schema theory, 138, 146
"template matching" in RC approach, 252
data-selection methods, xiii
Grünbaum's critique of, 175, 177
counterarguments to, 178–9
deconstruction, interpretation, and coherence, 90–1, 324n.
deductive reasoning
in commonsense psychology, 149
as evidence, 212
in Freud's approach, 51
in Lacan's approach, 69
vs. nondeductive reasoning, 56, 61, 90, 96
developmental lag (Gray), 45
doctrinal (theory-driven) approaches, 51–66. *See under* methodologic lag; methodology
as avoidable error, 56, 58, 303
countermeasures against, 103
critiques of, 60, 319n.
distorting effects of, 56, 57, 66
indoctrination, 52, 59–60
doctrinal interpretations, 293, 303
ways they betray themselves, 103
as form of methodologic lag, 50–60
Freud and, 51–2
Freud's antidoctrinal strategy, 52–3
general *vs.* specific theories, 58–9
Grünbaum's critique, 175, 177
vs. heuristic approaches, 56–7
in Kleinian and Kohutian approaches, 52, 60, 66
as "lingering ghost of positivism," 26
occasional necessity to use, 58
parallels with archaeologic decipherment, 130–1
positivist aspects of, 56
"refinding" of theory, 50
relation to "covariational judgments," 60
relation to reconstructions, 60
stereotyped nature of, 53
temptations to use, 57
theory-determined errors, 56
dream interpretation. *See* interpretation(s), of dreams
dual coding method and argument, 192–3

E

eclecticism, error of, 300–1
Edelson, M. *See also under* language-based models
narrative approach, 90–1
empathy
limitations of, 302–3
empathic failure, interpretive fallibility due to, 62
misused as evidence, 303
epistemology of interpretive inquiry, 34–40. *See also* justification; positivism; postpositivism; skepticism
complementarity, 20, 35, 307
covariational judgments, 60
dialectics, psychoanalytic, xiii–xiv
justifying measures, 218, 247–8, 286–7
multiple types of constructions, 40
naturalized, 41
specifying disanalogies, 36

epistemology of interpretive inquiry (*cont.*)
  theories
    general methodologic *vs.* specific clinical, 58–9
    heuristic use of, 56
    models of, 37
    nonstatement view of, 37
error-detecting and -correcting measures, 65, 304–9
errors, common avoidable, 299–303. *See also* biases; fallibility; Grünbaum's critiques
  enumerative inductivism, 300
  fallacies
    "and . . . and . . . and" (run-on interpretation), 300
    confirming consequent, 189
    doctrinal, 189
    eclecticism, 300–1
    focusing on dramatic event, 302
    focusing on early impression, 302
    genetic, 60
    post hoc, 199–201
    subjective, 302–3
    tour de force, 236
    transparency, 299
    use of empathy as evidence, 303
  Freud's overconfidence, 299–300
  heuristic shortcuts, 298
  misleading maxims, 299–301
  omnipresent possibility of, 189
  overreliance on theory, 293–4, 303
  overuse of single method, 302–3
  overvaluing observation, 301
exclusivist methodology. *See* interpretive approaches, monistic *vs.* pluralistic
externalism, 292

F

fallacies. *See under* errors, common avoidable
fallibility, interpretive, 296–8
  amount and complexity of data, 298
  error-proneness, uncertainty, and unreliability of clinical evidence, 215
  limitations of interpretation, 296–7
  limitations of interpreters, 217
  method effects, 217
  role of context, 297–8
  role of heuristic shortcuts, 298
  role of theory, 293–4
feedback, therapists' lack of systematic, 304
flexibility, importance of, 5, 19, 22, 25, 131–2, 310
foundationalism, 21, 25, 37
FRAME methodology, 229, 253
free association. *See under* Grünbaum's critiques
Freud, S.
  anticipated postpositivism, 5–6, 19, 28
  Brentano, intentionality, and, 153–5
  case histories, 7–8, 10, 87, 110–11, 118, 120, 158, 215, 250, 307
  devalued methodologists, 18–19
  on free association, 177
  on interpretive methods, 7–10
    attempted to make interpretations appear objectively certain, 7, 11–16
    definition of interpretation, 326n.
    equated interpretations with causal explanations, 12
    focused on fallibility of ancient methods rather than his own, 7, 11–16
    ignored investigations of interpretation in other fields, 16–18
    minimized role of, 7–10
    pluralistic justification, 192, 194–5, 223, 228, 232, 234, 236–7, 244
    positivist ideals *vs.* patient

needs, 3, 5–7, 11, 19–20
shifted task of interpretation to patient, 15–16
vague description of, 10–11
whole analysis needed for full interpretation of any fragment, 214
methodologic conflict, 3–4, 19–20
overconfidence, 299–300
on patients' introspections, 196
positivism and, 3–4, 19–20
sensitivity to criticism of his methodology, 18

G

gestalt approach
emergent characteristics, 100–1
emphasis on relations and patterns, 100
good form or figure, 100
"productive thinking," 101
relation to psychoanalysis and clinical interpretation, 101
"good enough interpretations," 65, 311–13. *See also* interpretive attitude
Grünbaum's critiques, 171, 206–9
consilience (convergence) argument, 194–6
critique, 194–5
dissenting counterarguments, 195–6
Freud's view, 194
free association, 177–80
critique, 177–8
dissenting counterarguments, 178–80
Freud's view, 177
indirect role in identifying prior events, 180
hermeneutic reformulations
critique, 204, 206
dissenting counterarguments, 204–6, 208–9
meanings and causes, 180–91
computational and teleologic arguments, 185
critique, 180–1
dissenting counterarguments, 182–91
Freud's view, 183–4
illustrative clinical vignette, 182
possible way of reconciling opposing views, 190–1
post hoc fallacy, 199–201
critique, 199–200
dissenting counterarguments, 200–1
recommendations for psychoanalysis, 206–7
repression theory
critique, 201–2
dissenting views, 202
Freud's view, 201
views supporting Grünbaum, 202–3
slips and dreams, 203–4
critique, 203
suggestibility problem, 175–7
critique emphasizing data contamination, 175
dissenting counterarguments, 175–6
unrecognized undercurrents of suggestibility, 177
tally argument, 191–4
critique, 191–2
dissenting counterarguments, 192–3
dual coding counterargument, 192–4
Freud's view, 191
treated patients' introspections, 196–9
critique, 196–7
dissenting views, 197–9
Freud's view, 196
Grünbaum's method of philosophical analysis, 171–4
eliminative inductivism, 172–3
examples of applying, 172

Grünbaum's method of philosophical analysis *(cont.)*
modern inductivist methods of validating causal hypotheses, 172
opposing counterarguments, 173–4
supporting views, 174

H
hermeneutic circle, 64
hermeneutics, 16–17, 103–6, 305, 310. *See also under* Grünbaum's critiques
Dilthey, 17
focus on part-whole relations, 104
illustrative application to clinical interpretation, 104–5
justification, 105–6, 205, 305–6
limitations of
circularity produces illusion of correctness, 64
strengths
aids understanding phenomena outside boundaries of individual schools, 310
does not claim to be consistently valid interpretive approach, 106
employs justifying approaches, 205
is nonreductive, 106
heuristics, interpretive, 295–6
advantages of, compared with doctrinal approaches, 56–7, 295
in discovery phase, 295–6
examples of, 295–6
Freud's use of, 52, 295
as guides to inquiry, 295
in justifying phase, 223
misuse of heuristic shortcuts, 298
parallels in other fields, 296
foregrounding, 113
template matching, 250, 252
thematization, 119
working backwards, 250, 295–6
holistic interpretive approach, 307
complementary to particularistic approach, 306
psychoanalytic interpretation involves both, 307
Hopkins' commonsense theory of clinical interpretation, 161–3
hypotheses, interpretive (alternative constructions), xiii

I
inductivism, 14, 38, 51
eliminative, 172–3
enumerative, 300
inference
central problem of psychoanalysis and interpretive methodology, 315n.
forms of
abductive, 162, 184–5
deductive, 51, 69, 149, 212
inductive, 14, 172
inference to the best explanation, 162, 185
"rational enough," 312
Freud's approach
deductive aspects, 51
failure to differentiate observations and inferences, 12
inductive aspects, 184–5, 211
inference to the best explanation in case histories, 185
infrequent references to interpretive inference, 14
shifted tasks of inference and interpretation to patient, 14
of latent contents, ix, 142, 162
relations between meanings and determinants uncertain, xii
uncertainties of, ix–x
unconscious determinants, xii, 162, 180
unconscious meanings, xii, 162
unsolved problems of, xi, 290–2

process of
within networks of induction *vs.* in isolation, 14
series of inferential steps *vs.* single inference, 216
relations to interpretations
both idiographic, 216
both theory-, method-, and perspective-bound, 217
midway between observations and interpretations, 216
information theory, interpretation and, 132, 340n.
initial impression bias, 302
intentionality, 152–3, 166, 330n.
definition, 152
Freud, Brentano, and, 153–5
relation to clinical interpretation, 155
relation to commonsense psychology, 152
interactive clinical approaches, xii, 292–3
continued need for interpretive understanding in, 293
interpretation(s). *See also* latent contents; *specific topics*
ancient methods, 7, 15–16
biases in. *See under* biases
choosing among competing, 305–6
circularity of. *See under* circularity problem
discovery *vs.* justifying phases of, 208, 235
doctrinal (theory-driven). *See under* doctrinal (theory-driven) approaches; methodologic lag; methodology
of dreams, 15–16, 203–4, 326n.
evidence against an, 64, 300
as explanation, 116, 322n., 336n.
as form of practice *vs.* theory, 34
Freud's view. *See* Freud, on interpretive methods
"good enough," 65, 311–13
justification of. *See also* justification
capability of, 219–20
clinical illustrations of, 249–82
Freud's approach to, 192, 194–5, 223, 228, 232, 234, 236–7, 244
individual methods, 223–48
intraclinical, 220–3
limitations of, 296–7
need for, 216–18
neglect of, 211
nonclinical comparisons. *See specific topics*
parallels with hermeneutic, 105–6, 305–6
posttherapeutic, 287–8, 306
problems of, 212–16
during treatment, 287–8
as method of inquiry, xi–xiii, 32–4, 289–90
nonclinical comparisons. *See specific topics*
origins of, in Freud, xiii–xiv
patients' responses to, 236–9, 288
posttherapeutic justification, 264–79, 287–8, 306
prerequisite knowledge needed for, xii
problems of. *See* biases; causal controversy; consensus problem; construction, uncertainty of; context, interpretive difficulties; damage control; doctrinal approaches; empathy, limitations of; errors; fallibility; Freud, on interpretive methods; Grünbaum's critiques; hermeneutics, limitations of; heuristics, misuse of; inference, of latent contents; justification, general aspects of
relations to higher level theories
lowest level theoretical statements of psychoanalysis, 212

interpretation(s) *(cont.)*
midway between observation and higher level theories, 216
only empirically testable theoretical statements, 215, 220–1, 247
other methods used to test higher level theories, 212
reliability, x, 5, 243–4, 279–80. *See also under* consensus problem
"rest on interpretations, rest on interpretations . . .", 15
role in interactivist approach. *See* interactive clinical approaches
scientific status of, 32–4, 211–12, 286, 288–90
Grünbaum's view, 172, 206
nature of interpretation, 288–9
need for model of justifying interpretations, 286
problems of establishing truth, 290
spontaneity of, 54–5
theory-independent, 53–6, 294
interpretive approaches. *See also under* Freud
doctrinal *vs.* data-driven, 50–60
method- *vs.* problem-oriented, 46–7
monistic *vs.* pluralistic, 46–50
overconfident *vs.* skeptical, 60–5
interpretive attitude, 309–13
flexible/postpositivist, 310
Freud's constructivist view, 312
"good enough" interpretations, 311–12
based on concept of "meaning types," 310–11
complete accuracy not necessary, 311
"most plausible" interpretation resonates with current dynamics, 311
supporting concepts of Ricoeur, Rubinstein, Hartmann, Eagle, 311–13
interpretive methodology improvable, 313
"modest" view of interpretation, 309, 312–13
truth claims limited by individual schools' concepts, 309
each conceptual system "a" way of knowing, 310
hermeneutic approach to surmount boundaries between schools, 310
interaction of contexts offers greater understanding, 309–10
"reality is views," 309
interpretive code, patients learning, 325n.
illustrated by speeding-up of recurrent dynamic cycles, 249, 264
interpretive heuristics. *See* heuristics
interpretive inquiry. *See also* epistemology of interpretive inquiry
characteristics of, 285–6
common errors in, 299–303
components and stages of, xii–xiii
difficulties and fallibility of, 7, 15–16, 296–8
limitations of, 26–8, 65–6, 309
postpositivist features of, 21–4, 286
as a scientific method, 32–4
interpretive methodology. *See* methodology
interpretive methods, xiii. *See also* checking, revising, and rechecking; construction; data processing; data selection; deductive reasoning; empathy; Freud, on interpretive methods; heuristics; inference; justification
methodologic problems of, ix–xi, 26, 69, 106–21, 175, 177,

212–17, 290–4, 296–8, 301–3, 309, 312
in other disciplines, 16–18, 143–6, 166–8
interpretive perspectives. *See also* Freud
advantage of pluralistic perspectives, 47
combined positivist and postpositivist, 28–32
positivist, 21, 25–8
Freud's positivism, 4
postpositivist, 21, 25–8
Freud's anticipation of, 5–6, 19, 28
interpretive technique, ix, xi
introspection, 47. *See also* Grünbaum's critiques, treated patients' introspections

J

justification, general aspects of, 38, 247. *See also* case study; case study method; checking, revising, and rechecking; clinical data; epistemology; error-detecting and -correcting measures; Freud, on interpretive methods; hermeneutics; heuristics; interpretation(s); interpretive inquiry
"bootstrap" methods, 38–9, 226
in case study method, 194–5, 221
clinical data and, 64, 128, 175–6, 215–16, 220, 221, 228–30, 233, 238–44, 247, 287–8, 303–4
crucial to science of psychoanalysis, 247
direct empirical evidence, 212
need for model of justifying interpretations, 286
epistemology of, 218, 247–8, 286–7
error-detecting and -correcting measures, 65, 304–9
Freud's pluralistic approach to, 192, 194–5, 223, 228, 232, 234–7, 244
hermeneutics and, 105–6, 205, 305–6
heuristics and, 223
intraclinical, 220–3
case study method, 221
circularity problem, 221–2
debates, 220–1
Freud's approach, 227
partitioning of data, 222
pluralistic approach, 222–3
limitations of, 297–80
necessity of, 216–18
debates, 217–18
reasons for, 218
posttherapeutic, 264–79, 287–8, 306
prestated criteria, 224–5
problem-solving approach to, 38
problems of clinical evidence, 212–16
circularity, 214–15
demonstrating latent contents, 213–14
nonobservable evidence, 213
objectivity problem, 214
paradigm specificity, 215
testability, 215–16
types of evidence, 212
relative probity of individual methods, 224
during treatment, 287–8
justification, individual methods of, 211–48
coherence, 234–6
circularity problem, 236
critique, 236
in discovery *vs.* justifying phases, 235
Freud's approach, 234
in "good hours," 235–6
popularity of, 235
cross-validation and convergence, 226–8
convergence of different methods, 226

justification, individual methods of *(cont.)*
cross-checking and integrating findings, 226, 228
cross-validation of independent data samples, 226
pluralistic aspects, 226–7
relative probity of different data and methods, 227–8
external methods, 244–6
clinical examples, 245
combined with intraclinical tests, 245–6
Freud's approach, 244–5
indirect prediction and postdiction, 230–2
pre- or postdicting classes of events, 232
problems of prediction, 230–1
justification by implication, 246
justification by observation, 246
critiques, 246
Freud's approach, 246
observation alone cannot justify hypotheses, 246
organized, interlocking microstructures, 228–40, 281
clinical illustrations, 264–75
French's recurrent dynamic cycles, 229
Freud's jigsaw puzzle model, 228
other microanalytic approaches, 229–30
supporting arguments, 228–9
pluralistic methods, 225–6
advantages, 226
clinical examples, 225–6
quantitative methods, 239–44
additional references, 338n.
Bayesian inference, 241–2
chi-square, 240–1
content analysis, 243–4
continuum of qualitative and quantitative methods, 240
repertory grid technique, 242–3
taxometric and theme-tracing, 241
time-series methodologies, 243
relative probity of individual methods, 224
repetition of themes and patterns, 232–3
debates, 233
rationale, 232
responses to interpretation, 236–9
critiques, 238–9, 288
Freud's approach, 236–7
related views, 237

K

kinesics, 118–19, 121–2
"nonverbal leakage," 118
parallels between kinesic and language structures, 122
repetitiveness, 121
Kleinian approach
as doctrinal, 52, 60, 66
as monistic and method-oriented, 48
knowledge, apodictic *vs.* assertorial, 25, 60–2
Kohutian approach. *See also* self psychology
as doctrinal, 52, 60, 66
as monistic and method-oriented, 46–7, 65–6
as overconfident and dogmatic, 62

L

Lacan, J. *See under* language-based models
language-based models of interpretation, 91–2. *See also* language-related parallels
action language, Schafer's, 76–8
clinical examples, 77
"language games" (Wittgenstein), 76
limitations and critiques, 77–8
nonpsychodynamic, 78
strictly rule-governed, 76

discourse model, nonrule-governed, 82–3
artificial intelligence model (simulated), 82
capabilities, 83
testing the model, 83
discourse model, rule-governed
history of discourse models, 78–9
incorporates "speech act" theory, 80–1
limitations of, 81
role of rule-governance in failure of, 81
rule-description *vs.* rule-ordering, 91
Freud's use of language, 67–8. *See also under* language-based models of interpretation, narrative models
figurative and illustrative comparisons, 67
language-based model of paranoia, 67
lapsus linguae model of psychoanalysis, 9
in processing clinical data, 67
reluctant to attempt theory of language, 68
"rules of interpretation" avoided, 68–9
linguistic model, Edelson's
based on Chomsky's linguistic rule-ordering, 74
interpretive competence based on linguistic competence, 74
limitations and critiques, 74–5
narrative models, 83–91
ambiguity in, 86
analogic, integrating, problem-solving, and structuring functions of, 86–8
constraints, minimal, 84
controversy regarding accuracy *vs.* coherence, 88–90
Edelson's narrative approach, 90–1
Freud's contributions to, 85
Freud's use of, 85
limitations and critiques of, 84, 88–9
narrative meaning, 86
psychoanalytic narratives, 86
radical constructivist views, 89–91
relation to observation, 84, 87
role of causality in, 84
single, initial, concrete, affirmative explanations in, 84–5
as strategy of processing voluminous data, 90
structuralist linguistic model, Lacan's, 69–73
based on relations of signifier (sounds) and signified (concepts), 69
emphasis on signifier, 69–70
examples, 70–2
limitations and critiques of, 72–3
neglects affects, 72–3
reduces complexity to few linguistic generalizations, 73
shortchanges developmental theory, 73
unconcerned with interpretive accuracy, 73
language-related parallels in nonclinical fields, 112–32
archaeological decipherment, 130–2
frequency of errors, 131–2
importance of flexibility, 131–2
overuse of theory, 130–1
parallels with clinical interpretation, 130–2
communication theory
importance and uncertainty of construction, 121, 144
importance of thematization, 119, 121

language-related parallels in nonclinical fields *(cont.)*
- kinesics, 121–2
- parallels with clinical interpretation, 119–23, 132–3, 144
- recoding, 119–21
- rhetoric, 122–3

linguistics, 112–13
- foregrounding, 113
- syntactical choices, 112–13
- syntactical cues largely subliminal, 113

literary theory and criticism, 126–30. *See also* myths
- clinical interpretation compared with New Criticism, 126
- dialectic-dialogic-interactive model, 127
- importance of details, 127–8
- integrating old and new information, 130
- literature and psychoanalysis, 327n.–329n.
- reading process and theory, 129–30
- repetition of contents, 128

psycholinguistics, 113–19
- analogies to clinical interpretation, 115–16
- concept of meaning, 115–16
- constructing *vs.* extracting meanings, 113
- data processing, 113
- dynamically conspicuous and key words, 116
- "lexical leakage," 116
- nonverbal behavior, 118–19
- ordinary conversation, 114
- rationale of freely hovering attention, 115
- speech act theory, 117
- ubiquity of paraphrase, 113–14
- verbal accompaniments, 117–18
- Vygotzky's "word meaning," 117

semiotics, 123–6
- clinical interpretation and, 124–5, 144, 326n.
- function of signs, 123
- interpretation of signs, 123
- relation to codes, 123–4
- repetition as signifying process, 125

lapsus linguae inquiry model, critique of, 9

latent contents, x, 16, 213–14. *See also* causal controversy; Grünbaum's critiques
- latent determinants, ix, 9, 40, 287, 291
- latent meanings, ix, 9, 16, 40, 287, 291
  - psycholinguistic aspects of, 115–17
  - whole (thematic) *vs.* part-meanings, 17, 104–5

linguistics. *See* language-based models of interpretation; language-related parallels

literary theory and criticism. *See under* language-related parallels

literature and psychoanalysis, 327n.–329n.

M

maxims, misleading, 299

meaning types, 310–13

meanings and causes, 291. *See also* causal controversy; Grünbaum's critiques

memory retrieval, 133–4. *See also under* parallels with nonclinical interpretive fields, cognitive science

mental content, 290–2. *See also* latent contents
- internal *vs.* external "locations" of, 292
  - both "locations" probable, 292
  - relation to intrapsychic *vs.* interactivist debate, 292

relation to causal controversy, 291
relation to representational states, 290–1
structural basis of, 291–2
abstract model theory, 291–2
sentential (language of thought) theory, 291
method effects, 297
method-oriented approaches, 46. *See also under* interpretive approaches; methodologic lag; positivism
vs. problem-oriented approaches, 46–50. *See also under* postpositivism
methodologic lag, 45–66
doctrinal, theory-driven, 50–60, 66
monistic and method-oriented approaches, 46–50, 65–6
overconfident, dogmatic approaches, 60–6
overgeneralized and rule-governed approaches, 69–82, 88–91
methodologic pluralism, 46–50, 222–3, 278–9, 288, 308–9
advantages, 308–9
alternative hypotheses, xiii, 64, 300
multiple revisions of hypotheses, 302
vs. exclusivism (monistic methodologies), 47
multiple interpretive methods, 308
multiple interpretive perspectives, 47
multiple justifying methods, 225–6, 308
Freud's pluralistic approach to justification, 223
multiple varieties of data, 227–8
parallels with other disciplines, 223
methodology, interpretive, xii–xiv. *See also* Freud, on interpretive methods; heuristics; interpretation(s); justification; methodologic pluralism
basic methodologic (core) concepts
Freud's interpretive system and, 59
preconceived conclusions avoided by generality of, 59, 66, 294
vs. specific clinical theories, 59–60, 66, 294
construal ("discovery") phase
advantages of ad hoc, ex post facto features, 53, 56
context-sensitive aspects of, 65
data-driven, 53–5
Freud's approach, original and later, 51–3
Freud's heuristic antidoctrinal strategy, 52–3
heuristic *vs.* doctrinal approaches, 50, 56, 66, 293–6
methodologic pluralism *vs.* monistic approaches, 46–50, 65–6
occasional necessary use of theory, 58
refinding theory, 50–1
skeptical *vs.* overconfident approaches, 60–5
stages of, xii–xiii
theory-determined errors in, 56
justifying phase. *See also* justification
alertness to discrepancies, 61, 64
checking-revising-rechecking constructions, 219
error-detecting and -correcting measures, 304–5
evidence, 212–16
Freud's pluralistic justifying approach, 223
illustrative case, 264–82
importance of details, 306
individual justifying methods, 223–47

methodology, interpretive *(cont.)*
intraclinical testing, 220–3
learning from error, 304–5
limitations of, 279–80
partitioning of data, 222
pluralistic use of multiple methods, perspectives, and varieties of data, 47, 222–3, 225–8, 308
posttherapeutic, 220–49
relative probity of individual methods, 224
during treatment, 219–20, 281
prerequisite knowledge and, xii, 139–40, 142–3
clinical and cultural competences, 139–40, 142–3
professional training and experience, 142–3
psychological-mindedness, 157
scientific sophistication, 142–3, 211
problems and limitations of
alternative interpretations, 214
circularity, 214
"interpretations rest on interpretations," 15
limited opportunity to improve accuracy, 304
paradigm-specificity of interpretations, 215, 279–80
soft pattern matches, 214
subjectivity, 214
therapeutic *vs.* propositional functions of interpretation, 215
uncertainty of constructions, 26, 106, 121, 297
use of one untested interpretation to test another, 238, 248
remedial strategies
alertness to discrepancies, 304
alternative hypotheses, 305, 308
damage control, 65, 304–5
disconfirming tests, 305
error-detecting and -correcting measures, 65, 304–9
expectation of errors, 304
holistic and particularistic perspectives, 307
importance of negative evidence, 300
learning from error, 304
posttherapeutic study of case record, 220–49
prestated selection criteria, 305–6
scientifically skeptical attitude, 304
small-scale microstructural evidence, 306
thematization, 307–8
use of multiple justifying tests and varieties of data, 306, 308
using all of the data, 304
motives, explanation by, 151
myths, interpretation of, 108–9

N

narrative models. *See under* language-based models of interpretation
naturalized epistemology (naturalism), 36–8, 41
neopositivist approaches, 29
New Criticism (literary), 126
New Paradigm (epistemologic), 35–9, 41

O

observation, 12, 87, 246
vs. inference, 12–13
overvaluing, 301
overconfidence, 60–6
dogmatic theoretic and therapeutic claims, 62
Freud's, 299–300
relation to confirmation bias, 302

P

parallels with nonclinical interpretive fields. *See also*

language-related parallels
cognitive science, 132–43
clinical expertise, 142–3
importance of extensive knowledge base, 139–40
memory retrieval, 133–4
problem-solving, 139–41
relations to clinical interpretation, 134, 138–43, 145–6
representations, 132–4
schema theory, 134–9, 145
relation- and pattern-oriented methodologies, 96–112
gestalt approach, 100–1. *See also* gestalt approach
hermeneutics, 103–6. *See also* hermeneutics
pattern model approach, 96–100. *See also* pattern model
structuralism, 107–12. *See also* structuralism
system theory, 101–3. *See also* system theory
part-whole concept, 100–1, 103–6. *See also* gestalt approach; hermeneutics; parallels with nonclinical interpretive fields, relation- and pattern-oriented methodologies
patients' responses to interpretations, 236–9. *See also* justification, responses to interpretation
pattern and theme repetition, 232–3
pattern matching, 96–100, 233
critiques of, 99, 323n.
pattern model, 96–100, 144
absence of general laws, 97
analogies important, 98
applicable to "loosely concatenated" theories like psychoanalysis, 96
critiques, 99–100
counterargument, 99–100
justification, 99
contextual validation employed continuously, 99
multiple check points, 99
networks of relations, 96
repetition important, 98
types of relations, 98
perceptual model, emphasizing "generate and test" cycles, 220
analogy with clinical interpretive process, 220
perceptual-motivational-emotional (PME) schemata, 193
perspectivism. *See* radical relativism
pluralism, methodologic. *See* methodologic pluralism
positivism, 25. *See also* interpretive perspectives, positivist
absolutism, 24, 30–1, 41
apodictic knowledge, 25, 60–2
Comte's, 4, 17
downfall of, 40
foundationalism, 21, 25, 37
Freud's, 3–4, 19–20
"lingering ghost of," 26–8, 40–1, 286
logical, 4, 41
method-oriented, 46
monistic, 46
postpositivist perspective combined with, 28–32
postpositivist perspective *vs.*, 25
reluctance to give up, 27–8
seeking certainty, 25, 60–2
post-hoc fallacy, 199–201. *See also under* errors, fallacies; Grünbaum's critiques
postdiction. *See* justification, individual methods, indirect prediction and postdiction
postpositivism. *See also* interpretive perspectives, postpositivist
assertorial knowledge, probabilistic, 25, 61–2
combined with empirical (positivist) methods, 28–32
data-driven, 25

postpositivism *(cont.)*
flexible, 22
foundationless, 21, 23, 25
Freud's anticipation of, 3, 7
pluralistic, 23
problem-oriented, 46–50
relativistic, 23–41
postpositivist interpretive attitude, 22–3, 25, 310
postpositivist interpretive models, advantages of, 65
postpositivist science, 25, 309
postpositivist shift (or "turn"), 40–1
resistance of psychoanalysis to, 41
pragmatism, 22
prediction. *See also under* justification, individual methods
vs. postdiction, 230–2, 337n.
processing of clinical data. *See* clinical data, cognitive processing of; data processing methods
progressive modification of interpretations, xiii, 276–9
psychoanalysis, science of
critiques of, 171–209, 211, 221
Grünbaum's recommendations for, 206–7
psychoanalytic schools
each claims (positivistically) to have the truth, 41
paradigm specificity of interpretations and their justification, 23–4
psycholinguistics. *See under* language-related parallels

R

radical relativism (perspectivism), 37–8
concept that "anything goes" methodologically, 37
counterargument proposes increased methodologic concern, 38
RC approach. *See* recurrent cycles approach
reconciliation of causal controversy, proposed, 190–1
reconstructions, 60. *See also* construction; interpretation(s)
recurrent cycles (RC) approach, 249–53. *See also under* case study, illustrative
basic dynamic cycle, 265–6
clinical records, 249–50
conflict-defense cycles, 252
cycle, original template, 265
cycle comparisons, 268–9
cycle lengths, 264
cycles, recurrent, 251
French's method, 249
modified, 249–53
justification, 272–6, 279–82
progressive revisions, 276–9
related approaches, 253
speeding-up of cycles, 251–2
template matching, 252–3
working backwards, 250–1
reflection on interpretive understanding, xiii
reformulating hypotheses, for communication to patient, xiii
relativism (perspectivism), 23, 30, 37, 41
vs. absolutism, 30–1
vs. certainty, 24, 41
reliability of interpretations, x, 279–80
consensus problem, x, 204, 238, 279–80
remedial strategies, 303–5. *See also under* methodology, interpretive
representations, shared concept of, 132–3
repressed, return of, 190
repression theory. *See under* Grünbaum's critiques
rhetoric, 122
rule-governed interpretive models,

74–6. *See also under* language-based models of interpretation, linguistic, action language, and discourse models

S

Schafer, R.. *See under* language-based models of interpretation, action language and narrative models
schema theory, 134–9, 145
 limitations of, 138–9
science, philosophy of, 21–5, 28–44, 172–4. *See also* positivism; postpositivism
 epistemology of interpretive inquiry, 34–40
  commonsense psychology model, 147–8, 150–3
  continental philosophies, 35
  debate about justification, 289–90
  Grünbaum's views, 172–4, 206–9
  increased recognition of interpretation, 32–4
  Klimovsky's views, 52
  mental content and, 290–2
  naturalized epistemology (naturalism), 36–9
  New Paradigm, 35–6
  pluralistic, 35
  Wittgenstein, 289
science, sociology of, 39–40
self psychology, 62–3. *See also* Kohutian approach
semantic differential method, 23
semiotics, 123–6. *See also* language-related parallels
sequences
 basic recurrent unit of narrative organization, 128
 in dreams, 252
 in RC approach, 250–1
 "sequences of sequences," 252
 in therapeutic process, 252
skepticism, 304. *See under* methodology, remedial strategies
speech act theory, 80–1, 117. *See also under* language-based models of interpretation, discourse model, rule-governed; language-related parallels, psycholinguistics
structuralism. *See also* language-based models of interpretation, structuralist-linguistic model
 focus on human mind, 107
 interpretation of myths, 108–9
 relation to clinical interpretation, 110–12
suggestion. *See also under* Grünbaum's critiques
 Freud's concern about, 14
system theory, 101–3
 emergent systems, 102
 importance of relations, 101
 parallels to clinical interpretation, 102–3
 "relations between relations," 101

T

tally argument. *See under* Grünbaum's critiques
technique, interpretive, ix, xi
testing behavior by patients, 49
thematization, 103, 119, 307–8
 as corollary of continuity principle, 307
theme-tracing method, 241
themes
 affective, 187
 as bridge between observable and unobservable evidence, 213
 causal controversy and, 181
  relation to other disciplines, 186
 central theme (whole meaning) of therapy session, 17, 307
  Grünbaum's critique, 178
 Core Conflictual Relationship

themes *(cont.)*
Theme (CCRT), 319n.
dynamic, 252, 295, 307
fallacy of combining dynamically different, 102
Freud's view, 53
informationally rich symbols and, 119
interpretive search for unifying, 103
detection of, 189
in justification, 213, 215–16, 224, 225, 232
parallel processing and latent, 115
purpose of, in narrative, 87
relation to extensive psychoanalytic database, 232
relation to inference, 142
relation to most plausible interpretation, 307
repetition of, 112, 232, 288, 301
in narratives, 87
strength of schemas and, 137
sequences, 252
single word as clue to latent, 116
unfocused listening and latent, 115
theory
general *vs.* specific, 58–9, 293–4
heuristic use of, 56
models of, 37
nonstatement view of, 37
overreliance on, 130–1, 303
doctrinal fallacy, 293
role in methodology, 293–4. *See also* doctrinal (theory-driven) approaches
theory-determined errors, 56. *See also* doctrinal (theory-driven) approaches
therapists, recommendations for, 304–5
transference compliance, detection of, 333n.
type conceptions, 310–12

U

uncertainty, x
of construction, 121

W

word meaning (Vygotzky), 117

For Product Safety Concerns and Information please contact our EU representative GPSR@taylorandfrancis.com
Taylor & Francis Verlag GmbH, Kaufingerstraße 24, 80331 München, Germany

www.ingramcontent.com/pod-product-compliance
Ingram Content Group UK Ltd.
Pitfield, Milton Keynes, MK11 3LW, UK
UKHW022005180926
475701UK00003B/199

* 9 7 8 1 1 3 8 0 0 5 4 0 2 *